CRITICAL COMPANION TO

Emily Dickinson

A Literary Reference to Her Life and Work

SHARON LEITER

Facts On File
An imprint of Infobase Publishing

for Darryl

That Love is all there is
Is all we know of Love,

Undated (Fr 1747)

Critical Companion to Emily Dickinson

Copyright © 2007 by Sharon Leiter

Facts On File, Inc.
An imprint of Infobase Publishing
132 West 31st Street
New York NY 10001

Library of Congress Cataloging-in-Publication Data

Leiter, Sharon.
Critical companion to Emily Dickinson: a literary reference
to her life and work / Sharon Leiter.
p. cm.
Includes bibliographical references and index.
ISBN 0-8160-5448-7 (acid-free paper)
1. Dickinson, Emily, 1830–1886—Handbooks, manuals, etc. 2. Women and literature—
United States—History—19th century—Handbooks, manuals, etc. 3. Poets, American—
19th century—Biography—Handbooks, manuals, etc.
I. Title.
PS1541.Z5L376 2006
811'.4—dc22   2005028123

Facts On File books are available at special discounts when purchased in bulk quantities
for businesses, associations, institutions, or sales promotions. Please call our Special Sales
Department in New York at (212) 967-8800 or (800) 322-8755.

You can find Facts On File on the World Wide Web at http://www.factsonfile.com

Text design by Erika K. Arroyo
Cover design by Cathy Rincon/Anastasia Plé
Cover image © Guillermo Cuellar. The image on the front of this book was printed with
permission of the artist and copyright holder, Guillermo Cuellar, of Amherst Massachusetts.
The original oil painting is entitled *Emily Dickinson—Her True Colors*.
Any duplication of this image without obtaining authorization is prohibited. All rights
reserved. More information about the image may be obtained from www.gcuellar.com.

Printed in the United States of America

VB Hermitage 10 9 8 7 6 5 4 3 2 1

This book is printed on acid-free paper.

CONTENTS

FOREWORD

The voice of the solitary
Who makes others less alone . . .
                              —Stanley Kunitz

More of Emily Dickinson's poems begin with "I" than any other word. Paradoxically, in the lyric this pronoun of self functions inclusively, rather than exclusively. The reader is invited to identify with the poem's speaker for the brief, intensified moment of the poem's unfolding. Although in most poems this lyric invitation is implicit, Walt Whitman states it outright and with typical confidence in the opening lines of "Song of Myself," recognizing that all the deeper emotional and spiritual transactions of his sequence derive from it:

I celebrate myself, and sing myself,
And what I assume, you shall assume
For every atom belonging to me as good
    belongs to you.

And 70 years after Whitman, William Carlos Williams even more boldly and baldly reminds his readers that the journey of the lyric "I" is one in which two travel together: "In the imagination, we are from henceforth (so long as you read) locked in a fraternal embrace, the classic caress of author and reader. We are one. Whenever I say 'I' I mean also 'you.' And so, together, as one, we shall begin." (*Spring and All*).

It may be odd to think of Emily Dickinson, one of our premier *isolatos*, extending such an intimate invitation. But has not she herself both claimed and generalized that pronoun when, in that dance of revelation and evasion that is her early corre-

spondence with Thomas Wentworth Higginson, she notes, "When I state myself, as the Representative of the Verse—it does not mean—me—but a supposed person"? And is she not also our greatest lyric poet, who, as Keats urged, proved her truths on her own pulse? Proven and tested for authenticity there, in the forge and hothouse of her own passions, these truths become "assumable" (to use Whitman's intriguing term) by readers, who give themselves over to her powerful experiences for the brief moment of the poem, who "become" her.

Dickinson's frequent use of "I" should not lead us to believe she is excessively egotistical or self-involved. Rather, it is the mark of a poet of the personal lyric—someone who writes an "I" poem about experience. Such a poem—the most common kind of poem or song composed in the world—is a means of coping, of incorporating the experience of disorder into the elaborate formal orderings of poetry. What makes the personal lyric such an important kind of poem in all sorts of cultures is that it represents a tool to help individuals survive existential crises. The disorders that are ordered by the personal lyric extend across the whole spectrum of human subjectivity, all the way from joy to despair, from love and delight to fear of death and madness. What all these disorderings have in common is the capacity to destabilize the individual self. By translating her joy or despair and her happiness or confusion into language and by ordering it into a poem, the poet restabilizes herself and gives her experience of disorder both shape and significance. Shakespeare described this process through which the poet both creates a poem and stabilizes a self:

> The poet's eye, in a fine frenzy rolling,
> Doth glance from heaven to earth, from earth
> to heaven,
> And, as imagination bodies forth
> The forms of things unknown, the poet's pen
> Turns them to shapes, and gives to airy nothing
> A local habitation and a name.
>
> (A Midsummer Night's Dream)

We could add that the "poet's eye" is also the poet's "I." Nor am I casually connecting Shakespeare to Emily Dickinson. Dickinson seems to me the equal of Shakespeare, though in a lyric mode. He created a hundred vivid characters moving through the world; she dramatized several hundred vivid emotional states in the course of her work. It is not that she showed us that her inner world of subjectivity (and ours by analogy) was rich and complex (we knew that), but that she showed us that odd and intense states of inner experience could be given voice and form. Keats, wishing near the end of his life not to only write poems but to "do some good," had come around to a grudging admiration of Wordsworth because he "thinks into the human heart." Keats even posited, in a wonderful image, that poets like Wordsworth, feeling "the Burden of the Mystery," were writing poems that were "explorative of the dark passages," and it is clear from Keats's image that these dark passages are corridors in the human mind, aspects of consciousness itself.

Keats wrote to his friend that, if they both lived long enough, they, too, might engage in such an exploration, to the benefit of mankind. Of course, Keats didn't live long enough, but Dickinson did. It is possible to think of her as exploring, with the huge body of her more than 1,700 poems, more dark passages than anyone before or since in English. She is like a great inner spelunker—her own mind and subjectivity a veritable Carlsbad Caverns of tunnels and chambers and strange spaces full of wonder and mystery and terror. She explores the inner world of her consciousness and the poems she sends back are reports of what she has discovered there.

In her poems, she gives us joy:

> Wild Nights—Wild Nights!
> Were I with thee
> Wild Nights should be
> Our luxury!
>
> (Fr 269)

She gives us love's anguish:

> I cannot live with You—
> It would be Life—
> And Life is over there—
> Behind the Shelf . . .
>
> (Fr 706)

She gives us despair:

> I measure every Grief I meet
> With narrow, probing, eyes—
> I wonder if It weighs like Mine—
> Or has an Easier size . . .
>
> (Fr 550)

She gives us the experience of enduring traumatic violence in the grim metaphor of a lightning strike that refuses to cease happening:

> It struck me—every Day—
> The Lightning was as new
> As if the Cloud that instant slit
> And let the Fire through . . .
>
> (Fr 636)

She gives us religious doubt:

> Those—dying then,
> Knew where they went—
> They went to God's Right Hand—
> That Hand is amputated now
> And God cannot be found—
>
> (Fr 1581)

Dickinson gives us all these things and invites us (challenges us) to identify with her—to "become her" for the brief experience of the poem. And by doing so, we as readers experience her triumph over disorder and confusion as our own. We experience her ordering of chaotic experience and passions into coherence as our own vicarious but real victory.

And so Emily Dickinson invites us into the world of her consciousness. It is an invitation that can seem a bit intimidating because she is so unre-lentingly intense. Sometimes, her invitation can even take the form of a challenge to the reader: "Dare you see a Soul at the 'White Heat'?" (from Fr 401)

No one I know in the history of the lyric was as passionate and various as Emily Dickinson when it came to dramatizing states of consciousness. But she is not an easy poet. She invites us to become her, to let our selves become her "I," but the invi-tation involves quite a leap—she is so smart, so passionate, so strange. She baffled her friends and family as much as she dazzled them. And her main literary correspondent, Thomas Wentworth Hig-ginson, was clearly intimidated by her genius.

Let me put it this way: Everyone around the young Emily Dickinson was walking in a somber, well-behaved way, but she was dancing. She was too smart, too ironic, too passionate and alive for the sober and narrow world she had to inhabit:

> They put me in the Closet—
> Because they like me "still"—
>
> Still! Could themself have peeped—
> And seen my Brain—go round—
> They might as wise have lodged a Bird
> For Treason—in the Pound—
>
> (Fr 445)

Those around her, who loved her and wished to keep her calm, could not shut her up. Like the bird in her poem, she was born for bigger things—and with her will and her imagination she was deter-mined to achieve them. The poet as a hero. Not a soldier in battle, but a consciousness, a mind bat-tling to stay alive and vital but also to control and order itself (that brain "going round" in its intensi-ties). She wrote most of her poems without hope of anyone seeing them, or, when she enclosed them in letters to friends and relatives, without much hope of people understanding them. But she stayed brave and productive—writing hundreds and hun-dreds of poems that only a few people read when she was alive, but that we now cherish.

Although Emily Dickinson has so much to share with us, most of us need help in making the leap from our own modest passions, thoughts, and sen-sations to Dickinson's more intense and eccentric ones. We are lucky to have such a guide as Sharon Leiter—an accomplished poet as well as a scholar, and someone who is both eminently sensitive and eminently sensible in her approach to Dickinson. She brings her closer to us by clarifying the stranger parts, giving us insightful interpretations of the most compressed material, giving us a feel for how Dickinson thinks and translates her thinking into words. In short, she brings Dickinson's poems and person closer to us, so the leap between her "I" and our own is not so huge. This is a great service, because to have a poet like Emily Dickinson as a part of our lives, to make her our own by coming to understand and love her poems, is to deeply enrich our own experience of what it means to be alive.

—Gregory Orr
Charlottesville, Virginia

INTRODUCTION

Days after Emily Dickinson's death on May 19, 1886, her younger sister Lavinia, from whom she had rarely been separated in her lifetime, discovered an unexpected Emily: hundreds of handwritten poems hidden in a box in her room. Lavinia had known that Emily wrote poems and had surely read some of them. But the sheer wealth of her finding stunned her; Lavinia was "actually trembling with excitement" when she came to Mabel Loomis Todd, who would later edit the poems, with her find. Since then, with each successive edition of her work, the world has discovered new Emily Dickinsons.

Because she never saw her work into print, the prejudices and tampering of early editors have had to be undone by later ones. Not until 1955, with the publication of Thomas Johnson's *Complete Poems,* was the poet's work available in its entirety, in a form closely respecting her original manuscripts. The process of discovery took a giant step further with the work of Ralph J. Franklin, who restored and published Dickinson's original manuscript books in 1981, thereby opening a new era of textual scholarship. One hundred and twenty years after her death, we are still finding new Emily Dickinsons.

And yet, she has been with us from the beginning of her journey into print. From the first volume of poems prepared by Mabel Todd and Thomas Wentworth Higginson in 1890, readers have responded intimately and urgently to the poems, demanding ever more of them. As Mrs. Todd wrote in her preface to the Second Series,

1891: "[Dickinson's] 'irresistible needle-touch' . . . piercing at once the very core of a thought, has found a response as wide and sympathetic as it has been unexpected even to those who knew best her compelling power." Words may have been changed, rhyme and line lengths altered, and arbitrary titles appended, yet the core—something of the magic and the power—of Dickinson's poetic vision survived all distortions. It was the enthusiasm of those readers of her first volume that led to the speedy publication of the second. The magnetic pull of the poems has been there from the first. It is no disparagement of the work of contemporary scholars to restore Dickinson to the reading public in her full authenticity to say that we already have the essential Emily Dickinson.

Dickinson's preeminent place in world literature rests, not merely on the sheer scope of her work—almost 1,800 poems, including more great poems than any other American poet before or since—but on its depth and breadth. She has been seen as the great poet of unfulfilled longing, of expectation that never attains its object, a misfortune she transformed into the blessing of "sumptuous destitution," a "Banquet of Abstemiousness." Yet this sense of a reality that must always fall short of desire and imagination was but one aspect of her vision.

A product of New England Calvinism who steadfastly refused to join the church, she wrote continually about God, wrestling with him, cajoling him, pleading with him, challenging him, reproaching him. Until the end of her life, she continued to ask her "flood question"—"Is Immortality true?" Although she scoffed at the primitive notion that heaven was "a Place—a Sky—a Tree," her questing mind burrowed into the grave and beyond, imagining heaven in endless guises: "the fair schoolroom in the sky;" a "small Town;" "a Tent" that wraps "its shining Yards" and disappears; an oppressive paradise, where "it's Sunday—all the time—/ And Recess—never comes—"; "my Delinquent Palaces—"; "what I cannot reach"—but most often, her own backyard, the earthly joys of love and nature that she preferred to whatever God's heaven might, or might not, be. Heaven haunted and eluded her. And it is the combined force of both her longing-inspired visions and her ineluctable doubts that makes her "religious" poems so powerful.

For all her conjured journeys to the "new Continent" of "Eternity," Emily Dickinson's most intrepid explorations were of what she called "the undiscovered continent" of the self. Her great obsession was with what she alternately called soul, self, spirit, mind, consciousness, me, heart, and brain—her approximate synonyms for the "hidden corridors" of the inner life. The shrewdness of her perceptions and her genius in articulating them continue to make even the most sophisticated of contemporary readers "feel physically as if the tops of their heads were taken off." Although she "thanked God" that "the Cellars of the Soul," "the loudest place he made," was "licensed to be still," she was a tireless translator of the inarticulate cries from those depths into the language of poetry.

Her ability to perform this feat depended, in part, upon her understanding that she could convey her awful and awe-inspiring truth only by indirection. In her most famous poem on "how to write," Dickinson advised:

Tell all the truth but tell it slant—
Success in Circuit lies

Thus, although she wrote from the depth of her own experience of love and loss, she was no "confessional" poet in the contemporary sense. Far from exhibiting the details of her personal life, she has left scholars forever guessing at the nature of the profound emotional trauma she experienced in her late twenties or early thirties; the identity of the great love(s) of her life; the reason(s) she chose not to publish her poetry; and the reason(s) she withdrew from society. She possessed the extraordinary ability to simultaneously distance herself from and make herself intimately accessible to the reader: to reveal herself while remaining hidden.

"When I state myself as the Representative of the Verse—it does not mean—me—but a supposed person," she told her literary correspondent, Thomas Wentworth Higginson (L 268). Indeed, she dramatized her inner life through a large cast of personae or "speakers": the child (sometimes "a boy") she both pitied and wished she could always remain, through whose eyes she expressed her "naive" perceptions; the "drunken" bee-poet; the dauntless bobolink-robin-singer, the sparrow with her precious crumb; the sun-worshipping daisy; the idolatrous lover; the Queen of Calvary; the exile from love; the triumphant wife without the crown; the sanctified woman in white; the mourner; the dying; the departed; the feaster at the banquet of abstemiousness; the semi-visible observer of the natural world; the exile from nature; the scornful suppliant of heaven; the invisible sibyl behind the wisdom poems that constitute fully half her oeuvre; nobody. Even so partial a listing reveals a gallery of opposites: the grandiose and the humble, victor and defeated, sufferer and survivor, believer and doubter.

What were these personae but the alternating voices of her multifaceted sensibility? Those who complain of her "inconsistency" fail to grasp that Dickinson's work mimics the contradictions of consciousness itself—particularly a probing, profound, and volatile consciousness such as her own. For a lyric poet, attempting in each poem to distill the essence of a single moment, there is nothing puzzling in the fact that one poem may "contradict" another. Dickinson has been charged with lacking a poetic "project," some grand vision of the human enterprise or overarching purpose for her poetry. Her great biographer, Richard Sewall, succinctly rebuts this accusation: "She is the poet of the passing insight, the moment of vision, the unitary experience. She had no social or political program and was inclined to smile at those who did" (*Life*, II, 714).

To this, critic Robert Weisbuch sagely adds that "you cannot define Dickinson by what she believes, but by what she keeps caring about, turning it this way and that" ("Prisming," *Handbook*, 221–222). Not only from poem to poem, but *within* a single poem, we see her searching mind taking a stance, then changing direction and turning against her original premise before a poem ends or trails off in a characteristic final dash.

Dickinson's "anti-project" has been enough to assure her status in the American canon and to continue to win her a devoted readership. At the same time, however, her poetry continues to arouse a certain discomfort. And, ironically, the source of this discomfort is the very thing that makes her great: her unprecedented use of the English language. From the outset, critics have distinguished between the poet's dazzling "thoughts" and her disconcerting style. Higginson embodied this approach, when he wrote, half apologetically, in his preface to the 1890 poems:

> The main quality of these poems is that of extraordinary grasp and insight, uttered with an uneven vigor sometimes exasperating, seemingly wayward, but really unsought and inevitable. After all, when a thought takes one's breath away, a lesson on grammar seems an impertinence.

Today critics see not only her grammatical "mistakes" but her oddities of capitalization and punctuation, her slant rhymes and "spasmodic" rhythms, as integral features of her poetics, a revolutionary attempt to engage every aspect of language in the interest of creating new meanings. Since Dickinson herself left no statement of her poetics, her intentions cannot be established in any definitive way; all that can be said is that, when we do assume that these "oddities" were conscious strategies, fascinating nuances of meaning emerge.

Higginson's artificial separation of form and content was long ago discarded by literary critics, in favor of an approach to poetry that recognizes form as a primary creator of meaning. "Where paraphrase is possible," wrote the great 20th-century Russian poet Osip Mandelstam, "the sheets have not been rumpled. Poetry has not spent the night." Anyone who has attempted to paraphrase a Dickinson poem, to reduce it to a simple, clean thought, knows that her sheets are indeed rumpled! For the poems' compressed, often jarring, disjunct forms, full of silences and absences, are part and parcel of their meanings. "My Business is Circumference," she informed Higginson, using her term for the far limits of human understanding. In her quest to stretch those boundaries, she was an intrepid deformer of language: chopping up words and adding to them, shrinking and expanding the spaces between them, destroying firm semantic connections, and replacing coherent sentences with floating units of meaning, capable of touching and repelling one another in a variety of ways. "I found the word to every thought / I ever had—," Dickinson noted in 1862, a bit of "boasting" we might forgive in light of the fact that she wrote 227 poems that year. She might have added that when she failed to find the word she sought in common usage, she invented it.

For all these reasons, even those who know and revere her work tend to find Emily Dickinson a "difficult" poet. While there are gems in virtually everything she wrote, striking, moving, unforgettable lines and phrases, grasping a full Dickinson poem requires a certain amount of work on the reader's part. The intent of the present volume is to serve as a critical companion, both to the poems themselves and to the engaged but perplexed reader attempting to enter the poems on a deeper level. In grappling with the fine structure of Dickinson's language, I have found my own invaluable companions. The first is my facsimile of Noah Webster's *American Dictionary of the English Language*, 1828 edition, the beloved "Lexicon" the poet not only consulted, but also read for pleasure. Within its pages, the 21st-century reader can learn not only what words meant in mid-19th century America but also what literary and cultural associations they held for Dickinson and her contemporaries. The second indispensable resource is Cristanne Miller's *A Poet's Grammar*, the best available study of Dickinson's language. Lucidly and concisely, Miller analyzes the poet's strategic use of grammar, syntax, rhyme and meter, punctuation, and capitalization, and illustrates her perceptions in a series of superb close readings.

I have written with the general reader in mind, high school and college students, as well as poetry lovers of all ages, making few assumptions about previous knowledge and keeping literary jargon to a minimum. At the same time, I believe that the detailed analyses of the poems will be of value to more advanced students of Dickinson as well. For despite the wealth of recent Dickinson scholarship, close readings of her poems are hard to come by.

In the difficult task of selecting from Dickinson's 1,789 extant poems those that are the greatest, most important, and most representative, I have tried to discern a "general consensus." The 575 poems selected by Dickinson's great editor, Thomas Johnson, in his *Final Harvest* were my starting point. I honed my sense of what should be included through reading the works of leading Dickinson scholars and noting the poems they found central to her oeuvre, as well as consulting the leading anthologies of 19th-century American poetry, to see what they include. The fact is, however, that apart from a small number of incontestable masterpieces, there is little consensus among editors, critics and anthologists as to what constitutes "the essential Dickinson." Scholar Gary Stonum points out the huge discrepancies among the poems included in anthologies—a situation that does not exist for other American icons such as Walt Whitman, Ralph Waldo Emerson, or Robert Frost. One reason for this may simply be the great number of superb poems Dickinson left us; another, no doubt, is her many-sidedness. With a breadth of insight into the human condition equaled, perhaps, only by Shakespeare, the appeal of Dickinson's work to different readers is bound to be subjective. While I have tried to choose all the poems that students commonly encounter today, I also made sure the selection would be representative of her scope— including poems on all her major concerns, in all her different voices, from all time periods. Beyond that, I have inevitably added those poems that I particularly, personally love. This can never be a bad thing for a critic, for what we love we are far more likely to understand.

Although focusing on the details and dynamics of a single poem does not provide a direct path to generalizations on Dickinson's beliefs or her poet-

ics, it is perhaps the most meaningful way of coming to know her. Certainly, it is the first approach a reader should take, before moving into the airy realms of theory. Within each analysis, I do bring in other "related" poems, in order to point to general concerns and poetic strategies. But I am aware that connecting Emily Dickinson's poems is a little bit like tracing constellations in the night sky. Within the vast and intricate corpus of her work, there exists a wealth of possibilities: pinpricks of light that take on specific shapes according to the vision of the observer. Other patterns could have been drawn.

Dickinson herself believed that each generation of readers refracts the poet's vision through its own "lens":

> The Poets light but Lamps—
> Themselves—go out—
> The Wicks they stimulate
> If vital Light
>
> Inhere as do the Suns—
> Each Age a Lens
> Disseminating their
> Circumference—
>
> (Fr 930, 1865)

In our present age, critics are reflecting Dickinson's light through a bewildering variety of lenses. There are those who see her as the last representative of the romantic tradition, while for others she is a precursor of modernism's fractured idiom and spiritual alienation. Still others, eager to correct the distorted image of Dickinson the isolated recluse, place her solidly in the midst of Victorian New England culture, a woman of a certain religious background and socioeconomic class. These scholars show us a Dickinson in touch with leading figures of the day and deeply affected by the events of her time, particularly the Civil War, which coincided with the years of her greatest poetic production. Feminist critics, plucking her from the context of the patriarchal society and literary tradition in which she has generally been seen, emphasize her involvement with women's social networks and women's literature. Dickinson has been subjected to posthumous psychoanalysis in which her precarious sexual identity and its effect on the poems have come under detailed scrutiny.

On the other end of the critical spectrum is the school of thought associated with respected scholar Robert Weisbuch, that biography has nothing to say about Dickinson's "sceneless" poems, which can and must be read on several levels simultaneously. If Weisbuch advises the reader not to "point" at any one narrow meaning, critic Sharon Cameron warns against "choosing" a specific variant for a poem, when the poet herself may have wished all her variants to be read as dimensions of a composite "meaning." Cameron's work belongs to the substantial body of textual scholarship that has emerged since the publication of *The Manuscript Books* in 1981. Another branch of textual research, associated with Martha Nell Smith, Doris Oberhaus, and Daneen Wardrop, has focused on the fascicles, Dickinson's hand-sewn booklets, as the poet's intended means of publication. While these critics see the fascicles as coherent units of meaning in which poems contradict and "balance" one another, others such as the preeminent editor R. W. Franklin believe the fascicles were merely a way for Dickinson to keep track of her rapidly growing stacks of poems and that their sequence in the fascicles is random.

These approaches represent only part of the explosion of scholarship emerging from today's thriving Dickinson industry. The reader in search of enlightenment can choose from those studies the ones that resonate with his or her interests and personal instincts about the poetry. In my annotated bibliography, I have tried to be of help by offering brief characterizations of the works I have found most meaningful. In developing my readings of the poems, I am indebted to the thinking of a number of disparate scholars. In exploring a poem, I frequently introduce their competing ideas and let them argue with one another. I have heeded the caution of Dickinson's most recent biographer, Alfred Habegger, who points to the "dubiousness of construing this profoundly one-of-a-kind writer by first enrolling her in any group at all" (*My Wars*, xii). The absence of any one theoretical axe to grind has given me the flexibility to pick and choose among critical approaches.

As an example, I don't take sides in the debate over whether biographical facts are relevant to understanding a poem. I believe that, while a good or great poem can never be wholly "explained" by biographical or historical events, some poems are clearly illuminated by knowledge of what was happening in the poet's life and world when she wrote it, while others are not. Thus, a poem such as "OURSELVES WERE WED ONE SUMMER—DEAR—" clearly refers to Emily's early love for Susan Huntington Gilbert Dickinson; to ignore the history of their relationship is to willfully turn away from an important dimension of the poem. On the other hand, a poem such as "THE BRAIN—IS WIDER THAN THE SKY—" is a philosophical reflection, rooted in the poet's concern about man's place in the world of God and nature; biographical details won't add to what we can understand without them. Similarly, I have applied the insights of feminist criticism in analyzing the many poems where they seem relevant, while omitting them when they seem contrived. In some poems, I have found plausible insights in even the much maligned psychoanalytic approach.

The subjectivity of this admittedly eclectic approach strikes me as far preferable to squeezing the poems into the procrustean bed of theory. There can be no such thing as an "authoritative and objective" reading of a Dickinson poem. For one thing, the authorities are always flat-out contradicting one another. This is the fault of lyric poems in general—slippery swimmers that elude any one conceptual net—and of Dickinson in particular. She is dense and enigmatic, complex and inexhaustible. What she wrote of "Eternity" applies as well to her poems:

> As if the Sea should part
> And show a further Sea—
> And that—a further

The aim of the present volume is to assist the reader in parting as many seas as seems necessary and desirable in order to find his or her own Emily Dickinson. As Weisbuch astutely comments, so capacious and many-leveled is her work that what a reader finds in it is to some degree a function of what he or she brings. Before reading my analysis of a poem, I advise the student to first read the poem aloud, listening for its tone and the rhythms of its thoughts, and formulating an initial sense of it. After that, he or she may want to go on to the recommendations for further reading that follow each entry or to turn to cross-referenced entries. I have cited the poems as they appear in Franklin's reading edition, now regarded as authoritative, while also giving the number of the poem in Johnson's earlier edition. I highly recommend purchasing one of these collections. Both are inexpensive—and indispensable for anyone who wishes to go beyond the selections of the popular anthologies.

How to Use This Book

The volume is organized into four parts. In Part I, an extensive biographical essay presents the fundamental known facts of Dickinson's life and writing career, as well as what is *not* known and continues to be the object of scholarly research and debate. Part II, the heart of the book, contains analyses of more than 150 of Dickinson's poems. Poem entries are given in alphabetical order, according to the first line of the poem, which, for purposes of this book, doubles as the poem's title.

Part III, "Related People, Places, and Topics," consists primarily of essays on biographical topics: the significant figures in Dickinson's life (her nuclear family, always the core for her, girlhood friends and relatives, teachers and presumed lovers, mentors, and canine companion), her home, the Homestead, the schools she attended, her church, and the predominant religious climate of the times. A poet who declared that she saw "New Englandly" could hardly be discussed without reference to her Puritan heritage, the Connecticut River Valley, her native Amherst, and the college that dominated its cultural and intellectual life. This section also con-

tains a number of essays on literary matters. Foremost among them is a discussion of Dickinson's surviving letters, the only prose we have of hers, and widely considered to be works of art in their own right. In addition to providing an incomplete but fascinating record of her thoughts, relationships, activities and concerns, they offer invaluable perspectives on the poems, for which reason I cite them frequently in my analyses. The three extraordinary "Master Letters," written to an unknown lover, receive separate treatment. I also include an extended essay on the history of publication and editorial scholarship, as well as entries on the essential elements of her language and style.

Part IV contains three appendices: a detailed chronology, including important life events and publication dates; a bibliography of Dickinson's works, including poems published during her lifetime and posthumous editions of her poems and letters; and an annotated bibliography of the most important books and articles on Dickinson and her work.

Any reference to a poem by Dickinson that is the subject of an entry in Part II and any reference to a person, place, or topic that is the subject of an entry in Part III is printed in SMALL CAPITAL LETTERS the first time it appears in a particular entry.

For a poet such as Emily Dickinson, who is constantly being rediscovered, it seems particularly appropriate that the image of her on the cover of this book should also be a rediscovery and a reinterpretation. In "Emily Dickinson—Her True Colors," Amherst artist Guillermo Cuellar has transformed the familiar black-and-white daguerreotype, Dickinson's only known likeness, into a new vision of what the chestnut-haired 16-year-old girl who posed for it might have looked like.

ACKNOWLEDGMENTS

Writing a book about Emily Dickinson is like standing within the circle of a rare and ever-changing light. More than anything else, the seemingly inexhaustible richness of her poetry, with its emotional depths and intellectual challenges, provided the sustained impetus and energy needed to complete a work of this kind. At the same time, I could not have written it without the collaboration and support of several individuals. First among these is my editor, Jeff Soloway. His enthusiasm, flexibility, and wisdom have been essential to this project from beginning to end. Receptive to the need for a critical companion to Dickinson's poetry, Jeff worked with me in defining and refining the shape such a book should take. I have benefited immeasurably from his advice and encouragement, his openness to new ideas, and his patience.

My husband, Darryl Leiter, has been my invaluable companion at every stage of my work. Sharing my love of Dickinson and excitement at the discoveries of each poem, evening after evening he played the role of the "general reader" for whom this book is written. Not only did he give me valuable perspectives on my analyses, but he also contributed his own astute insights. He shared my "pilgrimages" to Amherst and provided me with his sensitive photographs, many of which appear in this book.

I would like to thank the following individuals and institutions who generously made available to me images of Emily Dickinson and her world: Daria D'Arenzo and Margaret R. Dakin, Archives and Special Collections, Amherst College Library; Thomas Ford, Photographic Liaison for Houghton Library, Harvard University; Tevis Kimball, Curator of Special Collections, Jones Library; Cynthia Ostroff, Manager, Manuscripts and Archives, Yale University Library; Fiona Russell, Director, Amherst History Museum; and Jane Wald, Director, Emily Dickinson Museum.

Special thanks go to Tevis Kimball, for leading me to Guillermo Cuellar and his painting of Dickinson, which appears on the cover of this book; to my agent, Jodie Rhodes, for representing my interests so well; and to Cam Dufty, my reassuring and knowledgeable guide through the final editing phases.

During the years of research and writing I have been warmed by many friends "of higher temperature / For Frigid—hour of Mind—." Nancy Beardsley, Rita Lenn, Paula Leiter Pergament, and Jean Sampson listened and encouraged. Nancy Hurrelbrinck, Judy Longley, Kenny Marotta, and Susan Shafarzek read sections of the manuscript and shared their insights with me. Joan Saperstan and Josette Henschel extended their friendship and fine hospitality in Amherst.

Affectionate thanks go to my daughter and son-in-law, Robin and Sean Edwards, for their faith in me and to my little grandsons, Jacob and Andrew, for reminding me, as Emily knew, that "Blessed are they that play, for theirs is the kingdom of heaven."

PART I

Biography

Dickinson, Emily Elizabeth
(1830–1886)

"My life has been too simple and stern to embarrass any," Emily Dickinson wrote to her friend THOMAS WENTWORTH HIGGINSON in 1869 (L 330). In spite of this disclaimer, she has proven an elusive subject for biographers. Higginson noted the difficulty of capturing the poet when he wrote "you only enshroud yourself in this fiery mist & I cannot reach you, but only rejoice in the rare sparkles of light" (L 330a). Hers was not a consciously documented life. She kept no diary and left no memoirs. Her surviving LETTERS, only a fraction of her entire correspondence, are a rich source of information about her, but their cryptic style tends to obscure personal details.

Many of Dickinson's correspondents preserved her extraordinary letters, but at least as many lost or destroyed them. The only person who made a point of collecting facts about her, as if he knew her life would be important, was Higginson. Her letters to him are the most revealing, and his 1870 recollection of their first visit is the most cited source in biographies of the poet. While a wealth of research has been done, uncertainty remains about many vital facts of her life, including the exact dates of her manuscripts.

"'It is finished' can never be said of us," Dickinson observed (L 555). One hundred and twenty years after her death, scholars continue to search for revealing documents, despite the increasing unlikeliness of finding them. A range of new critical approaches has allowed readers to see the poet from fresh and revealing perspectives. Foremost among these are cultural studies, which deflate the myth of the "poet recluse," isolated from the social and political events of her times, and feminist studies, which view the role of gender as crucial to understanding the poet's life and work.

Emily Elizabeth Dickinson was born at 5 A.M. on December 10, 1830, at The HOMESTEAD, the brick mansion built by her grandfather, SAMUEL FOWLER DICKINSON, in 1813 on Main Street in AMHERST, Massachusetts. Her ancestors had come to the fertile western Massachusetts region known

This daguerreotype, made when the poet was about 16, is the only known photograph of Emily Dickinson. *(Amherst College Archives and Special Collections)*

as the CONNECTICUT RIVER VALLEY, in the 1630s to escape the corruption of the Church of England and find the freedom to practice their "purified" Calvinist religion. The line of Dickinson forebears that sprang from these early Puritans consisted of practical men and women, involved in the affairs of this world: settling and defending their new home, bearing and nurturing large families under severe conditions, becoming landowners and farmers, educators, lawyers, and civic leaders.

Grandfather Samuel had been a pillar of Amherst society, playing a leading role in the creation of its educational institutions and securing a position of social preeminence for his family. He was known by his fellow townsmen as "Squire" Dickinson, a role that combined property, privilege, and responsibility. But Samuel's fanatical zeal for his religiously inspired projects led him to overplay his hand. When he invested his personal wealth in the development of AMHERST COLLEGE, his finances grew increasingly shaky. In 1833, three years after the poet's birth, he went bankrupt and was forced to leave his beloved hometown for the inhospitable western lands of Ohio. Thus, Dickinson's family heritage contained a mixture of opposing elements: religious conservatism and secularism, social elitism and the specter of financial failure.

Emily Elizabeth was the second child of EDWARD DICKINSON, the oldest son of Samuel and LUCRETIA GUNN DICKINSON, and EMILY NORCROSS DICKINSON, the daughter of JOEL NORCROSS, a prosperous farmer and businessman, and BETSEY FAY NORCROSS, of nearby Monson. Marrying in 1828, the young couple learned they did not have secure possession of their new home, whose title Samuel owned. Rallying from what must have been a great shock, Edward, a promising young attorney, began working on various real estate deals and, by 1830, on the eve of the poet's birth, succeeded in buying the west half of The Homestead from Samuel. Thus, the poet's parents were enjoying a state of relative financial security when she was born, a hiatus between the uncertainties of their first two years of marriage and the economic difficulties Edward would face in the 1830s. In fact, Emily was born just nine months after Edward had purchased half of The Homestead, suggesting to Dickinson's latest biographer, Alfred Habegger, that she may have been conceived in celebration of that event.

Emily was a middle child. Her brother, WILLIAM AUSTIN DICKINSON ("Austin"), born in 1829, was a year older. In 1833, the year Samuel was forced to leave Amherst, Emily's sister, LAVINIA NORCROSS DICKINSON ("Vinnie") was born. Overwhelmed by the colicky baby, and with her husband distracted by renewed financial worries, Mrs. Dickinson sent two-and-a-half-year-old Emily to stay with her younger sister, LAVINIA NORCROSS, in Monson. The visit with her doting aunt was successful and yielded the earliest description of the poet:

> Emily is perfectly well & contented—She is a very good child & but little trouble—She has learned to play on the piano—she calls it the *moosic*. She does not talk much about home—sometimes speaks of *little Austin* but does not moan for any of you—She has a fine appetite

& sleeps well & I take satisfaction in taking care of her. . . . There never was a better child. . . . She is very affectionate and we all love her very much—She dont appear at all as she did at home—& she does not make but very little trouble.

The passage suggests that the toddler, probably receiving more lavish affection than she got at home, with the advent of a new baby, was thriving with her substitute mother. Aunt Lavinia missed her acutely when she returned home and remembered that "whenever any thing went wrong she would come to me."

If we are to judge from a statement the poet made when she was 40, such comfort was not generally available to her from her own mother. In 1870 Dickinson would tell Higginson, "I never had a mother . . . ," adding, "I suppose a mother is one to whom you hurry when you're troubled." Many have cited this statement as evidence of an early mother-daughter estrangement. Biographers have tended to see Mrs. Dickinson as an emotionally inadequate parent, inarticulate and nonintellectual, and a weak feminine role model to whom the poet was never greatly attached. "My Mother does not care for thought," Emily wrote to Higginson in her early 30s. Images of deprivation in Dickinson's childhood poems, in which she paints herself as "the slightest in the house," a desperate little being who is "locked up in prose" and "starved like a gnat" have contributed to the belief that Emily Dickinson had a "blighted childhood." Those who subscribe to this version of Dickinson's childhood apportion to Edward his share of blame as a gloomy, repressive, patriarchal figure, who thwarted his daughter's normal development.

Yet, while there were doubtless shadows in her childhood—her parents' financial insecurity, their anxieties about sickness and death, her mother's subservience to her husband's will—there were also certain "fundamentals" that made home and childhood sacred for Dickinson all her life. Both Richard Sewall, Dickinson's greatest biographer, and Alfred Habegger, her most recent one and the first to focus on the poet herself as she evolved from year

The house on North Pleasant Street where the Dickinsons lived from 1840 to 1855. This picture was taken c. 1870. *(The Todd-Bingham Picture Collection. Yale University Library)*

to year, rather than on the history of her relationships, dispute the notion of a deprived childhood.

Habegger asks us to consider "the parents' devotion to their first-born daughter and that daughter's attachment, adhesion to them" (*My Wars*, 76). Both Dickinson parents worked hard, Edward at his legal and civil affairs, Mrs. Dickinson at her strenuous housekeeping, but they did not impose heavy chores upon their children. Both were anxious and protective about the health of their progeny, and not without good reason, given the high child mortality rate of the times. Father, who considered

Emily especially frail, was constantly doctoring his offspring: ordering them to bed, plying them with medicines, and sitting up with them through the night. His ministrations became both an "accepted ordeal and a standing family joke" (*My Wars*, 78).

Father's oppressive concern extended to his anxious, fragile wife as well, whose activities he micromanaged, even when away on business. He constantly cautioned the children not to disturb or worry their mother, who had a lot of work and was often exhausted. She had suffered many deaths in her family, including her mother's in 1829, and may have been carrying the burden of repressed grief. Probably, the young Emily, a "good child [who] gave little trouble" (Sewall, II, 325) *did* feel constrained about running to her mother with her worries, a factor, Habegger suggests, that may have been an impetus toward psychological independence.

None of this, however, suggests that Emily was unloved, unloving or repressed as a little girl, and many things suggest the opposite. She appears to have been an affectionate, fun-loving, and witty child, responsive and thoughtful, who reveled in the company of both siblings and playmates. She was closest to her brother, Austin, an exuberant, sensitive, and intelligent boy, who engaged her in a conspiracy against parental stuffiness and injected a mood of general hilarity into the household. The odd man out in the sibling triangle was Vinnie, "the practical Dickinson," who did not share their sensibility. But Emily was affectionate and protective toward her little sister and, when Austin neglected the younger girl, Emily was sure to rebuke him.

There was order and discipline in the Dickinson home and if, as Emily claims in one poem, "They put me in a Closet—/ Because they liked me 'still,'" this liking may have reflected the parents' attempt to counteract the noise and bustle of their crowded living conditions. (Edward's finances enabled them to move to the roomy house on North Pleasant Street only when Emily was 10). In general, however, far from repressing her, her overworked parents may have ignored her to some extent. If she showed early signs of genius, nobody noticed. No one took note of her musical talent until she was 14, when Father bought her a piano.

Ever paradoxical, the same Dickinson who wrote of childhood as a prison often harked back to childhood's lost freedom. "When a Boy," as she put it, associating the free life with the privileges of boyhood, she was allowed to take long rambles through the woods, indulging her early passion for wildflowers. "Two things I have lost with childhood," she wrote after her mother's death in 1882, "the rapture of losing my shoe in the mud and going Home barefoot, wading for Cardinal flowers and the mothers reproof which was more for my sake then her weary own for she frowned with a smile."

When she was five, she entered a public primary school, which she would attend for the next four years, learning to read, write, spell and do simple arithmetic. Since her anxious parents kept her home if she was sick or the weather was bad, she was home a lot, a fact that may explain her

The Dickinson children, Emily Elizabeth, William Austin, and Lavinia Norcross, in a painting by O. A. Bullard, 1840. The artist exaggerated the children's resemblance to one another but was said to have accurately captured Emily's expression. *(By permission of the Houghton Library, Harvard University)*

later problems with spelling. Eager to make home a stimulating place, father subscribed to a leading children's magazine, *Parley's Magazine.* In an age when there was little children's literature, it must have been eagerly devoured by the Dickinson children. Their other reading fare included Isaac Watts's *Divine and Moral Songs for Children,* in one of which wicked children are torn to pieces by bears, and the leading children's evangelical monthly, *Sabbath School Visiter,* which featured stories of horrible deaths suffered by children both deserving and undeserving.

In 1840, a new world opened to the nine-year-old Emily when she entered upon her seven years of study at AMHERST ACADEMY, the secondary school for girls her grandfather Samuel Fowler had helped found. Despite sometimes extended periods of absence due to ill health, she flourished at the academy, which was allied with Amherst College and benefited from both its excellent senior staff and its young graduates who came to teach there. When Emily and Vinnie entered at the beginning of the fall term, there were about 100 girls enrolled, supervised by a "preceptress," who was responsible not only for her pupils' intellectual development, but also for their moral, social, and religious welfare. At the academy, Emily formed friendships she would cherish all her life. Her first intimate circle, "the five," coalesced in the fall of 1844 when Emily's beloved ELIZABETH C. ADAMS was preceptress. The other members were ABBY WOOD, HARRIET MERRILL, ABIAH PALMER ROOT, and SARAH TRACY. She was also close with JANE HUMPHREY, EMILY FOWLER, ELIZA M. COLEMAN, and SOPHIA HOLLAND. Sophia's death at age 15 in 1844 was a shattering experience for Emily. She was in Sophia's home when she died and insisted on being allowed to see her friend's face in death. Critics differ over whether her absorption was "normal," given the Victorian obsession with deathbed scenes, or morbidly excessive. In any case, her parents were sufficiently worried about her state of mind to send her for a month with Aunt Lavinia in Boston, a trip that seems to have lifted her spirits. The following year, Abiah, her closest friend, left to attend another

secondary school, and the two girls began their revealing correspondence.

Among her male teachers, Emily had an important, personal bond with young LEONARD HUMPHREY, the first of a small number of men in her life she would address as "Master," men older than herself to whom she turned for wisdom, counsel, or love. The deepest and most enduring influence, however, was that of EDWARD HITCHCOCK, the president of Amherst College, who was the guiding spirit of the academy during Emily's time there. An eminent geologist and a poet, Hitchcock was a man of God and science, who believed that the evidence of science, rather than contradicting religion, proved it. His inspirational love of nature and celebration of the New England landscape, which combined both a sense of its sublimity with precise observation, resonate with the nature poetry Dickinson would later write.

An outstanding student, she began in the English course but later enrolled in the esteemed classical course for two years. She took three and possibly four years of Latin, as well as history, ecclesiastical history, arithmetic, algebra, botany, and geometry, and classes in composition and declamation. Many years later, teacher Daniel Taggart Fiske remembered her at age 12 as

> a very bright but rather delicate and frail looking girl; an excellent scholar, of exemplary deportment, faithful in all school duties; but somewhat shy and nervous. Her compositions were strikingly original; and in both thought and style seemed beyond her years, and always attracted much attention in the school, and, I am afraid, excited not a little envy. (cited in Sewall, *Life,* II, 342)

If the academy offered Dickinson a stimulating intellectual and personal life, it also steeped her in an atmosphere of orthodox piety. Both textbooks and teachers were expected to ground their teachings in the soil of Christian faith, consistently relating specific subject matter to man's spiritual dimensions. The receptive student was then expected to undergo a religious conversion, a step young Emily did not take. The major REVIVAL that took place during the winter of 1846 made her

Silhouette of 14-year-old Emily, cut by Charles Temple, an Amherst College student from Turkey *(Amherst College Archives and Special Collections)*

anxious for the fate of her soul but failed to persuade her to declare her faith.

Her final term ended on August 10, 1847. The next month she became a live-in student at MOUNT HOLYOKE FEMALE SEMINARY in South Hadley, Massachusetts, seven miles from Amherst, where both her intellectual development and struggle with orthodox religion would enter a new phase. Most of what we know about Emily's year at the excellent secondary school for girls founded in 1837 by MARY LYON, comes from her correspondence with Austin and Abiah. Her intense homesickness ("you must remember that I have a very dear home . . . ," she wrote Abiah) was assuaged by visits from friends and family, as well as by frequent trips home, sometimes necessitated by illness. She adapted well and was in high spirits most of the time. Proud of the school, she energetically pursued its packed curriculum and did extremely well. She studied ancient history, chemistry, physiology, algebra, astronomy, and rhetoric, evoking both envy and irritation among fellow students by her original compositions. At 16, however, her lack of popularity with the boys distressed her. "Your *highly gifted & accomplished elder sister* is entirely overlooked," she wrote to Austin on Valentine's Day.

On the religious level, too, she was a misfit, one of a minority of students who was listed as "without hope" of finding Christ when she arrived, and who never improved her status. Just as she had in childhood and would continue to do as a young woman, Dickinson resisted considerable pressure to convert, or join the church officially. In her final semester, writing to the pious Abiah, Emily admits, "I have neglected the *one thing needful* when all were obtaining it. . . . I am not happy and I regret that last term, when that golden opportunity was mine, that I did not give up and become a Christian. It is not now too late . . . but it is hard for me to give up the world" (L 23, May 16, 1848). This was the first of innumerable times when, in poems and letters, Dickinson would proclaim her preference for the joys of this world over whatever the next might hold.

It was not unusual for students to leave Mount Holyoke after a single year and, when her father decided she should return home, Dickinson seems to have left quite willingly. A sour note was injected into her departure by the snub she received from Abiah, who, after not answering Emily's latest letter, appeared at the Mount Holyoke commencement in August but did not speak to her. Emily reacted with anguish and anger. "Why did you not come back that day, and tell me what had sealed your lips toward me? . . . if you don't want to be my friend any longer, say so, & I'll try *once* more to blot you from my memory." The rift was repaired, but similar avoidance on Abiah's part recurred over the years until, in 1854, their correspondence broke off. Their paths diverged, with Abiah going on to a traditional married life. The pattern of infatuation and subsequent disillusionment Emily experienced with this first bosom friend would be repeated in other close relationships with women. She demanded a great deal of her girlfriends: prompt and extensive replies to her own enthusiastic missives, which most were unable or unwilling to supply, and expressions of love and loyalty, which no doubt frightened some away, as they moved from girlish crushes into heterosexual courtship and marriage.

The loss of friends through this most ordinary route would be a source of sorrow and increasingly loneliness for her over the next several years. But when 17-year-old Emily returned to her parents' home, her formal education at a close, she entered a period of new intimacies and social delights. Amherst, with its vibrant college and frequent eminent visitors, offered rich opportunities for intellectual stimulation. And in her home library, she found what she called a "feast in the reading line." While it may have been true, as Dickinson once told Higginson, that her father preferred her to confine her reading to the Bible, realizing she would not, he supplied her with a rich variety of books. After the Bible, which permeated her consciousness as a "merry and wise book," whose characters were alive for her, no books were more valued by her than Shakespeare's, particularly his tragedies. She revered 19th-century English women writers, particularly Elizabeth Barrett Browning, Charlotte and Emily Brontë, and George Eliot. Ralph Waldo Emerson, Henry Thoreau and Nathaniel Hawthorne were vital presences to her. Of contemporary American novels, Ik Marvel's *Reveries of a Bachelor*, which argued in favor of choosing the "soul-culture" of books instead of dream-destroying marriage, and Henry Wadsworth Longfellow's *Kavanagh*, which describes a love between two young women, similar to what would develop between Emily and SUSAN HUNTINGTON GILBERT DICKINSON, made particularly deep impressions on her.

Particularly after she became a recluse, books, newspapers, and magazines were Dickinson's main conduit for learning about the world. She read voraciously, as if her life depended on it, and her judgment was sometimes questionable. While omitting the works of Walt Whitman, whom she had heard was "scandalous," as a young woman she lapped up the cliché-ridden sentimental literature of the time, with its bathetic death scenes and "pure little lives," works she called "not great, not thrilling—but sweet and true." Her famous last letter referred to a sentimental novel, *Called Back* (1883) by Hugh Conway.

Scholars speak of Dickinson's reading as representing her literary "affinities" rather than solid literary "influences," which are extremely hard to establish in her case. As Sewall notes, she was never the avowed disciple of anyone: "When she disclaimed the conscious use of 'a paint mixed by another person,' she distinguished herself from the tradition of learned poets who used whatever they wanted from their predecessors . . ." (*Life*, II, 669).

Helping her to shape her tastes as an adolescent was BENJAMIN FRANKLIN NEWTON, nine years her senior, one of her most important spiritual and intellectual mentors. She met him in her mid-teens, when he came to Amherst from his native Worcester to work in her father's law office for two years (1847–49). Newton visited the Dickinsons frequently and became her "gentle, yet grave Preceptor, teaching me what to read, what authors to admire, what was most grand and beautiful in nature, and that sublimer lesson, a faith in things unseen, and in a life again, nobler and much more blessed—" (L 53, 1854). Newton's UNITARIANISM stressed life's inherent dignity and the power of the sovereign mind's ability to transcend nature. It thus offered her a vision of immortality far more congenial than the Calvinist precepts of human depravity and an eternity dependent on the judgment of a wrathful God. When Newton left Amherst in 1849, they kept up a steady correspondence, none of which has been found. The loss of these letters is particularly unfortunate, given that they almost certainly would have shed light on Dickinson's development into a poet. Encouraging her poetic sensibility, Newton sent her a copy of Ralph Waldo Emerson's *Poems* (1847). She appears to have welcomed the Sage of Salem's vision of the poet as a figure of immense intuitive power, unafraid to challenge what passes for "common sense" and to be what others call "unintelligible."

Emily made other enriching friendships through Austin, then a student at Amherst College (1846–50). Most of the students and tutors who called on her and Vinnie were members of the Alpha Delta Phi Fraternity, the school's leading "secret society," to which Austin belonged. A group of outstanding young men, including William Cowper Dickinson, HENRY VAUGHAN EMMONS, GEORGE GOULD, and cousin JOHN LONG GRAVES, made the winter of 1849–50 in Amherst "alive with fun" for both Vinnie and 19-year-old Emily. Austin's close friend from preparatory school days, JOSEPH BARDWELL LYMAN, now a student at Yale, continued to regularly visit what he described as "that charming second home of mine in Amherst," romancing Vinnie and having long, intimate talks with Emily. Joseph found her "spiritual" and mentioned her, in a letter to his older brother in 1849, as an exception to the rule that women do not know how to make conversation: "Em. Dickinson is a year younger it is true but older . . . in mind & heart." Their spiritual connection would prove more enduring than his sensual infatuation with Vinnie.

The young people enjoyed long walks, sleigh rides, candy-pulling parties, and evenings of wine and animated conversation at the Dickinson'. Emily shared a passion for literature with most of these young men, particularly with Gould and Emmons. If there was a romantic side to any of these friendships, as was rumored about Gould, nothing came of them. Gould was believed to be the recipient of a comic prose valentine ("Magnum bonum") from Emily that appeared in February 1850, in *The Indicator,* the Amherst student literary magazine. Her first publication, it was a witty send-up of classical learning, biblical rhetoric, current political oratory, and discourses on romantic friendship. The identity of the "anonymous" author was no secret, since Emily, giving herself away, mentions in the verse her dog, Carlo, the black Newfoundland her father gave her that winter. Edward, who believed that women should stay out of the public spotlight, could hardly have been pleased by his daughter's flamboyant literary debut.

Whatever Father's reaction, Emily Dickinson was writing, exuberantly experimenting with style and voice. Habegger believes that she was "in a state of eruption, throwing off the rules her elders had pounded into her" (*My Wars* 230). The previous month, she had written her famous letter (L 29) to her uncle, Joel Warren Norcross. It is an extravagant piece of writing in which she describes a prophetic dream of apocalypse and retribution. In this tongue-in-cheek vision, Uncle Joel is horribly punished for the supreme crime of breaking his promise to write to his niece. If there was real rage behind the letter, as is probable, she had found "a way to structure certain thoughts that to express otherwise would have left her vulnerable in a way she was increasingly trying to avoid" (Sewall, *Life,* II, 385).

The following month, March 1850, she sent her first poem, another comic valentine, "Awake ye muses," to her father's law partner, Elbridge Gerry Bowdoin, a confirmed bachelor, adjuring him to "Seize the one thou lovest, nor care for *space* or *time!*" In 1852, the *Springfield Republican* published her "Sic transit" valentine (Fr 1). She was adept at imitating sermons and in the early 1850s, she wrote other comic valentines that made ironic fun of gender stereotypes and fuzzy clerical thinking. By the early 1850s, the nature of her "golden dream," that vague life ambition she had written of to her friend Jane Humphrey, was starting to crystallize.

At the same time, Emily was coping with the added household responsibilities thrust on her when her mother was stricken with "acute neuralgia." In addition to caring for the invalid, she took on cooking and baking, skills she would excel at and apparently enjoy all her life. (Her famous recipe for "Black Cake" has survived). In the same letter in which she boasted to Abiah about the "twin loaves of bread . . . born into the world under my auspices," she also exclaimed, "God keep me from what they call *households!*" (L 36, May 7 and 17, 1850). Emily is generally assumed to have found her timid mother uninspiring. But the relationship between mother and daughter was more complex. Like her mother, Emily made her home the stage of her life and eventually immersed herself in cooking, baking, and gardening, domestic skills at which her mother had excelled.

The early 1850s was also a painful time. Her two early mentors succumbed to illness at a young age: Leonard Humphrey in 1850, after a brief illness, and Ben Newton, in 1853, after a long struggle with consumption. She was devastated by both deaths. Without Newton, she was deprived of her only source of literary guidance and encouragement in those years. And each year she saw friends marry or graduate from the college and leave Amherst, adding to her sense of melancholy and abandonment.

Another source of her growing isolation was her continuing inability to join the church, as, by now, most of her friends and family had done. Yet if Emily sometimes envied the joyous faces of the converted, she was moving along her own path. In late 1850, she wrote to Abiah:

The shore is safer, Abiah, but I love to buffet the sea—I can count the bitter wrecks here in these pleasant waters, and hear the murmuring winds, but oh, I love the danger! You are learning control and firmness. Christ Jesus will love you more. I'm afraid he don't love me *any!* . . . (L 39)

She may have been alluding to romantic interests, to the development of "unorthodox" ways of thinking, or indirectly hinting at the life of the poet she was envisaging. To be a poet meant a bitter break with the "sweet girl christian" life she was brought up to live (Sewall, II, 389). During the powerful revival of 1850, Father and Vinnie converted; Mother had done so 20 years earlier. That left only Emily and Austin "standing in rebellion" within her immediate family. Then, in 1856, Austin, under pressure from his betrothed, defected. Although Dickinson would struggle with religious questions all her life, she never found it within herself to adopt the language and rituals of established religion. Despite the loneliness entailed by this principled stance, by age 30, Emily was steadfastly refusing, against the wishes of her overbearing, pious father, to accompany the family to church on Sundays.

In 1850, however, religious differences proved no obstacle to Emily's burgeoning friendship with Susan Gilbert, who had just converted. Although the two girls, born in the same year, had known one another for years, the death of Sue's older sister in July of 1850 brought them closer. For Sue, an orphan, who had dreamed of going to live with this beloved sister in Michigan, the loss was especially deep and bitter. With Sue's other sister, Martha, away in Michigan and unable to comfort her, Emily stepped in and established her own sisterly entitlement. At the same time, the dark-eyed, highly intelligent and charismatic Susan attracted several admirers among the Amherst College students, including Austin. When she impulsively left for Baltimore the following September to teach for a year, Emily wrote her a series of intimate, urgent letters. As Polly Longsworth notes, "Emily was quite literally in love with her" and what she sent her "were unmistakably love letters,

more persistently and lyrically romantic than what she was writing to other friends, although they did not far exceed the 19th-century tolerance for intimacy between unmarried females" (*Austin and Sue,* 92–93). The letters indicate how desolate Emily felt without her, though she may have been exaggerating when she expressed fears for her own sanity because of the intensity of her love. We don't know how Sue responded to this intensity, but in the spring of 1853, she became engaged to Austin.

Emily's romantic obsession with Susan was conducted safely through the mails, and appears to have remained within the realm of fantasy. It would be misleading to think of Dickinson as a lesbian, in the sense in which the word is used today, to denote not only sexual practice but also an identity. No such identity was possible for Dickinson (Pollak, *Anxiety of Gender,* 40). There was never any question of her stepping outside the family and social boundaries that defined her daily life and provided her economic security. Nor would she be disloyal to Austin. She acted as confidante and go-between to both Sue and Austin at first, trying to persuade herself that Sue's joining the Dickinson family would make her Emily's as well as Austin's. In fact, Emily would quickly find herself excluded from Austin and Sue's married intimacy and, as the years passed, increasingly estranged from her sister-in-law. She seems to have intuited these impending losses when she wrote to Austin in April 1853 of her loneliness for him, adding, "I wish we were children now. I wish we were *always* children, how to grow up I dont know" (L 115).

The summer after Austin and Sue became engaged, 22-year-old Emily embarked on an important new friendship. ELIZABETH LUNA CHAPIN HOLLAND and her husband, Dr. JOSIAH GILBERT HOLLAND, entered her life during the August 1853 Commencement Week celebrations of the college, when Emily's parents held their famous receptions. The couple came to dine with the Dickinsons in their Pleasant Street home and had, as Emily wrote to Austin, "Champagne for dinner and a very fine time. . . ." So well did they get on that Emily agreed to make a brief visit, together with Vinnie, the following month to the couple's home in Springfield, where Josiah served as literary editor for the *Springfield Republican.*

She reveled in the free-spirited atmosphere of their home, markedly in contrast with her own, reverberating with laughter, literary talks, and the harmony of Elizabeth's piano accompanying Josiah's fine tenor. Of equal importance was the Hollands' relaxed brand of religiosity. Like Dickinson, Dr. Holland rejected doctrine and his way of putting beliefs to the test of feelings authorized Emily to go on trusting her own feelings. She enjoyed herself so well that, despite her growing reluctance to travel, she accepted a second invitation the following September. So began a sustaining lifelong friendship, especially with Elizabeth Holland, seven years her senior, who became her closest friend. Ninety-four of the letters that Emily wrote to the Hollands have survived, most of them to Elizabeth, whom by 1860, she called her "Little Sister." With Elizabeth, an excellent

Sketch of Emily by her brother, Austin *(The Todd-Bingham Picture Collection. Yale University Library)*

listener, Emily found a rapport she lacked with her own mother and turned to her for motherly advice on all kinds of issues.

Yet another pivotal relationship appears to have begun in March of 1855, when Emily is believed to have met the REVEREND CHARLES WADSWORTH in Philadelphia, during a visit to the Colemans, whose daughter Eliza was Emily's close friend. Emily and Vinnie arrived from Washington, D.C., where they had spent three weeks with their father, who was then a member of the House of Representatives. The stay in Washington at Willard's Hotel had been a heady one, filled with numerous social engagements and an excursion to Mount Vernon that seems to have moved Emily more than the "scramble and confusion" of the capital. But Philadelphia would prove to be even more momentous. Although Emily makes no mention of it in her only surviving letter from Philadelphia, to Elizabeth Holland, since the Colemans were Presbyterians and belonged to the Arch Street Church, it is unlikely that she did not attend with them during her two-week stay and hear the famous minister preach.

This hypothetical meeting is the basis of the legend, perpetuated by Emily's niece, MARTHA DICKINSON BIANCHI, that in Philadelphia Emily "met her fate" when she fell in love with a married man. In Bianchi's romantic telling, rejected as simplistic by most commentators, the lovers nobly renounced one another and Aunt Emily dealt with her heartache by withdrawing from society. What we actually know of their relationship is sketchy. Wadsworth visited Dickinson in Amherst in the summer of 1860, a meeting that may be memorialized in her poem, "THERE CAME A DAY—AT SUMMER'S FULL—," in which the lovers briefly "wed" and swiftly renounce their earthly happiness for the promise of a reunion in heaven. Two years later, Wadsworth sailed with his family to San Francisco, where he took over a struggling congregation. So far as we know, Dickinson did not see him again until 1882, shortly before he died. Nothing of their correspondence to one another survives, with the exception of a brief, early note that poses more questions than it answers. Still, Wadsworth is probably the leading candidate for the man Emily called

"Master"—in poems and in three letters written between 1858 and 1861.

Shortly after Emily and Vinnie returned to Amherst in the spring of 1855, Father bought back The Homestead and proceeded to refurbish and expand the mansion that Dickinson would live in for the rest of her life. In November the family moved in, leaving the spacious wooden house on North Pleasant Street, where they had lived for 15 years. Both Emily and her mother missed the old house and Mother, especially, appears to have felt displaced. Her chronic depressive illness began at this time, placing long-term household pressures on both her daughters. Emily became her mother's caretaker, an event that probably reinforced her innate tendency to seclusion.

In January 1856, Emily wrote to Mrs. Holland, "Mother has been an invalid since we came *home* . . . lies upon the lounge, or sits in her easy chair. I don't know what her sickness is, for I am but a simple child, and frightened at myself" (L 182). Apparently feeling her own imbalance, she expresses the fear that her "own machinery may get slightly out of joint" and begs "someone" to "stop the wheel," should this occur.

Scant documentation exists for Dickinson's life between 1855 and 1858, the year she emerged as a full-fledged poet. This is particularly true for the year 1857, for which there is no surviving correspondence. This paucity of letters is only partly explained by the fact that two of her major correspondents, Austin and Sue, married in 1856 and settled in next door at The EVERGREENS. Father had built the Italianate villa for them as a powerful inducement for Austin to give up plans of moving to Chicago, remain in Amherst, and become his law partner. Thus, Emily found herself a lifelong neighbor of the brother she had considered her soul mate and the woman she loved. The psychological impact of this double loss has been the subject of much speculation about the nature of the crisis, possibly a nervous breakdown or even a full psychotic episode, that her family and friends carefully covered up.

In a letter to Uncle Joseph A. Sweetser in early summer of 1858, Emily alluded, somewhat cryptically, to a period of "darkness," which may refer to her mother's troubles as well as her own:

Much has occurred, dear Uncle, since my writing to you—so much—that I stagger as I write, in its sharp remembrance. Summers of bloom— and months of frost, and days of jingling bells, yet all the while this hand upon our fireside. . . . I cannot always see the light—please tell me if it shines. (L 190)

The most extensive case for a psychotic break (caused by early maternal deprivation) is made by psychoanalyst John Cody, in his highly controversial study, *After Great Pain: The Inner Life of Emily Dickinson.* The issue will probably never be resolved. Examining the slim evidence, Habegger concludes that Dickinson clearly experienced "severe and mounting troubles," but questions whether she "became any less capable of performing her usual functions, domestic and compositional" (*My Wars,* 327). What we do know is that many of Dickinson's subsequent poems ("I FELT A FUNERAL, IN MY BRAIN," "AFTER GREAT PAIN, A FORMAL FEELING COMES—," "PAIN—HAS AN ELEMENT OF BLANK—," and "There is a pain—so utter—," to name just a few of the most famous), reflect a period of extreme psychic disorientation.

We also know that she somehow survived the crisis and became a poet. Before 1858 there are only five known poems; in 1858, she wrote the first substantial group of poems, 43 in all, to enter her known oeuvre. That year she began organizing her work by transcribing poems onto sheets of stationary and sewing them into booklets or fascicles, a practice she would follow until 1865. (After this, she organized sheets of poems more haphazardly and did not bind them; these groups are now known as "sets"). She created 40 fascicles or, as they are called today, manuscript books, containing more than 800 poems. Although Dickinson sent many of these poems individually to friends and family, she never shared the booklets with anyone.

From the outset of her writing life, she evinced the ambivalence toward entering the literary marketplace that would result in the publication of only 10 poems in her lifetime. In 1861, she still nourished the hope of a larger poetic success, telling Sue, then her primary reader, critic, and mentor, "Could I make you and Austin—proud—sometime—a great way off— 'twould give me taller feet" (L 238). Yet the following year, in a letter to Higginson, she would deny any desire to publish. Sue and Austin would have valued her literary success, but Father, who believed that public exposure of a woman's achievements was unseemly, would surely have not. And Dickinson, the dutiful daughter, appears to have internalized some of his conservative philosophy. Moreover, as she would write in her famous poem, "PUBLICATION—IS THE AUCTION," compromising one's vision to please the public was anathema to her. Thus, by choosing not to publish she gained artistic freedom at the expense of social validation.

In 1858, in addition to some of her greatest poems, Dickinson wrote the first of three extraordinary letters to a man she passionately loved and addressed as "Master." She would write two more in 1861. The letters, which may have been part of a more extensive correspondence, show her in many moods: devoted, self-effacing, self-justifying, staking her claim to passion and acknowledging the futility of her love. Although some critics have speculated that "Master" was a fantasy, the quality of the emotion expressed in these letters is strongly suggestive of a searing, genuine experience. Scholars continue to speculate as to the identity of the beloved. While Habegger believes that Charles Wadsworth is the most likely candidate for Master, Sewall argues that Master can only have been the crusading editor of *The Springfield Republican*, the abolitionist and supporter of women's rights, SAMUEL BOWLES.

Bowles, extremely handsome, married, and with a propensity for forming relationships with talented single women, entered Dickinson's life in June of 1858 when he came to Amherst and was entertained by Austin and Sue at The Evergreens. Sue had become Amherst's foremost hostess, welcoming a roster of prominent figures, including Emerson, in 1857, to her elegant drawing room. (Emily apparently chose not to meet the great man face to face). Bowles became a frequent guest at The Evergreens at a time when Emily was an active participant in its lively social gatherings, joining in the stimulating conversations, playing the piano, and forming at least one more close friendship—with the lovely young widow, CATHERINE TURNER ANTHON.

As editor of a distinguished newspaper, Bowles might have become a channel to the publishing world. *The Republican* did publish a handful of her poems: "I TASTE A LIQUOR NEVER BREWED—," as "The May Wine"; "SAFE IN THEIR ALABASTER CHAMBERS—," as "The Sleepers"; "BLAZING IN GOLD AND QUENCHING IN PURPLE" and "A NARROW FELLOW IN THE GRASS" as "The Snake," which Sue pirated to him. Unattuned to either her language or her concerns, Bowles never became her literary champion, although Habegger believes that, if Dickinson had been less ambivalent about publishing, *The Republican* would have been open to her.

The nature of her intense relationship with "Mr. Bowles," as she always called him, continues to be the subject of scholarly debate. None of his letters to her survive and the dating of the surviving 50 letters and 35 poems she sent to him and his wife Mary is uncertain. Moreover, Dickinson's language in her letters to him is cryptic, even encoded at times. Not surprisingly, scholars have come up with radically different versions of what transpired between them.

For Sewall, "If her words mean anything at all . . . she was deeply in love with him for several years and never ceased loving him, at a distance, for the rest of her life" (*Life*, II, 473). Habegger takes a more cautious view. While characterizing Bowles as "possibly her most dynamic, volatile, and fascinating male friend," he believes that what she felt for him "wasn't love, or love exactly, but whatever it was it brought out some of her most intense writing" (*My Wars*, 375–6).

In early 1862, she sent him "TITLE DIVINE, IS MINE." with neither salutation nor valediction, only the concluding words: "Here's—what I had to 'tell you'—You will tell no other? Honor—is it's own pawn—" (L 250). Sewall suggests that the poem combines at least three interpretations that are not mutually exclusive: She is becoming Bowles's imagined wife, or sharing Calvary with him, or announcing her vocation to him, in the aftermath of "the agonizing failure of [their] friendship" (*Life*, II, 485). Habegger, however, interprets her sending of the poem as a way of confiding to Bowles her love for someone else, namely Wadsworth.

Whatever the precise nature of her feelings for Wadsworth or Bowles, both men were intensely important to her and both were receding from her in 1862. In April the frantically energetic Bowles left for a trip of several months to Europe, while Wadsworth sailed to San Francisco with his family in May. Austin and Sue, whom Emily had once called "my crowd," were now young parents, enmeshed in a married life that increasingly excluded her. In the view of many scholars, Dickinson survived her personal heartaches through the transforming power of her art. In the early 1860s, the poet, by now in semi-seclusion, began wearing the white dresses that symbolized her "betrothal" to the sacred cause of poetry. Since 1858, the beginning of her seven-year period of "flood creativity," she had been writing prolifically: 82 poems in 1859, 54 in 1860, and 88 in 1861. In 1862 she would write no fewer than 227.

Astoundingly, this was the year she reached out to Higginson, presenting herself as a novice and asking him to be her mentor. Begging Higginson, who had written an article in *The Atlantic Monthly*, "Letter to a Young Contributor," to tell her if her verse was alive, she enclosed four poems with her letter. She had a tendency to adopt a subservient tone when communicating with patriarchal male figures. But her pose may also be seen as a strategy for ensnaring the eminent man of letters in a literary conversation of which she was badly in need. In this, she succeeded. When Higginson, sufficiently intrigued, replied with inquiries about the poet, their lifelong friendship, conducted mostly through letters, began. He never understood her poetry and continually urged her to "normalize" her "spasmodic gait." For her part, she never took his advice, in spite of continuing to sign her letters to him, "Your scholar." If Higginson ultimately failed Dickinson as a literary critic, he nonetheless played a vital role in her life, providing her with a literary friend she could talk to. She read all his articles, which served as a point of departure for their literary discussions.

More than 70 of her letters to him have survived, and, despite a certain amount of posing, they are among her most revealing. Highly literary, thoughtful, and candid about the spiritual and artistic problems of her middle and later years, they tell us much of what we know about her. To Higginson she confided what she had told no one else, "explaining" both herself and her poetry. She presents herself as a loner, isolated within an uncongenial family whose companions are "the Hills—Sir—and the Sundown—and a Dog—" (L 261, April 25, 1862). In response to his inquiring why she writes, she tells him, "I had a terror—since September—I could tell to none—and so I sing, as the Boy does by the Burying Ground—because I am afraid—." The "terror" may refer to her learning about Wadsworth's imminent departure, or to the first hint of her subsequent eye troubles, or to some frightening nervous or mental disturbance. Apart from implying she had just begun to write, to cite this specific fear as *the* explanation for why she "sang" was surely misleading. Instead of the daguerreotype he requests, she sends him a self-portrait reflecting her vision of herself: "I . . . am small, like the Wren, and my Hair is bold, like the Chestnut Bur—and my eyes, like the Sherry in the Glass, that the Guest leaves—" (L 268, July 1862). Thus from the beginning, she both opened herself to him and enshrouded herself in that "fiery mist" of which he would later write.

Shortly after their correspondence began, Higginson, an ardent abolitionist who had been one of the secret supporters of John Brown's rebellion in Harper's Ferry, entered the Civil War as the head of the first regiment recruited from former slaves, in South Carolina. Writing to him then, Emily says only that she wished she had seen him before he became "improbable," adding "War seems to me an oblique place." As critic Shira Wolosky succinctly puts it, "One might say that Emily Dickinson disapproved of reality, and for excellent reasons" ("Public and Private," 107).

Sewall observes that, in her surviving letters to Higginson, "she all but ignored the stirring events of the time and said nothing at all about the great national causes with which he had for years been publicly identified—abolition, women's rights, the plight of the Northern poor" (*Life*, II, 535). Yet recent studies have disputed the view of Dickinson as indifferent to the great issues of her time in general and to the war in particular.

Wolosky argues that the Dickinson family tradition was one of involvement in public life and that Emily was in touch with people who were in touch with the world, including her father, Austin, Bowles, Lyman, Higginson, and Josiah Holland. Some of the most powerful political figures of the time not only visited the Dickinsons but also spent the night, including Massachusetts governor George N. Briggs. Dickinson was a regular, avid reader of newspapers and magazines, including *The Springfield Republican, The Atlantic Monthly* and *Scribner's Monthly.* Her poems include references to elections, economics, politics, and war, both as metaphor and historical reality. Her war poems, which question the justice of a God who permits so much suffering, include elegies for the war dead, particularly for Frazar Stearns, the son of Amherst College's president and a friend of the Dickinsons, who was killed in action on March 14, 1862. (*See* "It don't sound so terrible," Fr 384, "It feels a shame to be alive," Fr 524, "When I was small a woman died," Fr 518, and "Step lightly on this narrow Spot—," Fr 1227.)

Wolosky doubts that it is mere coincidence that more than half of Dickinson's poetic production coincides with the years of the Civil War, 1861–65. Her surviving correspondence for those years is marked by social consciousness, with at least 15 references to the war. They suggest how the carnage of war may have intensified some of her central concerns—the justification for suffering, life's ephemeral nature, the mystery of death, the delicate balance between society's demands and the integrity of selfhood, and the power of redemption through art. In a letter to her cousins, FRANCES AND LOUISE NORCROSS, she wrote:

> . . . Sorrow seems to me more general than it did, and not the estate of a few persons, since the war began; and if the anguish of others helped with one's own, now would be many medicines.
>
> 'Tis dangerous to value, for only the precious can alarm. I noticed that Robert Browning had made another poem, and was astonished—till I remembered that I, myself, in my smaller way, sang off charnel steps. Every day feels mightier,

Frazar Stearns, son of the president of Amherst College, whose death in the Civil War plunged Amherst into grief

and what we have the power to be, more stupendous. (L 298, 1864)

The late war years were a time of personal trial for Dickinson, when she experienced the disabling eye problem that she called "the only [woe] that ever made me tremble. . . . a shutting out of the dearest ones of time, the strongest friends of the soul—BOOKS." The ailment, which first appeared in September 1863, obliged the homebound poet to spend two extended periods in Boston, from late April to late November 1864 and from April to October 1865, under the care of a leading ophthalmologist. The precise nature of the illness remains a matter of speculation; we know only that the treatments she underwent were painful and that she was forbidden to read for a while and spent "part of the time in darkness." One happy outcome of the ordeal was her increasing closeness to her Norcross cousins, the daughters of Aunt Lavinia and Uncle Loring, who lived with her at

Mrs. Bang's boardinghouse in Cambridgeport, one mile from Harvard College. "Fanny and Loo," recently orphaned, were 17 and 23 at the time of Emily's first stay; they adored their older cousin (Emily was 33), who had first reached out to them following their mother's death, and returned her concern by ministering to her needs. Dickinson's candid, extensive correspondence with them is one of her most revealing, despite the censoring done by the cousins before allowing the letters to be published.

Upon her return home from Boston, her last venture into the world beyond Amherst, Dickinson's eyes slowly recovered. She never left the town again. Nor did she usually visit *in* the town, not even at The Evergreens. Nor did she freely receive visitors at home. The tendency to withdraw was there as early as 1854, when she told Abiah, "I dont go from home, unless emergency leads me by the hand, and then I do it obstinately, and draw back if I can" (L 166). As the years passed, her eccentric lifestyle became the object of local curiosity and speculation. When MABEL LOOMIS TODD, who would become Dickinson's first editor, arrived in Amherst in 1881, she wrote to her parents:

> I must tell you about the *character* of Amherst. It is a lady whom the people call the *Myth*. . . . She has not been outside of her house for fifteen years, except once to see a new church, when she crept out at night, & viewed it by moonlight. No one who calls upon her mother & sister ever see her, but she allows little children once in a great while to come in, when she gives them cake or candy, or some nicety, for she is very fond of little ones. She dresses wholly in white, & her

The poet's bedroom on the second floor of The Homestead *(Courtesy the Emily Dickinson Museum)*

mind is said to be perfectly wonderful. She writes finely, but no one *ever* sees her. . . .

For more than a century Dickinson scholars have wrestled with this riddle at the core of her life: What was the cause of her self-imposed seclusion? The legend of her disappointment in love, perpetrated by her niece Martha, was discounted by Vinnie, who insisted that her sister's gradual retreat from society "was a happening." Austin, too, saw his sister's withdrawal as "perfectly natural." While remarking that "at different times Emily had been devoted to several men . . . he denied that because of her devotion to any one man she forsook all others" (*Emily Dickinson's Home*, 374).

In her obituary of the poet, Susan Dickinson sees her seclusion as the suitable choice:

Not disappointed with the world, not an invalid until within the past two years, not from any lack of sympathy, not because she was insufficient for any mental work or social career— her endowment being so exceptional—but the "mesh of her soul," as Browning calls the body, was too rare, and the sacred quiet of her own home proved the fit atmosphere of her worth and work.

This notion is not far from the argument advanced by feminist critic Suzanne Juhasz, who perceives in Dickinson's withdrawal a conscious decision to live within the only realm where, as a woman in a male-dominated era, she had the freedom to fully explore reality: the "Undiscovered Continent," as she called it, of the inner life ("Landscape of the Spirit").

Others have seen her seclusion far less positively, as a manifestation of a psychological disorder. Dickinson's 1869 comment to Higginson, "I do not cross my Father's ground to any House or town," has been cited as evidence that Edward Dickinson's domination "thwarted" his older daughter's life and was responsible for what is regarded as "the tragedy" of her life. There is a high probability that she suffered from agoraphobia—fear of open spaces. She definitely suffered from extreme social shyness. At age 22, a letter to Austin describing the celebration of the opening of the Amherst-Belcher-town railroad, reveals her aversion to crowds and discomfort at the thought that "somebody would see me, or ask me how I did" (L 127).

Dickinson's 20 years of seclusion, between 1866 and her death in 1886, were by no means isolated. After 1866, her poetic production decreased and letters became her primary genre. They were her vehicles for cultivating intimacy with those who led their lives outside the boundaries of the household to which she had confined herself, a psychic space in which she could enjoy the sense of an exclusive bond with each correspondent.

From 1866 to 1869, she wrote only about 44 poems, less than in any one of the previous seven years. She was probably exhausted after her seven years of flood creativity, in one of which (1863) she wrote nearly 300 poems. But another factor was doubtless the absence of regular help in the Dickinson household in the period 1865–69. Emily was obliged to take on all the baking and dessert making, and so had less time for both social contacts and writing. This situation was alleviated in 1869 when a young Irishwoman named Maggie Maher took over as housekeeper, cook, and maid. She would work for the Dickinsons for the next 30 years, becoming a reliable and necessary figure for Emily. In 1870, Dickinson began writing more intensely, producing between 27 and 48 poems a year until 1884, when her final illness began.

In addition to her domestic duties and regular intercourse with Mother, Father, and Vinnie, who, like herself, had not married, Dickinson continued to read avidly, pursue her lifelong passion for gardening, exchange notes with Sue "across the hedge," and treat the children who played beneath her bedroom window to her baked delicacies. "I find ecstasy in living—the mere sense of living is joy enough," she told Higginson.

She also continued to receive a few members of her "select society," including Samuel Bowles, who visited periodically, and Thomas Higginson, who saw her twice, in 1870 and again in 1873. Higginson's account of his August 16, 1870, visit with her at The Homestead provides a unique portrait of the poet in her 40th year:

The Dickinson servants, about 1870, from left to right: Maggie Maher, Tom Kelley, and Margaret Kelley

A step like a pattering child's in entry & in glided a little plain woman with two smooth bands of reddish hair and a face . . . with no good feature—in a very plain and exquisitely clean white pique & blue net worsted shawl. She came to me with two day lilies which she put in a sort of childlike way into my hand & said, "These are my introduction" in a soft frightened breathless childlike voice—& added under her breath Forgive me if I am frightened; I never see strangers and hardly know what to say—but she talked soon & thenceforward continuously. . . . (L 342a and 342b)

Although clearly fascinated by her, he concludes: "I never was with anyone who drained my nerve power so much. Without touching her, she drew from me. I am glad not to live near her."

Dickinson also enjoyed visits with poet, novelist, and Indian rights advocate HELEN FISKE HUNT JACKSON. In 1870, after Higginson showed her some of Emily's poems, the two women began corresponding and soon developed a warm, late-blossoming friendship. "H. H.," as she was called, was unique in recognizing Dickinson as a "great poet" and reminding her of her duty to publish her work. She succeeded in persuading the poet to publish "SUCCESS IS COUNTED SWEETEST" in the anonymous 1878 anthology, A Masque of Poets, brought out by Roberts Brothers of Boston. Readers attributed the poem to Emerson, and publisher Thomas Niles offered to publish a volume of her verse, an invitation she did not pursue.

The early 1870s was also a time of losses. Childhood friend Eliza Coleman Dudley died of consumption in 1871, at age 41; Joseph Lyman succumbed to smallpox in 1872, at age 42. But her most shattering loss came on June 16, 1874, when Father died in Boston while attending the legislative session of the Massachusetts General Court. The cause of death was given as "apoplexy," although his family believed it was the morphine administered to him that killed him. Her description of their last afternoon together, to Higginson, in July 1874, reflects the spectrum of her complicated emotions for this domineering parent whose lonely life she had come to pity:

The last Afternoon that my Father lived, though with no premonition—I preferred to be with him, and invented an absence for Mother, Vinnie being asleep. He seemed peculiarly pleased as I oftenest stayed with myself, and remarked as the Afternoon withdrew, he "would like it not to end."

His pleasure almost embarrassed me and my Brother coming—I suggested they walk. Next morning I woke him for the train [to Boston]—and saw him no more. His Heart was pure and terrible and I think no other like it exists. I am glad there is Immortality—but would have tested it myself—before entrusting him. (L 418)

Devastated by his death, she stayed in her room during the funeral and did not attend the memorial service. She was shocked at her own reaction, telling her Norcross cousins, "I thought I was strongly built, but this stronger has undermined me. . . . Though it is many nights, my mind never comes home" (L 414). Two years later, she told them, "I dream about father every night, always a different dream, and forget what I am doing daytimes, wondering where he is" (L 559). In death, he remained an immense internal presence, a focus for the great questions about death and immortality that obsessed her.

Then, in 1875, Mother became paralyzed from a stroke on the anniversary of her husband's death. She would be an invalid for the rest of her life, with Vinnie and Emily nursing her. After she died on November 14, 1882, Emily wrote to Elizabeth Holland, "We were never intimate Mother and Children while she was our Mother—but Mines in the same Ground meet by tunneling and when she became our Child, the Affection came" (L 792, mid-December 1882). Her letters contain no relief, only shock and grief and a heightened sense of what her mother meant to her. In a poem memorializing her, "To the bright east she flies" (Fr 1603), she characterizes life without her mother as "Homeless at home."

The early death in 1878 of Samuel Bowles, whose unrelenting professional activity had undermined his health, was another severe blow. In the wake of this loss, Dickinson reached out as a fellow mourner to MARIA WHITNEY, the lovely and accomplished single woman with whom Bowles had enjoyed a long, intimate friendship.

That same year, she began her love affair with JUDGE OTIS PHILLIPS LORD. Eighteen years her senior and her late father's best friend, the portly, white-haired judge, feared and disliked by many for his ferocity in the courtroom, seems an unlikely amorous choice for the poet, who was in her late forties when their romance began. Placing the affair within the context of Emily's situation in the late 1870s, Sewall speculates that Lord "brought a release of spirit at a difficult time in her life, with her father gone, her mother a hopeless invalid . . . Bowles dead, Sue apparently long since lost . . .

Austin overworked and depressed, and her literary production and ambition well beyond their peak" (*Life*, II, 654).

Dickinson's surviving letters leave no doubt that she loved Lord and was loved in return. We know that she played with the idea of marriage and that Lord, in fact, made an offer. They never married, no doubt in large part because of the judge's failing health. Two months after his death of a stroke in March 1884, Emily had her first attack of the illness that she would suffer from for the next two years, until her death. The illness, which began

Otis Phillip Lord, the elderly judge with whom Dickinson fell in love in her late 40s *(The Todd-Bingham Picture Collection. Yale University Library)*

with fainting spells and edema, was long thought to be Bright's disease, a liver ailment; but more recent evidence suggests hypertension. Emily offered her own diagnosis when she wrote, "I have not been strong for the last year. The Dyings have been too deep for me, and before I could raise my Heart from one, another has come—" (L 939, autumn 1884). Her "Shepherd from 'Little Girl'hood" and "closest earthly friend," Charles Wadsworth, had died on April 1, 1882; Helen Hunt Jackson would die of stomach cancer on August 12, 1885, leaving her in stunned grief.

Dickinson's most devastating loss, however, was the death of her nephew THOMAS GILBERT DICKINSON ("Gib"), Austin and Sue's eight-year-old son, of typhoid fever, on October 7, 1883. On the night of his death, according to a plausible legend, she visited The Evergreens for the first time in 15 years. His father's idol and the adored "playmate" of his Aunt Emily, Gib was loved by all of Amherst. His death left his parents inconsolable. As Vinnie reported, "Emily received a nervous shock the night Gilbert died & was alarmingly ill for weeks" (cited in Sewall, 146). She was never wholly well afterward.

Evidently knowing she was dying, she wrote her last letter to Fanny and Lou Norcross in May 1886: "Little Cousins, Called back, Emily." The last phase of her illness was marked by paralysis and the "terrible breathing" of coma. Vinnie and Austin were with her when she died at about six in the evening on Saturday, May 15.

Sue washed and dressed the body in a white woolen shroud. The funeral, for which Emily herself had left instructions, was held on the sunny afternoon of May 19 in the presence of a few intimates. In the great parlor, Vinnie called each guest forward to view the body. For Higginson, her face in death held "a wondrous restoration of youth—she . . . looked 30, not a gray hair or wrinkle, and peace perfect on the beautiful brow" (Leyda, II, 475). Higginson read Emily Brontë's "No coward soul am I," telling those assembled that this "poem on Immortality was a favorite [of her] who has put it on—if she could ever have been said to have put it off." Later he noted in his diary, ". . . the sister Vinnie put in [the coffin] two heliotropes by

Emily Dickinson's grave, in Amherst's West Cemetery, is a place of pilgrimage for present-day admirers, who leave flowers. *(Courtesy of Darryl Leiter)*

her hand 'to take to Judge Lord.'" Then the coffin lid was closed and covered with sprays of violets and ferns. Pallbearers carried the casket through a rear door, then gave it to the servants who carried it across fields to the cemetery, keeping always in sight of the house. Dickinson was buried in a plot next to her parents, lined with ferns and pine boughs. Cascades of flowers were heaped on the casket as it was lowered.

After her death, Vinnie followed Emily's instructions and lost no time in burning her correspondence, a common practice of the times. In the course of making the bonfire she would later bitterly regret, she found masses of Dickinson's poems. Emily had not specified that they should be

The Dickinson family plot in West Cemetery, where Emily lies between her sister Lavinia's and her father Edward's graves. The fence in front of Emily's grave is adorned by flowers left by present-day pilgrims. *(Courtesy of Darryl Leiter)*

destroyed, and loyal Vinnie, who believed her sister was a genius, took on their publication as the mission of her life. Thus Dickinson's literary immortality began.

See also LETTERS; PUBLICATION AND EDITORIAL SCHOLARSHIP; MASTER LETTERS.

FURTHER READING

Martha Ackmann, "Biographical Studies of Dickinson," in *Handbook*, Grabher et al., eds., 11–23; Martha Dickinson Bianchi, *Face to Face*; Millicent Todd Bingham, *Emily Dickinson's Home*; Alfred Habegger, *My Wars*; Suzanne Juhasz, "The Landscape of the Spirit," *Critical Essays*, 130–140; Jay Leyda, *Hours and Years*; Vivian R. Pollak, "A Brief Biography," *Historical Guide*, 13–63; Richard B. Sewall, *Life*; Barton Levi St. Armand, *Emily Dickinson*; Cynthia Griffin Wolff, *Emily Dickinson*; Shira Wolosky, "Public and Private in Dickinson's War Poetry, *Historical Guide*, 103–131.

PART II

Poems A–Z

"A Bird came down the Walk—" (1862) (Fr 359, J 328)

This well-known early poem begins with a precise observation of nothing more profound than what its first line implies—a bird coming down the walk, biting an angle worm in half, letting a beetle pass. The narrator is there from the outset, observing, unbeknownst to the bird, and, in stanza 4, cautiously offering him a crumb. At least this is one possibility. As scholar Cristanne Miller notes, the line "Like one in danger, Cautious," an example of "syntactic doubling," may apply syntactically and logically to both the bird and the speaker (*Grammar*, 37–39). The bird is throughout referred to as "He" and the poet speaks of him, playfully, in human terms.

Insinuating herself into the dimensions of the bird's world, she speaks of "a Dew" instead of dew, "a Grass" instead of grass. Her desire to see him as kindred is undercut by the perception that his eating habits are distinctly nonhuman. The bird himself understands he is in a world not wholly his own. In stanza 3, the speaker focuses on the bird's "rapid" eyes that look like "frightened Beads," a noun-adjective pairing that makes him both comprehensible and alien. She admires the stirring of his "Velvet Head," yet the motion indicates the bird's uneasiness as he senses her approach.

Then, halfway through the fourth stanza, the poem takes off just as the bird does. We do not know whether the bird accepts the crumb from the speaker's hand or flies off without it. But as he takes to the air, his droll earthbound behavior gives way to the magic of his flight. By the end of the poem the speaker exchanges her tone of amused condescension for one of awe, as he flies off into a dimension in which she cannot reach him

And he unrolled his feathers,
And rowed him softer Home—

Than Oars divide the Ocean,
Too silver for a seam,
Or Butterflies, off Banks of Noon,
Leap, plashless as they swim.

Departing from precise observation, the speaker can only convey what she perceives by describing the bird in terms of a medium not his own: water. After he unrolls his feathers, he disappears from the poem to make room for the ecstatic images with which his flight is compared. In the vision of oars moving seamlessly through the ocean and of butterflies, making no splash as they leap into the water, the sense of something tiny disappearing in an immensity is idyllic rather than frightening: a blissful merging. The imagery moves from the ocean to the intimate banks of a small river or brook. The speaker conveys her enchantment (and enchants the reader) through the melodiousness of sounds (Oars and Ocean; silver and seam; seam and swim; Butterflies and Banks of Noon; Leap and the onomatopoeic plashless). The image "Banks of Noon" removes us from a literal, physical landscape altogether to an existential one, in which Noon, for Dickinson the moment when life is at its apex, is a leaping-off point into welcoming, navigable waters.

And yet there is a distinct note of longing in the speaker's evocation of this Eden, in which she participates only in imagination. The bird flies Home, just as she, presumably, returns to her own very different one. The natural and the human remain separate, a sense of things that pervades much of Dickinson's nature poetry.

See also "FURTHER IN SUMMER THAN THE BIRDS—," "THESE ARE THE DAYS WHEN BIRDS COME BACK—," and "WHAT MYSTERY PERVADES A WELL!"

FURTHER READING

Charles R. Anderson, *Stairway*, 132–133; Cristanne Miller, *Grammar*. 37–39; Robert Weisbuch, *Emily Dickinson's Poetry*, 137–138.

"A brief, but patient illness—" (1858) (Fr 22, J 18)

Until very recently, when R. W. Franklin published his reading edition of *The Poems of Emily Dickinson* in 1998, the latest and most authoritative version of Dickinson's collected poems, this poem was known to readers in a very different form. The earlier version, included in Thomas H. Johnson's *The Complete Poems of Emily Dickinson*, first published in 1957 (J 18), contained two additional sets of lines. The first was a quatrain at the very beginning of the poem:

The Gentian weaves her fringes—
The Maple's loom is red—
My departing blossoms
Obviate parade.

The second consisted of three famous lines, appearing at the very end of the poem:

In the name of the Bee—
And of the Butterfly—
And of the Breeze—Amen!

Both sets of lines appear in Franklin's edition as separate poems, Fr 21 and Fr 23 respectively.

In analyzing the poem in Franklin's shorter version, it is interesting to observe how it is changed by the omission of these seven lines. The opening omitted quatrain, a clear evocation of autumn, makes it instantly apparent to the reader that the subject of the poem is the death of summer: In metaphorical language, she tells us that the fringe-like petals of the gentian plant are decaying, the maple's leaves have turned red, and the poet's garden is dying, leaving her nothing to "parade." Without these four lines, the poem begins by giving the impression that *someone* has died after a brief illness. The sufferer had only an hour to prepare for what appears to be the swift, pitiless death of an *individual*. We think of a person, not a season, as being ill, preparing for death, being "below" and then joining "the angels." Moreover, by making the illness "patient," rather than the dying one, the poet, somewhat bitterly, implies that the deadly illness was willing to wait as long as possible to achieve its end.

Then comes the whimsical description of the funeral, and we are no longer sure of where we are. Of those in the "short procession" the first to be mentioned is the bobolink, the songbird whose distinctively bubbly song particularly delighted Dickinson. She wrote about it throughout her life in such poems as "We should not mind so small a flower," "Heart, not so heavy as mine," "I'll tell you how the Sun rose—," "The Way to know the Bobolink," "NATURE' IS WHAT WE SEE—," "The Bobolink is gone—," and "No bobolink—reverse his singing." She loved his jaunty, exhilarating song and associated him with joy, swagger, and with herself as the poet who keeps on singing, no matter what external disasters arrive.

The "Brave Bobolink" is a regular member of Dickinson's congregation in nature, a leading participant in the "alternative" house of worship she celebrates in her famous 1861 poem, "SOME KEEP THE SABBATH GOING TO CHURCH—" / I keep it staying at Home—/ With a Bobolink for a Chorister—/ And an Orchard, for a Dome—." In that poem, as in the one under discussion, she thumbs her nose at the formal Christian church and jubilantly proclaims that her heaven is on earth, in the simple delights of nature. In Fr 22 Dickinson is clearly having fun when she reports that the sermon was given by "An Aged Bee."

Then, in the next three lines, she grows sober as those assembled pray. When she says, "We trust that she was willing," she is referring to the willingness to die, based on submission to God's will. Note her use of this term in a letter she wrote to the minister of her first mentor, BENJAMIN FRANKLIN NEWTON, asking to know how he died: "He often talked to God, but I do not know certainly if he was his Father in Heaven—Please, Sir, to tell me if he was willing to die, and if you think him at Home, I should love so much to know certainly, that he was in Heaven" (L 153, 1854). Trusting that Summer accepted her fate, she prays that she and the other mourners may experience the same submissive spirit when their time comes.

The submissive mood changes abruptly, however, in the anguished cry of the last two lines, when she suddenly addresses the departed: "Summer—Sister—Seraph!" With these three two-syllable words, all stressed on the first syllable, she introduces an emphatic trochaic meter into this otherwise iambic poem. The line interrupts the poem's tranquil movement, injecting a heightened sense of loss and longing. Summer, which Dickinson often portrays as a woman, is both earthly Sister and Seraph—an angel of the highest order. The line places these three incarnations on an equal level. They are Dickinson's trinity, and her fervent wish is to rejoin them.

For readers of the earlier version, the poem concluded with yet another trinity, the Bee, the Butterfly, and the Breeze. Echoing the earlier images of Bobolink and Aged Bee, the poet's companions in mourning, she fervently invokes this trinity in what has appeared to many readers as a blasphemous parody of the Christian formula: "In the name of the Father, and of the Son, and the Holy Ghost." Dickinson is less interested in parody, however, than in asserting an alternate spiritual universe. For her, these simple natural elements—the bee and butterfly at work, the breeze that refreshed her and swayed the flowers as she worked in her summer garden—were not sacred in themselves, but her earthly conduits to the sacred nature of reality.

See also "LIKE SOME OLD FASHIONED MIRACLE," "'NATURE' IS WHAT WE SEE—," and "THESE ARE THE DAYS WHEN BIRDS COME BACK—."

FURTHER READING

Walter Hesford, "The Creative Fall of Bradstreet and Dickinson," 81–91.

"A Clock stopped—" (1861) (Fr 259, J 287)

In this masterful poem about death and its irreversibility, Dickinson's organizing metaphor is of man as a clock who ticks to his death. Although the speaker implies she is reporting on a death she has just witnessed, all personal details vanish as she explores a universal vision of what it means to be a human "clock" that has come to the end of his/its "Dial life." Scholar David Porter calls the poem "perhaps her most artful metaphorical excursion in the early period" (*Early Poetry*, 167). And, indeed, its fascination lies in the way Dickinson manipulates the metaphor, so that we can scarcely separate out three levels of existence: the mechanical, the human, and the metaphysical reality of death.

Emily Dickinson's watch, missing its hour hand *(By permission of the Houghton Library, Harvard University)*

In the first stanza, line 2, Dickinson is at pains to inform her reader that the clock that stopped is not one that sits on anyone's mantel, that is, she points to the fact that the clock is a metaphor for a life stopping. In this self-conscious gesture, the speaker betrays some anxiety that her subject be properly understood. Having made it, she goes on to develop the metaphor of a clock with a "puppet" (doll) on it that "bows," presumably when the hour strikes—a stronger image of the human/mechanical connection than a puppetless clock would have been. Note that it is "the puppet" (standing for the mechanism as a whole) that cannot be fixed by even the finest craftsman of Geneva, the capital of precision watchmaking. The master craftsman (the deity) may have created the clock, but he has no power to repair (resurrect) it.

In the second stanza, as the clock goes through its death throes, Dickinson continues to combine human/mechanical imagery to great effect. She belittles the clock by calling it a mere "Trinket," while at the same time making it capable of human "awe" as it experiences the moment of death. The "Figures" (numbers on the clock face) hunch with pain and quiver as "the Trinket" passes from time ("Decimals") into eternity ("Degreeless noon").

Biographer Cynthia Griffin Wolff points out that "Noon is a 'Degreeless' hour because when both minute and hour hand point to twelve, they are superimposed: there is no angle between them; they are separated by *zero* degrees" (*Emily Dickinson,* 192). While the same is true for midnight, had Dickinson written of "Degreeless midnight," the image would have lacked the further implication of (life) heat vanished from the day's center, when the sun is directly overhead. Moreover, Dickinson's choice of noon reflects her sense of that moment in the celestial cycle, developed in many other poems, as

> a token of the instantaneous, arrested present which is timelessness, or eternity, or heaven, when all accident or "grossness," is discarded and there is nothing but essence. . . . "Degreeless Noon" is the timelessness of death. (Sewall, *Life,* II, 681)

Having made its passage from life to death, the human "clock" is beyond either medical or mechanical help. (By "Doctor's" [*sic*] Dickinson undoubtedly means the plural, "Doctors"). God is reduced to a "Shopman" who can only "importune it," that is, urge it repeatedly to come to life again, to no avail. For the human "clock" has grown increasingly disembodied, its pendulum turned to snow, an image that rhymes and, in its coldness, resonates with "Cool—concernless No." In this memorable image, *No* becomes a noun, a force, the very principle of negation in a poem in which negation is a prominent feature, (note the neologisms "Degreeless" and "concernless"). "'No' is the wildest word we consign to Language," Dickinson wrote to her suitor, JUDGE OTIS PHILLIPS LORD (L 562). Miller speculates that this is because "*No* opens the doors that normal definitions close" (*Grammar,* 99). In this instance, *No* is a personification of Death, probably the most depersonalized one in all of Dickinson's writings. Perhaps the most famous of Dickinson's personifications appears in "BECAUSE I COULD NOT STOP FOR DEATH—," where death is a gallant suitor who takes the speaker on a carriage ride toward eternity. Here death has no outward form or action other than negating; death is nothing. On the linguistic level, the *noon* of "Degreeless noon" has broken down into its components: the word *no* facing itself. *Noon* is also contained in the double *o* of *cool*—a word that resonates with coldness (as warm life seeps away), which is another implication of "Degreeless."

This melding of sound groups and semantics continues in the fourth stanza, where *No* is literally a part of the repeated word *Nods.* In the first two lines it is *No* or death that nods from the "Gilded pointers" and "Seconds slim"—an image that both reinforces the external elegance of the mechanism and suggests the insubstantial nature of time. The last three lines are elliptical and might be paraphrased as follows: "*There are* Decades of Arrogance between / The Dial life—/ And Him—." This is the speaker's parting observation on the death of the human "clock," an attempt to give some perspective to the experience. "Decades of Arrogance" (exorbitant claims of rank, dignity, or power) must refer to humans, since human lifetimes are counted in decades. The image seems to point to the vanity and blindness of human beings, who will ultimately be humbled by "Degreeless noon." In Dickinson's world, *arrogance* was a word with strong biblical associations, as in Isaiah 13:11: "and I will cause the arrogance of the proud to cease." The last lines of this poem borrow the prophetic resonance, but within a very different religious context. For the "Him" of the final line, which *looks* like a traditional reference to God, actually refers to death or "concernless No"—a paradoxical god of negation. "The Dial Life"—is time measurable, within which man lives his misguided decades, before encountering Him. The neat, exact concluding rhyme of "slim" and "Him" seems to "rub in" the uncompromising message.

See also "FURTHER IN SUMMER THAN THE BIRDS—," "IT WAS NOT DEATH, FOR I STOOD UP," and "SAFE IN THEIR ALABASTER CHAMBERS—."

FURTHER READING

Sharon Cameron, *Lyric Time,* 104: Cristanne Miller, *Grammar,* 98–104; David Porter, *Early Poetry,* 167;

Richard B. Sewall, *Life,* II, 681; Cynthia Griffin Wolff, *Emily Dickinson,* 190–194.

"A Coffin is a small Domain" (1864) (Fr 890, J 943)

In this DEFINITION POEM, Dickinson uses geographical and spatial imagery to speak about death and immortality, time and timelessness. She begins with a paradox: The physical smallness of the coffin is able to contain something immeasurably vast: "A Citizen of Paradise." The image of the coffin or grave as a "Small domain" resonates with similar this-worldly or homey images found in her poems, where the grave is a bed, a room, an inn, a town, as in "AMPLE MAKE THIS BED—," "SAFE IN THEIR ALABASTER CHAMBERS—," "I went to Heaven—/ 'Twas a small Town—," "WHAT INN IS THIS," "the little Dwelling Houses rise" ("The Color of the Grave is Green"), "adjoining Room" ("I DIED FOR BEAUTY—BUT WAS SCARCE"), "Doom is the House without the Door—," and many others. Like these images, the democratic notion of a "citizen of Paradise" allows poet and reader to conceptualize the dead person in a familiar and comforting form: He or she is still a citizen, a member of a greater polity, someone with duties and rights, foremost of which is victory over death.

But in the second stanza, the poem breaks away from its original tone and message. The first line is a variant of the first line of stanza 1, but with an essential difference: In the phrase "restricted Breadth", it is impossible not to hear "restricted breath"—a diminished, disembodied transformation of the "citizen of Paradise." As if to counteract that somber vision, the next three lines assert the superior grandeur of the grave to all earthly—and solar—spaces. What are we to make of this hyperbolic assertion? Dickinson certainly loved the earth and celebrated nature as a holy temple (See "SOME KEEP THE SABBATH GOING TO CHURCH—"). Yet the mysteries of death and immortality held a greater sway over her imagination. She states this explicitly in the 1865 poem: "The Overtakelessness of Those/ Who have accomplished Death—/ Majestic is to me beyond/ The Majesties of Earth—" (Fr 894). At first glance, another assertion of the victory of immortality over the constriction of the grave, the second stanza is actually ambiguous: Is the grave so immense because of the immortality of the one whose body it contains—or because of the immensity of the grief of the mourner?

The question only deepens in stanza 3, where the coffin/grave has become a "small Repose," and the "citizen of Paradise" has reappeared in the more poignant, personal form of a "single Friend." The vision of the physical place of burial has shifted toward stillness, loss, immobility: from a Domain (full of life) to a restricted Breadth (a reduced space, the constricted breath of the dying), to repose (a nonspatial image implying the sleep of death). Although the verb is missing, the last two lines say that "To Him" who buries a friend *comes* "Circumference without Relief—/ Or Estimate—or End—." *Circumference* is a key word for Dickinson, which appears in her correspondence and in 17 poems. Circumference was central to her notion of poetry; it was her word for the poet's proper domain, a place where she encounters both revelation and the limits of knowledge. In this poem, *Circumference* implies the limits of what can be humanly known about death and eternity. This limitation is itself a state "without Relief," and in this sense, it is another dimension of grief for the dead friend. "Without Estimate" negates the poem's previous claim to define the relative dimensions of life, death, and immortality. The notion of "without end" has been transformed from "life without end" to "suffering without end."

The poem's initial attempt to affirm containment was reinforced by a regular meter and a rhyme scheme containing more regular rhymes than the slant or partial ones Dickinson often uses. In stanza 1, not two but three of the four lines rhyme exactly. Yet shape dissolves in the poem's final words and the final dash underscores this, giving a sense of openness. The attempt at a neat and satisfying definition falls apart and we are left with the tormenting mystery of mortality.

FURTHER READING

Sharon Cameron, *Lyric Time*, 236–38.

"A Dying Tiger moaned for Drink—" (1863) (Fr 529, J 566)

Among Dickinson's poems about thirst and hunger, this one is unusual, both for its exotic imagery, and for the fact that the speaker is not the one who is thirsting or hungering, but the one who tries to provide sustenance and fails. In the narrative of this poem, the tiger, a mighty, masculine beast, is dying of thirst in the desert. The speaker tries to bring him water, searches the arid place thoroughly, catches drippings from a rock in her hand and brings it to him, but she is too late with her meager offering. The tiger has died while she was searching for what could save him.

While tiger and speaker have been spatially separated in stanza 1, in stanza 2 they come together in the tiger's eyes. The phrase "mighty Balls" refers to the tiger's eyeballs. The choice of *balls* rather than *eyes* was probably based on sense and sound considerations. "Mighty balls" is a visual images whereas "Mighty eyes" are hard to envision; and the *m, b* and *l* sounds of "mighty balls" resonates with "My blame" and "his blame." Although "thick" in death (a reference to the eyes filming over), the tiger's eyes are still open: The speaker peers into these unseeing eyes and sees "A Vision on the Retina/ Of Water—and of me—." Despite its unusual imagery, this is one of Dickinson's deathbed scenes, in which the speaker strains to understand death by observing the experience of dying. The speaker has returned when the tiger is already dead, but the vision on his dead retina tells her what obsessed the tiger until his final moment: the object of his desperate need (water) and its location—just beyond his reach. The vision on the tiger's retina is also, of course, the vision of the speaker's failure to save him.

But in stanza 3, where she evaluates what happened, the speaker exonerates both herself—"who sped too slow"—and the tiger—who died while

help was on the way. Instead, what is to blame is "the fact that He was dead—." Does this strange assertion imply that blame lies in the fact that death exists at all? Or is this simply Dickinson's way of saying that there is no way to place blame in an impersonal and incomprehensible universe? To blame a "fact" is to blame both nothing at all—and everything, the very conditions of existence. At least one critic finds this stanza an unconvincing attempt at rationalizing the speaker's guilt: "The hardness of response, here, is a denial of feeling, a this-has-nothing-to-do-with-me statement. Yet the guilt is there, despite the denial. If there were no guilt, there would be no poem" (Pollack, 73). Pollack compares this poem with "I bring an unaccustomed wine," another poem in which the speaker tries unsuccessfully to minister to the dying, and concludes, "Inevitably, the starved self does not have the emotional or the practical resources to function as a nurturer" (72).

While the sense of personal failure and inadequacy as a nurturer is a central part of the poem, it does not exhaust its meanings. What we make of the poem depends on how we interpret the tiger and his relationship to the speaker. On the most literal level, the poem might be read as expressing her haunted sense of failure to convey some life-giving nurture to a powerful male figure in her life. Or as a powerful, masculine beast the tiger may represent the male-dominated world in which Dickinson lived, here rendered harmless by the fact that he is dying of thirst. By transferring her own helplessness in that world to the tiger, she brings about a sympathetic bond with him. But it is also possible, within the spare, primitive, dreamlike setting of the poem, that suggests a half-buried psychic landscape, to see the tiger as an aspect of the poet herself. In the poems in which the speaker herself is starving, and practicing the survival art of living on a crumb, she is a tiny creature—a bird, a sparrow, less than a gnat. To express that part of herself that desires hugely, cannot slake its need in the dry world in which it is stranded, *yet does not know how to starve and survive*, Dickinson uses the image of the powerful masculine tiger. His would-be rescuer, that part of the poet that interfaces with the world and tries to bring back what will keep the tiger/desire alive, is persistent but ineffectual. In Dickinson's world, survival depends on knowing how to do without. Clearly the sparrow has greater resources than the tiger.

See also "GOD GAVE A LOAF TO EVERY BIRD—," "I HAD BEEN HUNGRY, ALL THE YEARS—," "IT WOULD HAVE STARVED A GNAT—," and "UNDUE SIGNIFICANCE A STARVING MAN ATTACHES."

FURTHER READING

Vivian R. Pollak, "Thirst and Starvation," in *Critical Essays*, Judith Farr, ed., 62–75. Richard Wilbur, "Sumptuous Destitution," in *Critical Essays*, Judith Farr, ed., 53–61.

"After great pain, a formal feeling comes—" (1862) (Fr 372, J 341)

Emily Dickinson was an anatomist of pain. She used the word in no less than 50 poems, and its variants—agony, despair, grief, hurt, and suffering—countless times. Seeking to define the nature and course of the "ailment" she knew only too well, Dickinson took up the subject again and again, throughout her career, attacking it from different perspectives and in different states of mind, Not surprisingly, therefore, her writings on pain contain a spectrum of attitudes. In a poem such as "IF YOUR NERVE, DENY YOU," she counsels emotional intrepidity, the necessity of feeling to the utmost, in spite of pain and fear. Yet in numerous poems she writes of the emotional numbness that comes after "great pain" and is essential to personal survival.

In this poem, she describes this state of numbness with the oxymoron "a formal feeling," that is, a kind of ritualized "nonfeeling," fixed by custom or habit—the opposite of living, spontaneous emotion. Throughout the poem she evokes this state in terms of inorganic materials: "Wooden way," "Quartz contentment," "Hour of Lead." She conveys a sense of estrangement and lack of emotional integration through the personification

of the Nerves, the Heart, and the Feet, all elements of a feeling, active individuals that carry out their separate functions, but do not communicate with one another. The vision is similar to that of a poem written the following year, "I TIE MY HAT—I CREASE MY SHAWL—," in which a kind of mechanical behavior, the carrying out of "Life's little duties" replaces and attempts to disguise from others the death of a vibrant inner life. In "After great pain," Dickinson evokes a less functional, more severe state of estrangement, verging on spiritual death. Biographer Charles R. Anderson, who considers this work "her most remarkable poem rendering the extinction of consciousness by pain," suggests that the three stanzas "faintly shadow forth three stages of a familiar ceremony: the formal service, the tread of pallbearers, and the final lowering into a grave" (*Stairway*, 238). In a related poem of 1865, "I've dropped my brain—my soul is numb—," Dickinson writes "My nerve in marble lies." In this poem, her nerves are themselves tombs, receptacles for her dead ability to feel.

The "stiff Heart" is estranged from its own former capacity to bear great pain and has lost its ability to place the experience in the recent or distant past. The Feet are indifferent as to whether they "go round" on the ground, in the air, "or Ought"—on whatever other medium they may find themselves. The famous image of "A Quartz contentment, like a stone—" floats syntactically in the air, without a clear referent, appropriately since there is no solid entity to which it can attach itself. Dickinson, who had a solid basis in geology through her studies with EDWARD HITCHCOCK at the AMHERST ACADEMY, may have chosen "quartz" for its sound value, but she also knew that quarts is a very hard, crystallized mineral, that is, one that has grown fixed. "A Quartz contentment" is thus another permutation of the state of numbness, but with the added sense of something enviable. It is reminiscent of an idea she develops in a later poem, "How happy is the little Stone" (Fr 1569, 1882). The unfeeling stone is "happy" in the sense of "fortunate," precisely because it has no feelings.

The final permutation of this notion is the "Hour of Lead," lead being the "least elastic and sonorous of all the metals," as noted in Dickinson's lexicon. This is a time "Remembered, if outlived," but the way it will be remembered—as someone dying in a snowdrift experiences the process of losing consciousness—suggests the unlikeliness of survival, reinforcing the image of death ("Tombs") in stanza 1.

While the poem chillingly evokes the surrender to cold and stupor, Emily Dickinson, as we know, survived whatever personal ordeal motivated its writing. As for the nature of that ordeal, Dickinson scholars have long debated whether Dickinson went over the brink of madness at some point in her life or only teetered on it. Critic John Cody, who took "After great pain" as the title of his psychoanalytic study of Dickinson, has made perhaps the fullest case that the poet did, in fact, experience a mental breakdown. For him, the poem under discussion is a precise description of the acute phase of a psychotic illness, which, he believes, overcame the poet in the late 1850s, characterized by catatonia—a psychotic state of extreme inertia and stupor, as well as rigidity of the limbs ("The Feet, mechanical, go round—/ A Wooden way"). Cody presents an intriguing "reconstruction" of Dickinson's psychic history, in which the 1856 marriage of her beloved brother, WILLIAM AUSTIN, to the woman she depended on as a "mother-substitute," SUSAN GILBERT (DICKINSON), left Emily desolate and abandoned. He hypothesizes that her fragile "defense mechanisms" gave way, releasing repressed rage and unacceptable sexual impulses, which, in turn, led to a breakdown of her sense of reality. Since Cody published his work in 1971, numerous scholars have taken issue with his thesis. The objections of Dickinson's biographer Richard B. Sewall are representative of their arguments. He notes that no mention of the poet's breakdown has been found in the writings of her family and friends and that "Her production alone, with all the other things she had to do about the house, shows how firmly she kept her faculties under control during [this] time . . ." (*Life*, II, 491). (Cody anticipated this latter objection and argued in his book that psychotics are quite capable of writing coherent poetry).

While this irresolvable debate is likely to continue, it is largely irrelevant to the poem itself as it affects its readers. Whatever Emily Dickinson's personal experiences, this would not be the great poem it is if it did not speak to the aftermath of many kinds of "great pain." Dickinson's triumph was to have found universal imagery for the psychic experience she observed with such exactness. Robert Weisbuch, who likens this poem to Edvard Munch's famous painting of a "frozen scream," notes that Dickinson's poems about extreme suffering "say precisely nothing about Dickinson's unique experience. But they do afford an extraordinary comfort precisely because different people can bring their trouble to them. The poems in this sense are an autobiography not of Dickinson but of the reader" ("Prisming," 217).

See also "I FELT A FUNERAL IN MY BRAIN," "I LIKE A LOOK OF AGONY," and "PAIN—HAS AN ELEMENT OF BLANK—."

FURTHER READING

Charles R. Anderson, *Stairway of Surprise*, 238–239; John Cody, *After Great Pain*, 291–355; Kamilla Denman, "Emily Dickinson's Volcanic Punctuation," in *Critical Essays*, Judith Farr, ed., 192–193; Joanne Feit Diehl, *Romantic Imagination*, 44–48; Alfred Habegger, *My Wars*, 409; Richard B. Sewall, *Life*, II, 491–492; Robert Weisbuch, "Prisming," in *Handbook*, Grabher et al., eds., 216–217; Cynthia Griffin Wolff, *Emily Dickinson*, 468–469.

"A little East of Jordan" (1860) (Fr 145, J 59)

This early poem is a dramatization of the story of Jacob's wrestling with the Angel of God, as recounted in Genesis 33:24–32. This is a time of reckoning for Jacob, as he prepares to meet his brother Esau, whom he had cheated of his birthright many years before. Esau is advancing with an army of 400 men, and Jacob, plagued by guilt for his past deed, fears the worst. Jacob wrestles with "a man" whom he defeats and refuses to release until "the man" blesses him. God then reveals his identity and gives Jacob his blessing, together with a new name: "Thy name shall be called no more Jacob, but Israel: for as a prince thou hast power with God and with men, and hast prevailed" (33:28). Jacob is now defined by the role he plays, for Israel means "the one who wrestles with God." Jacob/Israel, in turn, performs an act of naming: "And Jacob called the name of the place Peniel: for I have seen God face to face, and my life is preserved" (33:30). The next day Esau arrives with his followers, but, to Jacob's boundless relief, he greets his long-lost brother peaceably, with tears of joy.

As biographer Cynthia Griffin Wolff notes in her important discussion of this subject, the story of Jacob and the Angel of God was the primary text for the REVIVALS that repeatedly swept through AMHERST during Dickinson's girlhood (*Emily Dickinson,* 144). For centuries Protestantism had viewed Jacob as a kind of Everyman figure. Like Jacob, Christians who hoped for salvation could win God's blessing, not by passive obedience, but by actively struggling with Him—and their own consciences. Although Emily Dickinson was never able to make the public commitment of faith expected of those who emerged from such God-wrestling, the story remained alive for her. Biographer Richard B. Sewall points out that, for Dickinson, "The Biblical characters, especially the Old Testament ones, lived . . . as vitally, and often as secularly, as any out of Shakespeare or her favorite novelist, Dickens" (*Life,* II, 698). She once wrote to her close friend, ELIZABETH LUNA CHAPIN HOLLAND, about an inner conflict she was having (about 1881): "Jacob versus Esau, was a trifle in Litigation, compared to the Skirmish in my Mind."

Dickinson's recasting of Jacob's story in this poem was heavily influenced by the new 19th-century sermon style, which was replacing the imaginatively restrained, doctrinally oriented Calvinist preaching of the past. This style, of which Emily's revered REVEREND CHARLES WADSWORTH was a master practitioner, was characterized by "diverting narrative, extensive illustrations, and even colloquial humor" (David S. Reynolds, "Emily Dickinson and Popular Culture," 168). Thus, in a sprightly storytelling style, Dickinson depicts the struggle as one between "A Gymnast and an Angel." The term *Gymnast* is not only an anachronism within the biblical context, it portrays Jacob as a physical being whose skill or merit is purely athletic: He undergoes a number of metamorphoses in the course of three brief stanzas: from "Gymnast" to "Jacob" to "cunning Jacob" to "bewildered Gymnast." The names Dickinson gives him track his stature: from nameless athlete to someone with a name, the legendary biblical figure, who then acquires an epithet denoting shrewdness, but who in his final appearance is once more demoted to a nameless athlete, utterly confused by what has happened to him. Thus, although Jacob triumphs and wins God's blessing, his triumph is somewhat dimmed by the sense that he has been a player in a drama he does not understand. The "Angel," who becomes a hungry angel in stanza 2, eager "To Breakfast—to return" and a "Stranger" in stanza 3, emerges as "God"—the final word of the poem. Thus, even as the two figures wrestle with one another, so do the meanings Dickinson assigns them, making the poetic outcome more ambivalent than the physical one depicted.

Critics have most often viewed this poem as a parable for her own "worsting" of an orthodox Christian God, whose terms—notably surrender of her own evolving judgments and sensibilities to a fixed doctrine—she could never accept. For Joanne Feit Diehl, it "takes as its subject a poet's birth, for it describes the struggle she thought essential before the individual imagination could *wrest* from God the power to create poems. . . . It is through discord, not harmony, through wrestling, not quiet affirmation, that Dickinson's Jacob witnesses the coming of a new day" (*Romantic Imagination,* 38–39). Biographer Thomas Johnson sees the struggle somewhat differently, as a "wrestling match" in which the poet strove to master the powerful creative force that possessed her.

Dickinson's later writing lends credence to this line of interpretation. Writing to THOMAS WENTWORTH HIGGINSON, the spring she died, after commenting on her illness and affectionately remembering him and his family, she writes playfully: "Audacity of Bliss, said Jacob to the Angel 'I will not let thee go except I bless thee'—Pugilist and Poet, Jacob was correct—." In this last letter to the man she called her mentor but who failed to grasp the nature of her poetic genius, she reversed the role of Jacob and Angel, and assumed the role of the one who blesses. For Dickinson's most recent biographer, Alfred Habegger, this passage indicates the poet's understanding that "her lyric vocation was a function of her essential lifelong struggle. Yielding to the nature of things no more than she had 'given up' to the Savior during the revivals of her youth, she asserted her own powers of 'pagan' ecstasy and sublime thought. She had been a defiant rule-breaker, and now, in her last defiant paradox, she declared that *that* was what made her 'correct'" (*My Wars*, 621).

In Genesis, God both blesses Jacob and wounds him in his thigh, giving him a permanent limp—an aspect of the story Dickinson knew well but chose not to include in her retelling. Significantly, although the gymnast of this poem is "bewildered" by his astonishing triumph, he emerges whole. Dickinson would return to the paradigm of two figures wrestling until dawn in her poetry many times (see, for example, "Two swimmers wrestled on the spar—" and Fr 221, "He was weak, and I was strong—then—"), but never with the sense of elation and amazement found here.

See also CONGREGATIONALISM and PURITAN HERITAGE.

FURTHER READING

Joanne Feit Diehl, *Romantic Imagination*, 38–39; Alfred Habegger, *My Wars*, 621; Thomas Johnson, *Emily Dickinson: An Interpretive Biography*, 74; David S. Reynolds, "Emily Dickinson and Popular Culture," in *Cambridge Companion*, 168; Richard B. Sewall, *Life*, II, 698–699; Cynthia Griffin Wolff, *Emily Dickinson*, 143–153.

"Alone, I cannot be—" (1862) (Fr 303, J 298)

This poem begins as if Dickinson, who had entered upon her years of seclusion, were answering the query, "How do you manage to be alone so much?" or "Don't you mind being alone so much?" She answers assuredly, with a boast, that she can never be alone, since she is in the constant company of "Hosts." We expect a poet to be visited by the Muse. Dickinson's muse, however, is no solitary, occasional visitor, but "Hosts"—a term whose basic meaning is "masses." If we interpret the poem as an expression of Dickinson's sense of poetic fecundity, then the word is indeed appropriate. In 1862, the year she wrote this poem, Dickinson also wrote 226 others (Fr 272 to 498). In claiming that the Hosts are "never gone," she is describing the never-ending stream of inspiration that possessed her during her years of flood creativity.

The term "Hosts" suggests the heavenly Hosts of angels and, indeed, an aura of divinity surrounds these visitors; but this is only the starting point of the extended definition of them that constitutes the rest of the poem. In lines 3 and 4 of the first stanza, "Recordless Company—/ Who baffle Key—," they become ethereal and mysterious. "Recordless" is a neologism, implying "not recorded, registered, imprinted, or remembered." The fact that they can enter without having a key suggests that they are bodiless. In contrast, the noun with which "Recordless" is paired—"Company"—suggests a royal or military retinue. Yet, the members of this retinue have neither robes nor names. Dickinson defines them *by what they are not*. In a characteristic strategy for suggesting meanings that are not encompassed by ordinary language, she uses negatives (no, nor, not) "to create a kind of negative definition . . . [which] illuminates the subject of a poem by specifying what it is not, or by contrasting it with more easily named experiences and phenomena" (Miller, 99). Thus, she tells us that her visitors are *not* palpable beings, clothed with robes or identifiable by individual names; they are *not* beings with any need for almanacs (calendars of the days, weeks, and months, with the times of rising and setting of the sun and moon). And they are *not* associated with any particular "climes" (climates or particular regions of the earth). They are independent of both time and place.

What we are told about them in positive terms is that they have "general Homes / Like Gnomes—." The phrase is striking for its linking of domestic and mythic imagery. In Dickinson's lexicon, gnomes are imaginary beings that inhabit the interior of the earth and are the guardians of mines and quarries. They are thus associated with the inner world and its buried riches. Significantly, Dickinson used the word to designate herself as a poet; she frequently signed her letters to her chosen literary mentor, THOMAS WENTWORTH HIGGINSON, "Your Gnome," alternating this signature with "Your Scholar." A secondary meaning of "gnome" is a maxim. Scholar Judith Farr suggests that Dickinson used the term for herself to indicate that her poetic gifts were "gnomic" (dealing in maxims) or aphorisms—pithy summations of general truth (*Passion,* 348, n46).

In the final stanza, the speaker gives two more indications of the nature of her visitors: Their arrival is known to "Couriers within"—the poetic receptors of inspiration who relay its presence to the soul, or to that part of the soul that makes poetry; and "they're never gone." Related thematically to the gold that falls continually in "I WAS THE SLIGHTEST IN THE HOUSE—" and to the sense of boundless inspiration that permeates "I TASTE A LIQUOR NEVER BREWED—," the poem expresses Dickinson's awareness of her poetic genius. Unlike the unbridled intoxication of the latter poem, however, this one is a cautious exploration of what can be known or said about the mysterious forces that possess her.

As in many of Dickinson's poems, she achieves closure and draws attention to her final, climactic statement by varying the basically simple metrical and rhyme scheme. In the final stanza, she abandons the regular iambic movement of the first two stanza, with their exact or partial rhymes. The third line, with its stark absence of rhyme, points up the stark reality of what is "not" known about the ever-present visitors. (Porter, *Early Poetry,* 118–119).

See also "I DWELL IN POSSIBILITY—," "IT WAS NOT DEATH, FOR I STOOD UP," and "THEY SHUT ME UP IN PROSE—."

FURTHER READING

Christianne Miller, *Grammar,* 98–104; D. Porter, *Early Poetry,* 118–119.

"A loss of something ever felt I—" (1865)   (Fr 1072, J 959)

This poem was written in 1865, one of the "flood years" of creativity, in which Dickinson wrote 229 poems; she was 35, no longer attending church, rarely venturing beyond the hedge of the family compound. In this poem, which critics have spoken of as an expression of religious doubt and statement of intellectual honesty, Dickinson recalls the sense of ineffable longing for something lost, an awareness that was always with her, inseparable from her consciousness. In stanzas 1 and 2, she envisions herself as a child Mourner—an image related to other poems about childhood deprivation: She was impoverished, bereft of something from the first. At the same time, she suggests a kind of inverse chosenness: The child Mourner's precocious understanding sets her apart from other children. She carries within her something hidden, a heresy she was too young to be suspected of. The lines suggest Wordsworth's "Intimations of Immortality," with its evocation of the child who arrives "trailing clouds of glory," that is, with knowledge of the divine, which fades as life goes on. In Dickinson's child Mourner, however, the emphasis is not on the glorious remnants of this knowledge, but on the sense of longing and loss. Her first *conscious* knowledge was of the *absence* of divinity. As in Wordsworth, aging is seen as growing into a "fainter" wiseness.

What she has lost is embodied as a place: "a Dominion," "my Delinquent Palaces," "the site of the Kingdom of Heaven." In lines 7 and 8, stanza 2, we encounter one of those moments when Dickinson's personal grammar can be confusing to the reader. Standard grammar suggests that the Dominion becomes "Itself the only Prince cast out." The Dominion itself is in exile—a more absolute and devastating estrangement than its being merely unavailable to the speaker of the poem. In a strange transformation of the biblical account of Lucifer, the Prince of Darkness, who is cast out of heaven, heaven itself is cast out of some higher, unspecified realm. What seems more likely, however, is that, grammatical irregularity aside, "it" refers to the child Mourner, who, alone, is cast out of the blessed kingdom. Such a notion resonates with Dickinson's frequent references to herself as "wicked," among the "bad ones," left outside the fold, deprived of Christ's love, in her letters to ABIAH PALMER ROOT written when she was struggling with her inability to make a public declaration of faith.

In stanza 3, this notion of personal blame is carried forward in the phrase "my Delinquent Palaces." Here the word "my" is crucial: By appropriating the Delinquent Palaces, she makes their "delinquency" hers, another allusion, perhaps to her failure to believe. This notion is carried a step further in stanza 4, where she gives the lost place the familiar, religious name, "the site of the Kingdom of Heaven." If the dominion/palaces become a grander thing—a Kingdom—they also grow paler, for the speaker is not looking for the Kingdom itself, but for its "site," evoking an archaeological site, where a vanished city *once* stood. "Site" also suggests "sight"—the desire to experience the Kingdom directly, to see it with her own eyes.

If the "soft searching" the speaker engages in is her writing, then in stanza 4, the Finger that touches her Forehead is the dawning realization that her chosen path will not lead her to the Kingdom. She suspects she is "looking oppositely," in the wrong place or in the wrong way—that her very act of looking, as Dickinson, the poet, with her bereft consciousness, "opposes" the possibility of finding the Kingdom. The metrical pattern reinforces this forlorn conclusion: Throughout, the poem is composed of lines of 4 iambs, with every first and third line ending with an extra stressed syllable. The last line, however, with its extra two syllables, one stressed, one unstressed, subtly shifts the rhythm, so that the poem seems to trail off wistfully, in a state of nonconclusiveness.

FURTHER READING

Thomas Johnson, *Emily Dickinson*, 125–126.

"Ample make this Bed—" (1864) (Fr 804, J 829)

In April 1883 Dickinson sent this poem, along with three others, to the publisher Thomas Niles, who wrote back expressing his pleasure in it. And, indeed, it is a moving work that evokes a direct, emotional response in the reader, despite the "logical" puzzles it presents. If we view it as a prayer, the question arises: To whom is it addressed? The first two lines of the first stanza and the entire last stanza are addressed to someone other than the dead, to the "maker" of the bed, though whether Dickinson is instructing the gravedigger or imploring God is uncertain. In fact, the notion of a specific addressee may be irrelevant, for the imperatives (make, make, be, be, let no) read as fervent wishes flung into the universe at large. Lines 3 and 4, on the other hand, can only be addressed to the occupant of the grave. The poem has been recited at graveside, both of numerous unknown individuals and of the protagonists of William Styron's novel *Sophie's Choice*.

Dickinson characteristically uses domestic images—rooms or a house—for the grave. (See "What Inn is This," "Safe in their Alabaster Chambers—," "Because I could not stop for Death—," and "I died for Beauty—but was scarce"). A single bed, however, is sparser and lonelier than a house or room; it creates a sense of the vulnerability and exposure of the deceased. The image of the bed was not unique to Dickinson, but was suggested by New England graves, which had headstones, sometimes called "bedbacks," and often footstones as well, and thus resembled beds. The bed/grave, in Dickinson's day, was associated with a common metaphor, namely that "the death of the righteous is but a brief sleep from which they will awaken" on Judgment Day (Wolff, *Emily Dickinson*, 340).

Dickinson begins with this image and uses it to affirm the value of the sleeper. She asks of an unnamed "maker" that all be "ample"—solid and comfortable. But how after all can a narrow grave be "ample" except in the spiritual sense of being large enough to accommodate the immeasurable worth of the sleeper? She asks that the bed be made with "awe," a sense of the mystery of death. A demanding housekeeper, she stipulates that the bed have a certain perfection—straight mattress, round pillow—for the perfect comfort of the dead and also, perhaps, to satisfy her own aesthetic need to shape the bed for its role in whatever comes next. In the poem's final, startling image, she demands that nothing "Interrupt this Ground." The phrase is arresting because of Dickinson's unusual use of the noun object "Ground" as a synecdoche (the use of a part of something to signify the whole) for waiting (a verbal form signifying process) that will take place within it. The phrase "Sunrise' yellow noise" is a striking synesthesia, merging the sun's light with sound into a single perception. For Dickinson, who counted the sun, as the quintessence of earthly light and vitality, among the things she most cherished (see "I RECKON—WHEN I COUNT AT ALL—"), this dismissive image is highly unusual. Even the joys of earth are mere "yellow noise" compared to the other sunrise underway, the dawning of eternal life, which will "break/ Excellent and Fair." On the other hand, the speaker's fear that the ordinary sunrise's yellow noise might interrupt this process is indicative of just how enticing the colors and sounds of this world are to her.

Dickinson's use of the traditional religious term—"Judgment"—for the unearthly sunrise is a crucial aspect of the poem. The Judgment of the wrathful Calvinist God of Dickinson's PURITAN HERITAGE, with its threat of eternal damnation, was repugnant to her. The Judgment in this poem, however, is of another kind—"Excellent and Fair." The poet states this as certainty, indeed, as her definition of Judgment. Appropriating the role of judge, she offers her own version of divine justice, decreeing a benevolent judgment for the deceased. In doing so, she rebels against the conservative theology of CONGREGATIONALISM, with its belief in an inherently sinful humanity and affirms the goodness of human nature. Since the language of the poem does not suggest a particular deceased, the inference is that such eternal reward is (or should be) universal.

For other poems in which Dickinson develops her personal vision of the Judgment, see "IT WAS NOT DEATH, FOR I STOOD UP" (Fr 355), "'Twas a long parting but the time" (Fr 621). "Departed—to the Judgment—" (Fr 399), "You're right—'the way is narrow'—" (Fr 249), and "Judgment is Justest" (Fr 1707). In the latter, the image of a "posthumous Sun" contrasts with the "Sunrise' yellow noise" of the poem under discussion.

FURTHER READING

Cynthia Griffin Wolff, *Emily Dickinson*, 329–331.

"A narrow Fellow in the Grass" (1865) (Fr 1096, J 986)

Since its first publication in *The Springfield Republican* on February 14, 1866, when editor SAMUEL BOWLES placed it on the first page with the title "The Snake," the solution to this "riddle poem" has been obvious to its readers. The true riddle for future commentators has involved the allusive subtext of the poem. Yes, the poem is about a snake, but what else is it about? In this ongoing discussion, sex (both heterosexual and homosexual), nature as a whole, sin, and death have been put forth as the "true" concern of the poem. For some, the poem is about the vitality of language, a tour-de-force of imagistic magic. As in so much of Dickinson's work, her specific yet resonant language, rooted in religious and literary traditions, yet strangely independent of them, lends support to all of these interpretations.

The speaker of the poem begins by addressing herself to a presumed listener/reader in the tone of a teacher and objective observer, offering a precise, visual description of the snake moving through the grass. By calling the snake a "Narrow fellow" she is being neither coy nor mysterious, but inviting the reader to think of this creature in unfamiliar terms. Instead of slithering, he rides, though on what invisible conveyance we can only conjecture. In the third line of stanza 1 the speaker interrupts herself in a chatty, informal tone and invites the reader in: "You may have met him? Did you not." In the version pirated by Emily's sister-in-law and confidante SUSAN HUNTINGTON GILBERT DICKINSON and published by Bowles, the line ends in a question mark, a change that agitated Dickinson and reinforced her fear of what editors might do to her work. She wrote to her literary mentor THOMAS WENTWORTH HIGGINSON, to whom she had previously expressed her reluctance to publish, in early 1866: "Lest you meet my Snake and suppose I deceive it was robbed of me—defeated too of the third line by the punctuation. The third and fourth were one . . ." (L 316). Scholar Martha Nell Smith incisively explains the significance of the change: "By emphasizing the break between the lines, the punctuation practically insists on a certain reading, whereas its omission makes the relationship between the two lines more indeterminate . . ." (*Rowing in Eden*, 12). "Did you not?" means simply, "You *have* met him, haven't you?" But, if lines 3 and 4 are read together, form reinforces meaning: Without the aid of punctuation at the end of line 3 or a transitional phrase such as "let me tell you," line 4 springs upon the reader with the suddenness of the snake's appearance.

Stanza 2 continues the evocation of the snake in exact, yet indirect terms, primarily as the movement it causes in the grass, which divides cleanly, as if a comb had run through it. The homey comb image may be seen as the speaker's attempt to "domesticate" the snake. Yet the stanza also offers ammunition to those who emphasize the poem's underlying sexual content and view it as an exercise in stimulating voyeurism. Karl Keller sees the "shaft" as a male erection that both shocks and attracts the speaker (*Only Kangaroo*, 268–269). The "Whip Lash / Unbraiding in the Sun" that "wrinkled And was gone—" when the speaker stopped to pick it up, easily lends itself to phallic interpretation. In a similar vein, John Cody sees the "alluring swamp" of stanza 3—the "Boggy Acre" as a metaphor for the female genitals. Within the context of his psychoanalytic interpretation, he relates the poem to what he sees as Dickinson's homosexual impulses, first directed toward her mother, and then to Sue Dickinson (*After Great Pain*, 437–438). (See Fr 1780, which begins "Sweet is the swamp with it's secrets, / Until we meet a snake" for a poem whose snake/swamp imagery is more obviously sexual than it is in the poem under discussion).

Whatever the symbolic meaning of the "Boggy Acre," it also reflects a precise observation of nature. Upon reading the poem, Bowles, who apparently underestimated the care with which Emily observed nature, remarked to Sue Dickinson, "How did that girl ever know that a boggy field wasn't good for corn?" "Oh, you forget that was Emily *'when a boy'!*" was the reply (Martha Dickinson Bianchi, *Face to Face*, 2). Sue was familiar with Emily's odd way of referring to her period of childhood freedom to roam barefoot through the woods

near her house, collecting specimens for her herbarium. Associating that unfettered wandering with the kind of freedom generally reserved for boys, she referred to herself as one. She first used the phrase in a letter to her brother WILLIAM AUSTIN, when she was 23: "Well, we were all boys once" (L 152, Jan 5, 1854). According to her latest biographer, Alfred Habegger, "Eventually, she looked backed at this free and fearless outdoor sauntering as a defining activity of her life 'when a boy'—a phrase that became indispensable to her after her habits of seclusion were established" (*My Wars*, 159–160). For example, in Fr 1538, "The Savior must have been," written in 1880, she writes: "The Road to Bethlehem / Since He and I were Boys / Was leveled." Thus, for Habegger, "the speaker in this tricky poem is *not* male but a woman who was once a boy."

Through the end of stanza 3, the snake is moving about its own business, not interacting with the speaker or threatening her in any way, vanishing as suddenly as it appeared. We have no indication this is a poisonous snake; indeed, since she stoops "to secure it," it is probably a harmless garden snake. Yet, two brief stanzas later, the snake has become a chilling, alienating presence. As stanza 4 begins, there is no hint that the poem is moving in that direction. The speaker assumes the simple, childlike persona of one on an equal plane with "Nature's People," for whom she feels "a transport / Of Cordiality." Only in the last two lines of the poem, in images of unexpected darkness, does the snake's life-stopping impact on the speaker suddenly emerge. It is possible to detect, as Cynthia Griffin Wolff does, hints of this emergence as the poem progresses. Wolff notes that "civilizing images"—the snake riding "as if there is a carriage," the grass divided as if by a comb—are gradually displaced as the speaker "moves beyond civilization and arable land," while at the same time moving "away from simple realism toward a portent of danger" (*Emily Dickinson*, 489–491).

What danger does the snake represent? Cody offers a psychoanalytically based interpretation, focusing on the homosexual issue. Hypothesizing that Emily identified with her father, Cody sees the speaker's account of how she often encountered the snake "when a Boy and Barefoot," as the appearance of the father to the "oedipal boy:"

> This fear of the snake is not for Emily Dickinson simply a fear of male sexuality per se. For her, as for the oedipal boy, the snake is the great deterrent to her encroachments upon the swamp—the female love object.

Another unavoidable association of the snake is with the tempter of Genesis: the snake as Satan or evil. While it is impossible for a Western reader *not* to make this association, there is little or nothing in the poem that develops this meaning. For Wolff, the fact that Dickinson does not connect the snake to its meaning within a theological universe or "any coherent system of symbols" limits the poem. She regrets that it is only "an isolated glimpse into an earthbound secret whose full extent cannot be charted and whose particulars emerge at such rare intervals that the essence of nature must remain forever hidden." (491). While Wolff considers this a failure of the poem, the sense of nature's inscrutability and indifference to human life, nature as a "Haunted House," is an integral and compelling dimension of Dickinson's worldview.

Whatever the significance of the snake to the speaker, its impact is fearsome and chilling. All the poem's attempts to view it in civilized, domestic terms break down at the end. Visual images give way to "Zero at the Bone." For Dickinson "Zero" is an image of death, associated with frost and belonging to the same semantic context as "Degreeless Noon," which lies beyond the "Dial life" of the everyday. The long *o* sound of *alone* and *Bone* at the conclusion produces a mournful mood that reinforces the sense of this "Zero."

See also "A CLOCK STOPPED—," "FURTHER IN SUMMER THAN THE BIRDS—," and "WHAT MYSTERY PERVADES A WELL!"

FURTHER READING

Martha Dickinson Bianchi, *Face to Face*, 26–27; John Cody, *After Great Pain*, 437–438; Alfred Habegger, *My Wars*, 159–160; Karl Keller, *Only Kangaroo*, 268–269; Cynthia Griffin Wolff, *Emily Dickinson*, 489–491.

"A nearness to Tremendousness—" (1864) (Fr 824, J 963)

Dickinson is the great cartographer of those regions of psychic pain and disorientation that lie outside the boundaries of both ordinary sensibility and conventional language. In poem after poem she describes the mind's strategies for survival both during and, more frequently, in the aftermath of great pain: numbness ("From Blank to Blank—," Fr 484; "There is a Languor of the Life," Fr 552); dreaming ("We dream—it is good we are dreaming—" Fr 584); continued possession in imagination ("IF I MAY HAVE IT, WHEN IT'S DEAD,"), the sustaining force of habit ("WE GROW ACCUSTOMED TO THE DARK—"); and the assertion of a life beyond the grave ("THERE CAME A DAY—AT SUMMER'S FULL—"). In Fr 824, Dickinson uses spatial imagery to suggest an agony whose nature (its manifestation and only "cure") is restless, even frenetic, and uncontainable motion.

In the first two lines of this poem, Dickinson, in a tone of bitter irony, notes that suffering "procures a nearness to Tremendousness," which lifts us above the trivial and puts us in touch with the essence of existence. She may have been thinking of the greatness of God, or, as she put it in a poem written the previous year, of "Death's tremendous nearness—" ("I TRIED TO THINK A LONELIER THING").

Yet over the course of the poem's brief expanse, the awesome connotations of "Tremendousness" are transformed into something very different: "Illocality"—a neologism by which the poet seeks to express a vacillating expanse in which she wanders blindly.

This transformation of meaning takes place gradually from line to line. In line 3, "Tremendousness" grows both vaguer (unstructured) and less knowable as it turns into "Boundlessness." At the same time "Agony," a word denoting extreme pain and associated with "the pangs of death and the sufferings of our Savior in the Garden of Gethsemane," becomes "Affliction," a less exalted concept with overtones of an external cause of suffering, whether "sickness, losses, calamity, adversity, or persecution," as in 'Many are the afflictions of the righteous' (Psalms, xxxiv). Agony "procures" proximity to tremendousness; it is a steep price but a measurable one that results in a measurable gain. Affliction, in contrast "ranges Boundlessness," that is, it "roves at large, wanders without restraint or direction." The sense of purposeful action gives way to one of purposelessness.

"Procures" and "ranges" are the only two verbs of action in the poem. In stanza 2, action gives way to the negative action of "cannot stay" and the stasis of "is." The poem is dominated by nouns of emotion: agony, affliction (twice), and contentment; and, even more heavily, by nouns of place/space: nearness, tremendousness, boundlessness, vicinity, suburb, acres, location, illocality. Although most of these are abstract nouns, they nonetheless allow the poet to make the existential spaces she invokes concrete. By means of them, she tries to tether the vastness, as if it were an immense balloon, to earth.

Yet the centrifugal, unsettling forces of emotion and language prove stronger. In the last line of stanza 1, the syntax loosens up, as the phrase "Vicinity to Laws" hangs indeterminately between what came before and what comes after it. Is Dickinson saying that Boundlessness exists in "Vicinity of Laws"—near them, but outside them? Or are "Vicinity to Laws" and "Contentment's quiet Suburb—" phrases in apposition—two ways of suggesting civilization and orderliness? Or is the former being defined as the latter? Similarly, "Affliction cannot stay" refers both backward to "Contentment's quiet Suburb" and forward to "In Acres." In that "cannot stay" there are faint but distinct echoes of the expulsion from Eden, the "quiet suburb" where Adam and Eve cannot stay, forced to leave for the boundless wilderness they "procured" with the agony of their disobedience.

The poem ends with one of Dickinson's anti-definitions: "It's Location / Is Illocality—." "Tremendousness" (greatness) has turned to "Boundlessness" (formlessness) and finally to "Illocality"—(a paradoxical "placeless place"). The awe evoked by "Tremendousness" has disintegrated into the anxiety of the unlimited and the ungraspable. Dickinson embeds her meaning into the very sounds of "It's Location / Is Illocality—." The two phrases mirror

one another, but inexactly, reinforcing the uneasy sense of blurred and unstable boundaries.

See also "AFTER GREAT PAIN, A FORMAL FEELING COMES—," "I FELT A FUNERAL, IN MY BRAIN," "I TIE MY HAT—I CREASE MY SHAWL—," "IT WAS NOT DEATH, FOR I STOOD UP," and DEFINITION POEMS.

FURTHER READING

Sharon Cameron, *Lyric Time,* 160–161; Robert Weisbuch, *Emily Dickinson's Poetry,* 154–155.

"A Pit—but Heaven over it—" (1863) (Fr 507)

In this striking, important poem, Dickinson situates herself existentially between two extremes, two immensities between which she balances precariously. Although the images that embody it may vary, this is a central place in the poet's psychic and spiritual life. It is indicative of a lifelong struggle to find her balance between faith and doubt, hope and despair, sanity and madness, and of a worldview in which the soul is continually balanced between two spiritual poles. One of the most famous poems in which this fundamental metaphor is developed is "I stepped from plank to plank—," in which she "walks the plank" of spiritual peril: "The Stars about my Head I felt / About my Feet the Sea—." Another is "BEHIND ME—DIPS ETERNITY—," which continues "Before Me—Immortality—/ Myself—the Term between—" and concludes "A Crescent in the Sea—/ With Midnight to the North of Her—/ And Midnight to the South of Her—/ And Maelstrom—in the Sky—."

Until R. W. Franklin's pioneering editing work with Dickinson's manuscript books, or fascicles, in the early 1980s, this poem was known to both scholars and general readers in a shorter, very different version. The earlier version, which appeared in Thomas H. Johnson's *Collected Poems,* was missing the last five lines, which Johnson had erroneously included in another poem, "I TIE MY HAT—I CREASE MY SHAWL—." It also contained a line, "Seed—summer—tomb" which is deleted in Franklin's new authoritative version. In reconstructing the fuller, original poem, Franklin has revealed a far more hopeful vision than earlier commentators were apt to discern. The closed, hopeless "circuit" from birth (seed) to tomb is replaced by a courageous and surprising strategy for overcoming terror.

In her discussion of the poem, Shira Wolosky finds "The poem . . . tries to ward off a terror already present. The heaven that should reassure her and make her position secure does not do so" ("A Syntax of Contention," 166). And yet, while the speaker is by no means secure, neither is she wholly uncomforted by heaven. In stanza 1, the word "Pit" appears only twice, while "Heaven" is mentioned four times, as the poet turns from one to the other and back again, as she struggles to reconcile these existential extremes, the heaven and hell, perhaps, of her inner life. The fact that heaven gets last mention suggests an unwillingness to let go of this pole of her reality. Moreover, although she cannot touch it, heaven surrounds her; it is above, beside her, and "abroad"—out in the open, at large. Note that there are no verbs in this stanza: the speaker is caught in a kind of paralysis as she registers her situation. Numbness and paralysis appear frequently in Dickinson's poems, for example, in "AFTER GREAT PAIN, A FORMAL FEELING COMES—" "I've Dropped My Brain—My Soul Is Numb," and "PAIN—HAS AN ELEMENT of BLANK," in which a failure to feel is the only mechanism the poet has at her disposal to survive unbearable pain.

In stanza 2, this paralysis continues: The only verbs that are introduced are in the form of infinitives in the conditional tense, that is, no action occurs, but what would happen *if* certain actions occurred is contemplated. The speaker can neither move (disrupt her precarious balance) nor look (be visually aware, vividly conscious) nor dream (be careless, unconscious), since any of these actions could cause her to plummet into the abyss. Her chances for survival are held up by a lone prop, not further identified, suggesting only how fragile is the barrier separating her from the pit. Verbs of any kind are absent from the stanza's final exclamatory line, suggesting her dismay, terror, and confusion in which all the poet can do is invoke the two opposing fates that beckon her.

Scholar Joanne Feit Diehl argues convincingly that Dickinson's Pit has an important origin in the blazing pit of Hell that played so central and fearsome a role in the thinking of the 18th-century revivalist preacher JONATHAN EDWARDS. Edwards's theological vision, with its punitive deity and conviction of the essential depravity of human nature, was anathema to Dickinson. Yet his fire-and-brimstone imagery was at the core of the PURITAN HERITAGE that embedded itself in her psyche. For Dickinson, however, the cosmic drama was internal. As Feit Diehl writes, ". . . in her abyss the flames are self-generated, created by the power of her own imagination. Furthermore, hers is an abyss that she tells us she can enter, and so it must be an internal, deeper part of the mind to which she descends and from which she emerges through the act of writing poems" ("Emerson, Dickinson, and the Abyss," 158).

Indeed, she tells us in the first line of stanza 3, "The depth is all my thought—." We may read this line as saying, "My thoughts are my hell, my pit" or "This pit is all in my imagination." Although both readings place the pit within, the difference is a significant one with respect to the speaker's chances of escaping it. In either case, she remains paralyzed and dares not ask her feet to carry her to safety, lest the slightest movement startle her and cause her to fall. (Note that "start" has the meaning of "startle"—its primary meaning in her Webster's—in both its appearances in this stanza.) In an image suggesting the immense discrepancy between her external life and her inner reality, she shows herself sitting "So straight you'd scarce suspect / It was a Pit—with fathoms under it."

At this point, the image of the pit vanishes from the poem and we are faced with three disjointed, puzzling lines. As Wolosky notes, "In a poem whose subject is disorientation and a consequent immobility, an avoidance of verbs and a staccato of images is not surprising. . . . [Her] disorientation is expressed in a form commensurate with it" ("Syntax of Contention," 167). If syntax mediates the sequential relations between successive words, the breakdown of syntax indicates a reality struggling for coherence. In the line, "It's Circuit just the same," what does "it" refer to? *Circuit* is a word Dickinson uses to describe both the daily round of temporal life and the indirectness of poetic language ("Success in Circuit lies"). If "it" is the Pit, she may be saying that, since the Pit, for all its terrors, "is all my thought" (only my thought), then it is "Circuit just the same," a terror based on the imagistic constructs of the imagination.

The next two lines, "Whose Doom to whom / 'Twould start them" makes more sense if we recognize their elliptical nature and attempt to fill in the missing words. The first line might read: "Whose doom [is known] to whom?" If so, the next line suggests that if "they" (another unclear referent) knew [of these dooms] they'd be startled. Fortunately for the reader, the four final lines of the poem are much more coherent. In them, the speaker considers her options for dealing with the reality she has evoked. One option is to tremble, but she rejects this. Instead, she introduces the new, startling image of a Bomb. Instead of a Pit, which may swallow her, she has been given a Bomb that may well explode in the Bosom to which she holds it. But the destruction potential in the bomb is calmed by her embrace of it. The syntax of the line also allows for the possibility that the "it" that is calmed by this action is not just the Bomb, but the poet's Bosom.

Thus far, the poem has been virtually absent of active verbs. In the third stanza, verbs exist, but either as the copula "is" or as denial of action, "I dare not ask." In its final two lines, however, the materialization of two active verbs, "held" and "holds"—the actions that "defuse" the mortal danger—is the signal of salvation. The word *Nay* is the crucial verbal gesture of the poem, asserting that this action is not relegated to the past, but is ongoing—the place where she now locates herself. Instead of teetering between the pit and heaven, she defines her "now" as embracing what is potentially explosive, holding it to her bosom. The lines imply an acceptance of inner turmoil, and its comforting integration within a larger, more loving self, at least in part through the transformative power of making poems. In the earlier version, which ended with a bleak evocation of the beginning, middle, and end of life, and our ignorance of our own fate, no such option was available.

See also "I FELT A FUNERAL, IN MY BRAIN," CIRCUMFERENCE POEMS, CONGREGATIONALISM, and PUBLICATION AND EDITORIAL SCHOLARSHIP.

FURTHER READING

Joanne Feit Diehl, "Emerson, Dickinson, and the Abyss," in *Modern Critical Views*, Harold Bloom, ed., 157–159; R. W. Franklin, "The Houghton Library Dickinson Manuscript 157," 245–257; Shira Wolosky, "A Syntax of Contention," in *Modern Critical Views*, 166–168.

"Apparently with no surprise" (1884) (Fr 1668, J 1624)

The murder of flowers was a subject that Dickinson brooded on all her life. Apart from writing, gardening was her great occupation and her identification with flowers—primarily simple ones like the daisy and buttercup—is found throughout her poems. Twenty years earlier, she wrote the famous poem, "A VISITOR IN MARL—," a riddle poem in which the "Visitor" is the frost, who caresses the flowers and, kissing them, kills them. In two other poems, "The Frost of Death was on the Pane—" (Fr 1130, 1866) and "The Frost was never seen—" (Fr 1190, 1870), she depicts the Frost as an unstoppable intruder who ruthlessly murders flowers. Given her devotion to gardening, her impassioned love for flowers and the fact that she lived in a harsh winter climate, it is not surprising that winter and frost were intimately tied in with her sense of a plundered world.

In "Apparently with no surprise," jotted down on the back of an envelope addressed to her aunt Elizabeth Currier, Dickinson implicates a disappointing deity in the death of innocents. Nature, too, is part of this indifference. The Sun, characteristically an emblem of warmth, light, and beneficent power, in a paradoxical play on words, "proceeds unmoved"; it is a mere mechanical servant to "an Approving God," who looks on as the beheading take place. Note that even the "happy Flower" is not "surprised." Apparently, it knows this is the way of things.

Critic Judith Farr notes that "Since the garden was her cherished metaphor for the world, the careers and fortunes of her flowers signified the bitter struggles of humanity" (*Gardens*, 116). This poem was written two years before Dickinson's own death, when she had experienced a series of recent losses—her mother, SAMUEL BOWLES, REVEREND CHARLES WADSWORTH, JUDGE OTIS PHILLIPS LORD, and, most devastatingly, her nephew GILBERT THOMAS DICKINSON ("Gib"), who died on October 5, 1884, of typhoid fever. Depending on when in 1884 it was written, this poem may have been motivated by the death of this beloved eight-year-old boy who was, struck down by an "accidental power" at his play. For the frost of this poem, like the child's death, comes prematurely, randomly, not as part of the natural cycle. In her startling image of the "blonde Assassin" Dickinson evokes the physical whiteness of frost while reversing the usual associations of whiteness with purity and assassins with darkness. For scholar Charles Anderson, whiteness, as in "Melville's famous chapter in *Moby-Dick* . . . is here invoked to symbolize the mystery of death" (*Stairway of Surprise,* 179).

A bleak and bitter vision of what we know, this is also a poem about what we do not know. As Anderson points out, Dickinson is "haunted by the suspicion that at its center nature is only automatic process, without any meaning of a sort the conscious mind can recognize. . . . 'Apparently' not only modifies the opening word but controls the whole poem. This is not necessarily the way things are, merely the way they appear to the mortal view. . . . Man, nature, and God are three entirely separate entities, moving in this poem like figures in a dream" (*Stairway,* 177–178).

See also "'NATURE' IS WHAT WE SEE" and "WHAT MYSTERY PERVADES A WELL!"

FURTHER READING

Charles Anderson, *Stairway,* 177–179; Wendy Barker, *Lunacy of Light,* 72; Judith Farr, *Gardens,* 10, 116.

"A Route of Evanescence" (1879) (Fr 1489, J 1463)

When Dickinson sent this much admired riddle poem to MABEL LOOMIS TODD as a way of thanking her for a painting of her "preferred flower of life,"

she wrote: "I cannot make an Indian Pipe but please accept a Humming Bird" (L 770). The nature of the exchange is particularly apt; for the poem is a word-painting in which Dickinson "makes" a mental construct of the hummingbird, related to the actual feathered creature, to be sure, but with an existence all its own. From beginning to end, this single eight-line stanza is a paean of delight in the appearance/disappearance of the tiny, multicolored bird. Dickinson evokes the miraculous hummingbird, whose wings flutter so rapidly as to be almost invisible, enabling the bird to hover in the air as it sucks the nectar from a flower, as "A Route of Evanescence." As it flits across the speaker's field of vision, the bird disappears. (In Dickinson's time, the word *evanescence* meant vanishing from sight and did not connote the sense of something transitory, as it does today). Dickinson extended this perception to all things beautiful, as she wrote to her old friend EMILY FOWLER (Ford) during this same period, "All we secure of Beauty is it's Evanescences—" (L 781, about November 1882).

The bird's "revolving Wheel" is doubtless a reference to the optical illusion created by its rapidly fluttering wings. (Dickinson considered the variants "delusive, dissolving, dissembling, renewing wheel"). Note how she uses extensive sound play within the poem's brief expanse. After introducing two *r* sounds in these first two lines, Dickinson heightens the music of the poem by repeating it in the next two, with their synesthetic images (combining two sense impressions) for the bird's colors. In "A Resonance of Emerald," the brilliant green color seems to be created by the bird's humming sound, while the phrase "A Rush of Cochineal" turns the red color of the bird into a jewel-like blur of speed. As critic Charles R. Anderson notes:

> No jewel offered quite the brilliance of this rare pigment used since ancient times to make especially vivid reds, like crimson and scarlet. To see this spot on the hummingbird's throat, the poet-spectator-reader must take the stance of the flowers themselves. (*Stairway,* 129)

And, indeed, this is where the poem takes us next. The "tumbled Head" of "every Blossom on the Bush" hums with *b, m,* and *mb* sounds. Note that *r, m,* and *b* sounds are all part of *hummingbird.* Having created this precise yet impressionistic word painting of vanishing bird-ravisher and ravished blossoms, the speaker drops from her enamored tone and remarks casually that what has "arrived" is the "Mail from Tunis—probably." Hummingbirds are, in fact, visitors from the south. But by making the bird a messenger—or perhaps even the message—from one of those exotic, distant lands, Dickinson expresses her sense that here is where ecstasy, something that seemed most real to her at a distance, truly resides. As a final homage to the hummingbird's remarkable power, she calls his flight "An easy Morning's Ride—."

Dickinson had made a previous attempt to capture the hummingbird in verse, 17 years earlier, in "Within my Garden, rides a Bird" (Fr 370, 1862), a far more discursive poem. Anderson considers the later poem more successful, comparing it to a Japanese haiku "in the conciseness of its notation" (*Stairway*, 127). Certainly "A Route of Evanescence" is perfect in its way; yet the earlier poem, in which the speaker and her dog debate whether the hummingbird actually existed or was the fruit of "the Garden in the Brain," also has its delights.

See also "A BIRD CAME DOWN THE WALK—" and "IT SIFTS FROM LEADEN SIEVES—."

FURTHER READING

Charles R. Anderson, *Stairway*, 127–132; Agnieszka Salska, *Walt Whitman and Emily Dickinson*, 147–148; Cynthia Griffin Wolff, *Emily Dickinson*, 483.

"As if the Sea should part" (1863) (Fr 720, J 695)

Emily Dickinson strove for an understanding of eternity all her life, exploring in poem after poem the vast mystery outside time that she sometimes envisioned as preceding the earthly span ("BEHIND ME—DIPS ETERNITY"), while at other times succeeding it ("BECAUSE I COULD NOT STOP FOR DEATH—"). While this poem ostensibly arrives at a definition of the mystery, its emphasis is not on conclusion, but on the ungraspable vastness of

a process that simply goes on and on. If this is Dickinson's vision of the end point toward which existence is moving, it is a vision, not of content, but of process.

Throughout the poem there are biblical echoes, notable for the way in which they depart from traditional religious meanings. The parting of the Sea is, of course, an image from *Exodus*: God's parting of the Red Sea, allowing the Hebrews to pass through, from slavery to freedom. Dickinson alludes to this miracle, but there is no God in her poem and no emancipation—only an ongoing series of discoveries. One Sea parts, only to reveal another. It may not be too far-fetched to detect echoes of Dickinson's favorite book of the Bible, *Revelations*, where the mystery at the core of existence comes closer with the successive opening of the seven *seals* (a word echoed in the parting of Dickinson's *seas*).

As the first stanza progresses, the process threatens to go on indefinitely, but Dickinson pauses at a significant number: "the Three / But a presumption be—." If this is her version of the holy Trinity, it designates not the three coexistent faces of the deity, but three successive stages of discovery, not stasis and finality, but movement and generativity. Moreover, this vast trinity—and this is the essential point—belongs to the mind: It is a "presumption." For Dickinson, the only universe we can know is within, and yet, lest we see this as a damning statement of human limitation, she continues to insist on the inexhaustible vastness of that inner realm.

In stanza 2, she strives to expand her notion through the image of "Periods of Seas." A period can mean a circuit, as in "the period of the Earth" as it rotates around the Sun. But it is most often used as a designation of time, so that the image suggests something akin to "eras/epochs of Seas," reaching beyond familiar, rational categories, to create the sense of a combined time and space enormity. And all this is merely the "Verge of Seas to be"—an instant prior to but on the brink of creation. The process threatens to go on indefinitely. Yet Dickinson does bring it to a conclusion in the poem's final line, arriving at a "definition" of Eternity. This definition, however, to paraphrase Dickinson, "is that definition is none." ("The Definition of Beauty is / That Definition is none—"). It is only a directional signal, pointing to the immeasurable and unreachable. Dickinson's DEFINITION POEMS characteristically begin with the concept defined ("Exultation is . . .," "Grief is . . ."). But, here the concept being defined is stated only at the end, which gives it the quality of an afterthought.

Syntax plays an important role in establishing the poem's emphasis. Note that the entire poem is a single sentence: The first seven lines constitute the dependent clause, the last line the independent clause. Yet, all the weight of the poem is on the hypotheticals, the "as ifs," while the "conclusion" is weaker, lamer, a mere wave of the hand. In addition, the rhyme reinforces meaning on the level of sound: a series of rhymes based on the long *e*, and not just rhymes but word repetitions: Sea, Sea, Three, be, Seas to be, Eternity. The long *e* syllables stretch out, creating a sense of unity, connection, and forward momentum. But the final word of the final line, which "should" rhyme, does not. "Those" dangles awkwardly and unconvincingly by itself, as the poem ends with a final dash. Critic Gary Lee Stonum points out that "By contrast the expected word, 'These,' would place eternity closer at hand and effectively capitulate to the insistent long *e* in 'Seas' and all of the poem's other rhyme words" (*Dickinson Sublime,* 183).

For Stonum, the eternity that *is* evoked in the poem as a whole is not one the poet—or anyone else, for that matter—would care to be close to, but an instance of the negative way in which Dickinson sometimes uses the term: "a blank, appalling endlessness that is devoid of vitality . . . vistas of monotonous endlessness" (*Dickinson Sublime,* 182). For scholar Robert A. Weisbuch, on the other hand, the endlessness has a far more positive connotation. Relating this poem to Dickinson's ever-changing and often contradictory approaches and attitudes to the mysteries that concerned her, of which "eternity" was the greatest, he writes, "The contradictions come together in complex understandings—we do sometimes get to a paradise, but as soon as we get there we find a 'further.'. . . We really do not want a final contentment, then, though we can hate the frustrations, because traveling is best" ("Prisming," 222). This interpretation is supported by other Dickinson poems that exalt dynamic endeavor above a static condition.

How does one "choose" between two such different interpretations? To a great extent, a reader will understand this poem on the basis of the tone he or she senses in it: despair at a blank emptiness or exhilaration at the prospect of an endless journey toward an ever-receding eternity. There is a neutrality to the sea imagery of the poem that focuses only on their number and vastness, indicating neither dark storm and depths nor sparkling expanses. Thus the reader's response may well depend on what she brings to the poem, that is, on whether she responds to the prospect of boundless horizons with horror or exultation. Certainly, many of Dickinson's own poems demonstrate that she herself welcomed the voyaging, notably "EACH LIFE CONVERGES TO SOME CENTRE," composed the same year as this poem, in which she declares that, should heaven be "ungained" by "A Life's low venture," there is always hope, since "Eternity enable the endeavoring / Again."

See also "A WIFE—AT DAYBREAK—I SHALL BE—," "BEHIND ME—DIPS ETERNITY," "CRISIS IS A HAIR," "EXULTATION IS THE GOING," "FOREVER—IS COMPOSED OF NOWS—," and "IT'S EASY TO INVENT A LIFE—."

FURTHER READING

Gary Lee Stonum, *Dickinson Sublime,* 182–183; Robert A. Weisbuch, "Prisming," in *Handbook,* Grabher et al., eds., 222.

"As imperceptibly as Grief" (1865) (Fr 935, J 1540)

This is one of Dickinson's finest poems on the movement of summer into fall, a transition that mattered deeply to her and always triggered feelings of loss. Dickinson's poetry is rich with testimony to her love of summer; it was for her the royal season of nature's lushness and fruitfulness, a time when life is most intense. In "I RECKON—WHEN I COUNT AT ALL—," she places the season on the highest rung of things she values, right after Poets and the Sun. In such poems as "LIKE SOME OLD FASHIONED

MIRACLE," "The Gentian weaves her fringes—" "THESE ARE THE DAYS WHEN BIRDS COME BACK—," and "FURTHER IN SUMMER THAN THE BIRDS—," she simultaneously celebrates summer, traces its disappearance, mourns it, and longs for a sense of inclusion in the "rites" of seasonal change that nature denies her.

Dickinson is the poet of the "imperceptible," who knew well that "CRISIS IS A HAIR" and "CRUMBLING IS NOT AN INSTANT'S ACT." She knew that enormous, fateful changes occur gradually, indeed with such stealth and subtlety that we notice them only afterward. A meticulous observer of natural and psychological processes, in this poem she traces the accumulating signs of summer's withdrawal. She measures alterations of sound in units of light ("A Quietness distilled / As Twilight long begun,") and of her own exclusion ("Or Nature spending with herself / Sequestered Afternoon—"). As these lines demonstrate, she mingles physical observation with metaphor in her quest to capture the many dimensions of summer's departure. The early autumn dusk is described precisely, as "drawing in" earlier. But Morning becomes a "foreign" guest, eager to leave and shining with "A courteous, yet harrowing Grace." The latter phrase is an oxymoron, since Grace should be the opposite of tormenting, but torment resides in the fact that Grace is departing.

The religious term—which Dickinson uses elsewhere in her evocation of summer's end—resonates with the second line of the poem, "The Summer lapsed away—." Dickinson's Webster defines *lapse* not only in physical terms ("to pass slowly, silently or by degrees . . .") but also in moral ones ("to slide or slip in moral conduct . . .") as well as religious ones ("to fall from a state of innocence, or from truth, faith or perfection"). Indeed, the notion of condemnation—the poet's condemnation of summer—hovers around this poem. In the first four lines she raises the idea of a betrayal too imperceptible to be called "Perfidy." And in the final lines, Summer is a beautiful woman making her "light escape / Into the Beautiful—." In this final evocation of the season she is embraced as "Our Summer" and apparently forgiven for escaping into the realm which is, after all, native to her: "the Beautiful." The phrase calls up the notion of an ideal realm, in which summer and other beautiful things continue to exist. But Dickinson, no heavy-handed philosopher, only suggests this in parting, and makes her own exit as lightly as the season she elegizes.

See also "A BRIEF, BUT PATIENT ILLNESS—."

FURTHER READING

Thomas Johnson, *Emily Dickinson*, 106–108.

"A solemn thing—it was—I said—" (1862) (Fr 307, J 271)

In this famous woman-in-white poem, Dickinson explores the dimensions of a life that beckons her but does not yet belong to her. Seeking a more direct, sensual experience of her life ideal, she ponders how it would "feel." How would the "bliss look?" Would the reality "feel as big" as what she sees hovering through the fog of her anticipation? The sense that reality never fully measures up to desire is central to Dickinson's worldview, appearing in such poems as "I HAD BEEN HUNGRY, ALL THE YEARS—," "UNDUE SIGNIFICANCE A STARVING MAN ATTACHES," "RENUNCIATION—IS A PIERCING VIRTUE—," and numerous others. In this poem, however, her inner voice tells her there would be no disappointment. Curiously, the poem is reported as something the poet "said" to an undisclosed listener. But the context of the statement is hidden. Is the speaker arguing with someone, defending herself? Whatever the initial impulse to speech, within the space of the poem, she moves from pondering to felt revelation—a swelling of horizons within her. In exchange for nothing less than the dropping of her life into the "plummetless purple well," she will win for herself a life that is by no means "small," no matter what the "Sages" of her own or previous times may say. With a characteristic blend of humility and self-aggrandizement, she proclaims the solemnity and largeness of her chosen path.

While we cannot look to Dickinson's life for "explanations" of her poems, it is impossible to read this one without considering its connection to the poet's habit, adopted somewhere in her early 30s (the exact date is not known), of wearing only white. Her first editor, MABEL LOOMIS TODD, in her much-quoted letter describing the figure the townspeople called the "myth of AMHERST," notes, "She dresses wholly in white & her mind is said to be wonderful." One of her white dresses, the only article of Dickinson's clothing that survived, can be seen at The HOMESTEAD. Believed to have been sewn sometime between 1878 and 1882, this patterned cotton house dress or wrapper was designed for daily life at home. It has "a loosely fitted waist, round collar, cuffs, and a pocket. . . . With its tucks and gores and edge lacing and mother-of-pearl buttons (in front), the dress looks ornate to modern eyes but was ordinary and unpretentious as compared to Gilded Age fashions, which were form-fitting and expensive and involved exacting procedures for sewing, wearing and maintaining" (Habegger, *My Wars*, 516). Habegger sees Dickinson's wearing of such dresses as "practical," since they required no corsets or expensive dressmakers and alleviated worries about colors running. But critic Susan M. Gilbert believes that the white dresses, with their tucks and ruffles, would have required extensive care. She hypothesizes that the poet was "not only conscious that her white dress made special demands on her life but conscious that the idea of her dress made special demands on her life" ("Wayward Nun," 28–29). Dickinson, writes Gilbert, "not only . . . transformed her life into art more readily than most other writers but also . . . more than most, she used her 'small' life itself as an instrument of her great art: even the most ordinary materials of her life, that is, became a set of encoded gestures meant both to supply imagery for, *and* to supplement the encoded statements of her verse" (30).

What does the poem itself reveal about the nature of the white dress and the demands it places on the poet? For Mrs. Todd, who entitled the poem "Wedded" in the 1896 edition, a "Woman white" was a bride. Yet the religious language and imagery of the poem, particularly in the first two stanzas, do not suggest a secular marriage. Further, as Judith Farr points out, it was not the custom for brides in the United States to wear white until the late 1870s. While many possible sources for the woman in white can be found in Dickinson's secular read-

One of the white dresses worn exclusively by the poet after the mid-1860s. The only one that has survived, it would fit someone about 5'1" to 5'4" in height. *(Emily Dickinson dress, property of The Amherst Historical Society, 67 Amity Street, Amherst)*

ing (Wilkie Collins's *Woman in White*; numerous gothic ghosts and pallid nuns; Elizabeth Barrett Browning's Aurora Leigh, who wears a "clean white morning gown," Miss Havisham, the bride deserted on her wedding night in Charles Dicken's *Great Expectations,* and Nathaniel Hawthorne's "Snow Maiden," who wears a "uniform of snow"), the most revealing reference occurs in Revelations, Dickinson's favorite book of scriptures: "Let us be glad and rejoice . . . for the marriage of the Lamb [Christ] is come, and his wife hath made herself ready . . . arrayed in fine linen, clean and white (19:7–8)." Farr notes that conventional Victorian novices and postulants, as well as some nuns, such as the Dominicans, wore white and suggests that Dickinson would have been influenced by "a spate of paintings depicting nuns at the moment of their marriage to Christ" which began appearing in the 1830s (*Passion,* 33). Indeed, in other poems such as Fr 818, "Given in Marriage unto Thee," written in 1864, she calls herself "Bride of the Father and the Son / Bride of the Holy Ghosts—."

If the white dress of this poem is the habit of a nun, what is the order to which the speaker hopes to belong? Does she believe that she is, literally, a bride of Christ? Although she says that God must "count her fit" to join this order, it is unlikely, in light of her refusal to join even her family's church, that Dickinson is referring to a Christian religious order. Instead, she appropriates the emblems of religious dedication to create her own sense of a sacred universe. Wearing an emblem of "blameless mystery" enables her to enact a profound sacrifice, the dropping of her life into the "plummetless purple well," in return for which she is rewarded with a miraculous, empowering bliss. Purple appears frequently in the poems; in addition to the hue of sunrises and sunsets, of flowers, and of the blood coursing through the human heart, it is the color of victory ("the purple Host" of "SUCCESS IS COUNTED SWEETEST"), of royalty, and of the royalty bestowed by death (the purple none can avoid in "One dignity delays for all" and the "full purple" state of the deceased in "Wait till the mystery of death"). In the manuscript of this poem, Dickinson gave "mystic" as a variant for "purple," suggesting other associations she had with the well. "Mystic" implies a direct communion with the divine, beyond the bounds of human comprehension. In an early poem, Dickinson wonders "By what mystic moor-

ing" the little boat of her life is to be found; she also uses it in "To die—takes just a little while" in an image of the dead as an "absent—mystic—creature." Thus, death, privilege, passion and mystery are all contained in the image of the plummetless well. The life that is dropped into it will not be returned until Eternity.

Indeed, in addition to its traditional associations with innocence and renunciation, "white" for Dickinson also signified despair ("that white sustenance") and death ("the White Exploit"). But the death the speaker undergoes in this poem may symbolize her reclusion or death to the world, while the well appears as a traditional emblem of artistic inspiration. (See also Fr 672, in which she symbolically dismisses a caller by appearing "Dressed to meet You—/ See—in White!"). Thus the "Woman white" is the artist who, by dropping her worldly life into the well, experiences the mystic illuminations of her vocation: the "Horizons" that swell within her. This "paradox of simultaneous self-discovery and self-loss" characterizes much of Dickinson's poetry in which she renounces a woman's ordinary joys (Gudrun Grabher, "Dickinson's Lyrical Self," 230).

See also "A WIFE—AT DAYBREAK—I SHALL BE—" "DARE YOU SEE A SOUL AT THE 'WHITE HEAT'?," "MINE—BY THE RIGHT OF THE WHITE ELECTION!," "ON A COLUMNAR SELF—," "TITLE DIVINE, IS MINE." FIRST CHURCH OF CHRIST, and MASTER LETTERS.

FURTHER READING

Judith Farr, *Passion,* 32–34; Sandra M. Gilbert, "Wayward Nun," 20–39; S. M. Gilbert and Susan Gubar, *Madwoman,* 613–621; Gudrun Grabher, "Dickinson's Lyrical Self," in *Handbook,* Grabher et al., eds., 229–231; Alfred Habegger, *My Wars,* 514–516; Robert Weisbuch, "Necessary Veil," in *Modern Critical Views,* Harold Bloom, ed., 94.

"A Spider sewed at Night—" (1869) (Fr 1163, J 1138)

This famous poem is Dickinson's most brilliant, condensed, and enigmatic vision of the "poet-Spider," working at night, as we know she did, with only the "light" of her own, inner vision. Like Dickinson, this spider sews, rather than weaves, as spiders are generally said to do. (See "Don't put up my Thread & Needle—" [Fr 681] for her self-portrait as master sewer).

In the two other poems in which she engages this theme, Dickinson's identification with the spider as artist takes a tragicomic turn. In an earlier poem, "The Spider holds a Silver Ball" (Fr 513, 1863), she stresses both the magic and insubstantiality of his art: "An Hour to rear supreme / His continents of Light—/ Then dangle from the Housewife's Broom—His Boundaries—forgot—." This same pathetic fate of the spider's art, at the end of a broom, is the thrust of a later poem, "The Spider as an Artist" (Fr 1373, 1873). The poet gently mocks him, while identifying with him in his obscurity: "Neglected Son of Genius / I take thee by the Hand—." But in "A Spider sewed at Night—," she gets beyond these easy associations, turning the spider's art into an emblem not of transience but of "Immortality."

Critic Charles R. Anderson correctly relates this poem to Dickinson's verse riddles. Pointing to the three-line stanzas with their triple rhyme scheme, and the brief lines of 3–2–3 accents, he sees the poem as "her incantation to cast a spell on the spider and make him yield up the secret of his web" (Stairway, 141). Each stanza contains its own riddle. In stanza 1, what is meant by "the Arc of White" upon which the spider weaves? Scholar Sharon Cameron considers the image indecipherable (Lyric Time, 6), while Anderson assumes it refers to the white filament of the web, a reasonable association, except that the spider does not weave upon his thread, but with it. As a visual image, the "Arc of White" fails to come into focus, but as a symbol it suggests a tabula rasa, the blank slate of existence, upon which the poet-spider sews his meanings. Thus, the first stanza insists on the complete absence of any outside assistance or direction for the spider's labors.

The second stanza speaks to the nature of what is being created. Is the spider sewing a "Ruff," a collar of fine muslin for a lady, or a "Shroud of Gnome," funeral clothes for an imaginary being associated with the interior of the earth? These two possibilities are not random: The first suggests the realm of romantic love, the second—death, poetry's two great themes. The lines might thus be interpreted as asking whether the poet/seamstress/spider is making a poem about love—or about death. The allusion to death grows more personal when we recall that Dickinson often signed letters to her literary friend THOMAS WENTWORTH HIGGINSON "your Gnome," a way of pointing to the dense, gnomic quality of her poetry.

But only the spider knows whether love or death is what he is weaving. In Anderson's view, both are "false leads," since "the design he makes is a sort of ritualistic expression of himself," in accord with "the modern scientific concept [apparently known to Dickinson] that the spider's web-building was an instinctive dance." Making his design "out of the dark secret of himself . . . he is the source of his own form" (Stairway, 142). In a double word play, the spider not only informs (forms) himself, he informs (communicates his creation to) himself of the nature of his creation as he does so. One may see this, as some critics have, as a solipsistic vision of poetry, in which all that exists or is knowable is the self. Or one may see it, as others have, as Dickinson's espousal of "art-for-art's sake," an art without intention or ability to teach others. But a third interpretation is that she is simply describing the unpremeditated nature of creativity, the way of the poet who "learns by going where she needs to go," to paraphrase the 20th-century American poet Theodore Roethke.

This pivotal line, "Himself himself inform—," an example of semantic doubling, plays a role in two different statements: Within the context of stanza 2, we read: "The spider himself informs himself of whether he is writing of love or death." But if we see it as a phrase spilling into stanza 3, then we read, "The spider informs himself of what he knows of immortality." Similarly, "Of Immortality" is part of the preceding phrase, as just noted, as well as being syntactically connected to the rest of stanza 3:

Of Immortality
His strategy
Was physiognomy—

Into this six-word stanza Dickinson has compressed more than one riddle. Switching from concrete one- or two-syllable words to abstract multisyllabic ones, she appears to be stretching her linguistic web in an attempt to stretch circumference, the far limit of the knowable, that poetry always seeks to transcend. A relatively minor puzzle is created by the preposition "of." If she had used "for" instead, we would be able to paraphrase the stanza as "His strategy for achieving immortality was physiognomy." Assuming that this was what Dickinson *did* mean, that is, that she was using "of" in an idiosyncratic way, we are still left with the larger puzzle: What did she mean by "physiognomy" and in what sense was it a strategy for achieving immortality?

The pseudo-science of physiognomy, defined in her Webster's as "The art or science of discerning the character of the mind from the features of the face," had been discredited by the time she wrote this poem. Nonetheless, Dickinson believed in her own demystified version of it, a conviction, expressed in many different ways in her poetry, that the external manifestation is indeed only a reflection of the internal essence. She states this directly in Fr 450, when she writes: "The Inner—paints the Outer—." Dickinson was fascinated by faces—the face of God, of the dying, the dead, the lover and the betrayer, the beggar and the saint—and "reads" them constantly in her poetry. Physiognomy claims to read the essence on the basis of the external. Dickinson strips the notion of mysticism and uses it as an analogy for the poet's art, her own strategy for immortality. With the image as its central tool, poetry is a way of grasping the invisible by means of the visible.

See also "IT SIFTS FROM LEADEN SIEVES—," "LIKE EYES THAT LOOKED ON WASTES—," "NOT IN THIS WORLD TO SEE HIS FACE—," "NOW I KNEW I LOST HER—," and "TO MAKE A PRAIRIE IT TAKES A CLOVER AND ONE BEE."

FURTHER READING

Charles R. Anderson, *Stairway*, 141–144; Sharon Cameron, *Lyric Time*, 5–6; Joanne Feit Diehl, *Romantic Imagination*, 92–93; Sandra M. Gilbert and Susan Gubar, *Madwoman*, 635–638; Agnieszka Salska, *Walt Whitman and Emily Dickinson*, 78–79.

"A Thought went up my mind today—" (1863) (Fr 731, J 701)

"She had to think—she was the only one of us who had to do that," LAVINIA NORCROSS DICKINSON said of her older sister, Emily. This poem's account of the repeat occurrence of a thought is testimony to the concrete, corporeal nature thoughts had for the poet. They were events, visitations, as much to be remembered (if not more so) than a visit from her Monson relatives.

Critic Robert Weisbuch has spoken of Dickinson as a poet who never stops thinking and who takes us with her as her thoughts advance, digress, or reverse themselves, as we read a single poem. Thus, a poem that begins with an assertion of faith, following its circuitous course, may end on a note of doubt. Or a thought may be turned inside out by the very language and images in which the poet states it.

In this poem, the content of the thought is irrelevant; indeed, the poet herself lacks "the Art to say" "definitely, what it was." What interests her instead is the passage of the thought through her mind: its mysterious arrival and equally mysterious departure. The language she uses for the thought's arrival suggests a physical being: The thought went up her mind (the mouse went up the clock). The speaker's tone is whimsical, and in a way, her telling is as "purposeless" as what is told in that child's nursery rhyme. The thought went up her mind. It struck the "chime" of remembrance. It came down again. Hickory dickory dock.

The speaker knows she has had this thought before but did not finish it. "I could not fix the Year—" she apologizes—as if anyone might reasonably expect she would. But the point of the poem is that, for her, the stray thought is important enough to be fixed with such attention. The coming and going of a thought is an event, an occasion both momentous and amorphous. It is as if she recognizes a face but cannot quite place where she's seen it before. Dickinson manages to capture both the soul's deep recognition of something that belongs to it—and the mind's inability to grasp the nature or significance of the thing:

But somewhere—in my soul—I know—
I've met the Thing before—
It just reminded me—'twas all—
And came my way no more—

That parenthetic "'twas all" is a key little phrase. It seems to dismiss the importance of the event, while at the same time making clear that, at the moment of mysterious recognition, it literally "was all." Beneath the matter-of-factness of the final line is an undertone of wistfulness for the vanishing of the elusive visitor.

See also "THE BRAIN—IS WIDER THAN THE SKY—," and "THIS WORLD IS NOT CONCLUSION."

FURTHER READING

Robert Weisbuch, "Prisming," in *Handbook*, Grabher et al., eds., 214.

"A Visitor in Marl—" (1863) (Fr 558, J 391)

This deceptively simple verse, which consists of one long, descriptive sentence, is one of a large number of Dickinson poems written in the form of a riddle. In his seminal essay, poet and critic Anthony Hecht notes that the poet used the riddle form, not because of "ladylike reticence, but rather a religious seriousness, however unorthodox, and a profound sense that neither life itself nor the holy text by which we interpret it is altogether intelligible, and both require a riddling mind or interpretive skill" ("Riddles," 162). At the conclusion of one of her famous riddle poems, "SOME THINGS THAT FLY THERE BE—," she asks "Can I expound the skies? How still the Riddle lies!" The poet's task was not to solve the riddle but to discern it and present it to the reader in all its irreducible mystery. One of her techniques, as in the poem under discussion, was to spend the length of a poem describing something in metaphors, leaving it to the reader to identify it.

Hecht points out that Dickinson had at her disposal two major but widely disparate literary traditions to validate her use of riddles: the Bible and children's nursery rhymes, such as those of "Mother Goose." In this poem, there are traces of both traditions. Stanza 1 introduces us to the make-believe town of Marl, a name choice with no apparent justification other than its humorous half rhyme with flowers:

A Visitor in Marl—
Who influences Flowers—
Till They are orderly as Busts—
And Elegant—as Glass.

The delightful strangeness of the word "influences" prepares the reader for a light-hearted fairy tale in which personified flowers have visitors (a breeze, perhaps?) capable of "swaying" their opinions.

This innocuous playfulness, however, turns deadly in the next two lines, where the half rhyme of the first two lines is followed by a jarring absence of rhyme. The poem's rhyme scheme might be written as: *aabc defe gehe,* where *a* = Marl and Flowers, *b* = Busts, which has no rhyme but whose vowel sound resonates with the e-rhymed words; *c* = glass, which has no rhyme, but whose final consonants resonate with the final consonants of "Busts"; *d* = Night, which has no rhyme; and *e* = sun and run (full rhymes), and gone and been (half rhymes). This pattern sets up expectations of musicality, but keeps jarringly diverging from it.

What Dickinson admired in flowers was neither their orderliness nor elegance. The word "Till" implies the relentlessness of the Visitor's influencing. Whatever else he has done, he has turned something soft, pliant, and living into hard inanimate objects and materials. Busts might be arranged in orderly fashion in a museum or, more likely, in a cemetery. And busts are frequently made of marble—the basis for the contraction "Marl." One meaning of "Marl" is a white chalky deposit employed for fertilizer. But Judith Farr has noted that Dickinson used the word in quite another sense, when she wrote to her beloved friend ELIZABETH LUNA CHAPIN HOLLAND in January 1875: "Mother is asleep in the Library—Vinnie in the Dining Room—Father—in the Masked Bed—in the Marl House" (L 432). "The Masked Bed" refers to her father's coffin, which may have been covered in silk or satin, "the Marl House," to his grave with its marble headstone. (*Gardens*, 10).

In the second stanza, the visitor is further described as a nocturnal one, who "Concludes his glistening interview" before the dawn. Once again, as with the word "influences," Dickinson's peculiar word choice is a source of both mystery and irony. What, after all, is a "glistening interview"? An interview implies some kind of reciprocal process, a meeting in which two parties participate, but this interview seems controlled by the visitor who "concludes" it. The notion of "glistening," followed by the caressing of the next line, have led some readers to interpret the Visitor as the dew. However, any such comforting notion is dispelled by the final stanza, particularly its last line. The first three lines of this stanza make the Visitor more palpable and sensual—his fingers touch, his feet run; instead of kissing their lips, he enters the "Mouths" of the flowers, who in Cynthia Griffin Wolff's words, are "ravish[ed] into oblivion." Death here, she continues, is "an eradication so thorough that both being and all recollection of it are utterly nullified" (*Emily Dickinson*, 314). There can be little doubt that the visitor is frost and that Dickinson is describing "the killing of her flowers, an event that always seemed to her like murder" (*Gardens*, 10).

In one of her most famous poems, "TELL ALL THE TRUTH BUT TELL IT SLANT—," Dickinson declares that in poetry, "Success in circuit lies." In this case, she uses the circuitous language of riddle to effectively dramatize a commonplace event—the killing of flowers by frost—and to endow the event with greater resonance. The poem is about flowers, but is it *only* about flowers? For some feminist critics, the visitor is a flesh-and-blood man whose kisses leave the poem's speaker in a state of suspended desire. More persuasively, Wolff points to underlying religious allusions, discerning in the frost's deadly "Interview" an ironic realization of the biblical promise of seeing God "face to face." Whether or not something this specific is implied, there can be no doubt that Dickinson implicated a disappointing deity in the death of innocents. In "APPARENTLY WITH NO SURPRISE" (Fr 1668), she tells how Frost, "The Blonde Assassin," beheads a "happy Flower" "at it's [sic] play—" while even the Sun, characteris-

tically an emblem of warmth, light and beneficent power, is "unmoved" and "an Approving God" looks on.

See also "A NARROW FELLOW IN THE GRASS," "A ROUTE OF EVANESCENCE," "HE FUMBLES AT YOUR SOUL," and "IT SIFTS FROM LEADEN SIEVES—."

FURTHER READING

Judith Farr, *Gardens*, 9–10; Anthony Hecht, "Riddles," in *Critical Essays*, Judith Farr, ed., 149–162; Cynthia Griffin Wolff, *Emily Dickinson*, 312–314.

"A Wife—at Daybreak—I shall be—" (1861) (Fr 185, J 461)

A defining feature of Dickinson's work is what has been called the "sceneless" quality of most of her poems (Robert Weisbuch, "Prisming," 200). Although she is a superb storyteller, Dickinson does not write poems that take as their starting point a specific occasion. The "scenes" that appear in them are not recreations of concrete situations, but mental constructs, shaped to illustrate or serve as an analogy for a spiritual state or perception.

At first glance, the poem seems to be an exception, presenting, in its four opening lines, a scene we can visualize: The speaker is a young woman in her bedroom, greeting the morning of her wedding day and anticipating the momentous transition from "Maid" to "Bride." As we read on, however, the clear signposts of where we are fall away and we are left in a landscape of multivalent symbols. *Is* this a woman awaiting her bridegroom, or a child awaiting death/eternity, or a child/woman awaiting eternity as one would await a bridegroom? Is this a love poem or a poem in which the speaker projects herself into the transitional moment between life and death?

The difficulty begins in lines 5 and 6, when the night that has passed and the day that is breaking take on symbolic overtones. The speaker addresses "Midnight" in a triumphant tone. She has passed from Midnight and proclaims her sure destination "Unto the East—and Victory." This is a strange way to speak of marriage, if that is in fact what the poem is about. By the time it has been thrice repeated, "Midnight" is no longer a temporal designation; likewise, the implications of "Daybreak" and "Sunrise" are transformed once they become "the East—and Victory."

Indeed, both "Midnight" and "East" are key words for Dickinson, emblems that she uses repeatedly in different contexts. In "BEHIND ME—DIPS ETERNITY—" (Fr 743, 1864), she envisions herself as "A Crescent in the Sea—/ With Midnight to the North of Her—/ And Midnight to the South of Her—/ And Maelstrom—in the Sky—." In this powerful image of existential crisis "Midnight" is the spiritual darkness of past and future surrounding the turbulent present. In "At last—to be identified—" (Fr 172, 1860), it is the starting point of an exhilarating journey beyond earth's boundaries, "Past Midnight—past the Morning Star—/ Past Sunrise—Ah, What Leagues there were—/ Between Our Feet—and Day!" And in "Good Morning—Midnight—" (Fr 382, 1862), which reverses the movement of "A Wife—at Daybreak," she comes home to Midnight, unwillingly, in defeat, after Day, of which *she* could never tire, has tired of *her*: "You are not so fair—Midnight/ I chose—Day—/ But—please take a little Girl—He turned away!" Here, "Midnight" signifies the loneliness and heartache of rejection and the darkness of a life of unreciprocated love.

Similarly, as biographer Richard B. Sewall notes, in poems from the beginning to the end of her career, "'East' is a word charged with symbolic significance, often with no regard to geography" (*Life*, II, 479). It may suggest paradise or heaven, as in the poem she wrote after her mother's death: "To the bright east she flies / Brothers of Paradise / Remit her home" (Fr 1603, 1883). Another striking example of this usage occurs in Fr 35, 1858: "Morning has not occurred! / That shall Aurora be—East of Eternity—One with the banner gay—One in the red array—*That* is the break of Day!" And in "Afraid! Of whom am I afraid?" (Fr 345, 1862), she identifies her own fearless spirit with the East of eternal life: "Of Resurrection? Is the East / Afraid to touch the Morn / With her fastidi-

ous forehead?" Elsewhere in her writing, East is her word for human passion, as in the poem, "Said Death to Passion," in which she expresses Death's victory as his taking from Passion "All His East" (Fr 984, 1865).

As they appear in "A Wife—at Daybreak—," both Midnight and East are many-sided, opposing symbols representing lovelessness and romantic passion, despair and triumph, spiritual darkness and redemption, death and eternity. As the symbolic poles that dominate the poem, they suggest new possibilities for other images in stanza 1: "Sunrise—Hast Thou a Flag for me?" On first reading, the "Flag" the speaker asks of sunrise seems only a way of referring to the bands of color that spread across the sky as the sun rises. But now it connotes something more—a banner of spiritual victory, the sign of the speaker's imminent admission to eternal life. The line "How short it takes to make it Bride" suggests the swiftness of a spiritual change, opening up the possibility that the speaker is about to become the "Bride of the Father and the Son / Bride of the Holy Ghost—" as she calls herself in "Given in Marriage unto Thee," (Fr 818, 1864).

The Call she hears at the beginning of stanza 2, and the Angels bustling in the Hall, seem to confirm this interpretation: The celestial beings are preparing for her, in the hallway of heaven. In this interpretation, the "childhood" she is leaving behind is earthly life. Barton Levi St. Armand identifies the "'Childhood's prayer' fumbled at by the speaker as *The New England Primer's* 'Now I Lay Me Down to Sleep,' with its Puritanical stress on the 'Lord' both keeping and taking the trusting souls of those young Elect who are 'willing to die.'" (*Dickinson and Her Culture*, 141).

The line "Softly, my Future climbs the Stair—" conveys the sealing of her fate that marriage signified to a woman in Dickinson's time. But the line also evokes the gentleness of Death the bridegroom or suitor whom Dickinson immortalized in "BECAUSE I COULD NOT STOP FOR DEATH—" and other poems. At the end, she calls what awaits her "Eternity." By adding "Sir," however, she leaves open the possibility that she is equating Eternity with the figure of a man. How do we decide whether Eternity is the metaphor for an earthly love, or vice versa? The last line doesn't help much, especially when we learn that the variant for "Master" in Johnson's earlier version of the poem was "Savior." But the very existence of the variant indicates that we don't have to choose, that the notions of a sacred and an earthly "marriage" were fused in Dickinson's imagination. In another famous "marriage" poem, "TITLE DIVINE, IS MINE," written the following year, in which she is now "Wife," sacred and earthly loves are similarly intertwined.

Yet the line, "Master [Savior]—I've seen the Face—before—" creates other riddles. Why would the speaker *not* have seen the Face before, if it belongs to her betrothed? The phrasing of this moment of recognition suggests that the Face does not belong to the Master/Savior—or, if it does, that the Face is only one "facet" of this larger being. Is this a terrible recognition—is it Death whose face she has seen before? Or is it the Face of God she has intuited but can only see when she has died and passed into eternity (See "NOT IN THIS WORLD TO SEE HIS FACE—"). Judith Farr suggests yet another possible layer of meaning, when she claims that the Face belongs to Emily's beloved friend and sister-in-law SUSAN HUNTINGTON GILBERT DICKINSON. Farr bases her conclusion on the evidence of another poem of 1861, "Dying! Dying in the night!" in which Jesus and everyone else fails her except for "Dollie," as Sue was known by her familiars: "I hear her feet upon the stair! / Death won't hurt—now Dollie's here!" (Fr 222). Farr notes that the stairway, which was a prominent feature of the architecture of The HOMESTEAD, was a "ready metaphor of sexual feeling, poetic elation, and natural fulfillment." Based on the poems Emily sent to Sue, Farr concludes that "Sue is her Eternity. By comparison, Christ himself pales" (*Passion*, 136).

See also "A SOLEMN THING—IT WAS—I SAID—," "MINE—BY THE RIGHT OF THE WHITE ELECTION!" and "REARRANGE A 'WIFE'S' AFFECTION?"

FURTHER READING

Judith Farr, *Passion*, 58, 136; Suzanne Juhasz, *Undiscovered Continent*, 116–119; Richard B. Sewall, *Life*, II, 479–481; Barton Levi St. Armand, *Dickinson and Her Culture*, 141; Robert Weisbuch, "Prisming," in *Handbook*, Grabher et al., eds.

"A word made Flesh is seldom" (Undated) (Fr 1715, J 1651)

This brilliant signature poem is Emily Dickinson's love poem and hymn of joy to words. If, in her poems to an earthly beloved, she frequently declares that her loved one's face "Would put out Jesus'—" here she equates the holiness of "a word made Flesh" to the incarnation of Christ and declares it immortal. The root of her concept is found in the opening words of the Gospel according to St. John, Dickinson's favorite New Testament author. "In the beginning was the Word, and the Word was with God, and the Word was God." When Christ appears among men, St. John writes: "And the Word was made flesh, and dwelt among us."

In the first three lines, the poet evokes the "partaking" of "a word made Flesh" as the Eucharist, the eating of the body of Christ, an initiation into knowledge of the divine essence, by which mortals partake of immortality. In the symbolic interpretation of this ritual, the bread and the wine, representing Christ's flesh and blood, remain physical entities but are elevated to spiritual vehicles of the divine. So, too, for words "made Flesh" in great literature.

This tasting of the divine occurs only "seldom" and is done with awe ("tremblingly"). Moreover, of these rare occasions, which probably include the partaking of the living words of great authors, as well as of the ones she herself selected for her poetry, many go "unreported." They remain within the silence of the soul, neither set down on paper nor proclaimed by voice to others. And yet, she says, if instinct serves her right, this ecstatic tasting is experienced by all of us, "To our specific strength—" (that is, it is precisely the nutriment we need and are capable of digesting). The phrase "ecstasies of stealth" suggests both that we sneak up stealthily on the experience and that its elusiveness is central to the ecstasy we experience in unveiling its hidden essence. In Dickinson's day, "stealth" also meant downright theft. If this was what she had in mind, then the "ecstasy" here is Prometheus's, as he steals the sacred fire of art from the gods.

In a prime example of how Dickinson's poems and letters are interconnected, the first line of stanza 2 reverberates with her famous question to THOMAS WENTWORTH HIGGINSON, the man she asked to be her mentor: "Are you too deeply occupied to say if my Verse is alive? . . . Should you think it breathed . . . I should feel quick gratitude" (L 260, April 15, 1862). Of course, since the poem is undated, we don't know whether poem or letter came first. What is certain, however, is that for Dickinson, a word "just begins to live" on the day it is articulated, as she wrote in one epigrammatic poem ("A word is dead, when it is said," Fr 278, 1862). In 1715, she proclaims, "A word that breathes distinctly / Has not the power to die."

Language is power, whether to bless or to curse, that extends indefinitely into the future. In "A Word dropped careless on a Page" (Fr 1268, 1872), a word's longevity may be pernicious:

Infection in the sentence breeds
We may inhale Despair
At distances of Centuries
From the Malaria—

With so potent a weapon in hand, the poet must take care to use it judiciously.

In "A word made Flesh," her emphasis is on language as a "cohesive" force, with the power to unite by its "consent" to live among us. The concluding six lines might be paraphrased: "If Christ, who was/was said to have been 'Made Flesh and dwelt among us'—could descend from his rank and dwell among us, in the same way words do, then 'a word that breathes distinctly could expire. But, since Christ does not/ or until he does—we have language instead, the closest we get, perhaps, to the

sacred." To understand these lines, we must read the word "condescension," not as we use it today, to imply a snobbish "looking down" at someone, but as it was used in Dickinson's day, to denote "a voluntary descent from rank, dignity or just claims." There is a hierarchy involved, in which man stands on a lower rung. In contrast to this improbable "condescension," language "consents," embracing us as equals.

In the final two lines, consenting language, "this loved Philology" surrenders to the poet and the pleasure she feels radiates from the very language she uses. "Philology" (like "condescension") spices the language of the poem with a multisyllabic, abstract, Latinate word. As a sound unit, it contains a brief joyous burst of song ("la-la") and twice echoes the "lo" of the *love* of words, which is its essential meaning. (Its second meaning, in Dickinson's Webster's, is "That branch of literature which comprehends a knowledge of the etymology or origin and combination of words . . . [that] sometimes includes poetry . . .").

Dickinson's poetry is replete with expressions of her passionate bond to language. One of the most direct and memorable is "Many a phrase has the English language—" (Fr 333, 1862), in which the language of the Anglo-Saxons is a word of love spoken by a Saxon lover, whom she adjures:

Say it again, Saxon
Hush—Only to me!

Related poems, in which Dickinson uses the Eucharist as her symbol of the inspiriting power of words are "Your thoughts dont have words every day" (Fr 1476, 1878) and "He ate and drank the precious Words—" (Fr 1593, 1882).

See also "I RECKON—WHEN I COUNT AT ALL—" and "MY LIFE HAD STOOD—A LOADED GUN—."

FURTHER READING

Charles R. Anderson, *Stairway*, 46–49; Cristanne Miller, *Poet's Grammar*, 171–173; Joseph Rabb, "The Metapoetic Element in Dickinson," in *Handbook*, Grabher et al., eds., 288–289; Robert Weisbuch, *Emily Dickinson's Poetry*, 35–36.

"A *wounded* Deer leaps highest" (about 1860) (Fr 181, J 165)

In this superb early poem, Dickinson explores the art of living with a hidden wound. Rather than adopting a confessional mode, the poet gives us a series of startling images, each of which adds new implications to what it means to be wounded. Dickinson's philosophical poems are never cold or cerebral; they convey the heat of lived emotion.

She does "hide" the biographical episode that motivated the poem behind her elliptical, rapidly alternating images, just as Anguish, in the final stanza, defends itself cautiously behind the armor of Mirth. At the same time, however, her images and diction boldly expose the depths and dimensions of the speaker's feelings and show her struggling with them. The italicized adjectives—*wounded, smitten, trampled* (underlined in the original manuscript)—convey heightened emotion and emphasize the unifying thread of humiliating injury caused by a violent act.

In the first stanza, she sets forth the notion of a mortal wound that gives rise to one last show of life force and superior agility. The speaker identifies with the high-leaping, wounded Deer, boasting that power is inherent in pain; the wound is a source of energy and artistic feats. But in line 2 she undercuts the strength of this assertion by attributing it to the Hunter, that is, she reports it as hearsay, rather than her own triumphant pronouncement. In line 3, the Deer's spectacular performance is further reduced by the dismissive "Tis but" (presumably the Hunter's way of putting it) the "extasy of death"—no miraculous enlivening, but the Deer's instinctive, final performance, before dying. Dickinson uses an older spelling of "ecstasy," similar to that used by her beloved Shakespeare, among others. The term denotes a state of being beside oneself, thrown into a frenzy or stupor with anxiety, fear, astonishment—or passion. The latter may well be what is implied; for, in Shakespeare's time, the trope of Hunter and Deer was commonly used to depict the ritual

of courtship. Moreover, "almost certainly it was Shakespeare who made her familiar with the Elizabethan pun for sexual climax—'death'" (Wolff, *Emily Dickinson,* 205). The stillness of the "Brake," (in this context, an area of dense undergrowth, shrubs, and brush) is thus as much a post-coital lull as the aftermath of death.

The second stanza "leaps" precipitously into new territory, leaving the Deer/Hunter imagery behind. In a frenzy imitating the Deer's "extasy," the poet flashes three discrete but parallel images before the reader, each followed by an exclamation mark conveying high emotion. Each deepens and develops the theme of wounding. In the image of the *smitten* Rock, Dickinson is alluding to the biblical story of Moses, who brought forth water for the Israelites in Sinai by striking a rock with his rod (Exodus 17:6). Traditionally, this is a tale of miracle and redemption: Moses, through the agency of his God, performs a miracle that overrides natural limits and allows him to bring forth a life-giving substance from dead rock. But, in her elliptical retelling, Dickinson shifts the focus to the "*smitten* Rock"—to the inanimate object struck by miracle—and to its fecundity. The blow enlivens and brings forth. It is hard not to read this line, with its ring of exultation, as an emblem of Dickinson's poetic art, "founded on thrilling loss, thrilled sublimation" (Farr, *Passion,* 182).

In the next line, shifting from the biblical to the material realm, she invokes the image of steel, another hard substance, which, for reasons unstated, has been "*trampled*"—a word that implies humiliation. But if the trampled steel is the degraded poet, then she is, literally, a coiled spring, filled with powerful, tumultuous emotions set to release. The cheek image adds yet other dimensions to the meaning of "the wound." Is the cheek red because it has been slapped? This is certainly implied. Is the cheek suffused with the heat of passion? This, too, is a possibility. In addition, however, the term "Hectic" denotes a hectic flush, the term used in Dickinson's time for the type of flush accompanying "consumption" (as tuberculosis was then known). Thus, the notion of an illness that creates a false sense of liveliness is added to the other dimensions (astounding performance and fecundity, humiliation, passion, repressed explosiveness) of the wound.

The final stanza shifts once more in tone and imagery. Coming down from the intense emotional ejaculations of stanza 2, it proposes a "cautious" strategy of concealment and survival:

> Mirth is the mail of Anguish—
> In which it cautions Arm,
> Lest Anybody spy the blood
> And "you're hurt" exclaim!

"Mirth"—deceptive clowning, the putting on of a merry show—is revealed as the armor ("Mail") defending Anguish from exposure before the eyes of others. This is a soldierly, stoic philosophy, very much in the New England and the Dickinson tradition. The poet's horror of exposure to the outside world is well known and recognized as a central factor in her reclusiveness. This poem demonstrates, however, that whatever Dickinson may have withheld from inspection by the world, she was excruciatingly aware of the depths of her painful emotions and of their power as wellsprings of her work.

FURTHER READING

Judith Farr, *Passion*, 182; Agnieszka Salska, *Poetry of the Central Consciousness*, 146–47; Richard B. Sewall, *Life*, I, 213; Cynthia Griffin Wolff, *Emily Dickinson*, 205.

"Because I could not stop for Death—" (1862) (Fr 479, J 712)

One of Dickinson's most famous and widely discussed poems, Fr 479 appeared in the first 1890 edition of her poems, edited by MABEL LOOMIS TODD and THOMAS WENTWORTH HIGGINSON. Higginson had given it the inappropriate title "The Chariot," thinking, perhaps, of an image from classical times that survived in Victorian paintings of Apollo, patron of the arts, carrying the artist to heaven in his chariot. (Farr, *Passion*, 329). The editors seriously disfigured the poem by omitting the fourth stanza; and Mrs. Todd "improved

on" the poet's exact rhyme in stanza 3, rhyming "Mound" with "Ground" instead. Not until the publication of Johnson's 1955 *Poems* were readers able to see the restored poem. Despite this, it had already been singled out as one of her greatest and continues to be hailed as a summary statement of her most important theme: death and immortality. As in all of Dickinson's complex works, however, the language and structure of the poem have left readers plenty of room to find varying and sometimes sharply opposed interpretations. At one end of the spectrum are those who view the poem as Dickinson's ultimate statement of the soul's continuance; at the other end are those who see the poem as intrinsically ironic and riddled with doubt about the existence of an afterlife; in the middle are those who find the poem indisputably ambiguous.

Scholars have suggested that Dickinson's carriage ride with Death was inspired by a biographical incident—the 1847 death of Olivia Coleman, the beautiful older sister of Emily's close friend ELIZA M. COLEMAN, who died of a tubercular hemorrhage while out riding in a carriage. But there are also abundant cultural sources for the image. The poem's guiding metaphor of a young woman abducted by Death goes back to the classical myth of Persephone, daughter of Ceres, who is carried off to the underworld by Hades. In medieval times, "Death and the Maiden" was a popular iconographic theme, sometimes taking the form of a virgin sexually ravished by Death.

Doubtless aware of these traditions, Dickinson made of them something distinctly her own. Not only did she transplant the abduction to the country roads of her native New England, she transformed the female "victim," not into a willing or even passionate lover of Death, but into an avid witness/participant in the mysterious transition from life to death, and from human time to eternity. The speaker never expresses any direct emotion about her abduction; indeed, she never calls it that. She seems to experience neither fear nor pain. On the other hand, there is no indication that she is enamored of Death: She is too busy to stop for him and it is he, the courtly suitor, who takes the initiative. But she does not resist. Death's carrying her away is presented as a "civility," an act of politeness. And she responds with equal good manners, putting away her labor and her leisure, too, that is, the whole of her life. What *does* draw her powerfully is the journey, which she observes and reports in scrupulous detail. The poem is her vehicle for exploring the question that obsessed her imagination: "What does it feel like to die?"

Note that there is a third "passenger" in the carriage—"Immortality"—the chaperone who guarantees that the ride will have an "honorable" outcome. Immortality is a promise already present, as opposed to the "Eternity" of the final stanza, toward which the "Horses' Heads" advance. Eternity is the ultimate transformation of time toward which the poem moves. In stanza 1, the speaker, caught up in this-worldly affairs, has no time for Death, but he slows her down. By stanza 2, she has adjusted her pace to his. Stanza 3, with its triple repetition of "We passed," shows them moving in unison past the great temporal divisions of a human life: childhood (the children competing at school, in a ring game), maturity (the ripeness of the "Gazing Grain") and old age (the "Setting Sun"). As the stages of life flash before the eyes of the dying, the movement of the carriage is steady and stately.

But with the pivotal first line of stanza 4, any clear spatial or temporal orientation vanishes; poem and carriage swerve off in an unexpected manner. Had the carriage passed the sunset, its direction—beyond earthly life—would have been clear. But the line "Or rather—He passed Us" gives no clear sense of the carriage's movement and direction.

It is as if the carriage and is passengers are frozen in time. The sun appears to have abandoned the carriage—as reflected in the increasing coldness that envelops the speaker. She is inadequately dressed for the occasion, in "Gossamer," which can mean either a fine filmy piece of cobweb or a flimsy, delicate material, and a "Tippet," that is, a small cape or collar. While tippets were commonly made of fur or other substantial materials, this one is of "tulle"—the fine silk netting used in veils or gowns. All at once,

the serenely observing speaker is a vulnerable physical presence, dressed for a wedding or ball, but "quivering" with a coldness that suggests the chill of the grave. A note of uneasiness and disorientation, that will only grow stronger from this point on, has been injected into what began as a self-assured journey. This is a stunning example of how "Dickinson, suddenly, midpoem, has her thought change, pulls in the reins on her faith, and introduces a realistic doubt" (Weisbuch, "Prisming", 214).

In stanza 5, the carriage "pauses" at "a House that seemed/ A Swelling in the Ground—," presumably the speaker's newly dug grave. The word "Swelling" is ominous, suggesting an organic, tumorlike growth. But there is no unified physical picture of what the speaker sees. In line 2, the ground is swelling upward. In lines 3 and 4, the House has sunk; its cornice, the ornamental molding just below the ceiling, is "in the Ground." The repetition of the word "Ground" stresses its prominence in the speaker's consciousness. It is as if all her attempts to hold on to the things of this world—the children at school, the grain, the setting sun, the cobweb clothing, the shapeless swelling of a House—have culminated in this single relentless image.

Then, in a leap that takes us to the poem's final stanza, the speaker is in a different order of time, where centuries feel shorter than the single day of her dying. This is the poem's only "description" of Eternity and what it implies is that life is immeasurably denser, fuller, weightier. Eternity has no end, but it is empty. Significantly, in the speaker's recollection of the final, weighty day, "Death" is not present. Instead, she invokes the apocalyptic vision of "the Horses' Heads" (a synecdoche for the horses) racing toward Eternity. But, for the speaker, seated in Death's carriage, the horses' heads are also an obstruction, "they are all she can see, or what she cannot see beyond" (Cameron, "Dickinson's Fascicles," 156). They point to the fact that the poem is an artifice, an attempt to imagine what cannot be imagined. "Toward Eternity—" remains only a "surmised" direction.

See also "BEHIND ME—DIPS ETERNITY—" and "I HEARD A FLY BUZZ—WHEN I DIED—."

FURTHER READING

Sharon Cameron, "Dickinson's Fascicles," in *Handbook*, Grabher et al., eds., 149–150, 156, and *Lyric Time*, 121–133; Judith Farr, *Passion*, 92–93, 329–33; Kenneth L. Privratsky, "Irony in Emily Dickinson's 'Because I could not . . . ,'" 25–30; Robert B. Sewall, *Life*, II, 572, 717–718; and Cynthia Griffin Wolff, *Emily Dickinson*, 274–276; Robert Weisbuch, "Prisming," *Handbook*, 216–217.

"Behind Me—dips Eternity—"
(1863) (Fr 743, J 721)

In this stark poem, considered to be among her greatest, Emily Dickinson attempts to define her life's coordinates on a "map" spanning the distance between Eternity and Immortality. But what begins on a note of certainty quickly degenerates into doubt and estrangement, and climaxes on a building note of disorientation and terror. In a poem in which, as Robert Weisbuch conceptualizes it, we are allowed to see the poet "thinking out loud," one image-thought gives way to others that carry their own contradictory messages and knock the poet off her original, intended course into a trackless realm.

Dickinson often used the words *Eternity* and *Immortality* interchangeably, as synonyms for time without end and life everlasting. Given that she is "the Term between" in stanza 1, which on one level refers to the time span of a mortal life, it is likely that the distinction she is making between the two words here is between the limitless time that preceded her birth (Eternity) and the immortality of the soul, promised by Jesus Christ, that awaits her after death. Carrying the idea further, she dismisses death as a mere wisp of gray cloud on the eastern horizon, that dissolves as the sun rises in the East—the symbol of resurrection. The stanza's final line, "Before the West begin," that is, before the sun's movement to the West (to sunset and death) begins, suggests that, in this new Day in heaven, there will be no movement westward, toward sunset and extinction. Time will have ceased. Thus far, we have what Cynthia Griffin

Wolff calls "the traditional Christian formula for passing from this world into the timeless realm of Heaven" (*Emily Dickinson*, 293). The one jarring note in this "Christian" stanza is the speaker's referring to herself as "the Term between"; not only does she fail to see herself as a child of God, she is a mere "term," something less than human, an element in a cosmic equation.

And in fact, in the second stanza, as she develops the theme of the promised Kingdoms, the neat conceptualization of stanza 1 gives way to doubt and estrangement. The tagged-on disclaimer "they say" at the end of line 1 is the first indication of her doubt. Moreover, the vision of heaven she evokes is not one that she—or we—would willingly embrace. While the royal imagery for God's kingdom is traditional, Dickinson's variations on this language gives it a cold, relentless quality. The Kingdom of God becomes a "perfect—pauseless Monarchy—," while God himself is rendered as a Prince, who, in a surprising image, is "Son of None." The blunt, internal rhyme reinforces the sense of emptiness. Spawned by nothingness, this Prince is an insular narcissist, forever reacting to himself alone, and duplicating himself: "Himself—His Dateless Dynasty—/ Himself—Himself diversify—/ In Duplicate divine—." This can only be read as a parody of the notion of God's unity. The plethora of "d" sounds "imitates" the divine duplication of the dateless dynasty, making audible what Wolff calls "the horrific proliferation of a house of mirrors" (293). A sense of claustrophobia begins to invade God's boundless kingdom, where even the Trinity generated consists of three identical, self-regarding entities. (For a radically different interpretation of this stanza as an "unabashed apocalypse," see Anderson, *Stairway*, 319–320).

It is little wonder that in stanza 3, the speaker flees back to her earthly dilemma in the present. The fact that the syntactic structure of this stanza parallels that of stanza 1 only highlights the difference between the opening and concluding "landscapes" in which she locates herself. To see this transformation more clearly, it is necessary to dwell for a moment on the unusual amount of alliteration, as well as repetition of words, and phrases, on which the poem is built. Initially, in stanza 1, the poet's delicate handling of this technique created a harmonious language that reinforced her optimistic vision. By stanza 2, however, the reader feels battered by the relentlessness of sound repetition (*perfect, pauseless, prince; dateless, dynasty, diversify, duplicate, divine*) combined with word repetitions ("Himself" occurs three times within two short lines). These repetitions create a sense of entrapment in "time eternal" that only intensifies when the poem shifts back to the "mortal span" of the present in stanza 3.

In the first two lines, the sense of meaningless "duplication" continues in the repeated word "Miracle." In stanza 1, what came behind the speaker ("Eternity") was different from what stood before her ("Immortality"). There was a progress from one state to the next, and consequently a sacred purpose to "the Term between," since it leads to Immortality. Despite the hopefulness inherent in the word "Miracle" the speaker is not uplifted by its surrounding presence. Disoriented, she stumbles awkwardly from one preposition to the next "behind—between—," and then vanishes altogether from the cosmic landscape, replacing herself with "A Crescent in the Sea." This startling switch in viewpoint signals, not an Olympian distancing, as some critics have suggested, but a terrified retreat from her own vision. Instead of herself, the fragile entity that finds itself in so dangerous a situation is the reflection of a quarter moon in the sea.

The East and West of time without end is now replaced by the North and South poles of this planet, of bounded temporality, where Midnight is a time of lonely terrors. Finally, as if this were insufficient peril, there is "Maelstrom—in the Sky—." In what has become a map of dislocation, the natural order has been reversed: The moon, which belongs in the sky, is in the ocean, the violent whirlpool of the maelstrom belongs in the ocean, but it is in the sky. In these images, there is an echo of Revelations 8, when apocalypse is loosed by the opening of the seventh seal, and earth, sky and ocean merge violently one into the other, e.g., "hail and fire mingled with blood and they were cast upon the earth" (8/7) . . . "And as it were a great mountain burning with fire was cast into the sea" (8/8) . . . "and there fell a great star from heaven, burning as

it were a lamp, and it fell upon the third part of the rivers" (8/10).

Thus, the poem never frees itself from eschatological concerns, even as it returns to the dangers of mortal life. "Miracle there may be," Dickinson seems to be saying, "and faint portents of the end of time, but now, in this present, I am surrounded by storm and darkness." It is "the Term between," her mortal life, that she must somehow survive.

See also "BECAUSE I COULD NOT STOP FOR DEATH" and "EACH LIFE CONVERGES TO SOME CENTRE—."

FURTHER READING

Charles R. Anderson, *Stairway*, 318–320; Sharon Cameron, "The Dialectics of Rage," in Harold Bloom, ed., *Modern Critical Views*, 115–117; Judith Farr, *Passion*, 311–313; Cynthia Griffin Wolff, *Emily Dickinson*, 292–295.

"Blazing in Gold and quenching in Purple" (1862) (Fr 321, J 228)

Under the title "Sunset," this poem was published in *The Springfield Republican* on March 30, 1864. Had Dickinson been in the habit of naming her poems, this title might have been given to a great many others as well. From youth to her final years, the dramatic spectacle of the setting sun, which spoke to her of both death and immortality, held a special place in her cosmology.

In this virtuoso early poem she personifies the sunset in a series of rapidly changing images. Like the ever-transforming light, the poet settles on no single visual image, but (like her leopards of light) leaps from one to another. Light is a regal gold and purple blaze in the first line, a leopard/leopards in lines 2–4, a humanlike figure capable of stooping low, touching and kissing her bonnet in lines 5–7, and in the final line, the departed "Juggler of Day."

Grammatically, the poem's single eight-line stanza is one sentence. The poem is structured as a series of participial phrases, which progress rapidly from vibrant acrobatics (blazing, leaping) to the gentle motions of decline and surrender (laying her spotted face to die, stooping low, and kissing the meadow farewell). These participles begin each line with a stressed syllable, setting up a dactyllic/trochaic rhythm that creates a sense of excitement. The departure of the light in the final line is the only action described, not as process, but in the past tense; the end of the drama is marked by a calmer rhythm: "And the Juggler of Day is gone." The spectacle of sunset has ended, revealing light's illusory nature. As scholar Charles R. Anderson puts it, "These are the illusions of time created by the great conjuror, not only day's juggler, but the juggler *of* the day" (*Stairway*, 154). He reminds us that in medieval times, the juggler was both imposter and magician. In another sunset poem of 1862, "They called me to the Window, for," (Fr 589), the Sun is "the Showman" who keeps "rubbing away" the visual illusions he creates.

The poet, too, is a conjurer, and there is an urgent quality to her many "tricks." Even within a single image, she "juggles" her images: many leopards leap to the sky, but only one lays "her spotted face to die" at the "feet of the old Horizon." With the death of the single leopard, the light grows tamer, becomes a country light that stoops "as low as the Otter's Window," touches the roof and tints the barn. (In two variants for these lines, the sunset bends to the FIRST CHURCH OF CHRIST, across the street from her home and to The HOMESTEAD's west-facing kitchen.

As biographer Cynthia Griffin Wolff notes, the thrust behind the fervent image-making of this and similar nature poems is the notion that "it is the poet's imagination, not God, that can give meaning to the natural world" (*Emily Dickinson*, 482), a notion Dickinson develops in Fr 557, the 1863 poem, "I Send Two Sunsets." In this droll rendering of the poet's "competition" with Day, she brags that she "finished Two [sunsets]—and several Stars—" in the time it took him to make only one sunset. While admitting that "His own was ampler," she notes that hers, the sunsets of poetry, are "more convenient / To Carry in the Hand—." However whimsical and self-mocking her words, the speaker's "rivalry" with the natural order and delight in her own powers are palpable.

In "Blazing in Gold," the sunset is feminine in all its metamorphoses, as it is in other of Dickinson's poems. In "She sweeps with many-colored Brooms," Fr 318, written that same year, the sun is a "Housewife in the Evening West" who trails shreds of purple, amber, and emerald behind her as she tidies up. In yet another 1862 poem, "The Day undressed—Herself—" the sunset is a brilliantly dressed woman who takes off her gold and purple clothing, "The Lady of the Occident" who retires "without a care—." The sunset may be male, however, as in the 1858 poem "The Guest is gold and crimson" (Fr 44), in which "he" is a luxuriantly attired nobleman. In her repeated attempts to capture what she calls in one poem "the Western Mystery" ("This—is the land—the Sunset washes—," Fr 297), she calls forth a dazzling array of metaphors.

Facsimile of "I send Two Sunsets—" (Fr 557, 1863) *(By permission of the Houghton Library, Harvard University)*

A major note running through all Dickinson's sunset poems, and in some cases, their sole impetus, is the sheer sensual delight the spectacle engenders. These include the long 1862 poem, "How the old mountains drip with sunset," in which fire images are subject to the flaring and ebbing transformations of the "Wizard Sun," yet another variant of the "Juggler of Day." In "The Sun kept stooping—stooping—low!" (Fr 182, 1860), the dense Armies of the sunset are "So Gay—So Brigadier—," they arouse "martial stirrings" within the speaker. "A slash of Blue! A Sweep of Gray!" (Fr 233, 1861) is little more than a series of exclamations on the changing colors of light as sunset is followed by sunrise, the speaker proclaims: "'Red Sea,' indeed! Talk not to me / Of purple Pharaoh—/ I have a Navy in the West / Would pierce his Columns thro'—";

In Fr 468 (1862), the setting sun turns the sky and clouds into "Whole Gulfs—of Red, and Fleets—of Red—/ And Crews—of Solid Blood." The poet calls this vision "a Drama—/ That bows—and disappears—," and indeed it was the drama of ending that the sunset primarily enacted for her. Similarly, "beautiful death" is the notion behind "Fairer through Fading—as the Day," in which the sun goes through its death throes and finally disappears with "an expiring—perfect—look—." In Fr 119 (1861), "If this is 'fading,'" the sunset's death is so glorious, she is quite willing to die in a similar "shroud of red."

In other poems, sunset is associated with both death and resurrection. Thus, in "An ignorance a Sunset" (Fr 669, 1863), sunset's "Amber Revelation" brings with it the hint of immortality. And in "The largest Fire ever known" (Fr 974, 1865), death and immortality hover around the repeated spectacle of sunset, evoked as "An Occidental Town, / Rebuilt another morning / To be burned down again."

In a later sunset poem, Fr 1366, 1875, the poet admits, "I'd rather recollect a Setting/ Than own a rising Sun. . . . Because in going is a Drama / Staying cannot confer." Indeed, Dickinson is the poet, not of birth, but of transience, death, and dying; not surprisingly, in only a handful of her poems does the sun rise without quickly setting again.

See also "BRING ME THE SUNSET IN A CUP—."

FURTHER READING

Charles R. Anderson, *Stairway*, 152–155, Cynthia Griffin Wolff, *Emily Dickinson*, 482.

"Bring me the sunset in a cup—" (1860) (Fr 140, J 128)

In this exuberant early poem, the speaker, with a delightful sense of entitlement, demands that nature's wonders be brought to her in digestible quantities and revealed to her in precise numbers. In the first three lines of stanza 1, she insists that nature be reduced to human, countable terms: the sunset in a cup, the number of "Dew" in the "morning's flagons." Images follow one another rapidly: The morning "leaps" (like the leopards of sunset in "BLAZING IN GOLD AND QUENCHING IN PURPLE"). In an image that alludes to the traditional vision of God the creator, she asks not *who* created the sky, but "what time the weaver sleeps / Who spun the breadths of blue!" Such numerical concerns continue to preoccupy the poet, a precise observer of nature, in the next stanza, in which she demands to know the number of notes in the "new Robin's extasy," the number of trips the Tortoise makes, the number of cups "The Bee partakes, The Debauchee of Dews!" Clearly this is a spring poem, animated by the speaker's exaltation in these small natural wonders. (In a poem of the following year, "I TASTE A LIQUOR NEVER BREWED—" Dickinson will refer to herself, in the drunkenness of poetic creation, as "Debauchee of Dews").

In the third stanza, however, as she continues her breathless, greedy list of inquiries ("Also . . . Also . . ."), she no longer asks "how many" but "Who created all this?" The speaker's questions will inevitably remind the Bible reader of those that God himself hurls at Job as a pointed way of reminding him of his inferior status in the sacred hierarchy. *I am the one who created all this,* God proclaims, *so who are you to question the justice of your fate?* While the allusion to Job is there, Dickinson's speaker appropriates the form of God's taunting, rhetorical questions, but utters them, in a tone of simple wonder at the glories of creation:

Also, Who laid the Rainbow's piers,
Also, Who leads the docile spheres
By withes of supple blue?

(Note that *withes* means willow twigs or a band consisting of twisted twigs). In the stanza's final whimsical image, she returns to the counting theme of stanza 1, making God into a careful accountant, tallying the number of stars:

Who counts the wampum of the night
To see that none is due?

But in the final stanza, the poem suddenly changes direction:

Who built this little Alban House
And shut the windows down so close
My spirit cannot see?
Who'll let me out some gala day
With implements to fly away,
Passing Pomposity?

The "Alban House" is a grave, and belongs to a series of images in which Dickinson perceives graves and graveyards as dwelling places. In this dramatic and unanticipated shift, the previously exuberant speaker, who has been rejoicing in life's wonders, speaks in the voice of one who has died. In the midst of her exhilaration, she has been reminded of the ultimate reality of death and a sudden doubt overcomes her. She attempts to recover her high spirits by evoking the "gala day" or resurrection. Beyond the pomposity of conventional religious rhetoric, she seems to say, there will be "implements," that is, some tool or mechanism built into creation, that will, indeed, see to the survival of her spirit. Yet this assertion is framed within the question of "Who," ending the poem on a note of that ambivalence that Dickinson characteristically brought to her "flood question": "Is Immortality true?"

See also "BECAUSE I COULD NOT STOP FOR DEATH—," "I DIED FOR BEAUTY," "SAFE IN THEIR ALABASTER CHAMBERS—," "THOSE—DYING THEN," and "WHAT INN IS THIS."

FURTHER READING

Ronald Wallace, *Clown*, 93–94.

"Come slowly—Eden!" (1861) (Fr 205, J 211)

This poem was included in the 1890 publication of Dickinson's work, *Poems*, edited by MABEL LOOMIS TODD and THOMAS WENTWORTH HIGGINSON, who was probably the one to entitle it, inappropriately, "Apotheosis." The bashful title, while accurate in a general sense—the poem *does* move toward a high point of glory—nonetheless camouflages the sexual nature of that ascent. Like "WILD NIGHTS— WILD NIGHTS" (Fr 269), written in the same year, the poem conjures the vision of sensual fulfillment through the image of the Garden of Eden. In Dickinson's time, the myth of Eden had been revived by American painters such as Thomas Cole, founder of the Hudson River School, whose paintings "The Garden of Eden" (1828) and "Expulsion from the Garden of Eden" (1827–28) created the image of a lost paradise, based on Latin American scenery (Farr, *Passion*, 226–227).

In the poem's first stanza, the "Eden" addressed by the speaker may be understood as both place (paradise) and beloved person. For it was not unusual in Dickinson's time to refer to someone as the place from which he hailed or was prominently associated. She sometimes referred to herself as "Amherst," and she called the love of her later years, JUDGE OTIS PHILLIPS LORD, "My Salem." With "bashful" lips, the speaker begs Eden to "Come slowly," so that she may savor and grow used to an unfamiliar pleasure. Thus the Eden of this poem is not a lost paradise regained, but uncharted territory, being experienced/explored for the first time.

The image she uses to evoke the pleasure she cautiously tastes, "Sip Thy Jessamines," refers to the jasmine; Dickinson adopts a spelling used by horticulturists. To 19th-century gardeners, "Poet's jessamine" was the name given to the plant's fragrant white flowers. Dickinson cultivated a jasmine, given to her by SAMUEL BOWLES, in her conservatory. Bowles is the man whom many scholars believe was the one Dickinson called "Master," her great love, and the one to whom this poem was written. Four years after his death, the poet sent a spray of pressed jasmine to his son, Samuel Jr., with the words: "A Tree your Father gave me, bore this priceless flower. Would you accept it because of him." This request is followed by a poem elegizing Bowles, which ends with the assertion that his "Immortality" is "Secreted in a Star," that is, the jasmine blossom (L 935, about 1884).

In this poem, however, the jasmine is clearly the flower of passion. The version of the name Dickinson uses for it, Jessamines—the only three-syllable word in the poem—conveys a languid sensuality. The sounds of that word—its *m* and *ns*—are picked up in the final stanza, particularly its last three lines (chamber hums, nectars, balms), but within a different picture entirely. Following a dash, the bashful speaker flits away into the safer, more manageable realm of metaphor, devoting the rest of the poem to the image of the bee—where what is overwhelming can be shaped and tamed. By means of this strategy, the poet engages an otherwise unbearable bliss. Dickinson, after all, is the poet who wrote that same year: "I CAN WADE GRIEF—/ Whole Pools of it—/ I'm used to that—/ But the least push of Joy/ Breaks up my feet—And I tip—drunken—" (J 61). Interestingly, the word "Balm," which in Dickinson's work connotes healing pleasures, occurs in this poem, too, and is associated with an unfamiliar—and to some extent, unwelcome—loss of control. From all accounts, the intensity of Dickinson's emotional responses in general was extreme, but, while she navigated the darker emotions—grief, loneliness, anger, terror—ingeniously, with acrobatic agility, she felt alarmingly unstable in the proximity of happiness.

She seems to have taken heart from the bee, an image that has a number of meanings in her poetry, but which she prominently associates with a spiritual inebriation (see "I TASTE A LIQUOR NEVER BREWED—"). The "gender reversal" entailed by her identification with the masculine bee does not imply anything with regard to the poet's sexuality; the image simply demands it. Snugly within the metaphor, she and the tardy Bee, who is "fainting" at first, after a bit of circling and procrastination, take the leap and, in a phrase whose music reinforces its meaning, are "lost in Balms," immersed in the healing ecstasy of love—and language.

FURTHER READING

Judith Farr, *Passion,* 225–227; Robert Weisbuch, "Prisming," in *Handbook,* Grabher et al., eds., 202–203.

"Crisis is a Hair" (1865) (Fr 1067, J 889)

This is one of Dickinson's most encoded, compressed DEFINITION POEMS. In her attempt to capture the essence of a powerful yet subtle inner experience, she enlists her full arsenal of linguistic and poetic innovations, including fractured syntax, a virtual absence of PUNCTUATION, extensive use of ellipsis, a complex pattern of imagery, and variations of rhyme and meter that reinforce semantic meaning.

Part of the poem's intensity derives from its short lines and use of predominantly one- and two-syllable Anglo-Saxon words, a feature that characterizes Dickinson's poetry as a whole. But she frequently varies the rhythm by inserting polysyllabic words of foreign derivation such as *retrograde, balancing, hesitate, Circumference,* and *Eternity* at the end of a line, or *ignorant* at the beginning of one. As Cristanne Miller notes, "the poet's polysyllables have the effect of emphasizing aurally the poem's general compression" (*Grammar,* 42). Their presence "loosens up" the rhythm, conveying a mood of uncertainty at certain key points: in stanza 2, in the line "*Ignorant* is it Life or Death"; in stanza 3, lines 3 and 4: "*hesitate* / In *Circumference,*" and in the poem's penultimate line: "That secures *Eternity.*"

The poem's key word, *Crisis,* is defined in the Webster's dictionary Dickinson once described as her only companion as follows: "1. In medical sciences, the change of a disease which indicates its event; that change which indicates recovery or death; 2. The decisive state of things, or the point of time when an affair is arrived to its highth (*sic*), and must soon terminate or suffer a material change." The language of the poem commingles both medical and nonmedical meanings; it offers no details that might pinpoint the precise nature of the crisis. What interests Dickinson are the *dynam-*

ics of the experience of crisis. She speaks here in the voice of the meticulous observer and strategist, determining her extremely limited options for action in the face of forces that move according to their own laws, beyond her control.

This military analogy—the ambush of something singular, fragile, and almost invisible (a Hair) by strong forces creeping toward it—dominates the first stanza. The poem is silent as to the nature of these forces; it does not tell us whether they are physical or spiritual, benevolent or malevolent, internal to the speaker or external to her. They may be life forces (the body's vitality, the energies of the soul), or something inimical to life, or both, that is, the opposed forces of life and death. All we are told is that they creep toward the Hair of crisis, then retreat past it. (As a verb, Dickinson's lexicon defines "retrograde" as "to go or move backward.")

Crisis is a Hair
Toward which forces creep
Past which—forces retrog[r]ade
If it come in sleep

If we assume that stanza 1 is a syntactic unit (a sentence), then the stanza may be taken to mean "If 'it,' that is, the moment of crisis (a Hair), comes while the person is sleeping, then forces will creep toward it and recede beyond it." This suggests the crisis of a physical illness, perhaps a fever breaking while the sufferer sleeps, followed by recovery, as the "forces retrograde." Admittedly, however, such an interpretation lends more specificity to the lines than they actually possess. If we assume that Dickinson knew what she was doing when she omitted punctuation and used spare, elliptical language, that is, that these "irregularities" are part of her "message," then we can only conclude that she intended her scenario of the Hair of Crisis to resist clear visualization. Instead, she invites us to enter an uncertain realm, where the movement of forces are only dimly—and threateningly—perceived.

The floating phrase "If it come in sleep" might just as well connect to the first lines of stanza 2:

To suspend the Breath
Is the most we can

In this case, a paraphrase of lines 4–8 might read: "If the crisis comes in sleep, all we can do is suspend our breath, since we are ignorant of whether the crisis will result in Life or Death, which, for now, are finely balanced." Scholar Jane Eberwein takes this approach, noting, "By representing the crisis as a hair, the poet emphasizes the fragility of the barriers protecting the circuit world, which can defend itself only by preternatural stillness . . ." (*Dickinson*, 177). By scarcely breathing, we may avoid setting off any of the tiny events, alluded to in stanza 3, that may trigger huge events.

In the third and fourth stanzas, as the poem shifts from the inner experience of crisis to the things that influence it, the syntax becomes more coherent. The minuscule events that can influence the outcome—"instant push" and "Atom press"—are what were then believed to be the smallest elements of time and space. The lines "Or a Circle hesitate / In Circumference" must be understood within the context of circle imagery in Dickinson's poetry. Circumference, a significant word in her vocabulary, has a number of interrelated meanings; essentially, it was her term for the boundary between what can be humanly known or experienced and what cannot. The circle or "circuit life" is the everyday realm of limited human experience, and, in Dickinson's thinking, the essence of being a poet was the gift of being able to move imaginatively beyond that limited world and stretch circumference just a little bit further. This privileged experience involved both ecstasy and terror. Thus, a "circle hesitating in circumference" might refer to a failure of nerve, confidence, or courage, preventing the circle (the poet) from transcending her own limitations.

In the fourth stanza, "It" refers to any of the factors just enumerated: Any slight temporal or physical pressure, any hesitation of the Circle can "jolt the Hand / That adjusts the Hair." The Hand is a metaphor for the individual's effort to control the crisis. But, as the jolt to the adjusting Hand suddenly magnifies into the event "That secures Eternity / From presenting—Here—," it becomes the Hand of God that determines individual fate. Dickinson's concept of a minuscule event setting in motion a series of larger events that result in a gigantic one resonates with contemporary "chaos theory," which posits that the motion of a butter-fly's wings can set off a chain of events resulting in a powerful storm. In this poem, the slightest "movement" can prevent "Eternity" from "present-ing Here—." Note how ingeniously rhyme rein-forces meaning: There is only a hair's breadth of a difference in sound between "Hair" and "Here."

If Eternity signifies death, as it often does for Dickinson, then the poem's ending alludes to how the very fragile forces that hold death at bay may be altered. But Eternity, for the poet, was also syn-onymous with heaven, immortality, or salvation. Which meaning is intended—and whether in fact Eternity, whatever its meaning, has been kept back, remains ambiguous. As critic Suzanne Juhasz notes, "Concentrating upon the nature of the balance itself, the poem is . . . purposefully ambiguous about what happens afterwards" (*Undiscovered Continent,* 62). Although the word *crisis* does not occur fre-quently in Dickinson (See "'Twas Crisis—All the length had passed—" [Fr 1093] and "Crisis is sweet and yet the Heart" [Fr 1365]), much of her poetry is structured upon the dynamics of crisis, a stance that endows her work with its peculiar dramatic intensity. In poem after poem, the poet experiences each moment of the processes of living or dying as a crisis toward whose turning point she irresistibly moves, all the while carefully observing its details and attempting to grasp its essence.

See also "CRUMBLING IS NOT AN INSTANT'S ACT," "I FELT A FUNERAL, IN MY BRAIN," and "I HEARD A FLY BUZZ—WHEN I DIED."

FURTHER READING

Jane Eberwein, *Dickinson,* 177, 196; Roland Hagen-buchle, "Precision and Indeterminacy in the Poetry of Emily Dickinson," 10–11; Suzanne Juhasz, *Undiscovered Continent,* 60–62; Cristanne Miller, *Grammar,* 40–43.

"Crumbling is not an instant's Act" (1865) (Fr 1010, J 997)

Written when Dickinson was 34, this DEFINITION POEM is an attempt to grasp intellectually the pro-cess leading up to some "crumbling" or "crash" that may have occurred at an earlier period in her life. Typically, the poem gives no hint of a specific epi-sode; only the sense of urgency in the speaker's need to reconstruct what happened betrays the probability that there *was,* in fact, an intensely per-sonal, traumatic experience behind the generaliza-tions. As in so many of her poems, she attempts to stand at a distance, in order to trace with utmost precision the subtle movements of the inner life.

Commenting on this underlying thrust of the poem, scholar Sharon Cameron writes: "If one could at least chart the stages whereby a thing passed into incomprehensibility, one might come to terms with the fact that the process itself and the loss with which it concludes is not sudden, as it appears, but has stages" (*Lyric Time,* 43). In this regard, Dickin-son is not so much contradicting what she says in "CRISIS IS A HAIR," that is, that the slightest event can mean the turning point between life and death, so much as she is describing the extended, insidious process leading up to that crucial moment.

The language of the opening stanza is scientific, the tone cool. There are a number of polysyllabic Latinate words and a prevalence of nouns. The only verbs are the copulas—the static verbs— "is not" and "are." This pattern continues in the second and third stanzas, so that the poem itself appears almost immobile, lacking in movement. What slow, subtle movement does occur is in the progression of meanings developed in the imagery. The gradual slippage that is "Crashe's law" is thus enacted by the poem itself.

Compression of meaning is intense in stanza 1, which is dominated by two-word combinations in which a noun is modified either by an adjective ("fundamental pause," "organized Decays") or by the possessive of another noun ("instant's Act," "Dilap-idation's processes"). What keeps the stanza from getting clogged by these densely packed phrases is the unexpected concepts they convey. Both "orga-nized Decays" and "Dilapidation's processes" are oxymorons, linking the notions of order and struc-ture to disordering and collapse of structure.

The second stanza turns from abstraction to visual imagery to continue the definition of "Crum-bling." The images chart a progression that is subtle at first. A cobweb is insubstantial and with a minor effort can be cast off; a cuticle is not much harder to remove (a thin coat of skin), but this one is made of dust. In the third line, however, the poem moves from passive coatings that dull the material they overlay to the image of a "borer"—an active agent of decay, something that makes holes in the very axis on which the self balances. In its final transformation, it becomes an "Elemental Rust," a state of decay inseparable from the material to which it adheres and thus virtually impossible to remove.

The third stanza returns to the abstract, nonvisual language of stanza 1, with its predominance of adjectives and possessive nouns modifying nouns: "Devil's work" and "Crashe's law." (Note that Johnson's earlier version reads "Crash's law.") Despite the lack of active verbs, there is a sense of incremental but definite movement into new territory. Words of order and disorder are linked ("Ruin is formal"), as in stanza 1, but "Ruin" is a more damning word than "Crumbling"; it points to the final stage of the process of crumbling. "Formal" belongs to the same semantic field as "law," an impersonal dynamic governing human affairs. Yet the phrase "Devil's work" introduces another, more personal note: Rather than denoting a literal belief in the Devil, it expresses the speaker's sense of being at the mercy of an evil beyond her control, one possessed of the supernatural patience that allows it to proceed slowly and consecutively. The rage she so tightly contains within the poem's formal strictures flares out in this phrase. Then, in the final two lines, she draws back and repeats with stronger emphasis her assertion of stanza 1: "Fail in an instant, no man did" and states her conclusion as a law of nature: "the beginning of a process contains and predicts its conclusion" (Cameron, *Lyric Time*, 43). A note of clarification: Historically, there is no such thing as Crashe's law, comparable to Newton's laws of motion. Dickinson often misplaces apostrophes and may have meant to place it after the "s" of the plural "crashes." What she clearly means is that crashes occur by virtue of gradual slipping. If such understanding returns a degree of intellectual control to the speaker, there is little comfort in its deterministic view. As biographer Cynthia Griffin Wolff sees it, the poem evokes a "movement through time that is undifferentiated and unshaped by God's mercy, every moment like every other, and each inching all of us irresistibly toward death" (*Emily Dickinson*, 234).

Dickinson's biographers have grappled with the issue of whether the poem is "evidence" of a previous emotional breakdown, an attempt to come to terms with a severe period of personal disintegration in her late 20s. While both Robert Sewall and Alfred Habegger concede the possibility that Dickinson may have experienced mental illness, each, in varying degrees, stresses her extraordinary ability to recover from her depressions, engage life, and overcome madness through the transcendent, integrative process of making poetry. The psychoanalytically oriented critic who has made the most extensive case for Dickinson's psychic disintegration is John Cody, who connects this poem to "the increasing imbalance in Emily Dickinson's personality that led to her collapse in her late twenties . . ." (*After Great Pain*, 260). Cody describes a long process, beginning in early adolescence with her depression (which she called a "fixed melancholy") following the death of her friend SOPHIA HOLLAND, that led to the "slipping" resulting in her psychic crash. He includes in his list of "undramatic but ominous harbingers of chaos" a host of symptoms including "depression, anxiety, estrangement, avoidance of gratification, extraction of pleasure from privation, preoccupation with death, withdrawal from social intercourse, agoraphobia, fear of loss of emotional control, preternatural awareness of the mind's unconscious depths . . . weakness of ego boundaries, and night fears" (261–262). While noting the impressiveness of Cody's analysis, Habegger cautions the reader to be wary of it, due to "the difficulty of reconciling such fragmentation with the integrative resourcefulness of the poet's work" as well as the fact that none of her contemporaries spoke of her as crazy (*My Wars*, 410–411).

See also "FOREVER—IS COMPOSED OF NOWS" and "I FELT A FUNERAL, IN MY BRAIN."

FURTHER READING

Sharon Cameron, *Lyric Time*, 43–44; John Cody, *After Great Pain*, 259–262; Cynthia Griffin Wolff, *Emily Dickinson*, 233–234.

"Dare you see a Soul at the 'White Heat'?" (1862) (Fr 401, J 365)

The year that Emily Dickinson wrote this poem she also wrote 226 others; the previous year she had written 88, and the following year she would write 295. With her own soul at the white heat of poetic creation, she could not resist throwing out the audacious challenge of the first line: "Have you the courage, dear reader, to witness me as I am, in the blinding glow of my creative passion? Will it hurt your eyes?" In another famous poem about poetry, "TELL ALL THE TRUTH BUT TELL IT SLANT—," she cautions, "The Truth must dazzle gradually / Or every man be blind—." Here, however, she exults in the dazzling "designated Light" her soul gives out and allows herself the satisfaction of knowing herself capable of an intensity and purity few are capable of either achieving for themselves or grasping in another.

The poem itself, of course, is a virtuoso example of telling things slant: an extended, complex metaphor of a blacksmith's forge, which, as the poet herself tells us, "Stands symbol for the finer Forge / That soundless tugs—within—." One might say that the metaphor of the forge is a commonplace, a rather obvious image for life as a searing, shaping process. Other poets had used it. Dickinson surely knew Henry Wadsworth Longfellow's 1840 poem "The Village Blacksmith," which concludes: "Thus at the flaming forge of life / Our fortunes must be wrought; / Thus on its sounding anvil shaped / Each burning deed and thought." In Longfellow's poem, the poet is a blacksmith, a conscious workman ("God's workman") who crafts his poems on the forge of life. Reading Longfellow's poem helps to define the uniqueness of Dickinson's forge metaphor, for both its point of view and its one-on-one correspondences are alien to her poetics.

As we would expect, Dickinson does not develop the metaphor in a simple, linear way, with a single meaning attaching to forge, flame, ore, and light. There is an unusual amount of repetition of key words, palpable in a poem of only 16 lines: ore (twice), forge (three times), blaze (twice), light (twice), as well as two pair of virtual synonyms (fire and flame, anvil and hammer). We may be sure that this is a conscious technique by means of which Dickinson both modulates the meanings of her metaphor and creates the sense of an evolving, self-influencing process. Within the first three lines of stanza 1, she sets up a contrast between white and red that goes beyond the physical reality to a symbolic plane. Red, she tells us, "is the Fire's common tint—." But red is also the color of passion, of blood, of the things that bind us to the imprisoning flesh (the "Scarlet prison"). White has many meanings in Dickinson, but is most often the symbol of purity and redemption. (See "MINE—BY THE RIGHT OF THE WHITE ELECTION!")

The next elements of the metaphor she introduces are "the vivid Ore" that "Has vanquished Flame's conditions—." By linking the concrete "Flame" to the abstract "conditions," Dickinson lifts "fire" to a principle, a state of existence with its own laws—to burn, destroy, incinerate. "Vivid" as the modifier of "Ore," the soul in its early, untested, unrefined state, also has two levels of meaning: On the physical level, it refers to the brightness and strength of the ore's original *vivid* color (red), while on the symbolic, it suggests the brilliance of a *vivid* imagination, a bright, strong spirit capable of transcending (vanquishing) "Flame's conditions."

The triumphant ore then "quivers from the Forge"—the next element of the metaphor, the larger "structure" in which the purifying process takes place. The word recurs in stanza 3 as "the finer Forge / That soundless tugs—within—," suggesting the action of the soul upon itself. It is a sensitive, silent, irresistible force that refines "these impatient ores"—presumably teaching them patience throughout the long, slow, difficult process. This process continues "Until the designated Light / Repudiate the Forge—." Thus, the "Forge" sets in motion a process that results in its own repudiation. What seems to be implied is that the "designated Light" emerging from the refining process is now wholly different and independent from the forge/force that has produced it. Through some undefined alchemy, it has transcended its origins, becoming something both separate from and greater than what has produced it. If this poem is about Dickinson's art, it appears to be saying that technique, conscious craft (the forge), shapes painful experience (another aspect of the forge) and that the light that the poem "designated" results in the distancing of the pain and the circumstances that caused it. Linguistic specialist Cristanne Miller points to another plausible related aspect of the forge metaphor, when she suggests that it "may apply to the cryptic compression and distortions of Dickinson's language. Ordinary language exists as unrefined ore, the unexamined life. It must undergo painful and unnatural or artful manipulation to become pure" ("'A letter is a joy,'" 35).

In counterpoint to the evolving "forge," images of light metamorphose throughout the poem. Fire with its "common tint" and vanquished flame gives way to "the Light / Of unannointed Blaze—" that emanates from the colorless ore that emerges from the forge. Scholar Sharon Cameron believes that "the bleaching out of color is not a reduction of desire" but "attests to the irrevocable 'Blaze' of life itself, the pure life of unconsecrated existence that comes from a force that breaks, burns, blows, and ultimately makes new" (*Lyric Time*, 199).

To be anointed is to be chosen, consecrated as a holy personage or a ruler anointed by God. But this blaze is unanointed; in Dickinson's universe, it emanates not from a divine presence but from the human soul. The image may also conceivably refer to the fact that the "blaze" of Dickinson's poetry was "unanointed" by the literary community. Whatever its specific reference, however, the image represents not the poet's defeat but her victory. When it recurs in the final stanza, "Blaze," the fire and light of genius, is one of the two instruments, by which the Forge does its refining, the other being the "Hammer" of life's blows. As biographer Richard B. Sewall notes, ". . . only when the soul is at the white heat can it be free of flame and 'repudiate the Forge' (its worldly existence). The stress is on the struggle for release, what [Herman] Melville would call 'the fine hammered steel of woe'" (*Life*, II, 709).

See also "OF BRONZE AND BLAZE—."

FURTHER READING

Sharon Cameron, *Lyric Time*, 198–200; Sandra Gilbert and Susan Gubar, *Madwoman*, 611–613; Cristanne Miller, "'A letter is a joy of earth': Dickinson's Communication with the World," 29–39; Agnieszka Salska, *Walt Whitman and Emily Dickinson*, 100–102; Richard B. Sewall, *Life*, II, 709; Helen Vendler, "The Unsociable Soul," 34–37.

"Did the Harebell loose her girdle" (1860) (Fr 134, J 213)

On its most obvious level, this celebrated poem, possibly conceived as a flirtatious reply to a lover's advances, is a revery on sexuality, desire, and the consequences of surrender. Dickinson's tone is whimsical in the first stanza as she rephrases the conventional wisdom: "Won't he respect her less if she gives in to him?" The "she" in this case is, of course, a flower: the harebell or bellflower, a plant with bell-shaped flowers, "a soft-fleshed white or blue ornamental perennial much loved in Victorian gardens" (Farr, *Gardens*, 185). The loosening of its "girdle" by this lovely bloom is an enticing image, indeed.

Throughout her life, Dickinson wittily explored sexuality through bee-flower imagery, taking a variety of perspectives. In the renowned "COME SLOWLY—EDEN," for example, the speaker identifies with the approach of the "fainting Bee" as he prepares to enter his intoxicating flower. In "The Flower must not blame the Bee—" Fr 235, 1861, the speaker advises the flower that it is she who has the onus of refusal and is obliged to inform the importunate bee "That seeketh his felicity / Too often at her door—" that she is "not at home." In a later poem, "Like Trains of Cars on Tracks of Plush," Fr 1213, 1871, she views the sexual encounter in more violent terms as the bee's "sweet Assault"; the flower is consumed, while the victorious bee flits off to his next conquest. As critic Joanne Feit Diehl notes:

This coy intrusion of society's conventions upon the natural union of bee and flower develops into an abiding mode in Dickinson's nature poems—the garden becomes a neutral landscape which may provide freedom from personal anxiety or, hiding behind a mock insouciance, an occasion to allegorize fear" (*Romantic Imagination*, 87).

In the poem under discussion, Dickinson restates the double standard of male/female sexuality through her bee/flower imagery. Since, however, nothing could be more natural than the "intercourse" of bee and flower, the poem parodies its own premise by taking the argument to an absurd level. Moreover, the second stanza implies that, not only will the flower/female be diminished by her surrender, but the Earl and Eden will be degraded as well. If we continue to read the poem in terms of erotic dalliance, then the language of stanza 2 suggests that "he" has attempted to persuade her by referring to her, or what awaits them, as "Paradise":

> Did the "Paradise"—*persuaded*—
> Yield her moat of pearl—
> Would the Eden *be* an Eden,
> Or the Earl—an *Earl?*

Having said this much, we are left with the question of what, if anything, is added to or changed in the poem's meaning by the abrupt shift of imagery in stanza 2, from bees and flowers, to paradise, moat of pearl, Eden, and Earl. For literary scholar Robert Weisbuch, the answer is just about everything. He points out that there are two full scenes posited in the poem: a country garden and the Garden of Eden; a partial sketch of a feudal castle with a moat and a knight; "and, if one reads the castle's yielding of the moat and the harebell's loosing of the girdle as sexual compliance, a metaphorized fourth scene, which is the female body" ("Prisming," 199). For Weisbuch, although the sexual meaning is certainly there, the second stanza introduces a theological dimension when "the bee is replaced by the Earl of Eden, which may be to say God." He thus proposes that the poem is asking, "If we could reach Heaven and be in the presence of God, wouldn't both Heaven and God somehow lose their supreme import, that is, no longer be Heaven (Eden) and God (Earl)?"

We might argue that the title of "Earl" has distinctly sexual connotations in Dickinson's work, as, for instance, in "THE MALAY—TOOK THE PEARL—," in which the speaker is herself the Earl, but loses the sexual prize (the pearl) to a primitive male figure, out of fear of the "sea" of sexuality. In "No matter—now—Sweet—," Fr 734, 1863, written from an androgynous point of view, becoming "Earl" designates the gaining of both royal power and sexual attractiveness: "No matter—now—Sweet—/ But when I'm Earl—/ Won't you wish you'd spoken / To that dull Girl?"

More persuasively, Weisbuch notes that Dickinson has put the word "Paradise" in quotes, suggesting that it stands for anything we want it to mean. For Dickinson, after all, Eden was in the eye of the beholder, as she wrote in a letter to her great friend, ELIZABETH LUNA CHAPIN HOLLAND: "Vinnie says you are most illustrious and dwell in Paradise. I have never believed the latter to be a superhuman site. Eden, always eligible, is peculiarly so this noon" (L 391, summer 1873). What was most eligible (in the sense of desirable) for Dickinson, however, was what was unattainable, as she tells us in Fr 310, 1862:

> "Heaven"—is what I cannot reach!
> The Apple on the Tree—
> Provided it do hopeless—hang—
> That—"Heaven" is—to Me!

In Dickinson's universe, then, asks Weisbuch, "will not whatever becomes ours, or known, lower itself in our esteem rather than elevating the seeker?" ("Prisming," 199). Thus, the harebell poem is about sexuality, religion, and the nature of human desire itself. To select any single meaning and exclude the others would be to "rob it of its vital versatility" (200).

See also "WILD NIGHTS—WILD NIGHTS!"

FURTHER READING

Joanne Feit Diehl, *Romantic Imagination*, 86–87; Judith Farr, *Gardens*, 175–213; Martha Nell Smith, *Rowing*, 54–56; Robert Weisbuch, *Emily Dickinson's Poetry*, 16–18, and "Prisming," in *Handbook*, Grabher et al., eds., 198–200.

"Each Life converges to some Centre—" (1863) (Fr 724, J 680)

In this complex, philosophical poem Dickinson explores the relationship between the "Centre," the central life goal toward which each human being strives, and the tortuous, uncertain process of the striving itself. The poem begins with an authoritative statement, but as it progresses, the poet's voice hesitates and becomes entangled in qualifications. Attempting to assert a linear movement toward something definite, it is repeatedly pulled back into a sense of tentativeness and doubt.

Stanza 1 begins with the assertion that there exists in each soul a central goal toward which it "converges." Intrinsic to the human spirit, whether articulated or not, "some Centre" exists for all of us. St. Augustine wrote, "God is a circle whose center is everywhere and whose circumference is nowhere." Dickinson's line has been interpreted by some critics in this light. Scholar Bettina Knapp, for one, believes that "The 'Centre' in the first stanza, considered as Principle or absolute Reality, refers to God. . . ." That each "Life Converges" . . . or moves toward a single point, approaching a limit as the number of terms increases without limit, signifies a universal and infinite presence" (*Emily Dickinson*, 138–139). Yet, this interpretation reads more into the line than its language justifies. Dickinson is asserting her belief, not necessarily in a deity but in a principle of striving that gives purpose to human life. There *may* be something higher that motivates this striving, but that idea is not developed in the poem. The phrase "Some Centre" is ambiguous. Is the "Centre" the same for everyone, or do we each have individual "centers"? Is it God toward which the soul strives, or its own, deeply personal vision of the good and the desirable?

Stanza 2 introduces a qualification to this universally sought center or goal: It, too, is in process. It is a goal—"Embodied scarcely to itself"—something that is still forming. Thus, the poem both asserts the definiteness of the soul's striving and

the dimly understood nature of the goal itself. The fragmented syntax of this stanza reinforces a sense of indefiniteness. For one thing, the lack of any punctuation but dashes allows for different readings. The line segment "—it may be—" is an example of syntactic doubling, that is, a phrase that can refer to what comes before and/or what comes after it. Thus, we may read: "It [the goal] may be scarcely embodied to itself" and/or "it [the goal] may be—/ Too fair / For Credibility's presumption / To mar—." Similarly, in stanza 1, line 2 "Expressed or still" may refer to either the preceding "Centre" or the subsequent "Goal." In these instances, the poem itself becomes a conception in the process of forming, sharing the semi-unarticulated nature of the center/goal. Beyond syntactic ambiguity, the language itself is puzzling. What does it mean that "It may be too fair for Credibility's Presumption to mar?" Something that is "credible" is somewhere between possible and probable, but it is a great deal less than certain. What Dickinson seems to be saying is that the goal may be so fair that even our skepticism, our presuming to judge it in terms of its logical credibility, cannot mar it.

In stanza 3, the goal, now no longer a center (movement inward) but a heaven (movement upward and outward), is further cast into doubt. Ellipsis and syntactic doubling contribute to the sense of uncertainty:

> Adored with caution—as a Brittle Heaven—
> To reach
> Were hopeless, as the Rainbow's Raiment
> To touch—

This stanza may be paraphrased: "We adore this goal with caution, since to reach a brittle heaven is hopeless, just as hopeless as touching a rainbow." A "Brittle Heaven" is one that may crack and crumble at the touch. If you get too close, grasp it too tightly, you may destroy it.

This idea is carried forward in stanza 4, which asserts that, despite the half-formed goal, our half-belief, and the fragility of our goal/heaven, we nonetheless continue to strive toward it. Moreover, it is the goal's distance that makes us persevere more surely—a sentiment that is fundamental to much of Dickinson's work. The phrase "How high" floats wistfully on its own, referring either to the preceding "Distance" or "The Sky" that doesn't materialize until two lines later. Using the solemn, biblical form "Unto," she asserts that the sky, though high, will be earned only by the Saints' slow diligence—attained as a reward only for that kind of steady, faithful striving.

In the final stanza, the poet both admits the possibility of failure and reaffirms the ever-present possibility of success:

Ungained—it may be—by a Life's low Venture—
But then—
Eternity enable the endeavoring
Again.

Again, the fragmented lines make the precise statement ambiguous. She may be saying that the goal may not be gained in a particular life, one that hasn't aimed high enough. Or it may be that life itself is a "low Venture." All depends on whether "a Life" means a particular life, or "any Life." In either case, we get another chance in eternity. This eternity, rather than a place of rest and reward, would be a strenuous place, where the soul goes on "Endeavoring." Note the use of the uninflected form of the verb ("unmarked for person, function, or tense") in the phrase "eternity enable" (rather than "enables") which makes the statement more universal (Cristanne Miller, *Grammar*, 65). The poem ends on a note of high affirmation. However, as Shira Wolosky incisively notes, "[the] conclusion would be more convincing if the poet had not . . . presented both goal and eternity as unattainable, as hopeless to reach as it would a rainbow" ("Syntax," 178). If life is a process governed by an end, both the nature of that end and its attainability remain in question.

The formal elements of the poem reflect and reinforce this tension between goal and process, certainty and uncertainty, order and disorder. Although the poem has an iambic tendency, especially in the short lines, it lacks a regular metrical pattern. Each stanza is built on the tension between alternating short lines (a goal, too fair, to mar, to reach, to touch, too high, the sky, but

then, again) and the longer lines, many of which contain polysyllabic words (converges, embodies, credibility's presumption, persevered, diligence, eternity, endeavoring). The long lines seem to reach out toward the goal, while the short ones pull back, imitating the halting, difficult progress of the Soul to "some Centre."

Further, as Wolosky points out, by inverting subject and complement, the poet's meaning remains hidden until the end of a stanza, for example, "Exists . . . A Goal" instead of "A Goal exists." She notes: "The prosody underscores the goal as that which governs process. It also underscores how tenuous relations between goal and process can be. Syntactically, inverted complements lead to confusion as to the subject left behind; conceptually, the significance of what has gone before depends entirely upon an end that remains beyond it and that seems unknown" (Ibid., 178).

To some extent, the poem's rhyme scheme and extensive sound orchestration create a "music" that works against the disordering elements of the poem. In the first three stanzas, alternating lines either don't rhyme at all or their final consonants echo one another: centre/nature, still/goal, fair/mar, heaven/raiment, reach/touch. Rhymes become more exact in the fourth and fifth stanzas, which reaffirm the value of striving: sky/high and then/again are exact rhymes, while distance/diligence, and venture/endeavoring are approximate rhymes, which repeat dominant sound patterns, such as *ev* and *en*. The poem contains a profusion of words with short *e* sounds at the beginning (*Expressed, exists, embodies enable, endeavoring, eternity*), as well as in the middle (*centre, every, credibility, heaven, venture, then,* and *again*). Note the frequent *en* and *ev* syllables. The long *e*, in *each, eternity, reach,* and *be,* forms a secondary pattern. In addition, *s* and *d* sounds occur frequently. This richness of sound orchestration, which compensates for the missing music of a regular metrical pattern, is a vital ordering principle that balances the poem's disorder.

See also "THIS WORLD IS NOT CONCLUSION," "UNDUE SIGNIFICANCE A STARVING MAN ATTACHES," and CIRCUMFERENCE POEMS.

FURTHER READING

Bettina L. Knapp, *Emily Dickinson*, 138–139; Cristanne Miller, *Grammar*, 64–70; Shira Wolosky, "A Syntax of Contention," in *Modern Critical Views*, 177–178.

"Eden is that old fashioned House" (Undated) (Fr 1734, J 1657)

In this subtle DEFINITION POEM, Dickinson meditates on the human failure to recognize Eden when we are in its midst. We only know we have lived in paradise when we can no longer return to it. At the same time, however, as in her 1862 poem "Heaven' is what I cannot reach!," she implies that the present transforms the meaning of what we have left behind, making it appear to our bereft eyes like paradise.

In Dickinson's time, the myth of Eden had been revived by American painters such as Thomas Cole, founder of the Hudson River School. His paintings, *The Garden of Eden* (1828) and *Expulsion from the Garden of Eden* (1827–28), created the image of a lost paradise, based on Latin American scenery (Farr, *Passion*, 226–227). Dickinson's familiarity with this revived myth is reflected in poems such as "COME SLOWLY—EDEN!" and "WILD NIGHTS—WILD NIGHTS," both of which conjure the vision of sensual fulfillment through the image of the Garden of Eden. There are no hints of this passionate Eden in the poem under discussion, however. What she invokes, instead, is the quiet paradise of everyday life: instead of an exotic paradise, a domestic one. For Dickinson, life was centered around the affairs of a house. She lived beneath her father's roof for her entire life, and played a central role in the managing of the household—baking, cooking, and gardening. As critic Sandra M. Gilbert notes, "Dickinson loved exotic place names . . . but nevertheless the news of those distances came to her at home, in her parlor, her kitchen, her garden" ("Wayward Nun," 27). In one well-known poem "Volcanoes

be in Sicily," Fr 1691, she contemplates "Vesuvius at Home."

It is not unusual for Dickinson to relocate paradise to her everyday world. Most often, however, she does this in the context of celebrating nature and the heavenly joy of participating in its "rites" as another "simple" creature. This is what critic Albert Gelpi called her concept of "Nature perfected to Paradise" ("Seeing New Englandly," 57). In "SOME KEEP THE SABBATH GOING TO CHURCH—," she triumphantly concludes her evocation of a Sunday "worship service" in her garden, amid the company of the bobolink and the bee, with the declaration, "So instead of getting to Heaven, at last—/ I'm going, all along." In another early poem, "As if some little Arctic flower," Fr 127—a parable about a lost, northern flower who wanders into "continents of summer," she writes, "As if this little flower / To Eden, wandered in—."

What is unusual in the poem under discussion is that the paradise-on-earth is not nature, but a house. Dickinson's poetic landscape is marked by houses of all sorts. She writes of the heavenly home and the House of the Lord. Her houses may represent shelter or comfort. Yet, they are often lonely or deserted and, most frequently, they are associated with death: either a house where a death has taken place ("There's been a Death, in the Opposite House," Fr 547), or, in poem after poem, the grave itself. (See, for example, "BECAUSE I COULD NOT STOP FOR DEATH—," "WHAT INN IS THIS," "SAFE IN THEIR ALABASTER CHAMBERS—," "I DIED FOR BEAUTY—BUT WAS SCARCE," "Who occupies this House?" [Fr 1069], "The Color of the Grave is Green—" [Fr 424], "Doom is the House without the Door—" [Fr 710], and "Too little way the House must lie" [Fr 902]).

In stark contrast, the house in this poem is a lost Eden. It is "old fashioned"—a word that appears in her poem about summer, "LIKE SOME OLD FASHIONED MIRACLE." The phrase expresses her wonder at an abundance she can scarcely credit and suggests that the summer past was the kind of real, honest-to-goodness miracle such as occurred in earlier, simpler, more faith-filled times. Thus, while what is "old fashioned" has a strong, nostalgic pull for Dickinson, the world it evokes is not accessible to her. From the very first line of "Eden is that old fashioned House," she stands outside it.

Dickinson was adept at using the archetype of Eden as a metaphor for many kinds of paradise and exclusion therefrom. Thus, Fr 437 begins:

> I never felt at Home—Below—
> And in the Handsome skies
> I shall not feel at Home—I know—
> I don't like Paradise—

This Eden strikes her as a lonely, restricted place, with a judgmental God she likens to a telescope, forever keeping a watchful eye on his subjects. The poem has an impish, defiant quality, quite different from Fr 1734, which is really about the unreachable past.

If the past is inaccessible in Fr 1734, this is, in part, because of its tenuous place in her consciousness. Not only does she not recognize the house for what it is while she dwells there, she can only return to it via an "unconscious" route, as in a dream. In its evocation of a dreamlike return to an abandoned house, and of a Door beyond which the speaker can no longer pass, this poem is related to "I YEARS HAD BEEN FROM HOME," written in 1862, which continues: "And now before the Door / I dared not enter, lest a Face / I never saw before / Stare stolid into mine / And ask my Business there—." This nightmare poem, written in Dickinson's dramatic mode and permeated with a sense of the surreal and the suspenseful, ends with the speaker fleeing in terror "like a Thief." Its emotional pitch is a far cry from the reflective sadness of "Eden is that old fashioned House." Yet both poems, through the central metaphor of the locked or vanished house, evoke the pathos of a lost era of time. In retrospect the vanished house may even seem like paradise.

See also "A LOSS OF SOMETHING EVER FELT I," "FOREVER—IS COMPOSED OF NOWS—," and "THOSE—DYING THEN."

FURTHER READING

Judith Farr, *Passion*, 226–227; Albert Gelpi, "Seeing New Englandly," in *Modern Critical Views*, Harold Bloom, ed., 57–58; Sandra M. Gilbert, "Wayward Nun," in *Critical Essays*, Judith Farr, ed., 25–26; Adrienne Rich, "Vesuvius at Home: The Power of Emily Dickinson," in *Shakespeare's Sisters: Feminist Essays on Women Poets*, Sandra M. Gilbert and Susan Gubar, eds.

"Exultation is the going" (1860) (Fr 143, J 76)

In this DEFINITION POEM, Dickinson takes the reader on a journey into a symbolic landscape: the journey of the "inward soul" into "deep Eternity." She defines exultation, not as arrival or fulfillment, but as "the going," the act of embarking on the seaward journey. Typical of many of her definitions, this one makes a noun ("Exultation") correspond to a verb or verbal form ("the going") instead of to another noun. From this simple core, the definition then expands in complex ways: "Exultation is 'going' in a particular landscape and direction" (Miller, *A Poet's Grammar*, 84–85, 97–98).

There is no lyrical "I" in this poem. Nonetheless, the speaker is clearly felt to be the "inward soul" of the poem, one whose native place is the Land, not the sea, not deep eternity. She makes this identification explicit in stanza 3, in the line "Bred as we, among the mountains." On one level, this is an allusion to the geographical reality of her life in the CONNECTICUT RIVER VALLEY, surrounded by mountains. In another famous poem, she writes, "I never saw the sea" (Fr 800, J 1052); in fact, her only chance to glimpse it would have been during one of her infrequent visits to Boston, and there is no record in her surviving letters that she did. But inwardness is also a complex metaphor: It connotes the native, safe but confining place, which must be left behind to journey toward Eternity. And that "place" is a spiritual one; after all, it is the soul that is inward. This suggests caution, timidity: a soul that does not habitually venture outward. But an inward soul is also one that *looks inward* for what it needs; it is capable of transcending physical limitations and knowing the world through imagination. This is precisely the assertion of Fr 800:

> I never saw a Moor—
> I never saw the Sea—

Yet know I how the Heather looks
And what a Billow be.

Thus, in "Exultation is the going" Dickinson escapes, via the inward soul's exertions, into an exhilarating inner journey. Significantly, in the most up-to-date edition of her complete poems (Franklin), this poem is preceded and followed by poems filled with cocoons, prisons, and the dream of escaping: "But I tug at my childish bars/ Only to fail again!" In "Exultation" she succeeds in imagining the escape; her focus is not on the bars that confine but on the landscape opening before her. She moves easily "Past the Houses," and thence "Past the Headlands," points of land, usually high and with a sheer drop, extending out into a body of water. Once the headlands separating water from land have been passed, the voyage into deep Eternity has begun. Eternity, one of the great concerns of Dickinson's poetry, is defined here only as the traveler's distant, ecstatic destination, an unknown, transcendent reality.

At this point, as stanza 3 begins, the journey/ definition appears to be interrupted by the speaker's question,

Bred as we, among the mountains,
Can the sailor understand
The divine intoxication
Of the first league out from Land?

Here, Dickinson's idiosyncratic grammar presents a difficulty. According to standard grammar, the modifying phrase "Bred as we, among the mountains" refers to the noun most closely following it: "the sailor." But the "we" is the speaker, the inward soul, the nonsailor. The intended sense of the stanza can only be "Can the sailor (who spends his life at sea) understand the divine intoxication felt by those of us who were bred among the mountains?" The question is rhetorical, an assertion that the sailor *cannot* understand what the inward soul is experiencing. "Exultation" (and its variant "divine intoxication") is thus further defined as something inaccessible to one for whom the sea is second nature. By shifting the poem's emphasis to the sailor, Dickinson contrasts those who have an abundance of something "divinely intoxicating," with those who have been deprived of it and

are experiencing it for the first time. In declaring that the intoxication of the deprived inlander is greater than what the sated sailor can understand, Dickinson reverts to a central theme of her poetry: the notion that deprivation brings a greater, truer appreciation of what is lacking (see "SUCCESS IS COUNTED SWEETEST").

Dickinson wrote many poems with references to boats as emblems of the solitary self on the broad sea of Life and Eternity. The same year that she wrote the poem under discussion, she also composed a darker one using the images of sea and sailor, in which she is turned back from a near encounter with Eternity: "Therefore, as One returned, I feel/ Odd secrets of the line to tell!/ Some Sailor, skirting foreign shores—/ Some pale Reporter, from the awful doors/ Before the Seal!" (Fr 132).

But "Exultation is the going" is fired by a joyous optimism: the inward soul is on its way; the voyage, however much delayed, is beginning. In both tone and imagery, it echoes a letter the poet sent to her friend ABIAH PALMER ROOT in younger days, when she was embarking on her lifelong journey of independent thought and creativity: ". . . The shore is safer, Abiah, but I love to buffet the sea—I can count the bitter wrecks here in these pleasant waters, and hear the murmuring winds, but oh, I love the danger! . . ." (L 39, late 1850). "The first league out from Land," however, is not a large distance—3 statute miles or about 4.83 kilometers. The traveler can still look back and see land. With the journey scarcely begun, the speaker is still in that thrilling state of expectation, which characteristically holds more satisfaction for her than reaching the desired goal.

FURTHER READING

Suzanne Juhasz, *Undiscovered Continent*, 132–137.

"'Faith' is a fine invention" (1861) (Fr 202, J 185)

This much-quoted quatrain has generally been read as Dickinson's economical critique of the brand of religious belief that ignores the evidence of science. As such, it reflects her time as a student at

AMHERST ACADEMY, where she was influenced by the thinking of EDWARD HITCHCOCK. For this eminent geologist, chemist, and man of religion, there was no contradiction between science and faith. He believed that, to the contrary, the findings of science only bolstered faith in a creator and an ordered creation.

The mocking speaker of this epigram is not so even-handed, however. She ridicules faith, both by putting it in quotation marks, and by defining it as "invention," a word drawn from the vocabulary of the field of investigation this kind of faith stands opposed to. The "Gentlemen who *see!*" are upholders of this rigid patriarchal religion, clergymen or theologians, and their "seeing" is clearly meant in the revelatory sense—to see spiritually, to see God's Truth. "See" is underlined in Dickinson's original manuscript, as if to mock the gentlemen's fervor for a vision that she dismisses as an "invention." That kind of seeing may be all right for such gentlemen, she implies, but let us have access to the vision of the microscope, in the event of an "Emergency." Let us keep the more useful inventions of science and modern medicine around, just in case. Critic Charles Anderson suggests that Dickinson's wit and irony in this poem are wholly the result of the way she plays off native Saxon words to describe the faith of the fathers and uses learned borrowings to describe the modern doubt. He writes: "The deliberateness of this contrast is shown in the skill with which she complicates the issues by throwing one unexpected Latinate word into the first line, so that faith becomes a mechanical thing . . ." (*Stairway*, 39).

For scholar David Porter, the poem implies that close investigation of the things of this world is what sustains one who does not accept the specious comfort of strong belief (*Early Poetry*, 160). Certainly Dickinson was such an observer, of nature, and of the inner landscape of thoughts and feelings. Biographer Richard B. Sewall offers a different interpretation, based on Dickinson's belief that faith must be "nimble," rather than complacent. He suggests that the poem is about the need for an ever-watchful eye, a "spiritual microscope" that continues to question, as hers did until the end of her life, the assumptions of one's faith.

Dickinson included this quatrain in a letter to her close friend, *Springfield Republican* editor SAMUEL BOWLES. In the letter, the verse is followed by these cryptic sentences:

> You spoke of the 'East.' I have thought about it this winter. Don't you think you and I should be shrewder, to take the *Mountain Road?*
> That *Bareheaded life*—under the grass—worries one like a Wasp. (L 220, about 1860)

Viewed within the context of this brief letter, with its oblique references to the "East," as the Resurrection was referred to, "the *Mountain Road*," the arduous pathway to God's realm, and the *"Bareheaded life,"* which clearly refers to death, the quatrain seems to be part of an ongoing religious discussion. While Sewall accepts this reading, he also sees a very different underlying concern in poem and letter: the issue of whether Bowles should publish her work:

> [S]he cannot live on the "faith" that somehow, someday, some editor will see her work for what it is and publish it. She has run out of patience; this is an "Emergency." Get a microscope! The 'East,' about which Bowles had spoken to her, may be the world of the Boston and New York publishers. But she urges Bowles not to wait for them. Would it not be 'prudent,' 'shrewder,' for her poems to take the "*Mountain Road*" (the path between the range of hills that separates Amherst and Springfield [the home of the *Springfield Republican*] for publication in the *Republican?* Time is running out. There may be a sense of urgency because of Bowles' health, which had been precarious for several years. "That *Bareheaded life*—under the grass—worries one like a Wasp." (*Life,* II, 478–479).

This interpretation may be a bit of a stretch (Sewall himself says only that it "may be valid"), yet it is worth remembering that Dickinson regularly employed code words and phrases with intimate correspondents such as Bowles and SUSAN HUNTINGTON GILBERT DICKINSON. She also incorporated her poems within her letters in such a way as to alter the meanings they had outside the letter context. Thus, what was originally a 16-word critique of the old religion might well have been used, in this letter, to express a very different crisis of belief.

See also "A WORD MADE FLESH IS SELDOM," "THOSE—DYING THEN," and LETTERS.

FURTHER READING

Charles Anderson, *Stairway,* 38–40; David Porter, *Early Poetry,* 160. Richard B. Sewall, *Life,* II, 478–479; Cynthia Griffin Wolff, *Emily Dickinson,* 248.

"Forever—is composed of Nows—" (1863) (Fr 690, J 624)

In this DEFINITION POEM Emily Dickinson envisions a "Forever" that is not only accessible but also present at every moment of life. She is not dealing here with what she called her "Flood subject" of whether there is an afterlife in the Christian sense—the soul's immortality. Instead, what concerns her is the heaven on earth, a sense of mortal time that partakes of eternity. In a two-line epigram written the same year, Fr 500, Dickinson captures the essential idea behind this poem: "Not 'Revelation'—'tis—that waits, / But our unfurnished eyes—." Revelation is already here—it is we who lack the vision to recognize it. "Forever—is composed of Nows—" belongs to a group of poems in which Dickinson locates heaven in the everyday world, where "commonplace objects and acts blaze into spiritual significance" (Weisbuch, "Prisming," 220). These include Fr 1734, where she writes, "EDEN IS THAT OLD FASHIONED HOUSE" / We dwell in every day / Without suspecting our abode / Until we drive away," and Fr 236, "SOME KEEP THE SABBATH GOING TO CHURCH—" where she worships among the flowers, birds and bees of her garden, declaring, "So instead of getting to Heaven, at last—/ I'm going, all along."

In a poem written the previous year, Fr 310, she notes with keen self-insight: "Heaven is what I cannot reach! / The Apple on the Tree—/ Provided it do hopeless—hang—/ That—"Heaven" is—to Me!" Here, Heaven is defined as the unattainable,

a vision that arises from a sense of inner emptiness and exclusion from paradise. Should she possess "the interdicted Land" it would cease to be Heaven. But in "Forever—is composed of Nows—," the poet describes another inner reality in which Heaven *is* attainable, not in any sudden or singular act of taking possession or transcending to another realm, but moment by moment.

In the first stanza, she declares time and eternity to consist of the same substance ("Nows"):

Forever—is composed of Nows—
'Tis not a different time—
Except for Infiniteness—
And Latitude of Home—

In this striking image, she evokes eternity in domestic terms, as a kind of celestial upgrade to a never-ending, more spacious home than the one she occupies on earth. Critic Robert Weisbuch suggests the core of this distinction when he notes that "If paradise is available for the right asking in every instant, it lasts only for an instant as well, and its departure makes a newly intolerable gloom of absence" ("Prisming," 220). But in the "Forever" of the poem under discussion, there is no such loss. This is the poet's vision of earthly paradise and in what follows she speculates on how we might get there.

What would be necessary, she tell us in stanza 2, is to give up the illusion that the smooth fabric of time can be artificially divided into separate, tiny snippets ("dates," "months," and "years") and thus open ourselves to the boundless continuity of sacred time. Dickinson describes this surrender as a dissolving and an exhaling, images that evoke the serenity of a self-forgetful yet life-giving merger with a greater whole. What such merging signified to Dickinson is suggested in letters to her sister-in-law, SUSAN HUNTINGTON GILBERT DICKINSON, in which she speaks of "forever" in a similar tone, using language that echoes that of this poem. "There is no first, or last, in Forever—It is Centre, there, all the time—," she wrote in 1864 (L 288) and in one of her last letters to Sue, she implored "Be Sue, while I am Emily—Be next, what you have ever been, Infinity—." This suggests that, in spite of her disappointment in Sue and the estrangement that had long existed between the two women, in Emily's inner world, Sue continued to represent a boundless, never-ending love. Is the "forever" of this poem, then, connected to the vision of a boundless love? This notion is supported by another poem written around this time, in which she writes of her "idolatrous" love as both time and eternity: "YOU CONSTITUTED TIME—/ I deemed Eternity / A Revelation of Yourself—."

In stanza 3, she continues to elaborate on what such uninterrupted time would be like, "Without Debate—or Pause—/ Or Celebrated Days—" and concludes that our years would be no different from "Anno Dominies." (Note that in Johnson's earlier version of the poem, he corrected the poet's misspelling and gives the correct "Anno Domini's"). "Anno Domini" or A.D., of course, indicates the Year of Our Lord commonly used in the kind of earthly calendar Dickinson advocates giving up. But she uses the word here in the reverse sense, returning it to its literal meaning of "God's years." This much is clear. The question that lingers, however, is whether the poet is as enthusiastic about this loss of distinctions as she appeared to be earlier in the poem. Would a life without debate or pause or days to celebrate be a relief or an unrelieved bore? These things, after all, represent the imposition of human perceptions and values on raw time, mental categories we are not really capable of dissolving. The poet surely knew this, and on another level would not have wished to dissolve them. Her poetic vision is one in which mental and temporal divisions, ceaseless inner debate, and awareness of time's passage play a dominant role.

Nonetheless, what she strove for in her poetry was an almost superhuman freezing of these inexorable processes that would allow her to penetrate to the eternal core of "Now." When she wrote this poem, Dickinson was in the middle of an extraordinary period of artistic fecundity; she would write 295 poems in 1863 alone, her most productive year. In writing these poems she must have experienced that expanded, heightened consciousness that comes to the artist in moments of transcendent creation. She had discovered the opposite of her universe of deprivation, one in which the moments were sufficient unto themselves. Dickinson's great

biographer Richard B. Sewall observes, "Much of what is often called the 'breathlessness' of Emily Dickinson's poems comes from the urgency of her attempts to arrest the moment, to catch and preserve its essence" (*Life,* II, 681). In this context, "Forever—is composed of Nows—" stands as a description, both of Dickinson's poetic oeuvre, consisting of some 1,789 separate "Nows," as well as of her life in poetry, as she experienced it.

See also "CRISIS IS A HAIR" and "I SHALL KNOW WHY—WHEN TIME IS OVER."

FURTHER READING

Richard B. Sewall, *Life,* 681; Robert Weisbuch, "Prisming," in *Handbook,* Grabher et al., eds., 220; Cynthia Griffin Wolff, *Emily Dickinson,* 234, 237.

"Four Trees—upon a solitary Acre—" (1863) (Fr 778, J 742)

This striking landscape poem, widely analyzed by Dickinson scholars, deals with the poles of certainty and uncertainty, order and disorder, design and randomness in the natural world. Instead of Dickinson's usual lyric "I," the speaker is an impersonal voice that reports what it observes while attempting to understand the relationship of the scene to a greater whole. The opening description gives the reader a bare minimum of particulars: Four trees are standing on an acre of ground. There is no hint that the number of trees has any special meaning, beyond the fact that this is the number that happens to be there. The poet does not tell us *why* the trees are there, whether they have simply sprung up or were left standing when the rest of the acre was cleared. Moreover, Dickinson, a learned botanist, chooses not to specify the type of trees. Nor do we know why the acre is "solitary." Whether we are meant to believe that there is nothing else *on* the acre or that the acre is in some way disconnected from its surroundings is unclear. None of these things are important to the speaker, who is intent on plumbing the larger meaning of what she sees.

And what she sees is twofold: The trees have neither design, nor order, nor function ("apparent action"), yet they "Maintain." Standing alone, on its own line, the word claims a central importance in the stanza. "Maintain" is a transitive verb, requiring a direct object; so, *what* do the trees maintain? Since the line trails off in a characteristic Dickinsonian dash, we must look to the next stanza for a clue. Do the trees maintain "The Sun" of the next line? If so, "The Sun" is being made to do double duty, as direct object of the preceding verb and as subject of the succeeding one: Four trees maintain the sun; the sun meets them (Miller, "Dickinson's Experiments," 252–255). A simpler, more satisfying interpretation is that the verb is being used intransitively, without a direct object. In this case, the poet is saying that the trees maintain themselves, that is, they endure. Since we know that "Do reign" was a variant for "Maintain," this seems a likely choice. The apparently random group of trees thus acquires a certain dignity and strength.

This interpretation frees the sun for the simpler role, in stanza 2, of meeting the trees, as does the wind. The trees dwell in a spare but sublime neighborhood, with God as their closest neighbor. The next stanza posits the interrelationship between trees and acre. Each, in its way, confers something essential upon the other: The acre gives the trees place, while the trees give the acre visual interest to the passer-by, the possibility of containing a shadow, and attraction to such inveterate tree climbers as squirrels and boys. Can the "Him" of the second line, which ostensibly refers to the Acre, also refer to God? If so, it is a God that is immanent in the humble, finite elements of creation coexisting on the "solitary Acre," with each part defining and sustaining the others.

This interrelatedness is the most that the speaker can assert. In stanza 4, she tells us that she cannot connect her observations to "the General Nature"—to a larger purpose or plan:

What Deed is Their's unto the General Nature—
What Plan
They severally—retard—or further—
Unknown—

The compression created by the absence of the verb *is* before "Unknown" enhances this sense of disjunction, and ends the poem on a note of wondering. The final dash contributes to the lack of definite closure. Throughout the poem, any sense of reassuring (orderly) musicality is undercut by the very partial rhymes (acre/action, design/maintain, by/Boy, nature/further, Plan/Unknown) and by the jolting effect of juxtaposed short and longer lines.

At the same time, there *is* a "design" inherent in the poem's structure. Despite their halting tone (enhanced by the absence of any punctuation but dashes), each of the four stanzas of this poem expresses a discrete thought. There is symmetry in the noun phrases that open each stanza (Four trees, The Sun, The Acre, What Deed) and in the two-syllable lines that close them (Maintain, But God, Or Boy, Unknown). In the key words *Maintain* and *Unknown*, the poem juxtaposes, without choosing between them, two realities—"The *fact* of the trees and the *mystery* of their ultimate function" (Farr, *Passion*, 295). Recognizing the limits of human knowledge, the poem lightens its burden of uncertainty with the leavening of wonder.

FURTHER READING

Judith Farr, *Passion*, 294–296; Cristanne Miller, "Dickinson's Experiments," in *Handbook*, Grabher et al., eds., 252–255.

"Further in Summer than the Birds—" (1865)
(Fr 895, J 1068)

In this haunting but difficult work, the poet evokes a delicate, defining moment in the calendar of the seasons, by placing the natural world within the context of the sacred. It is a poem about Grace (a word that appears twice in the poem) and its absence. Dickinson, who never accepted any specific theology, draws from the language of her Calvinist religion, Catholicism, and pre-Christian religion, and redefines them within a religious and poetic context wholly her own.

Since much of the difficulty of the poem arises from its specialized lexicon and irregular syntax, a stanza-by-stanza paraphrase can be helpful as a starting point for analysis. The poem begins enigmatically:

Further in Summer than the Birds—
Pathetic from the Grass—
A minor Nation celebrates
It's unobtrusive Mass.

A paraphrase of stanza 1 might read: "Long after the birds have arrived (or perhaps when they have already begun to leave), a minor nation performs its rite of communion, movingly, from where it resides in the grass." When Dickinson enclosed this poem with a group she sent to editor Thomas Niles, she referred to it as "My Cricket"—thus indicating the identity of the "minor Nation" that celebrates its "unobtrusive Mass." The first two lines modify the crickets. The poem begins with the odd phrase, "Further in summer" rather than the expected "later" to designate the moment when the crickets begin their song. *Further* denotes "distance from" and adds a spatial dimension to the time when the crickets sing; it suggests not just a specific moment but movement away from something—perhaps the full, unblemished moment when summer began and birdsong prevailed. The word "pathetic" is an important one, that some have interpreted as reflecting the poet's contemptuous attitude toward the crickets. But in Dickinson's day, the word was not used as we use it today, to signify the state of being pitiful or inadequate. Rather, it meant "affecting or moving the passions, particularly pity, sorrow, grief or other tender emotion" and was used with respect to a musical style. In another poem about Earth's music, Dickinson writes "The cricket is her [the Earth's] utmost/ Of elegy to me." The cricket's simple "elegy"—a mournful poem or funeral song—ranked very high for Dickinson. The fact that the cricket's pathetic (sad, moving) song rises from the grass, suggests that it is both humble (lowly) and fundamental; indeed, as lines 3 and 4 tell us, it is a form of religious communion. There is neither parody nor irony in this crickets' mass. (The fact that "mass" is a term deriving from Catholicism, rather than Calvinism, appears to have no theological sig-

nificance; Dickinson probably uses it here in its general meaning of communion with the divine.)

Stanza 2 might be paraphrased as follows: "No Ordinance can be seen, the state of Grace arrives gradually; as we gently accustom ourselves to it, we experience human loneliness in a way that enlarges that state." In Calvinist practice, Baptism and the Lord's Supper are designated as "ordinances," or sacraments, that is, established rites of ceremonies that confirm God's promise of eternal life. The line "No Ordinance be seen" has been interpreted as the absence of that promise—disappointment of the hope implied by the mass of stanza 1. But Dickinson says only that the ordinance is unseen, not that it is absent. Emanating from the grass, it is invisible, "unobtrusive." Unlike circumscribed ritual, nature's rites are "gradual," its Grace emerges through quiet process: "gentle Custom." (An earlier variant has "pensive Custom.") These positive attributes suggest that by "Enlarging Loneliness," Dickinson is not saying, as many have concluded, that she is made *more* lonely by the crickets' song, but that the *quality* of her loneliness changes, becomes larger, more inclusive in its meaning. It is a loneliness that goes beyond the personal to encompass something fundamental about nature and existence.

A paraphrase of stanza 3 might read: "This loneliness (or: this song, this Grace) is felt to be Antiquest at Noon. As August is burning low, this spectral canticle arises, in order to typify Repose." "Antiquest" may refer to the noun directly preceding it—loneliness—or to the "Grace" of the preceding stanza, or to the "Canticle" of this one. The absence of syntactic connection creates an indefinite reality, in which human loneliness and the crickets' song and gradual Grace are all implicated in the sense of ancientness. Rather than the time of the crickets' loudest singing, Noon is a metaphor for the intense midpoint of life, as it is in other Dickinson poems (See, for example, Fr 843, "It bloomed and dropt, a Single Noon—" and Fr 1060, "Noon is the hinge of Day—"). This hot, intense center of human life is contrasted in the following line with the sunset of the natural world ("August burning low"), when the "spectral Canticle" arises. In addition to meaning *any* song, "Canticles," for Congregationalists of Dickinson's day was the term used for the biblical Songs of Solomon. As opposed to that joyous affirmation of life, the crickets' "spectral" canticle may imply the long sleep of winter and death (Wolff, *Emily Dickinson*, 310). But the canticle is also "spectral" (ghostlike) because it and its source are not visible. It is an "invisible song" that celebrates an invisible process. The word "typify" has a specific meaning in Christian terminology: to represent by an image, form, or model, as in the sacrament of Baptism, where washing typifies the cleansing of the soul from sin by the blood of Christ. The implied sacrament here is not cleansing (Dickinson never accepted the doctrine of human depravity), but Repose. Whether Dickinson is referring to the death of nature, or humans, or human passion, the word suggests a gentle acceptance.

Stanza 4 can be paraphrased as follows: "The Grace (of the summer) has not yet been given back; the glow of summer is still unmarred; but a "Druidic difference"/Enhances Nature now—." The first line, "Remit as yet no grace," has also been taken to refer to the Canticle, that is, "The canticle has as yet brought no grace," But the following line, which clearly says that the glow of summer is not marred, makes the first paraphrase more likely. The change that has occurred in nature is not yet visible, but it is *felt*. Precisely *what* is felt depends on what the poet meant by "Druidic difference." We know that the Druids were ancient Celtic nations in Gaul, Britain, and Germany, who were known to worship the sun and were associated with primitive magic. But we don't know what Dickinson knew about or associated with them. This has allowed critics to see in these final lines whatever supports their concept of the poem's ultimate statement. Some see her referring to a primordial, pre-Christian culture in order to sever any links between her personal sense of divinity and conventional Christian theology. Biographer Cynthia Griffin Wolff, assuming that Dickinson was "familiar with the superstitious, bloodthirsty side of Druids," sees the image as a "correlative to the destruction that must follow the end of Indian summer." (*Emily Dickinson*, 311). The latter appears unlikely in view of the poem's final line, for the "Druidic difference / *Enhances*

Nature now—." Something positive has occurred. In the absence of more explicit references, the reader must be guided by the tone of the stanza, which is neither appalled nor agonized. It is a quiet ending, which simply observes than an enhancement has taken place. For David Porter, the poet is "not celebrating the change but calibrating it, dissecting it, placing it in no system. In the starkest modernist way, the poem is an analysis without an explanation" (Porter, *Modern Idiom*). Others have seen it as an expression of the loneliness of being human and isolated from nature, while yet others reach the opposite conclusion, viewing it as the affirmation of a poet, for whom nature speaks the indefinable but magical language of a transcendent reality.

See also "THESE ARE THE DAYS WHEN BIRDS COME BACK."

FURTHER READING

Cameron, *Lyric Time*, 182–184; Jane Donahue Eberwein, "Emily Dickinson and the Calvinist Sacramental Tradition," in *Critical Essays*, Judith Farr, ed. 89–104; Cristanne Miller, *Grammar*, 88–89; David Porter, *Modern Idiom*, 21–29, 107–108; Cynthia Griffin Wolff, *Emily Dickinson*, 309–311.

"God gave a Loaf to every Bird—" (1863) (Fr 748, J 791)

What did Emily Dickinson mean when she said that she had been given less in life? She had material comfort, family, and friendships; by the time she wrote this poem she knew she possessed great poetic talent. Perhaps she felt deprived of physical beauty, of a requited love, of literary recognition, or of a soothing and certain Christian faith. We can only speculate. Personal deprivation is a given in Dickinson's poetic universe—something she often takes for granted. Although God is prominently blamed in the first word of this poem, the speaker does not rail against the inequity of the portions allotted in life but merely states it matter-of-factly. In other poems about hunger, she is herself a bird with her crumb ("VICTORY COMES LATE—") or the companion of birds ("I HAD BEEN HUNGRY, ALL THE YEARS—"), sharing their crumbs; but here, even the birds have got it better than the speaker has: a whole loaf compared to her crumb.

> God gave a Loaf to every Bird—
> But just a Crumb—to Me—
> I dare not eat it—tho' I starve—
> My poignant luxury—

She goes on to explain that her "poignant luxury" is to possess the crumb, to touch it and thus have palpable evidence of the "feat—that made the Pellet mine—." In this line, the poet poses a riddle, teasing the reader to guess the nature of her feat. And, while the reader is free to guess (the feat of winning a crumb of love? of writing her poems?) all she can really know is that the self-protective poet has no intention of telling more. It is possible, however, that the feat is precisely *the ability to starve* that allows her to possess the pellet of bread. This contemplation of the desired object—the crumb—is her "Sparrow's chance" and she prefers it to the "Ampler Coveting—" of actually eating it. She presents this here as a matter of necessity: She has but this one crumb and so cannot afford to eat it. The mere knowledge that it is hers must suffice to keep her alive.

In the final stanzas, however, a vital transformation takes place. The poet turns her poverty and its severe limitations into a blessing, her own special form of wealth. Taking hyperbole in the opposite direction of the first two stanzas, she declares her boundless happiness, wealth, and sovereignty over "an Indiaman—An Earl"—images that takes us into the realm of the far-off and the fabulous. By learning how to starve, she has made herself independent of external circumstances. When others face a famine, she is oblivious to the lack of an ear of corn. She has her own plentiful board to draw from: the internal self-reliance she came increasingly to claim for herself (see "ON A COLUMNAR SELF—"). The stringencies of poverty lead to the art of abstaining, which, in turn, both builds internal resources and forces her to rely on them. Here, she enunciates a theme that became central to her worldview: Compared with the anticipation in imagination of the desired object, the reality

will always be disappointing. This is the "feast of abstemiousness" she will continue to celebrate in her poetry. (See "WHO NEVER WANTED—MADDEST JOY").

See also "IT WOULD HAVE STARVED A GNAT—" and "UNDUE SIGNIFICANCE A STARVING MAN ATTACHES."

FURTHER READING

Vivian R. Pollak, "Thirst and Starvation in Emily Dickinson's Poetry," in *Critical Essays,* Judith Farr, ed., 62–75; Richard Wilbur, "Sumptuous Destitution," in *Critical Essays,* Judith Farr, ed., 53–61.

"God is a distant—stately Lover—" (1863) (Fr 615, J 357)

This DEFINITION POEM is Dickinson's ironic take on God's contradictory distinction from and identity with Jesus Christ. The tone is detached and urbane, but, despite the "shocking" opening line, the message is not truly blasphemous. Dickinson struggled with belief all her life and rejected the doctrines of the Calvinist faith she inherited. But the Bible was an overwhelming presence in her imagination and she lived on intimate terms with its characters, turning them into everyday figures, with whom she argued or empathized, identified or disdained. God was no exception to this pervasive tendency. Throughout her poetry, she assigns him a plethora of earthly roles: burglar, banker, father, amputee, noted clergyman, bold person, old neighbor, merchant, jester, and experimental scientist, to name just a few.

In this poem Dickinson takes the figures of God and his Son into a familiar narrative of the Puritan New England past: Henry Wadsworth Longfellow's "The Courtship of Miles Standish." Her poem rests on an ingenious comparison: Miles Standish sends his friend John Alden as his envoy to court Priscilla, just as God sends his son to convey his message of love and redemption to his people. Priscilla ends up choosing John, just as Dickinson herself found God's envoy, Christ, a far more sympathetic figure than his father. As critic Agnieszka Salska sees it, Dickinson's "special regard for Christ is largely due to the fact that she sees Christ as co-victim of His Father's arbitrary plans" (*Walt Whitman and Emily Dickinson,* 51). Although there are poems in which she implicates Jesus in God's indifference (see Fr 377, "At least to pray is left—is left"), more often his suffering is the paradigm for human suffering ("ONE CRUCIFIXION IS RECORDED—ONLY—"), the "Tender Pioneer" of "Life—is what we make it—," who blazes the fearful path to Paradise.

In the poem's concluding two lines, Dickinson interjects a final irony. To cover his bets, as it were, God declares that he and Christ are one.

> Vouches, with hyperbolic archness—
> "Miles," and "John Alden" are Synonyme—

Thus, he has it both ways. But if God and Christ are one, the poem asks implicitly, then why was Christ "necessary" in the first place? Further, the shrewd God of this poem makes his claim with "hyperbolic archness," that is, he is wildly exaggerating—and cunning into the bargain.

See also "A LITTLE EAST OF JORDAN," "I NEVER LOST AS MUCH BUT TWICE—," and "THE BIBLE IS AN ANTIQUE VOLUME—."

FURTHER READING

Dorothy Huff Oberhaus, "'Tender Pioneer': Emily Dickinson's Poems on the Life of Christ," in *Critical Essays,* Judith Farr, ed., 105–118; Agnieszka Salska, *Walt Whitman and Emily Dickinson,* 51; Cynthia Griffin Wolff, *Emily Dickinson,* 272–274.

"Grief is a Mouse—" (1863)
(Fr 753, J 793)

In this well-known poem, Dickinson explores the faces of grief through a series of personifications: mouse, thief, juggler, gourmand, and, in the fourth stanza, tongueless martyr. Rather than developing a single metaphor, as she does in such DEFINITION POEMS as "EXULTATION IS THE GOING," "CRISIS IS A HAIR," and "EDEN IS THAT OLD-FASHIONED HOUSE," here she varies her personifications in order to come at her subject from different angles. What she describes are not the successive "stages of grief," but

the simultaneous maneuvers of a mind that is beset by grief and seeking to preserve itself. Strategies of elusiveness and avoidance of pain weave through the poem, until, in the final stanza, they culminate in the related but significantly different assertion of grief's principled silence.

The poem begins on a gentle note with Grief as a timid Mouse and the human heart a "shy House," where he hides behind the wainscot (wooden paneling that lines the walls of a room). The elusiveness of Grief the Mouse requires no elucidation for anyone who has experienced the mysterious comings and going of pain and realization of one's loss, following a death or other major bereavement.

The mood shifts abruptly in stanza 2, with the entrance of Grief the Thief:

> Grief is a Thief—quick startled—
> Pricks His Ear—report to hear
> Of that Vast Dark—
> That swept His Being—back—

We understand the more common metaphor of death as a thief, but what can Grief be stealing, unless it is peace of mind, a moment of blessed oblivion? Grief resembles a thief in the way he is startled by a sound in the dark. But what he hears, what pursues him, is the echo of the gunshot ("report") of death and loss: "that Vast Dark—/ That swept His Being—back—." The Thief's whole being is poised to detect the approach of this overwhelming darkness, threatening once more to engulf his entire being.

As she shifts from one metaphor to the next we sense the speaker's restless search for a satisfying vision; no single image wholly encompasses her meaning. This shifting accelerates in stanza 3, where she tosses out two metaphors. The Juggler must keep his pins (the emotions he keeps in a dynamic balance and distance from himself) moving through the air. Should his boldness and concentration slip for even a moment, "One—say—or Three—" of these "objects" will fall, painfully, upon the bruises he already has. These three lines ingeniously mimic the juggler's action: Their fractured syntax and hyphenated phrases show the poet maintaining her concentration with difficulty as she juggles her words. She then tosses off another image, one of thwarted emotional hunger, in a single line: Grief the Gourmand, that is, a glutton, who, ironically, has little ("spare") "Luxury."

From this evocation of scarcity the speaker leaps to the gruesome, passionate vision of the final stanza: Grief as a withholder, a tongueless martyr, who keeps his secret, even on pain of death. The speaker is doing more than describing here; she is advocating. By calling this version of Grief "Best," she is declaring her own tenacious determination to remain silent about her loss and pain. Note how the final word "now" brings a personal immediacy to Grief, indirectly announcing to the reader that behind the poem's universality lies the poet's specific grief, but one that she will never reveal. The neologism "tongueless" implies punishment and deformity: Grief has had his tongue cut out by a ruthless inquisitor; and yet, that inquisitor can only be the self, who is bound by a passionate conviction that silence must be maintained, at any cost. The speaker ends with what sounds like a challenge: Maybe Grief's ashes, after you've burned him, will reveal his secret. That's the only way you'll learn anything from him, since even torture on the rack "could'nt coax a syllable—now."

This ferocious determination to maintain control over her inner world is a recurring theme in Dickinson's work. The assertion "No rack can torture me—" begins another poem on the theme of preserving her soul's freedom. In many poems, she expresses the conviction that the soul's darkest layers, what she calls in one poem ("IT'S HOUR WITH ITSELF") "the Cellars of the Soul" should never be exposed to daylight, lest the external world shrink away in fear: "What Terror would enthrall the Street." In yet another work (Fr 1004), she speaks of a silence, "Which uttered, would discourage Nature / And haunt the World—." Her hyperbolic sense of what would be unleashed should the soul reveal its darkest moments is explored in "The soul has bandaged moments," when she invokes a moment of inner darkness: "The Horror welcomes her, again, / These are not brayed of Tongue—." In an early poem, "A Secret Told—," arguing for the wisdom of not confiding secrets, she observes, "A Secret—kept—That—can appall but One—."

Why the darkness of the inner world should have struck Dickinson as so appalling may be less a matter of the contents of that darkness than of an inherent reticence and sense of shame, that came to her by way of the PURITAN HERITAGE that influenced all the members of her family. In the memoirs she wrote after Dickinson's death, girlhood friend EMILY FOWLER (Ford) relates an anecdote that reveals the young Emily's revulsion at baring one's soul in public. Describing the Shakespeare club that she organized, Fowler writes: "[Dickinson] once asked me, if it did not make me shiver to hear a great many people talk, they took all the clothes off their souls. . . ."

For Dickinson, whose poems, paradoxically, create a powerful sense of intimacy in the reader, "Best Things dwell out of Sight / The Pearl—the Just—Our Thought" (Fr 1012). Yet she also knew that "Safe despair it is that raves—" and "Silence is all we dread. / There's ransom in a Voice—" (Fr 1300). Certainly one way of understanding the work of this prolific poet and letter-writer, for whom keeping her soul's secrets was a matter of honor and a condition for self-preservation, is to keep in mind her famous tenet, "TELL ALL THE TRUTH BUT TELL IT SLANT—." Through the indirect poetic language she constructed, with its verbal eloquence and fragmented awkwardness, its deeply resonant imagery and elliptical silences, Dickinson sought a way of balancing her opposing urges toward self-revelation and self-concealment.

See also "AFTER GREAT PAIN, A FORMAL FEELING COMES—."

FURTHER READING

Charles R. Anderson, "Despair," in *Modern Critical Views*, Harold Bloom, ed., 9–35; Cristanne Miller, *Grammar*, 1–19; Richard B. Sewall, *Life*, 38–41.

"Growth of Man—like Growth of Nature—" (1863) (Fr 790, J 750)

This seemingly abstract philosophical poem might serve as Emily Dickinson's credo and prescription for the "difficult ideal" of spiritual growth she strove toward in her life. As in so much of her work, she locates the existential center of gravity in the interior life of the individual. Critic Albert Gelpi has observed that the poet characteristically chose to emphasize the sphere of the self, rather than to acknowledge the reciprocity between world and self (*Mind of the Poet*, 95). While external influences in an individual's life may play the role that air and sun play for Nature, they merely "endorse" the process. Growth can be achieved only "Through the solitary prowess/ Of a Silent Life—." In these lines, Dickinson invokes the monastic ideal espoused by one of her favorite authors, Thomas à Kempis, whose book, *Imitation of Christ,* made a deep impression on her. Especially relevant are the chapters on "Solitude," "Silence," and "A Retired Life," in the last of which he quotes Peter 2:11: "If you will stand fast as you ought and grow in grace, esteem yourself as an exile and a stranger upon earth" (Ibid., 36).

Dickinson's own life was anything but silent. She was known as a brilliant conversationalist in her younger years. Even after she withdrew from society and began dressing exclusively in the white dresses that symbolized her identity as "Wayward Nun," she never observed a "rule of silence," but communicated with family, servants, and the few friends she consented to see. Not only did she write her nearly 1,800 poems, she kept up a voluminous correspondence with family, friends, and neighbors. If her life was "silent," it was so only with respect to the deepest layers of herself, the "Cellars of the Soul," "the loudest Place he made" which, thankfully, was "licensed to be still." ("IT'S HOUR WITH ITSELF"). For the poet who famously wrote "TELL ALL THE TRUTH BUT TELL IT SLANT—," hiding and revealing, silence and speech, were all part of a single process. The ability to maintain this extraordinary balance in the mysterious act of writing her poetry and letters was the "solitary prowess" she needed to attain the Silent Life.

In the third stanza, she presents the attainment of her "difficult ideal," not as a matter of genius or grace but of character.

> Effort—is the sole condition—
> Patience of Itself—

> Patience of opposing forces—
> And intact Belief—

The necessary virtues she cites are the traditional ones of her PURITAN HERITAGE: effort, patience, and belief. Yet, in their enumeration lie hidden messages. Dickinson, who recognized the enemies both within and without, knew that patience was required in dealing both with her own demons and with those individuals who opposed her. By the time she wrote this poem, more than one trusted confidant had fallen into the latter category. Neither SAMUEL BOWLES nor SUSAN HUNTINGTON GILBERT DICKINSON nor THOMAS WENTWORTH HIGGINSON, to each of whom she had shown her poetry, had understood it. Thus, the "intact Belief" she requires most likely refers, not to faith in God, but to belief in her own powers. Biographer Alfred Habegger, who calls this poem "a major statement [that] welds the idea of autonomy to vocation," notes that Fascicle 37 (1863), in which this poem appears, contains a number of poems that "repeatedly consider the inherent dignity of things that act independently" (*My Wars*, 481–482). Thus, in "ON A COLUMNAR SELF—," she rejoices in possessing "Conviction—That Granitic Base—/ Though none be on our side—."

This idea is buttressed in the final lines of the poem, which asserts that "no Countenance" assists the individual's growth. Dickinson was preoccupied with the image of the face; she uses the word 150 times in her poems, while "countenance" appears more than 20 times. Biographer Cynthia Griffin Wolff believes that the persistence of face images is traceable to a failure in the earliest relationship between the poet and her mother, EMILY NORCROSS DICKINSON: a "disruption of the nonverbal, face-to-face, eye-to-eye communication of the infant and its mother." Wolff posits that writing was for Dickinson a way to bridge a break in visual exchange and cites the many letters in which she expresses the longing to see her correspondent face-to-face (*Emily Dickinson*, 52–54). But "face" and "countenance" also have strong biblical associations, that is, they evoke the (usually inaccessible) face of God. The poet sometimes conflated personal and religious meanings of seeing face-to-face, as in a letter to Susan Dickinson of June 27, 1852, where she writes longingly, "Shall I indeed behold you, not 'darkly, but face to face' or am I *fancying* so, and dreaming blessed dreams from which the day will wake me?" (L 96). (The reference is to Corinthians I, 13:12: "For now we see through a glass darkly; but then face-to-face").

In light of all these associations, the poem's concluding statement that "Transaction—is assisted / By no Countenance—," while, on the one hand, a proud assertion of independence, also contains an undertone of desolation. Note how alone the individual is in the vision of this poem, an entity separate from nature, other human beings, and God. Self-sufficiency, the poem suggests, involves an essentially cold, businesslike relationship to the World. This is what Dickinson appears to be emphasizing by her use of terms drawn from the spheres of business and finance. In stanza 1, "Atmosphere and Sun endorse" growth, as one would endorse the back of a check, thus transferring monetary funds. The term injects a subtle note of irony, suggesting the analogy of inner growth and "growth of assets." In a similar vein, we are told that the "sole condition" for growth is effort and that "Looking on—is the Department / Of it's [growth's] Audience—," perhaps Dickinson's way of referring to those who read her poems. The final, chilling use of business/fiscal imagery, whereby she refers to the whole difficult, immense process of growth as "Transaction," seems defensive, a verbal strategy to distance or minimize or deny both its importance to her and the loneliness inherent in "no Countenance."

See also "I'M CEDED—I'VE STOPPED BEING THEIRS—."

FURTHER READING

Joan Burbick, "Emily Dickinson and the Economics of Desire," *Critical Essays*, J. Farr, ed., 76–89; Joanne Feit Diehl, *Romantic Imagination*, 42–43; Albert Gelpi, *Mind of the Poet*, 95; Alfred Habegger, *My Wars*, 481–482; Thomas Johnson, *Emily Dickinson*, 61–62; Thomas à Kempis, *Imitation of Christ*, 36; Cynthia Griffin Wolff, *Emily Dickinson*, 52–54.

"He fumbles at your Soul" (1862) (Fr 477, J 315)

This famous, fascinating, and difficult poem presents the reader with a double mystery: 1) Who or what is "He"? In other words, what is the poem about? 2) What do the last two lines mean and how do they relate to the rest of the poem?

Stanza 1 initiates the riddle:

He fumbles at your Soul
As Players at the Keys—
Before they drop full Music on—
He stuns you by Degrees—

At first reading, Dickinson seems to be describing the same kind of cat and mouse game she evokes in another poem written at this time, Fr 485, 1862—"The Whole of it came not at once—." In this brilliant anatomy of the cruel, stage-by-stage death of hope, she writes:

The Cat reprieves the mouse
She eases from her teeth
Just long enough for Hope to teaze—
Then mashes it to death—

Dickinson calls this "Murder by degrees," a phrase echoing line 4 of "He fumbles at your Soul": "He stuns you by Degrees—." But the imagery of "He fumbles at your Soul" is more suggestive and complex. Dickinson could be talking about religious conversion, death, sex, the experience of writing a poem (which she described as the art of stunning herself with "Bolts—of Melody!"), or even of reading a true poem (which made her "feel physically as if the top of [her] head were taken off").

The "He" of this poem begins as a piano player, then turns into a killer: a Zeus-like hurler of thunderbolts and a scalper—an archetypal image of terror from Dickinson's Puritan past. The pivotal image linking music to violence is "hammers"—the hammers of the piano, which, in another meaning, are also tools and instruments of violence. This development has been anticipated in stanza 1 by the lines "As Players at the Keys—/ Before they drop full Music on—," a bizarre image that turns music into a fearful assault. The fumbling, assaulting fingers are also sexual of course, and their "now fainter, now nearer, now slower" rhythm is suggestive of the buildup toward orgasm. The notion of religious conversion, in which the convert is struck by God's presence, is present in the notion of an "etherial Blow" that "Prepares your brittle nature," and reveals the soul in its nakedness. Common to all these possible meanings is the experience of being overwhelmed in a manner more fearful than pleasurable. Several critics have interpreted it as a veiled expression of Dickinson's fear of sex, or at the very least of "masculinity and masculine power, here embodied in the hell-fire preaching minister, or a Lover, or God Himself" (Cristanne Miller, *Grammar*, 114). Poet and feminist critic Adrienne Rich sees the masculine figure as the poet's own power externalized in an image compatible with a patriarchal society ("Vesuvius at Home," 105).

For critic Robert Weisbuch there is no need, and, indeed, no way, to pick the "right" interpretation from among all these intriguing alternatives. He believes that the specific identity of the master is irrelevant and deliberately ambiguous, since what concerns Dickinson is not the cause, but "the experiencing of the terrible moment." If "He" is the active figure, the pianist, blacksmith, scalper, and wind, the speaker is "the pounded piano, the tempered metal, scalped tree, and wind-pawed forest" (*Emily Dickinson's Poetry*, 98). The present tense implies an ongoing narrative: a pattern of event that continually recurs.

In the poem's final lines, Dickinson takes us into the primal forest where scalping is done:

When Winds hold Forests in their Paws—
The Universe—is still—

The "you" of the poem becomes a part of nature itself, a passive forest in the "paws" of the winds. This image of merged bestiality and etherealness is the culmination of the building series of images of violent possession. The stillness of the universe is portentous, but whether it portends peace or annihilation, the beginning or the end of something wonderful or fearful is not clear. For, as Miller notes, the poem dramatizes "a moment of anticipation and ambiguous fulfillment," both ecstatic and terrible in which these opposite meanings stand

in constant tension to one another (*Grammar*, 115–116).

Note that in Thomas Johnson's version, the poem is all one stanza except for the final unrhymed couplet, which stand alone as a kind of stunned coda. In the Franklin version, the two-line stanza trailing off in a dash, following three four-line stanzas, conveys a sense of incompleteness. This open-endedness leaves room for different readings for the last line: "The Universe still exists or still waits" or "The Universe is still some unstated modifier, such as "still silent, still cold. . . ."

See also "I WOULD NOT PAINT—A PICTURE—," PURITAN HERITAGE, and REVIVALS.

FURTHER READING
Cristanne Miller, *Grammar*, 113–118; Adrienne Rich, "Vesuvius at Home: The Power of Emily Dickinson," in *Selected Prose*, 105; Robert Weisbuch, *Emily Dickinson's Poetry*, 98–99

"'Hope' is the thing with feathers—" (1862) (Fr 314, J 254)

This well-loved poem is one of Dickinson's most famous DEFINITION POEMS. As in many of these verses, the poet defines an abstraction with a physical image. She explores a complex emotional phenomenon through the device of personification, a form of metaphor that allows her to imagine her relationship to the subject of the definition.

The personification she assigns to Hope in line 1 is only a partial one: a "thing with feathers" is not yet a bird, but some sort of object, not easily envisioned and defined only by the fact that it is feathered, that is, winged, capable of flight. It is a transient human experience, one that "perches" in the soul but does not live there. It "sings the tune without the words," that is, a song in which rational, lexical meaning plays no role, while melody (music, the music of poetry) is all. Finally, it "never stops at all." By this, Dickinson implies not that human soul is constantly buoyed by hope, but that hope itself has an independent existence as an eternal force in the universe.

Biographer Cynthia Griffin Wolff points out that, although "Christ and the 'Hope' that He gave to the world repeatedly figured in traditional emblems as a bird," modern readers "do not feel the presence of Christ in this poem" (*Emily Dickinson,* 478). In this context, it is worth noting that *hope* was an emotionally charged word in the religious struggles Dickinson experienced in her girlhood. During her year at the MOUNT HOLYOKE FEMALE SEMINARY, an institution that aimed to turn its students into devout Christians, 17-year-old Emily was classed among those who professed themselves as "without hope" of finding their Savior. In the poem under discussion, Dickinson draws from the images and lexicon associated with orthodox Christianity, but reinvents them within her own vision of what is sacred.

In stanza 2 the "thing with feathers" solidifies into "the little bird." Abandoning its perch within the soul, it is transformed from a docile, if persistent, songbird into a dauntless world traveler:

> I've heard it in the chillest land—
> And on the strangest Sea—
> Yet—never—in Extremity,
> It asked a crumb—of me.

Of course, it is really the soul that has been transformed by Dickinson into a landscape of storms, "chillest land" and "strangest Sea." The image of the brave little bird, whose song is heard most sweetly in the gale of human sorrows, verges perilously on sentimentality. But the poet breathes life into the metaphor by evoking the bird's mysterious self-sufficiency and generosity. The giving is all in one direction. In poems Dickinson wrote about hunger during this same period, the speaker is a bird among birds, sharing their crumbs and mastering the art of surviving on next to nothing. (See "VICTORY COMES LATE—" and "I HAD BEEN HUNGRY, ALL THE YEARS—"). Here, however, the bird of Hope is something separate from the speaker, and its song and warmth are received as a form of grace, without expectation or need of reciprocity. The final lines reverberate with a sense of awe and gratitude. Without alluding to a specific

episode, the poet persuades us "that a felt experience informs the definition" (Weisbuch, "Prisming," 216).

Throughout her writing life, Dickinson would continue to explore the nuances of hope as a thread in the complex fabric of human emotions. She wrote about hope in connection with fear ("WHEN I HOPED, I RECOLLECT," Fr 493, J 768, "When I hoped I feared," Fr 594, J 1181) and disappointment ("And this of all my Hopes / This, is the silent end," Fr 975, "This is the place they hoped before," Fr 1284). She described the soundless destruction of hope and used it as an occasion to assert the power of the mind to bear its "mighty Freight" and disguise its pain: "A great Hope fell / You heard no noise / The Ruin was within" (Fr 1187).

In two later poems, she once more attempts to define hope, but without the straightforward ebullience of the early definition poem. In Fr 1424, written in 1877, she declared: "Hope is a strange invention—/ A Patent of the Heart—/ In unremitting action / Yet never wearing out—." Like the "thing with feathers," this version of hope never stops. But it is a strange artifice, something invented by the heart. She goes on to call it an "electric adjunct"—a reductive, mechanical term and, in her concluding lines, speaks of its "unique momentum," which "embellishes" "all we own—." What at first reading appears to be a positive image soon reveals its skeptical, even bitter, underpinnings. For the word *embellishment* has the primary meaning of decoration and beautification; but it connotes artifice and falsity, distortion and self-deception.

In Fr 1493, written in 1878: "Hope is a subtle Glutton—" Dickinson gives us a personification diametrically opposite to the little bird who never asks a crumb of the one he warms and inspires. Note, however, that Hope is a "*subtle* Glutton." This Hope "feeds upon the Fair—," implying that it stays alive by focusing only on what is good or beautiful. If we observe it more closely, the poet goes on, we will note that, paradoxically, its gluttony implies great abstinence. What Hope abstains from is revealed in the second, concluding stanza: "His is the Halcyon Table—/ That never seats but One—/ And whatsoever is consumed / The same amount remain—." The price of Hope's "Halcyon" (tranquil) table is twofold: solitude and lack of fulfillment. Hope's "food" is available in unvarying quantity, neither increasing nor decreasing. By its very nature, Hope remains in a state of eternal stasis, never attaining the object of its desire. The same shrewd insight is expressed in a poem of 1873, "Could Hope inspect her Basis" (Fr 1282), where Dickinson concludes that the only "assassin" capable of destroying Hope is "Prosperity—." In other words, hope, once attained, is no longer hope but another state—one of satiety perhaps, but lacking hope's special exaltation. This notion that expectation is superior to actuality, a central one in Dickinson, was given perhaps its best-known formulation in the 1877 poem "WHO NEVER WANTED—MADDEST JOY," in which the poet warns against attaining the object of desire, "lest the Actual—/ Should disenthrall thy soul—."

See also "GOD IS A DISTANT, STATELY LOVER," "GRIEF IS A MOUSE," ABIAH PALMER ROOT, AMHERST ACADEMY, and REVIVALISM.

FURTHER READING

David Porter, *Early Poetry*, 147; Barton Levi St. Armand and George Monteiro, "Dickinson's 'Hope' is the thing with feathers," 34–37; Robert Weisbuch, "Prisming," in *Handbook*, Grabher et al., eds., 216; Cynthia Griffin Wolff, *Emily Dickinson*, 478.

"I am afraid to own a Body—" (1865) (Fr 1050, J 1090)

Emily Dickinson rarely used economic terminology to better effect than she does in this brilliant, incisive poem. In terms that cut through the fog of habitual perception, Dickinson confronts the sheer terror and strangeness of being alive:

> I am afraid to own a Body—
> I am afraid to own a Soul—

By using metaphors of ownership throughout the poem's two four-line stanzas she develops the conceit that the "I" of the poem can stand apart, somehow separate from her Body and Soul, the "Profound—precarious Property—" whose "Possession" is "not optional—" in this life.

Much of the terror of this mysterious, fragile enterprise of body and soul ownership arises from its inescapability. The possession of a Body and a Soul is the "Double Estate" that has been "entailed" on us, "unsuspecting Heirs," at the pleasure of an unnamed donor. The word *entail* in Dickinson's dictionary is defined as "1. To settle the descent of lands and tenements, by gift to a man and to certain heir specified, so that neither the donee nor any subsequent possessor can alienate or bequeath it . . . 2. To fix unalienably on a person or thing, or on a person and his descendants." By either definition, what is entailed can never be transferred to another. It is the lonesome burden thrust upon each of us at birth. In the poem's final two lines, she brilliantly encapsulates the glory and dread of consciousness:

> Duke in a moment of Deathlessness
> And God, for a Frontier.

In the brief "moment of Deathlessness" we are royalty, yet beyond that moment what lies before even so powerful a male self as a Duke is "God." In the first stanza, any mention of God as creator and giver of body and soul is conspicuously missing. Thus, in the context of the second stanza, the word evokes not so much the God of Judgment as the ultimate, unknown reality beyond. Dickinson's use of the image of a "Frontier" resonates with a poem written two years earlier, Fr 727, in which she refers to Jesus as "Tender Pioneer":

> Life—is what we make it—
> Death—We do not know—
> Christ's acquaintance with Him—
> Justify Him—though—

Unlike this one, however, "I am afraid to own a Body" is a comfortless poem. There is no one to go before and prepare the way for the next. Instead, each of us, from the prison of our individuality, must venture forth on her own.

See also "THIS CONSCIOUSNESS THAT IS AWARE."

FURTHER READING

Joan Burbick, "Emily Dickinson and the Economics of Desire," in *Critical Essays,* Judith Farr, ed., 76–88; Joanne Feit Diehl, *Romantic Imagination,* 25.

"I cannot live with You—" (1863) (Fr 706, J 640)

In this beautiful litany of loss, the best-known of Dickinson's love poems, the speaker moves through a series of states of being with her beloved, finding each one barred to her. Since she cannot live, die, be resurrected, be judged by God, lost or saved with him, they "must meet apart," in a place paradoxically defined as minuscule and vast, and nurtured by "that White sustenance—/ Despair—." In each hypothetical, rejected vision of meeting, the speaker unflinchingly juxtaposes the intensity of their love with the limiting reality confronting them.

In the first stanza, the poet rules out the possibility of actually living with her beloved on the grounds that "It would be Life—/ And Life is over there—/ Behind the Shelf." Read in isolation, the lines have the half-bitter, half-resigned quality found in so many Dickinson poems in which the speaker acknowledges hunger and deprivation as a primary condition of her existence. In works such as "GOD GAVE A LOAF TO EVERY BIRD—," "VICTORY COMES LATE—," and "WHO NEVER WANTED MADDEST JOY," satiety and fulfillment are elsewhere, out of reach, withheld from her.

However, as the first and second stanzas are joined by the enjambed lines, "Behind the Shelf / The Sexton keeps the key to—," another meaning for "Life is over there" emerges. For the "porcelain" a church sexton locks up is the vessel used for the ceremony of wine and bread of the Lord's Supper. The Life "Behind the shelf" thus refers to life eternal, which is symbolized by the Christian ritual. The speaker implies that she cannot live with her beloved because *that* would be Life, a fulfillment challenging God's paradise. This tension between earthly and eternal life runs through the poem.

As biographer Cynthia Griffin Wolff puts it, "the very nature of the lovers' excellence is a force that might disable God if it were permitted to exist" (*Emily Dickinson,* 419).

Dickinson used the image of a "porcelain life" earlier, in a letter to SAMUEL BOWLES, the crusading editor of the *Springfield Republican,* whom she revered, in which she asks about his and his family's health. Explaining her anxiety for them, she writes:

> I hope your cups are full. . . . In such a porcelain life, one likes to be *sure* that all is well, lest one stumble upon one's hopes in a pile of broken crockery. (L 193, late August 1858)

Here Dickinson takes the Psalmist's symbol of a life overflowing with blessings, "My cup runneth over," and transforms it into a complex image of both mortality and the destruction of romantic hopes (possibly hers for Bowles). In light of these associations, the "Sexton," "Putting up / Our Life— His Porcelain—/ Like a Cup—" becomes a deity indifferent to human happiness. Not only is the Cup fragile, it is devalued by the keeper of mundane orderliness: "Discarded of the Housewife—/ Quaint—or Broke—." The notion of broken lives/hopes is carried forward in the final evolution of the crockery image, "A newer Sevres pleases—/ Old Ones crack—," which suggests that the lovers' relationship is an old one.

Having thus "explained" why she and her lover cannot live together, the speaker goes on, in the next two stanzas, to say why they could not die together, perhaps in a suicide pact, as critic Vivian Pollak suggests (*Anxiety of Gender,* 182–183). Here the barrier is that "One must wait / To shut the Other's Gaze down—," that is, to perform the ritual of closing the eyelids of the deceased, and neither would be capable of waiting. "You—could not—" she tells her beloved, but whether this inability would stem from excess of grief or because he is much older and thus likely to die first, or some other reason, we are not told. As for the speaker, seeing him die would be impossible for her without dying instantly herself, claiming her own "Right of Frost—."

Judith Farr has written that this poem's "dark and harrowing logic has made it a model of poetic argument" (*Passion,* 308). The key word here is *poetic,* for it is difficult to see any simple logic in the argument of these stanzas. Since neither lover could wait, they might indeed die together. Moreover, as Pollak writes, there is no compelling reason "why a corpse needs to have its eyes closed, unless she is implying that she needs help with dying, and that her lover would be incapable of murder . . . (*Anxiety of Gender,* 183). For Pollak, the only way to see the stanzas as "internally consistent" is to assume that "the real problem is not her inability but her unwillingness to die herself or to cause her lover to do so." This is reading in a great deal, however. It seems simpler to assume that "logic" is secondary here to the logic of emotion, the speaker's simultaneous convictions that she could not live a moment if her beloved were dead, but that *any* shared experience, even the transition from life to death, would be denied them. In all her poignant "explanations" of why she and her lover cannot be together, the deep, immovable conviction of the impossibility of love's fulfillment precedes argument or evidence.

The next two stanzas, 6 and 7, form "the hinge upon which the verse turns from earth to heaven" (Wolff, *Life* 421). Dickinson has a number of poems in which she anticipates a reunion in heaven with a beloved denied to her on earth. Thus, in a related poem written the previous year, "THERE CAME A DAY—AT SUMMER'S FULL—," she describes the renunciation of an earthly love, but anticipates a union beyond the grave, in "*that* New Marriage—/ Justified—through Calvaries of Love!" In Fr 706, however, she devotes six stanzas to naming the obstacles to a reunion in heaven:

Nor could I rise—with You—
Because Your Face
Would put out Jesus'—
That New Grace

Just as in girlhood Dickinson found herself loving the world too well to declare for Christ during the Calvinist REVIVALS that regularly swept through AMHERST, so in this poem she rejects Jesus' glory as an inferior substitute for her earthly lover's. The lines resonate with a brief letter she sent, around 1877, to the radiantly handsome Bowles, possibly the beloved of this poem, whose relentless social

activism in spite of ill health endowed him for her with an aura of saintliness. Apparently acknowledging the receipt of a photograph, she writes, "You have the most triumphant Face out of Paradise— probably because you are there constantly, instead of ultimately—" (L 489). As Farr notes, the vision of the lover's countenance eclipsing Christ's recurs in the image patterns of the letters and poems Dickinson wrote to the man she called "Master." Without the radiance of her beloved ("Except that You than He / Shone closer by—"), she continues, she would be homesick in heaven. Homesickness, we should note, tormented the homebound Dickinson, whether on earth or in heaven, as she wrote, in 1862: "I never felt at Home—Below—/ And in the Handsome skies / I shall not feel at Home—I know—/ I don't like Paradise—" (Fr 437). Here, she is homesick for the "Life that never could be, an ordinary, domestic life infused with the radiance of his love" (Wolff, *Life* 421).

Then, too, she writes in stanzas 8 and 9, Judgment would come between them, since, although the beloved tried to serve Heaven, she, as his idolater, could not:

Because You saturated sight—
And I had no more eyes
For sordid excellence
As Paradise

Dickinson's heresy in dismissing God's gift of eternal life as "sordid" is consistent with "her lifelong recognition that she can love people (her friends, Sue, Master) more than God" (*Passion,* 126). Farr sees another version of this stance in the famous letter Dickinson sent to her future sister-in-law, SUSAN HUNTINGTON GILBERT (DICKINSON), that begins, "Sue—you can go or stay—" (L 173, about 1854), in which she "opposes to the idea of religion the burning reality of love. Dickinson imagines herself on the . . . Day of Judgment claimed by the Devil . . . while Sue, who loved Jesus Christ, is saved" (124).

Reading the next two stanzas, in which the speaker considers the possibilities that she might be saved and he lost, or vice versa, Pollak accuses the speaker of not "understanding the relationship between the attempt to serve heaven, in which she claims not to have participated, and the end product, grace" (*Anxiety of Gender*, 184). But Dickinson understood the relationship very well and is only denying her prospects for happiness in the next life from every conceivable perspective. The Heaven and Hell of the self are in any case what concern her, as she tells us when she writes that, if he were saved and she "condemned to be / Where You were not / That self—were Hell to me—."

In the final stanza, two lines longer than the others, as if to imitate the distance separating them, she drops the negatives and says not only what can happen, but also what must: "So we must meet apart—." Farr notes that "To 'meet apart with door ajar' is a concept taken from the very pattern of Dickinson's daily life in 1862. She met people behind doorways; she met them in letters; she met them by sending herself in spirit to their rooms" (*Passion*, 308). Within the space of the final stanza, the slender opening of the "Door ajar" between the lovers expands into three immensities: Ocean, Prayer, and "that White Sustenance—/ Despair—." Note how meaning is reinforced by sound in the progression from "Door ajar" to "Oceans are," to "Prayer," to "Despair," and how the very sounds of the word *Prayer* are reconstituted in the word *Despair*. For Dickinson, prayer was most often associated with the despair of knowing God is not listening, or, if listening, not caring.

In what sense does despair sustain her? Scholar Gary Stonum suggests that despair "can both sustain itself and be sustained by the lovers. In contrast to a consuming and apocalyptic presence, it can be prolonged without requiring the parties to be consumed" (*Dickinson Sublime*, 161). Despair sustains Dickinson's art as well, providing the emotional core of her love poetry. The sustenance it offers is *White*, a word she associated with death but also with the purity and integrity of her calling as a poet.

See also "IF I MAY HAVE IT, WHEN IT'S DEAD," "NOT IN THIS WORLD TO SEE HIS FACE—," "OF COURSE—I PRAYED—," "WHEN I HOPED, I RECOLLECT," MASTER LETTERS, and PURITAN HERITAGE.

FURTHER READING

Sharon Cameron, "The Dialectic of Rage," in *Modern Critical Views*, Harold Bloom, ed., 118–121; Judith Farr, *Passion*, 124–125, 306–308; Vivian R. Pollak, *Anxiety of Gender*, 181–184 Gary Lee Stonum, *Dickinson Sublime*, 160–161; Cynthia Griffin Wolff, *Emily Dickinson*, 417–423.

"I can wade Grief—" (1862) (Fr 312, J 252)

In this exploration of her own and the human capacity to bear grief and joy Dickinson begins and ends with a boast. Grief is her natural element, she tells us; she is a regular athlete when it comes to traversing "Whole Pools of it"—and keeping her head above water. We can interpret this as a revelation of a perverse innate disposition that made her more comfortable when she was miserable; but it may also be seen as a simple statement of fact. For, by the time she wrote this poem, at age 32, Dickinson *had* experienced—and survived—the deaths of such intimates as her close friend SOPHIA HOLLAND, and her mentors LEONARD HUMPHREY and BENJAMIN FRANKLIN NEWTON, as well as the deaths of neighbors and acquaintances, many of whom were young. She had also experienced the loss or waning of once intense friendships. Although shaken by these griefs, she had learned to live with them. But joy is a dizzying, unaccustomed medium for her. If grief is water, joy is air, a gust of wind whose "least push" makes her drunk and throws her off balance. Breezily defending herself against the smiles of the watching pebbles, she tells us it was only "the New Liquor" of joy that has affected her. Whatever new joy in her life sparked these words, there is no hint of it in the actual poem. This is deeply characteristic of her poems, which tell "all the truth" of her inner experience, without revealing the external circumstances involved. (See "TELL ALL THE TRUTH BUT TELL IT SLANT"). Thus, the "New Liquor" can stand for all and any joys. Dickinson speaks of herself as intoxicated in other poems, for example, in "I TASTE A LIQUOR NEVER

BREWED—," in which she appears in the throes of intense spiritual and emotional highs. She was, in fact, quite adept at "wading" her own particular brand of ecstasy, whether exultation in nature, in the writing of poems, or simply in the mystery of being alive.

In the lighthearted immediacy of the last two lines of stanza 1, we can feel the poet stepping off, however uncertainly, into a state of inebriated joy. But, along with the use of the first person, stanza 2 drops the theme of intoxication altogether. Indeed, in its shift of tone and focus, stanza 2 might be a separate poem altogether. There are, however, intimate connections between the poem's two halves. Dickinson believed in "leaving the soul ajar," that is, letting the experience she was exploring take her where it would. The fact that her poems often go in unexpected directions is part of their complexity and power.

Thus, in stanza 2, she generalizes from the personal, but universalized, experience of stanza 1. Joy is left behind, the tone becomes oracular and Pain is the subject. "Power is only Pain—/ Stranded—thro' Discipline," she proclaims, in one of her most famous and central statements. The first part of this borders on the common wisdom that hardship survived can strengthen the sufferer. But in the second half she develops this idea in a new direction. *Stranded,* in the edition of the dictionary Dickinson used, is defined as "driven on shore . . . as a ship, *stranded* at high water." The image is thus one of isolation and immobility. In this context, the stranding is a positive state: The ship of pain is under control. Unlike wobbly, out-of-control joy, it is anchored by the hanging weights of discipline. Through the will of the sufferer, it can be transformed into power—to endure or even to triumph through the alchemy of poetry.

In a final shift of imagery, the poet sees "Balm"— her term for healing pleasure—as a weakening gift, reducing Giants to mere men. In contrast, burdens create the strength to bear them. *Himmaleh* is a variant spelling of Himalayas, the Tibetan mountain range; it is the form Dickinson would have seen in S. Augustus Mitchell's *System of Modern Geography,* the text used at the Mount Holyoke

Female Seminary, which she attended. In a play of words that reinforces her meaning, she personifies *Himmaleh* as "Him," thereby shrinking both the word and the mountain range it refers to, making it something manageable:

> Give Himmaleh—
> They'll carry—Him!

"Him," also, of course, suggests that the gigantic burden carried is a man. This suspicion is heightened if we know that Dickinson wrote another poem that same year in which *Himmaleh* is personified: "The Himmaleh was known to stoop/ Unto the Daisy low—" (Fr 460, J 481, 1862). Daisy was the name she used for herself in her letters to Samuel Bowles, whom many scholars believe to be the beloved man she called Master. But any simple identification of Bowles with Himmaleh is ruled out by the fact that, in this poem, Dickinson makes the mountain range feminine: "Where Tent by Tent—Her Universe/ Hung Out it's Flags of Snow—" a possible allusion to the powerful woman she loved, her sister-in-law, Susan Huntington Gilbert Dickinson. The reader determined to nail Dickinson's poems firmly to the facts of her biography repeatedly encounters this kind of ambiguity.

Thus, this poem, in which the speaker at first appears to be taking her first unsteady steps under the influence of joy turns into an affirmation and celebration of the feats that pain makes possible. It belongs to that group of Dickinson's poems, prominently including "We never know how high we are/ Till we are asked to rise" (Fr 1197, 1871), which vaunt the power of the soul to grow into something mighty when faced with a great challenge.

FURTHER READING
Cynthia Griffin Wolff, *Emily Dickinson,* 214–216.

"I died for Beauty—but was scarce" (1862) (Fr 448, J 449)

Emily Dickinson came at the experience of death from numerous ingenious directions in her poetry.

In this poem, as in others such as "I HEARD A FLY BUZZ—WHEN I DIED—" and "BECAUSE I COULD NOT STOP FOR DEATH—," she asks the reader to accept the fiction that the speaker has already died. Thus, although "the poem's voice tells us what silences voice, it is still talking, is *after* its end relating its end" (Cameron, *Lyric Time,* 209–210). Dickinson employs this poetic strategy to reach what she calls CIRCUMFERENCE, the farthest limit of what can be humanly known, in this case, about the meaning of death.

In this poem, however, the poet has an additional concern: the relationship between human mortality and the ideals of Truth and Beauty. Both of these ideals occupy an exalted place in Dickinson's universe; both are eternal and exempt from analysis. Thus, she states of beauty in Fr 654: "Beauty be not caused—It is—/ Chase it, and it ceases—/ Chase it not, and it abides—." In Fr 797, she declares: "The Definition of Beauty is/ That Definition is none—/ Of Heaven, easing Analysis, / Since Heaven and He are one." And in Fr 1515, she says, "Estranged from Beauty—none can be—/ For Beauty is Infinity—." As for Truth, "Truth—is as old as God—/ His Twin identity / And will endure as long as He/ A Co-Eternity," she says in Fr 795; and in Fr 1495, "But Truth, outlasts the Sun—." Indeed, Truth is so brilliant that it "must dazzle gradually or every man be blind" (Fr 1263).

Although this poem gives no specifics as to *how* the speaker and her neighbor in the tomb died for Beauty and Truth, Dickinson's poetry as a whole gives evidence of *why* these ideals are worth dying for. She asks the reader to take as a given the principled deaths—and then tries to keep the ideals "alive" in death, through the conversation of the two "kinsmen." The victory is brief, however; time and death win. The earth silently conquers, wiping out both the speech and the memory or identity ("Our names") of the speakers:

> And so, as Kinsmen, met a Night—
> We talked between the Rooms—
> Until the Moss had reached our lips—
> And covered up—Our names—

There is a sharp shift in focus in the last two lines, as if the poet were unable to go any further in the direction of a continued conversation and is all at once overwhelmed with the sense of silencing and obliteration. She seems to be saying, somewhat cynically, that whatever the cause (or lack thereof) for which a person dies, the end result is the same. The sacrifice of dying for a high ideal is undercut by the "democracy" of death and time, which eventually cover up all traces of the idealists.

In this exploration of the relationship of Truth and Beauty (notions that encompass poetry, art, and imagination) to the perishing human lives they illumine, Dickinson may have been "replying" to two prominent literary treatments of that theme. The first is William Shakespeare's monody (personal lament) "The Phoenix and the Turtle," which concludes: "Truth may seem, but cannot be: / Beauty brag, but 'tis not she; Truth and beauty buried be." Dickinson's poem to some extent seconds this notion, although, for her, it is not Truth and Beauty that are buried, but their representatives.

The second precedent is John Keats's "Ode on a Grecian Urn" (1820), one of the English Romantic poet's great inquiries into the function of art and its relation to death, which concludes: "'Beauty is truth, truth beauty,—that is all/ Ye know on earth, and all ye need to know.'" In the second stanza of her poem, the speaker's neighbor in the tomb agrees with the first half of Keats's comforting declaration, saying "[Truth and Beauty] Themself are One—"; but as the body of her poetry testifies, this much knowledge of the human situation was far from all she found it necessary to know in this life.

Elizabeth Barrett Browning's "A Vision of Poets," which Dickinson knew and loved, has also been suggested as a likely source for this poem.

FURTHER READING

Joanne Feit Diehl, *Dickinson and the Romantic Imagination;* Josef Raab, "The Metapoetic Element in Dickinson," in *Handbook,* Grabher et al., eds., 273–295; Gary Lee Stonum, "Dickinson's Literary Background," in *Handbook,* Grabher et al., eds., 47.

"I dreaded that first Robin, so," (1862) (Fr 347, J 348)

In this work, which scholar Charles R. Anderson has called "her best poem on the theme of human suffering confronted by nature's gay parade" (*Stairway*, 224), Dickinson performs a virtuoso feat of tonal balance. While evoking her grief, her resistance to and alienation from spring's rebirth in striking imagery, she manages at the same time to undercut her dread and mock her own effrontery at imagining her individual woes could interfere with the "unthinking" rhythms of the seasons. The instrument of this complexity is the persona of the speaker, for whom nature's gentle "creatures"— robin, daffodil, bee—have an impact powerful enough to destroy her. They call to that part of herself that hopes and sings and begins again, and whose existence now provides too stark a contrast to the grief she feels. She is both a sufferer outside nature and one profoundly sensitive and therefore vulnerable to it.

How, otherwise, would it be possible for someone to "dread" the first robin? In a poem written the previous year, Dickinson announces "THE ROBIN'S MY CRITERION FOR TUNE—/ Because I grow—where Robins do—." This harbinger of spring is the very essence of her native music, a bird with whom she closely identifies. In 1861, she also wrote "I shall keep singing!" in which she herself is a robin: "I— with my Redbreast—/ And my Rhymes—," albeit one who will "take her place in summer" and will have a "fuller tune."

While dreading the first Robin, the speaker personifies the bird as "He," thereby drawing "him" closer to herself. And, indeed, in the next three lines of stanza 1, she admits she's mastered him, is getting used to him, and that he only "hurts a little." (She expresses a similar idea in an undated poem, Fr 1782, where not only the robin's bright song but the light of day are an insult to the dead: "How dare the robins sing, / When men and women hear / Who since they went to their account / Have settled with the year!—" . . . "Insulting is the sun / To him whom mortal light / Beguiled of immortality / Bequeath him to the night").

The emphasis on "first," repeated in stanza 2 in "that first Shout," is important, for the speaker understands that it is only the initial shock of nature's rebirth that she must withstand in order to dissipate its power to wound ("mangle") her:

I thought if I could only live
Till that first Shout got by—
Not all Pianos in the Woods
Had power to mangle me—

The "Shout" may be her way of referring to the Robin's song or it may refer to that mingled cry of birds and insects that she transforms into "Pianos in the Woods." The image is charming rather than fearful and, for Dickinson, who was herself an accomplished pianist and composer of melodies, it cannot have been a wholly alienating one. And so it goes in the next three stanzas: Despite the speaker's "dread," "hurt," the threat of being "mangled" or "pierced," the innocence and familiarity of what menaces her undermine the sense of terror. One suspects that the poet herself is aware of the incongruity of her hyperbolic dread with its commonplace and innocuous sources, and has knowingly injected into the poem a subtle note of self-irony.

Because, characteristically, the cause of the speaker's bereavement (a death? the failure of a love affair?) is never stated, it is possible to interpret it, not as a specific grief, but as the kind of chronic discomfort with happiness she speaks of in another poem of 1862: "I CAN WADE GRIEF—,/ Whole pools of it—/ I'm used to that—/ But the least push of Joy / Breaks up my feet—/ And I tip—drunken—." Thus, what disconcerts her about the daffodils is their "Yellow Gown," which is "So foreign" to her own way of dressing, presumably in either the black of mourning or the white dress that signified her renunciation of the world and dedication to her art. In his famous daffodil poem, "I wandered lonely as a cloud," William Wordsworth's sighting of a "crowd of golden daffodils" is a gift from nature he can draw upon in his imagination when his spirit is oppressed: "And then my heart with pleasure fills/ And dances with the daffodils." Far from dancing with the daffodils of her imagination, Dickinson's speaker wants to hide from them within the tall grass. The fear of being seen by others, which, by the time she wrote this poem, had already led her to seclude herself from all but family and the closest friends, has extended itself to the simple flowers she so covets and identifies with in other poems. In Fr 266, "What would I give to see his face?" she specifies both daffodils and bees, her companions in intoxication and sexual titillation, as subjects of her "Kingdom's worth of Bliss!" But here she wants nothing to do with their joyous message. She cannot even imagine what of relevance the bees might have to say to her.

However ardent the speaker's wishes that the whole gaudy, buzzing show would stay away, they have no impact on external events: "They're here, though; not a creature failed—," she states, deadpan, at the opening of stanza 4. There is little surprise in this observation, but more than a little self-irony in her designation of herself as "Queen of Calvary." The tone here is very different from the one she uses in "TITLE DIVINE, IS MINE," when she refers to herself, with real anguish, as "Empress of Calvary." For, as the poem moves toward closure, she has two kingdoms—Calvary and the natural world surrounding her, the "creatures" of her garden and nearby woods. And, although they have not shown her the "gentle deference" of staying away, they nonetheless "salute her" as they march past, to the rhythm of their "unthinking Drums." She acknowledges their greeting, by lifting the "childish Plumes" that "are the insignia of her royalty and of her grief, as in the purple plumes of traditional monarchy, and the black ones of hearse and horse in the funerals of her own day. Her recognition that both are childish is the mark of a certain stage of recovery, the awareness that at least her irrational terror is now dead" (Anderson, *Stairway*, 228).

Despite her dread of spring's flora and fauna, she doesn't quite succeed in banishing a note of reluctant delight in once more finding herself surrounded by them. They are, after all, as "unthinking" and delightful as small children, of whom Emily Dickinson was inordinately fond.

See also "FURTHER IN SUMMER THAN THE BIRDS—," "THESE ARE THE DAYS WHEN BIRDS COME BACK—," and "WHAT MYSTERY PERVADES A WELL!"

FURTHER READING

Charles R. Anderson, *Stairway*, 224–228.

"I dwell in Possibility—" (1862) (Fr 466, J 657)

As she does in another poem written that same year, "THEY SHUT ME UP IN PROSE—," Dickinson contrasts the word "Prose"—the natural language of everyday life, with all its looseness and limitations—to a state of unbounded freedom. In the latter poem, she finds this freedom in the spinning, birdlike flights of her "Brain"; here, she abandons the House of Prose for the House of Possibility—her metaphor for her life in poetry. Although it is a House, an enclosure, it is one with the utmost of openness: "More numerous of Windows—/ Superior—for Doors—."

In stanza 2, this House of Possibility first rivals the grandeur of nature and then merges with it. It has as many "Chambers as the Cedars"—an image that evokes the Scriptural verse "The trees of the Lord are full of sap: the cedars of Lebanon which He hath planted" (Psalms 104:16). The sap-filled limbs (Chambers) of the flourishing, majestic evergreens are an image of boundless vitality. The speaker claims this vitality for her House. Conspicuously lacking, however, is the sentiment of the verse's second half: praise to God who alone has planted and nurtured the cedars. Instead, Dickinson plucks the natural image, with its aura of divinity, from the biblical text and incorporates it into a "theology" of her own.

In the next image, we are presented with a paradox. For all its doors and windows, the House of Possibility becomes an impregnable fortress. "Impregnable of eye—" suggests that this is an internal, hidden dwelling, one that is inaccessible to ordinary vision and thus ensures the privacy of the one who dwells within it. Then, in the stanza's final image, this fortress of impenetrable mystery opens out again, as the House of Possibility is crowned with an "everlasting roof" wide as the world itself: "The Gambrels of the Sky." Gambrels are roofs with slopes on each side, of the sort traditionally used in barns. Thus, the image blithely transposes Amherst architecture to the domes of the heavens. Sap-filled cedars; impregnable fortress, everlasting roof of the sky. Note that consistency is not a factor in this grouping of imagery; rather, Dickinson stacks them to suggest the ineffable qualities of the state she is evoking. Together, they convey the shape and dimensions of her spiritual home.

The tone of intoxication is carried over into the final stanza, in which the speaker assures the reader she is not alone, but has "visitors." If her House is "fairer," these visitors are "fairest." All we have of them is this assertion; but they resonate with the ethereal "Hosts" who visit her continually in "ALONE, I CANNOT BE—," and with the shower of mint that falls ceaselessly into her basket in "I WAS THE SLIGHTEST IN THE HOUSE—," poems written during that same year of astounding poetic productivity. They are her mysterious and endlessly bountiful sources of inspiration, essential to the miraculous process in which she engages. The poem is rescued from boastfulness in the humble paradox of the last two lines, in which she defines her poetic vocation as "The spreading wide my narrow Hands / To gather Paradise—." In the final off rhyme of "his/Paradise," the rhyming vowel opens up, reinforcing the feeling of expansiveness. The image of "Paradise," picking up the celestial chord of "ever-lasting roof," seems both inevitable and wholly unexpected. Rarely if ever, has there been so intense an affirmation of the ecstasy of poetic creation.

See also "I TASTE A LIQUOR NEVER BREWED—."

FURTHER READING

Christopher Benfey, *Emily Dickinson and the Problem of Others,* 33–34.

"I felt a Funeral, in my Brain," (1862) (Fr 340, J 280)

This famous, dreamlike poem has spawned a wealth of widely varying interpretations. Biographer Cynthia Griffin Wolff has argued that the speaker is reporting, from beyond the grave, on what went on at her own funeral, describing the transition from life to death. As occurs in such powerful works as "BECAUSE I COULD NOT STOP FOR DEATH—," "I HEARD A FLY BUZZ—WHEN I DIED—," and "I DIED FOR BEAUTY—BUT WAS SCARCE," this speaker's aim is to discover "a strategy to hold identity together as the bland force of extinction systematically dissolves it" (*Emily Dickinson,* 221). For other readers, however, the dissolving process in "I felt a Funeral" is not death itself, but an experience akin to it, one of encroaching mental disorientation, that takes the speaker into realms for which there are no commonly shared descriptive words. Scholar Judith Farr sees the poem as a clinically accurate account of a fainting spell (*Passion,* 90–91), while critics Sandra Gilbert and Susan Gubar interpret death as a metaphor for madness and "psychic fragmentation." To buttress the latter argument, they and others have compared this poem with one written three years later, "I felt a Cleaving in my Mind—," which contains a similar verbal construction, but is "far more frank in its admission that madness is its true subject" (*Madwoman,* 627–628).

Another way to understand the role that death plays in this poem is to view it as both a metaphor for mental unraveling and as the very real, literal concern that leads to this dissolution. In this interpretation, the funeral in the speaker's brain is her obsession with what she called the "flood subject" of death and immortality. The question of what comes after death, pounding relentlessly in her brain, weakens the foundations of her inner world and sends her plunging downward. The poem's allegorical language, however, does not preclude other interpretations. A case could be made that the "funeral" commemorates the death of her hopes for love and acceptance from SAMUEL BOWLES, whom she seems to have loved at the time, or some other crisis in her personal or creative life. As is often the case with Dickinson, the language, imagery and structure of the poem resist being "tied down" to a single "situation." This is especially true in a poem such as this, where she is venturing into uncharted psychic realms, where the mind's usual structures are breaking down. "She seems as close to touching bottom here as she ever got. But there was nothing wrong with her mind when she wrote [this] poem," biographer Richard B. Sewall notes (*Life,* II, 502), reminding us that writing a poem such as this, about loss of consciousness and control, requires the highest degree of poetic mastery.

To counterbalance the speaker's increasing sense of disorder and loss of self, Dickinson makes extensive use of the ordering elements of poetry, including metaphor, rhyme, meter, sound play, and phrase repetition. In her attempt to make a coherent narrative out of a sense of incoherence, she employs the device of the *extended metaphor* in the first three stanzas, furnishing the funeral with mourners, a service, and the lifting and carrying away of a coffin. The funeral is an external image of her inner world; it never stands outside the speaker. "They" and "I" form an interconnected reality, "the Funeral, in my Brain," in which the speaker is "invaded" by the funeral but still is able to speak of herself and "the Mourners" in distinct terms. For the first 11 lines of the poem, "I" and "they" move in tandem, with the insistent, monotonous, maddening action of the mourners ("treading—treading," "beating—beating," creaking across her Soul with "Boots of Lead") bringing the speaker ever closer to internal dissolution.

Then, in line 12, as the coffin is being removed, the funeral metaphor breaks down and the poem tumbles into vaster, even less definable realms of absolute essences: Space, Being, Silence.

Then Space—began to toll,

As all the Heavens were a Bell,
And Being, but an Ear,
And I, and Silence, some strange Race
Wrecked, solitary, here—

Instead of a bell (the one customarily rung at Congregationalist funerals as the mourners disperse) tolling in her head, Space itself begins to toll. In the fourth stanza of this poem in which sounds play so great a role (treading, beating, creaking), it feels *as if* the Heavens have become one great producer of portentous sound (a bell), while Being (the speaker's?) is the receiver (Ear) of that sound. The relationship between the "Heavens," "Being," "I," and "Silence" is unspecified and unclear. If

the poem *is* about psychic fragmentation, then perhaps all these elements—sound and silence, unity and isolation (shipwreck)—are part of the speaker. As in a dream, they appear alien ("some strange Race") and unintegrated.

At this point, in a key image, the "Plank in Reason" breaks. The image takes us back to stanza 1 and the eroding floor of the poet's brain, being insistently tread by the mourners, which "Sense"—a word that denotes both perception and rationality—almost "breaks through," that is, falls through. Wolff makes the important observation that Dickinson's contemporaries would have caught her allusion to a prominent representation in mid-19th century conservative religious culture, in which a man, looking down at his Bible, crosses over the abyss between this world and heaven on a plank labeled "Faith" (*Emily Dickinson,* 230–231). Dickinson, unable to walk the plank of faith, substitutes a plank of reason:

And then a Plank in Reason, broke,
And I dropped down, and down—
And hit a World, at every plunge,
And Finished knowing—then—

The breaking of the plank of reason sends her plummeting into a downward journey that lends itself to two diametrically opposed interpretations. For some readers, the journey is a descent to hell; but hell, in the literal Calvinist sense, was not a concept that held any power over Dickinson. Far more likely, and more interesting in its implications, is that the speaker's descent is into psychological and spiritual depths. The breaking of the plank of reason frees her from the limits of that faculty. In the midst of her fall, Dickinson, tantalizingly, hits "a World at every plunge," suggesting some vast newly glimpsed knowledge.

For those who view the poem as a vision of mental extinction, to be "Finished knowing" is "simultaneously to see the utter depths of one's despair where no new experience of grief is possible, and also to lose the faculty of knowing at all, to have one's mind disintegrate" (Porter, *The Early Poetry,* 37). But it is also possible to read the phrase quite differently, that is, to say that the speaker "finished" (came to the end of her plunge) "knowing" something she did not know before. The dissolution of the mind's familiar supports and scenery has led to revelation. The intriguing little word *then* which concludes the poem may suggest that she knew something then that she no longer knows, that is, the revelation was fleeting. Or it may simply be a verbal signal that something else is to follow.

See also "MUCH MADNESS IS DIVINEST SENSE—."

FURTHER READING

Priyamvada Tripathi Anantharaman, *Sunset in a Cup*, 35–43; Judith Farr, *Passion*, 90–91; Gibson, "Poetry of Hypothesis," 232–234; Sandra M. Gilbert and Susan Gubar, *Madwoman*, 626–629; David Porter, *Early Poetry*, 37; Cynthia Griffin Wolff, *Emily Dickinson*, 219–236.

"If I may have it, when it's dead" (1862) (Fr 431, J 577)

This poem of desire for a lover's corpse has struck some readers as ghoulish, repulsive, and more than a little mad. But it is best understood as an exercise in conscious, bitterly ironic hyperbole, a desperate last bid for possession in death of the person denied to the speaker in life. The fantasy of possessing the lover's corpse is but one step beyond Dickinson's oft-repeated poetic statement that she can make a feast out of the crumb fate has allotted her. To read the poem literally or interpret the speaker's desire to "stroke" her lover's "frost" as an image of physical violation is to misunderstand its "necrophilia." At bottom, this is a poem about a woman dreaming of a secret rendezvous with her lover. That she conceptualizes it in these radical terms indicates the extent of her desperation.

Moreover, as scholar Judith Farr reminds us, the poem's fantasy was less alien to the Victorians than it is to contemporary readers:

Dickinson's was an age in which the dead "lived" in mausoleums, where—as in the case of Queen Victoria visiting Albert entombed in Frogmore—their survivors might come to sit awhile or even brew a cup of tea. This was an age in which the young Emerson, who could

stand his loneliness no longer, dug up his wife Ellen's body by lantern light so that he might hold it in his arms again (*Passion*, 97).

For Vivian Pollak, a further justification for the fantasy of lover as corpse is that it allows the speaker to transcend her fear of heterosexuality. The corpse is perceived as a disembodied lover, made sexually inaccessible by death (*Anxiety of Gender*, 159). Such an interpretation, while plausible and intriguing, depends on biographical assumptions that lie outside the poem. Joan Burbick, on the other hand, derives the poem's logic from the text itself:

For the fulfillment of desire, death is required. A middle space between earth and Paradise, the grave becomes a sanctioned meeting place for love ("Economics of Desire," 86).

The notion of death as the only "place" she can possess her lover is an extension of Dickinson's fatalistic belief that, "For each extatic instant/ We must an anguish pay / In keen and quivering ratio / To the extasy—" (Fr 109, 1859). That ratio is central to this poem in which the speaker pays the ultimate price of his death for her "extatic instant" with her lover's corpse.

In her great love poem, written that same year, "I CANNOT LIVE WITH YOU—," Dickinson despairingly eliminates, one by one, the "spaces" (life, death, heaven) in which the lovers might meet. Here, she conceives a new one: the brief interval between physical death and burial. As she immerses herself in this hypothetical scenario (her lover is, after all, not really dead, and the speaker doesn't know for a certainty whether the deciding authority—fate, perhaps, or "society"—will grant her wish), her enthusiasm increases: from contentment to bliss to an almost unimaginable joy:

Until they lock it in the Grave,
'Tis Bliss I cannot weigh—
For tho' they lock Thee in the Grave,
Myself—can own the key—

Think of it Lover! I and Thee
Permitted—face to face to be—
After a Life—a Death—we'll say—

For Death was That
And This—is Thee—

In the third stanza, she reverses dictionary meanings, declaring the life without him as a form of death, compared to which "This" (the imagined possession of his corpse, at this moment, within the space of the poem) "—is Thee." Having imagined their reunion in this stanza, she drops the chilling, albeit appropriate pronoun "It." As she switches to the exclusive use of "Thee," she brings her lover back to life, replacing his corpse with the beloved himself. Thus, "It"—the body or, perhaps, the new thing he has become—serves as the instrumentality of her possessing him, after which the lover is restored to a "Thee."

United with the beloved now, in stanzas 4, 5, and 6 she confides to him what it was like for her when he died, describing "how the Grief got sleepy," a state akin to freezing to death as her senses grow numb. This is the retreat from the pain of consciousness she describes in "AFTER GREAT PAIN, A FORMAL FEELING COMES—," when "The Nerves sit ceremonious, like Tombs—." She describes the way that she made wordless signs to him across the barrier separating life and death, so that he might notice her. She offered him the encouragement of a smile to show him that—"When the Deep / All Waded," that is when the abyss between life and death has been crossed, looking back, their earthly sufferings, "those Old Times—in Calvary," will seem like play. For Dickinson, who called herself "Queen of Calvary," the crucifixion of Christ was not a unique event, but the prototype for human suffering in general and the torments of love in particular. Reading backwards, we find echoes of Jesus in the tomb in the lines in stanza 2: "For tho' they lock Thee in the Grave, / Myself—can own the key—." As owner of the key, the speaker is like God: the poet ruling her own creation.

In the final stanza she asks forgiveness of the beloved for keeping him from burial. The grave may come slow, but it comes all the same. All she has with him is the brief interval between death and burial, and all she really does during this period is to look at him. The phrase "to stroke thy frost" could conceivably refer to actually touching, making love to the corpse. But note that the bliss of this stroking "Outvisions Paradise." Once more, as in so much of Dickinson's work, the eye-to-eye, face-to-face encounter with the beloved is the ultimate ecstasy.

See also "I LIVE WITH HIM—I SEE HIS FACE—," "NOT IN THIS WORLD TO SEE HIS FACE—," "ONE CRUCIFIXION IS RECORDED—ONLY—," and "THERE CAME A DAY—AT SUMMER'S FULL—."

FURTHER READING

Joan Burbick, "Emily Dickinson and the Economics of Desire," in Critical Essays, Judith Farr, ed., 84–86; Judith Farr, The Passion of Emily Dickinson, 96–97; Cristanne Miller, Grammar, 81–82; Camille Paglia, Sexual Personae, 624, 660–665; Vivian R. Pollak, Anxiety of Gender, 159.

"If your Nerve, deny you—" (1862) (Fr 329, J 292)

In this poem, Dickinson exhorts herself to transcend fear and indulge what Robert Weisbuch calls "the dangerous, authentic feeling" ("Prisming," 222). It belongs with such poems as "I CAN WADE GRIEF—," in which the poet speaks with the voice of authority, claiming for herself or urging upon herself the spiritual discipline to rise above her own emotional limitations.

The vitality of this wisdom poem arises in part from Dickinson's awareness of the divisions of the inner life and her ingenuity in finding ways for language to express them. Nerve is another term for courage. But it also denotes the components of the nervous system—the physical underpinning of emotional responsiveness. Thus, it is a word that combines references to the biological and the spiritual (courage). In line 1, "you" (which may refer to either the speaker or the reader, or both) is the larger self, capable of "going above" the powerful, complex entity that is "your Nerve." In its faith in the power of the spirit over the physical and instinctual, this is a religious poem. However, the "steadying" force behind the steadfast spirit is not God, but the Grave.

In lines 3 and 4 the poet declares with wry humor that He, that is, "your Nerve," can steady himself by "leaning against the Grave." She is suggesting, not that death is the solution to fear, but that *awareness* of death is the greatest incentive to overcoming fear and living life to the fullest. Stanza 2 develops this idea:

That's a steady posture—
Never any bend
Held of those Brass arms—
Best Giant made—

The phrase "Never any bend," an instance of Dickinson's use of syntactic doubling, seems to float in midair; it can refer to either the line before or the line following it. Thus, the elliptical second stanza might be paraphrased as follows: "Leaning against the grave is a steady posture, without any bending. Whoever is held by the Brass arms of death (which never bend), is made into 'Best Giant.'" In its meaning as a metal alloy, brass is a visual image suggesting something bright and shiny. The second meaning of "brass" in Dickinson's lexicon is "impudence, a brazen face." Death's "impudence," the fact that it will not go away but holds us in its inescapable embrace, makes it a powerful impetus to transcend whatever inner timidity keeps us from engaging reality. In contrast with the exact rhyme patterns of the first and third stanzas, the suspended rhyme of this central stanza, together with its choppy syntax, reinforces the jarring, painful message.

In the concluding stanza, "your Nerve" has been replaced by "your Soul." The difference is a significant one. "Your Nerve" "denies you," that is, turns away from you altogether, refusing to even recognize whatever painful, difficult thing you know and feel. "Your Soul," on the other hand, merely vacillates, "see-sawing" between denial and recognition, fear and courage. Dickinson's remedy for this is to "Lift the Flesh door—," implying that the Soul's shortcomings are rooted in the wants of the flesh. The image of a "Flesh door" is bizarre and grotesque, suggesting, on the physical level, some kind of penetration behind the surface of the flesh. Behind the flesh door is a room, analogous to Dickinson's "haunted chamber" of the mind, where

the body keeps its secret. As it turns out, the secret is contemptible. The Flesh is a "Poltroon," defined in Emily's dictionary as "an arrogant coward . . . a wretch without spirit or courage." All it cares about is breathing (oxygen), staying alive on the most basic level. The speaker expresses her disdain for this creature in the poem's final words, "Nothing more—." She wants her wavering soul to aim higher, to free itself from the animal of the body that cares for only the most rudimentary survival.

In its valuing of the lived experience, no matter how painful, this poem expresses one side of a duality that runs through Dickinson's work. She was aware of the inevitability of numbness in the aftermath of great pain, when "The Nerves sit ceremonious, like Tombs—" and of the value of temporary numbness in helping the individual to navigate the most acute stages of loss and grief. But she was also driven by the desire to be fully conscious, an impulse deeply embedded in her concept of the poet as one who travels to the far limits of circumscribed human awareness, thereby stretching those boundaries a bit further. In this role, as scholar Joanne Feit Diehl has remarked, "the need to confront her version of reality precludes any desire to defend her bruised spirit" (*Romantic Imagination,* 114).

See also "AFTER GREAT PAIN, A FORMAL FEELING COMES—," "ONE NEED NOT BE A CHAMBER—TO BE HAUNTED—," and CIRCUMFERENCE.

FURTHER READING

Sharon Cameron, *Lyric Time,* 155–156; Joanne Feit Diehl, *Romantic Imagination,* 114–155; David Porter, *Early Poetry,* 165; Robert Weisbuch, "Prisming," in *Handbook,* Grabher et al., eds., 222.

"I had been hungry, all the Years—" (1862) (Fr 439, J 579)

This is one of the strongest of Dickinson's many poems dealing with thirst and hunger. About 10 percent of her poems contain images of food and drink, yet although their number is relatively small, they are among the poet's finest works. In these poems, which incorporate "the basic tensions of her experience. . . . [t]he Dickinson persona concentrates its energies on redefining the normal meaning of starvation and repletion and in the process attempts to redefine and recreate the self" (Vivian Pollak, "Thirst and Starvation," 67). The poem is structured as a narrative, with a simple plot: The perennially hungry speaker dines at last and finds the experience to be other than what she expected. She feels odd and ill and loses her appetite. The first thing the 31-year-old poet tells us is that she had been "hungry all the Years—," presumably throughout childhood and girlhood. This is all we know of the hunger, that it has been a constant in the speaker's life. We are never told *what* she is hungry for; the speaker does not explore this issue and seems to accept it as an unquestioned condition of her existence. The reader, of course, is free to suggest the source of the poet's hunger, and many have done so. Some have suggested the absence of maternal love or love of the passionate, romantic variety, as the most likely meaning of her hunger. Others have pointed to her exclusion from the literary world, while still others have understood the poet's hunger as a function of her exclusion from the religious community surrounding her. If the bread and wine of the poem allude to communion, then, consuming them would mean to become a part of the religious structure Dickinson resisted. While none of these interpretations can be excluded, the condensed, allegorical language of the poem works against the selection of any one meaning:

> I had been hungry, all the Years—
> My Noon had Come—to dine—
> I trembling drew the Table near—
> And touched the Curious Wine—

The event that changes the speaker's life is presented as an appointed rightful occurrence in a life. Like Sunrise and Sunset, the other pivotal diurnal moments that Dickinson repeatedly evokes in her poetry, Noon is a time of the soul: the intense center of the soul's "day," when the sun is at its highest point. Whether something has changed *within* the speaker or in her external circumstances to bring her to this point is not revealed. But the speaker appears to approach it willingly, trembling

with anticipation as she touches "the Curious Wine—." The word "Curious" tells us the speaker is unfamiliar with wine's intoxication. (It is indicative of the protean nature of Dickinson's speaker that, in earlier poems, she has appeared as a "little Tippler" [Fr 214] who, like the Bee, "lives by the quaffing" [Fr 230]. In these and other poems, wine is her image for a rare and intense spiritual intoxication.)

The speaker of this poem, however, is an abstainer, a deprived outsider. If, in her actual, external life, Dickinson returned home to an ample dinner, which she, as an excellent cook and baker, had helped provide, in the poem she is a poor waif, pressing her nose against the window of others' bounty, with no expectation of sharing it. In stanza 3, she shifts from wine to bread imagery, which allows her to contrast the "ample Bread" with the "Crumb" to which she is accustomed. In a poem written the previous year, "VICTORY COMES LATE—," she is a sparrow, who knows how to make do with her crumb. In this poem, she sees herself as a human being who is nonetheless accustomed to dining with the birds. This is a significant shift in persona, yet she makes it reluctantly—and reverts to less than human stature—a mountain berry—in the next stanza. As Pollak points out, a mountain berry transplanted to a road will die: "The self has been so completely defined by its starvation that food threatens to destroy it. The speaker cannot, in the end, conceive of the relaxation of restrictions as enabling growth and change. Thus she resists food in order to survive" (Ibid., 71).

Yet, the speaker of the final stanza has not died:

> Nor was I hungry—so I found
> That Hunger—was a way
> Of persons Outside Windows—
> That entering—takes away—

The newness of plenty has hurt her, made her feel ill—an accurate description of the effect of too much food or liquid on a person dying of thirst or starvation. But, at the end of the poem, she has survived. She has learned something about hunger and lived to tell about it. One may say that what Dickinson has "learned" is what she already knew and expressed in a poem such as "'Heaven'—is what I cannot reach!" (Fr 137). If "Heaven" is defined in this way, then reaching it automatically makes it "not Heaven." The inability to find the same intensity of joy in the reality as she found in imagining that reality was a defining feature of her psyche. Dickinson would write longingly to friends of her desire to see them, then refuse to see them when they appeared on her doorstep. But whatever the personal "pathology" behind this poem, it contains a profound truth about the nature of human hunger, which rarely survives the experience of satiation. As poet Richard Wilbur puts it, "Once an object has been magnified by desire, it cannot be wholly possessed by appetite" ("Sumptuous Destitution," 56).

The open-endedness of the final line seems to ask, "What am I going to replace hunger with? Is satiety worth the price of relinquishing hunger? Am I capable of satiety? Will I grow accustomed to it?" Although this poem provides no answers, Dickinson's subsequent writing indicates that the paradox that "to gain is to lose" became an ever more meaningful truth in the spiritual journey that led her to her later formulation of the "Banquet of Abstemiousness." (See "WHO NEVER WANTED—MADDEST JOY.")

See also "A DYING TIGER MOANED FOR DRINK—," "GOD GAVE A LOAF TO EVERY BIRD—," "IT WOULD HAVE STARVED A GNAT—," and "UNDUE SIGNIFICANCE A STARVING MAN ATTACHES."

FURTHER READING

Barbara Antonina Clarke Mossberg, "Emily Dickinson's Nursery Rhymes," in *Feminist Critics Read Emily Dickinson,* Suzanne Juhasz, ed., 45–66; Vivian R. Pollak, "Thirst and Starvation in Emily Dickinson's Poetry," in *Critical Essays,* Judith Farr, ed., 62–75; Richard Wilbur, "Sumptuous Destitution," in *Critical Essays,* Judith Farr, ed., 53–61.

"I heard a Fly buzz—when I died—" (1863) (Fr 591, J 465)

Although deathbed scenes obsessed the Victorian imagination, they were not generally presented through the eyes of the one who has already died.

Yet this is precisely the point of view that the startling first line of this poem invites the reader to accept. Not a word is said about where the speaker is, while telling of how she died, not even the bare allusion to the centuries of Eternity that concludes, "BECAUSE I COULD NOT STOP FOR DEATH—," another great poem about the transition from life to death. If, in that poem, Dickinson explored the moment of dying in images of movement and destination, in this one she clings to the final moments of stillness (repeated twice), stasis, and expectation in *this* world. With open-eyed determination, she pushes her imagination—and the reader's—to the extreme limits of what a dying person might perceive.

The poem merits comparison with another written in 1863, "I'VE SEEN A DYING EYE," in which the speaker watches in frustration as the eye of the dying person searches desperately for something it dimly sees, and then closes "Without disclosing what it be/ 'Twere blessed to have seen—." Only by putting herself in the place of the dying one can the poet satisfy her hunger to know. But there is nothing obviously blessed about what she sees; and it is the lack of any transcendent vision at the final moment that makes this poem so disturbing. Critics have tended to see it as a stark vision of human limitation that concentrates on the "final bitter deprivation" of the circumscribed ability to penetrate the meaning of mortality (Eberwein, *Dickinson,* 219).

But Dickinson is determined to stretch understanding to its limits, and in this pursuit she explores the gradations of sound, as well as light. In stanza 1, sound—the "Buzz" of the "Fly"—is heard against the "Stillness of the Room"; and this stillness, in turn, is perceived as similar to the stillness "Between the Heaves of Storm—," suggesting that something momentous is about to occur. The word "Stillness" contains both silence and lack of movement; it evokes the stillness of death.

Dickinson then uses images of disembodiment to further the poem's powerful sense of estrangement. In stanza 2, which alludes to those standing around the deathbed, we never see a whole person; instead we have disembodied "Eyes around" and "Breaths":

The Eyes around—had wrung them dry—
And Breaths were gathering firm
For that last Onset—when the King
Be witnessed—in the Room—

Similarly, in stanza 3, the speaker signs away a "Portion" of herself. Fractured grammar also contributes to this effect: In line 1, stanza 2, it makes no sense to read "The Eyes around" as the subject of the phrase "had wrung them dry," since "them" can only refer to those Eyes. We can only conclude that there is an omitted subject, that is, "grief" or "weeping" had wrung them dry. Dickinson enhances the sense of a floating reality by setting off the phrase with dashes.

Then, briefly, the poem admits the elements of a conventional deathbed scene: the religious expectation of the bystanders that the King, presumably the King of Kings, will be witnessed in the Room by the dying speaker; and the speaker's willing away of her earthly treasures. The Fly intervenes at just this moment, but its appearance is presented as sequence, not causality.

There interposed a Fly—
With Blue—uncertain—stumbling Buzz—
Between the light—and me—

The fortuitous appearance of a blue-bottle fly—the most ordinary, everyday annoyance—sharply undercuts the expectation of a divine apparition. With the appearance of the fly, ordinary perception once more breaks down. Dickinson uses synesthesia, the merging of visual and aural sensations (the Buzz is blue and it stumbles uncertainly), to get at what the dying person perceives. The Windows, "the apertures of the house, darken just as do those of her body's house, her eyes" (Farr, *Passion*, 310). When light fails so does life; the speaker observes it with minute precision as it disappears. The final words "see to see" inch the reader closer to the perception of the final moment. They seem to imply two levels of perception, with the second "see" denoting physical vision, while the first suggests a state prior to that, a certain modicum of life force, perhaps, required for visual perception to take place.

The phrase "see to see" is also the culmination of the poem's complex sound play. It echoes the repetition of "Stillness" in stanza 1, and it is the last of the series of sibilants, or hissing sounds (*s*, *sh*, *z*) that run through the poem, building up to the Fly's "Buzz." The consonant cluster *st* appears in "*st*illness" [twice], "*St*orm," "la*st*," and "*st*umbling"; the *s* sound—in all of the previous words, plus "*s*Onset," "witne*ss*ed," "*s*igned," "a*ss*ignable," "interpo*s*ed," "uncertain," and "*s*ee to *s*ee." The *z* of "Buzz" occurs twice. But "Buzz" is also part of another sound group that includes "*b*e," "*b*lue," "*b*etween" (twice), and "*B*reaths." A smaller group of *k* sounds belong to two words denoting certainty: "*K*ing" and "*K*eepsakes." The *f* first seen in "*F*ly" recurs in "*f*irm," in "*F*ly" again, and then in "*f*ailed." Note, too, that the inexact rhymes in the first three stanzas give way to the regular rhymes "me" and "see" in the final stanza, creating a tenuous sense of closure, at variance with the openness of "see to see—."

While there are those who see the fly as a statement of nihilism that ridicules the notion that death is transcendence, others see the image as more ambiguous. For all its mindless uncertainty, the fly is a symbol of blind, persistent life, and as such, worth clinging to until the very final instant of consciousness.

See also CIRCUMFERENCE.

FURTHER READING

Jane Eberwein, *Dickinson*, 219; Judith Farr, *Passion*, 310; Clarence L. Gohdes, "Emily Dickinson's Blue Fly," 423–431; A. Robert Lee, "'This World Is Not Conclusion': Emily Dickinson and the Landscape of Death," 217–232; Vivian R. Pollak, *Anxiety of Gender*, 193–198.

"I know that He exists" (1862) (Fr 365, J 338)

This poem about God's existence has all the characteristics of a soliloquy, in which Dickinson speaks to herself, following her initial thought where it takes her and ending up at a very different place from where she began. Immediately after her initial firm declaration of faith, she locates the God whose existence she is sure of "in silence." He cannot be heard and, as the next two lines tell us, he cannot be seen:

> He has hid his rare life
> From our gross eyes.

God's hidden nature is not presented as a reproach; it is a function of the unbridgeable distance between "his rare life" and "our gross eyes," the poet declares. Yet, it is difficult not to detect a note of sarcasm in her humility.

As if to ward off whatever doubt or anger she may have let slip out, she hastens to assure herself in stanza 2 that God's hiding is only a game— a child's game of hide-and-seek—and that such "play" lasts just an instant, the "instant" of mortal life, presumably. God is fond of men, and only hides himself briefly so that his "ambush" may enhance the bliss of seeing him with the element of surprise. God is a benevolent prankster.

But in the next stanza, the note of distrust implicit in the word "ambush" bursts into full-scale terror:

> But—should the play
> Prove piercing earnest—
> Should the glee—glaze—
> In Death's—stiff—stare—

The speaker suddenly realizes that there's a hitch, a potential problem with the game. What if God's hiding should go on for too long and prove to be an insurmountable absence? What if it is not play at all, but "piercing earnest," as the human "playmate" would discover when her expectant "glee" glazes "in Death's—stiff—stare—"? Through this stark image, the speaker is struck by the realization that death without resurrection may be the outcome of the game. Whatever "belief" she has does not assuage her terror.

In the poem's final stanza she asks herself, If there is no resurrection, but only death, wouldn't God's "jest" have gone too far? Wouldn't God be jesting at man's expense? The speaker has come *almost* full circle from her initial assertion that He exists. She does not deny that He exists: There is a jest—which presumes someone who is jesting. But God is not mentioned. In fact, the word God

is never used in the poem, an "absence" that reinforces, on the linguistic level, the lurking suspicion of an absent deity. In the poem's question "Would not the jest—/ Have crawled too far!" the act of this hypothetical deity is represented as animal- or insect-like—something that "crawls." It is a strange image that is difficult to visualize but conveys the speaker's revulsion. As E. Miller Budick succinctly notes, "the poem concludes with an awful shudder that effectively denies all of the comfortable assumptions of Christian idealism on which the poem is built" (*Emily Dickinson*, 93).

It is instructive to compare this poem to one written the following year, "IT'S EASY TO INVENT A LIFE—," in which Dickinson's sense of God's capriciousness and essential indifference to man is present from the outset. Certainly, such feelings of bitterness and frustration at her inability to reach a distant, inscrutable God constitute a major thread in Emily Dickinson's poetry of searching. However, as Robert Weisbuch points out, the poet expresses a contradictory worldview in other poems, in which she asserts as a matter of faith that she will overcome all limits and complete her quest. He cites, for example, Fr 199, "Tho' I get home—how late—how late / So I get home—'twill compensate," and concludes, "You cannot define Dickinson by what she believes but by what she keeps caring about, turning it this way and that ("Prisming," 221–222).

See also "I SHALL KNOW WHY—WHEN TIME IS OVER—" and "OF COURSE—I PRAYED—."

FURTHER READING

E. Miller Budick, *Life of Language*, 92–93; Thomas Johnson, *Emily Dickinson*, 152–153; Fred D. White, "Emily Dickinson's Existential Dramas," in *Cambridge Companion*, 101; Robert Weisbuch, "Prisming," in *Handbook*, Grabher et al., eds., 221–222.

"I like a look of Agony" (1862) (Fr 339, J 241)

The apparently perverse sentiment of the first line of this well-known poem invariably produces a shock; the reader reflexively recoils from a speaker who freely admits that she likes to witness the manifestations of terrible pain. But the speaker quickly redeems herself in the next line by explaining that what she values in "a look of Agony" is its authenticity—a quality, Dickinson was coming to believe, that could only be gained through suffering:

I like a look of Agony,
Because I know it's true—

In her willingness to pierce through the niceties of polite discourse and embrace an apparently "immoral" stance to get at authentic experience, Dickinson anticipates a key feature of modernism. One thinks of the early 20th-century Russian poet Vladimir Mayakovsky, who begins his poem, "A Few Words about Myself" with the taunt, "I love to see how children die." In a similar vein, American poet Sylvia Plath writes of how well she attempts suicide: "Dying / Is an art, like everything else. I do it exceptionally well. / I do it so it feels like hell. / I do it so it feels real" ("Lady Lazarus"). Numerous other examples might be cited.

In Dickinson's poem, the surest proof of genuine knowing is to be found in the evidence of the body. She expressed this notion in her famous definition of true poetry, contained in an early letter to the man she asked to be her mentor, THOMAS WENTWORTH HIGGINSON:

If I read a book [and] it makes my body so cold no fire could ever warm me I know *that* is poetry. If I feel physically as if the top of my head were taken off, I know *that* is poetry. These are the only way I know it. Is there any other way? (L 342a).

Daneen Wardrop, in her study of this poem within the context of the Gothic elements in fascicle 15, where Dickinson placed it, relates this sense of the body as barometer of the real to the poet's attraction to Gothicism, with its "jitters and hair-raisings." Dickinson knew that "the Gothic operates on bodily reflexes—convulsions and throes, and the beads of sweat on the forehead." ("Gothic in Fascicle 16," 147).

The obsession with death and its physical manifestations is another central feature that made Gothic literature so congenial to Dickinson. In the second stanza the idea of "Agony" swiftly becomes the absoluteness of death, taking us to suffering's most extreme consequence. Note how the poem floats free in the space of imagination; it is not tied to a particular death. At the same time, however, there is precise observation of what happens on a dying face: "The eyes glaze once—and that is Death—." Dickinson, whose poetry was driven by the need to understand death and its aftermath, seems to be saying, "Here is a simple way of knowing what death is, without any way of being deceived." Thus, the "sham" she rejects may not refer to the falsity of human beings in their emotional and social lives, but to false representations of death. The implication is that all the rest—the peaceful expressions on the face of the dead, the promise of Immortality—is sham.

The poem takes us from "Agony" to "homely Anguish," suggesting gradations of suffering. In Dickinson's lexicon, the two words may be used synonymously, but *agony* is a more extreme, all-encompassing state, "pain so extreme as to cause writhing or contortions of the body," on a par with "the sufferings of our Savior in the Garden of Gethsemane." In contrast, *anguish* "may be a more localized pain." Here, "homely Anguish" strings beads of perspiration on the forehead of the dying person. One implication of the word "homely" is an insistence on simplicity, in contrast with the false glitter of ostentatious jewelry. There may also be a hidden allusion to the crown of thorns placed on Jesus' forehead. The striking image, like so much else in this poem, resonates with the Gothic vision, which is built upon "the psychological fact that what can scare the most remains what is closest" (Ibid., 144).

See also "I CAN WADE GRIEF—," "I FELT A FUNERAL, IN MY BRAIN," "'TIS SO APPALLING—IT EXHILIRATES—," and PUBLICATION AND EDITORIAL SCHOLARSHIP.

FURTHER READING

Christopher Benfey, *Emily Dickinson*, 88, 91–92; M. L. Rosenthal and Sally M. Gall, *Modern Poetic Sequence*, 69–70; Daneen Wardrop, "Emily Dickinson and the Gothic in Fascicle 16," in *Cambridge Companion*, 142–164.

"I like to see it lap the Miles" (1862) (Fr 383, J 585)

In Emily Dickinson's best-known poem with a social theme, the unnamed "it" of the first line is generally recognized to be the railroad, which made its entry into AMHERST in 1853. Emily's father, EDWARD DICKINSON, a local civic leader, had a passion for bringing the railroad to Amherst and played a major role in this historic event. In her letter of May 16, 1853, to her brother, WILLIAM AUSTIN DICKINSON, she proclaims a simple delight in the revolutionary innovation: "While I write, the whistle is playing, and the cars just coming in. It gives us all new life, every time it plays. How you will love to hear it, when you come home again!"

But her letter to Austin the following month, describing the festive day of June 9, 1853, when a train full of celebrating passengers arrived from New London, Connecticut, to honor the completion of the Amherst and Belchertown Rail Road, shows her distancing herself from the general opinion: "The New London Day passed off grandly—so all the people said—it was pretty hot and dusty, but nobody cared for that. Father was as usual, Chief Marshal of the day, and went marching around the town with New London at his heels like some old Roman General, upon a Triumph Day. Carriages flew like sparks, hither, and thither and yon, and they all said t'was fine. I spose it was—I sat in Prof Tyler's woods and saw the train move off, and then ran home again for fear somebody would see me, or ask me how I did." (L 1, 254).

Apart from revealing an affectionately ironic attitude toward her father, a tone she often adopted in her letters to her brother, the passage offers a striking example of her aversion to crowd scenes. She once called an AMHERST COLLEGE commencement "some vast anthropic bear ordained to eat me up." This is not to say she took no pleasure in the railroad. In this poem, written almost a decade later, she clearly exults in the power of the train.

Dickinson conveys her vision of the train through an ingenious use of syntax, metaphor, and tone. Syntactically, the entire poem consists of a single sentence, with the subject-predicate "I like to see" followed by an extended train (pun intended) of objective complements describing what "it" does. In this way, the poem may be said to be "about" itself, that is, to mimic the motion of its subject. From its initial phrase, with a momentary halt to fuel itself in line 3, the poem, like the train, accelerates into its journey, gathering steam and growing ever wilder, until its sudden stop. Dickinson's use of dashes mimics the jerkiness of the locomotive's movement.

The use of the pronoun "it" instead of a noun such as "train" or "locomotive" makes a kind of riddle, challenging the reader to "guess" the subject, but it becomes obvious soon enough. That the poet will not dignify her subject by naming it may also suggest her emotional distance from it; but, above all, the use of "it" creates the neutral ground, the blank slate on which she then builds the many-layered reality of the train through a series of metaphoric transformations.

In stanza 1, "it" is a monstrous animal-like figure, a devourer of landscapes, drinking briefly at its proper watering hole ("at Tanks") before stepping off into stanza 2, a giant capable of reducing the grandeur of mountains to mere rubble ("a Pile of Mountains"). Rushing forward, "it" acquires the human vices of contemptuous intrusiveness (peering into the Shanties of the poor), and ruthlessness, violating the quarry (in an image of penetration which, taken together with the subsequent crawling, hooting, neighing and subsiding, suggests a sexual interpretation) to accommodate its own needs.

In stanza 3, the tone becomes more playful, suggesting that affectionate irony Dickinson habitually expressed toward that advocate of the railroad, her own revered father, who, like the train at different times, could appear to his daughter as highly impressive ("prodigious"), arrogant ("supercilious"), and intrusive:

To fit its sides
And crawl between
Complaining all the while

In horrid—hooting stanza—
Then chase itself down Hill—

As the poet *hears* the train as well as sees it, this virile, powerful figure transforms into a pathetic one that crawls, complains, and chases its own tail, a bad poet, whose stanza offends the ear.

In the fourth and final stanza, as the train—and the poem—race to a stop, the metaphoric shifts speed up and become more startling: "It" is likened to a horse whose neighing recalls Boanerges—a term used to denote a thundering orator. The simile "prompter than a Star" to describe the train's stopping, in line 15, suddenly opens up the poem's sphere of allusion: The train's ingenuity is compared—and judged superior—to the workings of the celestial order itself. While the comparison is ironic, it also contains an uneasy sense, carried forward in the next line, that this momentarily "docile" creature is also, in some undefined way, "omnipotent." it may have arrived at "its own stable door"—but will it enter?

Thus, the poem's complex images contradict the straightforward "I like to see" with which it begins. Dickinson transforms the product of technology into a creature of the animal kingdom, something organic, "natural" and more familiar, yet not entirely reassuring: an immense, contradictory, amusing, greedy, ear-jangling, all-powerful, obedient, out-of-control, eerily punctual beast. If the poem is a way of both celebrating and imaginatively "taming" this beast, it also conjures the disturbing image of the servant-machine that may become the master.

FURTHER READING

Wendy Martin, *American Triptych,* 134–35.

"I live with Him—I see His face—" (1863) (Fr 698, J 463)

The desire to see the beloved face, to meet face to face and eye to eye, and the anguish of being deprived of this supreme fulfillment are guiding obsessions of both Dickinson's love poetry and her religious lyrics.

Just as in the Bible, God's face is hidden, so for Dickinson, in a poem such as "NOT IN THIS WORLD TO SEE HIS FACE—," the earthly beloved's face is denied her in life. Her hunger for this face is such that, in "IF I MAY HAVE IT, WHEN IT'S DEAD," she blissfully envisions a face-to-face rendezvous with her lover's corpse. Relentless in her quest to see and in some manner to possess his face, Dickinson is ingenious in her varied creations of a poetic "space" in which the meeting can and does take place. In the despairing "I CANNOT LIVE WITH YOU—," a reunion of the lovers can occur only within the paradox of "meeting apart." With its ringing, repeated assertions that she lives with him, sees him and hears his voice, this poem may on first reading appear far more positive. Yet though the tone of one poem is despairing and the other triumphant, the message of both is the same: Only within the inner space of emotion and imagination can the lover, who is, in external reality, always absent, be possessed.

In the opening line, with its double spondees (metrical feet with two stressed syllables) creating a sense of rapt urgency, the poem reads like the declaration for Jesus Dickinson was never able to make as a girl, when a series of highly emotional religious REVIVALS swept through AMHERST. In stanza 3, she declares:

I live with Him—I hear His Voice
I stand alive—Today—
To witness to the Certainty
Of Immortality—

Yet she is declaring, not for Christ's promise of eternal life, but for the immortality of a love that exists only as she internalizes it, the one taught her "the lower Way" by Time.

The question that pursued her all her life was the one she posed to SAMUEL BOWLES in 1858, "Do you think we shall 'see God'?" (L 193) and was still asking 34 years later when she wrote to the Reverend Washington Gladden in 1882, "Is immortality true?" (L 752). In Fr 698 she gives her own answer, not as a theologian, but as a lyrical poet. What is "heresy" from the view of orthodox religion was for Dickinson a revitalization of a traditional religious concept. As scholar Jane Donahue Eberwein astutely observes:

Dickinson revitalized the concept of sacrament to include those imaginative processes by which the poet—recognizing occasions of grace in the natural world, within her own consciousness, and in her relationships with other people—demonstrated the multifarious ways in which spirit surcharges matter, thereby giving symbolic expression to her hope for immortality ("Emily Dickinson and the Calvinist Sacramental Tradition," 104).

The other "transfigured" religious underpinning to this love poem is the image of the speaker as a nun in her cloister. In a number of famous poems, Dickinson creates what scholar Sandra M. Gilbert calls "the ironic hagiography . . . of a New England nun" ("The Wayward Nun," 22). The "nun" of this poem stands outside the world's conventions and God's judgment. Freely admitting that, "No Wedlock—granted Me—," she ends by asserting her conviction, found in many of her poems, "That Life like This—is stopless—/ Be Judgment—what it may—."

In the first three lines of stanza 1, she presents herself as one who no longer leaves her room "For Visitor—or Sundown," in order to remain always in the beloved's presence. Her refusal to "receive" Sundown may signify that she no longer participates in the cycle of the days, since she lives with her beloved in an immortal space. Strikingly, however, the word following "Sundown" is "Death's" and the next four lines are devoted to recognizing that only death has a greater claim to privacy with him than she does, because "He"—the pronoun now signifying death rather than the beloved—"Presents a Claim invisible—." We do not know whether Death's claim is potential or has already been made, in which case the lover with whom she shares immortality has already died.

When considering this poem in light of Emily Dickinson's life, it is tempting to view it as "evidence" of the legend perpetuated by her niece, MARTHA DICKINSON BIANCHI, that her withdrawal from society was precipitated by a great, unconsummated love affair with a married man, which both renounced for honor's sake. What is important to remember, however, is that the poem itself is a reconstruction after the fact, in which Dickinson was creating her own myth. It tells us something of what obsessed her in her reclusive state, but little about what compelled her to adopt it in the first place.

See also "A SOLEMN THING—IT WAS—I SAID—," "TITLE DIVINE, IS MINE," and PURITAN HERITAGE.

FURTHER READING

Jane Donahue Eberwein, "Emily Dickinson and the Calvinist Sacramental Tradition," in *Critical Essays*, Judith Farr, ed., 89–104, and "Is Immortality True?" in *Historical Guide to Emily Dickinson*, 67–102; Judith Farr, *Passion*, 44–46; Sandra M. Gilbert, "The Wayward Nun," in *Critical Essays*, Judith Farr, ed., 20–39.

"I'm ceded—I've stopped being Their's—" (1862) (Fr 353, J 508)

This poem, written at age 32, is Dickinson's declaration of independence. The poem is notable for its lack of ambiguity; its clear affirmation does not change from the beginning to the end of poem, but only accretes nuances of meaning. In it, she puts away the identity given to her at birth, along with childhood and its games:

I'm ceded—I've stopped being Their's—
The name They dropped opon my face
With water, in the country church
Is finished using, now,
And They can put it with my Dolls,
My childhood, and the string of spools,
I've finished threading—too—

Given Dickinson's love of children and her pleasure in their unspoiled spontaneity, her renunciation should probably be read as a rejection of that part of childhood that was conditioned and "unconscious." Baptism in this poem, in addition to its literal meaning as a religious sacrament, is also emblematic of all that was imposed on her as an unknowing child.

In CONGREGATIONALISM, the Calvinist religion in which Dickinson was raised, Baptism was one of two recognized sacraments (the other being the Supper of the Lord). It involved a cleansing ritual of sprinkling the child with water and represented a symbolic promise to children of church members, who were "baptized into future repentance and faith" (Eberwein, 94). (Interestingly, Emily's father, EDWARD DICKINSON, was not yet a professed member of the church at his daughter's birth in 1830 and would not become one until 20 years later. Her mother, EMILY NORCROSS DICKINSON, became a church member in July of 1831.) Baptism alone was not considered sufficient to purify what Calvinism believed to be the intrinsic depravity of human nature. When Emily's parents had her baptized as an infant, they were expressing their hope—and the church's—that she would eventually, as a young adult, experience converting grace and be purified. Thus, the "They" in this poem, refers, not just to Dickinson's parents, but to the larger Amherst religious community. During Emily's girlhood, the series of religious REVIVALS that swept through the CONNECTICUT RIVER VALLEY placed her under severe community pressure to make a public profession of her faith in Christ. Over the years, she watched her family and closest friends join the fold, while she herself was unable to make a sincere commitment. By the time she was 30, she had stopped attending Sunday services with her family at the FIRST CHURCH OF CHRIST, preferring to keep the Sabbath at home, "With a Bobolink for a Chorister/ And an Orchard for a Dome"), as she wrote in a famous poem of 1861 ("SOME KEEP THE SABBATH GOING TO CHURCH—").

But what Dickinson is repudiating in this poem is something broader than religious orthodoxy. Its nature can best be seen by examining what she chooses in its stead. (Note that the word "choose" appears twice, in addition to the word "choice"). When it was published in the 1890 *Poems*, Dickinson's first editors, MABEL LOOMIS TODD and THOMAS WENTWORTH HIGGINSON, entitled the poem "Love's Baptism," thus suggesting what some subsequent readers have assumed, that the "second Baptism" the speaker enters into is marriage. For those who espouse this view, the fact that Dickinson had *not* married poses no obstacle, since, in her poetry, she speaks of herself as a "wife," in connection with a secret love affair. More to the point is scholar Jane Eberwein's observation that neither Dickinson nor her church thought of marriage as a sacrament; moreover, while baptism and marriage are both name-giving ceremonies, the latter involves changing the last name—not the baptismal first name—and may be perceived as erasing a woman's identity rather than awarding her a grander one.

The language in which she evokes her "second Rank," the one she chooses freely, specifies wholeness and fullness ("Called to my Full—The Crescent dropped—/ Existence's whole Arc, filled up,"); self-sufficiency ("Adequate—Erect,"); and royalty ("supremest name," "small diadem," "just a Crown"). The "supremest name" for Dickinson is that of Poet, her preferred crown, the poet's laurel wreath. (See "I RECKON—WHEN I COUNT AT ALL—" first poets then the sun). And being a poet involves both choice and surrender. The opening words, "I'm ceded"—imply that she is a territory that has been surrendered from one authority to another. The paradox of this passivity and simultaneous assertion of an active role is encapsulated in the phrase "consciously, of Grace." Her inner change involves elements of both will and destiny. She has made a conscious decision; but she is able to do this, in great part, because of the unearned gift or grace of her poetic genius.

Dickinson wrote this poem at the beginning of her years of "flood creativity," when she was coming into her full powers as a poet. Her emancipation is not only from religious language, but also from all "languages" and fixed worldviews that might constrain the truth of her creative vision. She celebrates her enhanced sense of selfhood in a number of other "poet-poems" of this period, including "I shall keep singing. . . ." (1861, Fr 270); "Put up my lute!" (1862, Fr 324); "One life of so much consequence!" (1841, Fr 248); "ON A COLUMNAR SELF—" (1863, Fr 740); "THE SOUL SELECTS HER OWN SOCIETY—" (1862, Fr 409); and "MINE—BY THE RIGHT OF THE WHITE ELECTION!" (1862, Fr 411).

FURTHER READING

Eberwein, "Emily Dickinson and the Calvinist Sacramental Tradition," in *Critical Essays,* Judith Farr, ed., 94–96.

"I'm Nobody! Who are you?" (1861) (Fr 260, J 288)

For Dickinson's great biographer, Richard A. Sewall, "I'm Nobody!" is not one of the poet's stronger works. Objecting to its "sentimental pose," he finds the poem "coy, or cute," but a great improvement over the poem by Charles Maccay, "Little Nobody," printed in the *Springfield Republican* in January 1858, which he believes she "reduced" in her poem. "Although the frog and the puddle are hardly new to proverbial wisdom," Sewall concedes, "she rejuvenates the cliché" (*Life,* II, 675).

Whatever its artistic limitations, "I'm Nobody!" is a Dickinson favorite. Since its first publication in 1891, this poem, with its rejection of popular measures of success and celebration of the superior joys of obscurity, has had an immediate appeal to readers. Dickinson speaks in the voice of her "child persona," a poetic strategy, which allows her to speak truths inadmissible in adult society. As biographer Cynthia Griffin Wolff astutely notes, "Only the conspiratorial invitation of youth could so consistently beguile readers into answering 'yes' to the question . . . 'Are you—Nobody—too?' She uses this 'Everyman figure of the child' to convince readers that they are in league with the speaker against the grown-up world" (*Emily Dickinson,* 184). Further, since we know that Emily Dickinson was, in fact, far from Nobody, but a poet who would be recognized as one of the greatest of all time, there is an additional "just wait and see" satisfaction in identifying with her. Surely, the poet herself, while lacking this knowledge of her posthumous acclaim, nonetheless had written enough poems by this time to recognize that, in light of her gift, she was "Somebody."

Why did the 30-year-old Emily, an educated and respected member of the AMHERST community and daughter of the town's leading citizen, speak of herself as a nonentity? While the answer to this question has several dimensions, one important factor was surely Dickinson's sense of herself as a woman in mid-19th-century New England society. Under the law, she was, indeed, a Nobody. Her revered, patriarchal father, EDWARD DICKINSON, believed that, while women should be educated, a "proper woman" would maintain a low profile, confining her influence to the private sphere. Within the Dickinson household, it was Emily's older brother, WILLIAM AUSTIN, whose achievements (including his writing) were lionized. The options open to women were severely limited and the primary one, marriage, seemed already closed to her. As a writer, she had not found the comprehending reader nor the literary recognition she still desired at this stage of her life. Moreover, even if she had successfully published her work, she might have been drawn to strategies for negating herself. As scholar Gudrun Grabher has noted, the image of the little girl was a popular one with women writers of Dickinson's day: "Because their unique female presence had to remain invisible, women writers had to turn to specific images in order to make themselves heard, while denying their presence as a female subject" ("Dickinson's Lyrical Self," 231).

What is distinctive about Dickinson's "small" persona, however, is the way in which she uses it to create her own alternate sense of significance and potency. She may be "the slightest in the House," yet as such she is also the recipient of a divine bounty that falls into her basket (Fr 473). She may be Nobody, but her obscurity allows her a vital inner freedom. As scholar Robert A. Weisbuch observes, "For Dickinson, the simple desire for a private life contains . . . the life principle of a protean ego, free to identify with its moving thoughts as they move forward . . . [she] forsakes the froglike certainty of a public Somebody to become a [being] voyaging in the hope of finally achieving the status of a Somebody at the Source" (*Poetry of Emily Dickinson,* 172–173).

In addition to this existential dimension, the poem contains social implications that are less obvious than has often been assumed. Who are the Somebodies on which the poet heaps her scorn? Readers have tended to view "I'm Nobody!" as a defense of the little man as opposed to the power-ful. Stanza 1 reads:

> I'm Nobody! Who are you?
> Are you—Nobody—too?
> Then there's a pair of us!
> Don't tell! they'd advertise—you know!

In the version of the poem used by Dickinson's early editors, line 4 of stanza 1 reads, "Don't tell! they'd banish us—you know!" The fact that banishment was traditionally a punishment for dissent against tyranny gave added weight to the argument of those who saw this as an essentially democratic poem. In the later versions of editors Thomas Johnson and Ralph W. Franklin, however, the notion of banishment is no longer present. Although the poet's own "final" choice cannot be established, Franklin believes his and Johnson's version is more "appropriate to the sense," since "to a nobody who wants to remain a nobody, being advertised is a worse fate than being banished" (*Editing*, 135).

If Dickinson is not defending the oppressed and marginal, whom is she defending? Critic Domnhall Mitchell believes she is affirming the ethos of her elite social class, with its "preference for observation above involvement" ("Emily Dickinson and Class," 197). Focusing on the use of the word "Bog" and its derogatory association with the Irish in 19th-century Massachusetts, Domnhall concludes, "Rather than expressing sympathy for the disenfranchised, the speaker expresses both anxiety and contempt for the democratic system that gives 'bog-trotters' access to political and cultural influence" (197). While Dickinson's father was himself a politician on both the state and national levels, he was of the patrician variety, as opposed to what Betsey Erkkila calls "the noisy 'public' culture of democracy—of stump speech and camp meeting—" that was in the ascendancy ("Dickinson and the Art of Politics," 151). These scholars see the poem as antiegalitarian or, at best, expressing anxiety about the new public culture, from whose vulgarity and crudeness the poet emphatically distances herself.

See also "GROWTH OF MAN—LIKE GROWTH OF NATURE—," "I WAS THE SLIGHTEST IN THE HOUSE—," "IT WOULD HAVE STARVED A GNAT—," and "PUBLICATION—IS THE AUCTION—."

FURTHER READING

Jane Eberwein, *Dickinson*, 61–62; Betsy Erkkila, "Dickinson and the Art of Politics," in *A Historical Guide to Emily Dickinson*, 151; Ralph W. Franklin, *The Editing of Emily Dickinson*, 135; Gudrun Grabher, "Dickinson's Lyrical Self," in *Handbook*, Grabher et al., eds., 230–231, 237. Domnhall Mitchell, "Emily Dickinson and Class," in *Cambridge Companion*, 197–199; Vivian R. Pollak, "Introduction," in *A Historical Guide to Emily Dickinson*, 4; Richard A. Sewall, *Life*, II, 674–5; Robert A. Weisbuch, *Poetry of Emily Dickinson*, 172–173.

"I never lost as much but twice—" (1858) (Fr 39, J 49)

This famous early poem prefigures the enduring ambivalence toward God that would characterize Dickinson's writing. The speaker has experienced a third loss "in the sod," that is, a death of someone dear to her, and stands before the deity in a posture of destitution and reproach. Imaging her loss in financial terms, she is a beggar. God is a criminal—a thief. He is, in addition, a banker, a "thrifty Deity" like the one in "IT'S EASY TO INVENT A LIFE—," who is too economical to confer eternal life on mortals. And yet—and herein lies the power of the poem—he is also "Father." As scholar David Porter notes, the poem's "success is in the stark rendering of the gamut of emotional responses to bereavement," including grief, bitterness, resignation, and, finally, humility (*Early Poetry*, 164). Yet, as in "I KNOW THAT HE EXISTS," the suspicion that God is a cheat and a manipulator, a malicious jester, is not dispelled.

The poem contains Dickinson's sense of being cheated by God, as well as her sense of continued blessing. For, between the first two deaths and this one, she has been (continuing the financial imagery) "reimbursed—":

> Angels—twice descending
> Reimbursed my store—

Note that she attributes the reimbursement, not to God, but to descending angels—beneficent aspects of the divine, whose only "theological" connotation is that they are "not God."

Critics such as Barbara Mossberg have seen the poem as expressing the correlation in the poet's mind between her own and her heavenly father, both of whom create dependence upon themselves, while at the same time "sadistically refus[ing] to satisfy her needs" (*Emily Dickinson,* 113–115). Others have seen the deity of this poem as Dickinson's "archetypal male figure," powerful and excluding, at whose door she stands as a supplicant.

See also "GOD GAVE A LOAF TO EVERY BIRD—," "GOD IS A DISTANT, STATELY LOVER—," and "THOSE—DYING THEN."

FURTHER READING

Joan Burbick, "Emily Dickinson and the Economics of Desire," in *Critical Essays,* Judith Farr, ed., 76–88; Sharon Leder and Andrea Abbott, *Language of Exclusion,* 141–143; Barbara Mossberg, *Emily Dickinson,* 113–115; David Porter, *Early Poetry,* 164.

"I never saw a Moor." (1864) (Fr 800, J 1052)

This deceptively simple work may be Dickinson's most often memorized and best-known poem. It is generally perceived as a statement of simple faith: It isn't necessary, the poet declares, to physically perceive something in order to *know* it, by means of imagination and faith. For this poet of the inner landscape, the "knowing" that came through intuition and imagination was every bit as true—and more so—as that gleaned through the evidence of the senses.

She had never walked the wild moors that were featured in the novels of her beloved authors, Charlotte and Emily Brontë. We may question the literal truth of her assertion that she never saw the sea. After all, she visited Boston as a girl and surely saw the harbor. In a delightful poem, Jean Balderstan puts these words into the mouth of Maggie Maher, the Dickinsons' longtime servant and Emily's confidante:

But sure she saw the sea;
at Boston Harbor, when a girl.
Seemed teacup more than sea, she said.

"Maggie" is surely right; whatever glimpse "Miss Emily" had of the Atlantic was not the open sea, which in her poetry symbolizes so many immensities: the unknown regions of the mind, death, art, eternity, and sexuality.

The first stanza expresses one of Dickinson's essential truths. But what of the second, in which she retains the verbal pattern ("I never . . .") but changes the subject from imagination to faith?

I never spoke with God
Nor visited in Heaven—
Yet certain am I of the spot
As if the Checks were given—

The disclaimer of lines 1 and 2 is pure Dickinson. For, if this poet never ceased to call upon God or imagine a heaven, her poetry insists that "'Heaven' is what I cannot reach" and "Heaven is so far of the mind." It is the unqualified certainty of the last two lines that makes us wonder: Are we to take them literally, or is the poet playing with us? Is the statement ironic? Certainty of heaven's very existence, much less its precise location, is hard to find in Dickinson. Even when she begins a poem with the assertion "I KNOW THAT HE EXISTS," she ends on a note of agonized doubt. Of course, we need not demand consistency of Dickinson on the "flood subject" of immortality. Doubt and faith alternate in all her writing and she may very well "mean" precisely what she says. Indeed, the brevity of the poem and its apparently sustained tone argue for this interpretation.

A key to the poet's intent may be found by examining her use of the puzzling word "Checks" as a marker of heaven's spot. They may simply indicate "checks" on a map. However, scholar Barton Levi St. Armand relates them to the "Rewards of Merit" handed out in schools and Sunday schools and sees the line as a parody of the 19th-century association of commodity with religious commitment.

See also "THOSE—DYING THEN" and "TO MAKE A PRAIRIE IT TAKES A CLOVER AND ONE BEE."

FURTHER READING

Jean Balderston, "'Miss Emily's Maggie' Remembers," in *Visiting Emily: Poems Inspired by the Life and Work of Emily Dickinson*, 1; Barton Levi St. Armand, "Heavenly Rewards," 219–238.

"I reckon—When I count at all—" (1863) (Fr 533, J 569)

In this famous poem, which has been called "her clearest, most composed statement of the function of the poet" (Sewall, *Life*, II, 486), Dickinson sets out her hierarchy of cherished things. It is a short list, as she herself notes, but its four "items" provide a powerful shorthand for understanding her sense of the relationship between poetry, nature, and immortality.

In the first stanza she affects a casualness ("When I count at all—"), implying she is rarely preoccupied with such questions as her ultimate values. Yet, she rattles them off decisively and appears to know with a certainty both their order of importance and when "the List is done—." In the second stanza she peruses the list and realizes that it is only necessary to name "Poets," since they contain within themselves all the other items. In stanza 3 she describes how Poets subsume the Sun and Summer. But she cannot deal so easily with the "Further Heaven" and devotes stanza 4 to what amounts to a disclaimer of all she has said before, revealing that Heaven would be number one on her list, if only it were attainable.

The claim for "Poets" as the most precious and powerful forces she knows is an extravagant one, with more than a touch of bravado in it. Before she could proclaim it so confidently, Dickinson had to free herself from any doubts as to the "rightness" of her own poetry. In Dickinson's AMHERST, poets who were not inspired by Calvinist orthodoxy were viewed as "dangerous" by even so enlightened a teacher as EDWARD HITCHCOCK, the eminent geologist, whose worldview permeated the atmosphere and curriculum at AMHERST ACADEMY when Emily was a student there. Moreover, she had yet to find a reader among her intimates or those she called "mentor" who understood what she was trying to do in her poetry.

But by 1863, in the midst of her period of "flood creativity," Dickinson had found her internal truth about the power of poetry in general, and her own poetry in particular. The sun was for her the mighty regulator and embodiment of life, light, consciousness, and intensity; and summer was the sun's most intense season, a time of "miracle"—beauty and fruitfulness—that she celebrated repeatedly in her poetry. But these natural phenomena are ephemeral: The sun sets and summer passes. As one scholar notes, "The poet's power depends upon an ability to vanquish process . . . only imagination can create a sun which makes faint the fiery star that renders all others invisible," (Diehl, *Romantic Imagination*, 90–91). The unsetting sun and perpetual summer of the poetic imagination were Dickinson's most cherished possessions, her best hope for transcending time and decay, the only heaven available to her.

As for the other heaven, the "Heaven of God," her wistful longing for it is palpable, as stanza 3 trails into stanza 4; but she calls it "the Further Heaven"—the Christian God's promise of immortality—undeniably beautiful, but remote:

And if the Further Heaven—

Be Beautiful as they prepare
For Those who worship Them—
It is too difficult a Grace—
To justify the Dream—

The use of the plural pronoun *they*, and possessive *their* in the first two lines of stanza 4 may well confuse the reader. In stanza 3 "they" refers to "Poets." In stanza 4, however, "they" can logically refer only to the "Further Heaven." A paraphrase would read, "The Further Heaven is beautiful as *it* prepares for those who worship *it*."

Dickinson often uses singular and plural pronouns inconsistently, making the referent ambiguous. Cristanne Miller and other students of

Dickinson's poetic grammar persuasively argue that this is a conscious technique, an additional tool for creating meaning. In this case, the plural has the effect of making "Further Heaven" a collective noun, containing within it all the members of the heavenly kingdom.

Dickinson calls "the Further Heaven" "too difficult a Grace—/ To justify the Dream—," implying that Grace is something that can be achieved through human efforts. In the Calvinist theology she was raised on, Grace *cannot* be achieved; it depends wholly on the will of an inscrutable God. Thus, this formulation takes some power away from God and gives it to man. Why, then, does Dickinson find it so difficult? Surely not because she was unwilling to make the effort; spiritual laziness was not a characteristic even remotely associated with her. If this poem suggests no answer, another poem does. In "A LOSS OF SOMETHING EVER FELT I—," she writes of feeling bereft since earliest childhood of any knowledge or sense of "the Site of the Kingdom of Heaven—." In her poetry as well as in her letters, particularly those written during the many religious REVIVALS of her girlhood, when she witnessed the joy and peace in the faces of those who had "found Christ," Dickinson honestly and painfully acknowledged her simple inability to do so. That kind of certainty eluded her, although she continued to search for it all her life. In Sewall's judgment, ". . . the 'Dream' was always there. Immortality was the 'Flood subject.' And it was the pursuit of this that gave form and coherence to her life and to her work" (*Life*, II, 724).

See also "A WORD MADE FLESH IS SELDOM," "I DWELL IN POSSIBILITY—," "LIKE SOME OLD FASHIONED MIRACLE," "THE POETS LIGHT BUT LAMPS—," "THESE ARE THE DAYS WHEN BIRDS COME BACK—," "THIS WAS A POET—," CIRCUMFERENCE, CONGREGATIONALISM, and PURITAN HERITAGE.

FURTHER READING

Joanne Feit Diehl, *Dickinson and the Romantic Imagination*, 90–91; Cristanne Miller, *Grammar*, 61–63; Josef Raab, "The Metapoetic Element in Dickinson," in *Handbook*, Grabher et al., eds., 273–295; Richard B. Sewall, *Life*, II, 486–487, 724.

"I shall know why—when Time is over—" (1861) (Fr 215, J 193)

At the core of this moving poem is the desire to believe that human suffering has a meaning, a purpose, that will be revealed in eternity. The poem's power is in the manner of its telling; instead of merely stating her belief in neat assurances, the speaker engages her imagination in the creation of a scenario in which all will be explained. Thus, as in so many of her greatest and most intriguing poems, what Dickinson gives us is a picture of her own thoughts as they unravel, invariably leading her in unexpected directions.

Ironies abound from the beginning, for the first line's assertion that enlightenment will come is immediately undercut by the realization that by the time is does—"when time is over"—she will no longer "wonder why." Her present wondering is, after all, no mere intellectual curiosity, but a deep need born of her present suffering, a function of her mortal life. Yet, she will be enlightened only when she has passed into eternity and it is too late for such knowledge to assuage her anguish. In the next two lines Christ is evoked as a conscientious schoolmaster, who will not overlook any pain but will give weight to "each separate anguish" and explain the meaning of it. The "fair schoolroom of the sky" is an enchanting phrase, but a naïve way of envisioning spiritual enlightenment, one that Dickinson herself (as opposed to the speaker of the poem) would not have subscribed to. In her speaker, however, she creates a childlike persona who clings to the hope that everything can be simply and satisfactorily explained.

In stanza 2, she anticipates that Christ will tell her "what 'Peter' promised." This may be a reference to Peter's denial of Christ: "Jesus said unto him, Verily I say unto thee, That this night, before the cock crow, thou shalt deny me thrice. Peter said unto him, Though I should die with thee, yet will I not deny thee" (Matthew 26:34–35). Peter, of course, then goes on to fulfill Jesus' prophecy and betrays him. The line thus suggests that the speaker too has been betrayed and that this is the source of her present anguish.

A second possibility is that the promise Dickinson had in mind was Peter's promise of salvation in the Epistles. She may have been referring to the words of Epistle I: "But the God of all grace, who hath called you unto his eternal glory by Christ Jesus, after that ye have suffered a while, make you perfect, stablish, strengthen, settle *you*" (5:10). The promise is explicitly mentioned in Epistle II: "Whereby are given unto us exceeding great and precious promises: that by these ye might partake of the divine nature" (Epistle II, 1:4). For those who believe in and practice charity, temperance, patience, and godliness, Peter promises: "For so an entrance shall be ministered unto you abundantly into the everlasting kingdom of our Lord and Saviour Jesus Christ" (1:11).

Given the explicitness of Peter's promise, one wonders what more it is that the speaker expects Jesus to tell her. It may simply be a reiteration of the promise, which receives added weight when it comes from Christ's lips. As Dickinson tells us in another poem, Fr 727, "Life—is what we make it—," "Just his own endorsement—/ That—sufficeth Me—." In this poem Christ's credibility stems from his role as "Tender Pioneer," the one who has led the way to immortal life, through his suffering, death, and resurrection. Similarly, in "I shall know why" it is the speaker's "wonder" at Christ's "woe" that she sees as a transforming force. In her article on Dickinson's poems on the life of Christ, Dorothy Huff Oberhaus notes that the poet was engaged throughout her life in imaginatively recreating the traditional material of the Scriptures. In the accounts of the Evangelists, Christ suffers and dies for the sins of humanity. In this poem, rather than having her sins absolved through Christ's suffering, the speaker anticipates that her memory of pain will be erased by his "woe." Her witnessing of Christ's suffering will be so overwhelming that her own will seem insignificant and she will "forget it." Or so she would like to believe. In fact, her attempt to project herself into that future moment of forgetting is undone in the poem's final line: "That scalds me now—that scalds me now!" Whatever she may learn in a time-out-of-time is eclipsed by the inten-

sity of her present suffering. Her intention is to find comfort in Christ's image and example, yet the relentless honesty of her own poetic process leads her back to the undeniable reality of her pain.

As opposed to the numerous evocations of God in Dickinson's poems as a stingy, careless, indifferent, and malicious deity, personified as a "King who does not speak" (Fr 157), a "banker," a "burglar," a powerful "papa above" (Fr 151), "a distant lover" (Fr 615) and an egotistical "jealous God" (Fr 1752), Christ occupies a more positive place in her religious universe. He is her prototype for human suffering and compassion, most frequently invoked in terms of his crucifixion and promise of redemption. She identifies with him, portraying herself as "Queen" and "Empress of Calvary." She turns to him in times of need, although he, like God, eludes her, as in Fr 377: "At least—to pray—is left—is left—/ Oh Jesus—in the Air—/ I know not which thy chamber is—/ I'm knocking everywhere—."

See also "EACH LIFE CONVERGES ON SOME CENTRE—," "ONE CRUCIFIXION IS RECORDED—ONLY—," "THERE CAME A DAY—AT SUMMER'S FULL—," and "TITLE DIVINE, IS MINE."

FURTHER READING

Joanne Feit Diehl, *Romantic Imagination*, 102–103; Dorothy Huff Oberhaus, "'Tender Pioneer': Emily Dickinson's Poems on the Life of Christ," in *Critical Essays*, Judith Farr, ed., 105–118.

"I should have been too glad, I see—" (1862) (Fr 283, J 313)

In this poem, Dickinson struggles with a devastating disappointment. With its autobiographical motivation hidden, the poem reads as a statement of the universal human struggle to accept the reality of suffering. Centered on the image of the Crucifixion, the poem vacillates between rebellion and the attempt to submit to God's will; the dominant voice, however, is one of bitter irony: "Of course, this joy could not have been mine! I would have just been too happy, too lifted above the usual conditions of my life."

I should have been too glad, I see—
Too lifted—for the scant degree
Of Life's penurious Round—
My little Circuit would have shamed
This new Circumference—have blamed—
The homelier time behind—

Circuit and CIRCUMFERENCE are words she often uses almost synonymously, to designate the indirect route the poet must take to get at her truth (see "TELL ALL THE TRUTH BUT TELL IT SLANT—"). But Dickinson's *Circumference* also means the farthest limit of human knowledge or experience, often reached through the medium of poetry. It is this meaning of *Circumference* that is used and contrasted with the "little Circuit" of the speaker's everyday experience in this poem. The "new Circumference," which would have stretched the existential boundary of her life and made her scorn the earlier one, has been lost. Note how, through the use of extreme compression, grammatical logic is distorted. We would expect "my little Circuit" to be the subject of both "would have shamed" and "[would] have blamed." However, since Circuit and "the homelier time behind" are the same, this would make no sense. Instead, Dickinson has "Circumference" serve as both direct object of "shamed" and subject of "would have blamed." In other words, she is saying in those last three lines of stanza 1: "The expanded scope of my new [glad] life would have made the "little Circuit" of my previous "homelier" life appear shameful to me."

This is a relatively long Dickinson poem. The four six-line stanzas allow the poet to approach from different angles the implications of her drumming refrain "I should have been too glad—I see," and its variants. Despite the syntactic and logical linking the refrain provides, this poem, like all Dickinson's best work, is still highly elliptical. The first omission is that of a first explanatory clause: "If *this* had happened to me, been given to. . . ." Dickinson never tells us just what happiness was denied her. Passion—fulfilled, earthly love—is an obvious candidate; and water imagery (the Coast) *is* associated with passion in some poems (See "WILD NIGHTS—WILD NIGHTS!" and "SHELLS FROM THE COAST MISTAKING—").

But she also uses images of the sea to speak of venturing into a dangerous, exhilarating unknown, sometimes suggestive of poetry or eternity (See "EXULTATION IS THE GOING," and "I STARTED EARLY—TOOK MY DOG—"). Another possibility, then, is that Dickinson is talking about religious salvation, election by God to the ranks of the redeemed. This interpretation seems unlikely, however, both on the basis of the poem's internal evidence, and in view of the fact that, by 1862, Dickinson's struggle to formally accept the tenets of her Calvinist religion was essentially behind her. Although she may never have ceased wondering about her decision, when the other Dickinsons attended Sunday services at the FIRST CHURCH OF CHRIST, Emily opted to stay at home.

Nonetheless, her earlier struggle with the punitive Calvinist God is very much a part of the poem. In stanza 2, she speaks of the experience she has missed as one that would have rescued her and dimmed "the Fear" that had previously allowed her to say the "scalding" prayer she knew so well: "*Sabacthini.*" Dickinson evokes the image of Jesus on the cross, pleading. "Eli, Eli, lama sabacthani? My God, my God, Why hast Thou forsaken me?" (Matthew 27:46). Jesus' outcry, only too familiar to her in the past, is "here"—once again, in the aftermath of loss—"Recited fluently."

At the core of stanza 3 is the vision of a jealous God, who forbids anyone to love Earth above Heaven, rules by fear, and will not grant the palm of victory without the Calvary of pain:

Earth would have been too much—I see—
And Heaven—not enough for me—
I should have had the Joy
Without the Fear—to justify—
The Palm—without the Calvary—
So Savior—Crucify—

The first five bitter lines are capped by the line "So Savior—Crucify—." Is the speaker, in a sudden about-face from defiance to submission, telling God to crucify her? If so, why does she address God as "Savior" when she is invoking God in his role as crucifier of the Savior? Another possibility is that Dickinson, who often used religious terms secularly and "assigned Christ's proper role to the beloved man she called Master" (Farr, *Passion*, 211), is addressing the lover who rejected her as "Savior," telling him in short, "If I can't have you, I may as well be dead, so go ahead and crucify me."

In the final stanza, Dickinson restates the theme she had articulated in earlier poems, such as "SUCCESS IS COUNTED SWEETEST," and "A WOUNDED DEER LEAPS HIGHEST," and would sound again in later works such as "WHO NEVER WANTED—MADDEST JOY" and Fr 1482, "Forbidden Fruit a flavor has": Deprivation is the source of the keenest appreciation of what one lacks. In her first metaphor for this notion, she invokes the garden of Gethsemane, where Christ prayed, "O my Father, if it be possible, let this cup pass from me; nevertheless not as I will, but as Thou wilt." (Matthew 26:39). But she makes this archetypal site of submission to God's will an image of deprivation, the dry land ("Reefs") that makes one yearn for the Coast. In reality, there are no reefs of rocks or coral in Gethsemane, which is near Jerusalem, an inland city. Dickinson, who must have known this, is taking liberty with the geographic facts, moving Gethsemane closer to the desired "Coast beyond," as if reinforcing the meaning "So near and yet so far."

The final three lines contain images—banquet, wine, bleating lamb—that have associations with the Passover feast (the paschal lamb), which preceded Jesus' withdrawal to Gethsemane and his crucifixion. But there are other relevant biblical allusions that Dickinson may be playing with, substituting her own philosophy of suffering and survival for the miraculous vision of the Scriptures. In Dickinson's world, it is not Jesus who creates the banquet, multiplying fishes and loaves of bread—but the hunger of beggars. It is not Jesus who "vitalizes" wine (turning water into wine at the marriage in Cana), but the thirst of those who have no wine.

In the poem's final line, she makes yet one more metaphoric leap, introducing a different idea entirely. The image of the bleating sheep of faith may be her final image for Jesus on the cross, asking his God why He has abandoned him. But it almost certainly also represents the remnant of faith within the poet, still begging rather pathetically to under-

stand why she must suffer. In this line, Dickinson tells us that all the half-believed "explanations" in the poem, particularly the frantic justifications of the last two stanzas, *are* the bleatings of faith, seeking an elusive answer.

See also "ONE CRUCIFIXION IS RECORDED— ONLY—."

FURTHER READING

Judith Farr, *Passion*, 178–244.

"I should not dare to be so sad" (1871) (Fr 1233, J 1197)

In this poem we hear the voice of Dickinson, the anatomist of suffering and survival, mapping our inner divisions and transformations, as we move from engagement to retrospection. The poem is built around the notion that the willingness or ability to suffer over an extended period of time requires a superhuman strength and courage. The speaker perceives that "to be so sad," as she quietly describes her suffering, is a matter of choice that requires a certain heroism: the daring to be aware and sensible of one's pain.

Biographer Alfred Habegger sees this poem as a backward glance at "her combined misery and heroism of the early 1860s" (*My Wars*, 531). While plausible, such an interpretation depends on external biographical considerations. The poem itself has a characteristic Dickinsonian omitted center, an absence of any hint as to the cause of the speaker's suffering. Here the poet is not interested in a specific circumstance, be it a failed romance or some other grievous loss, but in the process by which one self looks with awe and incomprehension at what another self has endured:

> I should not dare to be so sad
> So many Years again—
> A Load is first impossible
> When we have put it down—

As she does in one of her most famous poems, written in the same year, Fr 1197, she recognizes that we are made by circumstance:

We never know how high we are
Till we are asked to rise
And then if we are true to plan
Our statures touch the skies—

This is a very different poem from the one under discussion, sunnier and more idealistic about the possibilities of human stature. Yet both works insist that there is a reservoir of available strength that allows each of us to be a "Giant" or a "King." Generalizing from her own experience, she declares human beings capable of rising to the occasion, and that this expansion is part of a "plan," a blueprint inherent in our natures. Note that, in "I should not dare to be so sad," the speaker switches from "I" to "We" after the first two lines. As a "wisdom poem," however, Fr 1233 clearly draws its emotional authenticity from the speaker's deeply lived personal experience.

The poem tells us that the whole notion of "an impossible burden" is a conceptualization made by temporal distance, after the fact. When we are engaged in bearing the impossible load, we do not think about its difficulty or the risk involved, because all our energies are consumed in the effort of bearing it. Only afterward do we see what we have borne. Dickinson goes a step further, however, implying that we literally *become someone else* when we have no further need to muster superhuman strength. Then a split occurs between the Giant at the other side of the divide between past and present, the one who bore the impossible burden, and the present self, defined as "we who never saw" the Giant. Through these personifications Dickinson conveys the impenetrability of the divide between our separate selves over time.

The poem ends with the puzzling assertion that, when the Superhuman withdraws, the "we" of the present begins to perish. Is this because we are then returned to the human, mortal realm? Did the strength to bear that much suffering confer an immortality that has now been withdrawn? Does the realization of what we have borne slowly kill us, after the fact? Or is the notion that, with our finest hour, our heroic period of sadness behind us, our lives begin to decline?

See also "AFTER GREAT PAIN, A FORMAL FEELING COMES—," "I TIE MY HAT—I CREASE MY SHAWL—," and "WE GROW ACCUSTOMED TO THE DARK."

FURTHER READING

Alfred Habegger, My Wars, 531–532.

"I started Early—Took my Dog—" (1863) (Fr 656, J 520)

Emily Dickinson was a hypnotic storyteller, yet the connection between her compelling narratives and anything we might recognize as everyday reality becomes increasingly tenuous the closer we get to them. Robert A. Weisbuch, the scholar who developed the idea that Dickinson's poems are essentially "sceneless," tells of the frustration of a colleague who asks, "Why can't we view the poem as describing an actual visit to the sea by a little girl accompanied by her dog?" Weisbuch answers, ". . . because, sir, mermaids don't really exist" ("Prisming," 203).

Indeed, this poem, which fairly begs for symbolic analysis, has a dreamlike, fairy tale quality from the outset. The girl and her Dog set out to "visit" the Sea, as if it were a house—a situation that recurs in many poems in which the speaker confronts a house, or perceives herself as a house, both terrifying and compelling. "I YEARS HAD BEEN FROM HOME," and "ONE NEED NOT BE A CHAMBER—TO BE HAUNTED—" are prominent examples of this archetypal encounter. Dickinson did in fact have a dog given to her by her father, a large black Newfoundland named CARLO, who accompanied her on her walks. But the Dog of the poem is more than a representation of him. Note that the Dog is never mentioned again after the first line. He is a "liminal" or threshold figure, that is, one who exists at the boundary of known experience. The Dog helps the girl make the transition from her inland home to the edge of the Sea, but once she comes in sight of the Sea, he disappears and the drama that ensues is between the girl speaker and the successive manifestations of the Sea.

The first of these are the Mermaids, who emerge from the "Basement" of the oceanic house to view the strange visitor. While the speaker seems to take their appearance in stride, it is they who, presumably, do not know what to make of her. These alluring, dangerous creatures, half-woman, half-fish, are static "previews," as it were, of the larger, surging element from which they emerge. Their residence in the "Basement" clearly signifies that they are creatures of the depths, the unconscious, perhaps, with all its creative and destructive potential. For psychoanalytic scholar John Cody, they represent "the id," that is, the force of primal, irrational desires, while the Frigates are "ego defenses that are alarmed by this dallying with the unconscious . . . [and] offer her a solid deck of reality before she is engulfed" (*After Great Pain*, 306). Since the Frigates are "in the Upper Floor"—the surface of the Sea as well as the "higher" conscious levels of the personality—Cody's identification of them with the rational, reality-oriented forces of the ego is quite plausible. But the ego misunderstands her, perceives her as a mere "Mouse—/ Aground—opon the Sands—," rather than a complex feminine being, deeply ambivalent toward the danger she herself has come to meet. Cody, who believes that Dickinson suffered a psychotic break in the early 1860s, sees the Sea as "representing the vast unconscious . . . and drowning in it representing the loss of one's psychic integrity in psychosis" (Ibid., 307). But this interpretation ignores the attractiveness of the sea; the sense of psychic disintegration is terrifying, not attractive. The encounter of girl and sea in this poem is more in the nature of a flirtation that temporarily gets out of hand:

> But no Man moved Me—till the Tide
> Went past my simple Shoe—
> And past my Apron—and my Belt
> And past my Boddice—too—

The speaker makes no bones about the fact that the Tide/Sea is a symbol for the masculine principal. Noting how he overruns her "simple Shoe," she perpetuates her childlike persona, a conceit that allows her to evade nascent sexual impulses. But the Sea himself clearly recognizes that she is a woman and proceeds to envelop her body, piece by piece. The speaker half-denies the sexual nature of what is happening by substituting clothing—Shoe, Apron, Belt, Boddice (*sic*)—for body parts, but the import of this inundation is obvious enough.

What is striking is the disproportion between the Sea's enormity and power and the speaker's sense of insubstantiality: "And made as He would eat me up—/ As wholly as a Dew / Opon a Dandelion's Sleeve—." These lines reverberate with a passage the young Emily wrote to her future sister-in-law, SUSAN HUNTINGTON GILBERT (DICKINSON), more than a decade earlier. In it she compares women who marry to flowers who were "at morning, *satisfied* with the dew, and those same sweet flowers at noon with their heads bowed in anguish before the mighty sun; think you these thirsty blossoms will now need naught but—*dew*? No, they will cry for sunlight, and pine for the burning noon, tho' it scorches them, scathes them; they have got through with peace—they know that the man of noon, is *mightier* than the morning and their life is henceforth to him. . . . I tremble lest at sometime I, too, am yielded up" (L 93, early June 1852). In this passage the mighty sun has the role of the sea in the poem, but the dynamics are the same: The fragile feminine consumed by the overwhelming power of the male.

And just as the young Emily trembled at this prospect, the girl speaker of the poem flees:

> And then—I started—too—
> And He—He followed—close behind—
> I felt His Silver Heel
> Opon my Ancle—Then My Shoes
> Would overflow with Pearl—

Even so, the glimmer of desire remains, for the remnants of the Sea's touch upon her ankle and shoe are evoked in magical, lustrous terms: his "Silver Heel," his "Pearl." She escapes him by reaching the "Solid Town," which Weisbuch sees as representing "both the conventions of society that would deny the irrational and the sanctions of the sane self that protect against exposure to aspects of our internal wildness that would topple sense" ("Prisming," 204). Here the Sea, knowing no one and recognizing the limits of his power, turns from seducer to gallant courtier, bows to her "with a Mighty look," and withdraws. Yet that "Mighty look," in a final Dickinson twist, tells us that he is far from vanquished; there will be other confrontations, with perhaps different outcomes.

Interpreting this poem as a symbolic evocation of a thrilling, threatening brush with sexuality by no means rules out other meanings. Many critics have viewed the Sea as death, while others have seen the image of the Tides as representative of the fluctuating currents of creativity. The gulf between unconscious and conscious life, dream and waking, are certainly suggested in the separate realms of fluid Sea and Solid Town. Weisbuch does justice to the breadth of Dickinson's symbolism when he says that the Sea of this poem "is the symbol of all the experiential unknowns and of all the denied irrational urges. . . ." ("Prisming," 204).

See also "AS IF THE SEA SHOULD PART," "BEHIND ME—DIPS ETERNITY—," "EXULTATION IS THE GOING," and "WILD NIGHTS—WILD NIGHTS!"

FURTHER READING

John Cody, *After Great Pain,* 305–307; Clark Griffith, *Long Shadow,* 18–24; Cristanne Miller, *Grammar,* 70–74; Agnieszka Salska, *Poetry of the Central Consciousness,* 92–94; Robert A. Weisbuch, "Prisming," in *Handbook,* Grabher et al., eds., 203–205.

"I taste a liquor never brewed—" (1861) (Fr 207, J 214)

One of Dickinson's best-loved works, this poem enchants with its imagery and sustained tone of exultation. One of six poems published in different issues of the *Springfield Republican,* under the editorship of Dickinson's close friend, SAMUEL BOWLES, it appeared on May 4, 1861, under the title "The May-Wine." Like the other five, it was considered to be "if not conventional, at least accessible . . . [and with a subject] that appears to be within the prescribed limits for "lady poets" (Wolff, *Emily Dickinson,* 245).

Despite its relative forthrightness, however, the poem leaves room for varying interpretations.

Readers have differed over whether the poet is exulting in summer or in the joys of the creative process. For scholar David Porter, who sees nature as the source of ecstasy, "The ultimate triumph of her virtuoso performance is that she sings the scandalous behavior of the speaker . . . in the stately rhythms of the common meter of hymnody" (*Early Poetry,* 171). Wolff, on the other hand, argues that the ". . . exhilaration of creativity that is the subject of [this poem] is captured in the swaying, country dance, the reel" (*Emily Dickinson,* 187).

> Inebriate of air—am I—
> And Debauchee of Dew—
> Reeling—thro' endless summer days—
> From inns of molten Blue—

Certainly, the speaker glories in nature: the air, the dew, the endless summer days, the startling image of skies as "inns of molten Blue," a celestial alehouse made of brilliantly glowing color. Yet the central image of "a liquor never brewed"—an example of Dickinson's way of defining the indefinable through negative characterization—evokes an intoxicant that is *not* made from what is found in nature. In an earlier variant, line 3 reads "Not all the Vats upon the Rhine." By exchanging the vats for Frankfort berries, the poet shifts the emphasis to the natural ingredient itself, pointing to the stuff from which the "liquor" is *not* made, not only the process. Her "liquor" comes from "Tankards scooped in Pearl," such as can be found only in the imagination.

In stanzas 3 and 4, the speaker turns from her present state of inebriation to a self-assured prediction that she will continue to imbibe indefinitely. If Dickinson often identifies with the bee, here she surpasses him, transgressing the limits set by the natural cycle, the "Landlords" of time who evict the bee from the depleted foxglove flower and cause the butterflies to turn away from their emptied "drams." To compensate for nature's diminished intoxicants, not only will the speaker continue drinking, she will "but drink the more!"

The last stanza explodes in hyperbole. Some readers have seen the wild exaggeration as a part of the poem's comic perspective, while others have seen an *absence* of perspective in the grandiosity of the speaker's self-portrait. The invocation of seraphs and saints may be her way of saying she'll go on drinking until she dies. Or, it may be Dickinson's take on the common expression "till Kingdom come," implying "forever." Rather than a serious religious allusion, the heavenly figures are called in so that the "Little Tippler" may mock the purity of their "Snowy hats" and scandalize them as they peer from their windows. Everyone will be looking at me, the poet declares, amazed at my audacity! Whatever "self-centeredness" the stanza contains is surely balanced by its comic spirit. And there is another important facet to the speaker's boasting. As Suzanne Juhasz points out, ". . . her intoxication is more than fun; it is also a sign of power. In this poem, lack of control, diminutive stature, are coyly representative of their opposites, as the final audacious image . . . indicates." (*Undiscovered Continent*, 106–108). The poem is thus strongly related to other evocations of her poetic powers, written during this same time period, including "ALONE, I CANNOT BE—," "I WAS THE SLIGHTEST IN THE HOUSE—," "I DWELL IN POSSIBILITY—," and "THEY SHUT ME UP IN PROSE—."

If Dickinson's abandonment to ecstasy in this poem connects her to romanticism, it is an aspect of her work tempered by other, opposing elements in her nature. As Sewall notes, "She was always wary of excess, even joy. . . . She was too Puritan, too severe with herself, too spiritually anxious to allow herself for long the luxury of the Romantic sensibility" (*Life*, II, 714–715). More characteristic of her stance is the little poem beginning, "Partake as doth the Bee, Abstemiously" (Fr 806), as well as the numerous poems she wrote about the virtues of abstinence. In "The soul has bandaged moments—" (Fr 360), an anguished poem written the following year, she refers to moments of intoxicated abandon as "moments of Escape . . . As so the Bee—delirious borne." For this consummate poet of the separate moments of the Soul, "the Little Tippler['s]" joyful inebriation is but one shifting pattern in a rich and complex kaleidoscope of moments. It is interesting to compare this early poem with one written two years before her death, in 1884 (Fr 1630), "A Drunkard cannot meet a Cork," in which the complex of images in Fr 207 ("reeling," "the Bumble Bee," "liquors") recurs.

Here Dickinson affirms her earlier exuberance: "The moderate drinker of Delight/ Does not deserve the Spring—." But it has been transformed into the exoticism of memory. "Jamaicas of Remembrance stir / That send me reeling in—."

See also "I CAN WADE GRIEF—," "I HAD BEEN HUNGRY, ALL THE YEARS," "UNDUE SIGNIFICANCE A STARVING MAN," and "WHO NEVER WANTED—MADDEST JOY."

FURTHER READING

Suzanne Juhasz, *Undiscovered Continent*, 106–108; David Porter, *Early Poetry*, 187; Josef Raab, "The Metapoetic Element in Dickinson," in *Handbook*, Grabher et al., eds., 290–291; Richard B. Sewall, *Life*, 714–715; Cynthia Griffin Wolff, *Emily Dickinson*, 187, 245.

"I tie my Hat—I crease my Shawl—" (1863) (Fr 522, J 443)

This is one of Dickinson's greatest poems on what critic David Porter calls "the living in the aftermath," perhaps her most crucial poetic concern ("The Crucial Experience," 280). How do we continue to live "after great pain," when some irrevocable loss has occurred or after "a great hope" has died? How do we "grow accustomed to the dark"? How do we continue to exist after we have died? What part of us survives, what does it perceive, and where does it abide?

The poem has often been read as the soliloquy of a woman who continues to simulate her social role in her domestic realm, although the inner woman is lost, her true inner existence "stopped" by an unnamed event. Despite its bleakness, it is a poem of survival. I go on living, the speaker says, focusing on the tiny details of my duties, as if they were infinite, performing them precisely. The poem reminds us that, except during periods of illness, household duties formed the substance of her daily life, with reading and writing fit in at the far corners of night and early morning. Here we get a rare glimpse of Dickinson performing those daily tasks.

In the first line, the speaker adjusts her hat and shawl, apparently as she prepares to leave the house, perhaps to call on friends, something Dickinson was doing very little of by 1863. But in stanza 2, there is an abrupt shift of scene:

> I put new Blossoms in this Glass—
> And throw the Old—away—
> I push a petal from my Gown
> That anchored there—I weigh
> The time 'twill be till six o'clock—
> So much I have to do—
> And yet—existence—some way back—
> Stopped—struck—my ticking—through—

Objective time is disconnected from the narrator's broken inner clock, her subjective sense of time. We now see her throwing away old flowers, replacing them with new, all in a rote manner. She moves mechanically through her chores. Were the flower-adoring Dickinson herself in a more feeling state, she would not be discarding even old flowers indifferently. The detail of pushing a stray petal from her gown suggests a putting away of any trace of love. The petal has "anchored" on her gown. It is heavy, like the time she "weighs" "till six o'clock." Her pretense of busyness ("So much I have to do—") makes the stunning honesty of the stanza's last lines all the more effective.

The speaker is a broken clock that can fix the point when existence stopped only vaguely. Note that these elliptical lines, replete with ambiguous dashes, can be read in different ways:

1) Existence itself stopped some way back and [as a consequence] struck my ticking through.
2) Existence some way back stopped and struck. My ticking [is] through. Here, existence is a clock that strikes the hour, in this case, its last.
3) Existence some way back stopped and struck my ticking; my ticking is through. In this reading, we have a case of what Cristanne Miller calls "syntactic doubling," in which "my ticking" is both the object of the verb "struck" and the subject in the sentence, "My ticking [is] through."
4) Some way back existence stopped my ticking, by striking it through. This version makes

existence the malevolent instrument that stops the speaker's ticking.

These possible readings point to a lack of clear connection between the cessation of existence and the striking of the speaker's ticking; perhaps the best way to view them is as two different images for the same notion of a (spiritual, emotional) death.

After the death of the "I," the speaker switches to first person plural for the rest of the poem, turning the private confession into a wisdom poem in which she generalizes her experience to comment on the ways of humanity:

> We cannot put Ourself away
> As a completed Man
> Or Woman—When the errand's done
> We came to Flesh—upon—

As "we," the speaker immediately takes on a moral authority. We *cannot* "put Ourself away," that is, commit suicide, even though there's no further purpose to life, now that the errand we were born for is done. Whether the religious stance against taking one's own life or a personal survival instinct is behind this injunction is not clear, but the speaker's certainty that this is not an option *is*.

There is much that is puzzling in these lines. Why, for instance, does Dickinson speak of not putting ourselves away "As a completed Man / Or Woman"? What is the significance of the pointed reference to gender? Scholars Suzanne Juhasz and Cristanne Miller suggest that "the poem specifies gender as the act that keeps us in culture. It gives us an identity: it makes of us a 'Man' or 'Woman'" ("Performances of Gender," 116). Most mysterious is the nature of the "errand done" "We came to Flesh—upon—." The first question concerns the identity of the errand (a belittling term) we were born to accomplish. Some critics have suggested that life itself is the errand. But love, which Dickinson once proclaimed her life's "business," seems a better candidate, since it would explain the reference to the completed man and woman. Then there is the question of whether the errand has been completed or merely attempted unsuccessfully. Is she saying that she has achieved fulfillment, but it is now behind her, or that she has lost the possibility of achieving it? The poem does not answer this question definitively. Vivian Pollak suggests that "perhaps these two possibilities can be reconciled if we assume that ... *What* happened no longer matters ... her mind continues to function, but it contemplates the death of ambition." Pollak's guess is that "Probably the speaker attributes her spirit's death to the loss of someone who once appeared to symbolize her psychological salvation. . . ." (*Anxiety of Gender*, 204).

Turning her eyes to the future, she anticipates that there may be "Miles on Miles of Nought—" ahead of her, in which she must engage in the "stinging work" of simulating the actions of one who is still spiritually alive. She must hide herself from the "Too telescopic eyes" of Science and Surgery, both of which would dissect her, the first intellectually, the second physically. The intrusiveness of those eyes must not "bear on us unshaded—," a line that recalls what she would write, almost a decade later, about the necessity of an oblique method in writing poetry, "Too bright for our infirm Delight / The Truth's superb surprise" ("TELL ALL THE TRUTH BUT TELL IT SLANT—"). That the "unshaded" truth of a human life must be concealed from probing eyes at all costs was a basic tenet of her poetic practice and, in this sense, another dimension of the "simulation" she espouses in this poem.

The line "For their—sake—Not for Our's—" has usually been interpreted as expressing an altruistic sentiment, that is, that we pretend for the sake of others. But critic Fred D. White believes that "their" refers to Science and Surgery and sees the line as a knowing comment that "science serves its own needs—not our deepest human needs" ("Emily Dickinson's Existential Dramas," 99).

In the final line, the speaker admits that the scrupulous exactness with which she carries out her tasks is, in fact, for her sake, since it keeps her from losing her sanity ("senses"). Going through the motions of "normal life," pretending one is alive, somehow persuades, not only others, but the pretender. White suggests that the last line also refers to "believing in our human senses enough to forego the need for a supernatural *raison d'être*" (99). The poem's final note of resignation is mixed with a clear-eyed determination. There is nothing more to look forward to, but she will faithfully do

"life's labor"—a phrase that evokes not the concrete tasks of daily life but the perseverance that life demands of us, which is its most demanding challenge.

Readers who encounter this poem in Thomas Johnson's *Collected Poems* will find five additional lines, just before the final stanza, after the phrase "not for Our's":

> 'Twould start them—
> We—could tremble—
> But since we got a Bomb—
> And held it in our Bosom—
> Nay—Hold it—it is calm—

In his later editing work, R. W. Franklin found that they belong instead to "A PIT—BUT HEAVEN OVER IT—." But many published analyses of the poem have been based on this earlier version and so have focused on the speaker's underlying rage (the bomb), which she tries to keep from exploding. This has led to the conclusion that Dickinson is saying that rage must be repressed, if the speaker is to stay sane.

See also "I SHOULD NOT DARE TO BE SO SAD," "AFTER GREAT PAIN—A FORMAL FEELING COMES—," and "WE GROW ACCUSTOMED TO THE DARK—."

FURTHER READING

R. W. Franklin, *Editing of Emily Dickinson*, 40–46; Suzanne Juhasz and Cristanne Miller, "Performances of Gender in Dickinson's Poetry," in *Cambridge Companion*, 115–116; Cristanne Miller, *Grammar*, 37–39; Vivian Pollak, *Anxiety of Gender*, 202–206; David Porter, "Crucial Experience in Emily Dickinson's Poetry"; Fred D. White, "Emily Dickinson's Existential Dramas," in *Cambridge Companion*, 98–99.

"I tried to think a lonelier Thing" (1863) (Fr 570, J 532)

Seeking to escape loneliness, the speaker of this poem attempts to turn loneliness itself into a companion. The dominant emotion conveyed is not the passive, protracted misery of loneliness, but the excitement and desperation of breaking through to an uncharted and forbidden realm, where her "Duplicate" dwells. Dickinson explores the phenomenon of inner duality in such poems as "I never hear that one is dead" (Fr 1325), "ME FROM MYSELF TO BANISH—," and "ONE NEED NOT BE A CHAMBER—TO BE HAUNTED—." Those poems develop the notion of an unknown, hidden self, inimical to the conscious self. The poet fears the hidden self and tries to escape it. But in Fr 570, she hungrily seeks a double that mirrors rather than opposes the self she already knows. There may be terror in the act of uncovering "Horror's Twin," yet her purpose is not to terrify herself with this alter ego, but to find comfort in him.

Yes, "him." The masculinity of the duplicate emerges only in the last stanza, but it emerges prominently, with mention of "His Hand," "he" and "him" within four lines. What are we to make of this "male identification"? Psychoanalytic critics see it as proof of her confused sexuality, while others point to it as evidence of Dickinson's androgynous nature. She was, it is true, a poet who more than once referred to herself as a "boy" and it is clear that she loved at least one woman. There may, however, be another reason for the maleness of the speaker's suffering twin. In the pervasive religious culture of her time, which held a powerful sway over her imagination, the archetypal image of lonely suffering was Jesus. The final stanza, with its visions of clasping his hand, and of mutual pity, strongly suggests the lonely figure on the Cross.

The poem is an attempt at transcendence, to go not above suffering, but further into it than she has ever been. Paradoxically, only by digging deeper into her imagining of loneliness can she hope to find relief from it, by uncovering a co-sufferer, even worse off than herself:

I tried to think a lonelier Thing
Than any I had seen—
Some Polar Expiation—An Omen in the Bone
Of Death's tremendous nearness—

Dickinson uses the word "polar" to connote a spiritual as well as physical coldness, a remoteness associated with death, so the phrase "Polar Expia-

tion" implies expiation by dying; death is mentioned directly in the very next phrase. Of course, Dickinson isn't going to tell us what particular sin, if any, she imagines expiating in this way. She merely tosses the suggestion of guilt into the darkness she must navigate—along with death and loss ("Retrieveless things")—in order to "borrow" her Duplicate.

At this point, the double is still a thing, located "Somewhere / Within the Clutch of Thought—." But in the next lines it becomes sentient, "one other Creature / Of Heavenly Love—forgot—." The phrase is reminiscent of the way the poet spoke of herself in a youthful letter to her friend ABIAH PALMER ROOT: "I'm afraid he [Jesus] don't love me *any!* . . ." (Letter 39) The 19-year-old Emily who wrote this rather prided herself on being a rebel, outside the fold. But in this poem, written by the 32-year-old Emily, the sense of an absolute abandonment is palpable.

In stanza 4, as the speaker plucks at the partition separating herself from her Duplicate, she calls it "Horror's Twin," suggesting that they are both monstrosities, too awful to be revealed to the world at large. Yet, in the poem's dense imagery, this monstrous twin is also a fellow prisoner, who dwells in the opposite cell:

I plucked at our Partition—
As One should pry the Walls—
Between Himself—and Horror's Twin—
Within Opposing Cells—

The image suggests the famous "scene" in "I DIED FOR BEAUTY—BUT WAS SCARCE," in which the deceased speaker and the one "who died for truth" talk to one another all night through the walls of their adjacent tombs. In the final stanza of "I tried to think a lonelier Thing," the notion that they might pity one another grows so strong as to seem an irresistible "Luxury," like the "poignant luxury" of owning and touching her single crumb in "GOD GAVE A LOAF TO EVERY BIRD—." So exciting is this prospect that "I almost strove to clasp his Hand," she says. "Almost" is the crucial word. In the end, the journey inward to the twin-in-suffering remains unconsummated. Some unbridgeable, unstated barrier to communication remains. Dickinson's fundamental sense of the loneliness of the self ("Adventure most unto itself / The Soul condemned to be—") prevails.

This poem begs comparison with one written in the same year, "I measure every Grief I meet" (Fr 550), in which the poet describes a more successful attempt to overcome pain's isolation. Although she is still looking for a mirror of her own pain, she is looking for it, "With narrow, probing eyes—" in the eyes of others. With an almost scientific curiosity, she seeks to weigh and measure the suffering of others, cataloguing different types of grief, and skeptically speculating on time's healing power. She knows she can't be sure of what she's seeing in the eyes of other sufferers, but nonetheless finds value "In passing Calvary—/ To note the fashions—of the Cross—/ And how they're mostly worn—/ Still fascinate to presume / That Some—are like my own—." In affording her "A piercing Comfort," this attempt to overcome her isolation is more successful than the one described in "I tried to think a lonelier thing." Yet both efforts ultimately fail to overcome the barrier to communication. The speaker is deprived of the healing mutual self-revelation she seems to desire yet knows how to seek only in her mind.

See also "ONE CRUCIFIXION IS RECORDED—ONLY—" and "THIS CONSCIOUSNESS THAT IS AWARE."

FURTHER READING

Jane Eberwein, *Dickinson*, 55, 57; William Shurr, *Emily Dickinson*, 89.

"It's easy to invent a Life—" (1863) (Fr 747, J 724)

Once more, as in "I KNOW THAT HE EXISTS," Dickinson conjures the image of a carelessly "playful" God, wielding his power with sublime indifference to human suffering. In stanza 1, he is a facile inventor and prankster, for whom "Creation," which may refer either to the act of creating or to the created universe, is "but the Gambol" (defined in Dickinson's lexicon as a "sportive prank") of God's "Authority." In the second stanza, the vision grows darker: God can "efface" a life with the same ease

as he created it. The poet pretends to justify a "thrifty Deity" who is too economical to confer eternal life on mortals. She (barely) conceals her bitterness behind the abstract formality of three Latinate words: Deity, Eternity, and Spontaneity—of which the last is a striking example of the quality it defines. By defining a human life as "Spontaneity" Dickinson suggests that it is no more than the Deity's momentary whim; at the same time, however, she points to the free play of human consciousness, which contrasts starkly with the relentless determinism she characterizes in the final stanza:

> The Perished Patterns murmur—
> But his Perturbless Plan
> Proceed—inserting Here—a Sun—
> There—leaving out a Man—

Both expressing and containing her withering irony in a sputtering spray of alliteration (Perished Patterns, Perturbless Plan, Proceed), she returns to the opening picture of God as an arbitrary inventor, for whom the insertion of a Sun or omission of a Man represents nothing more than a design shift. She thus mocks God's so-called "plan." For such a deity, the dead are no more than "Perished Patterns" whose "murmuring" he may hear but chooses to ignore. In the poem's final line, however, Dickinson uses her own term for such effaced entities, reminding the reader that what she is talking about and God is treating so cavalierly is "a Man." Another meaning as well seems to be implied in the last two lines. The insertion of a Sun, in addition to alluding to God's creation of the cosmos, also suggests that aspect of his plan that involved incarnating his son as a man. Thus, Christ's journey on earth becomes just one more act of an arbitrary deity.

In Emily Dickinson's early education, dominated by the thinking of EDWARD HITCHCOCK, God was viewed as the "Supreme Scientist of the universe," whose face could be discerned in the splendid mathematical patterns and natural laws of his creation. God's direct relationship with mankind was to be discerned in what Hitchcock called "the wheels of Nature," just as his direct communication with mankind was found in the Bible. It is this vision that Dickinson stands upside down in this poem, accepting the basic premise, but, as Cynthia Griffin Wolff writes, seeing in these divine manifestations "principally malice, capriciousness, and the terrifying drive toward extinction" (*Emily Dickinson,* 344). Wolff sees in the "sloppy" God-inventor of this poem a perversion of the image of the inventor that held so heroic a stature in the minds of 19th-century Americans. She interprets the "Perished Patterns" as extinct species such as the dinosaurs who once populated the CONNECTICUT RIVER VALLEY, whose fate geologists had unearthed by Dickinson's day. In this light, the poem implies that the "thrifty" deity may very well choose to extinguish mankind when "He doesn't like them or they fail to function in quite the way he had Hoped," rather than let them use up space in his creation (347).

See also "I KNOW THAT HE EXISTS," "I SHALL KNOW WHY—WHEN TIME IS OVER—," "OF COURSE, I PRAYED—" AMHERST ACADEMY, CONGREGATIONALISM, MOUNT HOLYOKE FEMALE SEMINARY, and PURITAN HERITAGE.

FURTHER READING

Cynthia Griffin Wolff, *Emily Dickinson,* 344–347.

"It's Hour with itself" (1871) (Fr 1211, J 1225)

In this brief, psychologically penetrating poem, written in the aphoristic style that characterized her later work, Dickinson defines a "law" of the inner life: the injunction against revealing the subterranean depths of "the Spirit" (here used interchangeably with "the Soul") to the external world. As psychoanalytic critic John Cody has observed, "the deepest self-knowledge must be hidden from the view of others. It is obvious from the context that the kind of self-knowledge referred to is not the self-awareness that a realistic person builds up through self-observation and ordinary introspection" (*After Great Pain,* 309). Characteristically, the poet offers no hints as to the specific contents of the Spirit's depths, other than their terrifying, burdensome quality. The reader is free to surmise,

as Cody does, that she is alluding to "the dark and troublesome side of human nature associated with sexuality, madness, and murder as they are manifested as agents of the unconscious." Rage, despair, grief, "forbidden" love, the sheer strangeness of the mind and emotions—all are reasonable candidates.

We can only guess, however, for this poem about the iron rule of reticence strictly adheres to its own precept. At its core is no single hidden secret, but the inner law that forever isolates the spirit, the unbridgeable chasm between the depths of the soul and the external world. Note that "Countenance" *cannot* disclose, even if it were so inclined. An image that expresses the duality of the self, "It's Hour with itself" is a temporal confrontation, when the Spirit is alone with itself, and knows its own depths. The implication is that this confrontation is of limited duration and that it occurs repeatedly.

Despite its generalized nature, the poem is neither cold nor abstract, but conveys, through spare, striking imagery, the speaker's horror at the "Subterranean Freight"—a phrase that anticipates Freud and the modern psychology of the subconscious—that lurks in the "Cellars of the Soul." Dickinson often compares Mind, Brain, Soul, Spirit, Consciousness, or Self to houses, rooms, or corridors, sometimes likening the self and its many aspects to a house with many chambers. As critic Suzanne Juhasz notes, Dickinson's "architectural vocabulary usually portrays the mind as an enclosed space, its confinement responsible for power, safety, yet fearful confrontation" ("The Landscape of the Soul," 138). Thus, in "ONE NEED NOT BE A CHAMBER—TO BE HAUNTED—," the poet declares, "The Brain has Corridors—surpassing Material Place—" and speaks of a confrontation with the hidden self as far more terrifying than encountering an "Assassin hid in our Apartment."

Dickinson's sense of the horror of the inner world may seem hyperbolic in a world such as ours in which people routinely reveal themselves, not only to family and friends, but to strangers—therapists, journalists, and even national television audiences. It is difficult for us to imagine what, after all, could be so terrible that one could not reveal it under any circumstances. In the poet's Puritan-haunted, Victorian New England, however, not only a host of subjects, sexual and otherwise, but the very act of that kind of self-revelation, were taboo. And, since the psychic power of what is not spoken aloud inevitably amplifies in the isolated spaces of the mind, Dickinson's "Subterranean Freight" had ample opportunity to assume enormous weight and terror. Note, too that this terror, if unleashed "would *enthrall* [author's italics] the Street," that is, would both fascinate and enslave it; as one suspects, it enthralled the poet herself.

In the powerful closing image, in which she merges religious and legal terminology, the poet expresses her relief that the "loudest Place he made / Is licensed to be still." Instead of reproaching God the Creator for making the terrible "Cellars of the Soul," she thanks God the Lawgiver, for authorizing (licensing) it to remain silent. Yet the irony behind her apparent gratitude, as well as a world of unspoken implications, are contained in the image of "the loudest Place." Beyond the sound perception of others, this "Place" clamors within the poet herself, dominating her perception of reality. It suggests screams of pain, cries of anguish or anger. At the very least, "loudest" indicates the insistence and intensity of the Cellar's claim upon the poet.

Cody cites another poem written in that same year, Fr 1234, in which Dickinson writes of "the deepest Cellar / That ever Mason laid—" and cautions the reader (and herself) to avoid being pursued by "its Fathoms." He comments that "a glimpse into the hidden depths of personality should be avoided because it exposes one to the danger of being overwhelmed." This, he notes, could lead to psychosis (310). But "It's Hour with itself" suggests that Dickinson, rather than avoiding the Spirit's hour with itself, regularly experienced it—and survived. Its loudness suggests a voice, which in turn suggests that this hour was a vital source for her, the necessary darkness that fed her poetry.

See also "ME FROM MYSELF—TO BANISH—."

FURTHER READING

John Cody, *After Great Pain*, 309–312; Suzanne Juhasz, "The Landscape of the Soul," in *Critical Essays*, Judith Farr, ed., 138.

"It sifts from Leaden Sieves—" (1862) (Fr 291, J 311)

This is one of Dickinson's most famous riddle poems. If she had been given to naming her poems, she might have entitled this one "The Snow," as she indeed alluded to it when she sent a copy to editor Thomas Niles ("I bring you a chill gift—My Cricket ["FURTHER IN SUMMER THAN THE BIRDS"] and the Snow," L 813). But a title would have worked against the main thrust of the poem—not simply to set a riddle before the reader, but to evoke the forever transforming, unfixable nature of the snow. To name it would be to undermine the intention of going beyond names to the mysterious essence of a phenomenon. Dickinson does this by conjuring a series of metaphors for snow, until the snow itself becomes a metaphor for any magical and ephemeral reality.

In this virtuoso display of metaphor-making, the snow becomes increasingly disembodied. "It" begins its transformations in the domestic realm, sifting through the leaden sieve of the storm clouds:

It sifts from Leaden Sieves—
It powders all the Wood—
It fills with Alabaster Wool
The Wrinkles of the Road—

For Dickinson, who became the baker of the household, the sieve—a utensil for separating flour from bran, or the fine and the coarse of any pulverized substance—was a particularly apt image. The fine substance thus obtained "powders" the wood of houses, barns, and fences, like flour on a wooden board. Thus far, the imagery is simple and visual. But in the next two lines, the poet gives her imagination greater rein, turning "It" into "Alabaster Wool," an image that merges the hard, white, smooth, cool material of which gravestones are made (see "SAFE IN THEIR ALABASTER CHAMBERS—") with the soft, irregular, warm material of which sweaters and socks are knit. This substance, with its complex associations, fills the "Wrinkles of the Road," making it young again.

In stanza 2, "It" becomes increasingly animated, airborne, and disembodied. In the first two lines, alternately moving in opposite ways, it turns into a flock of birds, first scattering, then "condensing." "It" then becomes the somewhat vague "Juggler's Figures"—balls or pins, presumably—that "situates / Upon a baseless Arc—." What holds the figures aloft has no material base, but is sustained by momentum and mystery.

In stanza 3, "It" is defined not by nouns but by verbs delineating simultaneous movement and stasis: "It" traverses yet halts, disperses and stays. In the final image of "It" curling "itself in Capricorn—/ Denying that it was—," the snow has withdrawn to a distant stellar constellation, a curling wisp of smoke perhaps, or an ornery cat, so far away as to leave the speaker in doubt as to whether it has visited at all. She chooses Capricorn, a goat with a fish tail, the tenth sign of the Zodiac, which represents the winter solstice. By this time, although we have doubtless "guessed" the answer to the riddle, "snow" is a great deal more than snow; it has become the deeper riddles of nature's endless metamorphoses and the uncertainty of human perception.

In his illuminating article on Dickinson's pervasive use of the riddle "as almost a technique," critic and poet Anthony Hecht traces her models to both the Bible and to the body of children's fairy tales and verse with which she was familiar. Other riddle poems include "Who is the East?" (Fr 1085), "It sounded as if the Streets were running" (Fr 1454), "She slept beneath a tree" (Fr 15), "The Guest is gold and crimson" (Fr 44), "A ROUTE OF EVANESCENCE," "A NARROW FELLOW IN THE GRASS," "A VISITOR IN MARL—," and "HE FUMBLES AT YOUR SOUL." When she sent these riddle poems to her correspondents, Dickinson sometimes enclosed a concrete object—a cocoon, pine needle, and some apples—as an "answer" to the riddle. While she doubtless enjoyed the intellectual play of these exercises, the fundamental notion of a riddle went deep into her nature, to her sense of existence as the greatest riddle of all. As she writes in the conclusion of "SOME THINGS THAT FLY THERE BE—" (Fr 68), she writes: "Can I expound the skies? / How still the Riddle lies!" A good part of her greatness lies in her never losing sight of the stillness of the Riddle, while continuing to come at

it from as many angles as her remarkably fruitful imagination could envision.

Dickinson had a considerably longer, earlier finished version of this poem, which develops the notion of the snow as an annihilating force; a much darker work, it entirely lacks the playfulness of this one.

FURTHER READING

Anthony Hecht, "The Riddles of Emily Dickinson," in *Critical Essays*, Judith Farr, ed., 149–162; Cynthia Griffin Wolff, *Emily Dickinson*, 435, 437, 482–483.

"It was not Death, for I stood up," (1862) (Fr 355, J 510)

One of Dickinson's most agonized and complex explorations of an inner state, this poem has been the subject of much critical scrutiny. Some see in the poem indications of religious despair, while at the other end of the spectrum are those who ferret out symptoms of severe mental illness. Whatever their differences, however, most scholars agree that Dickinson is here engaged in the attempt to define what cannot be defined, to name what has no name, to give form to what is formless. This is evident from the first word of the poem, "It"—"a blank around which the poet draws the boundaries for a phenomenon she cannot name . . . [a] kind of hole in knowledge. . . ." (Miller, *Grammar*, 76).

In her effort to describe an overwhelming inner state for which she has no ready designation, the poet leans heavily on the use of negatives:

It was not Death, for I stood up,
And all the Dead, lie down—
It was not Night, for all the Bells
Put out their Tongues, for Noon.

It was not Frost, for on my Flesh
I felt Siroccos—crawl—
Nor Fire—for just my marble feet
Could keep a Chancel, cool—

By a process of elimination, she pares away all the things that this state was *not,* in order to get at what it *was*. The result, however, is anything but a sense of clarity, for the poem is structured on an elusive "logic." For one thing, there is a lack of parallelism among the negated options: While death is an existential state, night is a period of time, and frost and fire are extreme temperature sensations. Further, the speaker, even in her negations, is confused and prone to contradicting herself. Rather than sticking to her negative assertions, the poet partially retracts them in stanza 3: "And yet, it tasted like them all." She goes on to say how "It" "tasted" like death, night, and frost, but not how it tasted like fire. This imbalance contributes to the unpredictable feeling of the poem and deprives the reader of a coherent structure to hold on to. Instead, Dickinson leaps from one stunning image to the next, creating new puzzles with each supposedly "explanatory" line.

Thus, in stanza 1, she eliminates the possibility that she is dead, but who are all the dead who are lying down? The image of the bells suggest she may be in a church or nearby in a churchyard cemetery. The number of times the bells toll is offered as proof that "It was not Night," but noon. However, as critic Sharon Cameron points out, since "chimes at noon sound indistinguishable from those at midnight," the speaker betrays her own confusion (*Lyric Time*, 49–50). In the image of the bells that "Put out their Tongues, for Noon," the "Tongues" can be visualized as the clappers in the bell; this is a grotesque image, suggesting gleeful mockery of the poet's state, as if the bells were spitefully sticking out their tongues at her. Furthermore, while the bells toll for "Noon," a symbol for Dickinson of life at its highest intensity, often connoting love, fulfillment, happiness, and heaven, the tolling of bells, especially in light of the preceding lines, is also associated with death. Thus, death, denied in the first line, still hovers within the borders of the stanza.

The second stanza repeats the "It was not . . . for . . ." structure of the first, supposedly eliminating "Frost" and "Fire" as explanations of the speaker's state. (Note how Dickinson re-enlivens a stock phrase: instead of having her "flesh crawl" with disgust or terror, she feels Siroccos—extremely hot, southern winds—crawling on her flesh). Yet the

two negations negate one another: She knows it was not frost because she felt on fire, it was not fire because she was so cold—her "marble feet" alone "Could keep a Chancel, cool—." A chancel is the part of the choir of a church between the altar or communion table and the railing that encloses it. Why would it be hot, difficult to cool? Noting that a chancel is supposed to be located in the ecclesiastical east of a church, scholar John Cody speculates: "East is the direction of sunrise and therefore suggests . . . approaching light and warmth. . . . By extension then, the chancel is the most 'warmly' located part of the church. But the poet's mere presence is sufficient to chill it" (*After Great Pain*, 327). Charles Anderson suggests that we are meant to see the poet kneeling at the chancel rail, "beyond which sacrament and conviction are at white heat." The word "tasted" in the following stanza leads him to speculate that the sacrament being enacted is the Eucharist ("Despair," 29). Critic Joanne Feit Diehl, while agreeing that "[t]he ceremonies of the altar, the 'Chancel,' indicate that the moment is sacramental," sees no sign of redemption in the experience that is evoked (*Romantic Imagination*, 117).

In the third stanza, "tasted" may simply imply how visceral the speaker's experience was, or perhaps that it has left an aftertaste of all the things (death, night, frost, fire) it supposedly "was not." For, in the remainder of the poem, she continues to "taste" them, exploring new images of death, night, and frost (but not fire). The sense that she was dead returns in her sense that she was like "The Figures I have seen / Set orderly, for Burial." The horror implicit in "Set orderly" arises from the sense of indifference toward the dead, who are manipulated as unruly objects that must be brought under control. The passive voice, which evades the issue of *who* is doing the ordering, enhances this sense of the dead as objects, which is developed in stanza 4. In images of enclosure and suffocation, the speaker sees her life as "shaven" and "fitted to a frame." If this is meant to be an image of a body placed in a coffin, it is a terrible one, in which the body itself has turned to wood. Moreover, this coffin is locked with a key, a detail Anderson explains by noting that "spirits are locked in bodies, and since coffin and corpse are one here, her vital life 'could not breathe without a key' to release it from the body of this despair" ("Despair," 28).

Line 4 of stanza 4 returns to the image of night, negated in stanza 1, since the bells indicated it was noon. She now admits "And 'twas like Midnight, some—" And this midnight, as we move into stanza 5, is like the stoppage of time, like space staring all around. We are no longer in a church, and whether it is day or night is no longer relevant. The most fundamental dimensions by which the mind orients itself—time and space—are disappearing. In the next two lines, as she tells why her unnamable state "tasted" of frost, time ("first Autumn morns") and space (the frozen ground) are restored. The "Grisly frosts" that "Repeal" the "Beating Ground" descend like a grim judgment from on high. The image is a complex one and cannot be contained within any one picture. The ground is "repealed," as laws are, in this case the law of life. At the same time, the ground is likened to a beating heart that is stilled.

In the sixth stanza, the speaker drops all these partial analogies to what she experiences, finding its closest resemblance in "Chaos." The universal indifference and ruthlessness that has been suggested in previous images here finds expression in the words "cool" and "stopless"—a typical Dickinsonian neologism, formed by adding a suffix to an established word. By turning the noun *stop* into a negative modifier, she creates a new meaning, endowing the notion of "not stopping" with a terrible momentum. Then with increasing concreteness she embodies this meaning in the images "No Chance," "No Spar (ship mast)," "No Report of Land," all images of what might stop or interrupt the "stopless Chaos," if they existed. The final line presents one final puzzle: Why "Despair"? Wouldn't "Report of Land" justify hope? In her elliptical way, Dickinson seems to be saying just that: Yes, to the sailor lost at sea, a report of land *would* justify hope; and only where hope can exist is despair possible.

See also "I FELT A FUNERAL, IN MY BRAIN," and "THERE'S A CERTAIN SLANT OF LIGHT."

FURTHER READING

Charles R. Anderson, "Despair," in *Modern Critical Views*, Harold Bloom, ed., 26–29; Sharon Cameron, *Lyric Time*, 48–51; John Cody, *After Great Pain*, 326–328; Joanne Feit Diehl, *Romantic Imagination*, 117–118; Cristanne Miller, *Grammar*, 78–80, 100–101.

"It would have starved a Gnat—" (1862) (Fr 444, J 612)

This stark evocation of childhood deprivation belongs with such poems as "I WAS THE SLIGHTEST IN THE HOUSE—" and "I HAD BEEN HUNGRY, ALL THE YEARS—," written during the same year. For Dickinson, who was 31 when she wrote these poems and in the thick of her period of "flood" creativity, these fictionalized narratives seek to define the emotional essence—if not the literal facts—of her early years. Taken both individually and as a whole, they draw a childhood interior characterized by extreme smallness, hunger, and helplessness.

Of the various speakers in Dickinson's hunger poems, this one is the most diminished and dehumanized. Elsewhere, the speaker is a sparrow ("VICTORY COMES LATE—") or the dining companion of birds ("I had been hungry, all the Years"). In the nightmarish imagery of this poem, not only is she smaller than a gnat, but she is attacked and surrounded by parts of creatures (the "Claw" of hunger), by a bloodsucking worm ("Leech") and a fire-breathing reptile of myth and fairy tale ("Dragon"). Though infinitesimally tiny, she has the appetite of a "living child." Her dilemma lies in precisely this mismatch between her needs and her resources:

> Nor like the Gnat—had I—
> The privilege to fly
> And seek a Dinner for myself—
> How mightier He—than I!

The speaker is powerless. Not only is she forced to live on less than what would sustain a gnat, she is without the gnat's resources to find its own food—or to dash its life out on the windowpane and be released from "beginning again." The latter is an ambiguous phrase, which may refer simply to awakening day after day and once more engaging in the quest for nourishment. Or it may be interpreted as a reference to an afterlife—something a gnat need not worry about, but whose prospect here does not comfort the speaker. Still, suicide beckons as a desirable, but never fully embraced, alternative to the constricted life she is forced to live, just as it does at the conclusion of "I was the slightest in the House": "And if it had not been so far—/ And anyone I knew / Were going—I had often thought / How noteless—I could die—."

Although the poem is a bitter accusation, an expression of rage, contained by the grotesque imagery, the identity of the accused is noticeably absent. While the most obvious candidates are Dickinson's parents, some readers have suggested that God is the sadistic and withholding adult; certainly Dickinson evokes—and reproaches—the deity in similar terms in other poems (see "I NEVER LOST AS MUCH BUT TWICE—," "GOD IS A DISTANT, STATELY LOVER," "OF COURSE—I PRAYED—," and "IT'S EASY TO INVENT A LIFE—."). Others, pointing out that the Gnat is masculine, have seen the whole poem as a comparison between "He" and "I" and speculated that writing about herself as child was Dickinson's way of talking about being a woman in her male-dominated world. Emphasis is on what He *could* do and what the feminine "I" could *not*. The word *not* appears with greater frequency in Dickinson's work than any words but articles, a few prepositions and *and, it, is, that*. The pattern reveals her way of getting at the nature of her experience indirectly, "or through multiple, competing perceptions" (Miller, *Grammar*, 101). In this poem, "the female self is seen as the negative space that allows the positive pattern to merge" (Fulton, "Her Moment of Brocade," 24–25). Another, related supposition is that the poem reflects a state of being that has followed the poet into adulthood, an expression of the poet's inability "to extinguish such inevitable hungers as the desire for literary recognition and for sexual gratification, or to renounce them" (Pollack, "Thirst and Starvation," 71).

In light of these possible readings, it would be reductive to see the poem as "evidence" of parental (and particularly maternal) deprivation. Although Dickinson did once write, "I never had a mother . . .," she wrote in her letters in positive, affectionate terms of home and parents with far greater frequency. The poetic truth she had to tell about her childhood and the more complex reality of her early years should not be confused. In her childhood poems, she was creating a myth of her personal origins, full of "exaggerated and fabulistic elements" (Habegger, *My Wars*, 406). Against this persona she would define the self-reliant "Columnar Self," the self-nurturing poet she was striving to become. It is interesting to compare her vision of herself as a starved child with the mature Dickinson's nurturing relationship to children. According to her niece, MARTHA GILBERT DICKINSON BIANCHI (Mattie), who lived next door, "Aunt Emily stood for *indulgence*" (*Face to Face*, 6). The poet, who devoted many daylight hours to baking and cooking for her family, would be remembered by the neighborhood children as the lady at an upstairs window who frequently lowered a basket of gingerbread to them as they played outside the house.

See also "A LOSS OF SOMETHING EVER FELT I—," "GOD GAVE A LOAF TO EVERY BIRD—," and EMILY NORCROSS DICKINSON.

FURTHER READING

Nina Baym, "God, Father, and Lover," in *Puritan Influences in American Literature*, Emory Elliott, ed., 193–209; Martha Dickinson Bianchi, *Face to Face*, 6: Alice Fulton, "Her Moment of Brocade," 9–44; Cristanne Miller, *Grammar*, 98–104; Vivian Pollak, "Thirst and Starvation," in *Critical Essays*, Judith Farr, ed., 62–75.

"I've seen a Dying Eye" (1863) (Fr 648, J 547)

Like many Victorians, Dickinson was fascinated and, to some degree obsessed, by deathbed scenes. As a girl of 15, she had insisted on being admitted to the presence of her dying friend SOPHIA HOLLAND. Told that Sophia was near death, wrote the adolescent Emily, "Then it seemed to me I should die too if I could not be permitted to watch over her or even to look at her face." Later in her life, this urgency to experience the moment of passage from life to death found expression in some of her greatest poems, including "I HEARD A FLY BUZZ—WHEN I DIED—" and "BECAUSE I COULD NOT STOP FOR DEATH—." What she called "the flood question" ("Is Immortality true?") led her imagination repeatedly to the death chamber, and in her so-called "proleptic" poems she wrote from the perspective of one who has already died.

In "I've seen a Dying Eye" Dickinson uses the device of synecdoche, the representation of a whole by one of its parts. Her evocation of "a dying eye" representing a dying person proves dehumanizing in this instance, casting the deathbed scene in a grotesque light. Images of the eye or eyes are ubiquitous in Dickinson; like images of the face she often uses them to express the desire for direct communion with a beloved human being. Here, however, she does something very different. The speaker sees the Eye, but the Eye is involved in its own frantic drama:

I've seen a Dying Eye
Run round and round a Room—

This Eye suggests nothing so much as a demented rodent of some sort racing desperately in circles. It is "In search of Something—as it seemed"—a goal, perhaps clear to the Eye, but vague to the speaker. This vagueness then overcomes the Eye itself, which becomes "Cloudier," then "obscure with Fog," and in a final grim image "soldered down." For scholar Jane Eberwein, "A kind of anger smolders in this poem about the cruel insensitivity of the dead to the questions of the living whom they are luring toward circumference, without giving adequate insight into the journey's goal" (*Dickinson*, 212). The anger is reflected in the speaker's total lack of sympathy for the disembodied Eye and her refusal to perceive the dying person to whom it belongs. Her only regret is that it has shut down without revealing its secret: "what it be / 'Twere blessed to have seen—." This last line is ambiguous. We never know, not only *what* the Eye has seen, but *whether* it has seen the thing for which it searched. This tormenting indeterminacy is reminiscent of the ending of "I Heard a Fly buzz—when I died":

And then the Windows failed—and then
I could not see to see—

In this equally terrifying work, the dying Eye belongs to the speaker, and there is every indication that it has seen nothing more illuminating at the moment of death than a blue-bottle fly.

See also "I DIED FOR BEAUTY" and "I FELT A FUNERAL, IN MY BRAIN."

FURTHER READING

Jane Eberwein, *Dickinson*, 212; Bettina L. Knapp, *Emily Dickinson*, 122–126; Vivian Pollak, *Anxiety of Gender*, 106–107.

"I was the slightest in the House—" (1862) (Fr 473, J 486)

Although the candid and seemingly spontaneous voice of this poem may tempt the reader to view it as an actual description of Dickinson's childhood, the known facts of the poet's early years argue against so literal an interpretation. Emily may have had the frailest health in the family, but in her prime she worked as vigorously as the others did, rising the earliest, and going to bed latest. Her room may have been the smallest in the house, but she was not alone there. She shared it with her younger sister LAVINIA (Vinnie) and, possibly, when she was a small child, with her brother, WILLIAM AUSTIN. Emily was anything but a reticent child. She had intimate and boisterous times with both lively siblings and enjoyed a reputation among her childhood friends as "a talker and a tease." Her chatty, exuberant early letters, and the many times she expressed her love of home in the letters of her youth and maturity, create a different picture altogether of her "real" childhood. (Sewall, *Life*, II, 330).

If the poem is not "autobiographical" in the usual sense of the word, however, it is still "about" the 31-year-old woman who wrote it. Dickinson is reimagining her early years in order to understand the path that has led her to become a poet. Looked at closely, the poem is less about deprivation than about the carving out of her own "place," in which sparseness, solitude, and reticence are requisite conditions for attaining unending riches. In calling herself the "slightest," she implies that she was the least important, as well as the physically smallest. Yet she presents herself as playing an active role in "taking" the smallest room, and arranging its symbolic contents into a kind of poet-monk's cell. Her lamp (light, vision), her book (reading, the company of other poets), her geranium (the inspiration of homey nature), and her basket (her ear, her poet's receptivity) represent all the things she needs in order to "catch the mint / That never ceased to fall—." Looked at in this way, the speaker's room is not only adequate, but also ideal for her purposes. Although mint is a fragrant herb, and something one would collect in a basket, *this* mint comes from "above" in an endless shower. The word *mint* also designates a place where money is coined, as well as the coins produced at such a place, and it is likely that these meanings, with their associations with wealth and fabrication, are what Dickinson had in mind. At night, tucked away inconspicuously in her spare room, she is ideally stationed to receive the bounty of invention (inspiration, poetry) continually falling her way. At this point, the apparently naïve speaker stops to recall whether she owned anything else, before saying she is sure that "this was all," thus underscoring her material poverty.

In stanza 3, her attention shifts to another element of her monastic childhood, its devotion to silence:

I never spoke—unless addressed—
And then, 'twas brief and low—
I could not bear to live—aloud—
The Racket shamed me so—

What was the shame of living aloud for this poet who revered words and lived by self-expression? Judith Farr sees it as an expression of "the guarded and secretive life of a persona embarrassed by the noise and triviality of shared community; one who therefore depicts herself living most enjoyably and creatively at night or just before sunrise" (*Passion*, 52). Although she wrote to her mentor, THOMAS WENTWORTH HIGGINSON, of her embarrassment when people talked aloud about "Hallowed things" (L 415, August 1862),

Dickinson herself spent a lifetime writing of what was sacred to her. But manner and circumstance were all-important in her ability to do so. She once commented to her friend EMILY FOWLER (Ford) on a meeting of the "Shakespeare club" to which she belonged, asking her "if it did not make me shiver to hear a great many people talk, they took all the clothes off their souls" (Jay Leyda, *Years and Hours,* vol. 1, 133). Rejecting the "racket" of public discourse, Dickinson insisted on the privacy of communication, once reproaching a friend for addressing a letter to both herself and her sister, Vinnie. By creating a highly compressed and enigmatic poetic style, she managed to tell her truth "slant," without revealing her naked soul.

The imagined child of this poem, however, has not yet found her way; shamed by the noise around her, she feels her insignificance and thinks how she could die "noteless." Picking up the theme of the speaker's slightness, the word suggests that she may die without having uttered a note, or, perhaps, without having been noticed. Sewall, who sees this poem ostensibly about childhood as reflecting "many of the attitudes of her maturity," suggests that the line expresses her thought that she might die unrecognized as a poet (331). In the poem's final lines, the naïve speaker admits that death seemed too far away and that she would not have been willing to go without the company of anyone she knew. In her image of the child who is afraid to go alone to death, she injects a "contradiction"—a recognition of her human relatedness, which is absent from the rest of the poem.

It is interesting to compare this poem with "THEY SHUT ME UP IN PROSE—," in which the child speaker is locked up and made to be "still." Although stillness, here, has a *negative* meaning, the underlying image of a child enclosed in a small space, in which she nonetheless finds her own extravagant freedom, is similar to the vision of this poem. The poem is one of several written at this time, including "ALONE, I CANNOT BE—," and "I TASTE A LIQUOR NEVER BREWED—," in which the poet celebrates her creative "riches."

See also "A LOSS OF SOMETHING EVER FELT I," "I DWELL IN POSSIBILITY," and "IT WOULD HAVE STARVED A GNAT—."

FURTHER READING

Farr, *Passion*, 52; Jay Leyda, *Years and Hours*, vol. 1, 133; Richard B. Sewall, *Life*, II, 330–331.

"I would not paint—a picture—" (1862) (Fr 348, J 505)

In this well-known poem, Dickinson declares her preference for being an enamored receiver of art rather than a creator. She had already created hundreds of "stunning" poems by the time she wrote this, so there is a good measure of disingenuousness in her stance. But the pose allows her to revel in the nature of art and to celebrate the complex joys of both reader (viewer, listener) and poet (artist, musician). In three roughly parallel stanzas of eight lines each, she addresses painting, music and poetry, respectively. Dickinson was a skilled cartoonist and accomplished pianist who composed original pieces, as well as a lover of the visual arts and of music. So she had some experience as maker and receiver in all three artistic realms.

In stanza 1 she declares:

I would not paint—a picture—
I'd rather be the One
It's bright impossibility
To dwell—delicious—on—

Although the lines are ostensibly about visual art, they comment directly on Dickinson's verbal art. No painter of representational pictures, she makes of her poems vehicles for summoning "bright impossibility," the vivid presence of what is absent, the omnipresence of nothingness, the sumptuousness of destitution. In line 4 of this poem the language grows sensual and continues in that vein for the next four lines in which the speaker wonders "how the fingers feel" that create such "sweet torment" and "sumptuous Despair." These are no masochistic musings but an expression of what critic Judith Farr calls "the pleasure of feeling the poignancy of life, captured in art" (*Passion*, 154). Dickinson is describing the paradox whereby

art in general, and lyric poetry in particular, transforms suffering and enables us to transcend it. The "rare—celestial—stir—" of the artist's fingers is both sexual and exalted.

In the second stanza, she declares, "I would not talk, like Cornets—." The most likely meaning for *cornet* is the first listed in her dictionary, a musical instrument shaped like a trumpet; used in armies and on occasions of joy. In a biblical reference with which she was doubtless familiar, "David played before the Lord on cornets" (Samuel, vi). Rather than produce this joyous, triumphant music, she would rather be uplifted by it, an "endued Balloon" that floats upward "Through Villages of Ether—." The phrase refers, not to ether as anesthetic, but to the concept of the ether, the pervasive fluid medium of the universe, belief in which held sway in Dickinson's day. The meaning of the uncommon word "endued" becomes clear when we note that Dickinson's variants for it were "upborne, upheld, sustained." What upholds her is the cornet's "lip of Metal," which is also defined as "The pier to my Pontoon—." Thus, balloon becomes pontoon, an appropriate boat image for one drifting through the liquid ether. The cornet's music sends her floating high above the earth and keeps her tethered to it—a brilliant metaphor for yet another mysterious power of art.

In the final, most provocative stanza, the speaker declares that she would rather be the owner of the Ear listening to poetry than the poet. The speaker, whose identity is as "owner" of an Ear, is "Enamored—impotent—content—" in her passive role, in which she has "The License to revere." This disjunct syntax makes it virtually impossible to choose whether the next line, "A privilege so awful," refers to what precedes it (the license to revere), or to what follows ("the Art to stun myself / With Bolts—of Melody!"). "Awful," in its primary meaning of "striking with awe, filling with profound reverence; as the *awful* majesty of Jehovah," might apply equally to both. Thus the wavering of distinct boundaries on the syntactic level mirrors the semantics of the final lines in which the speaker hypothesizes herself as both stunner and stunned, Zeus hurling his thunderbolts and the lesser god or mortal struck by them. This sense of poetry's violent impact was characteristic of Dickinson, who once wrote, "If I feel physically as if the top of my head were taken off, I know *that* is poetry."

What would be the cost of such a double ecstasy, she asks. Dickinson uses the word *Dower,* which can simply mean a gift, but which has other highly suggestive meanings. According to Dickinson's lexicon, the most common meaning of the word was "that portion of the lands or tenements of a man which his widow enjoys during her life, after the death of her husband." But it can also mean "the property which a woman brings to her husband in marriage" or the opposite—"the gift of a husband for a wife." The possibilities of interpretation, depending on which definition one chooses, are dizzying! And all of them point to a subtext of sexuality beneath the poem's language and imagery. Sexual implications virtually leap out at the reader. In stanza 1, there are the artist's arousing fingers and the one in whom it arouses a "sweet torment." The phallic cornet of stanza 2 "upholds" the round, feminine balloon. "His" metal lip is a pier to "her" pontoon. The masculine Poet pours his essence into "her" vaginal Ear. And what could be more phallic than his thunderbolts? The final image has been called "autoerotic" by some critics, "an orgasmic moment that combines the phallic 'Bolts' with the more feminine (in its pleasing tunefulness) 'Melody'" (Juhasz and Miller, "Performances of Gender," 125). Biographer Cynthia Griffin Wolff is tuned in to the sexual imagery, too. But she interprets it as a "tongue-in-cheek assertion of the necessarily 'androgynous' nature of the Poet" (*Emily Dickinson,* 171–172), and particularly of the woman poet, who must possess the active, assertive, penetrating, aggressive qualities conventionally thought of as "masculine."

The primary role of sexual imagery, however, is to point to the ecstasy and intensity of the aesthetic experience. If Dickinson rejoices in the receiving role in this poem, it is not necessarily because she wished to "avoid responsibility" for the creative act, as some have suggested. As many of her poems testify, the passion she experienced as a reader was in some ways equivalent to what she knew in the act of writing. For one who called a book "the Chariot / That bears the Human Soul—" the act of receiving art was a sublime experience, and, as any artist

knows, a more reliable one than wresting art from the void, or the self, or the quixotic muse.

See also "I RECKON—WHEN I COUNT AT ALL—" and "THERE IS NO FRIGATE LIKE A BOOK."

FURTHER READING

Judith Farr, *Passion,* 253–255; Farr, "Dickinson and the Visual Arts," in *Handbook,* Grabher et al., eds., 65; Suzanne Juhasz and Cristanne Miller, "Performances of Gender," in *Cambridge Companion,* 123–125; Vivian R. Pollak, *Anxiety of Gender,* 249–250; Gary Stonum, *Dickinson Sublime,* 83–84; Cynthia Griffin Wolff, *Emily Dickinson,* 171–174.

"I Years had been from Home" (1862) (Fr 440, J 609)

In this narrative dream poem, Dickinson attempts to cross a threshold that in the end proves too fearful, causing her to flee in panic. Even if we did not know that the poet never left an actual, physical home, but lived in one of two houses all her life, the imagery of the poem makes clear that this is a psychic landscape, a Home of the inner world, to which she cannot return. The obstacles she encounters in this dramatization are all within her: fears and imaginings she cannot quite overcome. She never does open the door, but instead *imagines* the "Face" and the stolid stare that would greet her if she could conquer her terror. She gets as far as placing her hand upon the latch before fleeing "like a Thief." Thus, although she starts out by claiming her right to enter—she has "left a Life" within this Home—the poem ends on a note of guilt, implying an inward knowledge that she is *not* entitled to reenter it and claim what she has come for. Dickinson's sensibility was keenly attuned to the inexorable flux of time and the way that the past excludes us from our former lives. She understood this to be an insidious process that occurs without our conscious knowledge. In "I could not prove the Years had feet—" (Fr 674), she recognizes that she has somehow outgrown "the Self I was," which, though "competent" to her in the past, no longer fits the larger self she has become. She is able to "smile Opon the Aims / That felt so ample—Yesterday," while recognizing that "Today's—have vaster claims—." In "EDEN IS THAT OLD FASHIONED HOUSE," she evokes the House of the past as a lost paradise, recognized for what it was only after she has left; when she tries to return, she finds that it has vanished. In these poems, whether she regards her moving on with satisfaction or regret, as a process of growth or of loss, there is a sense of integration of past and present: the speaker sees where she has come from and regards it with a measure of acceptance.

This is not the case in the poem under consideration. Fear is the predominant emotion as she attempts a confrontation with a past that is capable of overwhelming her. Characteristically, Dickinson speaks in symbolic rather than autobiographical terms of the dilemma confronting her. She gives us a Door, a Face, a Latch, a Hand, a Floor—with nothing more specific to indicate whether it is the very existence of an alien past that is fearful or something particular contained in that past.

The image of the awful Door, which frightens her as other more ostensibly frightening things in her life have not, is central to the poem. It contains echoes of the Door of Revelations, Dickinson's favorite book of the Bible, "the awful doors / Before the Seal" she evokes in "Just lost, when I was saved!" (Fr 132). Within this context, the strange Face she fears to encounter suggests the Face of God—a presence from which Dickinson often felt herself to be excluded. This is not to say that the poem is *about* God and the Doors to eternity, but that Dickinson uses apocalyptic imagery to suggest the psychic enormity of this failed attempt to cross a threshold. In the key third stanza, where Home and Door dematerialize into a visionary moment, the speaker leans on "the Awe," which implies fear of something mighty and wondrous:

> I leaned upon the Awe—
> I lingered with Before—
> The Second like an Ocean rolled
> And broke against my ear—

Transforming a preposition into a noun, she lingers with "Before"—the past encountered on the metaphysical plane. In the image of the "Second"

that "like an Ocean rolled / And broke against my ear—," she conveys the deep, boundless impact of the moment of recognition. Remembering her ability not to "wince" at "Consternation" that engulfed her in the past, she tries to laugh it off—but what emerges is a "crumbling laugh":

> I laughed a crumbling Laugh
> That I could fear a Door
> Who Consternation compassed
> And never winced before.

She summons the courage to place her hand upon the Latch, but fearing "Lest back the awful Door should spring / And leave me in the Floor—," she carefully withdraws her fingers. As she flees, in the final lines, she holds her ears, in terror of hearing the awful sound of time again. What is the significance of this unusual phrase, "in the Floor," with its implied parallel of "in the ground"? Is this a hint that the speaker, who receives no answer to her (imagined) question of whether the Life she left "remains" in the Home, is speaking from beyond the grave? Or is the blow that would leave her "in the Floor," should the Door to the past spring open, the existential shock of encountering oneself as someone alien? Biographer Alfred Habegger takes the latter view, seeing the poem as being about the mind's avoidance of the past. He points out that "Ten years later when Dickinson was writing her cycle of poems about the fearsome house of memory, she opened the manuscript book containing this narrative and revised it—the only pre-1865 poem she is thought to have reworked in 1872." (*My Wars*, 533).

A radically different view is contained in John Cody's classic psychoanalytic study of Dickinson. Cody views the poem as a confession of how the poet fled sexuality. In his interpretation, the poet may have been "Home"—an image signifying "happiness, belonging, sheltering love, and sexuality" in early childhood (*After Great Pain*, 136). In the poem, she returns to claim adult consummation. She stands at the threshold of her affective life and argues with herself about whether she has the right to it. When she realizes "that the tender love she wants can only be had in conjunction with sexuality," she hesitates and flees (137). He suggests that touching the Latch is "a faltering and terrified sexual gesture" and that what she flees from is homosexual love, since "the 'latch' is more fittingly a female phallus" (138).

However ingenious and plausible Cody's thesis may be, it unnecessarily narrows the poem to a single possible meaning. The retreat from a threshold, whether figurative or literal, that leaves the speaker estranged is, after all, a recurrent theme in Dickinson. While sexual consummation may be one dimension of this experience, it is only one of the "multitudes of meaning" to be found in the poem. As critic Robert Weisbuch cautions, "assigning the poem to one aspect of experience will rob it of its vital versatility" ("Prisming," 199–200).

See also "A Wife—at Daybreak—I shall be—," "Forever—is composed of Nows—," "I cannot live with You—," "If your Nerve, deny you—," and "One need not be a Chamber—to be Haunted—."

FURTHER READING

John Cody, *After Great Pain*, 129–144; Alfred Habegger, *My Wars*, 532–537; Robert Weisbuch, "Prisming," in *Handbook*, Grabher et al., eds., 197–223.

"Like Eyes that looked on Wastes—" (1863) (Fr 693, J 458)

In most of Emily Dickinson's poems to the woman she loved, widely assumed to be her girlhood friend and later her sister-in-law, Susan Huntington Gilbert Dickinson, Susan is the unattainable beloved who exists within a realm to which the speaker has lost access. She is "the Pearl—/ That slipped my simple fingers through," the luxuriant woman of "Your Riches—taught me—Poverty," who moves on to heterosexual love, while the speaker stays behind. She is the forfeited jewel in "The Malay—took the Pearl—," the flown bird in "I have a bird in spring." In this poem, however, instead of an inequality between the poet and the woman she loves, the speaker declares a grim identity: Both she and the face she looks upon are locked into the same fate, with

"Infinites of Nought" stretching like a wilderness before them.

In the first stanza, Dickinson piles on images of nothingness:

Like Eyes that looked on Wastes—
Incredulous of Ought
But Blank—and steady Wilderness—
Diversified by Night—

These lines can be read in two ways: 1) The eyes can't believe in *anything but* blank, wilderness, etc. 2) The eyes can hardly believe what they are seeing—nothing but blank, wilderness, etc. The first reading is by far the most damning, implying a total spiritual devastation.

The eyes are disembodied. Only in the next stanza do we learn that what is being likened to the eyes staring at wastes is "the face I looked opon—." This is an unusual poetic strategy. We would expect the "eyes" alone to be present, as a synecdoche (a representation of the whole by a part) for the woman. See, for instance, Dickinson's image of "the Horses' Heads" (a synecdoche for the horses) racing toward Eternity in "Because I could not stop for Death—." By making the eyes a simile for the face and developing the image over several lines, Dickinson gives them an eerie, parallel, but independent existence; they are the poem's most powerful image of unrelieved existential emptiness.

In another startling twist, we learn in the last line of stanza 2 that "the waste" that the face is looking upon is the speaker. And she can do nothing to help, since "the Cause was Mine," that is, she is the cause of the face's misery. They are both locked in a "Compact of Misery," "As hopeless—as divine—," what critic Judith Farr sees as "their reciprocal gaze [which] describes the mirror by which many 19th-century painters portrayed Sapphic love" (*Passion*, 161).

As the final stanza mournfully concludes, there can be no absolution for either of them, presumably for their forbidden sexual desires for one another:

Neither—would be absolved—
Neither would be a Queen
Without the Other—Therefore—
We perish—tho' We reign—

They can neither be absolved of their illicit desires nor joined in marriage, as the term *Queen* clearly signified for Dickinson. See, for example, "Ourselves were wed one summer—dear—," in which the speaker recalls the brief time when "We were Queens in June." Despite the frustration of this conclusion, it is less bleak than the poem's beginning: The emptiness has been transposed into another context, in which, instead of "Infinites of Nought," we at least see the outline of two suffering women. The paradox that, although neither will be a Queen, yet each will "reign," suggests that each woman, autonomous in her pain, will reign over her own desolate kingdom of frustrated passion.

This poem about two individuals, each divided against herself, resonates with other Dickinson poems about the divided self, such as "Me from Myself—to banish—," and "One need not be a Chamber—To be Haunted—."

See also "Now I knew I lost her—."

FURTHER READING

Judith Farr, *Passion*, 160–163, 166–167; Vivian A. Pollak, *Anxiety of Gender*, 144–145.

"Like some Old fashioned Miracle" (1862) (Fr 408, J 302)

Much of Emily Dickinson's work is bound to the seasons of the year. She lived in the midst of an imposing natural environment, surrounded by mountains, in an age when people were highly vulnerable to the weather. As a precise observer of nature and devoted gardener, as well as a student of botany and other natural sciences, she was acutely attuned to the nuances of New England's dramatic seasonal cycle. In one of her first known poems "Frequently the woods are pink—" (Fr 24, 1858), after describing a series of visual changes in the landscape over the course of a year, she assumes the voice of her naïve speaker, in order to convey her wonder at the process: "And the Earth—they tell me / On it's axis turned! / Wonderful rotation—By but twelve performed!" Dickinson wrote

about all of the seasons, and she wrote about them all of her life. As Habegger notes,

> As Dickinson gradually restricted herself to her father's house and yard, the plants, birds, insects, and surrounding hills that she had closely observed became increasingly symbolic. They announced the seasons, and the seasons came to be emblems of the phases of psychic existence. (*My Wars*, 161)

Of the four seasons, summer occupies a place of special prominence in her poetry, not merely because of the number of times it is named or evoked, but because of its preeminence in her value system. In a famous poem, in which she "lists" the things she most cherishes, she writes: "I reckon—When I count at all—/ First—Poets—Then the Sun—/ Then Summer—Then the Heaven of God—/ And then—the List is done—." And a prime indicator of the supremacy of poets is the fact that "Their Summer—lasts a solid Year—." If summer is a "psychic phase," then Dickinson seems to be saying that poets live all year round in the state of intensity and fecundity associated with the physical season.

As a poet writing about summer, however, Dickinson was painfully aware of the season's ephemeral nature. In several of her summer poems, the speaker is either hungrily awaiting the "miracle" or reflecting on its passing. In "It will be Summer—eventually," she writes of how the world will hum and blossom, "Till Summer folds her miracle—." In the poem under discussion, summer *is* over and, as the poet remembers it, it appears to her to have been "Like some Old fashioned Miracle." The phrase expresses her wonder at an abundance she can scarcely credit and suggests that the summer past was the kind of real honest-to-goodness miracle such as occurred in earlier, simpler, more faith-filled times.

As the summer recedes, however, its reality grows increasingly hard to hold on to. The "Affairs of June" seem "an infinite Tradition," that is, something handed down by word of mouth, as fairy and folk tales are. (The image echoes one from a great, earlier poem, "These are the days when Birds come back—": "The old—old sophistries of June—/ A blue and gold mistake," where the theme of a deceptive reality associated with summer's "miracle" is developed). Dickinson offers as examples of the ongoing "Tradition" Cinderella's bay horses; Robin Hood's companion, the skilled archer Little John, who appears in Sir Walter Scott's historical romance *Ivanhoe*; Lincoln Green—the name of the cloth of the outlaw band's simple livery; and Bluebeard, the legendary wife-killer. The specific content of these tales is probably less important than the fact that they were familiar to readers of Dickinson's day—all commonly known fictions, with some degree of "miracle" associated with them. Note, too, that in her selection of details, Dickinson is enjoying the sound play created by the repeated consonants, *g*, *l*, and *b* combinations, and the repeated syllable *in* (*In*finite, *Cin*derella, *Lin*coln) and its partial echo in *Green*. The rich sound orchestration continues, particularly at the beginning and end of the first two lines of stanza 3 (Her Bees, Her Blossoms, Hum, Dream). Its effect is to aurally recreate the vital hum of the season.

As the poem progresses, the idea of summer as an insubstantial fiction, rather than as a miracle, predominates. In stanza 3, the memory of bees and flowers is "like a Dream," yet so intense, bringing such painful elation, we almost believe the reality is still present. In the final stanza, Dickinson develops the aural imagery introduced in the bees' hum:

> Her Memories like Strains—Review—
> When Orchestra is dumb—
> The Violin in Baize replaced—
> And Ear—and Heaven—numb

Summer's opulence is compared to an orchestra that has fallen silent; its "violin" (the birds, perhaps, transposed into the voice of poignancy) has been put back into its coarse, woolen ("baize") casing. Note how "baize" is an exact homonym for the "bays" of stanza 2; their meanings, however, are diametrically opposed, bay horses suggesting vigorous movement, the baize casing symbolizing the coffin in which summer's voice is laid to rest. The last line evokes the numbness of universal grief. The human "Ear" becomes the organ of an "unfeeling" bereavement. Even "Heaven" is stunned. Thus, the summer in this poem transforms from miracle to tradition to fiction to dream to numbness, receding to an increasingly vague state of unreality. What

began as a celebration of what has been has turned into a lament for what has gone.

The many nuances of Dickinson's sense of the hottest season can be further explored in such poems as "Summer for thee, grant I may be" (Fr 7), "When roses cease to bloom, sir" (Fr 8); "I know a place where Summer strives" (Fr 363); "She died at play" (Fr 141); "A soft sea washed around the house" (Fr 1199): "A something in a summer's Day" (Fr 104); "Summer laid her simple Hat" (Fr 1411); "Summer has two beginnings" (Fr 1457); and "'Twas here my summer paused" (Fr 1771).

See also "A BRIEF, BUT PATIENT ILLNESS—" and "FURTHER IN SUMMER THAN THE BIRDS—."

FURTHER READING

Judith Farr, *Gardens*, 282–287; Alfred Habegger, *My Wars*, 161, 369.

"Me from Myself—to banish—" (1863) (Fr 709, J 642)

Dickinson's poetry was a continual, amazingly varied assault on the mysteries of the inner life, an attempt to grasp its workings through language. Soul, Self, Spirit, Brain, Mind, Consciousness, Heart, Me—all were variant terms she used to designate the mystery of the quintessential self. The word *soul* or *souls* appears 141 times in the poems. She addressed, defined, relied on, and exulted in her soul, gambled with it, brought it to a white heat, and saw it scalped naked. She took the precise measure and weight of her brain and held funerals in it. So vast to her was the terrain of inner life that she counseled the explorer Hernando de Soto "Explore thyself!" and assured him that he would only then find the "Undiscovered Continent."

Frequently, her emphasis is on the soul's sovereignty, as in "THE SOUL SELECTS HER OWN SOCIETY—." This is the "imperial soul" that makes its own rules and sets its own boundaries; it is the "Columnar Self," a solid, unitary structure, upon which the poet can rely. As in the thinking of Ralph Waldo Emerson, it is the inner spark attuned to the divine. Dickinson celebrated this soul, closely identified with the self that loved passionately and wrote poetry, and gloried in its faithfulness and consistency.

But she also had a keen and tormenting awareness of the soul's duality—an inheritance, perhaps, from her Puritan past—and explored it from many perspectives. She knew that "The Soul unto itself / Is an imperial friend—/ Or the most agonizing Spy—/ An Enemy—could send—" (Fr 579). The divided soul was most often for her a place of ambush and hidden terrors, as in "ONE NEED NOT BE A CHAMBER—TO BE HAUNTED—." She was painfully aware of the inseparability of the soul from its dark "double," declaring, "Of Consciousness—her awful mate / The Soul cannot be rid—" (Fr 1076).

In the poem under consideration, she speaks of the self's duality as "Mutual Monarch," positing what was called in Greek tragedy an *agon*—a conflict between morally equal forces. The tone of the poem would be cerebral—a speaker working out a problem in logic—were it not for the elliptical syntax that gives it a sense of emotional urgency, even anguish. The omission of words is necessary in order to pare the elements of the speaker's dilemma down to a few and to isolate the two primary antagonists, "Me" and "Myself." In the first stanza, the speaker is "Myself" (also identified with "My Fortress") while "Me" is the "Other" (also identified as "All Heart"). In the second stanza, Dickinson reverses the terms, calling herself "Me," while the "Other" is "Myself," as well as "Consciousness." The interchangeable terms *suggest* that "Me" and "Myself" are the same. Finally, in the third stanza, their identity is made explicit, as both become "Me":

> And since We're Mutual Monarch
> How this be
> Except by Abdication—
> Me—of Me—?

"The effect is to intensify the situation, the pain, the impossibility of victory . . . enemy and friend are one . . . self-consciousness means precisely the encounter of the self with itself, and . . . this is a perpetual struggle" (Juhasz, "Landscape," 140). The battle between opposite and equal sides of the self has been developed as a physical assault of a fortress, a struggle for supremacy that can never be resolved. The answer to the speaker's question— "How have I peace [?]"—is that she cannot have it; instead she is compelled to live with the ongoing tension of warring impulses, perceptions, and beliefs.

Dickinson famously explained, in a letter to her mentor THOMAS WENTWORTH HIGGINSON, that the "I" of her poems was not herself but a "supposed person." Not only does this statement reveal her awareness of the divisions within herself; it indicates her recognition of the changeable "speakers" of the lyric poem—artifices created by the poet—as natural vehicles for her disparate selves. Dickinson's complex and capacious soul was divided between belief and doubt, desire and renunciation, ecstasy and grief, rebellion and submission, hope and despair, passion and numbness, bitterness and gratitude. She was incapable, as this poem clearly states, of making herself less of a poet by making herself a more consistent one. As Weisbuch notes, ". . . this is a poet who will not stop thinking. One final meaning of the dash seems to be its implication that any thought is liable 'to be continued.' To expect settled truth from Dickinson is to wish for a contradiction in terms" ("Prisming," 219).

See also "THIS CONSCIOUSNESS THAT IS AWARE" and JONATHAN EDWARDS.

FURTHER READING

Judith Farr, *Passion*, 83–88; Joanne Feit Diehl, "Emerson, Dickinson, and the Abyss," in *Modern Critical Views*, Harold Bloom, ed., 145–159; Suzanne Juhasz, "Landscape," in *Critical Essays*, Judith Farr, ed., 130–14; Robert Weisbuch, "Prisming," in *Handbook*, Grabher et al., eds., 197–223.

"Mine—by the Right of the White Election!" (1862) (Fr 411, J 528)

What one makes of this poem, which consists exclusively of exclamatory assertions of ownership, very much depends on how one interprets the tone of the poem.

> Mine—by the Right of the White Election!
> Mine—by the Royal Seal!

For biographer Cynthia Griffin Wolff, the poem merges the voices of the child saying "Mine, mine!" and that of the saint, in an ongoing property dispute with an unidentified antagonist. She sees it as a usurpation of "God's mystical language of the Covenant, the Apocalypse, and Salvation . . . to the aggrandizement" of the self (*Emily Dickinson*, 198). While this is a minority view—most critics see the tone as ecstatic and triumphant rather than antagonistic and greedy—Wolff's approach does point to an underlying sense of desperation beneath the speaker's apparently regal, absolute assertions.

For Wolff, the central question of the poem is *who* the speaker is arguing with and she concludes that "the only worthy opponent of such a Voice is God Himself" (197). Whatever distinction she is claiming for herself, Wolff stresses, she is claiming that it belongs in her own domain rather than God's. Most readers, however, have perceived the speaker's appropriation of religious categories as a means of conferring the highest order of sanctity on what she is experiencing. The lack of a clear referent for the repeated incantation "Mine!" makes the poem elusive and open-ended.

For David S. Reynolds, the doctrine of election here is "totally detached from its sacred referent and fused with the human psyche" ("Emily Dickinson and Popular Culture," 171). He points out that the poem consists of mixed references, in which "negative images reminiscent of sensational literature that featured prisons, death, and blood" ("Scarlet prison," "Bars," "Veto," "Grave's Repeal") are fused with affirmative, ecstatic religious imagery ("White Election," "Vision," "Confirmed," "Delirious Charter!") (188).

At the other end of the interpretive spectrum, Jane Donahue Eberwein sees a unified linguistic source and a wealth of relevant meanings within Dickinson's Calvinist background, as well as in biblical symbolism. She explains the "White Election" as the right of the saints in Revelations, who are privileged to wear white, and links the "Royal Seal" to the traditional Puritan metaphors of covenant theology: "A bargain has been struck for the speaker with God. The contract committing her soul to him and granting assurance to her of immortality has been sealed by Christ through his atonement" ("Emily Dickinson and the Calvinist Sacramental Tradition," 92). She notes that Dickinson evokes whiteness as the sign of the highest level of divine martyrdom in another well-known poem, Fr 328: "Of Tribulation—these are They, / Denoted by the White." Eberwein goes on to elucidate the "Scarlet prison—/ Bars—cannot conceal!" as Christ's empty tomb, proof to the elect of "the Grave's Repeal" (93–94). This is her "Delirious Charter"—the title to eternal life. In this light, the poem is seen as the poet's assertion that she has achieved grace and the promise of immortality.

Eberwein concedes, however, that Dickinson may only have been imagining what it would be like to experience such grace. And, indeed, Dickinson's biography gives no reason to think she could be referring to an actual religious conversion. As a very young girl, Dickinson experienced a short-lived, illusory sense of communion with Christ, which left her wary of her own impressionability and eager to avoid the pressure to again succumb to it during the successive religious REVIVALS that marked her girlhood. Unable to publicly declare her acceptance of Christ, she remained outside the FIRST CHURCH OF CHRIST in AMHERST that the rest of her family attended. By the time she wrote this poem, she had taken a position with respect to Christianity from which she would not diverge, although she seems never to have totally relinquished the wish for such divine grace.

Yet another possibility is that the "White Election" Dickinson experienced had nothing to do with traditional religious ecstasy, whether attained or imagined, but was her way of speaking about her coming into her poetic gift. In the poems and letters of this period, Dickinson expressed the urgent realization that, given the failure of her important friendships with SAMUEL BOWLES and SUSAN HUNTINGTON GILBERT DICKINSON, her survival depended upon her ability to "reform her life according to the creative powers surging within her" (Sewall, *Life*, II, 485–486). The following year she wrote "I RECKON—WHEN I COUNT AT ALL," in which she exalts "Poets" to the highest rung of her ladder of sacred values, while concluding wistfully that traditional religious grace remains unattainable to her: "And if the Further Heaven—/ Be Beautiful as they prepare / For Those who worship Them—/ It is too difficult a Grace—/ To justify the Dream—." When Dickinson wrote "Mine—by the Right of the White Election!" she was in the midst of her period of "flood creativity." If her poetic vocation is the election celebrated in this poem, then both "Vision" and "Veto" are hers: the right to envision the world according to her own lights, as well as to alter or even reverse that vision, though it may entail relinquishing "her own cherished hopes" (Robert Weisbuch, "Prisming Emily Dickinson," *Handbook*, 215). The state of "White Election" is thus not a painless one. If, as critic Charles R. Anderson suggests, the scarlet prison represents "the heart, as the seat of worldly attachment" (*Stairway*, 208), the "bars" of its contradictory desires will have to be breached again and again. The perceived stridency of the poet's territorial claim may thus reflect the continual struggle underlying her triumph.

The fusion of secular/religious meanings that characterizes this poem, as well as common language and imagery, is found in "TITLE DIVINE, IS MINE!" which is generally considered to be the companion poem to Fr 411. At the conclusion of that poem, written a year earlier than this one, the speaker, who has rejected ordinary wifehood in favor of the title of "Empress of Calvary," veers off on a note of uncertainty, asking, "Is this the way?" In Fr 411, fired by an intense conviction of inner rightness, she does not ask this question.

See also "A SOLEMN THING—IT WAS—I SAID," "I DWELL IN POSSIBILITY—," and "THEY SHUT ME UP IN PROSE—."

FURTHER READING

Charles R. Anderson, *Stairway*, 206–210; Jane Donahue Eberwein, "Emily Dickinson and the Calvinist Sacramental Tradition," in *Critical Essays*, Judith Farr, ed., 92–94; David S. Reynolds, "Emily Dickinson and Popular Culture," in *Cambridge Companion*, 188; Richard B. Sewall, *Life*, II, 484–486; Cynthia Griffin Wolff, *Emily Dickinson*, 196–198.

"Much Madness is divinest Sense" (1863) (Fr 620, J 435)

Although the first line of this poem seems to raise the time-honored idea that poetry and madness are somehow linked, Dickinson has other concerns in this brief, incisive work. She was no "mad poet," and she is speaking here, not as an advocate for the irrational, but as a knowing social critic. Note that she does not speak of all madness, but of "much," that is, of a certain kind of "madness," which, as the rest of the poem makes clear, involves believing or doing something that offends the majority. The underlying concept is not far from the modern psychological idea that "normality" and "deviance" are, to a large degree, socially defined.

Rather than a definition of madness, the poem is a reaction to the ways in which society treats nonconformity; it is an angry poem, under strict, poetic control. Despite the dashes that give the poem a look of fragmentation, it is constructed logically, without the many ellipses that can make it difficult to recreate thought and syntax in a Dickinson poem (see PUNCTUATION). It consists of short sentences, with the end of a thought coinciding with the end of a line. If the straightforward argument it presents is not necessarily "logical," it is nonetheless based on clear-eyed perception, what is obvious to a "discerning Eye." But it also presents the judgment of a wider experience, which sees that majority rule prevails in all things ("as all"). The line "to a discerning Eye" takes on special prominence because it is an instance of what scholar Cristanne Miller calls "syntactic doubling," that is, it refers both to the line before and the line after it:

Much Madness is divinest Sense—
To a discerning Eye—
Much Sense—the starkest Madness—

Note how sounds, predominantly those in the initial position in a word, or sound groups, reinforce meaning: Sanity is expressed in words with s, n—sane/assent/sense, while madness is expressed in words with d, m—dangerous, demur, much madness, Majority. These two sound groups merge in the key phrases "divinest sense" and "starkest madness," In this way, the sound pattern "imitates" the apparent paradox that madness and sanity are one.

In these few terse lines, Dickinson takes her stand against the rigidities of the conservative society that surrounded her in AMHERST. When she wrote them, she was a woman of 33; she had not married and her years of self-imposed seclusion had begun. She no longer attended the FIRST CHURCH OF CHRIST on Sundays, with her family, all of whom had made a public declaration of faith in Christ. She was the only holdout. She knew just how "wide and deep the chasm was between her and what she called the World" (Sewall, II, 487) and must have been aware that others viewed her askance. Years earlier, she had written to her beloved friend, ELIZABETH LUNA CHAPIN HOLLAND, "Pardon my sanity, Mrs. Holland, in a world *insane* . . ." (L 185, early August 1856). With the Hollands, who believed in a kinder, sunnier God than the punishing Calvinist deity, Dickinson felt freer to explore ideas and feelings that marked her as deviant in mainstream Amherst. Three years later she expressed the theme of her loneliness with respect to the sane majority in a letter to her friend CATHERINE TURNER ANTHON: "Insanity to the sane seems so unnecessary—but I am only one, and they are 'four and forty,' which little affair of numbers leaves me impotent" (L 209, late 1859). Behind the humor, there was a somber realization that what she ironically calls "insanity"—which was nothing less than her unique poetic vision—was a profoundly necessary thing to her.

In future years, even so devoted a friend as THOMAS WENTWORTH HIGGINSON, who valued her poetry without fully understanding it, would speak of her as "my eccentric poetess," and "my partially cracked poetess at Amherst." While Dickinson would have no awareness of these particular comments, she knew in general that she was regarded as odd. The poem under discussion may be seen as her "reply" to those who would see her in that light. It belongs to that group of watershed poems, written during the same prolific period, including "I'M CEDED—I'VE STOPPED BEING THEIRS—" and "ON A COLUMNAR SELF—," in which she finds the strength to declare her independence from both the conventional aesthetic tastes and religious persuasions of her time.

FURTHER READING
Cristanne Miller, *Grammar*, 37–39; Richard B. Sewall, *Life*, II, 487.

"My life closed twice before it's close;" (Undated) (Fr 1773, J 1732)

One of Dickinson's most frequently quoted works, this undated poem is deeply *epistemological* in its concerns, that is, it explores the nature of human knowledge. What and how can we know about death and its aftermath? Like all of Dickinson's philosophical poems, however, this is no dry intellectual inquiry, but a cry from the aggrieved heart, struggling to understand personal experience in terms of universal truth. Although we don't know which specific deaths she is referring to (she experienced the loss of many friends and mentors in her life, from her early adolescence onward), the biographical facts are less important than what the poet makes of them. The power of her opening line derives from the use of the words "closed" (verb) and "close" (noun). In the second usage, she refers to her own death, in the first—to the impact of the death of two friends or loved ones on her life. She is saying that it was as if she herself had died when they died. (Note that she uses the incorrect form of "it's"—the contraction rather than the possessive [its], a mistake she frequently made).

The formal elegance of that first line is carried forward in the cool tone of the next three lines: the impersonal voice ("it yet remains to see") and the euphemistic "Immortality" (for death) and "a third event" (for a third death). Indeed, the word *death* does not appear in the poem. It is as if the idea (and the experience of it) is so great, the poet must carefully step around it.

Note the enjambment between stanzas, that is, the spilling over of the description of the "third event" into the second stanza: "So huge, so hopeless to conceive" as the two previous deaths. The word *hopeless* has a double meaning, referring to both the impossibility of understanding and the emotional hopelessness of the bereaved. Then, after telling us what she cannot grasp, Dickinson tells us what she *does* know, in the powerful two-line aphorism with which the poem ends:

> Parting is all we know of heaven,
> And all we need of hell.

Heaven and hell become one in the parting of death, which tells us nothing of what comes after, while revealing to us the terrible extent of our pain. Dickinson serves up this stark vision of human fate in lines of such polished perfection that it somehow becomes bearable. In addition to employing exact rhymes (see/me, befell/hell), she uses sounds to create haunting repetitions in stanza 2: the sighing sound of *h* in "huge," "helpless," "heaven," and "hell," the pairing of *n* and *h* sounds in "know of heaven" and "need of hell," and the resonance of "befell" and "hell" with the word "all," which appears twice.

The poem is a moving example of Dickinson's "determination to confront the full barrenness of human fate" and to perceive it as "not a personal grievance, but a universal tragedy" (Wolff, *Emily Dickinson*, 148).

FURTHER READING

Cynthia Griffin Wolff, *Emily Dickinson*, 148.

"My Life had stood—a Loaded Gun—" (1863) (Fr 764, J 754)

One of Dickinson's most haunting, enigmatic, and debated poems, Fr 764 has come to be viewed as the great analytic challenge for Dickinson scholars attempting to prove their mettle. There are any number of interpretations the interested reader can consult, as notable for their scope as for their ingenuity. Scholar-poet Susan Howe has centered an entire book, *My Emily Dickinson*, on a reading of this poem. For Robert Weisbuch, this "particularly magnificent, capacious, and demanding poem" is

the premier example of how Dickinson's endlessly expansible poems resist any reduction to a single meaning.

There are certain basics all readers can agree upon: The poem is built around the single extended metaphor of an "alliance" between a masculine figure and the speaker, a "Master" and a "Loaded Gun":

> My Life had stood—a Loaded Gun—
> In Corners—till a Day
> The Owner passed—identified—
> And carried Me away—

The Master empowers the Gun, removing it from the corner where it was languishing, and takes it hunting, thus allowing it to embark upon its mission of killing. The Gun, which revels in its destructive powers, in turn, protects the Master from any and all threats. Indeed, this is its sole purpose. The language of the poem is simple and direct, and the story is clear. But what do Owner/Master and Loaded Gun represent? How one answers this central question will determine how one answers the second mystery: What is the solution to the riddle of the final stanza?

> Though I than He—may longer live
> He longer must—than I—
> For I have but the power to kill,
> Without—the power to die—

Weisbuch asserts that the poem's greatness depends on "forgoing a single identification of the relationship between gun and owner/master" ("Prisming," 206):

> I don't mean that anything goes interpretively or that the poem is a Rorschach inkblot. I do mean that the poem gets egregiously robbed if you see the gun-to-owner relation simply as that of a believer to her god or as a lover to her adored beloved or even . . . as language personified in relation to the poet who shoots and masters it. The poem can absorb these meanings . . . but it is the play among the possibilities that makes the poem. . . . (Ibid., 207)

For Weisbuch, the encompassing idea of the poem "concerns the delusions of borrowed power and the resultant despoiling of potentially harmonious and loving connections." This, he believes, is the only way to explain the sudden switch from celebration to complaint in the final stanza: "the speaker-gun comes to understand its own error of uncritical servitude" (Ibid., 208). The monomaniacal speaker begins by celebrating loyalty and power; she ends by understanding the delusion of achieving self-realization through subservience. The gun may live longer than the owner may in the sense of mere existence, as inanimate objects do, but it is not alive in any meaningful sense, as the owner is. This is the fate "of anyone who gives away their own will and attempts to gain power by becoming the instrumentality of another, whether that other is another person or a mastering ideology" (Ibid., 208).

Weisbuch suggests that, in light of this overall interpretation, the poem can also be seen as a description of a particular kind of love relationship. And, indeed, the largest group of analyses takes this direction. Thus, Judith Farr believes that the poem is one of the many written to the man Dickinson called "Master." She relates it to an 1862 poem, Fr 349, "He touched me, so I live to know," where the speaker begins to "live" when Master touches her or carries her away. Farr points to an 1865 poem, Fr 1042, "'Twas my one Glory—" as evidence that, for Dickinson, being owned by the beloved was part of her ecstatic language of love (*Passion*, 242–243). She stresses the speaker's pleasure in the comradely intimacy between the gun (Emily as the "boy" she called herself on several occasions) and her Master. Yet, when it comes to the last stanza, Farr has no way of making it consistent with her positive interpretation and admits that it appears to be a revelation of the limits of women under patriarchy.

Cristanne Miller's analysis, with its emphasis on the speaker's rage, presents a more consistent overall vision of the poem. She sees it as "an adolescent fantasy about coming of age that breaks down before what should be its happy conclusion—powerful adulthood—revealing the flaw in its initial fiction but perhaps also the extreme limitation the speaker feels in her life choices" (*Grammar*, 123). Perceiving this limitation in cultural/historical terms, Albert Gelpi sees the poem as an expression of "the psychological dilemma facing the intelligent

and aware woman, and particularly the woman artist, in patriarchal America." He notes that the speaker kills her own feminine side (the doe) to adopt male destructiveness ("Deerslayer," 122). Developing this theme, Susan Howe writes:

> Women of Dickinson's class and century existed in a legal and financial state of dependence on their fathers, brothers, or husbands that psychologically mutilated them. Excluded from economic competition (hunting), they were forced to settle for passive consumerism. For a Puritan nature, happiness is based on the sacredness of the work ethic. (*My Emily Dickinson*, 84)

Vivian Pollak is another critic who views the poem as an exploration of rage, in which ". . . the speaker cooperates with a demonic male who appears to invest her with authentic social power" (*Anxiety of Gender*, 150). But Pollak's understanding of the roots of the rage embodied in images of gun and volcano is psychological rather than social. She perceives an "oedipal structure" at the core of the poem: neutered female gun, masculine owner, and maternal female (the doe and the Eider duck, an image of maternal devotion, who lines her nest with feathers plucked from her own breast). The speaker-gun hunts the doe and rejects the Eider duck's nest in favor of guarding her master. For Pollak, this points to the object of her fury as another woman, "a composite sister-lover-mother" figure, who, in Dickinson's real life, fundamentally disappointed her and deprived her of essential nurture. The "owner" is an empowering, yet destructive, male principle, the "animus." She suggests that, in the mountains echoing her omnipotence, the explosive smile, the fiery "Yellow Eye" and "emphatic Thumb"—all "orgiastic figures"—"eroticized death and thanatized love have been perfectly commingled . . ." (152). She interprets the gun's inability to die in the Shakespearean sense of the inability to consummate sexual love. But she adds, "More crucially, rage split off from its origins is unable to comprehend its generation and thus can achieve no final catharsis or death" (153).

Some readers, such as David Porter, Thomas Johnson, and Robert Weisbuch, have seen the poem in very different terms, as about the poet and the transformation of language. Other writings of Dickinson hint at this connection. Thus, in the undated poem Fr 1715, "A Word made Flesh" we find the lines: "A Word that breathes distinctly / Has not the power to die." The gun-life might then refer to the word (the poet) before it (she) is "empowered," that is, transformed through the power of poetry. As Weisbuch puts it, "The life-gun is language shot off, creatively, to describe the world; the hunting of the second stanza is not to be taken literally but as a capturing of meaning . . ." ("Prisming," 109). This use of violent imagery is characteristic of Dickinson's other statements on the power of poetry, as when she told THOMAS WENTWORTH HIGGINSON:

> If I read a book [and] it makes my whole body so cold no fire ever can warm me I know *that* is poetry. If I feel physically as if the top of my head were taken off, I know *that* is poetry.

Even closer in imagery, years later, in a letter to her cousin LOUISE NORCROSS, she wrote, "An earnest letter is or should be life-warrant or death-warrant, for what is each instant but a gun, harmless because 'unloaded,' but that touched 'goes off'?" (L 656, early September 1880). What does this approach say about the final stanza? The gun's power to "kill" may be the power of poetry, which is immortal, that is "Without—the power to die—." Yet, this interpretation is satisfactory only if the final stanza is spoken in a tone of triumph rather than complaint, and the speaker's desire, "He longer must—than I—," unmistakably conveys dismay.

Another fascinating and original interpretation is suggested by biographer Cynthia Griffin Wolff, who writes that, in answer to the riddle of the last stanza, "Who am I?" an Amherst audience of Dickinson's day would have answered that the gun is death and the owner/master is Christ. Wolff explains that Death "may" live longer than Christ, for Christ died on the cross, yet "Christ 'must' live longer than death, for the righteous cannot be raised from their graves unless Christ first vanquishes death" (*Emily Dickinson*, 443).

Wolff concludes her reading with the heretical suggestion that this poem may be so difficult to explain, not because no reader has yet found the key, but because the poem itself may not be fully successful. Otherwise stated, the poem may embody a confusion the poet had not sufficiently resolved for herself. We cannot know what Dickinson intended when she wrote this poem or to what extent she was aware of her intentions. What can be said, however, is that the poem's structure, language, and symbols provide its readers with fertile and rewarding grounds for exploration, without surrendering the irreducible mystery that is poetry's essence.

FURTHER READING

Charles R. Anderson, *Stairway*, 194–198; Sharon Cameron, *Lyric Time*, 65–74; Judith Farr, *Passion*, 241–244; John Cody, *After Great Pain*, 399–415; Margaret H. Freeman, "A Cognitive Approach to Dickinson's Metaphors," in *Handbook*, Grabher et al., eds., 265–269, 271–272n18; Albert Gelpi, "Emily Dickinson and the Deerslayer," in *Shakespeare's Sisters*, Sandra M. Gilbert and Susan Gubar, eds., 124–134; Sandra M. Gilbert and Susan Gubar, *Madwoman*, 607–612; Sandra M. Gilbert, "The Wayward Nun," in *Critical Essays*, Judith Farr, ed., 25–26; Susan Howe, *My Emily Dickinson*; Adrienne Rich, "Vesuvius at Home: The Power of Emily Dickinson," in *Critical Essays on Emily Dickinson*, Paul J. Ferlazzo, ed., 175–195; Vivian R. Pollak, *Anxiety of Gender*, 150–155; Robert A. Weisbuch, "Prisming," in *Handbook*, Grabher et al., eds., 205–211; Cynthia Griffin Wolff, *Emily Dickinson*, 441–446.

"'Nature' is what We see—" (1863) (Fr 721, J 668)

Dickinson's DEFINITION POEMS tease the reader with the expectation of certainty but end up suggesting a second complex reality to define the first. In this poem's attempt to define no less a phenomenon than "Nature," she creates that complexity through dialogue. In the first three lines of the first two stanzas, one voice declares what "Nature" is in terms of specific perceptions. Then, in the fourth line of these stanzas, an answering voice says "Nay," and insists upon a definition that depends not on the senses but on the human impulse to assign larger meaning to things. Critic Charles Anderson hypothesizes that the poet places "Nature" between quotation marks in order to suggest that what we see and hear is not the whole truth, but only "the outer shell that contains the essence" (*Stairway*, 93).

Thus, in the first stanza, the assertion that "'Nature' is what We see" is followed by an enumeration of things seen and then contradicted with, "Nay—Nature is Heaven—." One suspects that this euphoric generalization arises from the final item on the poet's list, "the Bumble bee," which is for Dickinson associated with summer and flowers, inebriation and sexuality. But even before the intrusion of the second voice, the flow of items on the list strains against too literal an identification of nature with what we see. In line 2, the speaker betrays her inability to stay with pure visual perception by leaping from "The Hill" to "the Afternoon"—a complex, temporal concept, encompassing far more than any one sense or even all the senses together take in. In line 3 the leaps from the small to the cosmic and back to the small in line 3 (Squirrel—Eclipse—the Bumble bee—) contain an implicit meditation on nature's varied magnitudes. The dashes contribute to the sense that the overwhelmed speaker is picking things out of the air from the vast array of natural phenomena.

Something similar happens in stanza 2, in which we are told, "'Nature' is what We hear—." Lines 2 and 3 contrast the small and the homey (Bobolink, Cricket) with the mighty and threatening (Sea, Thunder). The bobolink is one of Dickinson's most beloved songbirds, a rowdy, exultant singer with whom she identifies, while the cricket, as she says in one poem, is the earth's "utmost / Of elegy to me," associated with prayer (see "Nature—the Gentlest Mother is," and "FURTHER IN SUMMER THAN THE BIRDS—"). As in stanza 1, it is the list's final item, the cricket, that seems to spur the assertion of the opposing voice, "Nay—Nature is Harmony—." Anderson observes that since the variant to "Harmony" was

"Melody," Dickinson is not necessarily implying that all things coexist in universal harmony (*Stairway*, 93).

By now the two-voiced speaker, with her propensity to define according to her most recent perception, has proven herself an unreliable source of rock-hard wisdom. What she has proven herself to be is, instead, a poet, drawn to concrete observation but ultimately enamored of metaphor. Dickinson says as much in the third, concluding stanza:

> "Nature is what We know—
> But have no Art to say—
> So impotent our Wisdom is
> To Her Sincerity—

Wisdom is impotent to articulate what we know, on the nonverbal level, about "Her Sincerity." In this concluding phrase, which both personalizes and personifies nature, what the poet may be suggesting is nature's pure manifestation of itself, unmediated by human interpretation. Thus, like Beauty, "The definition of Nature is that Definition is none." As in many of her finest poems on this major theme, no matter how great her joy in nature or how close she stands, Dickinson's speaker remains a stranger to the natural world.

See also "SOME KEEP THE SABBATH GOING TO CHURCH—," "THESE ARE THE DAYS WHEN BIRDS COME BACK—," "THIS IS MY LETTER TO THE WORLD," and "WHAT MYSTERY PERVADES A WELL!"

FURTHER READING

Charles Anderson, *Stairway*, 92–93; Robert Weisbuch, *Emily Dickinson's Poetry*, 67–68.

"Not in this World to see his face—" (1862) (Fr 435, J 418)

This brief meditation on deprivation and the consolations of religion offers a glimpse into the poet's mind at work, as she wrestles with the terms of her existence. Rather than offering certainty or conclusion, Dickinson invites us to view the process by which her mind shuttles between alternatives.

Thus, in the first stanza of this two-stanza poem, the speaker seeks comfort for her inability to see a beloved face, in the promise of eternal life; in the second, she rejects this consolation, blithely bequeathing eternity to someone more "learned" than she, if only she can have this world.

The first two lines of the first stanza, with their naïve understatement and violation of grammatical parallelism ("Not in this World to see his face—/ Sounds long . . .") establish a childlike persona. She is momentarily consoled when she "reads the place" where "this," that is, this life, is said to be only a prelude to another. Dickinson juggles book imagery to create her meanings. The "book" that tells her of the life to come is the Bible, or another religious text. Eternal life is itself a book, "Unopened—rare— Opon the Shelf—/ Clasped yet—to Him—and me—." The following year Dickinson would write her great poem of love's impossibility, "I CANNOT LIVE WITH YOU—," in which she uses "shelf" imagery again in connection with eternal life. But in both poems, what is "upon" or "behind" the shelf is inaccessible. In contrast to this infinitely valuable but unattainable book of eternity, she sets the "Primer." In its first usage in stanza 1, the Primer signifies the prelude to eternal life; as such, it is of little importance. But the import of this word is transformed in stanza 2 when it becomes "My Primer," an elementary book for teaching children to read. It is this simple book—the poem's metaphor for earthly life— that the speaker declares she prefers to any other book, however wiser it may be. The "simplicity" of the speaker is, of course, deceptive, a device that gives Dickinson an excuse for her audacity in preferring this world to the next. The child persona can get away with the heresy, since her love of her "A—B—C" is only natural:

> Might some one else—so learned—be—
> And leave me—just my A—B—C—
> Himself—could have the Skies—

Yet the "child's" preference was one that both the adolescent and mature Dickinson confessed to innumerable times in her poems and letters. In a youthful letter to her close friend ABIAH PALMER ROOT she spoke of her love of the world as an impediment to her accepting Christ. And many poems speak, with varying degrees of anger and despair, of God's distance or absence. As Judith Farr observes:

> The attainment of the face of God, the 'beatific vision' of his nature, was the Christian's proper end and certainly the end of the Christian artist. . . . Thus *not* to see Gods face in this world constitutes the primary deprivation of those who believe, or want to believe. (*Passion*, 44)

The absent face of this poem, however, may just as well belong to an earthly beloved. Dickinson's love poetry is filled with evocations of her lover's face; indeed, her greater attachment to this world often took the form of declaring her beloved's face more radiant than God's or Christ's. In Fr 395, so holy is his face that she plans on "carrying" it with her when she dies and using it, that is, her love for him, as her passport to heaven:

> The face I carry with me—last—
> When I go out of Time—
> To take my Rank—by—in the West—
> That face—will just be thine—

But, precisely because the lover's face is "godlike," and the speaker's feelings for him "idolatrous," Dickinson's poetry often does not allow us to decide which "deity" the speaker refers to. For example, in Fr 266, "What would I give to see his face?" she declares she would give her life for "'*One hour*—of her Sovereign's face'!" The beloved's face is absent, sometimes because he is traveling in distant places, or because she has somehow offended him, but most often because life itself, with all its unspoken limiting circumstances, denies her the ecstasy of his presence.

See also "A WIFE—AT DAYBREAK—I SHALL BE— ," "I LIVE WITH HIM—I SEE HIS FACE—," and "OF COURSE—I PRAYED—."

FURTHER READING

Judith Farr, *Passion*, 43–44; William Shurr, *Marriage*, 75; Shira Wolosky, *Emily Dickinson*, 150–152.

"Now I knew I lost her—" (1872) (Fr 1274, J 1219)

In this haunting poem, Dickinson evokes the moment when she realizes she has lost the woman she has loved. When she wrote this poem, its likely subject, Dickinson's sister-in-law, SUSAN HUNTINGTON GILBERT DICKINSON, had been married for 16 years, borne two children, and was living a life in society utterly at variance with Emily's celibate, increasingly inward and reclusive existence. In light of this, Emily's realization that she has lost Susan must certainly have come earlier. But Dickinson is speaking here, not of the outward course of their lives, but about a profound inner distance that signals the loss of love itself. Sue is not literally gone—she is still living in the "adjoining" house across the hedge, at The EVERGREENS:

> But Remoteness travelled
> On her Face and Tongue.

Through this paradoxical image, the poet creates a sense of absence/distance in ceaseless movement in the other woman's expressions and in her words. It contains an allusion to the restless Susan's love of travel, which the homebound Dickinson transforms into the sign of Susan's spiritual evasions. She is

> Alien, though adjoining
> As a Foreign Race—

In these lines, Emily decisively repudiates the Susan of one of her earliest poems, "One Sister have I in the house—" (Fr 5. 1858): the woman, "a hedge away," whom she celebrated as her true sister. She recognized that her sister-in-law sang "a different tune" from that sung by the family she has joined: "Herself to her a music / As Bumble bee of June." But the different music of the bumble bee and of June delighted Dickinson, as did the young Sue's. Anything but "alien" to the poet's soul, she claims her as her chosen star "From out the wide night's numbers—/ Sue—forevermore!

In "Now I knew I lost her—" Sue's alien nature implies not only distance from the speaker, but her homelessness as she traverses a "Latitudeless

Place." In the following stanza she forlornly registers that "Love's transmigration" has "somehow" come, despite the fact that the Universe and its elements are unaltered. The three meanings of *transmigration* in Dickinson's Webster indicate the rich suggestiveness of this word choice: "the passing of men from one country to another . . . the passing of a thing into another state, as of one substance into another . . . the passing of the soul into another body. . . ."

In the long final stanza the poet adjures herself to remember that "Nature took the Day" for which she had paid so much. Scholar Judith Farr suggests that the lines "probably allude . . . to the fact that Sue's heterosexual nature, whatever it is that moves women toward men, stole the Sue that Dickinson's love paid for" (*Passion*, 167). But Dickinson may have been alluding to something even more fundamental in Susan than her sexuality: a spiritual flaw within her essential nature.

As if she can no longer bear to contemplate her loss, in the five concluding lines she shifts to a public voice that meditates on the folly of attempting to restore what has been lost:

> His is Penury
> Not who toils for Freedom
> Or for Family
> But the Restitution
> Of Idolatry.

Although she is speaking "generally," the lines are a veiled admission that she has not given up hoping all these years. The notion of restitution implies the return of some thing or right of which one has been unjustly deprived. Emily has lived in the conviction that Sue rightfully belonged to her. Only now does she see the penury such emotional toil has earned her.

If we were to attempt to construct a poetic history of Dickinson's disillusionment with Susan, her beloved woman, it would prominently include, "She dealt her pretty words like Blades—" (Fr 458, 1862):

> How glittering they shone—
> And every One unbared a Nerve
> Or wantoned with a Bone—

She never deemed—she hurt—
That—is not Steel's Affair—

In this poem, Susan is already alien, a creature made of steel not flesh and blood, who lives by different rules than mere mortals. She is contemptuous of their "vulgar grimace in the Flesh—," to which the speaker replies, "To Ache is human—not polite—."

The following year, she wrote "It dropped so low in my regard" (Fr 785), widely interpreted as about Susan, in which the dehumanized "it" drops and goes to pieces "on the Stones / At bottom of my mind—." For her disillusionment, she denounces not Fate but herself "For entertaining Plated Wares / Opon my Silver Shelf—."

Ten years later, in "Art thou the thing I wanted?" (Fr 1311, 1873), she has difficulty in believing she could ever have desired something so unworthy and bids it, "Be gone—my Tooth has grown—."

There are other poems that might have a place in this history of disaffection, including "The most pathetic thing I do" (Fr 1345) and "Cosmopolites without a plea" (Fr 1592). Yet, even if we were to gather them all into a single damning document, they would not tell the full story. "With consistency a great soul has simply nothing to do," wrote Ralph Waldo Emerson. The same year that Dickinson wrote of her utter loss of regard for what she had once valued in the relationship, she composed "Precious to me she still shall be" Fr 751, in which she vows continued devotion, "Though She forget the name I bear—/ The fashion of the Gown I wear—/ The very color of My Hair—." And in Fr 752, she evokes Susan as "Ah, Teneriffe—Receding Mountain—," brilliant and regal, "Still clad in Your Mail of Ices—/ Eye of Granite—and Ear of Steel—," with whom "We're pleading still—."

Two years before she died, in 1884, she implored her, "Be Sue—while I am Emily—/ Be next—what you have ever been—Infinity" (L 912). Apparently, long after the everyday reality of Sue had utterly disappointed, Dickinson retained a place within herself where she kept alive the ideal of what Sue had once been or seemed to be.

See also "LIKE EYES THAT LOOKED ON WASTES—" and "OURSELVES WERE WED ONE SUMMER—DEAR—."

FURTHER READING

Judith Farr, *Passion*, 165–167; Vivian R. Pollak, *Anxiety of Gender*, 142–143; Richard B. Sewall, *Life*, I, 197–214.

"Of all the Souls that stand create—" (1862) (Fr 279, J 664)

In this extraordinary poem, Dickinson celebrates her performance of the central mystery of love: the selection of a single human soul from the vast pool of possibilities. She who could not claim exclusive right to any single human being in her external life, who stood outside the marriages of those she loved, could, in her poetry, passionately assert her selection of and fidelity to her One.

She declares that she has made her choice with a rhetorical flourish, using the term "stand create" instead of the simpler "created." Moreover, she has "elected," rather than "selected" this soul, much as the Calvinist God she was raised to believe in elects those souls who will receive his grace. Dickinson offers no more reason for her choice than the impenetrable Calvinist deity. She does not enumerate the special virtues of the soul she has chosen. What moves her to speech is the need to declare her eternal commitment to the choice she has made. Thus the poem moves toward the culminating verbal gesture, in an imagined afterlife:

Behold the Atom—I preferred—
To all the lists of Clay!

But an "Atom" has no individuality. What is really being celebrated is the speaker's devotion.

The uncertain syntax of the poem, however, obscures a central point: Is the speaker saying that she will declare her choice *even* in the next life, or that she will not be able to make her announcement *until* the next life? The distinction is pivotal: In the former case, the evocation of an afterlife underscores the enduring nature of the commitment. In the latter, the afterlife is a vision of liberation, when she will finally be able to speak her love, as she could not in her earthly life. While both dynamics are in play, the vision of a purer, less encumbered state of being dominates the center of the poem.

Of the poem's 12 lines, the first two and last two consist of the speaker's declaration that she has selected one soul. In the eight middle lines, four future conditions are posited, in which fetters and veils will be cast away, making visible the naked, triumphant spirit. In the first, "When Sense from Spirit—files away—," assuming that *Sense* refers to the physical senses, body and soul separate at death. Dickinson used the verb *file* in another poem written that same year, Fr 305, "What if I say I shall not wait!," in which it has the meaning of sloughing off mortality: "What if I file this mortal—off—." Yet, Dickinson may have intended a pun here on another meaning of *Sense,* that is, "common sense." At death, the speaker will be able to abandon the sensible caution of not revealing a love that would be socially objectionable, for another woman or for a married man. This is clearly implied in the following line; "And Subterfuge—is done—."

In the next two lines she envisions a future in which past and present "Apart—intrinsic—stand—." Then, in a Shakespearean phrase, the longed-for future becomes a time when "this brief Drama in the flesh" will be "shifted like a Sand." In her eagerness to shrug off these mortal coils, the speaker departs from Dickinson's far more characteristic desire to remain in this world, whatever heaven may have to offer. Even in a poem such as "THERE CAME A DAY—AT SUMMER'S FULL—," in which the lovers have to wait for eternity to be together, the hope of a reunion in the next life is overshadowed by the "Calvaries of Love" endured in this one. In "Of all the Souls that stand create," Dickinson reaches for a materialization of the next world, and, if what she sees is somewhat vague—Figures that show their royal Front, a mist clearing—her images do convey a certainty that the royalty of the spirit, hers and her beloved's, will be revealed.

As the mist parts, the speaker, who has now imaginatively projected herself into the afterlife, asks the reader to behold what she does: "the Atom—I preferred—/ To all the lists of Clay!" In this stunning, unexpected image, the "Soul" of line 1 has become

an "Atom." One might see this, as some critics have, as the poet's failure to extract the beloved from the realm of materiality. But the image is a triumphant one, capturing the paradox that what is a mere atom in the vastness of the physical universe is everything to the speaker in the soul's realm.

This poem demands comparison with "THE SOUL SELECTS HER OWN SOCIETY—," which also speaks to the soul's discrimination. "I've known her—from an ample nation—/ Choose One—," Dickinson writes in that verse, also composed in 1862. Yet the soul's selectivity is evoked negatively, as an exclusion of others, and its conclusion is ominous, suggesting a rigidity and a shutting down of the heart. In contrast, Fr 279 is exuberant, ending with a joyous exclamation of fidelity. Its regular hymn form (alternating four and three foot iambs) and *abcb defe ghih* rhyme scheme reinforce the triumphant message. The poem it resonates with is "*One life of so much consequence!*" (Fr 248, 1861), where Dickinson continues: "Yet I—for it—would pay—/ My soul's *entire income*—/ In ceaseless—salary—." This one life is her "*one Pearl, my Gem . . . Intact—in Diadem!*" In all her poems about the soul's selectivity, images of royalty are prominent. Thus, she concludes this one: "The life is thick—I know it! / Yet—not so dense a crowd—/ But *Monarchs*—are *perceptible*—/ Far down the dustiest Road!"

See also "I CANNOT LIVE WITH YOU—," CONGREGATIONALISM, and PURITAN HERITAGE.

FURTHER READING

Charles R. Anderson, *Stairway,* 192–193; Cristanne Miller, "How 'Low Feet' Stagger," in *Feminist Critics Read Emily Dickinson,* Suzanne Juhasz, ed., 139–140, 154n13; Richard Wilbur, "Sumptuous Destitution," in *Critical Essays,* Judith Farr, ed., 59–60; Cynthia Griffin Wolff, *Emily Dickinson,* 413.

"Of Bronze—and Blaze—" (1862) (Fr 319 J 290)

In this well-known poem, the speaker is propelled into an altered, exalted state of mind by looking at the night sky. Most critics assume that "the North" is a reference to the northern lights, also known as the aurora borealis, spectacular displays of colored light that occur in the night skies around the poles and in northern regions, as a result of solar particles interacting with atmospheric gases. Biographer Cynthia Griffin Wolff, who points out that the North is where God generally keeps His kingdom in Dickinson's work, suggests a significant dimension to the image. She notes, however, that in this poem, "The only thing we can know is the display, which may or may not portend a Presence behind it" (*Emily Dickinson*, 432–433).

Thus, in the luminosity evoked in the first line, it is possible to see a faint reflection of the burning bush of the Book of Exodus, in which God simultaneously reveals and hides himself from Moses. But, if there is a voice that issues from this blaze it is one of indifference to everything but its own glory. The single-syllable words "Bronze" and "Blaze," with their buzzing *b* and *z* sounds, create an almost abstract effect of gleaming color, fire, and tumultuous motion, without identifiable form or boundaries. Lines 3 through 6 evoke an indifferent phenomenon, personified as a "being" who is self-obsessed, regal, and wholly adequate unto itself:

> So adequate—it forms—
> So preconcerted with itself—
> So distant—to alarms—

In the line "So adequate—it forms—," Dickinson uses a transitive verb, "to form," which requires a direct object, intransitively. The meaning here may be reflexive, that is, the bronze and blaze phenomenon "forms itself." But an added effect of this usage is to suggest that the essence of the phenomenon is the process of forming; it is a dynamic, sublime beauty whose sole purpose is self-creation and self-perpetuation. It is *not* the "indifferent Universe," since it is indifferent *to* the Universe as well as the speaker, but something more specific. "Preconcerted" in Dickinson's lexicon means something that has previously been settled, and thus follows its own laws, impervious to anything else. The embedded/root word "concert," with its connotations of music and harmony, carries forward the idea of self-willed, sublime beauty.

Note that lines 6 and 7, "An Unconcern so sovereign / To Universe, or me—," refer to both what precedes and follows them. They describe both the attitude of the bronze and blaze phenomenon and the attitude that rubs off on the speaker. Her "simple spirit" is infected with "Taints of Majesty," an oxymoron, linking low with high, soil or stain with shining grandeur. The phrase encapsulates the speaker's ambivalence toward this change in herself. The next two lines show her expanding to "vaster attitudes" and then immediately taking herself down a peg.

> Till I take vaster attitudes—
> And strut opon my stem—
> Disdaining Men, and Oxygen,
> For Arrogance of them—

She portrays herself as a flower on a stem; this is a self-mocking image, given the restrictions to any free movement, much less strutting, a stem imposes. While Dickinson's frequent self-identifications with flowers in her poems and letters usually point to qualities that she admires, here the flower-speaker's "Arrogance" and disdain of "Men, and Oxygen," once more, express ambivalence. Declaring one's independence from "Men" may reflect an admirable self-sufficiency, but disdaining oxygen can only be fatal for a flower.

In the shorter second stanza, Dickinson introduces a new element into the interplay of the night sky's grandiose beauty and her own simple spirit: her own "Splendors," which, she boasts, are "Menagerie." If her "Splendors" are her poems, then the word "Menagerie," used here as an adjective, refers to their number and variety, while also suggesting that they are alive and wild (since "menagerie," as a noun, is a place where wild animals are kept). She continues:

> But their Competeless Show
> Will entertain the Centuries

Whose competeless show is meant, her poems' or the northern lights'? Some critics opt for the poems/splendors as the referent of "their." Since "splendors" immediately precedes the referent, this is the grammatically correct interpretation. But Dickinson's grammar regularly ignores standard usage. Other scholars, such as Roland Hagenbüchle and

Agnieszka Salska, find an ambiguity, in that 'competeless show' can refer to either the northern lights or the permanence of her own work or both. In "completeless," a neologism formed by adding the suffix "less" to an existing verb, Dickinson follows her frequent practice of turning a verb into an adjective by adding a suffix. One of the mechanisms by which her language attains its distinctive strangeness, the neologism is a form of compression of meaning. "Competeless" evokes the idea of a contest while simultaneously declaring that there *is* no competition. Yet this boasting is undercut by the belittling notion that "they" (whether her splendors/poems or the northern lights) are a mere "show" that "entertains" the centuries. Given her high idea of poetry, it seems unlikely that she would speak of them in this way. The northern lights, on the other hand, are beautiful, but sterile, diffusing a light, unlike the sun's, that cannot nurture life.

Whatever the identity or the limitations of "their competeless show," what matters to the poet is that "they" are immortal, while she is not. An immense sadness enters the poem with the thought that she will be "long ago." By transforming an adverbial phrase that usually modifies an action ("they parted long ago") into an adjective, she essentially *becomes* the faraway past. In the isolation of her mortality, she (her grave) is "An Island in dishonored grass." "Dishonored" contrasts starkly with the grandeur she has just been experiencing; it suggests, not only that she will not be honored in anyone's memory, but also that there is something shameful about death. The only ones who will be aware of her grave are the humble daisies, an image that picks up the idea of the speaker's "simple spirit" and of the speaker herself as a flower. Dickinson wrote frequently of the small, gentle, ubiquitous daisies; she called herself "Daisy," and identified herself with the flower's vulnerability and dependence on the powerful sun.

Recently, critics have discussed this poem within the context of an important new approach to Dickinson's work, which views each poem in terms of its placement in her fascicles. Sharon Cameron, a pioneer in this approach, points out that this poem appears in fascicle 15 directly before "THERE'S A CERTAIN SLANT OF LIGHT," a poem that recognizes the distance between nature and the human response to it. For Cameron, this poem acts as a retort, making clear "that the natural perspective is not the person's perspective and never can be" ("Dickinson's Fascicles," 155). But "Of Bronze—and Blaze—" makes that point, too. There are three major elements/realizations in the poem: the grandeur of the northern lights (nature's immortality), the poet's myriad splendors (her poetry's immortality), and the "Island in dishonored grass" (her personal, physical mortality). None of the three predominates. The subtlety and brilliance of the poem lies in the way that Dickinson keeps these realities in motion around one another, letting each reflect upon and modify the impact of the others.

The poem exhibits a classic alternation in Dickinson's self-image. Both poems and letters are replete with assertions of grandiosity and significance, of authority/self-sufficiency and submissive/dependence. In a poem (Fr 450) written the same year she composed this one, she offers a keen insight into this duality: "The Outer—from the Inner / Derives it's magnitude—/ 'Tis Duke, or Dwarf, according / As is the central mood—." Pitted against nature's cold majesty, these warring aspects of her self-perception—"Duke" and "Dwarf"—battle for predominance, without a clear victor.

See also "I RECKON—WHEN I COUNT AT ALL—," "ON A COLUMNAR SELF—," and MASTER LETTERS.

FURTHER READING

Sharon Cameron, "Dickinson's Fascicles," in *Handbook*, Grabher et al., eds., 152–155; Judith Farr, *Gardens*, 39–40, 110–112, 191–192, and *Passion*, 194–195; Roland Hagenbüchle, "Sign and Process: The Concept of Language in Emerson and Dickinson," 59–88; Cristanne Miller, *Grammar*, 59–63; David Porter, *Early Poetry*, 52–53; Agnieszka Salska, *Walt Whitman and Emily Dickinson*, 80, 176, 183; Gary Stonum, "Dickinson Against the Sublime," 32–35; Cynthia Griffin Wolff, *Emily Dickinson*, 432–434.

"Of Course—I prayed—" (1863) (Fr 581, J 376)

This bitter poem is striking for its unquestioning acceptance of God's existence and equally firm conviction of his indifference:

He cared as much as on the Air
A Bird—had stamped her foot—
And cried "Give Me"—

In another poem written that year, Fr 632, Dickinson writes of the dismal consequences of losing one's faith: "To lose one's faith—surpass / The loss of an Estate—/ Because Estates can be / Replenished—faith cannot—." She goes on to say that one inherits faith when one is born, but once it is lost it cannot be recovered, and afterward: "Being's—Beggary." Despite her lifelong struggles with belief, particularly with respect to the question of whether there is an afterlife, Emily Dickinson seems to have believed intensely in God, but not in his mercy.

The conversational opening of this poem reads like a reply to someone who has asked the speaker whether she has sought solace in prayer. Critic William Shurr believes that the person in question was CHARLES WADSWORTH, the charismatic Presbyterian minister who may have been the man she addressed in letters and poems as "Master," a likely person to have urged her to turn to prayer (*Marriage*, 142–43). Whatever the identity of Dickinson's implied interlocutor, only the first five lines are addressed to him or her, the rest of the poem to God himself.

The thrust of the poem is a denial of Jesus' promise of a loving response to prayer: "Ask, and it shall be given you; seek, and ye shall find . . . for everyone that asketh receiveth; and he that seeketh findeth. . . . Whatsoever ye shall ask in my name, that will I do, that the Father may be glorified in the Son. If you shall ask anything in my name, I will do it (Matthew 7:7–8; John 14:13–14). More than once in her poetry, Dickinson "dismisses prayer as an act of desperation: we resort to it only because face-to-face communication is impossible" (Cynthia Griffin Wolff, *Emily Dickinson*, 262). Thus, in Fr 623, she writes, "Prayer is the little implement / Through which Men reach / Where Presence—is denied them. / They fling their Speech / By means of it—in God's Ear—." In another poem on her attempt to pray, Fr 377, the divine presence is hard to locate: "At least—to pray—is left—is left—/ Oh Jesus—in the Air—/ I know not which thy chamber is—/ I'm knocking everywhere—." And in an undated poem, Fr 1768, in which she speaks of a "disappointing God," she declares: "There comes

an hour when begging stops, / When the long interceding lips / Perceive their prayer is vain."

Dickinson's disillusionment with the efficacy of prayer did not prevent her from recognizing the grounds for gratitude to God: "My Reason—Life—/ I had not had—but for Yourself—." But she declares these gifts insufficient and uncharitable on the part of the giver. She would have been better off if God had left her "in the Atom's Tomb," an oxymoron in which the two words, linked by the sound unit "tom," combine to form an image of the fundamental unit of life as a container for death. In the Atom's tomb, she would have remained, "Merry, and nought, and gay, and numb"—another oxymoron that defies logic but expresses the poet's sense of the blessedness of not feeling. The theme of numbness recurs in her poems, as a merciful state in a world of unbearable pain. (See "AFTER GREAT PAIN, A FORMAL FEELING COMES.") Here she suggests that nonexistence might be preferable to the pain-filled existence to which God's indifference has condemned her. Dickinson's great biographer, Richard B. Sewall, writes of this poem: "She never made a starker statement of a deprived existence" (*Life*, II, 501). Indeed, in a famous poem of deprivation, Dickinson paints herself as one who has been excluded from God's bounty: "GOD GAVE A LOAF TO EVERY BIRD— / But just a crumb to me. . . ." In the demeaning self-image of the poem under discussion she imagines that God sees her as a bird stamping her foot on the air and crying, "Give me!" So insignificant is her request to God, he sends her not even a crumb. In the pun of the final line, in which she declares nonexistence preferable to "this smart Misery," she conveys both the "Smarting" pain of her condition and its basis in her "smart," (intelligent, keen) apprehension of the nature of reality.

See also "I SHALL KNOW WHY—WHEN TIME IS OVER—," "IT'S EASY TO INVENT A LIFE—," "OF GOD WE ASK ONE FAVOR, THAT WE MAY BE FORGIVEN—," and "ONE CRUCIFIXION IS RECORDED—ONLY—."

FURTHER READING

Richard B. Sewall, *Life*, II, 501; William H. Shurr, *Marriage*, 142–143; Cynthia Griffin Wolff, *Emily Dickinson*, 262.

"Of God we ask one favor, that we may be forgiven—" (1885) (Fr 1675, J 1601)

Emily Dickinson was not a respecter of doctrines and the Calvinist doctrine of innate sin, with its belief in a vindictive God lording it over a depraved humanity, was always repugnant to her. In this ironic poem, written the year before her death, when she was ill and bowed by a series of terrible losses, she resurrects those orthodox religious constructs only to dismiss them once more, with renewed bitterness.

The first thing to be noted is that God remains a presence for her, albeit a distant and inscrutable one. From the first line Dickinson makes her disappointment in God clear. Whereas earlier she might have prayed for blessings and rewards—the survival of a loved one, a fulfilled love, the grace of religious faith—now the only "favor" she asks is to be forgiven. Although she doesn't say so explicitly, there is an underlying sense that life has been a punishment, filled with griefs. Why have we/I been punished so? she seems to be asking. And her answer is that we can only presume that God knows, since "The Crime, from us, is hidden—." The surface humility of these lines thinly masks an accusation against God and a profound skepticism that *any* crime could justify the suffering inflicted on humanity.

The poem's central image is the paradoxical one of a humanity "Immured the whole of Life / Within a magic Prison." We are limited in our knowledge, our freedom, and our capacity for attaining what we desire. Dickinson was acutely aware of these limitations and was constantly rattling the bars, if not in the external circumstances of her life, then in her poetic stretching toward what she called CIRCUMFERENCE, the far limits of what poetry can ascertain. But even in this reproachful poem, she is too honest to deny life's ecstasy. The prison is a "magic" one, filled with miracles and wonders. This was the poet who once declared, "I find ecstasy in living—the mere sense of living is joy enough." Dickinson's joy keeps her from total nihilistic despair.

For whatever her disappointment in God's failure to relieve or redeem human suffering, she loved God's world, the earthly "Happiness" that all her life overshadowed the desire for God's heaven, as she declares in the poem's final lines. As a 16-year-old girl, writing to her best friend, ABIAH PALMER ROOT, she recalled a fleeting period of religious belief and confessed "But the world allured me & in an unguarded moment I listened to her syren song. From that moment I seemed to lose my interest in heavenly things by degrees." This preference for earthly things to heavenly ones became a lifelong theme for Dickinson, developed in some of her greatest poems. She always felt that her earthly happiness was an affront to God—the beloved's face "outshone Jesus'" and his love offered her salvation without the pangs of Calvary. By evoking this "reprehensible" happiness at the end of this poem, Dickinson may be doing more than characterizing the human condition; she may be suggesting that the very love of his world is our greatest crime against a jealous God.

See also "I CANNOT LIVE WITH YOU—" and "I SHOULD HAVE BEEN TOO GLAD, I SEE—."

FURTHER READING
Shira Wolosky, *Emily Dickinson*, 117–118.

"On a Columnar Self—" (1863) (Fr 740, J 789)

This is one of a series of poems, including "I'M CEDED—I'VE STOPPED BEING THEIR'S—," "Put up my lute!," and "I shall keep singing!," written between 1861 and 1863, in which Dickinson affirms her sense of inner rightness as a poet and independence from external judgment.

By the time she wrote it, she had already sought responses to her poetry from her literary sister-in-law, SUSAN HUNTINGTON GILBERT DICKINSON, from SAMUEL BOWLES, the editor of *The Springfield Republican*, as well as from THOMAS WENTWORTH HIGGINSON, the editor of *The Atlantic Monthly*, all of whom gave her qualified praise and advice she ultimately rejected.

In Dickinson's time, the great advocate of self reliance was, of course, Ralph Waldo Emerson. However, this proclamation of self-sufficiency reflects the influence of JONATHAN EDWARDS, the great 18th-century Calvinist preacher, whose thinking was central to Dickinson's PURITAN HERITAGE, many of whose spiritual stances she adopted, even as she rejected its theology. Edwards was the great spokesman for the "spirit of sublime self-reliance," who argued passionately for ignoring society's judgments in favor of one's own sense of moral and spiritual rectitude, Dickinson's poetry continually asserts that the essential human reality—the source of genuine experience, whether blissful or painful—is internal: the domain of the self-reliant, resourceful spirit. In the struggle for inner integrity, Dickinson's own greatest resource was her poetic imagination, "the moment of perception, of vision, that imparted to her such a different and unique message" (Seawall, *Life,* I, 24–25).

She develops her notion of self-reliance, in the first two stanzas of this poem, through the architectural image of the self as an unbreakable column. Dickinson, who had studied with the eminent geologist EDWARD HITCHCOCK at AMHERST ACADEMY, was familiar with the mineral world and knew what she was saying when she selected granite, a very hard stone, for the base of her column. The image suggests not rigidity but the unbreakable nature of the base itself and, by extension, of its bond with the shaft. Significantly, the poem does not develop the image of the shaft itself, the vertical section of the column that may rise to great heights. What she can amply rely on is "Conviction—That Granitic Base"—the source of poetry. Conviction, as she uses the word, is not mere thought or idea, but idea grounded in the deepest layer of the spirit. In Dickinson's case, the shaft of the column, consisting of the poems themselves, was rent by conflicting emotions, contradictory impulses, and fluctuating beliefs. They did not express an undivided, harmonious whole, nor did they need to, so long as the base held.

In stanza 2, line 4, and the first two lines of stanza 3, she abandons the architectural metaphor and reverts to a more common image for self-sufficiency: the individual versus the crowd:

Though none be on our side—
Suffice Us—for a Crowd—

Ourself—and Rectitude—

She uses the plurals "our," "Ourself," and "Us" to refer to *any* individual. The first image is of an unsupported self; the second—of a self supported by Rectitude. The hint of self-righteousness in this phrase, so uncharacteristic of this poet who was vehemently averse to doctrine and smugness of any kind, has led some readers to interpret the entire poem as an ironic commentary on those who claim virtue as their exclusive domain.

But the two lines that follow it place the poet's "Rectitude" in an altogether different light: "And that Assembly—not far off/From further Spirit—God—." Here the poet reaches out for a greater authority—the source of her self-sufficiency that is *outside* her. Sewall sees in these lines the poet's attempt to reconcile "those two disparate phases of her being: her love of the God of her fathers and her belief in herself." (*Life,* I, 390). Any reconciliation, however, is incomplete, and, to the extent that it takes place at all, depends upon an intermediate entity, "that Assembly." The way Dickinson breaks the line creates an ambiguity: "that Assembly—not far off" suggests that she is alluding to the heavenly saints, whom she will encounter in an afterlife. But then the enjambment occurs, introducing the idea that "*the Assembly* is not far from God." This suggests that she has in mind the assembly of poets, among whose ranks she counted herself, and which she placed at the apex of all she valued (see "I RECKON—WHEN I COUNT AT ALL—"). In evoking the Assembly that is not far from God, who is "furthest Spirit," Dickinson ends the poem with a paradox. God is both close to her, or at least to those she reveres and counts herself part of, and God is distant. A quality of wistful longing enters the poem, giving it a vital resonance that removes it from any suspicion that it was meant ironically.

FURTHER READING

Sharon Leder and Andrea Abbott, *Language of Exclusion,* 50–51, Richard B. Sewall, *Life,* I, 390.

"One Crucifixion is recorded—only—" (1863) (Fr 670, J 553)

In this well-known poem Dickinson internalizes the Crucifixion of Jesus Christ, taking it out of the realm of history and myth and into the province of unseen, personal suffering. There have been and continue to be many crucifixions since Christ's, she declares, the quiet martyrdoms of countless unknown individuals, whose sufferings no one may have witnessed, but which carry the same overwhelming pain.

Playing with the word "Centre," Dickinson places her key idea at the very center of the poem: "Gethsemane—/Is but a Province—in the Being's Centre—." On one level, this is but a variation of her general conviction that *all* authentic experience lies within. Dickinson is, after all, the poet who advised the explorer Hernando de Soto, "Soto! Explore thyself," reminding him that the mind is the true "Undiscovered Continent" (Fr 814), and who, in a letter to her great friend ELIZABETH LUNA CHAPIN HOLLAND, spoke of "the Landscape of the Spirit." Emily Dickinson granted spatial dimension to the mind and made it the setting for her most significant experience.

For the intensely private Dickinson, there may even have been something indecent about "One Calvary—exhibited to stranger—." When still in her 20s and mixing in society, she once asked her friend EMILY FOWLER (Ford), "if it did not make [her] shiver to hear a great many people talk, they took all the clothes off their souls. . . ." It was a point of honor for her to conceal the depths of her pain, and an enormous relief that the "Cellars of the Soul" were "licensed to be still" ("IT'S HOUR WITH ITSELF").

In this poem, she democratizes crucifixion, envisioning every human life as containing a Calvary. Why there are as many Calvaries as "peninsulas" is mysterious. Dickinson may have chosen the word since, on the level of sound, it resonates with "Persons" and "Province," and semantically it suggests the isolation of a landscape surrounded by water on three sides—almost an island. There is nothing in the least exotic or heroic about such everyday crucifixions, which take place in a "Judea" too near to offer the high adventure of a journey or "Crusade's Achieving."

In the final stanza, Dickinson restates the contrast between the hidden nature of these nearer, newer crucifixions of the many and the public nature of Christ's with the words "Our Lord—indeed—made Compound Witness." The word "Compound" may allude to the fact that Christ's death "made witness" to more than one thing; that is, he gave his life as evidence of God's love and of his transformation of death. It may also mean that there were many witnesses and that his death was offered on behalf of many. Biographer Cynthia Griffin Wolff makes the ingenious suggestion that Dickinson was using the word "compound" in the financial sense: "like compound interest upon a loan, piling up credit upon credit as years pass and increasing numbers of people who find it relevant to their own experience" (*Emily Dickinson*, 457–458).

While Dickinson's vision of human suffering in this poem is thus clear enough, the question of the poem's religious implications remains. Does it belittle the Passion, reducing it to no more than human suffering without the supernatural redemptive power that adheres to it in Christian thinking? Critic Robert Weisbuch reflects the views of most Dickinson scholars when he asserts that Dickinson finds Christ's crucifixion "unique only in that it was made historically public" (*Emily Dickinson's Poetry*, 80–81) and that Christ is no longer the center of time for her. Wolff argues that ". . . when the notion of the Divinity loses its hold on our imagination . . . Christ becomes noteworthy not because He was divine, but because He was human; the meaning of Calvary is defined not by transcendent values, but by earthly ones. . . . The word 'Crucifixion' becomes no more than a trope for extraordinary pain" (*Emily Dickinson*, 457).

Taking an opposing position, scholar Dorothy Huff Oberhaus denies that Dickinson is merely bending biblical imagery to describe her own psychic state. Noting that "Dickinson keeps the Crucifixion of Christ before the reader's attention throughout the poem," she points out that the shape of the poem "is that of the typic cross, its long pentameters and tetrameters the upright post, its short alternating dimeters and monometers the transverse piece" ("Tender Pioneer," 113–114). Oberhaus identifies Dickinson's internalization of biblical texts as characteristic of the great poets of the Bible, including "the epitome of Christian poets," George Herbert (115), whose work Dickinson knew and loved. She bases this view on the observation that biblical poetry tends to move "from inner to outer, from heaven to earth, to the human heart."

While there is no denying that the figure of Christ played a vital role in Dickinson's inner universe, Oberhaus focuses on the poems in which he is sympathetically evoked, as "tender pioneer," "larger lover," or "docile gentleman." Christ, the sacrificed son, was undoubtedly closer to her than was God the distant, arbitrary, and indifferent father. But if Dickinson often turns to him in hope or desperation, she also finds him elusive: "Jesus— in the Air," as she calls him (Fr 377), "I know not which thy chamber is—/ I'm knocking everywhere—." Christ's primary significance to her, as Oberhaus herself points out, is as the sufferer of the Crucifixion, not the Hope of the Resurrection. She identifies herself as one of "Christ's faint Confederates" and alludes to herself as "Empress" and "Queen of Calvary." Another striking instance of this is found in Fr 1760, in which she identifies with Jesus as one who has "drunken without companion . . . the strong cup of anguish." In that poem, which begins with the line "Proud of my broken heart, since thou did'st break it," as in "One crown that no one seeks" (Fr 1759), Dickinson embraces suffering as a kind of triumph and evokes Christ as an emblem of triumph over suffering, "stigma deified."

See also "I LIKE A LOOK OF AGONY," "I SHALL KNOW WHY—WHEN TIME IS OVER—," "OF COURSE— I PRAYED—," and "TITLE DIVINE, IS MINE."

FURTHER READING

Suzanne Juhasz, "The Landscape of the Spirit," in *Critical Essays,* Judith Farr, ed., 130–140; Dorothy Huff Oberhaus, "Tender Pioneer": "Emily Dickinson's Poems on the Life of Christ," in *Critical Essays,* Judith Farr, ed., 113–115; Richard B. Sewall, *Life,* II, 691–692; Robert Weisbuch, *Emily Dickinson's Poetry,* 80–81; Cynthia Griffin Wolff, *Emily Dickinson,* 456–458.

"One need not be a Chamber—to be Haunted—" (1862) (Fr 407, J 670)

In this poem, Dickinson explores the terrain of a divided soul in a new language, tense and immediate, engaged in the very process of fearful discovery. To achieve this, she co-opts the image of the haunted house or chamber, a staple of the Gothic literature that she knew well from her reading of Anne Radcliffe and the Brontë sisters. These tales of the macabre and supernatural characteristically took place in haunted castles, graveyards, ruins, and wild picturesque landscapes and were permeated by a sense of mystery and impending horror. Here, contrasting exterior with interior dangers, Dickinson uses this imagery as a foil for the far greater horror of a hidden self. The apparatus of Gothic terror—its ghosts, abbeys, and hidden assassins—are mere child's play compared to the reality of the enemy within:

> One need not be a Chamber—to be
> Haunted—
> One need not be a House—
> The Brain has Corridors—surpassing
> Material Place—
>
> Far safer, of a midnight meeting
> External Ghost
> Than it's interior confronting—
> That cooler Host—

Dickinson's poetry repeatedly claims a reality for the interior world that is equal to or greater than that of the material world. In a large number of poems, often centered on the image of a house, she asserts that life's greatest riches—truth, freedom, joy, self-respect, creativity, security—are only to be found within (see "I DWELL IN POSSIBILITY—," "ON A COLUMNAR SELF—," "THEY SHUT ME UP IN PROSE—"). But there is also a dark side to the inner realm. As scholar Suzanne Juhasz notes, Dickinson's "architectural vocabulary usually portrays the mind as an enclosed space, its confinement responsible for power and safety, yet also for fearful confrontation" (138). Dickinson was acutely aware of the duality of the inner life. As she says elsewhere, "The Soul unto itself / Is an imperial friend—/ Or the most agonizing Spy / An Enemy—could send—" (Fr 579).

Here she looks at the dark side of that interior realm: at the self of "Corridors," at the "cooler Host," armed, concealed, the self behind the self. The precautions "the Body" takes—borrowing a revolver, bolting a door—are powerless before "a superior spectre—/ Or More—." That scary "Or More—" in the final line creates a sense of fearful suspense, the suspicion that there is something so awful waiting, the mind cannot quite imagine it. Just what that may be we are never told. Dickinson was anything but a confessional poet, inclined to share precise biographical details with her readers. What is frightening is not the *content* of what is hidden but *the very fact* that it is hidden or "repressed," as we would say in modern psychological jargon. What "Should startle most" is the awareness that what is concealed is not something "out there" but a part of our own being: "ourself behind ourself." Sigmund Freud might well have used this poem as an epigraph to his writings on the subconscious.

In a later poem (1874), "I never hear that one is dead" (Fr 1325), Dickinson reprises this theme, dispensing with the Gothic dramatization:

I do not know the man so bold
He dare in lonely Place
That awful stranger Consciousness
Deliberately face—

Fearful as the confrontation might be, however, as a poet, Dickinson herself chose to deliberately face the awful stranger, to enter the haunted chamber of the self. She once wrote a one-line letter to her literary mentor, THOMAS WENTWORTH HIGGINSON, "Nature is a Haunted House—but Art—a House that tries to be haunted" (L 459A, 1876). Like nature, which for Dickinson recedes further from one's grasp the closer one approaches, the far reaches of human consciousness are ulti-

mately unknowable. Yet the artist's task, indeed her compulsion, is to create "a House that tries to be haunted," that is, to go as far as possible into the realm of the knowable, thereby recreating the experience of awe and mystery. Despite her healthy respect for the perils of self-confrontation, she was continually drawn to what Weisbuch calls "the dangerous authentic feeling" (222), urging both herself and her reader: "IF YOUR NERVE, DENY YOU—/ Go above your Nerve—" (Fr 329, J 292).

See also "ME FROM MYSELF—TO BANISH—," "'TIS SO APPALLING—IT EXHILIRATES—," "WHAT MYSTERY PERVADES A WELL!" and CIRCUMFERENCE POEMS.

FURTHER READING

Joanne Feit Diehl, "Emerson, Dickinson, and the Abyss," in *Modern Critical Views*, Harold Bloom, ed., 145–159; Suzanne Juhasz, "The Landscape of the Soul," in *Critical Essays*, 130–140; Robert Weisbuch, "Prisming," in *Handbook*, Grabher et al., eds., 197–223.

"Ourselves were wed one summer—dear—" (1863) (Fr 596, J 631)

In this poem, spoken to a beloved woman, Dickinson looks back to the summer of their love from a present in which each woman has sealed a bond with someone else. Although this was not one of the poems sent to her, most scholars assume that it is addressed to her girlhood friend and later sister-in-law, SUSAN HUNTINGTON GILBERT DICKINSON, Three different unions are interwoven within its four stanzas. The first is the "marriage" of the speaker and the beloved woman "one summer." The second is the beloved woman's marriage to a man, described as her "Vision" or "crowning" in June. In point of fact, Susan and Emily's brother, WILLIAM AUSTIN DICKINSON, were married on July 1, 1856. Dickinson's "adjustment" of the date reveals something of her method, in which autobiographical particulars are subsumed in universal imagery. Similarly, in the poem's third union, between the speaker and a subsequent love, this new beloved is described only as "Some one carrying a Light—," who overtakes her "in the Dark—/ Where You had put me down—". By the time she wrote this poem, Dickinson had apparently experienced a great passion for a male lover, whom she called "Master." In scholar Judith Farr's interpretation, this poem offers testimony that "it is the anger and pain occasioned by being jilted by the female lover (who marries) that drive the speaker to accede to Master's rescuing love" (*Passion*, 110). Although we know nothing more about the individual in question, images of a light bearer are frequently present in Dickinson's evocations of the beloved man. "I—too—received the Sign—," she declares, in a line that resonates with her famous 1861 poem, when she calls herself "The Wife without the Sign" ("TITLE DIVINE, IS MINE"). For the speaker's "wifehood" is of quite a different nature from the other woman's:

'Tis true—Our Futures different lay—
Your Cottage—faced the sun—
While Oceans—and the North must be—
On every side of mine

'Tis true—your Garden led the Bloom,
For mine—in Frosts—was sown—

Knowing what we do of Emily's and Susan's lives, it is difficult not to read these lines as Dickinson's contrasting of Sue's legal wifehood and subsequent bearing of children with her own veiled and illicit love, which can bear no fruit. Sue's is a sun-filled, domestic fate, while the speaker's is surrounded by the vast wilderness of "Oceans"—vaster, more mysterious, but comfortless and infinitely more frightening. For critic Vivian Pollak, the imagery evoking the speaker's fate "symbolizes a lesser triumph over sterility, because she never effectively renounced her love for Sue, transferred her affection to anyone else, or recovered from Sue's betrayal of her" (*Anxiety of Gender*, 142). While Sue's lifelong primacy for the poet is debatable, in this poem at least the female beloved continues to dominate the speaker's consciousness. In the final two lines, her thoughts return her to the brief season when they shared the same royal status. The lingering anguish

of her loss is palpable, as she once more, as in the first two lines, juxtaposes the summer when they were "Queens" and the June when the beloved woman was "crowned," while she was dethroned.

See also "LIKE EYES THAT LOOKED ON WASTES—" and "YOU CONSTITUTED TIME—."

FURTHER READING

Judith Farr, *Passion*, 110–111; Vivian A. Pollak, *Anxiety of Gender*, 141–142.

"Pain—has an Element of Blank—" (1863) (Fr 760, J 650)

Some of Dickinson's most incisive poems are explorations of the nature of pain and its variants: affliction, agony, anguish, despair, grief, loss, misery, and suffering. She came at the subject from many directions, enlisting her genius as thinker and image-maker to approach its nature, its power, and the process by which it transforms human consciousness. Far from narrowly cerebral, her "meditations" on pain are suffused with the passion and authenticity that can only have come from deeply felt experience. In composing them, she must have transcended, at least momentarily, both the chaos and blindness she identified as pain's markers.

When Dickinson explores pain in spatial terms, as she does in "A NEARNESS TO TREMENDOUSNESS—," she conceives of it as something without boundaries: "It's Location / Is Illocality—." When she approaches the subject in temporal terms, she sees pain as something that both contracts time and expands it (Fr 833, 1864): "Gamuts of Eternities / Are as they were not—," she writes in that poem, expressing the essential idea of "Pain—has an Element of Blank—." As scholar Sharon Cameron conceives it, Dickinson expresses her defeat by pain as a breakdown of temporal sense: "'Blank—' is the renunciation of temporal category, the lapse of memory that makes the present the be-all and end-all, the defunct imagination that cannot be required to think beyond what is" (*Lyric Time*, 162).

Dickinson wrote several poems on the "blankness" entailed in suffering. In some, such as "I TIE MY

HAT—I CREASE MY SHAWL—," a kind of blankness is inherent in the numbing, saving power of daily routine. In others, including "From Blank to Blank—" (Fr 484), "There is a Languor of the Life" (Fr 552), and "There is a pain—so utter—" (Fr 515), feeling is "swallowed up" when the sufferer can tolerate no more. The ensuing blankness, while a form of death, is also a tool of survival, at least temporarily, during the moments when pain is so new and so acute the soul could not bear it without a good deal of blunting.

The notion of an "Element of Blank" seems contradictory, until, as Cameron notes, it turns out that it is the *only* element of pain: a self-immersion so complete it can conceive of nothing beyond itself. Dickinson conveys this by equating the Pain and the person/sufferer; indeed, imagistically, she replaces the sufferer with his pain. For it is Pain that takes over the person's role of remembering and anticipating a future—and finds itself incapable of doing either:

It has no Future—but itself
It's Infinite contain
It's Past—

Note that she accords it (Pain) not an "Infinity," but only an "Infinite"—a word that can be used as a noun, but which, in this case, functions as an adjective: "It's Infinite Past." (Note, too, that Dickinson incorrectly uses the contracted form "it's" for the possessive). What Pain has is an "Infinite Past," a hell-on-earth in which the same torment endlessly repeats itself.

In the final line and a half, she employs an ellipsis, omitting the subject-predicate, "Pain is," before the complement ". . . enlightened to perceive. . . ." The effect is to stress the predominance of process. The word "enlightened" is used ironically, for what Pain is "enlightened" to perceive is only more of itself. As Cameron observes, "The last line is also a play on the sense of 'Period—' as end, here duration and absolute finality being hideously interchangeable" (*Lyric Time,* 162).

See also "AFTER GREAT PAIN, A FORMAL FEELING COMES—," "I FELT A FUNERAL, IN MY BRAIN," "I LIKE A LOOK OF AGONY," and "THE HEART ASKS PLEASURE—FIRST—."

FURTHER READING

Charles Anderson, "Despair," in *Modern Critical Views,* Harold Bloom, ed., 9–35; Sharon Cameron, *Lyric Time,* 161–162; Cynthia Griffin Wolff, *Emily Dickinson,* 470–472.

"Publication—is the Auction" (1863) (Fr 788, J 709)

By the mid-19th century, writing had shifted from a leisure pastime into a paid profession subject to the laws of the market, and a writer's reputation depended on an unpredictable literary economy. Dickinson's famous poem, a high-minded refusal to subjugate her creative vision to the demands of this literary marketplace, is both a personal declaration and a sermon. Her Puritan forebears used economic analogies to speak of divine things, in order to demonstrate that "this world is a sign for the next world and material success a sign for spiritual grace" (Shira Wolosky, "Being in the Body," 137). Dickinson takes this tradition in an altogether different direction. By applying the language of economic transaction to poetry and publication, she evokes the debased state to which spiritual activity is reduced when it becomes entangled with materiality and thus subject to a world whose values are not its own.

The speaker's moral passion dictates the formal elements of the poem: its emphatic trochaic meter (feet of one stressed, one unstressed syllable), unusual in her verse; the sputtering broken syntax, to be examined below; and above all, the pattern of imagery built upon a tension between the language of economic transaction ("Auction," "invest," "sell," "Parcel," "Merchant," and "Price"), and the vocabulary of the spiritual realm ("Mind of Man," "White," "White creator," "Snow," "Royal Air," "Heavenly Grace," "Human Spirit," and "Disgrace"). Binding these two semantic groups is the voice of the speaker, with her elitist, royal "we," who pretends to speak for humanity as a whole in her moral judgments and imperatives.

Because this poem was written in the midst of the Civil War, readers have assumed that the opening image of an auction is an allusion to a slave market. Certainly, a parallel between the merchandising of literature and the trade in human beings is present in the poem's fundamental tenet that the value of a human being cannot be measured by economic yardsticks. Whether Dickinson was making a consciously antislavery statement is more doubtful, however, particular in light of her repeated usage of the word "White" in stanza 2 to signify holiness and spiritual integrity. Critic Domhnall Mitchell believes that Dickinson's image refers to the practice, common in her day, of auctioning the goods of someone who is bankrupt, in order to defray a portion of his debts. He suggests that "publication for Dickinson is equivalent to a public stripping of assets and dignity, in the sense that it calls into question the social and/or literary status of the person doing the publishing/selling" ("Social Class," 199).

Supporting this interpretation is the caveat in lines 3 and 4 of stanza 1, following the opening declaration, that poverty (alone) justifies "so foul a thing" as publishing. Yet immediately after conceding that the poor may be excused, she retreats a step in the first word of stanza 2, "Possibly." She in any case would not stoop that low even if she were poor:

Possibly—but We—would rather
From Our Garret go
White—unto the White Creator—
Than invest—our Snow—

To paraphrase, the speaker would prefer to live in a garret all her life and die/meet God in a state of innocence than to soil her innocence / gift ("Snow") in financial dealings. Identifying her soul with divinity, she will go "White—unto the White Creator." The Nobility of this stance is somewhat lessened when we consider that Dickinson was *not* poor. As the daughter of a wealthy man, she never lived in a garret or was forced to write for money. The poem demeans those, like her literary friend HELEN FISKE HUNT JACKSON, who did.

Nonetheless, though it involved no financial sacrifice, Dickinson's refusal to publish *was* principled, and her indignation in this poem is real. Its vehemence seems to build in stanzas 3 and 4, as she struggles, not entirely successfully, to give it form. The fractured syntax and unconventional verb forms makes these stanzas confusing. Stanza 3 may be paraphrased as follows: "Thought comes from God ('Him who gave it') and belongs first to him and, secondarily, to the one who gives thought a material form, that is, who incarnates thoughts in words ('Him Who bear / It's Corporeal illustration')." By the latter, she can only mean the poet, here referred to with the same designation ("Him") as the deity. The word *bear* suggests that the poet suffers this act, much as Christ suffered his incarnation. The use of the uninflected verb forms *belong* and *bear,* rather than the correct *belongs* and *bears* may indicate the poet's desire to suggest the universality of these acts.

The reader may have a difficult time in following the poem's logic when, after this unconventional verb usage, there is a dash and, in the final word of line 3, a shift from the declarative to the imperative form: "—sell / The Royal Air // In the Parcel—Be the Merchant / Of the Heavenly Grace—." At first (and possibly second) reading, the sanctioning of these "economic activities" seems to contradict all that the poem has been saying. But these are the "permitted," unavoidable reductions of the divine spirit as it passes through the intermediary of the poet. The Parcel of the poem can only contain a bit of the Royal Air; the merchant-poet can only be the middleman of Heavenly Grace, in that his work only passes it on by reflecting it. Dickinson is saying that the divine spirit cannot help but be reduced in the transaction from the ineffable to the effable. It is only the Human Spirit that must not be reduced "To Disgrace of Price" by subsequent artistic compromise.

Dickinson had not always taken this view. Judging from her early correspondence, as a young poet she entertained hopes of publication and subsequent fame. But by the time she wrote this poem, she already had some idea of what she would encounter in the publishing world. She was disillusioned by the "mangling" (by alterations made to suit popular convention in rhyme and imagery) of her poems in the *Springfield Republican* in 1861 and 1862. In a letter to THOMAS WENTWORTH HIGGINSON, whom she had petitioned to become her literary mentor, she reported. "Two Editors of Journals [possibly SAMUEL BOWLES and JOSIAH HOLLAND, of the *Republican*] came to my Father's House this winter—and asked me for my Mind—and when I asked them 'Why,' they said I was penurious—and they would use it for the World" (L 261, April 25, 1862). When Higginson advised her to delay publishing, she assured him that publishing was "as foreign to my thought, as Firmament to Fin—" (L 265, June 1, 1862). The disavowal rings somewhat hollow, however, in light of the fact that she had written to him in response to an article advising young poets on how to publish. Initially, then, she vacillated in her repudiation of worldly fame.

Her ultimate stance against publishing was motivated by many factors, almost certainly including her father's extreme disapproval of women who showed a public face. As her genius matured, so did her notion that internal standards of worth and fame were the only ones that mattered. Thus, in an 1862 poem, Fr 481, "Fame of Myself, to justify," she declares: "All other Plaudit be / Superfluous—." Fifteen years later, she was of the conviction that "To earn it by disdaining it/ Is Fame's consummate Fee—" (Fr 1445, 1877). As a poet for whom writing was a high spiritual calling, she shared her work with her "select society" of intimates. Critics such as Martha Nell Smith have proposed that, both in her LETTERS and in her creation of manuscript books or fascicles, Dickinson was engaging in her own form of publication.

See also "A NARROW FELLOW IN THE GRASS," "I'M NOBODY! WHO ARE YOU?" EDWARD DICKINSON, and PUBLICATION AND EDITORIAL SCHOLARSHIP.

FURTHER READING

Charles R. Anderson, *Stairway*, 66–70; Domhnall Mitchell, "Emily Dickinson and Class," in *Cambridge Companion*, 199–202; Shira Wolosky, "Being in the Body," in *Cambridge Companion*, 136–138.

"Rearrange a 'Wife's' Affection!"(1861) (Fr 267, J 1737)

This declaration of eternal, immovable devotion was recorded on the same sheet as Fr 266, "What

would I give to see his face?" The Dickinson family refused to publish it and destroyed the original, although fortunately not before Dickinson's first editor, MABEL LOOMIS TODD, made a copy of it. By their action, the family made clear their view of the poem as a scandalous revelation of a hidden love affair.

Critic Jane Eberwein suggests that the poem could be read as "a dramatic monologue addressed by a secretly pledged 'wife' to her skeptical 'husband' who may even be trying to escape from their tie by questioning her continued love" (*Dickinson*, 106). The physically grotesque images of stanza 1 declare the kind of transformation the speaker would have to undergo before her "'Wife's' Affection" could be altered. The notions of having her brain dislocated and her "freckled Bosom" amputated, while growing a man's beard are more than hyperbolic fancies, the most extreme tests she can think of to demonstrate her fidelity. They say pointedly, "I could feel differently about you only if I stopped being a sentient being and a woman." The passive voice, in which "they" do these things to her casts her in the role of love's unswerving martyr, prefiguring the theme of mingled devotion and pain that is developed later in the poem.

In the second stanza, she commands both her spirit and flesh, her "unacknowledged clay," to "blush," perhaps because of all that "Seven years of troth" have taught them about love, both spiritual and carnal. If "seven years" were the length of an actual relationship in the poet's life, it would have begun in 1854. Biographer Alfred Habegger, who believes that CHARLES WADSWORTH, the hypnotic Presbyterian minister, was the great love of Emily Dickinson's life and the man she called "Master" in poems and letters, tries to connect the time designation to her first meeting with him. He writes, "If we move [the date of the poem] to early 1862 and take the seven years literally—two big ifs— the originating event (heavily fantasized) could be assigned to March 1855, when Dickinson was in Philadelphia" (Habegger, *My Wars*, 414), where she met Wadsworth.

Judith Farr, on the other hand, who believes this is a poem written to Master, identifies the beloved man as SAMUEL BOWLES, who came into Dickinson's life almost four years later, when he began to be a regular visitor at The EVERGREENS. Farr makes no attempt to connect the "seven years" to Bowles in any literal sense, and, indeed, it seems far more likely that Dickinson's use of the phrase is symbolic. She is probably alluding to the biblical story of Jacob who works for Laban for seven years, in order to obtain his beloved: "And Jacob served seven years for Rachel; and they seemed unto him *but* a few days, for the love he had to her" (Genesis 29:19). Seven years is the biblical time span of indentured labor required to "earn" the beloved. It is interesting to recall that Jacob is deceived by Laban, who gives him his eldest daughter, Leah, instead, and requires him to work yet another seven years for Rachel. Is Dickinson implying that her seven years of troth (fidelity) have not brought her what she was promised? In any case, this "Troth" of loyalty and its faithful execution is here contrasted with Wifehood—not in quotation marks this time, as in line 1, but used in the literal sense of wifely status, which the speaker, of course, does not have.

In the next three stanzas, a series of nouns define the many facets of that troth: "Love," "Trust," "Constancy," "Anguish," "Burden," "Secret." In every line of the third stanza constancy is linked to pain (constricting, searing, without anything to dull it):

Love that never leaped it's socket—
Trust intrenched in narrow pain—
Constancy thro' fire—awarded—
Anguish—bare of anodyne!

This love is wedged into a "socket," some hollow place in her being that would yawn emptily without it. In one more image evoking physical mutilation (a dislocated bone or gouged-out eye), Dickinson suggests that the love is trapped in her; it has "never leaped it's socket," that is, burst free of its inner confines into external expression.

In stanza 4, the emphasis shifts to love as a triumphant burden. In a permutation of her self-image as "Empress of Calvary" (*see* "TITLE DIVINE, IS MINE") she evokes the crown of "Thorns" she wears during the day, which may signify daytime as well as her earthly life, and the diadem she exchanges it for after *Sunset,* signifying both night and eter-

nity, when she has passed beyond mortal eyes to another life. By comparing her sufferings with those of Christ, she suggests both nocturnal trysts with the beloved and divine transfiguration after death.

The hidden nature of her love is carried forward in the last stanza, in the key line: "Big my Secret but it's *bandaged*—" What is bandaged is wounded, but covered, contained, not visible to the eyes of others. The speaker can live with it, albeit in anguish. The line "It will never get away" picks up the idea that her love is imprisoned within her soul, "it's Weary Keeper," who will carry it with her "through the Grave" to her beloved "husband." (Note that Dickinson changes the referent of "thee" in this final line; in the second stanza "thee" refers to her "spirit" and "unacknowledged clay"). Habegger offers a unique interpretation of the poem's "daring fifth stanza" as suggesting a kind of emotional pregnancy, "where the betrothed speaker, seduced and abandoned, big with her secret, leads it as a small child to a heavenly reunion with her lover" (414).

To the end of her days, Emily Dickinson doubted the reality of life beyond death. Nonetheless, the consoling hope of a reunion beyond the grave with a beloved denied her in this life was a leitmotif of many of her love poems. Notably, in "THERE CAME A DAY—AT SUMMER'S FULL—" the mingled notions of "troth," wifehood, and love's crucifixion recur: "Sufficient troth—that we shall rise—/ Deposed—at length—the Grave—/ To *that* New Marriage—/ Justified—through Calvaries of Love!"

Finally, there is another important level of meaning suggested by the poem's imagery. The speaker of this poem exchanges her thorns for a crown at sunset, and it was at night that Emily Dickinson turned the key to her room and entered into the vast, secret kingdom where she wrote her poetry. Thus, the constancy Dickinson celebrates here may signify her consoling devotion to her art. Sandra M. Gilbert relates the "bandaged secret" to the white dress Dickinson wore from the early 1860s until she died, which symbolized her retreat from external affairs into the world of her poetry. She writes, "Through this artful bandage, this cloth that both shrouds and stanches, conceals and reveals, the mysterious poet of transformation converts absence into presence, silence into speech, in the same way that Christ, through *his* mysteries, converted thorns into jewels, bread and wine into flesh and blood, death into life" ("Wayward Nun," 31–32).

Biographer Robert B. Sewall also sees the poem as a pledge of fidelity to the poet's inner quest. He notes that the image of thorns comes, "not so much from the Gospels as from *The Imitation of Christ*" by Thomas à Kempis, a book that exhorted readers to "Despise the world" and "Take refuge within the closet of thine heart." (*Life*, II, 692). For Dickinson, who was deeply influenced by this work, fidelity that is its own reward, whether to one she loved or to her poetry, was a pivotal enabling idea that she returned to frequently in such poems as "A SOLEMN THING—IT WAS—I SAID," "A WIFE—AT DAYBREAK—I SHALL BE," and "I CANNOT LIVE WITH YOU."

See also "ONE CRUCIFIXION IS RECORDED—ONLY."

FURTHER READING

Jane Eberwein, *Dickinson*, 106–108; Judith Farr, *Passion*, 232–233; Sandra M. Gilbert, "Wayward Nun," in *Critical Essays*, Judith Farr, ed.; Alfred Habegger, *My Wars*, 299, 413–425; Richard B. Sewall, *Life*, II, 688–694.

"Rehearsal to Ourselves" (1863) (Fr 664, J 379)

In this famously shocking poem, Dickinson employs paradox and hyperbole to construct her challenge to an insupportable loss. "Rehearsal" in this instance does not mean anticipation of or preparation for a future "performance," but the reliving, through memory, of what has already been: "a Withdrawn Delight." She calls the great self-torturing pleasure this gives "a Bliss like Murder—/ Omnipotent—Acute—." Paradoxically, there is boundless, intense, blissful power in the act of "killing oneself" over and over again with the reminder of what one has lost. Hyperbolically, both the loss and the act of remembering it are presented as "murders," for in the last line the speaker, generalized as "We," says that she has died. But in the original murder, she was the passive victim of whoever withdrew

the delight; since Dickinson uses the passive "withdrawn," the actor is never named. In the subsequent, repeated murders of memory, however, she is the omnipotent murderer, who does herself in over and over again. The "Bliss like Murder" the speaker feels as she repeatedly stabs herself with the dirk (dagger), in part, conveys the murderous anger she feels at her deprivation.

Why is it that "We love the Wound"? Are we simply masochists or, more complexly, sadomasochists? It is easy to see such perversions in this line, but to do so is to miss a far deeper source for valuing pain: Without the memory/rehearsal of the wound, we are emotionally dead—without even the memory that we have died. Reviving the wound is the only way we have to feel, to stave off the state of numbness "After great pain," which Dickinson evokes in some of her finest poems, including two written the same year as "Rehearsal to Ourselves." In Fr 760, "Pain has an Element of Blank," she describes the kind of anguish that "cannot recollect / When it begun—Or if there were / A time when it was not—." Similarly, in Fr 515, she describes "a pain—so utter—" "It swallows substance up—/ Then covers the Abyss with Trance—/ So Memory can step / Around—across—upon it—." Memory, as personified in this poem, walks like a person "in a Swoon," and the speaker acknowledges the prudent self-preservation in such avoidance. In a startling image, in which Memory becomes a skeleton, she tells us that full consciousness of pain would "drop Him—Bone by Bone—." By comparison, "Rehearsal to Ourselves" is a feistier poem, insisting that wounds and repeated self-mutilations are preferable to a living death. Dickinson's poetry repeatedly proclaims her unending fidelity to what she loves. In the absence of that love object, she will remain faithful to the memory of losing it:

> We will not drop the Dirk—
> Because We love the Wound
> The Dirk Commemorate—Itself
> Remind Us that We died—

The final stanza is complicated by grammatical and syntactic peculiarities. For one thing, Dickinson uses the uninflected forms of the verbs, "commemorate" and "remind" instead of the grammatically correct "commemorates" and "reminds," a usage that may suggest a universality to the action in question. Second, the lines "The Dirk Commemorate—Itself / Remind Us that We died—" are examples of what scholar Cristanne Miller has dubbed "syntactic doubling," in which a word or phrase may play a role in more than one syntactic unit (*Grammar,* 67). Is "commemorate" an uninflected verb or an adjective? Is it the predicate of the syntactic unit, or modifier to the subject? In other words, either of the following paraphrases is possible: "The Dirk commemorates itself, reminds us that we died." Or: "The commemorate[d] Dirk, (which is the wound) itself reminds us that we died."

Does "Itself" refer to the dirk or to the wound? Critic Sharon Cameron points out that if "Itself" refers to the wound, "the recollection is still fatal, but it is not, as in the first, futile. Since the fatality is caused by the loss—rather than by the recollection of the loss—it is compensated by being also caused by the "Bliss" associated with the loss, and inevitably recollected at the same time." For Cameron, Dickinson's use of dashes, instead of conventional punctuation, makes it impossible to resolve this question: "The dashes permit, even insist on, these overlapping, disparate meanings, suggesting both the futility of recollection and its compensations." ("Dickinson's Fascicles," 146). Memory as life-source and as murderer is one in the same.

FURTHER READING

Sharon Cameron, "Dickinson's Fascicles," in *Handbook,* Grabher et al., eds., 14; Sharon Cameron, *Lyric Time,* 143–144; Cristanne Miller, *Grammar,* 67.

"Remorse—is Memory— awake—" (1863) (Fr 781, J 744)

In this powerful DEFINITION POEM, Dickinson explores one of the fundamental human emotions in universal terms, but through language and imagery that convey the pain of lived experience. In discussing the poem, biographer Richard B. Sewall associates it with regrets arising from her early love for SUSAN HUNTINGTON GILBERT DICKINSON, and its painful evolution. "At the center of Emily Dickinson's being," he writes, "must have been the gnawing realization of an early mistake in judgment, hers as well as Austin's; a youthful affinity that came to nothing; the lifelong suffering to which that mistake had condemned her brother; and the tension and anxiety it had brought them all" (*Life,* I, 233). The speculation is intriguing as it reflects on the poet's life. Yet, like so much of Dickinson's work, and particularly her large number of wisdom poems, this poem transcends whatever specific experience may have motivated it and stands as a self-contained statement.

"Statement," however, is no doubt too pat a term for the encoded, evolving definition rendered. The first two stanzas develop an internal drama, in which Memory plays the central role, while the third shifts the discussion to God's role and responsibility. While those seeking consistency in Dickinson's poetic thought will be disappointed, readers willing to accept Robert Weisbuch's suggestion that Dickinson is a poet who never stops thinking and shows us the movement of her thought will find this a fascinating journey.

We gain some insight into Dickinson's method by asking, "How would the poem be different if she had written, "Remorse is evoked by awakened memory, when we vividly recall past acts"? Presented in this expository way, the thought conveyed is nothing more than thought, devoid of emotional resonance. By personifying Remorse and Memory and the Presence of Departed Acts, the poet creates the drama of a startling and painful awakening in the middle of the night. Instead of being told that the speaker's own sleep has been disturbed, we are given an image, parallel to and probably motivated by that disturbance. Memory, which has been sleeping, is jarred by the arrival of unexpected visitors at window and door. The "Parties all astir—" in this house of the soul may be merely "interested parties" or, as Dickinson's dictionary records, "disputants" on "opposite sides" of an issue. The agitation and inner conflict stirred by the sudden arrival, as well as a sense of immediacy, are enhanced by the use of dashes, in place of a connecting verb ("Her Parties *are* all astir *as they see* "A Presence of Departed Acts—"). Of course, the lack of logical connection also leaves open the possibility that the disputing parties *are* the departed acts themselves. Instead of a neat, one-to-one correspondence between images and what they represent, Dickinson achieves a sense of upheaval and disorientation.

Thus, in stanza 2, although the implication is that the Departed Acts have broken into the house and lit the fire by which the soul's past may be read, the events are told in passive voice:

> It's Past—set down before the Soul
> And lighted with a match—

Ostensibly, the match of memory has the benign purpose of making the soul's past easier to read ("Perusal—to facilitate—"). The phrase can only be tongue-in-cheek, since if the past is a paper to be read then setting a match to it will ignite a conflagration. The second purpose of the match, "And help Belief to stretch—" may simply allude to the soul's enhanced ability to see—and thus to believe—the painful truths of memory. But another, more terrible meaning is suggested in the poem's final line, when Remorse is equated with Hell.

For in the third and final stanza, the nocturnal scene vanishes in flame and a new definition of remorse is given, far darker than the first. Remorse is an incurable disease that "Not even God—can heal—." In this final twist of thought, God is not merely helpless to cure the disease; he is helpless because he has caused it. If we assume that the God of this stanza is the traditional sin- and guilt-obsessed Christian deity, then there is no mystery as to why remorse is his "Institution." But remorse is not wholly identical with guilt (the knowledge of one's wrongdoing); it is rather the *feeling* incited by guilt. Dickinson's *Webster's* defines it as "the keen pain or anguish excited by a sense of guilt; compunction of conscience for a crime committed." It is closer to regret or self-reproach, and the "crime" in question may be no more than a mistake in judgment or a misguided emotion. On the experiential level, remorse results from wishing we could do something differently from the way we have done it. Yet life, God's "Institution," is so structured that we don't get a second chance. The speaker's bitterness toward God is related not to any theological association of God and sin but to the tormenting manner in which he has arranged existence. Thus if remorse is hell, as the poem's final definition insists, it is one of Dickinson's definitions of "hell on earth." One thinks of the famous final couplet of "MY LIFE CLOSED TWICE BEFORE IT'S CLOSE;" ("Parting is all we know of Heaven / And all we need of Hell"). As in the lines in "I CANNOT LIVE WITH YOU—" where she envisions separation from the beloved who is saved in the next life, while she is not, the hell she dreads is the internal one ("That self—were Hell to me—").

Guilt, on either the religious or psychological plane, has no substantial place in Dickinson's poetry. (Indeed, to discern its presence, one would have to take John Cody's psychoanalytic approach and see her poems of renunciation as veiled expressions of self-punishment motivated by oedipal guilt for her murderous impulses). For those who prefer to take Dickinson at her word, it is difficult to discern the pervasive presence of guilt. Thus, an 1863 poem, Fr 793, "My Soul—accused me—and I quailed—" is less a meditation on guilt than on the soul's autonomy in determining its own worth. And in a later poem, Fr 1660, 1884, "Who is it seeks my Pillow Nights—," she dismisses "Conscience," with its warnings of the traditional Hell ("the phosphorous of God") as "Childhood's Nurse."

The year before she died, Dickinson wrote, with thinly disguised bitterness:

> Of God we ask one favor, that we may be
> forgiven—
> For what, he is presumed to know—
> The Crime, from us, is hidden—
>
> (Fr 1675, 1885)

Hers is not a poetry of guilt, but it *is* memory-haunted and saturated with the presence of loss. Awareness of the impossibility of returning, of redoing, or repossessing comprised a dreaded but frequently revisited circle in her personal inferno.

See also "EDEN IS THAT OLD FASHIONED HOUSE" and "I YEARS HAD BEEN FROM HOME."

FURTHER READING

Sharon Cameron, *Lyric Time*, 35–36; Richard B. Sewall, *Life*, I, 233; Robert Weisbuch, *Emily Dick-*

insⁿ *Poetry,* 2–3, 119; Shira Wolosky, *Emily Dickinson,* 77–78.

"Renunciation—is a piercing Virtue—" (1863) (Fr 782, J 745)

In this searing DEFINITION POEM, Dickinson explores the price of "renunciation" in short, halting lines, that give the sense that she is moving with difficulty, unwillingly, from one thought to the next. Although there is no stanza break, the poem has a two-part division, each of which spins out a single sentence definition: "Renunciation—is a piercing Virtue," and "Renunciation—is the Choosing." The words "piercing Virtue" evoke the image of Christ on the cross and introduce the notion of sacrifice of this world for a higher reality. This theme is continued in the next lines: "The letting go / A Presence—for an Expectation—/ Not now—."

"Not now—" may also be read as a plea for postponement of "The putting out of Eyes—," a "renunciation" even worse than relinquishment of the present for the expectation of an unspecified future reward. To Dickinson, blinding was a particularly horrible form of self-mutilation. Her world-observing, book-reading eyes were her most vital connections to life. She was forced to give up reading for eight months in 1864, because of eye problems that developed in September 1863, and later wrote of this restriction as "the only [woe] that ever made me tremble. It was the shutting out of the dearest friends of the soul—BOOKS. The Medical man . . . might as well have said, 'Eyes be blind,' 'heart be still'" (Sewall, *Lyman Letters,* 76).

Her horror at this sacrifice is quickly muted in the next lines, where she turns to natural imagery: "Just Sunrise—/ Lest Day—/ Day's Great Progenitor—/ Outvie." These lines express a recurrent theme in her life and work—her sense that "Day"—*this* world in its full glory—is more alluring than God, its Creator, and his promise of a life to come. As a young girl, she wrote to her friend ABIAH PALMER ROOT, "it is hard for me to give up the world" (L 23, May 16, 1848). And it was a

stance she never really changed. Later in life, she would write, "the only Commandment I have ever obeyed [was]—'Consider the lilies.'" (L 904, June 1884). For Dickinson, the only way *not* to feel the superiority of day was not to experience it, to be satisfied with sunrise (beginning, expectation).

Dickinson's poems frequently celebrate sunrise as an exhilarating moment of creativity and dawning light, and expectation as a state of being that is superior to fulfillment. But in this poem, "Just Sunrise—" and the trade-off of the present for expectation painfully diminish the speaker. In the second segment, she uses the word "itself" three times, instead of "myself" or "oneself," both diminishing and neutering herself, the female speaker. Further, "Renunciation—is the Choosing / Against itself—/ Itself to justify / Unto itself—" expresses a complex psychological state. It implies recognition of an inner duality—a self divided, choosing against itself, in order for one part to "justify" itself to the other. In addition to dehumanizing the speaker, the three repetitions of "itself" create a sense of entanglement and confusion, and of a "choice" that leads to the impoverishment of language.

In the condensed final three lines, the speaker specifies "when" (under what circumstances) renunciation becomes necessary. They might be paraphrased as: "when larger, other-worldly concerns make this-worldly vision seem smaller." Her attempt to accept this is undermined, however, by the language she uses. "Larger function" is a flat, mechanical term for eternity, while having "Covered Vision—Here—" is in any case superior to having your eyes put out. As a description of limited human perception, the phrase has a wistful quality, further emphasized by the open-ended final dash. Thus, through imagery, grammar, line length, punctuation, and elliptical syntax, the poem creates a sense of deep conflict, a tension between the speaker's surface message (acceptance of renunciation) and her underlying emotions (pain, a sense of personal mutilation and diminution).

Critics have offered varying interpretations of the specific meaning of *renunciation* in this poem. Some have suggested that the choice posed is between the glory of this world ("Day") and God ("Day's Great Progenitor—"). Other readers have seen this poem as an expression of the poet's painful giving up of "her role in society in order to be worthy of her own creative talents" (Juhasz, 129–131). Still others view the poem from a feminist historical perspective, as an accurate description of "the *effects* of a system of restraint endemic to female sexuality in the nineteenth century," which required "physical and mental wounding" (Burbick, 83). Dickinson's habit of telling her truth "slant," as she put it, using spare, elliptical language and syntax and universal imagery, leaves the door open for all these possibilities.

See also "WHO NEVER WANTED—MADDEST JOY."

FURTHER READING

Joan Burbick, "Economics of Desire," in *Critical Essays*, Judith Farr, ed., 76–88; Susan Juhasz, *Undiscovered Continent*, 129–131; Richard B. Sewall, ed., *Lyman Letters*.

"Safe in their Alabaster Chambers—" (1859) (Fr 124, J 216)

This poem is one of several in Dickinson's oeuvre, including "I DIED FOR BEAUTY—BUT WAS SCARCE" and "WHAT INN IS THIS" in which she visualizes the dead in their underground dwellings in relation both to the world of the living and the world to come. In "A COFFIN—IS A SMALL DOMAIN," she calls the deceased "A Citizen of Paradise," while in this poem the dead are identified as "the meek members of the Resurrection." The biblical allusion here is to the Beatitudes, where Christ bestows his blessing on particular virtues: "Blessed are the meek: for they shall inherit the earth" (Matthew: 5:1–5). Yet the poem contains no vision of this reward, and the only "earth" the dead seem to inherit is the tiny parcel in which they are buried.

There is irony in the notion of their "safety" within their alabaster bedrooms, with their "Rafter of Satin, and Roof of Stone." The stanza is richly orchestrated, with its saturated *s*, *t*, and *r* sounds (Safe, alabaster, sleep, untouched [twice], Resurrection, rafter, satin, roof stone), its interspersed *m* sounds (Morning, meek, members), and echoing long and short *a*'s (safe, chambers, alabaster, satin, rafters), in addition to the repetition of "Untouched." The effect would be one of soothing harmony, were it not counteracted by the inexact rhyme "noon/Stone" which interrupts the musicality and injects a note of uneasiness. Does the exclusion of the dead from earthly time imply that their realm is now eternity, or is that promised "Morning" and "noon" of their immortality unreachable as well?

To seek an answer, the reader must look to the second stanza, and here his difficulties begin, since Dickinson wrote no less than four versions of the concluding verse. As she gained experience in composing her fascicles or manuscript books, she left an increasing number of variants. While the version given by Franklin was recorded in fascicle 6, she recorded three alternative second stanzas in fascicle 10. Many scholars are of the opinion that there is no way to determine which version Dickinson preferred, or even *if* she had a preference. But clues to her judgment can be found in the history of the poem's circulation.

Emily sent the original 1859 version to her beloved friend and sister-in-law, SUSAN HUNTINGTON GILBERT DICKINSON, whose literary opinion she greatly respected. It contained this second stanza:

Light laughs the breeze
In her Castle above them—
Babbles the Bee in a stolid Ear,
Pipe the sweet birds in ignorant cadence—
Ah, what sagacity perished here!

When Sue found this stanza inadequate, Emily composed a second version, sending her a note with the hope that "Perhaps this verse will suit you better." It begins:

Grand go the Years,
In the Crescent above them—
Worlds scoop their Arcs—
And Firmament—row—

Facsimile of "Safe in their Alabaster Chambers"
Dickinson sent to her sister-in-law, Susan Dickinson,
who had disapproved of the second stanza. She wrote
"Perhaps this verse would suit you better—Sue—
Emily." *(By permission of the Houghton Library, Harvard University)*

But Sue regally declared herself "not suited with the second verse," insisting that the first stanza was complete in itself:

> It is remarkable as the chain lightening that blinds us hot nights in the Southern sky, but it does not go with the ghostly shimmer of the first verse as well as the other one. . . . Strange things always go alone. . . . You never made a peer for that verse, and I *guess* you[r] kingdom doesn't hold one.

Sue was no better pleased with the other two alternatives Emily sent her with the query, "Is *this* frontier?" But when she arranged with editor and close friend SAMUEL BOWLES for the poem to be published in the *Springfield Republican,* Sue sent the first "babbling bee" version. The poem appeared on March 1, 1862, under the title, "The Sleeping," with "regularized" punctuation, capitalization, and line breaks.

What Emily's feelings were about the publication is not known. However, when she first wrote to THOMAS WENTWORTH HIGGINSON, the man she would style her "mentor," on April 15, 1862, she enclosed the poem with the second stanza beginning, "Grand go the Years—." By this time she was no longer asking Sue to critique her work. She told Higginson: "The Mind is so near itself—it cannot see distinctly—and I have none to ask—." The many critics who regard this version as superior to the rest see its inclusion with the letter to Higginson as evidence that Dickinson did, too. Dickinson's latest editor, R. W. Franklin, selected this version for *The Poems of Emily Dickinson: The Reading Edition,* as her "latest full effort."

Turning to the variants themselves, we find in both the "babbling bee" version and "Grand go the years" the same underlying notion of nature's indifference to the dead. In the earlier variant, we are in a spring or summer world, just above the grave, amid familiar Dickinsonian imagery of breezes, bees, and birds. Cynthia Griffin Wolff sees in this a double irony: Not only is lighthearted nature insensitive to what is below, but spring, a time of rebirth and symbol of resurrection, has no transcendent connotations for the dead. The "sagacity" that has "perished" is "the ancient discipline of natural theology, which found evidence of God's goodness and love scattered throughout the natural world" (*Emily Dickinson,* 318). In this version, the poem ends with an ironic commentary on the "falseness of Christ's promises and the natural symbols that are said to portend them."

In the later variant, the perspective opens up as the poet reaches out to distant dimensions, both spatial and temporal, placing the "Alabaster Chambers" of the dead against the background of the cosmos and human history. She sets both time and the planets whirling in enormous cycles above the still graves. The sublime tone is heightened by the biblical word *firmaments*: the immense arc of the heavens, suggesting the planets as they rotate, or, as they do in this image, "row." When history is introduced, the motion changes to a falling one. "Diadems—[the crowns of royalty] drop / And Doges [rulers of Italian principalities—Venice and Genoa—during the Renaissance]—surrender—." Then, in the final two lines, we are returned to stillness, one that is both "soundless" and frozen. Crescents and arcs shrink to dots on a two-dimensional disc, suggesting snow falling on snow, perhaps over the winter graves. The image, which is not easily visualized, evokes an existential coldness rather than a physical one. As the "dots" fall silently, they disappear into a flat, frozen realm, just as the dead vanish in the frost of time and universal indifference. The exact rhyme at the end, row/snow, reinforces the chilling conclusiveness of the image. The absence of the dead in this stanza, the very fact that the "meek members of the Resurrection" are not mentioned again, deepens the sense that the dead are untouched, not only by time, but by the eternity they have been promised.

While most readers see the poem in these bleak terms, at least one respected scholar sees greater ambiguity. Cristanne Miller believes that, "In this poem, Dickinson clearly compares the world of the dead in stanza one with that of the living in stanza 2, but she leaves the reader to determine the point of the contrast" ("Approaches," 226).

See also "BECAUSE I COULD NOT STOP FOR DEATH—" and PUBLICATION AND EDITORIAL SCHOLARSHIP.

FURTHER READING

Cristanne Miller, "Approaches to Reading Dickinson," 223–228; David Porter, "Early Achievement," in *Modern Critical Views*, Harold Bloom, ed., 74–75; Cynthia Griffin Wolff, *Emily Dickinson*, 316–321.

"Shells from the Coast mistaking—" (1863) (Fr 716)

This poem belongs to the cycle of "pearl" lyrics, which include "YOUR RICHES—TAUGHT ME—POVERTY," "THE MALAY—TOOK THE PEARL—," and "Removed from accident of loss," associated with

Dickinson's beloved woman, SUSAN HUNTINGTON GILBERT DICKINSON. Each of these poems approaches the image of the Pearl from different perspectives, but in all of them the pearl is inaccessible: lost, claimed by another, or obtainable only at the "cost of a life." In "Shells from the Coast," however, the Pearl at last becomes accessible; indeed, she offers herself, but at the wrong "Age" of the speaker's life.

A paraphrase might read: "I misunderstood the nature of 'Shells from the Coast'—that is, I cherished them as if they were 'all.' But at a later stage in life, I found myself with a Pearl. Why have you come so late, I murmured, I no longer need you. For that very reason, the Pearl responded, my time with you is just beginning."

The overall tone of the poem is light and worldly: The speaker "happen[s] to" "entertain" the untimely Pearl. This mood darkens at the end, however. The pearl's announcement sounds ominous, almost like a threat, or, as Judith Farr suggests, a spell, witchcraft—one of Dickinson's definitions of love (*Passion*, 151). The poem's ending asserts that only when one no longer wants something does one get it. From another perspective, it suggests that having too much need is a sure way to lose a thing. Loosen up a bit and it will come to you. This is the same dynamic she points to in a later poem: "To earn it by disdaining it/ Is Fame's consummate Fee—" (Fr 1445, 1877). The explanation Dickinson offers for Fame's perverse behavior is that "He loves what spurns him—." This is close to the ironic principle the pearl declares: "Therefore—the Pearl responded—/ My Period begin." "Just because you don't want me, my time in your life is beginning."

The part of Dickinson's life that she had considered over when Sue came into her life was her adolescent period of girlhood crushes, in which she turned to friends such as ABIAH PALMER ROOT, ABBY WOOD, and JANE HITCHCOCK to meet her intense needs for love and intimacy. Her letters to these female friends, while well within Victorian limits of propriety, were filled with expressions of devotion and loneliness, coupled with demands for reciprocity that none of these young women were able to meet, especially as they entered into relationships with men. Thus, in the imagery of this poem, they proved to be hollow "Shells from the Coast." The coastal waters are too shallow for the pearl-bearing shells she desires. To find these, she would have had to venture further out, into deeper waters.

By the time the Pearl chances to enter the speaker's life, the time for seeking pearls (love's fulfillment) in shells (girls) has passed—or so the socially conventional side of her declares. She *should* be beyond this, though apparently she is not. Farr suggests that "My need of thee—be done" may be an example of the "Dickinsonian continuing subjunctive, and, possibly, an expression of determination: *May* my need of thee be done'" (*Passion*, 152). Thus, the "dialogue" between speaker and Pearl is really an interior argument between two sides of the speaker: the side that expresses conventional, "mature" expectations, and the side that recognizes the power of this "regressive" love.

When Dickinson wrote this retrospective poem, many years after the onset of her passionate friendship with Sue, she was a 31-year-old woman who had experienced a great love for a man she called "Master." Her friend Susan Gilbert was now her sister-in-law, a wife and mother, and Amherst's most celebrated hostess. Yet Dickinson would continue to write about her love for Susan all her life. The "period" of the Pearl, having begun when its "appropriate" time had already passed, would be an enduring, irradicable "age" in the poet's emotional life.

See also "LIKE EYES THAT LOOKED ON WASTES—," "OF ALL THE SOULS THAT STAND CREATE—," and "YOU CONSTITUTED TIME—."

FURTHER READING

Judith Farr, *Passion*, 151–152.

"She rose to His Requirement—dropt" (1864) (Fr 857, J 732)

In this portrait of the conventionally married woman, her sacrifice and rewards, her expectations, and unspoken disillusionment, Dickinson indicts Victorian marriage as a trap that deprives the wife of her selfhood. Its opening lines establish the essential terms of the marriage contract:

> She rose to His Requirement—dropt
> The Playthings of Her Life

It is the husband who sets the terms of the married woman's life, and she who must "rise" to his demands and standards. Read by itself, the poem's first stanza seems straightforward enough. But the notion that the woman ascends to a higher moral level to take on "the honorable Work" of woman and wife is subtly undermined in that stanza and undercut in the following two. In considering the opposition of "Requirement" and "Playthings" (mature duty versus childish frivolity), we would do well to remember how important play was to Dickinson. For Dickinson the poet, the play of language and imagination was primary. She believed that her father's tragedy was his inability to play, and she once wrote, "Blessed be those who play, for theirs is the kingdom of heaven." Something in her recoiled from adult womanhood and made her wish she could remain a child. In a famous letter to her friend SUSAN HUNTINGTON GILBERT DICKINSON (who later married Emily's brother, WILLIAM AUSTIN), she anticipated with a mixture of fascination and dread the prospect of being consumed by the blazing sun of a husband's demands. Certainly, she had ample opportunity to observe in her parents' marriage a union in which the man's requirements dominated.

Thus, although she speaks of "honorable work," the essence of honor for Dickinson's married woman is sacrifice and self-effacement. Ironically, her apparent "ascension" to his "Requirement" entails the loss of those things that expand and uplift her life: "Amplitude" (a quality of breadth, size, magnitude), "Awe" (a word Dickinson associated with the mystery and miracle of life), "First Prospective" (her initial expectations of what her married future would hold), and the "Gold" of love, that "wears away" as it is used. This is a substantial list of missing elements in a life, but the wife never speaks of these things. In the final stanza, Dickinson compares her reticence to the silence of the Sea that "develops" both the precious Pearl and the incidental Weed, but reveals nothing of "the Fathoms" that produce such mixed "results."

For herself, Dickinson chose a different "wifehood," chaste, mystical, and inseparable from the poetic calling that enabled her to set her own "Requirement" and to retain her "Playthings" as essential tools of her art.

See also "A WIFE—AT DAYBREAK—I SHALL BE—" and "TITLE DIVINE, IS MINE."

FURTHER READING

Vivian R. Pollak, *Anxiety of Gender*, 161–163.

"Some keep the Sabbath going to Church—" (1861) (Fr 236, J 324)

This lighthearted declaration of independence from church-centered religious worship has been popular among readers since THOMAS WENTWORTH HIGGINSON and MABEL LOOMIS TODD first published it in the 1890 *Poems*. It shows the 31-year-old Emily, who had resisted strong social pressures to formally convert to Christianity throughout her girlhood, in a mood of self-confident, good-natured mockery. Unable to make her public declaration of faith in Christ, not only had she become the only holdout among family and friends, but by the time she was 30 she also had stopped accompanying her family to services at the FIRST CHURCH OF CHRIST.

The poem is built on a series of whimsical substitutions of nature's delights for the staples of church ritual. For "Chorister" she has the bobolink, the songbird whose distinctively bubbly song she particularly enjoyed. She wrote many poems about the bobolink, celebrating the bird's jaunty, exhilarating song and associating him with joy, swagger, and with herself as the dauntless singer. She herself wears the uplifting "Wings" of her spirit instead of the white ritual gown, identifying herself, as she often does in her poems, with songbirds and honey bees:

Some keep the Sabbath in Surplice—
I, just wear my Wings—

And instead of tolling the Bell, for Church,
Our little Sexton—sings.

This is her earthly heaven, the simple natural world around her, and she hears God's word more clearly here than in church. God, of course, assists in this by apparently keeping his sermon short but sweet. By calling God a "noted Clergyman," she assumes an intimacy with the deity and brings him down to earth. If this seems blasphemous, it is worth noting that Dickinson called the deity less flattering and stranger things in other poems: "a distant, stately Lover," "Papa Above!" and "Burglar! Banker—Father!" among others.

Given such unorthodoxy of thought and imagery, how shocking was this poem to conventional, educated readers of Dickinson's time? Not very, it would seem. The fact that Dickinson included it in a group of poems she sent to her new mentor, Higginson, at the beginning of their correspondence, in July 1862, indicates that she knew it would not offend him. Dickinson's biographer, Richard B. Sewall, who dismisses the poem as "a tuneful bit of 'natural religion,'" speculates that she may have been "testing Higginson's humor, or perhaps, in view of her delight in Higginson's nature essays, she was telling him in a way suited to his taste how much nature meant to her" (*Life*, II, 558). The poem was apparently in tune with popular taste, since it was one of the handful of poems published in Dickinson's lifetime. It appeared in the short-lived journal of her cousin Charles Sweetser, *The Round Table*, in March 1864. Whether Dickinson or someone else submitted it is not known. And it was sufficiently uncontroversial for Higginson and Todd to include it in the 1890 *Poems*.

As David S. Reynolds persuasively argues in his study of the influence of popular culture on Dickinson's work, the poet's contemporaries would have found the humor and irreverence of this poem already familiar through the new religious style that evolved between 1800 and 1860. He notes, "popular sermon style, which had in Puritan times been characterized primarily by theological rigor and restraint of the imagination, came to be dominated by diverting narrative, extensive illustrations, and even colloquial humor" ("Popular Culture," 168).

Dickinson, who attended many sermons by the leading preachers of the day during her girlhood in AMHERST, where they came to speak both at the church and at the college, would have been familiar with this evolution. She was conversant with the sermons of the Presbyterian preacher REVEREND CHARLES WADSWORTH, who corresponded with her and whom she may have loved. (Many scholars believe he is the man to whom she addressed her passionate MASTER LETTERS). A leading innovator and master of the new sermon style, Wadsworth came into her life in 1855, at precisely the time she was beginning to write seriously. It is likely that the new preaching offered her both "permission" and a rhetorical vehicle for her natural iconoclasm and wit. For Reynolds, the poem is "a clever adaptation of the new antebellum religious style: not only does it shift worship from church to nature and sing praise to short sermons, but it actually converts God into an entertaining preacher obviously trained in the new sermon style" (Ibid., 171).

See also "A BRIEF, BUT PATIENT ILLNESS," CONGREGATIONALISM, PURITAN HERITAGE, and REVIVALISM.

FURTHER READING

David S. Reynolds, "Popular Culture," in *Cambridge Companion*, Wendy Martin, ed., 169–172; Richard B. Sewall, *Life*, II, 558.

"Some things that fly there be—" (1859) (Fr 68, J 89)

In this famous early poem, Dickinson points to the "riddle" that most engaged her as a poet: the "flood subject," as she called it, of the soul's continuance after death. Neither the things that fly (in either the sense of moving through the air or passing quickly) nor the things that stay—the pain of loss, the landscape, or that which by definition stays (Eternity)—move her to write. Her characteristic use of compression and ellipsis make the first two tercets into riddles. If we were to expand their final lines, filling in the "missing words," they might read: "I will write no elegy for passing things"

(line 3) and "I don't feel compelled to write a poem about the things that stay either" (line 6).

Flying or staying things, in and of themselves, are insufficiently interesting. Instead, what intrigues her and motivates her art is paradox. As scholar David Porter notes, she concisely articulates here the theme that dominates her work, "the quest of the speaker's mind for reconciliation of the paradoxes in nature and in the mind ... the process of mind in its perpetual effort to reconcile and to unify, to bring to acceptable terms the perception of things that fly and things that stay" (*Early Poetry*, 30–31). Thus, what does engage her is the riddle of those that, "resting, rise," that is, the riddle of the Resurrection:

> There are that resting, rise.
> Can I expound the skies?
> How still the Riddle lies!

How can we bridge the gap between time and eternity? Dickinson offers no solution to the riddle. The act of stating the paradox moves her to recognize the limits of even the magic of her poetry. She cannot "expound the skies," that is, reduce either nature or the supernatural to mental concepts.

The poet's task, as poet and critic Anthony Hecht points out, was not to solve the riddle, but to discern it and present it to the reader in all its irreducible mystery. Her many "riddle poems" emerged from her deep sense that life is not altogether intelligible. Hecht writes:

> The last line is a riddle all by itself, and may refer either to the soul or to God. In either case, it seems to insist that the living are denied any sure sign of their salvation ("Riddles," 155–56).

Another possibility is that the riddle referred to is death, for it lies "still" before her, like the incomprehensible body of the deceased, after the soul has departed.

See also "A VISITOR IN MARL—" and "IT SIFTS FROM LEADEN SIEVES—."

FURTHER READING

Anthony Hecht, "Riddles," in *Critical Essays*, Judith Farr, ed., 149–162; David Porter, *Early Poetry*, 31–32, 83–84.

"Split the Lark—and you'll find the Music—" (1865) (Fr 905, J 861)

This famous poem perfectly illustrates critic Robert Weisbuch's claim that the richness and complexity of a Dickinson poem is lost when the reader "points" at a single level of meaning rather than allowing all possible meanings to coexist. If we ask what this poem is about, several answers quickly suggest themselves: the music of poetry, the music of love, defloration and sex, fidelity, power, and victimization. Is the poem a servile invitation to the lover to take her life (or her virginity), if that will persuade him of her loyalty? Or an angry reproach to this doubting Thomas (God? a lover?) for requiring such crude, brutal proofs? A boastful declaration of the wealth she possesses and will bestow on the beloved? All these things at once?

In light of Dickinson's frequent identification with songbirds such as the robin and bobolink, it is no great leap to assume that the lark she invites her addressee to bisect represents herself as poet. The speaker's invitation to the addressee, to destroy the songbird in order to find its music, is scathingly ironic. If you need to kill me to find the music, she says, go right ahead. The irony, of course, lies in the fact that, once "Bulb after Bulb, in Silver rolled" are found, the bird will be incapable of releasing them, or creating others. The oddness of this image lies in the mixing of bird and plant imagery. By daringly commingling these two realms, Dickinson is reaching for the necessary metaphor. For, a bulb, as Dickinson the master gardener well knew, represents potential life. She knew, as her *Webster's* specified, that "the bulb underground is what the bud is on stem or branches." Thus, the bulbs rolled in silver represent life potential lovingly wrapped in the silver of song. Judith Farr has shown that bulbs, for Dickinson, were also emblems of the beauty of the risen body (*Gardens*, 25). The potential for not only life but for immortality is destroyed by the brutal separation of the living bird from its song.

Scholar Judy Jo Small points out Dickinson's concern, shared with the romantics, with the inef-

fable power of music, which she treasured for its suggestiveness and resistance to analysis. She suggests that this poem is essentially a satiric reproach to one who demands certainty, is "stupidly insensitive to sublimity," and turns logical analysis into "a murderous dissection" ("A Musical Aesthetic," 212). Dickinson likens such a skeptic to Thomas, the disciple who would not believe in Christ's Resurrection until he had fingered his wounds. As critic Charles Anderson notes, the skeptic appears in a related poem, "To hear an Oriole sing" (Fr 402, 1862), in which the poet argues with a skeptical ornithologist who insists that "The 'Tune is in the Tree—.'" The poet replies, "'No Sir! In Thee!'" insisting that the hearer's perception, not the physical bird alone, creates the music. The doubting Thomas of "Split the lark" is allowed to prove his thesis by vivisecting the bird—with deadly results:

Scarlet Experiment! Sceptic Thomas!
Now, do you doubt that your Bird was true?

Anderson suggests that Dickinson's doubting Thomas may also allude to Sir Thomas Browne, who carved up a corpse to find the seat of his soul (*Stairway*, 101).

Biographer Cynthia Griffin Wolff takes the reference to Thomas differently, as an allusion to God's faith (or lack thereof) in man. In her provocative analysis, the poem is "about the Lord's vindictiveness toward poets" (*Emily Dickinson*, 362). God himself is the "Sceptic Thomas," demanding material proof of his subjects' loyalty, and the "Scarlet Experiment" of this Christian God, ironically, is akin to the examination of the entrails of sacrificed animals by pagan priests to predict the future. Wolff sees other allusions to God's brutal experiments: the loosed Flood in which he drowned his creatures and the split lark itself as a symbol of Christ's crucifixion.

At the same time, it is impossible not to see a rich undercurrent of sexual allusions in the poem: the defloration image of the split lark, the suggestions of orgasm in the image of the silver-rolled bulbs, the flood of virginal blood and/or passion. One controversial scholar, William Shurr, has even suggested that the poem refers to a painful abortion. The great achievement of this and so many of Dickinson's poems is that they are sufficiently universal and illustrative as to allow the reader any of these interpretations—or all of them at once.

See also "THE ROBIN'S MY CRITERION FOR TUNE—."

FURTHER READING

Charles Anderson, *Stairway*, 99–102; Judith Farr, *Gardens*, 23–25; William Shurr, *Marriage*, 36, 151, 181; Judy Jo Small, "Musical Aesthetic," in *Critical Essays*, Judith Farr, ed., 212; Robert Weisbuch, "Prisming," in *Handbook*, Grabher et al., eds., 197–223; Cynthia Griffin Wolff, *Emily Dickinson*, 362–363.

"Success is counted sweetest" (1859) (Fr 112, J 67)

In this poignant early poem, one of Dickinson's most famous, the poet conveys her tragic sense that hunger creates value and that those who lose a prize "comprehend" its worth more fully and deeply than those who attain it. Although the lyrical "I" is missing in these indelible lines on frustrations and life's inequities, the speaker is firmly bound to the perspective of those who are defeated.

This is one of the few poems to be published in Dickinson's lifetime. Dickinson sent it in her fourth letter to THOMAS WENTWORTH HIGGINSON in July 1862. It was not Higginson, however, but his and Emily's mutual friend, the well-known writer HELEN FISKE HUNT JACKSON, who pressured the poet to allow her to submit it to one of the No Name volumes of contemporary verse published by Roberts Brothers of Boston. Jackson began importuning her for a contribution in 1876, offering to submit Dickinson's work in her own hand. "Surely, in the shelter of such *double* anonymousness . . . you need not shrink," she wrote. Faced with the aggressive Jackson's repeated requests for this "personal favor," Dickinson apparently gave in. The poem appeared in late 1878, in *A Masque of Poets,* occupying a prestigious place at the end of the volume's shorter poems. The editor-in-chief, Thomas Niles, a promoter of women's writing, sent Dickinson a letter thanking her for the contribution, "which for want of a known sponsor Mr. Emerson has generally had to father."

Little is known about Dickinson's reaction to the publication, other than that, when SUSAN HUNTINGTON GILBERT DICKINSON recognized the lines and told Emily of her discovery, Dickinson went "so white" that her sister-in-law regretted having spoken (Martha Dickinson Bianchi, *Face to Face*, 30). Was she flattered that people thought the great Ralph Waldo Emerson had written the poem—or annoyed that anyone else should receive credit for her work? Most interestingly, what was her response to the editorial changes made in the published poem by Niles or someone else in his office? Did they confirm her opinion that "PUBLICATION—IS THE AUCTION / Of the Mind of Man"? Without ruining the poem, the changes substantially weakened it, by altering passages that did not conform to contemporary tastes. Despite the fact that, in its grammar, rhythms and rhyme scheme, the poem is "smoother," more conventional, than much of her other work, it apparently still left room for editorial "improvement," In line 2, "who" is changed to "that," probably for alliteration. A more serious change occurs in line 3, where "a" becomes "the," making the article refer to the specific nectar, "success," and thereby depriving the *nectar* of its other possible meanings. In line 4, the insertion of "the" before "sorest" by adding another syllable to the line, changes its emphatic rhythm to a lilting one. The editor changed the word "clear" in line 8 to "plain," perhaps because he objected to its repetition in line 12. Finally, and most damagingly, the powerful final line 12 is changed to "Break, agonizing clear." The editor may have thought "Break" was less jarring than "burst." And, by substituting the new line for "Burst agonized and clear!" he is making crystal clear that it is the listener who is agonized, not the distant strains of triumph (Sewall, *Life,* II, 584). But in so doing, he loses the musicality of the line. Moreover, the ambiguity of the original line, in which agony and clarity can belong to both the dying listener *and* the music of victory, suggests a more complex picture, in which victory, too, contains agony, perhaps because of the price paid to attain it. Finally, the separation of "agonized and clear," conveying two simultaneous perceptions, each of which enhances the pain inherent in the other, is far stronger than "agonizing[ly] clear."

Analysis of this poem demonstrates how Dickinson's work cannot be read in a linear way, as "about" one thing, but gives rise to a constellation of meanings. After the aphoristic opening lines that state the psychological premise, the idea of "sweetness" as satisfaction becomes the sensual sweetness of "a nectar," thus broadening the possibilities of meaning. "To comprehend a nectar" (as opposed to more expected verbs such as "enjoy" or "appreciate" or "revel in") implies the deeper appreciation of intelligence *rooted in* feeling ("sorest need"), a dependence she would later codify in the 1875 poem "The mind lives on the heart" (Fr 1384). Thus, in the first stanza, success shifts in meaning to satiety, failure to unslaked hunger.

When the poem moves on to military imagery in the next stanza, the meaning of success shifts once more—to victory. "He who ne'er succeeds" becomes first the hungry bee, and then the vanquished soldier. Probably drawing on religious, biblical traditions, Dickinson uses military imagery in a number of poems to talk about spiritual battles. In this instance, the masculine, military imagery is not motivated by the occurrence of any actual battle; the Civil War was two years off when Dickinson wrote this poem. As in many of her poems, there is no direct connection between the scene she draws and an actual event in her life. The imagery stands in its own right, contributing its distinctive overtones to the existential reality she is exploring. She refers to the victors as "the purple Host." Rather than denoting a specific uniform, purple connotes royalty. But the word *Host*, which also has a religious meaning very familiar to Dickinson, suggests a heavenly royalty, that is, a triumphant Host of Angels. The phrase may also refer, as some have proposed, to the royal company of published poets. Or it may allude to those who triumph in love. (Emily had originally sent this poem to Sue in 1859, "with an obvious bearing on their friendship" [Sewall, *Life*, II, 387].) Dickinson *did* identify with those defeated by such victors. She was excluded from the realm of the Angels by her inability to accept orthodox doctrine, from the company of recognized poets, and from the paradise of lovers allowed to live out their love in *this* world. She may be talking about any one of these things—or about all of them at once.

What the poem tells us is that defeat endows one with a special perception. Defeat and its variants, hunger, wounding, exclusion, and deprivation, are all channels of spiritual clarity. By shifting the adjective "forbidden" from "the distant strains of triumph," which it logically modifies, to the ear of the defeated, she makes of that sense organ a special instrument of perception—one that hears with a clear recognition of both the value of what is desired and the pain of not attaining it:

As he defeated—dying—
On whose forbidden ear
The distant strains of triumph
Burst agonized and clear!

See also "A WOUNDED DEER LEAPS HIGHEST."

FURTHER READING

Robert Weisbuch, "Prisming," in *Handbook,* Grabher et al., eds., 197–223.

"Sweet Mountains—Ye tell Me no lie—" (1863) (Fr 745, J 722)

On the simplest level, we can view this poem as an expression of Dickinson's reverence for the natural beauty of the region in which she lived. The mountains surrounding AMHERST were a daily presence in her life and her communion with them in this poem reflects the spirit of EDWARD HITCHCOCK, the influential educator of her AMHERST ACADEMY days. A scientist and a religious man, Hitchcock, for whom nature's grandeur and orderliness were evidence of God's loving and intelligent plan, praised those mountains in exalted, semireligious terms. While this poem takes such reverence as its starting point, it moves in a unique and "heretical" direction, integrating the familiar mountains into what Sandra

Mountains surrounding Amherst, Massachusetts *(Courtesy of Darryl Leiter)*

M. Gilbert calls "the ironic hagiography of . . . a New England nun" ("Wayward Nun," 22).

At the core of Dickinson's poem is a hymn of praise to the mountains for their faithfulness to her and a reciprocal pledge of her fidelity to them. The first thing she praises is their honesty: "Ye tell Me no lie." What is it that makes the mountains honest? They cannot "speak" in the ordinary sense of the word; they speak by merely being. What they are they are, imposing nothing upon her beliefs she cannot confirm with her own senses.

In the second line, she praises the mountains for not denying her, or she beseeches them not to, thereby evoking the figure of Jesus denied by his disciples:

Never deny Me—Never fly—
Those same unvarying Eyes
Turn on Me—When I fail—or feign,

If she is Christ, the mountains now become her nonjudgmental witnesses, observing with "unvary-ing Eyes" her failures and pretenses. She receives greater forbearance, greater forgiveness from the feminine Mountains than she would from the masculine, punishing Calvinist God. They see her when she takes "the Royal names in vain" without changing "Their far—slow—Violet Gaze—." While we don't know precisely what Dickinson has in mind by these "Royal names," we do know they are a substitute for "God's name," some ultimate value of her own with which she replaces the Christian deity.

This notion of alternate worship becomes full-blown in the second stanza, when she addresses the "Sweet Mountains" as "My Strong Madonnas," transforming the physical image—the nurturing breasts of old, rounded mountains—into a vision of powerful and sacred female presences. She asks them to continue to cherish her, calling herself "The Wayward Nun—beneath the Hill—." She is "Wayward," presumably, because she serves the Mountains rather than the traditional figures of

Christian worship. In her youthful letters to friends such as ABIAH PALMER ROOT and JANE HUMPHREY, Dickinson, who could never bring herself to formally accept the Calvinist religion she was born into, referred to herself as bad, deviant, and outside the fold.

The reader may also find it somewhat "wayward" for a woman of Puritan background to speak of her spiritual life in terms of such Catholic figures as Madonnas and nuns. However, as scholar Judith Farr notes, in the Victorian literary and painterly tradition there were many depictions of nuns. Even in Calvinist New England there was a fascination with Madonna art and even some Calvinist fathers such as EDWARD DICKINSON presented their daughters with pictures of the Virgin Mary. Dickinson would write another poem the following year, "Only a shrine, but Mine—" (Fr 981), which "can only be called a prayer to the Virgin Mary" (*Passion*, 36), in which she develops the concept of herself as a nun:

> Madonna dim, to whom all Feet may come,
> Regard a Nun—

But in the poem under discussion, the Madonnas the poet serves are mountains. Dickinson appears to be engaging in "nature worship," placing herself in the romantic tradition in literature and painting by declaring herself a vestal of Pan. Such a stance is not characteristic of her work, where nature is most often a "mystery" from which she is excluded. In the work of the Hudson River and Luminist painters of her time mountains represented what was permanent in nature and therefore were revered, Farr points out.

Of course, the identification of mountains with salvation in the Judeo-Christian religion goes back to the Psalmist: "I lift up my eyes unto the mountains. Whence cometh my help? My help cometh from the Lord." Dickinson leaves out the final element (the Lord) and sees her help as coming from the mountains themselves. She vows her service to them and evokes her "latest Worship" as the moment when the day has faded and she lifts her eyes to them a final time. Thus, for Dickinson, who distrusted doctrine and insisted on knowing the world in her own terms, perception itself was an act of devotion.

See also "A SOLEMN THING—IT WAS—I SAID—," "SOME KEEP THE SABBATH GOING TO CHURCH—," "THESE ARE THE DAYS WHEN BIRDS COME BACK—," CONGREGATIONALISM, and CONNECTICUT RIVER VALLEY.

FURTHER READING

Judith Farr, *Passion*, 36–37; Sandra M. Gilbert, "Wayward Nun," in *Critical Essays*, Judith Farr, ed., 20–39.

"Tell all the truth but tell it slant—" (1872) (Fr 1263, J 1129)

This is one of Dickinson's most famous "metapoems," or poems about poetry, widely considered to be a key statement of her philosophy and way of writing. Ostensibly written as an advice poem, it is really a revelation of herself as a canny, self-aware craftsman and psychologist of the human soul.

The poem's first two lines contain the core idea:

> Tell all the truth but tell it slant—
> Success in Circuit lies

The quality of "slantness" or indirection permeates every aspect of Dickinson's poems and letters: the elliptical nature of her imagery, her use of disjunction and compression, and her manipulation of syntax and PUNCTUATION. Her use of "Circuit"—a circuitous or roundabout approach—turns many of her best poems into riddles the reader is challenged to solve. Circuit is the path to the center the reader must travel to reach what can be known about the center. One way to understand this is to assume that Dickinson believed that Truth in any pure form was basically unknowable; it could only be approximated. Thus, "she uses a slanted perspective that might reveal what would otherwise remain hidden" (Josef Raab, "Metapoetic Element," 284–285).

But Dickinson offers another explanation in lines 3 to 6: Truth must be revealed indirectly, gradually, in order to protect against its "too bright" dazzle. In "contrast to the more common nineteenth-century portrait of the poet as a wielder of lightning, like Zeus, Jove, or Thor, whose bolts announce his omnipotence and divinity" (Miller, *Grammar,* 16–17), Dickinson sees the poet as a mother whose role is to insulate her children/ readers from the lightning's head-on impact. By offering them "kind explanations," she allows them as much of the Truth as they are capable of absorbing.

This notion is saved from being condescending to the reader by the poet's inclusion of herself in the ranks of those in need of such protection. "The Truth's superb surprise" is too bright for "*our* infirm Delight" (author's italics). One is reminded of Robert Frost's famous dictum: "No surprise for the writer, no surprise for the reader." To convey a hidden truth to the reader, the poet must first experience it herself. And she, too, must be taken unawares. From this perspective, Dickinson's "slantness" is not just a strategy to conceal the particulars of her life, it is the essence of lyric poetry. By transmuting the unbearable into the bearable, a poem awakens the reader to the "Truth."

The thorny question naturally arises: what did Dickinson mean by "Truth"? The mere fact that she capitalizes the word does not mean she is referring to "Truth with a capital T"—some absolute understanding of existence—since, after all, she regularly capitalizes proper nouns. Still, the potentially blinding truth of the poem's final line *does* have religious overtones. In a poem written in 1875, "To pile like thunder to its close" (Fr 1353), she writes, "For none can see God and live—." Yet, this poem is not about religion, but about love and poetry, which Dickinson equates with one another ("—the two coeval come—") in that, like God, neither can be experienced directly with impunity. Words rarely have a clear, single referent in Dickinson. Her Truth encompasses the full constellation of insights vouched her into the mystery of the human condition.

The poet told THOMAS WENTWORTH HIGGINSON, during his first visit to her in 1870, "If I read a book [and] it makes my whole body so cold no fire can ever warm me I know *that* is poetry. If I feel physically as if the top of my head were taken off, I know *that* is poetry" (L 342a). Dickinson's experience in

encountering true poetry corresponds to the Truth/ Lightning of this poem; it is immediate, powerful, dangerous and potentially deadly. But its surprise is also "superb," for it provides a precious opportunity to expand our sense of what it means to be alive. Or, as Dickinson told Higginson during that first meeting, "Truth is such a *rare* thing it is delightful to tell it."

See also CIRCUMFERENCE POEMS.

FURTHER READING
Cristanne Miller, *Grammar,* 16–17; Josef Raab, "Metapoetic Element," in *Handbook,* Grabher et al., eds., 273–295.

"The Bible is an antique Volume—" (1882) (Fr 1577, J 1545)

If this witty poem were all a reader knew of Dickinson's relationship to the Bible, he might conclude that the poet viewed that sacred book with a mixture of amusement and contempt. In point of fact, however, both Old and New Testaments were powerful literary influences for her; she knew them like the back of her hand and was constantly citing them from memory in her correspondence. Biographer Richard B. Sewall points out that, for Dickinson, "The Biblical characters, especially the Old Testament ones, lived . . . as vitally, and often as secularly, as any out of Shakespeare or her favorite novelist, Dickens" (*Life,* II, 698). She once wrote to her close friend, ELIZABETH LUNA CHAPIN HOLLAND, about an inner conflict she was having (around 1881): "Jacob versus Esau, was a trifle in Litigation, compared to the Skirmish in my Mind."

The secular version of the sacred book that she develops in this poem was influenced by the new 19th-century sermon style, which was replacing the imaginatively restrained, doctrinally oriented Calvinist preaching of the past. This style, of which Emily's revered REVEREND CHARLES WADSWORTH was a master practitioner, was characterized by "diverting narrative, extensive illustrations, and even colloquial humor" (Reynolds, "Popular Culture," 168). Thus, when she calls the Bible an "antique Volume," she is by no means dismissing it. Dickinson loved "ancient volumes," as she attested in an 1863 poem where she calls them "A precious—mouldering pleasure" (Fr 569). Here, however, she assumes an ironic stance implying that "antique" signifies antiquated, out of date, "Written by faded Men."

This is the rebellious Emily, who refuses to be cowed by solemnity and insists on translating the Holy Book into up-to-date, "relevant" terms. By calling Eden "the ancient Homestead" she is punning, that is, evoking the word in its general sense as well as the name of the Dickinson family mansion. Satan, Judas, and David are recast in secular social roles, while sin becomes something others must resist—a jab at the hypocrisy of preachers:

> Satan—the Brigadier—
> Judas—the Great Defaulter—
> David—the Troubador—
> Sin—a distinguished Precipice
> Others must resist—

As the last lines tell us, however, the main target of Dickinson's irony—what she objected to in the Bible and in her Calvinist religion in general—was its condemning attitude: the vision of a wrathful God who punishes an essentially sinful humanity. She tended to see human beings as more sinned against than sinning and her own lyric gift led her to "sing" rather than denounce:

> Orpheu's Sermon captivated—
> It did not condemn—

Like Orpheus, her "Sermon" was a song. Recall that Orpheus is the figure in Greek mythology who was presented with a lyre from Apollo, with which he made such enchanting music that he charmed the wild beasts and made the trees and rocks move. When his wife Eurydice was killed by a serpent bite, he descended to the underworld and enchanted its rulers with his music. They told him he could take Eurydice back to earth with him, provided he would not look back on her until they arrived. At the last moment he succumbed to temptation, looked back, and thus lost her forever. As a figure who speaks to us both of the immortal power of art and of mortal limitations, Orpheus would have been a particularly compelling hero to Dickinson.

The fact that she sent this poem in a letter to her 22-year-old nephew, EDWARD DICKINSON ("NED"), possibly when he was ill and home from college (L 753, about 1882), may explain the references to boys who believe and boys who are lost. Ned may have been wrestling with some of the religious questions and pressures that plagued Dickinson as a student at MOUNT HOLYOKE FEMALE SEMINARY

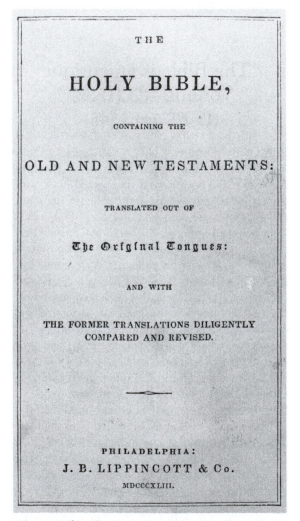

THE

HOLY BIBLE,

CONTAINING THE

OLD AND NEW TESTAMENTS:

TRANSLATED OUT OF

The Original Tongues:

AND WITH

THE FORMER TRANSLATIONS DILIGENTLY
COMPARED AND REVISED.

PHILADELPHIA:
J. B. LIPPINCOTT & Co.
MDCCCXLIII.

Title page of Emily Dickinson's Bible *(By permission of the Houghton Library, Harvard University)*

where there were intense annual REVIVALS, in which students were pressured to accept Christ and publicly declare their faith. Aunt Emily may have been urging him to step back and view the oppressive "religious question" with a healthy measure of humor.

See also "A LITTLE EAST OF JORDAN," "OF GOD WE ASK ONE FAVOR, THAT WE MAY BE FORGIVEN—," "SPLIT THE LARK—AND YOU'LL FIND THE MUSIC—," and "TWO SWIMMERS WRESTLED ON THE SPAR—."

FURTHER READING

Wendy Martin, *American Triptych*, 137–138; Dorothy Oberhaus, *Emily Dickinson's Fascicles*, 12; David S. Reynolds, "Popular Culture," in *Cambridge Companion*, 168–172; Richard B. Sewall, *Life*, II, 696–699.

"The Brain—is wider than the Sky—" (1863) (Fr 598, J 632)

In Dickinson's vocabulary of the inner realm, the words *brain, mind, consciousness, self, spirit,* and *soul* are used more or less interchangeably. At times, the poet draws a sharp distinction between *mind* and *heart,* insisting that mind without heart is anemic and lifeless. ("The Mind lives on the Heart / Like any Parasite—", Fr 1384).

Elsewhere, she declares "The Heart is the Capital of the Mind" (Fr 1381). But "brain" was in general not a sterile image for her but a proud one, the essence and glory of being alive. Dickinson's poetry repeatedly claims a reality for the interior world that is equal to or greater than that of the material world. In poem after poem, she asserts that life's greatest riches—truth, freedom, joy, self-respect, creativity, and security—are only to be found within.

"The Brain—is wider than the Sky—" is both a celebration of human consciousness and a virtuoso demonstration of its ability to "contain" the world outside within its frame of reference. In the first two stanzas, the poet playfully devises ways to compare and measure first brain and sky, then brain and sea, and finds the brain the larger, more capacious and absorbing element. Like sky and sea, the brain is "Blue," the color of vastness:

> The Brain is deeper than the sea—
> For—hold them—Blue to Blue—
> The one the other will absorb—
> As Sponges—Buckets—do—

In the final stanza, however, the poet turns her attention from the visible, natural world to the transcendent reality of God and the terms of her comparison grow more complex. Devising another fanciful method of measurement ("Heft them—Pound for Pound—"), she finds that the brain is not greater, but equal to "just the weight of God—." Abandoning the weight metaphor, she then declares that if they differ, it will be "As Syllable from Sound—." This intriguing simile may be read in different ways. If God is Sound, the pervasive, undifferentiated element of which the shaping syllable of a human mind is made, then the brain is superior to God in its complexity, though unable to exist without God, the source. On the other hand, what if God is the Syllable and the Brain is Sound? After all, "In the beginning was the Word"—a single syllable, perhaps. In this reading, the brain, as the "sound" that evolved from that first syllable, would be a mere echo of the divine. Two very different meanings thus emerge, which the poem's compression and ambiguous syntax do not allow us to resolve.

Most commentators proceed on the assumption that the poem identifies God with sound. As biographer Cynthia Griffin Wolff conceptualizes it, "Syllables are concocted from sound and contain them; the brain has been created by God, but nonetheless contains Him" (*Emily Dickinson*, 462). Scholar Gary Stonum takes a similar approach:

> . . . a syllable does partition the continuum of sound, transforming the aural presence into a cognitive form and thus distancing it in the way any mediation does. On the one hand, then, the analogy credits the brain with transforming, taming, or humanizing the awful presence of God. On the other hand, sound and hence presence is the source and the energy that drives language, perhaps even drives us to language,

just as God is the creator of the human mind, and so the transformation into syllable is an example of human weakness. (*Dickinson Sublime*, 101)

Critic Charles Anderson goes a step further and reads the poem as speculating that nature as well as God may exist *only* in the mind. Anderson perceives this in a positive light. For him, "The effect of the poem is not to minimize the importance of God, or nature, but to magnify the value of the consciousness" (*Stairway*, 300). But Wolff raises the crucial issue of the loneliness of the conscious self in such a conception of reality. She writes:

[T]he self that has been thus empowered is paradoxically limited, for every significant other self has been obliterated through absorption.... The voracious 'Brain ... will contain ... You' along with everything else, and without another separate and distinct self in either the transcendent or the immanent realm, what is the value of this arrogation of authority? (*Emily Dickinson*, 462–463)

Indeed, in at least one other poem, Dickinson expresses the loss entailed by the brain's authority: "Perception of an Object costs / Precise the Object's loss—," she wrote in 1865 (1103). In two brilliant stanzas, she articulates the relativistic vision of contemporary physics that "The Object absolute, is nought—." Far from rejoicing in this, she knew the inherent frustration of being limited to subjectivity, without the possibility of knowing reality in any absolute sense. Perception tells us all we are capable of knowing, she writes, "And then upbraids a Perfectness / That situates so far—." Somewhere then, in the corners of all-powerful perception, lurks the belief in that unperceived Perfectness.

See also "THIS CONSCIOUSNESS THAT IS AWARE."

FURTHER READING

Charles Anderson, *Stairway*, 300–301; Gary Stonum, *Dickinson Sublime*, 100–101; Robert Weisbuch, *Emily Dickinson's Poetry*, 161–162; Cynthia Griffin Wolff, *Emily Dickinson*, 462–463.

"The Bustle in a House" (1865) (Fr 1108, J 1078)

Emily Dickinson lived in a world of fixed social and cultural traditions and duties and, while they did not constitute the substance of her inner life, they provided her a supportive framework in times of grief. The act of moving, however mechanically, through the external motions of daily chores and obligations helps her to "keep her senses on" at a time when she has gone dead internally. Thus, in Fr 1108, the "Bustle" associated with death rituals and funeral preparation is both avoidance of the stark reality of loss and tonic for the grieving.

In an instance of powerful understatement, she calls the domestic flurry of keeping a grieving household afloat the "solemnest of industries," drawing her image, as she often did, from the realms of finance and factories thriving in the masculine world surrounding her. By alluding to women's work in this way, she makes a subtly feminist statement about the importance of such work. Not only is theirs the "solemnest" occupation, but it is "Enacted opon Earth"—as sacred rituals are enacted.

This drawing together of the domestic and the divine is repeated in the second stanza, in which the House becomes the Heart:

The Sweeping up the Heart
And putting Love away
We shall not want to use again
Until Eternity—

In this imagistic transformation, focus shifts from the external tasks to the internal one of acceptance and survival. This is not an expression of the efficient putting away of love. It expresses rather what biographer Cynthia Griffin Wolff calls "the incalculable value of quotidian domestic activities." Wolff writes:

Perhaps this insight could issue only from a "Wife": so many small, unobtrusive homely acts are recollected here. To an outsider, the juxtaposition of "Bustle" and "The Morning after Death" might seem macabre; mourning, weeping, fainting into prostration—surely these attitudes would be more suitable to the occasion. Yet ... every mother knows that even "after Death" the business of living must be expedited, lest those who sorrow grieve too strenuously. Thus such "Bustle" becomes a way of "Sweeping up the Heart," not denying unhappiness or bereavement, but learning to contain them by affection for the family that remains." (*Emily Dickinson*, 485)

See also "I TIE MY HAT, I CREASE MY SHAWL—."

FURTHER READING

Cynthia Griffin Wolff, *Emily Dickinson*, 484–485.

"The Drop, that wrestles in the Sea—" (1861) (Fr 255, J 284)

The image of the sea is a constant in Dickinson's poetry, a multivalent symbol for the immense, the submerged, and the unknown, capable of arousing both terror and ecstasy. In her early poems, the sea is more than once a symbol of fulfillment in love, with the beloved the larger, encompassing element with whom the diminutive, subservient female speaker wishes to merge. In one poem, "My River runs to thee—," she asks the Blue Sea to welcome her and let her fetch brooks for him. In "The Drop that Wrestles in the Sea," the speaker's size is minuscule compared to the Ocean's, yet she wrestles with him and engages him in polite debate. Her final plea, "Me?" seems to be begging some concession from the all-encompassing element, though whether she wishes him to possess her or to recognize the separateness of her "Me" remains ambiguous.

In the first stanza, it is not clear whether the fact that the drop "forgets her own locality" is a cause of anxiety at losing one's personal boundaries—or of bliss in the self-forgetful merging with a beloved. The word "wrestles" suggests not only a struggle with the sea but an inner struggle with what is happening to her. In stanza 2, she engages in a cryptic debate, playing with the words "small" and

"all." She knows herself to be "an incense small—." Incense is an aromatic substance burnt in religious rites as an offering to a deity, which in this case is Poseidon, a fact we know because his wife Amphitrite, goddess of the sea in Greek mythology, is later mentioned. But lurking behind this meaning is the shadow of the verb "to incense," that is, to make angry or "to kindle to violent action." The argument the Drop makes to the Sea is "logical" and guarded, yet it contains an undertone of angry frustration at her relationship to the Sea's "all":

> Yet small, she sighs, if all, is all,
> How larger—be?

This condensed, elliptical argument makes it difficult to choose between at least two readings. Speaking from her smallness, she may be questioning her ability to give anything: "If you are already all, how can I give to you, make you larger? Of what use/importance am I to you?" This is the question Dickinson would ask in a later poem, Fr 1370 (1875):

> Unto the Whole—how add?
> Has 'All' a further realm—

On the other hand, she may be speaking from a resentful sense of being marginalized: "If you are all, what's left for me to be? How can I grow, become larger?" In the first reading, the Drop only wishes to serve the Sea. In the second, she competes with him, demanding, "How can I be larger when you're the whole show?" Her "incense small" may thus refer not only to her own anger but also to her desire to provoke the Sea to some more openly aggressive response than the smile he gives her.

Dickinson continues to use puns to suggest double meanings. In the line "The Ocean, smiles at her conceit," a "Conceit" is both an idea (the argument she has been making to him) and a high, self-flattering opinion of oneself (her belief that she could compete with him). He may be smiling in amusement at her cleverness—or condescendingly at her arrogance.

The ambiguities continue in the final lines. What does it mean that she forgets Amphitrite? Does it imply that, forgetting that Poseidon already has a beloved wife, she pleads take "Me" as wife?

Or, is what she has forgotten Poseidon's brutal acquisition of Amphitrite, whom he stole from her father's home, raped, and condemned to live in his dark, uncongenial kingdom? In this case, the poet suggests that the Drop has forgotten the overwhelming loss of self awaiting her, should the Ocean choose her.

The light, polite tone of the poem, with its regular multiple rhymes, repeated, simple rhyming words (small, small, all, all, Thee, be, Me) creates a deceptive surface that cloaks these dark underpinnings.

For biographer Cynthia Griffin Wolff, the "mannerly conflict" between Drop and Sea has misled critics who see it as a love poem, whereas it is, instead, a wrestling match between God and a mortal woman who has turned to him through religious conversion. Wolff writes, "If God is truly infinite, then He needs no 'Drop,' for infinite plus any increment, however large, is still infinity unchanged. Divinity cannot be glorified or altered in any way by the acquisition of one small soul" (*Emily Dickinson*, 272). In this reading, the Drop is telling the Sea that losing her will have no effect on him and thus he should let her go; she is trying to save herself from losing her psychic identity in him. Although she gets the last word, albeit courteously framed as a request, the Ocean's smile reveals his expectation of victory, because he is remembering how he overpowered Amphitrite. While Wolff's explanation is plausible, it does not explain why Dickinson would drag in a pagan myth to talk about the Christian god. For critics who see this as a love poem, the mention of the Ocean's wife is precisely the clue that the relationship between a man and a woman is being alluded to.

In poems and letters, throughout her life, Dickinson wrote of the prospect of merging with a beloved in varying (and often mixed) moods of ecstasy and dread, with the humility of one who worships another, as well as with the pride of one who knows her powers. In a famous passage written to her future sister-in-law SUSAN HUNTINGTON GILBERT DICKINSON, she contemplates the day when she and Sue will be "yielded up" to marriage, comparing them to blossoms destined to be consumed by the mighty sun: "They know that the man of noon, is *mightier* than the morning and their

life is henceforth to him" (L 93, early June 1852). While this passage is generally cited as evidence of Dickinson's fear of heterosexuality, it exudes an excitement and craving for the dangerous intensity of marriage.

Ultimately, Dickinson did not have to pay the feared/desired cost that union with another might exact of her. In the life she shaped within her father's house, she grew in her separateness and her sense of who she was. Comparison of "The Drop that wrestles in the Sea" with another "dialogue with the sea" poem written 11 years later reveals her sense of what such separateness costs. "The Sea said 'Come' to the Brook—" (Fr 1275, 1872) is another parable of larger and smaller waters, only here, instead of Sea and Drop we have Sea and Brook, a far more substantial entity. The Brook begs the Sea to let it grow, but the Sea refuses, saying, "then you will be a Sea—I want a Brook—." The second stanza skips to a later time when, it is clear, the Brook did not obey, for it is now a sea itself. The original sea, which wanted a brook, now tells the brook-turned-sea to go away. The latter objects, "I am he / You cherished." But the original sea, while addressing the new sea respectfully as "Learned Waters," tells him "Wisdom is stale—to Me." By coming into your own, you may lose your appeal to him, who cherished you when you were a lesser being, capable only of merging your identity in his.

See also "HE FUMBLES AT YOUR SOUL" and "TWO SWIMMERS WRESTLED ON THE SPAR—."

FURTHER READING

Judith Farr, *Passion*, 215; David Porter, *Early Poetry*, 101; Cynthia Griffin Wolff, *Emily Dickinson*, 271–272.

"The Heart asks Pleasure— first—" (1863) (Fr 588, J 536)

In this great poem of diminishing expectations, Dickinson's powers of suggestion and compression are at their height. Characteristically, she offers no hint of the underlying disappointment motivating her words. Instead, she writes a wisdom poem, applying to "the heart" in general, but with the unmistakable authenticity of lived experience. Economically, painstakingly, she traces the step-by-step transformation of thwarted desire to the wish to be "excused" from pain, to be numb, to sleep, and, finally, to die.

The sense of despair, of being at the mercy of powerful, external forces is present from the outset in the image of the heart as a supplicant or beggar, one who asks. This humbleness of the heart is carried forward in the notion of asking an "excuse" from pain, as if the heart were a schoolgirl pleading to avoid some unpleasant requirement. But this, too, is refused, for, in its next request, the heart is a patient, asking for "those little Anodynes," that is, medicines that relieve pain or induce sleep. For Dickinson, not given to drink or chemical painkillers, the word likely refers to "life's little Duties" that "hold our Senses on," of which she wrote in "I TIE MY HAT—I CREASE MY SHAWL—," another, longer poem about the aftermath of heartbreak. The desire for numbness then deepens into the desire for sleep, and then for death:

> And then—if it should be
> The will of it's Inquisitor
> The privilege to die—

While the power of whom she has asked all these things has remained implicit until this point, that power is now referred to as "it's [the heart's] Inquisitor." (Note that Dickinson, incorrectly, always used "it's" for the possessive, as well as for the contraction). With the reference to the Catholic Inquisition, God is invoked as the all-powerful torturer, of whom she requests, with undisguised bitterness, the "privilege to die—."

Emily Dickinson, who has been characterized as the poet of the aftermath, often speaks of the numbness necessary to survive great pain. In Fr 1119, "Pain has but one Acquaintance," she portrays death as pain's "tender" assistant." In Fr 584, she gives thanks for life as a sleepwalker: "We dream—it is good we are dreaming—/ It would hurt us—were we awake—." In "From Blank to Blank" (Fr 484), she is glad to be sightless, declaring, "'Twas lighter—to be Blind—." In Fr 515, pain itself is the benevolent creator of its antidote:

"There is a pain—so utter—/ It swallows substance up—/ Then covers the Abyss with Trance—." In these poems, numbness is an immediate response to great pain. But in the poem under discussion, it is unclear whether the turning away from feeling, from consciousness, and ultimately from life itself, is a rapid process following a single loss or one that stretches out over decades of continual disappointment. The implication of the latter interpretation is that *any* heart will suffer enough over the course of a lifetime to ultimately desire its own death.

See also "AFTER GREAT PAIN, A FORMAL FEELING COMES—" and "PAIN—HAS AN ELEMENT OF BLANK—."

FURTHER READING

Shira Wolosky, *A Voice of War*, 99–100.

"The Malay—took the Pearl—" (1862) (Fr 451, J 452)

This much discussed, allegorical poem is built upon a sexual triad: the Pearl—the object of desire, which is taken from the Sea; the Malay, who takes the Pearl home to his Hut; and the Earl, who desires the Pearl but, too afraid of the Sea to take action, can only watch helplessly as the Malay bears his prize home.

Spoken by the angry, cheated Earl, the poem's syntax quickly breaks down, giving the narrative a breathless, disconnected quality. A paraphrase might read: "The Malay took the Pearl, Not I, the Earl. I feared the unsanctified sea too much to touch it [the Pearl]. Or: I feared the sea [too much]. I was [too much] unsanctified to touch it. While I was praying I might be worthy of the destiny [of owning the Pearl], the swarthy fellow swam and bore my jewel home, Home to the Hut! What a [different] lot [the pearl would have had] had I taken her. The pearl is worn on [the Malay's] dusky breast, while I hadn't considered an amber vest good enough to place it on. Or: I hadn't considered that vest of amber [his dusky breast] fit. The Negro never knew that I, too, wooed the Pearl. Gaining or losing [being undone] the Pearl was all the same to him."

Although some have argued that the poem is a universal allegory, most critics believe that it must be understood in biographical terms, as an expression of Emily's (the Earl's) loss of SUSAN HUNTINGTON GILBERT DICKINSON (the Pearl), the woman she loved, to her brother WILLIAM AUSTIN DICKINSON (the Malay), who married Susan in 1856. When the two people she loved most became engaged, Emily at first acted as mutual confidante and intermediary, rejoicing that Susan, as her "sister," would be a permanent part of her life. But once Sue and Austin established their conjugal life at The EVERGREENS, her fantasy of a loving alliance among the three of them soon gave way to the reality that she stood outside their intimacy. In a poem written in 1863, Fr 658, she writes of her exclusion directly, without the veil of allegory: "'Tis true—They shut me in the Cold—/ But then—Themselves were warm." In this verse, the poet asks God to forgive them, as she herself has, insisting, "The Harm They did—was short—."

In contrast, "The Malay took the Pearl," written a year earlier, is bitter and despairing, permeated with regret for an unlived life. The speaker/Earl blames both himself and the Malay for his fate, while viewing the Pearl as the passive prize whose fate has been determined by the outcome of the rivalry between the two male figures:

> I—feared the Sea—too much
> Unsanctified—to touch—
>
> Praying that I might be
> Worthy—the Destiny—
> The Swarthy fellow swam—
> And bore my Jewel—Home—

This is but one of a number of poems, including "One life of so much consequence!" (1861, Fr 248), "YOUR RICHES—TAUGHT ME—POVERTY," "SHELLS FROM THE COAST MISTAKING—," and "Removed from Accident of Loss" (1862, Fr 417), in which Susan is embodied as Emily's precious, shining, perfect pearl. In the latter poem, another expression of sexual rivalry, the "Brown Malay" is evoked as one unconscious "Of Pearls in Eastern Waters—/ Marked His—."

It is this absence of awareness arising from his instinctive nature that earns the Malay the Earl's disdain. Despite the Malay's victory, the aristocratic Earl/speaker views this man of action as primitive, an inferior. While Dickinson's evocation of a "dusky," "swarthy" "Negro" as the Earl's rival reflects the stereotypes of her time of dark-skinned "natives," it also allows her to make an aesthetic contrast between the Malay's darkness and the Pearl's brightness. Moreover, by making the rival a dark, exotic male, the speaker stresses her difference from him, ostensibly one of color and nationality, but really one of sex. Why a Malay? The reason may be found on the level of sound: the Malay is the male, the only true male in the poem. In addition, Judith Farr traces the roots of the Malay figure to Thomas De Quincey's *Confessions of an English Opium Eater,* a work Dickinson obtained for the family library. In De Quincey's book, a Malay appears in dreams and conducts the author to exotic places where he is punished for some 'deed' by being buried alive or drowned. Thus, the Malay in both the poem and the *Confessions,* is an enemy with whom the speaker/narrator does not communicate directly.

Dickinson's Malay is unaware that the Earl, too, has "wooed" the Pearl, as no doubt Austin was unaware when he carried Sue "Home to the Hut!" that Emily had wooed Sue. In the final lines, the crude Malay is portrayed as more or less indifferent to his prize: "To gain, or be undone—/ Alike to Him—One—." And yet, whatever his insufficiencies, the Malay/male is the one who is naturally entitled to the Pearl. As Farr observes, "[T]he Malay simply claims the speaker's pearl. Yet [Dickinson] never says he steals it. Though she is filled with anger and contempt to think so, the pearl is the Malay's by right. It is his 'destiny' as a male to have it" (*Passion,* 150).

In contrast, the Earl's "masculinity" is a poetic construct, which empowers the speaker by allowing "him" to legitimately woo the Pearl. In a poem written the following year, Fr 734, the speaker asks an unidentified woman, "No matter now—Sweet—/ But when I'm Earl—/ Won't you wish you'd spoken / To that dull Girl?" Imagining herself an "Earl," instead of a girl, she feels confident in her power to win over a woman who would not have noticed her earlier. As critic Vivian R. Pollak notes, however, this psychological sex change is not altogether successful, and the speaker is "forced to witness the triumph of raw physical acquisitiveness over her Puritanical self-restraint" (*Anxiety of Gender*, 156). The reason the Earl fails to act in this poem is his fear of the Sea, a complex image that has many meanings in Dickinson's work. Here it may represent the speaker's unconscious, the unknown depths of female sexuality, or, more generally, the unknown. The sea is one of her metaphors for Sue, and thus, Farr interprets, "the sea is Sue as Unknown in the fullness of her sexuality" (*Passion*, 150). Pollak suggests an alien environment, nature, and death as other possible meanings (*Anxiety of Gender*, 156).

A very different reading has been suggested by scholar Robert Weisbuch, who believes that Dickinson's poems should not be "pinned down" to any one situation, biographical or otherwise. He sees the poem as a traditional allegory, in which the Earl's failure exemplifies the moral "that nothing will come to the man who waits in selfish fear—not wealth in any real sense of the word, not paradise, not beauty, not a realization of the meaning of things. . . . The poem devalues a pious passivity, an unengaged intellect, in comparison to a passionate activity, an involvement with experiential risk" (*Emily Dickinson's Poetry*, 57). Farr heartily disagrees with Weisbuch's reading; for her, the poem contains no moral and does not recommend risk, but is rather "an angry statement of fact" (*Passion*, 149).

Pollak, too, challenges Weisbuch's approach, asserting that "The Pearl need not be Sue, the Malay need not be Austin, and the Earl need not be Emily. Yet however generalizable the situation depicted, the poem is informed by the sexual temptations of Dickinson's experience . . ." (*Anxiety*, 156). As a "searching parable of insufficient courage," the poem, she suggests, is built on a psychoanalytic symbolism, in which the Pearl is the ideal self, the Earl is paralyzing conscience, and the Malay-Negro is the admired and despised id. Summarizing the poem's impact, she writes, "Dickinson satirizes the primitiveness of male dominance, fears the sea-change of homosexual conquest, and laments an unlived life" (*Anxiety of Gender*, 156).

Dickinson returns to the theme of unsuccessful competition with a male figure in a poem written the following year, Fr 596 "OURSELVES WERE WED ONE SUMMER—DEAR—." Here, however, the tone is elegiac rather than angry. The speaker admits that she and the beloved woman have taken different paths in life, while nostalgically recalling: "And yet, one Summer, we were Queens—/ But You—were crowned in June—." In the poem immediately following this one, Fr 597, the pearl/sea motif undergoes a transformation. The Pearl is no longer important because a wealthy, powerful male figure has come on the scene, not as rival, but as gift-giving lover: "'Tis little I—could care for Pearls—/ Who own the Ample sea— / Or Brooches—when the Emperor—/ With Rubies—pelteth me—."

See also: "I STARTED EARLY—TOOK MY DOG—" and "BEHIND ME—DIPS ETERNITY—."

FURTHER READING

Judith Farr, *Passion*, 147–151; Vivian R. Pollak, *Anxiety of Gender*, 155–156; Robert Weisbuch, *Emily Dickinson's Poetry*, 57–58.

"The missing All, prevented Me" (1865) (Fr 995, J 985)

In this poem Dickinson stands on its head the conventional wisdom, "Because I had the most important thing I could not bother about the little things I didn't have." Instead, she declares:

> The missing All, prevented Me
> From missing minor Things.

Her ability to rise above minor losses comes from *lacking* the most important thing. *Not having* is a positive good, a source of inner freedom.

In his classic essay on Dickinson, poet Richard Wilbur remarks that in this poem "she conveys both the extent of her repudiation and the extent of her happiness" ("Sumptuous Destitution," 61). Indeed, the poem is a simultaneously wry and poignant account of personal deprivation so extensive ("missing All") that only the end of a world or the extinction of the Sun could sufficiently rouse her curiosity so as to distract her attention from the work at hand. Dickinson's use of hyperbole ("The missing All") is not "exaggeration" in the usual sense, but a means of conveying how the loss feels to her. She underscores the substantiality of her deprivation by turning the participial phrase into a nominal one: "The missing All" is a concrete thing or force. Characteristically, Dickinson does no reveal what she has lost in its particularity but generalizes it to express not something abstract but its essential, subjective meaning. Whatever "its" specific content, it is "All" to her: the one thing compared to which nothing else matters.

Critics have wrestled with this "All," in the attempt to justify so extreme a statement. Thus, for example, J. V. Cunningham has written, "Only loss of salvation justifies such hyperbole" ("Sorting Out," 455). Yet, who is to say what another person's "All" may be? Given what we know of Dickinson—her spirited argument with traditional concepts of God and salvation, her passionate longings—it seems far more likely that she was talking about the loss of a SUSAN HUNTINGTON GILBERT DICKINSON or a CHARLES WADSWORTH or a SAMUEL BOWLES. For the reader, however, what makes the poem powerful is the recognition of a kindred "disproportion" in his or her own inner life: that one thing whose loss would make all other losses trivial.

Dickinson presents deprivation of so extreme a nature as a boon, bringing both emotional insulation and philosophical perspective. She does not, in modern parlance, sweat the small stuff but keeps her head down and concentrates on her work. We may assume she is working on her poetry. For, through her poetry, she transformed "the missing All" into what she calls, in one poem, "The Banquet of Abstemiousness."

By writing of this state of being in the past tense, she implies that this is how things were at one time, not necessarily how they stand now. The poet stands at a distance and observes herself during this period; we are not to assume she remained "above it all" forever. This explains why, as scholar Sharon Cameron notes, "The distinctive feature of [the poem] is its impersonality . . . this is loss acutely seen and objectively rendered" (*Lyric Time,*

171). Formally, the poem is written in Dickinson's predominant hymn form, with alternating lines of four and three iambs. In the last line, however, the rhythm is broken. The line is shorter than the others, with a five-syllable word, and has only two stresses: "For curiosity." These features, together with the final period, contribute to the sense of curt dismissal with which the poem ends.

See also "GOD GAVE A LOAF TO EVERY BIRD—" and "WHO NEVER WANTED—MADDEST JOY."

FURTHER READING

Sharon Cameron, *Lyric Time,* 170–171; J. V. Cunningham, "Sorting Out," 455; Richard Wilber, "Sumptuous Destitution," in *Critical Essays,* Judith Farr, ed., 61.

"The only news I know" (1864) (Fr 820, J 827)

Fr 820 offers one of Dickinson's most memorable self-conceptualizations as poet-seer, the recipient of "Bulletins from Immortality." Creating a persona who has virtually no interface with ordinary life, she employs hyperbole to convey the truth of where her being centers and what it means to "receive" poetry. By couching her revelations and visions as "Bulletins" and "Shows," she slyly underscores the gap that separates her from those who concern themselves with more ordinary news flashes and spectacles. The conceit of apparent self-effacement ("the only news") thinly veils the underlying assertion of superiority by a speaker whose sole concern is with ultimate realities.

The poem in no way represents her actual life, in which she read the *Springfield Republican* regularly and listened avidly to news of the world from friends who traveled widely and were engaged in the world's business. Dickinson took a lively interest in AMHERST gossip, and in the news of her friends' and relatives' lives, which came to her both through word of mouth and letters. A talented raconteur and satirist, especially in her younger years, she reveled in the passing on of commonplace bulletins. All of this, however, is irrelevant to the concerns of this poem: an insistence upon the poet's spiritual obsessions: Immortality, Eternity, God, and Existence.

The phrase "Bulletins all Day" takes on special meaning when one considers that Dickinson must have felt bombarded by poetic inspiration and ideas at the time she wrote this poem. She was, in fact, slowing down—from almost 300 poems the previous year to a mere 100 in 1864. By ordinary standards, however, this still qualifies as a period of intense creative absorption and productivity. Moreover, the serious problems she was having with her eyesight that year, which curtailed her activities and, worst of all, prevented her from reading, no doubt made her feel isolated and more than ever intensely focused and dependent on her inner "news."

This poem invites comparison with one written the previous year, "THIS IS MY LETTER TO THE WORLD," in which she also presents herself as a conveyor of universal messages ("The simple News that Nature told / With tender Majesty") to a vast audience ("Sweet—countrymen"). In contrast to the positive and loving characterization of the "message" in that poem, "Bulletins from Immortality" and "Shows" that are "Tomorrow and Today—/ Perchance Eternity—" are starker and more mysterious. Dickinson often used the words *Eternity* and *Immortality* interchangeably, as synonyms for time without end and life everlasting, the limitless time that precedes birth and the resurrection of the soul, promised by Jesus Christ, that awaits after death.

For scholar Dorothy Huff Oberhaus, reading the poem in the context of Dickinson's 40th fascicle, in which it is the lead poem, the "only news" the speaker knows is unambiguously from Christ, "who is referred to or addressed or speaks himself in every poem but one of this fascicle" (*Dickinson's Fascicles*, 26). Oberhaus's conviction that Christ is the sender of the Bulletins is based on her analyses of the two poems that follow it in the fascicle as recollections of Jesus' words. She sees the poem's clarity of form reinforcing its clear meaning: "With its four crisp, concise tercets, the first poem itself resembles a 'Bulletin'" (Ibid., 41). Upon closer examination, however, the "Bulletin" yields an uncertain content. The speaker begins confidently enough, conclud-

ing the first stanza with a decisive period—unusual punctuation in the middle of a Dickinson poem. In the second stanza, however, she calls the "Shows" she sees "perchance Eternity." Since "perchance" can mean either "by chance/accident" or "perhaps," Dickinson may mean either that she occasionally stumbles over Eternity or that what she sees may be Eternity, but she cannot say with certainty.

Stanza 3 returns us to firm ground with the assertion, "The only one I meet / Is God—." But this is followed by a very different statement:

—The Only Street—
Existence—This traversed

If other news there be—

With the dash separating "Existence" from "This," syntax breaks down and connections become uncertain. Her actual location—the only street available—is not Eternity but Existence, which she must "traverse" before she can discover whether there is any other news. The lines may be paraphrased as: "Once I traverse this street of existence, that is, when I have died, if there's other news, that is, news of life eternal, I'll let you know about it." Thus, the poem's ending seemingly contradicts its confident beginning. The contradiction may be only apparent, however, since the speaker has only said that she receives "Bulletins," which generally convey the "breaking news" of discrete events, without disclosing their larger implications.

The history of this poem offers an interesting example of how Dickinson's poems take on new meaning in the context of different letters. She incorporated the first stanza in a letter sent to THOMAS WENTWORTH HIGGINSON in early June 1864 (L 290), from Cambridge, Massachusetts, where she was undergoing treatment for her eye problems. She has received a note from him, indicating that he has been wounded in the war, and begins her letter, "Are you in danger—I did not know that you were hurt. Will you tell me more? Mr. Hawthorne died." This "bulletin" of the great writer's death obviously stuns her and resonates with her fears for Higginson's life. She then tells him about the confinement and isolation imposed by her illness and its treatment, saying that she nonetheless manages to "work in my Prison, and make Guests [poems] for myself—." She prefaces the first stanza of Fr 820 with the words, "I am surprised and anxious, since receiving your note—." In this context, the lines read like an apology and convey a sense of being lost, blind, and out-of-touch with vital news about a beloved friend.

See also: "Behind Me—dips Eternity—," "I dwell in Possibility—," and "I was the slightest in the House—."

FURTHER READING

Charles Anderson, *Stairway*, 201; Sharon Cameron, "Dickinson's Fascicles," in *Handbook*, Grabher et al., eds., 151; Dorothy Huff Oberhaus, *Emily Dickinson's Fascicles*, 25–26, 40–44; Richard B. Sewall, *Life*, II, 636.

"The Poets light but Lamps—"
(1865) (Fr 930 J 883)

In this great poem, Dickinson builds upon the Latin aphorism *ars longa, vita brevis* (art is long, life is short) to create a unique vision of poetry's immortality: Not only do true poems live after their creator has died but they are transformed by the succeeding generations that read them. Dickinson's metaphor for the writing of poems is the lighting of lamps, an apt one given the prominence of vision and light in her poetry. The metaphor is also one of many instances in which she introduces women's work (sewing, sweeping, gardening) into her verses. For, as biographer Cynthia Griffin Wolff points out, women were in charge of keeping the lamps lit in 19th-century Amherst, a vital task that kept the household from being plunged into cold and darkness (*Emily Dickinson*, 207).

In the first two lines, as the poets light their lamps and "Themselves—go out—", they seem to transfer their light to the lamps. Reinforcing this notion, the very word "poets" disappears from this verse as the light of the poems/lamps takes over. If the "poets" reappear at all, it is in the final phrase, "their Circumference," where "their" refers to both the poet and her poems, now merged.

In the second stanza, Dickinson carries her lamps from the house in which they were first lit into the immense spaces of future ages, where they "Inhere as do the Suns—." "To Inhere" in her lexicon is defined as "to exist or be fixed in something else." Thus, to say that the lighted wicks of the poems/lamps are as "inherent" (fundamental, integral) to existence as suns are to the cosmos is to affirm that poetry is warmth and light, essential to life itself.

But poems will inhere only if they are "vital Light"—living light. The image resonates with Dickinson's famous question to Thomas Wentworth Higginson, "Are you too deeply occupied to say if my Verse is alive?" She believed that a true poem had to breathe, and her concept of a word, the basic unit of a poem, was of something that takes on life only when it is "spoken" in the body of a poem. In 1862, she had written, "A word is dead, when it is said / Some say—/ I say it just begins to live / That day" (Fr 277).

Such a word goes on living and, like all living things, changing. In this poem, change occurs when the poem's light passes through the lens of each age:

Each Age a Lens
Disseminating their
Circumference—

A lens may change the direction of light, magnify or diminish it. Dickinson describes what each lens does by the phrase, "Disseminating their / Circumference—." The use of a five-syllable and a four-syllable word, after all the mono- and disyllabic ones, creates the outward-moving flow of sound the poet is evoking, while the final dash reinforces the sense of openness.

Dickinson's succession of light images—lamps, suns, "circumference"—opens up, too, into successive meanings. If suns are a cosmic expansion of the lamps' light, then circumference is the furthermost reach of their light. Dickinson used the word *circumference* repeatedly in both poems and letters, endowing it with a number of related meanings. In 1862, she wrote to her mentor, Thomas Wentworth Higginson: "Perhaps you smile at me. I could not stop for that—My Business is Circumference—"

(L 268). She wrote this during her most productive and inspired period, as a poet who would not be deterred from her task, even if others ridiculed her for pursuing what she perceived as the essence of poetry, "circumference."

The term expresses a belief that the periphery of the circle is the poet's proper domain; it contains two concepts that were central to her idea of poetry. The first is "slantness": The poet cannot reach the "center," that is, the Truth of human experience, head-on, but must circle around it, exploring it indirectly from varying perspectives. She sometimes uses the word "circuit" to express this aspect of circumference. The second meaning has to do with limitation: Circumference is the outer limit of the circle of human experience, the boundary separating what is knowable from what is unknowable. While recognizing the existence of such a boundary, the poet's "business" is to explore the far limits of what can be known, reaching within herself and employing all the resources of language to stretch that boundary a bit further. The inherent mystery and ambiguity the poet captures through her pursuit of circumference is precisely what allows her poem to be seen anew by successive ages.

In this poem's closing image, Dickinson uses the word "disseminating" for what each age does to circumference. Disseminating is what bees do: spreading, fecundating, scattering seed for growth and propagation. But it is also what preachers, prophets, philosophers, and poets do when they disseminate the truth or Gospel. Thus, the word draws together the notions of biological and spiritual propagation. By linking this many-leveled scattering to the "stretching" inherent in circumference, Dickinson demonstrates the very essence of circumference: the use of language to suggest a mystery not contained in language itself.

See also "I RECKON—WHEN I COUNT AT ALL—," "TELL ALL THE TRUTH BUT TELL IT SLANT—," "THIS WAS A POET—," and CIRCUMFERENCE POEMS.

FURTHER READING

Joseph Raab, "Metapoetic Element," in *Handbook,* Grabher et al., eds., 283–293; Cynthia Griffin Wolff, *Emily Dickinson,* 207.

"There came a Day—at Summer's full—" (1862) (Fr 325, J 322)

Unlike the great majority of Dickinson's poems, this famous and much-debated narrative appears to contain a specific "scene" from the poet's life: a day within the summer solstice, June 21 and 22, when a love is consummated and virtually simultaneously renounced. Appropriately, within this season of weddings, a "marriage" takes place, yet its only "future" is in the life to come. The poem is Dickinson's most complete expression of this central theme of a reunion with the lost beloved in God's heaven, a vision evoked in other poems of this period (see "REARRANGE A 'WIFE'S' AFFECTION!").

Recent biographers have suggested that the poem may commemorate a farewell meeting, perhaps with REVEREND CHARLES WADSWORTH (although his 1860 visit was in March), perhaps with SAMUEL BOWLES, who often attended the August commencements of AMHERST COLLEGE, in which the Dickinson family played a prominent role, or even with BENJAMIN FRANKLIN NEWTON, her first "tutor," who saw her poetic gift and died prematurely in 1853 (Sewall, *Life,* II, 552; Habegger, *My Wars,* 413). At the same time, they caution against too literal a reading. In addition to being a love poem, it may be seen as "a religious dedication, the mystical marriage of the soul to Christ. Or, in an interpretation that unites the romantic and the religious. . . . [t]he poem may be Emily Dickinson's way of dramatizing her ultimate determination to be a poet. . . . In this reading, the poem commemorates the moment of rebirth . . ." (Sewall, 552, 553).

What is striking about this poem, as compared with others proclaiming the speaker's spiritual "wifehood," is its tone of assured belief, so different from the tormented ambiguity that runs through other works on this theme. While it may not conform exactly to Wordsworth's definition of poetry as "emotion recollected in tranquillity"—the anguish is palpable in the final image—the poem is told in past tense, as a story, with a certain degree of distance and acceptance conveyed through its fairly regular metrical and rhyme patterns, its coherent syntax and sequencing of events. There is no undertone of doubt that the promise will be fulfilled. Yet the faith Dickinson expresses here is far from a conventionally orthodox one. By her "deft fusion of the language of love with the vocabulary of Christianity," as Sandra M. Gilbert points out, Dickinson "converts the Christianity she had begun to reject as a seventeen-year-old Mount Holyoke student into a complex theology of secular love" ("Wayward Nun," 25). Within Dickinson's sacred universe, she and her lover are "sealed churches" and their erotic communion becomes a sacrament.

Since summer was for Dickinson the beloved season of nature's intensity and fruitfulness (see "LIKE SOME OLD FASHIONED MIRACLE"), "Summer's full" suggests the very apogee of fecundity. The day is "Entirely for me—" as few things were in a life marked by frustrated desire to possess her loved ones exclusively. She is unaccustomed to such days, more suited "for the Saints—," yet it is earthly fulfillment that is heavenly to her and, within the course of the poem, she and her lover are redefined in sacred terms and deemed worthy vessels of it ("sealed churches"). In stanza 1, nature, the "Day—at Summer's full" resonates with and represents the speaker's inner state; by stanza 2, however, nature moves in its usual round, as if nothing extraordinary were occurring in her soul:

The Sun—as common—went abroad—
The Flowers—accustomed—blew—
As if no Soul the Solstice passed—
That maketh all things new.

This is not nature in harmony with human emotions, but indifferent to them (see "I DREADED THAT FIRST ROBIN, SO,"). "The 'solstice' of the speaker's transforming love is literally a moment outside of time: 'the point . . . at which the sun stops or ceases to recede from the equator'" (Wolff, *Emily Dickinson*, 413).

In stanza 3, this sacred time, "scarce profaned—by speech," is a moment of rebirth into a new dimension, characterized by external silence and holiness. For the poet "the symbol of a word" was itself a sacred thing, but here it is superfluous, like the "Wardrobe of Our Lord" during a Sacra-

ment, when the bond between God and man is reaffirmed. Both are outer shells, unnecessary at this moment of pure sacred being. Then, in the pivotal fourth stanza, which stands at the precise center of the poem, consummation occurs, but in the context of compressed, multilayered religious language, as the lovers themselves become sacred entities to one another:

Each was to each—the sealed church—
Permitted to commune—this time—
Lest we too awkward—show—
At "Supper of the Lamb."

The image of the "sealed church" may simply imply that the lovers' separate, tightly closed souls were opened to one another, "Permitted to commune." But the scriptural resonance of the phrase is impossible to ignore. In Revelation, Dickinson's favorite book of the Bible, the Lamb, representing Christ, is the only one capable of breaking open the sealed book that reveals the future. Moreover, the fourth line is a clear allusion to Revelation 19:9: "Blessed *are* they which are called unto the marriage supper of the Lamb." Through these verbal resonances, the union of the lovers is connected to their future in the Resurrection and to their worthiness as members of the spiritual elect—notions that recur in the poem's final stanza.

But the image of "sealed churches" also contains an important sacramental meaning, which helps to clarify this stanza. Jane Eberwein notes that Dickinson was familiar with the phrase as representing all those elected by God to participate in the two sacraments recognized by CONGREGATIONALISM: baptism and the Lord's Supper. (In Calvinism, a sacrament is a seal of the covenant by which God affirms his promise of salvation to the elect). In Dickinson's time, there was an ongoing debate on who was worthy enough to be eligible for this spiritual elite. Here, she declares that she and her lover each constitute a community of the elect and that "they have ordained a new sacrament to consecrate their private promise of fidelity" (Eberwein, "Calvinist Sacramental Tradition," 92). Eberwein supports the view that the lover is Jesus, "since sacraments involve the sealing of a bond between man and God" (Ibid., 93). This interpretation becomes shakier, however, when we remember that Dickinson regularly identified her earthly lover/Master with Christ/Savior. The stanza is more coherent if the speaker and an earthly lover are the ones "Permitted to commune this—time—," perhaps to gain a little practice and thus avoid being "too awkward" when they meet again at "Supper of the Lamb," that is, at the Resurrection.

In stanza 5, however, eternity is only a hope as they are cast back into fleeting, earthly time that slips away though they clutch at it greedily. The summer day of sun and flowers has vanished and in its stead is a boundless sea, emblematic, perhaps, of life itself and suffering, where, looking back at one another, they sail on separate ships "Bound to opposing Lands—." In stanza 6, the speaker describes the end of the lovers' meeting as the moment "when time had failed—/ Without external sound"—as if time itself had silently taken on mortality. Instead of an exchange of rings, the lovers then "bind" one another's crucifixes—emblems of their pain and of their faith. Scholar Judith Farr explains the term "bound" by noting that "[W]hen a Victorian novice took final vows, her crucifix was often 'bound' or fastened on her breast as a sign of Christian witness, but also of her calling as the spouse of Christ (*Passion*, 306). In Dickinson's appropriation of this custom, "the speaker and another act as sponsor and sponsored in taking up the cross to wear" (306). They are each Christ figures, who, as the final stanza affirms, will endure "Calvaries of Love" in order to merit "that New Marriage" that will come when the Grave has been "Deposed," and they have been reborn into eternal life.

The early publication history of this poem is illustrative of the complexity of determining which of different variants is the "authoritative version" of a Dickinson poem. The poet made at least three different copies of the poem, each of which differs from the others. She sent one to THOMAS WENTWORTH HIGGINSON on April 25, 1862, accompanying Letter 261. She bound a second version, containing a number of cancellations and alternative wordings into one of her manuscript books (fascicle 13). She sent yet another version to her sister-in-law, SUSAN HUNTINGTON GILBERT DICKINSON. Scholars are uncertain whether a copy in the Amherst Col-

lege library is the "lost" copy she sent to Susan, or yet another variant (Martha Nell Smith, "Dickinson's Manuscripts," 114). Susan placed a copy in *Scribner's Magazine* (August 1890), under the title "Renunciation," that omitted stanza 4, and gave the word *sail* instead of *Soul* in stanza 2. To refute this version, Higginson and MABEL LOOMIS TODD, who had printed it in the 1890 *Poems* as "Renunciation" reprinted it in the 1891 *Poems*.

See also "A WORD MADE FLESH IS SELDOM," "I CANNOT LIVE WITH YOU—," "I SHOULD HAVE BEEN TOO GLAD, I SEE—," and PUBLICATION HISTORY AND EDITORIAL SCHOLARSHIP.

FURTHER READING

Millicent Todd Bingham, *Ancestor's Brocades,* 149; Jane Eberwein, "Emily Dickinson and the Calvinist Sacramental Tradition," in *Critical Essays,* Judith Farr, ed., 92–93, 96; Judith Farr, *Passion,* 304–306; Susan M. Gilbert, "Wayward Nun," in *Critical Essays,* 25; Alfred Habegger, *My Wars,* 412–413; Richard B. Sewall, *Life,* II, 552–555; Martha Nell Smith, "Dickinson's Manuscripts," in *Handbook,* Grabher et al., eds., 113–114; Cynthia Griffin Wolff, *Emily Dickinson,* 412–413.

"There came a Wind like a Bugle—" (1883) (Fr 1618, J 1593)

Throughout her writing career, Dickinson called upon the wind as a necessary and versatile image to embody her sense of the world. The wind is the subject of at least 10 other poems (Fr 123, Fr 494, Fr 621, Fr 796, Fr 802, Fr 1152, Fr 1160, 1216, Fr 1441, and Fr 1703), as well as a regular cast member in Dickinson's natural dramas, particularly those involving storms. As we would expect of so nonformulaic a poet, she endowed the wind with a wealth of connotations. In her early verse, "windiness" is a quality associated with cosmic unpredictability, randomness, and adversity: "Grant me, Oh Lord, a sunny mind—/ Thy windy will to bear!" (Fr 123). For Dickinson, who wrote of the wind in different tones, ranging from apocalyptic to tongue-in-cheek, the wind was primarily a transformative power, violent, passionate or playful, destructive or creative, bestial, humanized, or cosmic and ethereal. The wind's power is often portrayed as masculine, but also as an invisible force ("A Wind that rose though not a Leaf / In any Forest stirred—"). For, of course, the wind is breath, the universe's breath, and the poet's. Recall that Dickinson was the poet who wanted to know if her verse "breathed." While Dickinson's wind is doubtless an inheritance of the Romantic tradition (think of Shelley's "Ode to the West Wind"), she developed it in a direction distinctly her own.

The "Wind like a Bugle" of this poem is a close relative of Dickinson's martial winds (see Fr 1164, "The Winds went out their martial ways"), but with cosmic connotations. The bugle-wind is Gabriel's trumpet announcing—not God's—but Dickinson's "flying tidings," which emerge only in the poem's final unexpected lines, surprising the reader and opening the poem out beyond the limits of ingenious metaphor:

How much can come
And much can go,
And yet abide the World!

The wind announces not peace on earth, but the World's endurance, despite its great and continuous losses. The "World" may be interpreted literally as planet or cosmos, or as the inner world of the poet or of anyone who has lived a certain span, as the 52-year-old woman who wrote this poem had.

From the first line, "There came a Wind like a Bugle," with its subtle biblical undertones, Dickinson's syntax and language raise the events she describes to mythical status. This is an annunciation and the images at the center of the poem suggest that the message is one of chaos: a world in a state of violent flux. One device used to suggest chaos is synesthesia, that is, the description of one kind of sense perception using words that describe another kind of sense perception. Thus, both "Green Chill" and "Emerald Ghost" are images that merge the wind with the greenery (grass, trees) it sets in motion. Note that the wind is "a Green Chill upon the Heat"—this is a summer storm—and the image evokes a natural order turned upside down: "Green Chill" and "Emerald Ghost," as well as the words "so ominous" and the barring of windows and door against an encroaching doom, introduce several notes of Gothic horror into the narrative.

The wind is a shape-changer: a bugle, a snake "quivering through the grass," a "Green Chill" and "Emerald Ghost." Then comes the lightning, or, in Dickinson's memorable phrase, "The Doom's Electric Moccasin," an image evoking the "Indian" menace of her PURITAN HERITAGE. In the next set of images (lines 9–12), the world has grown alien, breathless and uprooted: "a strange Mob of panting Trees," fences, houses, rivers—all fleeing:

On a strange Mob of panting Trees
And Fences fled away
And Rivers where the Houses ran
Those looked that lived—that Day—

By inverting the syntax of those lines and splitting the verb, that is, placing subject and verb ("Those looked that lived—that Day—") before the preposition and three lines of indirect objects ("On a strange Mob," etc.) Dickinson disorients the reader, making the poem "imitate" the chaos it evokes. A sense of portentousness is evoked by the words "that Day," which suggests a legendary event looked back upon from a great distance.

Having thus brought on what scholar Charles Anderson has called "the poetic end of the world," Dickinson reverses herself and proclaims its survival. There is no argument or "reason" for why this should be so; it is simply a declaration of the poet's observation, her inner knowledge. This poet, who allows us to hear her "thinking aloud," invites us to make the leap with her.

See also "HE FUMBLES AT YOUR SOUL."

FURTHER READING

Charles Anderson, *Stairway*, 136–137; Joanne Feit Diehl, *Romantic Imagination*, 156–159.

"There is no Frigate like a Book" (1872) (Fr 1286, J 1263)

One of Dickinson's most beloved poems, Fr 1286 is a celebration of the transporting joy of reading and its sustaining role in the poet's life. Dickinson wrote it when she had been living in seclusion for more than a decade and reading books and journals had become her primary connection to the world beyond her native AMHERST. Even before her retreat from society in her early 30s, she had traveled little; her only trip outside of New England was to Washington, D.C., and Baltimore in 1855. Thus this reclusive poet likens books to ships that take her "Lands away." A "Page / Of prancing Poetry—," she declares, is better than any "Courser," In this sense, the poem is emblematic of her approach to experience in general: It is not the outer journey, but the inner one that counts, the exploration of what she called the "Undiscovered Continent" (Fr 814).

This nonmaterial aspect of the journey offered by a book is what makes it democratically available to rich and poor alike. Note that the book is both the journey itself ("Traverse") and the transporting vehicle (the "frugal" "Chariot / That bears the human soul"). Intriguingly, in Dickinson's work, death is the other "democratic" experience, as in the early poem, "One dignity delays for all—" (Fr 77, 1859), in which she says of death:

Coach, it insures, and footmen—
Chamber, and state, and throng—

The chariot bearing the soul is most often death's, as in her great poem, "BECAUSE I COULD NOT STOP FOR DEATH—." The "Traverse" of this poem is reminiscent of her poems of "the transitus" between life and death, such as "It was a quiet way—" (Fr 573), in which she imagines herself borne away "With swiftness, of Chariots" toward eternity. As an image for the experience of reading a book, Dickinson reverses the meaning of the democratic chariot and makes it a symbol of spiritual/imaginative expansiveness, the "immortality" available to all.

Dickinson's own poetry, with its complex and sometimes jarring rhythms, does not always "prance." This poem, however, with its regular meter and exact concluding rhyme "Toll"/"Soul") does. Compressed, spirited, and inspiring, it demonstrates the artistic frugality of which it speaks.

See also "UNTO MY BOOKS—SO GOOD TO TURN—."

FURTHER READING

Gary Lee Stonum, "Dickinson's Literary Background," in Handbook, Grabher et al., eds., 44–60.

"There's a certain Slant of light," (1862) (Fr 320, J 258)

When MABEL LOOMIS TODD published this poem in the 1890 *Poems* under the rubric of nature poems, she set a precedent that would be followed by editors for more than half a century. Todd may have seen it as a straightforward response to winter, similar to the Victorian nature poetry that was fashionable at the time; it was among several poems that led Todd to consider Dickinson's work "Impressionist." (Farr, *Passion*, 263). While it remains Dickinson's most frequently anthologized landscape poem, critics now recognize that the poet was engaged in something very different from a word painting of nature in this poem. As she minutely explores the impact of a "certain Slant" of afternoon winter light, Dickinson reveals the way human emotions are affected by subtle physical perception, on a level beyond rational argument. The slant of light is its own argument, undeniable and unteachable.

The winter light of this poem "oppresses," not as a passing mood, but as a permanent deformation of the soul, a knowledge that, once admitted, can never be removed. Speaking of Dickinson's work as a whole, scholar Charles R. Anderson notes that "[s]he . . . separates the lesser pains that will heal from the greater pains that will not and chooses the latter as her special concern, noting with precision their qualities and above all their effects" ("Despair," 10). Anderson considers Fr 320 Dickinson's finest poem on "the protean condition of despair" (Ibid., 30). Dickinson's astonishing feat in this poem is that she somehow transforms light, an image deeply embedded in the human psyche as an emblem of joy, hope, happiness, and salvation, into the "Seal" that signifies existential despair and locks it within the soul. Her certainty of the universality of this experience, reflected in her use

Amherst in the snow *(Courtesy of the Jones Library, Inc., Amherst, Massachusetts)*

of the plural "we," has been justified by her many readers who have reacted to the poem with a shock of recognition.

The transformation begins in stanza 1, where Dickinson uses synesthesia, the merging of images dependent upon different senses, to evoke the light's impact:

> There's a certain Slant of light,
> Winter Afternoons—
> That oppresses, like the Heft
> Of Cathedral Tunes—

By describing the emotional impact of the light (a visual image) as akin to the heft (a tactile image) of Cathedral tunes (an aural image), she forces the reader into unfamiliar associative territory, while deepening the sensual reality of the experience. Dickinson's earliest editors did the poem a disservice by replacing *Heft*, a provincial word that,

in her lexicon, denotes something ponderous that requires great effort to lift, with the neutral word *weight*. The oppressive, ponderous tunes belong not to a familiar "church," but to an imposing "Cathedral," evoking the quality of organ music resonating through great empty spaces. Farr suggests that *Heft* "conveys the difficulty of lifting up the heart, of believing in what cathedrals stand for." She makes a further, intriguing connection between this poem and the paintings of cathedrals by the English painter John Constable, which were well-known in Dickinson's region. Juxtaposed to Constable's "cathedrals bathed in light" and his notion that painting was both poetry and prayer, this poem stands as an ironic antithesis (*Passion*, 265).

For the very next words, "Heavenly Hurt" link the notions of ecstasy and pain. The phrase, with its repeated *h* sound (picking up the *h* of *Heft*), has the breath release of a sigh. It can be read in several ways. On one level, the phrase implies that the hurt *feels* heavenly, sublime. Anderson relates it to, "the curious conjoining of ecstasy and despair that pervades most of her writing" ("Despair," 32), comparing it to such lines as "A perfect—paralyzing Bliss—/ Contented as Despair—" (Fr 767). But another unavoidable connotation is that the hurt is *sent* by heaven. In what way? Is it that God wounds us? That the very longing for heaven hurts us? That we are hurt by the absence of heaven? That the hurt we feel is "heavenly" in the sense that it is unending, eternal? The fact that "We can find no scar" implies not only that the hurt is not physical but also that we cannot find an emotional scar, either. This wound is at the same time too subtle to be identified and limitless; it leaves no finite, visible scar. It pervades the psyche; for the place it has altered is "Where the Meanings, are—," including the sense of whether life has any meaning at all. Cultural critic Barton Levi St. Armand characterizes the moment evoked in this poem as Dickinson's "negative crisis conversion to unbelief" (*Culture*, 239).

In the first line of stanza 3, "None may teach it—Any—," *it* clearly refers to "Heavenly Hurt," although *it* refers to the light, in stanzas 2 and 4. Dickinson's first editors "smoothed out" the line to read "None may teach it anything." Indeed, this seems the most likely meaning, although other interpretations are possible. Sharon Cameron sees it as an example of how Dickinson is "not choosing how particular words are to be read" and gives three different readings: (1) "None may teach it—[not] Any[one else]—"; (2) "None may teach it—Any[thing]" [it is not subject to alteration]; (3) "None may teach it—[to] Any[one else]—" ("Dickinson's Fascicles," 147).

Dickinson is describing a wound that cannot be influenced from outside and thus remains forever fixed. She might be talking about the kind of recalcitrance modern psychology associates with untreated neurotic syndromes. But, although many of Dickinson's discoveries about the inner life anticipate what modern psychology would uncover, she lived within a different, more spiritual universe of reference. For her, the wound was the "Seal Despair," a biblical reference to the seven seals of

Revelations. Dickinson's "eighth seal" belongs with the plagues that are sent to afflict mankind. By alluding to an apocalyptic, visionary text, Dickinson suggests a cosmic dimension to her experience. But her "vision" does not go beyond itself, that is, it leads to nothing but the psyche's awareness of its own pain, as it endures the "imperial affliction" (a variant of "Heavenly Hurt"), whose source is the insubstantial "Air." This is the poem's central insight: the paradox that we live in the iron grasp of the ungraspable, so that our deepest convictions are shaped by subtleties of perception of which we are scarcely aware.

In the fourth stanza the poet returns to the surface level of a winter afternoon and draws the natural world into her sense of things, employing a "pathetic fallacy" (the poetic device that attributes human feelings to nature). The listening landscape and shadows holding their breath share the poet's apprehension and awareness that something momentous is coming ("It" is once again the "certain Slant of Light"). The effect of these lines is to heighten the sense of mystery and suspense, which culminates in the poem's stunning final image: "When it goes, 'tis like the Distance / On the look of Death—." The absence of the "certain Slant of Light" is still a terrible presence. The image contains two attempts to place Death at a distance; it says both "it's not Death but the *look* of death" and "it's not the look of death but the *distance* on the look of death." But the effect of such distancing is to bring death palpably close. It evokes both "the staring eyes of the dead [and] the awful 'Distance' between life and death. . . . The final and complete desolation of the landscape is the precise equivalent of that 'internal difference' which the action of the poem has brought about" (Anderson, 32).

See also "IT WAS NOT DEATH, FOR I STOOD UP."

FURTHER READING

Charles R. Anderson, "Despair," in *Modern Critical Views*, 28–33, Sharon Cameron, *Lyric Time*, 100–103, and "Dickinson's Fascicles," in *Handbook*, Grabher et al., eds., 147, 152–155; Judith Farr, *Passion*, 263–265; Joanne Feit Diehl, *Romantic Imagination*, 54–55; Barton Levi St. Armand, *Emily Dickinson and Her Culture*, 239.

"The Robin's my Criterion for Tune—" (1861) (Fr 256, J 285)

One of her most famous poems, this is Dickinson's succinct recognition of what we might today call (with a pompousness she would disdain) "cultural relativism." Our sense of what is beautiful and essential in nature, she says, is a function of where we are born and live, what we are used to. The poem is about hearing and seeing, about "discernment" and its limits. It is also about Dickinson's perception of the basis of her poetic art.

Significantly, Dickinson, who was a skilled pianist, composed her own music and was familiar with the work of Mozart, chooses the common robin as her "Criterion for Tune." Indeed, the robin flits in and out of her poetry with some frequency. This harbinger of spring is the very essence of her native music, a bird with whom she closely identifies. In 1861, she also wrote, "I shall keep singing!" in which she herself is a robin: "I—with my Redbreast—/ And my Rhymes—," albeit one who will "take her place in summer" and will have a "fuller tune." In "I DREADED THAT FIRST ROBIN, SO," he is the sound and symbol of hope itself, a reminder she "dreads" as she traverses a season of personal grief. To the end of her life, she would celebrate him as "a Gabriel / In humble circumstances—" (Fr 1520). In that 1880 poem, it is once again the robin's steadfastness and his regional identification that she stresses:

He has the punctuality
Of the New England Farmer—
The same oblique integrity,

At the same time, however, she lauds his "Silvan Punctuation"—a reference to the more universal and mysterious rhythms of the woods. As a practitioner of her own "wild" system of punctuation, she proudly identified with him. Note, for instance, the omnipresent dashes and the unusual placement of commas in this poem, creating, now

a sense of breathlessness, now an unexpected pause:

The Robin's my Criterion for Tune—
Because I grow—where Robins do—
But, were I Cuckoo born—
I'd swear by him—
The ode familiar—rules the Noon—

Like the common bird, the common flower is Dickinson's standard and image of herself. She referred to herself as "Daisy," both in poems and in her missives to an unknown beloved, the MASTER LETTERS. The daisy represents both humbleness and fidelity, as in "The Daisy follows soft the Sun—" (Fr 161). Buttercups were the flowers she said she wanted to have at her funeral and they were bestowed on her in abundance in the meadow she was carried across to her grave.

My vision is shaped, the poet says, by these humble phenomena. The falling nut is the essence of October, the sign of death and the mechanism of rebirth; there is no winter without the snow.

Just so we know what this simplicity means, however, in a final twist she makes it clear that she is in good company:

The Queen, discerns like me—
Provincially—

The idea of narrowness or limitation is subtly transformed into one of aristocracy, individuality, and judgment. To "see New Englandly" and "discern provincially" are variants of the same action. But "discern" emphasizes the element of judgment and discrimination. To discern, in Dickinson's Webster's, is "to separate by the eye, or by the understanding"—the very essence of the creative act.

See also "SOME KEEP THE SABBATH GOING TO CHURCH—."

FURTHER READING

Alfred Gelpi, "Seeing New Englandly," in *Modern Critical Views*, Harold Bloom, ed., 37–64; David Porter, *Early Poetry*, 86–87; George H. Soule, "Emily Dickinson and the Robin," *Essays in Literature*, 67–82.

"These are the days when Birds come back—" (1859) (Fr 122, J 130)

Dickinson sent this poem, along with another, related poem she had written that year, "Besides the autumn poets sing," to her intimate friend and editor of the *Springfield Republican*, SAMUEL BOWLES, in 1859. They were copied on separate pages, as samples of her work, rather than incorporated into the body of the letter—a clear, if subtle, indication that she was asking him to regard them in a professional light. Despite the high quality and relative conventionality of these verses, which should have made them acceptable to a conservative publisher, Bowles "failed to take the hint" and made no offer to print them (Sewall, *Life*, II, 476). Fr 122 would not be published until the 1890 *Poems*.

Along with the more obscure but no less haunting "FURTHER IN SUMMER THAN THE BIRDS—," written six years later, Fr 122 is a complex evocation of the days of late summer. Poets have always been drawn to late or Indian summer and autumn because of the unavoidable association of the dying of nature, which will be "resurrected" in spring, and the dying of human beings, for whom resurrection is less certain. For Dickinson, who was obsessed by the transition between life and death and devoted some of her greatest poems (see "I HEARD A FLY BUZZ—WHEN I DIED—" and "BECAUSE I COULD NOT STOP FOR DEATH—") to what it might feel like to die, this transitional time was especially compelling. Just as in her poems of human dying, in her late summer poems Dickinson is at pains to capture the precise, perceptual quality of the transition. For most of the poem, she stands outside the process— a sensitively aware, and undeceived, yet passionate and ecstatic observer. At its conclusion, she strives to enter into the mystery it represents.

For the poem's speaker, late summer is both an intoxicating fraud and a "Last Communion in the Haze." She is "almost" but never fully taken in by the illusion that summer has returned. No sooner does the poet announce the return of the birds in line 1 than she undercuts the import in line 2:

"A very few—a Bird or two." Riches are momentary and quickly recognized as paucity. She is like the Bee, a creature with whom she often identifies, who is not "cheated" (a word she uses in its meaning of "deceived") into believing that summer has returned. The unspoken implication is that the bee, in the absence of the flowers and their nectar, is unlikely to misinterpret the renewed warmth.

In stanza 2, she uses an unusual form of synesthesia, in which an image combines the impressions of two different senses, such as sight and hearing (for example, the "blue Buzz" of the Fly in Fr 591):

These are the days when skies resume
The old—old sophistries of June—
A blue and gold mistake.

In "sophistries of June" and "blue and gold mistake" aspects of reasoning and judgment are linked to the season. The sophistries, that is, fallacious reasoning, sound in appearance only, belong to the lush month of June. The "mistake" is the "blue and gold" of the skies. Through these images, deception and beauty, error and intoxication are merged into an indissoluble whole. It is important that the sophistries are June's, that is, even in June, when summer is fresh and in its glory, its beauty is a form of deception. The repetition of *old* may be there for the meter, but it conveys a sense of weariness with those well-worn sophistries. Thus, what is recapitulated in late summer—not the actual season, but the hopes and desires it engendered in the human heart—was misleading in the first place. Moreover, in stanza 4, faint but undeniable signs tell this keen observer that autumn is on the way.

Then, in the final two stanzas, a dramatic shift of tone occurs, as the speaker fervently begs permission to participate in this "Last Communion in the Haze" of late summer days. She asks to participate "as a child," a simpler perception than that of a reasoning adult, but one more enmeshed in the physical world and more susceptible to wonder. Her supplication is addressed, not to God or Christ, but to nature as it exists in this particular moment. Dickinson never accepted the terms of her religion and later in life remembered herself as a child, "fleeing from Sacrament" (L 412, May 1874). But, in speaking of nature's "sacred emblems," "consecrated bread," and "immortal wine," she uses the language of the Calvinist sacramental tradition and transposes it into the world of nature. The perceptions of the first stanzas suddenly open up to a larger apprehension of the sacredness of what is occurring. What was a "fraud" to the birds and bees, briefly enticed by the seeming return of summer, here becomes a mystery, in the sense of something sublime:

Thy sacred emblems to partake—
Thy consecrated bread to take
And thine immortal wine!

The word *emblem,* in addition to its religious meaning (for example, baptism as an emblem of spiritual cleansing) also denotes a picture that presents one thing to the eye and another to the understanding. In a moment of recognition, the seasonal transformation reveals itself in its sacred dimension. The mostly regular rhyme scheme, the repetition of words ("Thy," "Thy," "Thine") and rich sound orchestration (*Sacrament, summer, sacred, emblems, consecrated, immortal*) contribute to a harmonious, devotional tone, giving the final moments of the poem a mood, not of disappointment, but rather of exultation.

See also CONGREGATIONALISM.

FURTHER READING

Charles R. Anderson, *Stairway,* 164–167; Jane Eberwein, "Emily Dickinson and the Calvinist Sacramental Tradition," in *Critical Essays,* Judith Farr, ed., 99–101; Timothy Morris, "Dickinson's Style," 26–41, 36–40; Ernest Sandeen, "Delight Deterred by Ecstasy," 489; Cynthia Griffin Wolff, *Emily Dickinson,* 307–309.

"The Soul Selects her own Society—" (1862) (Fr 409, J 303)

In this famous and much-debated poem, Dickinson employs the ingenious strategy of making the relationship of ruler and society a metaphor for the life

of the soul. The poem has challenged readers with the question: Who or what, precisely, does the Soul Select? Is it her own company, that of an earthly lover, or of Christ? For some readers, the poem is a formal declaration of the reclusive life that the 32-year-old poet had already adopted when she wrote this poem, an affirmation of what moved her to shut the door on virtually everyone who came to visit her in the second half of her life. Others see it as an affirmation of herself as a writer, who chooses her own sensibility above those of obtuse critics. For those who view the poem as an expression of the exclusiveness of a passionate love, the choice between an earthly lover and Christ is a difficult one, since Dickinson often characterized the man she loved as Savior. Dickinson's manner of telling her truth "slant" allows for all these interpretations and more. On one level, this work may be seen as one of Dickinson's DEFINITION POEMS, in which the Soul is defined, not in terms of what it *is*, but of what it *does*. The Soul, in this poem, has essentially two interconnected "actions"—selecting (select, choose) and excluding (shut, close):

The Soul Selects her own Society—
Then—shuts the Door—
To her divine Majority—
Present no more—

The absence of any hint as to *why* the Soul chooses as it does is itself a statement: The Soul rules, but what rules *it*—or *her*, as the poem would have it—is unknown. (The Soul is feminine in many cultural and religious traditions, including the Greek [Psyche] and Hebrew [Shekhina]; here, its femininity brings it closer to the feminine speaker). Thus, on one level, the poem is a statement of the inherent irrationality of human attachments. The fact that the speaker establishes "the Soul" as an entity separate from herself supports this interpretation. In the final stanza, she reports the Soul's action as something she has observed in the past ("I've known her"), hinting that even she (the speaker) finds the Soul's behavior astonishing or extraordinary in some way.

Another possibility, however, is that the Soul's choice is divinely inspired. The word *Soul* points to the relationship of the human spirit to God, that is, it is a spark of the divine. Before we can conclude that the Soul of this poem partakes of divinity, however, we must navigate a syntactic ambiguity. In stanza 1, line 3, "To her divine Majority—," is one of those troubling instances of "syntactic doubling," that is, it may refer to either of the lines surrounding it. Stanza 1 may be read to mean "The Soul, after selecting her own society, shuts the door, and is no longer present/available to her divine majority." In this case, "her divine Majority" is outside the soul and is shut out by the soul—a sarcastic way of referring to those who would presume to rule the soul, be they religious, moral, or literary "authorities." This is consistent with other poems in which Dickinson uses the term "the Majority" in its conventional meaning and presents it as a bullying force from which the individual must protect herself. For example, in "MUCH MADNESS IS DIVINEST SENSE—," she writes scornfully, "Tis the Majority in this as all prevail. . . ." However, stanza 1 can also be paraphrased as follows: "The Soul, after selecting her own society, *shuts the door to her divine majority.* She is no longer present." Because the rulings of the Soul prevail, a power that usually belongs to the majority, *she* is now the "majority." And a divine one, at that—God-inspired.

"Divine majority" also suggests the divine right of kings, a notion that resonates with the image of the soul as "Queen Recluse" that permeates the poem. In late November or early December 1862 SAMUEL BOWLES visited the Dickinsons, but Emily refused to see him. In January 1863, Emily's offended friend wrote to her brother WILLIAM AUSTIN, archly asking him to convey "to the Queen Recluse my especial sympathy—that she has overcome the world." Whether or not she had Bowles's letter in mind, Dickinson makes the Soul in this poem a queen, visited by chariots and emperors who kneel before her. The low gate is the barrier between the Soul and what she would exclude. Although the "lowness" of the gate to the Soul and the simple Mat before it suggest humility, the Soul rejects both the powerful Emperor and the owners of chariots. Are these angels' chariots, waiting to drive her to paradise, or the carriages of wealthy socialites? The poem offers no enlightenment on this point.

What are stressed are the Soul's exclusivity and her lack of feeling for any person or thing but the One she has chosen. In stanza 2, the word "Unmoved" appears twice. In stanza 3, the "Valves of her attention" close, turning attention into a heart, and the heart into stone. The poem closes on this chilling image of the consequences of the Soul's selectivity: instead of the joy of communion, numbness and entrapment. The unstated implication is that the One the Soul has chosen has not chosen her, suggesting an unrequited earthly love.

Yet another, fascinating dimension to this poem, linked to Dickinson's Calvinist religious upbringing, has been suggested by Anthony Hecht, who sees in it "an unstated but implied parallel. As the soul is to its society (absolute, arbitrary, ruthless) so is God in His election and salvation of souls. . . . We play at God; it is characteristically human of us to do so" ("Riddles," 157).

See also "I'M CEDED—I'VE STOPPED BEING THEIR'S—," "ON A COLUMNAR SELF—," CONGREGATIONALISM, and PURITAN HERITAGE.

FURTHER READING

Judith Farr, *Passion,* 84–85; Alfred Habegger, *My Wars,* 446–451; Anthony Hecht, "Riddles," in *Critical Essays,* Judith Farr, ed., 157; Cynthia Griffin Wolff, *Emily Dickinson,* 198–200.

"They shut me up in Prose—" (1862) (Fr 445, J 613)

In this defiant, triumphant poem, written during one of Dickinson's years of flood creativity, she declares that an unspecified "they" has no power to confine her. Like, "I WAS THE SLIGHTEST IN THE HOUSE—," it records not the external realities of her childhood years (it is doubtful she was ever actually confined to a closet) but a vision of the path she has taken from early confinement to her present state of inner liberation. "They" might be her close but patriarchal family, in which her father and her brother, WILLIAM AUSTIN, enjoyed far greater opportunities and freedoms than those available to the women in the household. "They" might also refer to AMHERST society in general, with its pressure to conform to conservative social and religious standards that she found stultifying. As a schoolgirl at AMHERST ACADEMY and later as a student at the MOUNT HOLYOKE FEMALE SEMINARY, Emily had stood outside the fervor of religious REVIVALS, and as time went on, she found herself increasingly isolated among friends and family members who had made their public declaration of faith in Christ. She perceived herself as an outsider and, apparently, others did, too. In a letter to Emily's loyal friend and cousin JOHN LONG GRAVES on October 4, 1854, the poet's childhood friend ELIZA COLEMAN wrote, "I know you appreciate her. . . . I think few of her Amherst friends do." She found allies among a few "literary" friends, but most of these relationships proved transitory and, ultimately, she was thrust upon her inner resources to escape from "Prose."

In this poem Dickinson uses the word "Prose," the conventional, loosely structured language of everyday life, as she does in "I DWELL IN POSSIBILITY—," as a designation for a linguistic and spiritual world whose very terms imprison her:

> They shut me up in Prose—
> As when a little Girl
> They put me in the Closet—
> Because they liked me "still"—
>
> Still! Could themself have peeped—

The repetition of the word "Still!" from the speaker's own lips mocks the foolishness of "their" attempt to still her, but it also highlights the word and its association with death. Had "they" been capable of seeing her "Brain—go round"—her seething, vital inner life—they might have understood the futility of their efforts. The speaker uses a metaphor to "explain" why she cannot be locked up: "They might as wise have lodged a Bird /For Treason—in the Pound—." Her use of the word "Treason" is significant, implying that Dickinson knew that her unique sense of life and unorthodox approach to religion *were* treasonous from the standpoint of society. By likening herself to a bird, the speaker is saying that walls can't confine a crea-

ture so minuscule and capable of flight. But she is also saying that birds are beings of another sort than humans; the concept of "treason" does not apply to them. Birds do not make moral decisions; like poets, their song is inborn.

Moreover, the idea of imprisoning such a being is absurd. The third elliptical stanza might be paraphrased as follows: "Just as a Bird (Himself) simply by willing it, can rise as easily as a star and look down on captivity—so can I—." In an earlier variant, line 3 reads "Abolish his Captivity"—a more abstract image than the "looking down" perspective of the bird but one that emphasizes that she is a "law unto herself," rising above the restrictions others try in vain to impose on her.

See also CONGREGATIONALISM and PURITAN HERITAGE.

FURTHER READING

Barbara Mossberg, *When a Writer Is a Daughter,* 3–4, 107–109.

"This Consciousness that is aware" (1864) (Fr 817, J 822)

This poem merges two of the central concerns of Dickinson's poetry: the nature of consciousness and the transition from life to death. Her work is permeated with a tormenting awareness of the duality of consciousness—or soul, self, mind, brain, heart—as she variously called it. She knew that "The Soul unto itself / Is an imperial friend—/ Or the most agonizing Spy—/ An Enemy—could send—" (Fr 579). The divided soul was most often for her a place of ambush and hidden terrors, as in "ONE NEED NOT BE A CHAMBER—TO BE HAUNTED—." She was keenly aware of the inseparability of the soul from its dark "double," declaring "Of Consciousness—her awful mate / The Soul cannot be rid—" (Fr 1076). Elsewhere she writes "I do not know the man so bold / He dare in lonely Place / That awful stranger Consciousness / Deliberately face" (Fr 1325). Yet Dickinson herself possessed the courage to imaginatively confront the soul at its most fearful moment, as *it* confronts its own annihilation.

In this poem consciousness is both divided and utterly alone. It is divided not by inner conflict, but by a dual awareness: of life and of its own death. Paradoxically, only consciousness will be aware of its own unawareness, if indeed that is all death is. Dickinson's poetic imagination was constantly grappling with the enigma of death and, to an even greater extent, with the experience of dying. Some of her greatest poems, including "BECAUSE I COULD NOT STOP FOR DEATH," "I HEARD A FLY BUZZ— WHEN I DIED—," and "I DIED FOR BEAUTY—BUT WAS SCARCE" deal with "traversing the interval"— the transition from life to death.

Unlike those works, the poem under discussion does not recreate this transition in a dramatic scenario but reflects, in a tone of stoic acceptance, on the "testing" each individual consciousness must ultimately undergo. Emphasis is on the utter aloneness of consciousness. Not only will it be the one aware of death; it will have the added burden of awareness of its aloneness as it traverses "the interval/Experience between."

Note that the language here is abstract, creating a tone of objective neutrality. Death is designated as the "Most profound experiment / Appointed unto Men—." By using the passive voice, Dickinson avoids having to specify "who" or "what force" has appointed this experiment. By using terms such as "adequate," "properties," "make discovery," borrowed from the scientific lexicon, she strives for an unemotional tone. But this "objective" language quickly becomes elliptical, calling attention to itself with its compressed and tangled syntax. By designating consciousness with the word *itself*, the poet diminishes it, turning it into a neutral thing. Moreover, *itself* occurs no less than three times, twice as "unto itself," in the first three lines of stanza 3, in such a way as to create a sense of self-entanglement or entrapment.

> How adequate unto itself
> Its properties shall be
> Itself unto itself and None
> Shall make discovery—

A plausible paraphrase of stanza 3, consistent with what the poem as a whole seems to be saying, might read: "The discovery of whether the proper-ties of a particular consciousness are adequate to deal with the transition from life to death will be revealed to consciousness itself and to none other." In this interpretation, consciousness is both the discoverer and the discovery. Even in this it will be alone. Whatever the self learns will die along with it. There is no one watching, praising, or disapproving. Critics such as Wendy Martin see in this poem an expression of a post-Christian mentality, where "consciousness replaces Christ and self-awareness supersedes salvation" (*American Triptych*, 117).

In the final stanza, Dickinson switches the metaphor from "experiment," and "test of mettle," to one of "adventure"—implying openness, possibility. As Juhasz notes, "death is the object of the great adventure, but the adventure itself is the act of knowing, the business of consciousness" (*Undiscovered Continent*, 163). Yet, the positive nature of this adventure is undermined by the notion that the soul is "condemned" to it. Once more the passive voice allows the poet to circumvent the question of who or what is doing the condemning. There is no deity either to blame or to lean on, only the "single Hound" of the self's own identity. The image of the dog is one of faithfulness, inseparability; Dickinson herself reveled in the companionship of her dog, CARLO, her large black Newfoundland. The dog of the poem, however, is a "hound," a word that carries overtones of being "hounded." The image also suggests the contrast between this lone companion/identity in the journey from life to death with Cerberus, the terrible many-headed dog with the tail of a serpent who guards the entrance to Hades. In Dickinson's personal mythology, external monsters give way to stark existential realities. For her, there was none starker—not even death—than what she called, in an undated poem (Fr 1696), "That polar privacy / A soul admitted to itself—." (Note that the volume of poetry published by Dickinson's niece, Martha Dickinson Bianchi, in 1914, was entitled *The Single Hound*).

See also "I FELT A FUNERAL, IN MY BRAIN," and "ME FROM MYSELF—TO BANISH—."

FURTHER READING

Joanne Feit Diehl, *Romantic Imagination*: 134–135; Suzanne Juhasz, *Undiscovered Continent*, 161–163;

Wendy Martin, *American Triptych*, 117–118; Cynthia Griffin Wolff, *Emily Dickinson*, 466–467.

"This is my letter to the World" (1863) (Fr 519, J 441)

From the time that THOMAS WENTWORTH HIGGINSON selected this poem as the "Prelude" to the 1890 first edition of Dickinson's *Poems*, readers have perceived it as the poet's characterization of her poetry as a whole. Indeed, the metaphor of poet as letter-writer is particularly apt for a poet who regularly enclosed verses in her LETTERS or sent them as letters themselves. One of her most popular poems, Fr 519 is formally uncomplicated, with its emphatic rhyme scheme (Me/Majesty, see/Me) and regular iambic meter; and it presents a sympathetic (some would say pathetic), accessible, Dickinson, who, though ignored by "the World," remains the carrier of Nature's "simple News." "Here are the dimensions and significance of my work," the poet seems to be saying. "For the sake of Nature whom you love, love me, her spokesman, as well."

Yet the poem's upbeat "message" is misleading in many ways and uncharacteristic of the great body of her work. The artless pose the speaker assumes can by no means be taken at face value. For one thing, "the World" did write to Emily Dickinson. Far from the unknown, neglected figure she makes herself out to be, she had numerous correspondents to whom she confided her poetry and who responded to it. These included her sister-in-law and confidante, SUSAN HUNTINGTON GILBERT DICKINSON, who commented on her work regularly, Higginson, an eminent writer whom she engaged as her literary "mentor" in 1862, and *Springfield Republican* editor SAMUEL BOWLES, who, if not wholly attuned to her work, was happy to read and publish some of her "little gems."

Second, and most important, "her letter to the World" was no direct transcription of Nature's message, but an artful and agonized exploration of the interrelationship of nature, God, and man. The "News" she conveyed from nature was anything but simple. Certainly, Dickinson's poetry contains celebrations of Nature's "tenderness" ("I'll tell you how the sun rose—" [Fr 204], "Nature the Gentlest Mother is" [Fr 741]) simplicity ("SOME KEEP THE SABBATH GOING TO CHURCH—," "'NATURE' IS WHAT WE SEE—"), and "Majesty" ("She sweeps with many-colored brooms" [Fr 318], "BLAZING IN GOLD AND QUENCHING IN PURPLE," "SWEET MOUNTAINS— YE TELL ME NO LIE—"). Yet the greater part of her nature poetry—greater in both number and quality—explores the essential mystery of nature, its fundamental separation from and chilling indifference to the human condition. This is the vision of "WHAT MYSTERY PERVADES A WELL!":

> But nature is a stranger yet;
> The ones that cite her most
> Have never passed her haunted house,
> Nor simplified her ghost.

In this poem of 1877 Dickinson might be rebuking the younger speaker of "This is my letter to the World" for her overly sunny and simplistic point of view. Yet it would be inaccurate to conclude from this that Dickinson's sense of nature grew darker and more complex only as she matured. A poignant sense of personal exclusion from nature's mysteries and sacred rituals is already present in such early poems as "THESE ARE THE DAYS WHEN BIRDS COME BACK—" (1859), "OF BRONZE—AND BLAZE—" (1862), and "FURTHER IN SUMMER THAN THE BIRDS—" (1865).

One can imagine Dickinson in 1863, her greatest year of "flood creativity," when she produced 295 poems, writing "This is my letter to the World" in a burst of exultation as she sensed her extraordinary powers. She is, after all, the poet of the moment, loyal to the truth of each discrete experience; in this specific instance, in a mood of euphoria, she celebrates herself as a direct and universal conduit of "Nature."

Some critics, however, take a darker view of the poem. Both Sharon Cameron and Paul Crumbly, based on readings of Dickinson's holographic manuscript rather than the "print translation" of the poem, suggest that this "is not necessarily a poem about a benign telling of nature's secret" but rather than "the secret being told is ominous." (*Choosing Not Choosing*, 33). Noting that Dickinson's use of dashes indicates disjunction, Crumbly interprets her as saying that, instead of Nature communicating words to the world through the poet, "Nature is part of a 'World' that never wrote to her" ("Dialogic Voice," 107). In his reading, Nature's message was sent to others whose "hands I cannot see." He perceives in the poem a dialogue between the voice of conventional viewpoint, offering clichéd descriptions of nature's benign influence on human life, and the poet's arguing voice that expresses anger and disappointment in a world that never wrote.

This interpretation, while intriguing, may be reading too much into what is, after all, one of Dickinson's more sentimental poems. Note her adjectives and adverb: "Simple," "tender," "Sweet," "tenderly." These word choices, together with the poem's musicality, create a sense of unambiguous affirmation. And it is difficult to detect anything ominous in the poem's final appeal: "For love of Her—Sweet—countrymen—/ Judge tenderly—of Me." With a characteristic mixture of self-effacement and grandiosity, the poet asks to be identified with all that is most lovable in Nature itself.

Biographer Richard B. Sewall notes that Dickinson's exhortation to her "Sweet—countrymen" is "American and democratic" (*Life*, II, 713). The Civil War was raging when she wrote this poem, and political and war news were foremost in people's minds. Dickinson *did* write Civil War poems, but this is not one of them. Yet, despite the distinctly political ring of this appellation, the "News" she wishes to convey to her compatriots is not narrowly political. By addressing the American public at large and referring to what she knows as "News" she is challenging the common hierarchy of values and implying that what she knows is infinitely more important than what can be read in the newspapers. This is the same "news" she refers to in a poem of the following year: "THE ONLY NEWS I KNOW / Is Bulletins all Day / From Immortality." For Dickinson, the mystery of existence itself was the "news," beside which all other events paled. This is the news William Carlos Williams wrote of almost a century later, perhaps with Dickinson's lines in mind: "It is difficult / to get the news from poems

/ yet men die miserably every day / for lack / of what is found there" ("Asphodel, That Greeny Flower").

Finally, Dickinson's address to a larger public in this poem hints at the hopes for a larger fame she still harbored or, at least, felt herself worthy of. Noting that this poem was included in the fascicles, more than 800 poems gathered together in hand-sewn booklets between 1858 and 1865, Betsy Erkkila writes:

> Perhaps Dickinson addressed an imaginary community; or perhaps she imagined her poems being passed from hand to hand among a select republic of 'country' men as some 600 of her poems were during her lifetime. Or perhaps by publicizing the 'News' of her writing to some of the most powerful social and cultural figures of her time, she anticipated that her poems would eventually reach a larger "World" of countrymen. . . . ("Dickinson and the Art of Politics," *Historical Guide*, 149).

See also HELEN FISKE HUNT JACKSON and PUBLICATION AND EDITORIAL SCHOLARSHIP.

FURTHER READING

Sharon Cameron, *Choosing Not Choosing,* 33; Paul Crumbly, "Dialogic Voice," in *Handbook,* Grabher et al., eds., 106–108; Betsy Erkkila, "Art of Politics," in *Historical Guide,* 148–149: Cristanne Miller, *Grammar,* 9; Richard B. Sewall, *Life,* II, 713–14.

"This was a Poet—" (1862) (Fr 446, J 448)

Since Dickinson never wrote an *ars poetica*, we must turn to her poems for her concept of the nature of poetry and the task of the poet. "This was a Poet—" is her most extended development of the subject. Either a tribute to "the Poet" as a universalized figure or an epitaph to a particular, unnamed poet who has died, it reflects the 19th-century tendency to glorify the artist as a mighty and heroic figure.

The poem contains two different visions of the poet's power. In the first two stanzas, he is a "distiller" of "amazing sense":

From Ordinary Meanings—
And Attar so immense

From the familiar species
That perished by the Door—

As she does in a poem written in 1863, "Essential Oils—are wrung—" (Fr 772), Dickinson likens poetry to perfume or "Attar," the precious fluid that is pressed out of the rose. In the process, the rose is destroyed. The notion is similar to that expressed in another great poem about poets, Fr 930:

The Poets light but Lamps—
Themselves—go out—

In the next two stanzas, Dickinson gives us the poet as "discloser" of the immortal pictures hidden in nature and in our mundane lives. Infinitely rich, he is unaware of his riches—a Mozart who easily, unconsciously creates. So sufficient is he unto himself, he would scarcely notice should he be robbed. In the concluding lines Dickinson virtually deifies him when she says that he exists "Exterior—to Time—."

Scholar Inder Nath Kher interprets Dickinson's Poet in a wholly positive light when he writes:

In the creative process the poet arrests the flow of our perishable existence. He creates pictures of immortality, and when these rich visions are disclosed to us in the form of images and metaphors our daily world fades by contrast into ceaseless poverty (*Landscape of Absence,* 118).

Yet several other critics have detected in Dickinson's evocation of the Poet undertones of sarcasm and competitiveness. They point out the mingled admiration and rivalry in the speaker's observation that the attar distilled by the Poet was "so immense":

We wonder it was not Ourselves
Arrested it—before

By condemning us "by Contrast—/ To ceaseless Poverty—," this Poet, far from enhancing his readers,

underscores their inadequacy. The sentiment resonates with that found in "YOUR RICHES—TAUGHT ME—POVERTY," where the speaker's recognition of the power of the sensual, heterosexual woman makes her painfully aware of her own powerlessness.

Furthermore, scholars have suggested, does not the phrase, "Himself—to Him—a Fortune" imply smugness and narcissism? Perhaps, but there are numerous instances in which Dickinson wrote of herself as poet in the same way, as one who needs no external riches or support, but possesses an irreducible inner wealth, as in "ON A COLUMNAR SELF." The tension and ambiguity of this poem arises, however, from the fact that, although she ascribes the wealth to a male poet and assumes the role of humbled reader, the very existence of the poem makes clear that she, too, is a poet.

Both Gary Stonum and Cristanne Miller see the image of the dominating male at the core of this poem. Stonum associates the Poet with the dominating Masters in Dickinson's poems, while Miller sees this portrait of a Poet who seems to create effortlessly, without sacrifice, as Dickinson's image of male privilege. She writes, "As younger sister of a favored son and as a consciously female poet, Dickinson might well differentiate herself with some resentment from the poet who creates unconsciously and with ease, the man of ceaseless, inherited cultural wealth" (*Grammar,* 120). Miller finds evidence for Dickinson's ambivalence in the awkward syntax that undercuts her praise. She suggests that the opening lines, "This was a Poet—It is That" is both awkward and reductive of the Poet's humanity, observing that Dickinson might at least have written, "It is He." This interpretation has been challenged by Judith Farr, however, for whom the phrase "'It is That'" reflects Dickinson's "definition of the poet as a nearly suprapersonal asexual force" (*Passion,* 324). The lines can be read both ways. What seems clear is that, whether or not Dickinson intended such ambiguity (something we can never know) it wove itself into the fabric of this poem.

See also "A SOLEMN THING—IT WAS—I SAID—," "ALONE, I CANNOT BE—," "DARE YOU SEE A SOUL AT THE 'WHITE HEAT'?," "I DWELL IN POSSIBILITY—," and "I RECKON—WHEN I COUNT AT ALL—."

FURTHER READING

Judith Farr, *Passion*, 323–324; Inder Nath Kher, *Landscape of Absence*, 118; Cristanne Miller, *Grammar*, 118–122; Josef Raab, "The Metapoetic Element in Dickinson," in *Handbook*, Grabher et al., eds., 291–292; Gary Lee Stonum, *Dickinson Sublime*, 12–14.

"This World is not conclusion" (1862) (Fr 373, J 501)

The movement of this poem recalls the maxim of Sir Francis Bacon, which begins, "If a man will begin with certainties, he shall end in doubts. . . ." In its opening line, Dickinson's "oracular voice" confidently declares that there is an afterlife; but in the final couplet, what she asserts is the inability of any numbing agent (such as religion) to still the painful gnawing of doubt.

Although there are no stanza breaks, the poem is divided, by both tone and idea, into four-line units. The first four lines are serene and visionary:

This World is not conclusion.
A Species stands beyond—
Invisible, as Music—
But positive, as Sound—

Dickinson uses the word *Species* not in its zoological or biological sense, but with the lesser-known meaning, found in her lexicon (Noah Webster's 1828 *American Dictionary of the English Language*), of a "visible or sensible representation." "Invisible, as Music," but sensible to the ear of the spirit, what comes after this World (she used "Sequel" instead of "Species" in an earlier variant), is "positive," that is, as her Webster defined it, "capable of being affirmed." Dickinson the artist, who played the piano and composed music in her youth, knew that music was "real"; the science student in her knew that the existence of sound could be physically demonstrated. Thus, in these lines, art and science are called upon to affirm a single, hopeful tenet of faith. If there is anything in this first quatrain to suggest the uncertainty to follow, it is the PUNCTUATION.

A period (the only one in the poem) finalizes the first line. From then on, however, the great majority of lines end in dashes, giving the poem a sense of openness that works against the initial certainty.

In line 5, there is no clear referent for "it." *What* "beckons" and "baffles"? Have the previous four lines, which seemed to proclaim a certainty, been only an alluring puzzle? Is there, as Cynthia Griffin Wolff writes, a pun on the word "Conclusion," with a second meaning of "the close of a debate or argument"? This would imply a second meaning to line 1: No conclusion about the existence of an afterlife can be made on the basis of what is knowable in this world (*Emily Dickinson*, 269). This is clearly the import of the second quatrain:

It beckons, and it baffles—
Philosophy, don't know
And through a Riddle, at the last—
Sagacity, must go—

The arguments of Philosophy (or, as her use of the plural *don't* implies, Philosophers) are powerless to know, and even "Sagacity," the faculty of readily discerning truth from falsehood, must "go through," that is, experience, the Riddle of death. Note Dickinson's use of punctuation as a stylistic element: By placing grammatically incorrect commas after "Philosophy" and "Sagacity," she interrupts the flow of the lines in which they occur (much as she does with dashes), making them "hesitate" uncertainly.

The third quatrain continues the theme of the Riddle or puzzle, shifting emphasis from intellectual attempts to *solve* the mystery of eternity to spiritual attempts to *gain* it. Note that "it" in line 9 refers to the "Riddle," while "it" in line 10 refers to eternal life. The image of martyrs ("Men [who] have borne/ Contempt of Generations") segues naturally into that of the Crucifixion. In a striking instance of syntactic doubling, "And Crucifixion" is the direct object of both the preceding phrase (men have borne contempt of generations and crucifixion) and of the succeeding phrase (men have shown crucifixion). By the latter phrase, Dickinson suggests that men have raised up the vision of the crucifixion in order to gain the certainty of a resurrection.

From these solemn images, the poem leaps without transition, in the fourth quatrain, to the image of a frivolous Faith, evoking the debased nature of faith in Dickinson's own time. Faith is a confused, resilient but clueless, blushing young girl, capable of social embarrassment, who plucks at twigs of evidence and seeks direction from a weathervane. In the first two lines of the final quatrain, the tone of ironic mockery sharpens. What the "Pulpit" offers is superficial, extravagant gesture, in response to which the "strong Hallelujahs" rolling from the congregants appear mindless. Their noise bounces ironically off the positive "Sound" of line 4, the image Dickinson uses to suggest the way in which eternity may be known.

Throughout this poem, Dickinson has relied on dashes to "create a suggestion that the mind at work in the text is unfettered by normal rules of logical procedure" (Miller, *Grammar*, 51). Her most audacious logical leap is the final one, in which she turns from the world to the soul. Suddenly, both speculation and social satire give way to an image of spiritual pain that makes the poem direct and personal. The "I" of the poet, although not explicit, is palpably present. Coming as it does right after the image of a church service, "Narcotics" implies the numbing effect of a superficial religion. For Dickinson, the narcotics are ineffective against the pain of the tooth eating away at the interior. The riddle remaining to solve is the identity of this Tooth. In light of the poem's concerns, the nibblings of doubt seem a likely meaning. Additionally, however, Dickinson, who was a great reader of Shakespeare, may have had in mind his image of "the tooth of time" (*Measure for Measure*, V, i, 45). The poem, which began so triumphantly confident, thus ends on a note of painful, ongoing uncertainty. The oracle's voice has given way to the sufferer's.

That the "Tooth" continued to nibble at Dickinson's soul is clear from a letter she wrote less than three years before she died, after the death of her eight-year-old nephew, THOMAS GILBERT DICKINSON ("Gib"):

"Open the Door, open the Door, they are waiting for me," was Gilbert's sweet command in delirium. *Who* were waiting for him, all we possess we would give to know—Anguish at last opened it, and he ran to the little Grave at his Grandparents' feet—All this and more, though *is* there more? More than Love and Death? Then tell me it's name! (L 873, late 1883, to Elizabeth Holland)

See also "THOSE—DYING THEN."

FURTHER READING

Jane Eberwein, *Dickinson*, 227–228; Cristanne Miller, *Grammar*, 49–54; Cynthia Griffin Wolff, *Emily Dickinson*, 269–270.

"Those—Dying then" (1882) (Fr 1581, J 1551)

Throughout her life, Dickinson explored her struggle to come to terms with the Christian God, in her poems and letters. She called God, on different occasions, "Papa Above," "a distant, stately Lover," "Burglar, Banker, Father," and the "thrifty Deity," who cannot afford to endow his spontaneous creations with Eternity, to name just a few of the epithets, primarily challenging or reproachful, that she created for him. In this late poem, however, she turns to the question of what has happened to the general state of religious belief in her time. Critic Roger Lundin links Dickinson with Melville, Dostoevsky, and Nietzsche as among "the first to trace the trajectory of God's decline" throughout the Western world (*Art of Belief,* 4). More specifically, as Jane Eberwein notes, the poem speaks to Dickinson's reaction to changes in New England's religious culture in the middle and late decades of the 19th century ("'Is Immortality True?'" 67).

Perhaps because Fr 1581 comments on a historical trend, it lacks the agitated quality of Dickinson's more immediate poems on religious doubt, written in the first person ("I SHALL KNOW WHY—WHEN TIME IS OVER—," "OF COURSE—I PRAYED—"). Instead, she embeds the powerful image of a wounded, absent God in fairly regular iambic meter, to create a mood of controlled resignation. For Eberwein, the poem calls to mind imagery from the mid-1860s, when Dickinson envisages Truth dying on the same day that God does, to be "borne away/ From Mansion of the Universe / A lifeless Deity" (Fr 795). But the earlier poem evokes the death of God only to assert its impossibility. Truth will live as long as God does, the poem says, since Truth, like God, is deathless. In "Those—dying then," God is as good as dead: mutilated in a way that deprives him of his power to save, and in hiding. With his amputated Right Hand, he resembles the multitude of Civil War veterans that were a common sight in post-bellum America, deformed and debilitated by the horror of what they had experienced.

In a letter she wrote to her friend and literary adviser, THOMAS WENTWORTH HIGGINSON, Dickinson offers a clue to the episode that may have motivated her image:

> When a few years old I was taken to a Funeral, which I now know to be of peculiar distress, and the Clergyman asked, 'Is the Arm of the Lord shortened that it cannot save?'
>
> He italicized the 'cannot.' I mistook the accent for a doubt of Immortality and not daring to ask, it besets me still. (L 503).

The clergyman was alluding to Isaiah 59:1: "Behold, the Lord's hand is not shortened, that it cannot save," a commonly cited text, particularly among Abolitionists, at the time. Thus, the amputated arm signifies, above all, a negative answer to the question Dickinson asked another clergyman the same year she wrote this poem, one she had asked all her life: "Is Immortality True?" (L 752a). For Dickinson, this was the "Flood subject" (L 319) and the only truly essential one posed to her by religion.

Impotence is combined with absence in the God of this poem. It is instructive to compare it with "I KNOW THAT HE EXISTS," written 20 years earlier, in which the speaker struggles with her tormented desire to believe in a God playing a perverse game of hide-and-seek:

> I know that He exists.
> Somewhere—in silence—
> He has hid his rare life
> From our gross eyes.

In the earlier poem, the speaker is willing to make excuses for God's hiddenness, to see the cause in his entirely justified unwillingness to reveal himself to an unworthy humanity. There is a disjunction between the divine and the human that has to do with human limitation. In the poem under discussion, no justification is offered; instead the poet simply states what she perceives as an incontrovertible fact. By using the passive voice—God's Hand is amputated—she avoids the issue of who or what is to blame for the amputation.

Looking outside the poem, however, scholars have found no dearth of causes for God's disfiguration. As biographer Cynthia Griffin Wolff observes, "the drift away from God was generational, the phenomenon of an increasingly secular America" (*Emily Dickinson*, 451). In the New England of Dickinson's childhood and youth, Calvinist Christianity permeated daily life and impassioned REVIVALS were a regular part of communal life. By the last decade of the poet's life, even orthodox AMHERST was a far more secular place. There were a number of cultural and religious trends that destabilized belief, including romanticism, with its extreme assertion of the self and the value of individual experience; Ralph Waldo Emerson's transcendentalism, with its this-worldly emphasis on the supreme value of the heart's spiritual awakening; Darwinism's secular explanation of creation; the theological rethinking spurred by the new European biblical scholarship known as Higher Criticism, and, in the United States, the devastation of the Civil War. By the time of Dickinson's death in 1886, being an agnostic or even an atheist was neither unusual nor very difficult to justify intellectually.

What were the consequences of this widespread loss of faith? This is the question Dickinson addresses in the poem's second stanza. Not only has the certainty of heaven vanished, but "Behavior" in this world has become "small." There is a practical need for faith, to give us larger lives, bigger behavior, to make us nobler, more moral beings. The word "abdicate" suggests a throne that is relinquished; we are no longer kings. But the speaker finds this unacceptable:

> Better an ignis fatuus
> Than no illume at all—

The Latin *Ignis fatuus,* sometimes translated as "will-o'-the wisp," literally means "foolish light," and signifies any misleading or deluding goal. It refers to the phosphorescent light sometimes seen at night above marshy ground and thought to be caused by the combustion of methane rising from decaying vegetable matter. An "ignis fatuus" can be a misleading light to follow in the darkness, but given the available choices—delusion or darkness—the speaker chooses delusion. The choice is a practical one. What remains in the absence of God is a vision of right behavior that originated within the spiritual/moral context of a God-ruled universe. Eberwein points out that this stance resonates "with her father's piety that valued faith as an impetus to those virtues that promoted personal prosperity while advancing Christ's kingdom" ("Is Immortality True?" 95). Dickinson's generation must be satisfied with only the first of these desirable outcomes.

The poet's personal journey toward doubt began early in her life and probably had more to do with her intrinsic nature than with social trends. As a schoolgirl, she was incapable of making the public declaration of faith that would have admitted her to the church, and in her final years she was no further along the path to certainty. Playfully, in a letter to her suitor, JUDGE OTIS PHILLIPS LORD, she says that "on subjects of which we know nothing, or should I say *Beings . . .* we both believe, and disbelieve a hundred times an Hour, which keeps Believing nimble" (L 750, April 30, 1882). The following year, after describing the death of her beloved eight-year-old nephew, Gib (THOMAS GILBERT DICKINSON), she cries in anguish to her closest friend, ELIZABETH LUNA CHAPIN HOLLAND, "All this and more, though *is* there more? More than Love and Death? Then tell me it's name!" (L 873, late 1883). What comfort she had she herself described as "the Balm of that Religion / That doubts—as fervently as it believes" (Fr 1449, 1877).

See also CONGREGATIONALISM, JONATHAN EDWARDS, PURITAN HERITAGE, REVIVALISM, and UNITARIANISM.

FURTHER READING

Jane Eberwein, "'Is Immortality True?'" in *Historical Guide,* 67–102; Roger Lundin, *Art of Belief,* 4; James McIntosh, *Nimble Believing,* 3; Cynthia Griffin Wolff, *Emily Dickinson,* 451.

"'Tis so appalling—it exhilirates—" (1862) (Fr 341, J 281)

In this powerful and disturbing poem, Dickinson's concern is the relationship of suspense, with its components of dread and hope, to certainty:

> Tis so appalling—it exhilirates—
> So over Horror, it half captivates—
> The Soul stares after it, secure—
> To know the worst, leaves no dread more—

The poem captures a psychological paradox: that the certainty of knowing "the worst", no matter how "over Horror" that reality is, brings the exhilaration of release and liberation. By beginning with a "'Tis" that has no previous referent, Dickinson gives the opening line an unanchored quality: we are in the middle of something extreme—both appalling and exhilarating—but what? The poem seems to be about death, and most commentators have interpreted it in this way. Others however, have suggested that the poem is about facing the reality that she is not loved by the man (or woman) she loves. The language of the poem is universal enough to justify this interpretation as well. Whether "the worst" is death, lovelessness, or some other devastating disappointment, confronting it is better than anticipating it.

The paradox is sharpest if what "exhilirates," that is, makes cheerful, enlivens, is death. (Note that Dickinson misspells "exhilarate", as well as "yours" and "woe." While Franklin prints the poem with these errors, Johnson chooses to eliminate them, apparently considering them merely errors, not stylistic devices meant to contribute to the impact of the poem). Dickinson was not "in love" with death, as some have claimed, but she was obsessed with it. As one who defined her "business" as "circumference," that is, reaching toward the far limits of the poet's ability to know, she spent much of her poetic career pushing her consciousness as far as it could go into the inaccessible realms of dying and being dead.

In 1862, one of her "flood years" (1861–1865), when she wrote no fewer than 227 poems, Dickinson explored the fear of death in several other poems. In one, she is full of bravado: "Afraid! Of Whom am I afraid?/ Not Death—for who is He?/ The Porter of my Father's Lodge/ As much abasheth me!" (Fr 345). In others, she explores the same paradox that lies at the core of the poem under discussion: "The difference between Despair/ and Fear—is like the One/ Between the instant of a Wreck—/ And when the Wreck has been—" (Fr 576). "When I hoped I feared—/ Since I hoped I dared. . . . He deposes Doom/Who hath suffered him—" (Fr 594). Eleven years later, she returned to the same theme: "While we were fearing it, it came—/ But came with less of fear/ Because that fearing it so long/ Had almost made it fair—. . . 'Tis harder knowing it is Due/ Than knowing it is Here" (Fr 1317).

In the poem under discussion, Dickinson pushes this idea a stage further—"knowing" leads, not just to relief, but to a kind of frenzied gaiety. As we move through the poem, we feel the *struggle* to conquer dread, rather than the certainty of conquest. In line 2, although "it" is more extreme in its essence ("over Horror"), its impact is lessened (only half captivating). And by lines 3 and 4 the poet has adopted a calm, oracular tone and message: the soul is secure, dread is no more. (Johnson prints a variant for line 4: "A Sepulchre, fears frost, no more." This is a starker image: the price of freedom from dread is becoming a tomb). In the five stanzas that follow, this idea is developed through imagery that qualifies and transforms the original message in striking ways. In stanza 2, the ungrammatical commas slow down the lines and contribute to a sense of hesitancy. Far from smugly proclaiming

her certainties, the speaker experiences the process of coming to terms, both the relief ("How easy") and the pain of being "sawed" by suspense. And far from escaping torment, she simply finds it easier to bear:

> To scan a ghost, is faint—
> But grappling, conquers it—
> How easy, Torment, now—
> Suspense kept sawing so—

The lines contrast the "faintness" of scanning (scrutinizing, critically examining) "a ghost" with the physicality of grappling with it. The image of "grappling" recurs in stanza 5 as "wrestling." Both were key words in the religious REVIVALS that surrounded Dickinson in her youth, evoking the central revivalist text of Jacob wrestling with the Angel of God. Here, the speaker is wrestling, not with God, but with death or the terror of death. For Dickinson, this "irreverent . . . usurpation of the language of revivals" (Wolff, *Dickinson*, 223) describes a heroic spiritual stance. For those without such spirit, who still hope, there is always the pablum of prayer. Dickinson, who, in "TELL ALL THE TRUTH BUT TELL IT SLANT—" recommends an indirect path to revelation ("The Truth must dazzle gradually/ Or every man go blind") here asserts the value of confronting a Truth that is bald and cold— "But that will hold—." Although the referent of "that" is unclear, the meaning seems to be that *this* truth endures.

To this point, the poet has asserted that fear—not Death—is what may be conquered. In stanza 4, in the striking line "Looking at Death, is Dying—" she goes further and says that we die—or begin to die—when we look at death. The line has no simple or single interpretation. Some have seen it as describing a rehearsal for death. The imaginative act of confronting one's own death is as close as we can come to "dying" while still alive. The rest of the stanza is bitterly ironic: See how easy it is to die, to become less animate than inanimate things!

Then, following the brief refrain of stanza 5 in which the poet tells herself that others can wrestle with doubt and belief but her own struggle is over and welcomes the coming of "woe," the poem's tone shifts once more. In the compressed evocation of what "It"—presumably the imagination's confrontation with death—brings about, there is a manic note that bespeaks anything but the "security" the Soul was supposed to have found. Throughout this poem, Dickinson has used a series of similar, but not identical nouns for fear: horror, dread, torment, woe, fright, and terror, each with a different nuance of meaning. For example, horror compounds fear with hatred or disgust; fright is usually sudden, violent and temporary, whereas dread is a longer, more continuous experience. In the poem's final lines, words for fear—Fright and Terror—are linked to two different words for freedom: Fright is at *Liberty* and Terror's *free*:

> It sets the Fright at liberty—
> And Terror's free—
> Gay, Ghastly, Holiday!

Since it is unlikely that Dickinson, for whom every dash and syllable had weight, meant to repeat the same idea in different words, we must look for what distinguishes these phrases. While "terror" denotes extreme fear, it can also mean *the cause* of fear or dread. Dickinson's dictionary told her that "Death is emphatically styled *the king of terrors*." It is possible, then, that in the penultimate line Terror is the *cause* of Fright, that is, Terror is Death, free to do as it wills. This would "deny" the earlier statement that the Soul that confronts death conquers fear. The poem has come full circle, from dread eliminated to fright running rampant. The final line, with "Ghastly" sandwiched in between "Gay" and "Holiday," compresses the poem's central paradox. By capitalizing all three words—both adjectives and noun—and separating them by commas, Dickinson puts them on an equal plane. The jolting meter of that line—with its two initial pounding stresses—creates a sense of dissonance and unease.

In the fascicle in which this poem appears, it follows "I FELT A FUNERAL, IN MY BRAIN," which describes a hallucinatory state in which the speaker cannot grasp a frightening reality. Critics have suggested that this poem in which Dickinson confronts the "worst" represented a cure for that dreamlike state. What is certain is that the experience of confronting what "appalled her," was an exhilarating one, awakening her to the realities that stimulated her poetic impulses.

See also PUNCTUATION.

FURTHER READING

Inder Nath Kher, *Landscape of Abscence*; Greg Johnson, *Emily Dickinson*, 154–55; Cynthia Griffin Wolff, *Emily Dickinson*, 323.

"Title divine, is mine." (1861) (Fr 194, J 1072)

Emily Dickinson sent this poem in 1862 to her close friend SAMUEL BOWLES, with whom she had been corresponding for at least four years. She sent it with no salutation but added tersely, "Here's— what I had to 'tell you'—You will tell no other? Honor—is it's own pawn—" (L 250). For unknown reasons, she never copied this poem, widely considered to be one of her best, into the fascicles or sewn manuscript packets, in which she preserved her work. She did, however, give a version of the poem to her sister-in-law, SUSAN HUNTINGTON GILBERT DICKINSON, in 1865.

Dickinson's biographers disagree over whether the poem was sent as a confession of the poet's love for Bowles, the worldly, married editor of the *Springfield Republican,* and a long-time intimate of the Dickinson family, or whether she was confiding in Bowles about her feelings for REVEREND CHARLES WADSWORTH, the charismatic Presbyterian minister, whom she first met on a visit to Philadelphia in 1855 (Habegger, *My Wars*, 422–424). Bowles and Wadsworth are the leading candidates for the beloved man Dickinson addressed, in letters and poems, as Master.

While the identity of the "husband" to whom Dickinson declares herself to be "Wife" can never be known with certainty, the figure in the poem becomes something more—or other—than an earthly man. On some level, the "husband" is absent in this work, which proclaims, instead, the identity of the speaker *in relation* to someone or something else. For biographer Robert Sewall, there are three aspects to this identity, neither of which negates the others: the imagined wife of Samuel Bowles, denied her in reality; the Bride of Christ, who shares Calvary with him; and a woman who confers upon herself the "Acute Degree of Poet" (*Life*, II, 484–486).

In its merging of divine and earthly love, and the high vocation of poetry, it is of a pair with another great poem, written that same year, "MINE—BY THE RIGHT OF THE WHITE ELECTION!" Indeed, it is impossible to disentangle these two levels in many of the marriage and love poems, for Dickinson's imagery takes the reader in both directions at once. Thus, the speaker's opening words, "Title divine, is mine," can be read as her claiming entitlement to eternal life, to her status as the Bride of Christ, or as her raising to the level of divinity her title as earthly "wife." She lacks the external "Sign" of earthly wifehood: "the Swoon," of sexual surrender and the ring received in the double ring ceremony, "Garnet to Garnet—/ Gold—to Gold—." What she does have, however, is an exalted, painful status, "Acute Degree conferred on me," and the ironic married title, at once self-humbling and self-aggrandizing, "Empress of Calvary," a royal spiritual rank that neither has nor requires a visible "crown" to signify it.

> Title divine, is mine.
> The Wife without the Sign—
> Acute Degree conferred on me—
> Empress of Calvary—

The image of Calvary was a highly charged one for Dickinson, appearing in her poetry as an emblem of mingled agony and promised spiritual grace. In a poem of 1862, "THERE CAME A DAY—AT SUMMER'S FULL—," she remembers the wordless culmination and renunciation of a great earthly love and ends with the hope that she and her beloved will rise from the grave "To *that* New marriage—/ Justified—through Calvaries of Love!" (Fr 325). And in yet another poem of what she calls "bereaved acknowledgment," written in 1862, Fr 347, "I DREADED THAT FIRST ROBIN, SO," she calls herself "The Queen of Calvary." A poem such as Fr 670 (1863), "ONE CRUCIFIXION IS RECORDED— ONLY—," makes clear Dickinson's unorthodox use

of the word: her sense that there are many calvaries and that, in the lives of ordinary, suffering human beings, "There's newer—nearer Crucifixion" than the one recorded in the New Testament.

As "Empress of Calvary" the speaker asserts the immensity of the pain of *not* being an earthly wife and makes the defiant gesture of embracing it. Indeed, critic Sandra M. Gilbert sees this poem as a supreme instance "of anguish converted into energy." ("Wayward Nun," 29). Nonetheless, Dickinson cannot help lingering on the "signs" of what has been denied her, identifying with "the Swoon / God gives *us* Women" and devoting two lines to the evocation of the double ring ceremony. Until this point, wifehood seems desirable, but with the line "Born—Bridalled—Shrouded—" it takes on negative meaning. Judith Farr understands this line as a shorthand for Dickinson's own, ironic, "Tri [triple] Victory," implying that "as soon as she felt passion she renounced it" (*Passion*, 180). Similarly, psychoanalytic critic John Cody sees the line as an expression of Dickinson's sense of her great love affair as something extremely brief but uplifting, which passed "decisively and irrevocably" (*After Great Pain*, 368). Thus, the love would be "Shrouded" just as soon as it was born and consecrated. This assumes, however, that the lines *do* refer to the speaker, a conclusion the poem's elliptical syntax does not allow us to make with certainty. Given the lines that precede and follow it, it seems more likely that they refer to the women who swoon, exchange wedding rings, and say "My Husband." Thus, in the word "Bridalled" Dickinson may be punning on the word "bridled": Like a wild pony, the young unmarried woman is tamed and constricted. "Shrouded" implies that marriage is either a form of living death or a state that leads directly to death. The sequence of events "bridal veil to shroud" was no melodramatic notion; Dickinson was well aware of the large number of women who died during childbirth in her day, including a beloved sister of Sue Dickinson.

Is this, then, an anti-marriage poem? Biographer and critic Cynthia Griffin Wolff can see it no other way, "so bitterly does it capture the smugness with which some women flaunt their married state." In the image of the wife, "'Stroking the Melody,' perhaps by saying, 'My *husband* says . . .'" Wolff discerns the poet's undisguised contempt for ordinary wives (*Emily Dickinson*, 396). She notes that the poet was too aware of the pitfalls of marriage to prefer it to a life dedicated to one's "true vocation." If, however, "Title divine" expresses Emily Dickinson's decision to marry her art and achieve the divine identity of poet, in the final questioning line, the emphatic certainty of the poem's beginning gives way to doubt:

Is this the way—

Ambivalence toward her own "title" as opposed to that of the ordinary wife has been present throughout the poem, and as the poet wistfully, desperately "thinks aloud" in its final line, it only deepens.

See also "A WIFE—AT DAYBREAK—I SHALL BE—," "GOD IS A DISTANT, STATELY LOVER," and "I SHOULD HAVE BEEN TOO GLAD, I SEE—."

FURTHER READING

Charles R. Anderson. *Stairway*, 200–211; Sharon Cameron, "Dialectics of Rage," in *Modern Critical Views*, Harold Bloom, ed., 124–126; John Cody, *After Great Pain*, 366–369; Judith Farr, *Passion*, 178–180; Susan M. Gilbert, "Wayward Nun," in *Critical Essays*, 26–27; Alfred Habegger, *My Wars*, 422–424; Dorothy Huff Oberhaus, "'Tender Pioneer,'" in *Critical Essays*, Judith Farr, ed., 105–118; Robert Sewall, *Life*, 484–486; Cynthia Griffin Wolff, *Emily Dickinson*, 396–397.

"To make a prairie it takes a clover and one bee,"
(Undated) (Fr 1779, J 1755)

In this famous aphoristic poem, Dickinson declares the power of the imagination to create a world. The poet begins by stating that only "a clover and one bee" are required in order to "make a prairie." She repeats this meditatively in the next line, indicating the slowing down of her thought by the commas after *clover* and *bee*, before adding, "And revery," as if this were a mere afterthought. She

then seems to "realize" that this third element, revery (imagination), is the essential one, both necessary and sufficient—"if bees are few." In the playful rhyme scheme, the only word that doesn't chime is "revery"—emblematic of the fact that imagination goes its own way.

In what sense can the contention of the first line be true? Certainly not in a literal one. As scholar Suzanne Juhasz points out, "A prairie in the world of nature cannot be composed from one clover and one bee, but the idea of prairie can" (*Undiscovered Continent*, 50). The *image* of a prairie can be created in the human mind by just one or two components of it. Dickinson is describing what takes place through use of the poetic device of synecdoche, the representation of a whole by one of its parts. She goes an important step further, however, in asserting that even the actual, material components are not necessary. In Juhasz's words, ". . . since the mind can also think of an object that is unperceived, in that sense it creates the object before perception" (*Undiscovered Continent*, 50).

Thus, on one level, this poem is Dickinson's statement about what is essential in the making of a poem. Critic Joseph Raab, in his study of Dickinson's metapoetics, that is, her ideas about the nature of poetry, discusses this poem in connection with an undated poem (Fr 1749), which begins "By a departing light / We see acuter, quite." Raab notes that for Dickinson, "Only when the light of the imagination takes precedence over the actual daylight can the mystery of human existence be illumined" ("The Metapoetic Element," 282). This does not negate the fact that Dickinson was an acute observer of the details of the outer world, a feature of her work that has been noted by many commentators. It simply means that she was not content to stop at the level of observation. For Emily Dickinson, as for the renowned 20th-century poet Marianne Moore, the challenge for genuine poets was to create "imaginary gardens with real toads in them" ("Poetry").

This declaration of the independence of the inner world from the material world is reminiscent of one Dickinson's best-known, most frequently memorized poems, Fr 800, "I NEVER SAW A MOOR":

I never saw a Moor.
I never saw the Sea—
Yet know I how the Heather looks
And what a Billow be—

In both poems, she evokes landscapes that were not part of her experienced world. She had never seen the prairies of Kansas or walked the wild moors that were featured in the novels of her beloved authors, Charlotte and Emily Brontë. (She probably *did* see the sea, or at least the Boston harbor during one of her visits to that city.) Still, she insisted, these experiences were not unavailable to her; for this poet of the inner world, the "knowing" that came through intuition and imagination was every bit as true—and more so—as that gleaned through the evidence of the senses.

See also "I DWELL IN POSSIBILITY—," "THE BRAIN—IS WIDER THAN THE SKY—," and "THE ONLY NEWS I KNOW."

FURTHER READING

Suzanne Juhasz, *Undiscovered Continent*, 49–50; Joseph Raab, "Metapoetic Element," in *Handbook*, Grabher et al., eds., 282–283.

"Two swimmers wrestled on the spar—" (1861) (Fr 227, J 201)

Emily Dickinson sent this enigmatic, allegorical poem to her close friend and confidant, SAMUEL BOWLES, prefaced by the words: "I cant explain it, Mr. Bowles." The contemporary reader might well echo this sentiment, for the poem raises more questions than it answers:

"Two swimmers wrestled on the spar—
Until the morning sun—
When One—turned smiling to the land—
Oh God! the Other One!

Since a spar is a round piece of timber used for the topmasts of ships, the opening image is one of shipwreck, with two swimmers struggling to stay afloat, wrestling either one another or the waves of the sea. Given this basic scenario, what is the poem about? Who are the two figures and what does the term "swimmers" designate? Why were they wrestling? What is the meaning of the smiling victory of the one and the defeat of the other?

For someone immersed in biblical culture, as Dickinson was, the image of two figures wrestling until the dawn is an inescapable allusion to the story of Jacob wrestling with "a man" who proves to be God. "And Jacob was left alone; and there wrestled a man with him until the breaking of the day" (Genesis 32: 24). This text occupied a central place in the poet's imagination. In "A LITTLE EAST OF JORDAN," she recreates the story of Jacob explicitly. In many other poems she alludes to it through the use of resonant words such as "wrestle," "grapple," and "strive," as Cynthia Griffin Wolff notes, "each one of which, in Dickinson's world, carried the association of a 'struggle with faith' or 'a struggle with the Lord'" (*Emily Dickinson*, 145).

Jacob's wrestling with God was of enormous importance in the Calvinist concept of "conversion" through the acceptance of Christ, a commitment Dickinson herself wrestled with as a girl and young woman. During the successive REVIVALS that swept through AMHERST during the 1840s and 1850s, "sinners" were expected to engage in an agonizing struggle with God and their own consciences. They were wrestling for high stakes: release from the terrors of disease and death and the promise of resurrection. The price they paid for these blessings was the fundamental revision of the sense of self that accompanied submission to a will greater than their own. While Dickinson's entire family and her closest friends eventually succumbed to the spell of these highly emotional public events, the poet herself, apparently finding the price too high, never did.

In light of this refusal, Wolff sees "Two swimmers wrestled on the spar—" as "Dickinson's contrary, *rebellious* interpretation of mankind's wrestle with belief and trust in God." For this biographer and critic, "the swimmer who has chosen the world and turns to 'land' is 'smiling; the swimmer who has turned his hope to God has become no more than an empty face with blinded eyes" (*Emily Dickinson,* 145). This interpretation is plausible, however, only if we ignore the intense despair that permeates the poem, from the anguished exclamation, "Oh God! the Other One!" to the final image of "hands—beseeching—thrown!" The weight of the poet's sympathies is clearly with the one who is defeated.

If the poem *is* about the struggle for religious faith, it would seem to reflect a sense of horror at the fate of one who does not believe, the lost "shipwrecked man" characterized in a sermon by REVEREND CHARLES WADSWORTH, the charismatic Presbyterian minister whom Dickinson revered. In "The Great Query," using imagery that resonates with that of "Two swimmers wrestled," he writes, "to the poor, lost soul *there shall be no tomorrow* . . . the spar will be washed away from the grasp of the shipwrecked man ere the sun rise up again to shine upon his sea-tossed head" (Sewall, *Life,* II, 457). The lone boat voyaging on the "sea of life" was a popular image in the painting and writing of Dickinson's day; as a girl she had employed it to speak of her fear of spiritual damnation: "I feel that I am sailing upon the brink of an awful precipice, from which I cannot escape & over which I fear my tiny boat will soon glide if I do not receive help from above" (L 11, March 28, 1846, to ABIAH PALMER ROOT).

In "Two swimmers wrestled," not only does the drowning man receive no help from above— even the "stray" passing ships ignore him. In this light, the tragic sense of the poem has to do, not with the fate of the nonbeliever, but with the nature of existence. The vision is one of total helplessness in a random universe in which God, nature, *and* man are indifferent to the pleas of the sufferer. We don't know whether the "smiling" swimmer has caused the death of the other or whether he has simply failed to reach out to save him. In either case, the mercy that is beseeched is not given. Unlike the Jacob story, God is not present at all in this narrative—two *men* wres-

tle—except in the speaker's cry of horror, "Oh God! the Other One!"—a formula devoid of its original meaning.

While religious interpretations find fertile ground in this poem, they are not the only ones that critics have discerned. Judith Farr sees the verse as an expression of despair at the poet's loss of her intense friendship with SUSAN HUNTINGTON GILBERT DICKINSON. In this interpretation, it is Sue, her sister-in-law, who turns smiling toward the land, "a safe marriage perhaps; [while] the other, herself . . . becomes a grotesque face . . . begging for love as she dies." Farr, who believes that Samuel Bowles was the Master, to whom Dickinson dedicated much of her great love poetry, hypothesizes that Dickinson sent him the poem "as a revelation of her earlier relations with Sue. . . . Suggesting such desperate passion to Bowles might have had the effect of transferring her love to him more easily" (*Passion,* 192). Whatever the circumstances in Dickinson's life that may have motivated the poem, the suggestive spareness and universality of her language takes it beyond the narrowly autobiographical. On the metaphysical level, it is an evocation of man's tragic isolation in an uncaring universe, a vision of merciless struggle in which only "the fittest" survive. On the psychological level, the poem can be seen as a dramatization of the divided soul, pitted against itself (Ward, *Capsule of the Mind,* 47), a theme Dickinson repeatedly explored in some of her most incisive existential poems, including "ONE NEED NOT BE A CHAMBER—TO BE HAUNTED—" and "ME FROM MYSELF—TO BANISH—."

See also CONGREGATIONALISM, JONATHAN EDWARDS, MASTER LETTERS, and PURITAN HERITAGE.

FURTHER READING

Priyamvada Tripathi Anantharaman, *Sunset,* 103–107; Joanne Feit Diehl, "Emerson, Dickinson, and the Abyss," in *Modern Critical Views,* Harold Bloom, ed., 156–157; Judith Farr, *Passion,* 192, 202–203; Richard B. Sewall, *Life,* II, 457–458; Theodora Ward, *Capsule of the Mind,* 47; Cynthia Griffin Wolff, *Emily Dickinson,* 139–147.

"Undue Significance a starving man attaches" (1863) (Fr 626, J 439)

Among the poems Dickinson wrote on the theme of starving, during the early 1860s, in the midst of her most spectacularly prolific period, this one has the quality of summation. It stands in contrast to narrative poems such as "I HAD BEEN HUNGRY, ALL THE YEARS—" or "IT WOULD HAVE STARVED A GNAT—," in which the poet tells the agonizing personal story of a woman/bird/child who is obliged to exist on the most minimal sustenance, teeters on the edge of extinction, but learns the art of survival. Here, the perspective shifts back and forth between the arguments of a removed, "objective" speaker and the perceptions of the "starving man."

> Undue Significance a starving man attaches
> To Food—
> Far off—He sighs—and therefore—Hopeless—
> And therefore—Good—

The first two words are abstract and judgmental, while the syntactic inversion gives the line a formal quality. Juxtaposed to this long line, the minimal second line, "To Food—," two syllables of generalized nourishment, devoid of smell, taste, color, shape, or texture, seems to confirm its posited insignificance. In contrast to the flowing coherence of these lines, which form a single sentence uninterrupted by dashes, the next two are broken by dashes and elliptical. They have a disconnected quality that mimics the thought process of the starving man, who "sighs" that the food he desires is "Far off" and so he cannot hope to obtain it, and because he cannot obtain it, it is "Good." The poet might be making fun of the starving man's logic, but, as the following stanza reveals, she wholly agrees with him.

The cool, philosophical voice returns in the first three-and-a-half lines of the second stanza, which can be paraphrased as follows: "Partaking of food relieves our hunger, but makes us realize that the food we eat (receive) is no longer spicy (its spices have flown away)." Had Dickinson used conventional punctuation, there would be a period after

"Receipt." In the final, wistful one-and-a-half lines, "It was the Distance—/ Was Savory—," she sums up, in a synesthetic image that merges the sense of taste and physical space, her enduring insight that, indeed, what is far off, what we cannot hope to obtain, is what is "good." Looked at from a slightly different perspective, she is saying, "Once an object has been magnified by desire, it cannot be wholly possessed by appetite" (Wilbur, "Sumptuous Destitution," 56).

Unlike "A DYING TIGER— MOANED FOR DRINK—," this is not a tragic poem. The hypothetical starving man gets to eat in time. But only his physical needs are satisfied, not his hunger for "Spices," those stimulating ingredients that add relish to a dish, and which Dickinson often referred to in her poetry. Not only is desire obtained less pungent than desire anticipated; sated and unsated hunger are different experiences altogether. Dickinson reaches a similar conclusion in "I had been hungry, all the Years," in which she learns "That Hunger—was a way/ Of persons Outside Windows—/That entering—takes away—." And Dickinson is loath to part with her hunger, because it alone is capable of allowing her to fully perceive the value of what she hungers for. In the famous early formulation of "SUCCESS IS COUNTED SWEETEST," she announces, "To comprehend a nectar—/ Requires sorest need."

Dickinson's insight that unwilled deprivation leads to heightened perception of what is desired evolved into the paradox that something or someone can only be truly possessed through willed renunciation. This affirmation, which turns victimization into active choice, is one of the fundamental tenets of Dickinson's poetic universe. A short list of other food and drink poems, in which the explores this theme, would include: "Who never lost are unprepared" (Fr 136); "Water, is taught by thirst" (Fr 93); "To learn the Transport by the Pain" (Fr 178); "I TASTE A LIQUOR NEVER BREWED—"; "Exhiliration is within" (Fr 645); "A Prison gets to be a friend" (Fr 456); "Deprived of other Banquet" (Fr 872); "The Luxury to apprehend" (Fr 819); "To disappear enhances" (Fr 1239); "Art thou the thing I wanted" (Fr 1311); and "I took one Draught of Life" (Fr 396).

The fact that Dickinson returned to the theme of possession through renunciation again and again in her poetry is an indication of her ongoing struggle to turn the disappointing realities of her life into spiritual victories. On one level, her disappointments were the result of external circumstances. There were real, fundamental limitations in her life—her celibacy and her obscurity as a poet chief among them—which she had somehow to learn to live with. But it is also the case that her inner nature—her emotional and imaginative intensity and her neediness, ensured that certain realities (primarily those involving social relationships) would always let her down. This explains how Dickinson could write passionately to a friend of her desire for a meeting, then refuse to see that friend when she appeared in the Dickinson drawing room.

Critics differ on whether Dickinson's "notion that anticipation is always superior to fulfillment and that fantasy is the only fulfillment" is an enriching or limiting aspect of her worldview (Pollack, "Thirst and Starvation," 68). Pollack sees it as not only limiting, but at variance with the concern of her poetry as a whole "for observing and gratifying the urgent thirsts and hungers of the instinctive self" (Ibid., 68). For Wilbur, it is an enhancing force, allowing the poet to "live in a huge world of delectable distances" ("Sumptuous Destitution," 59). In either case, it was a sense of life that would endure. Fourteen years later, in "WHO NEVER WANTED—MADDEST JOY," she would write, "The Banquet of Abstemiousness/ Defaces that of Wine—." This is Dickinson's full-scale celebration of, what she called the "piercing Virtue" of renunciation. Yet, as the brief poem concludes, it becomes clear that her "choice" of abstaining is based on a "principle" over which she has no control: "Within it's reach, though yet ungrasped/ Desire's perfect Goal—/ No nearer—lest the Actual—/ Should disenthrall thy soul—."

See also "RENUNCIATION—IS A PIERCING VIRTUE—" and "VICTORY COMES LATE."

FURTHER READING

Vivian R. Pollak, "Thirst and Starvation," in *Critical Essays,* Judith Farr, ed., 62–75. Richard Wilbur, "Sumptuous Destitution," in *Critical Essays,* Judith Farr, ed., 53–61.

"Unto my Books—so good to turn—" (1863) (Fr 512, J 604)

If there is a single experience Dickinson celebrates without qualification it is the reading of books. She begins this poem with an artless expression of satisfaction that embodies both a sigh of relief, as she turns away from mundane labors, and a catch in the throat of pleasurable anticipation. At first, she tries to perceive her longing for a book during the course of her workday as the "Banquet of Abstemiousness" she would later declare superior to indulgence, which always disappoints. But abstinence from books is only "half-endeared" by such thoughts. For, unlike the other experiences she craved and feared would disappoint her (love, friendship, fame), she knows that reading does not. Beloved books

Enamor—in Prospective—
And satisfy—obtained—

Books are "Banquettings to be," anticipation of which injects "Flavors" and "Spices" into the hours when she must be away from them. She likens herself to "Retarded Guests," that is, late guests, who cheer themselves with thoughts of the bounty awaiting them. In the realm of books, Dickinson is no longer the bird who has received "just a crumb" from a depriving God but one who regularly feasts. She described her ordeal in 1864–65, when a disabling eye problem prevented her from reading, as "the only [woe] that ever made me tremble . . . a shutting out of the dearest ones of time, the strongest friends of the soul—BOOKS." In this poem, she calls her books her "Kinsmen of the Shelf," with kid (leather) countenances.

Dickinson wrote this poem while the Civil War was raging and her sense of books as a refuge from the "Wilderness—without—," where men were dying, is prominent in the third stanza, where she proclaims:

But Holiday—excludes the night—
And it is Bells—within—

Spiritual nurture and companionship, refuge from a brutal world: precious as these gifts were, they did not exhaust Dickinson's store of imagery for what books provided her. In her famous later poem, "THERE IS NO FRIGATE LIKE A BOOK" (Fr 1286, 1873), this reclusive poet likens books to ships that take her "Lands away." A "Page / Of prancing Poetry—" she declares, is better than any "Courser." A book is democratically available to rich and poor alike, the "frugal" "Chariot that bears the human soul." Intriguingly, in Dickinson's work, death is the other "democratic" experience, as in the early poem, "One dignity delays for all—" (Fr 77, 1859), and the chariot bearing the soul is most often death's, as in her great poem, "BECAUSE I COULD NOT STOP FOR DEATH—." As she uses these images for the experience of reading a book, Dickinson reverses their meanings to express the "immortality" available to all.

In another poem of 1863, "A precious—mouldering pleasure—'tis" (Fr 569), Dickinson rhapsodizes on the pleasures of encountering "an Antique Book—In just the Dress his Century wore—." Maintaining the personification throughout seven stanzas, she makes clear her delight in both the physicality of the "Vellum Heads" of old books and their ability to transport her to a time when Sappho lived and Beatrice wore the gown Dante would "deify":

> When Plato—was a Certainty—
> And Sophocles—a Man—

The poem reflects her avid intellectual curiosity, a desire to compare notes on mutual themes, to know what ancient scholars were most interested in and "What Competitions ran—." In her culminating image, the antique book takes on a transcendent dimension. An antique volume is one that "lived—where Dreams were born—," probably a reference to ancient Greece, the cradle of Western civilization. The word "Dreams" in this context suggests mankind's long endeavor, through literature and philosophy, to grasp the essence of human life. For Dickinson, the quester, the "truth" the ancient book confirms, is not any specific dream-content, but the supreme value and honorable heritage of dreaming.

See also "GOD GAVE A LOAF TO EVERY BIRD—" and "WHO NEVER WANTED—MADDEST JOY."

FURTHER READING

Jack L. Capp, *Emily Dickinson's Reading, 1836–1886*; Richard B. Sewall, *Life*, II, 668–705; Gary Lee Stonum, "Dickinson's Literary Background," in *Handbook*, Grabher et al., eds., 44–60.

Elizabeth Barrett Browning. Dickinson kept this portrait, as well as one of George Eliot, both of whom she revered, in her room. *(By permission of the Houghton Library, Harvard University)*

"Victory comes late—" (1861) (Fr 195, J 690)

This is one of the earliest poems among the many in Dickinson's oeuvre that use the imagery of thirst and starvation to explore the realms of emotional and spiritual deprivation. The word "Victory," in connection with the themes of death and deprivation, contains echoes of Dickinson's 1859 poem, "SUCCESS IS COUNTED SWEETEST," where the meaning of victory is perceived with greater clarity by the dying and defeated soldier than by the victor. In this poem, Dickinson makes no claims for the blessings of deprivation. Rather, the potentially reviving liquid of victory comes too late to save the victor, whose "freezing lips" are "Too rapt with frost," that is, who is already dead. "Rapt" implies both enchantment and ecstasy; the belated victor cannot be saved because she has succumbed to her enthrallment to "frost," or deprivation.

Thus, in the poem's first images, death is the result of deprivation, and an "economical" God is to blame, a God whose Table is spread so high that the speaker cannot reach it unless she dines "on Tiptoe." (Note that she uses the plural "We" and "Us" to refer to herself, as she does frequently in her poems; she may, however, also be implying "the likes of us," that is, the sparrows she goes on to identify herself with). In the final bird images, however, deprivation does not lead to death: The sparrow survives on its crumb. The poet puts forth a natural hierarchy of entitlement: Sparrows, whose little mouths require crumbs, Robins, who are large enough to dine on cherries, and Eagles, who enjoy more substantial fare. The leap from Dickinson's quintessential songbird, the robin, to the large, predatory eagle, whose "Golden Breakfast" may very well include sparrows and robins, is significant. The complexity of the image is enhanced when we recall that, for Dickinson, the word "Golden" had special meaning. When she was 19, she wrote to her friend ABIAH PALMER ROOT that she was "dreaming a golden dream," and to her special confidante JANE HUMPHREY she wrote about a new mysterious joy in her life, using the metaphor of a "golden thread." In this poem, however, the glory inherent in goldenness belongs to the huge and powerful ones who consume smaller birds, such as the speaker-sparrow. Note the ominous word *strangle*—with its implication of murder. Thus, read in the context of Dickinson's work as a whole, the image implies that what "strangles" the smaller bird is the appropriation of that "golden reality" that she had coveted for herself.

As Sparrow, she is on the lowest rung. She would choke if she had to swallow anything larger than a crumb. She implies that there is a certain "rightness" in her allotment. She is one of those whose "little mouth" is fit only for crumbs. The implication is that "that's the way things are," and God is not to blame: He merely implements this natural order. Furthermore, "God keep his Oath to Sparrows." The irregular grammar of this phrase—"God keep" instead of "God keeps"—calls attention to itself. We don't know whether the poet is making God plural, or if she means the line to be read as possibility rather than certainty: "May God keep his Oath" or "God [may] keep his Oath. . . ." The allusion is to the biblical notion that God is aware of the fate of even the most inconsequential of his creatures: "Are not two sparrows sold for a farthing? And one of them shall not fall on the ground without your Father" (Matthew 10: 29). In the context of the poem as a whole, however, the allusion seems to be an ironic hint that God's attention to the sparrow's fall is not altogether benevolent: Sparrows, which receive little love, *know how* to starve. More than a function of mouth size, starving is an art; the pitiless terms of their loveless existences demand that they acquire it.

The fact that Dickinson was only 30 when she wrote this poem, with the possibility of love and literary success still before her, raises the question of why it was already too late for "victory" to touch her. Scholars speculating on the reason for so devastating a sense of deprivation have turned to Dickinson's family life and to the feminine culture in which she lived. In his psychoanalytic discussion of Dickinson's oral imagery, John Cody develops the theory that the poet suffered a total emotional breakdown just before her great creative period of 1858–65, due largely to maternal deprivation in childhood. Vivian Pollak, making a feminist cultural interpretation, relies on the evidence of Dickinson's letters to argue that "the strategy of shrinking vital needs to the point where crumbs and drops must suffice developed as a defense against the sexual politics of Victorian America, especially as represented by the Dickinson family . . ." ("Thirst and Starvation," 64). In her formative years, it was her brother WILLIAM AUSTIN who was revered as the family's literary light, while younger sister Emily duly embraced a subservient, demeaning role: "I feel quite like retiring, in presence of one so grand, and casting my small lot among small birds and fishes—"

she wrote him, thinly concealing her jealousy (L 45, June 29, 1851). Dickinson was not one to directly confront the powerful males in her life and challenge their entitlements. Instead, in her poetry she strove to develop a self-reliant persona, capable of subsisting on mere "crumbs" from the outside world. The strategy proves only too successful; for when greater nurture comes her way, she is too accustomed to deprivation to respond to it.

See also "GOD GAVE A LOAF TO EVERY BIRD—," "I HAD BEEN HUNGRY, ALL THE YEARS—," "IT WOULD HAVE STARVED A GNAT—," and "ON A COLUMNAR SELF—."

FURTHER READING

John Cody, *After Great Pain*; Vivian R. Pollak, "Thirst and Starvation," in *Critical Essays*, Judith Farr, ed., 62–75. Richard Wilbur, "Sumptuous Destitution," in *Critical Essays*, Judith Farr, ed., 53–61.

"We grow accustomed to the Dark—" (1862) (Fr 428, J 419)

In this sad, inspiring poem, we hear the voice of Dickinson the survivor. Using the analogy of making one's way home from a neighbor's house on a dark night, she discloses her vision of the aftermath "of larger—Darknesses—/ Those Evenings of the Brain—." Dickinson may be alluding to mental breakdown, depression, heartache over the end of a love affair, or grief for someone's death. There is nothing in the language of the poem that points to any specific circumstances. Indeed, one of the poem's triumphs is its universality. Dickinson manages to use light and darkness, the most traditional, overworked images of hope and despair, and their variants (life and death, good and evil, knowledge and ignorance, salvation and damnation) and to make them new. So perfect a fit is her analogy of external to internal light and darkness, and so unsentimental her conclusion, that the reader is brought to a fresh, clear-eyed recognition of how we go on living in the aftermath of sorrow.

The five-stanza poem is structured symmetrically. In the first two stanzas, the analogy is intro-

duced, and the drama of "adjustment" to the dark encapsulated in a single image:

> A Moment—We uncertain step
> For newness of the night—
> Then—fit our Vision to the Dark—
> And meet the Road—erect—

In stanza 3, the speaker makes explicit her analogy to "Those Evenings of the Brain" when neither moon nor star appear in the inner sky. Although Dickinson might have ended the poem there, we must be grateful she did not, for the last two stanzas add the essential subtlety to her vision. Returning to her solitary figure in the night, she details her struggle with the surrounding darkness. A note of comedy enters in the image of the "Bravest" hitting their foreheads smack into a tree. To survive, one must grope and injure oneself in the process. Indeed, the whole process of survival is mysterious. Since "Perception of an Object costs / Precise the Object's loss—" (Fr 1103), we have no way of knowing whether objective reality or subjective vision has changed:

> But as they learn to see—

> Either the Darkness alters—
> Or something in the sight
> Adjusts itself to Midnight—
> And Life steps almost straight.

Without the little word *almost* the poem would be diminished, for it conveys the recognition of inexorable loss. Life will never be "straight" again; we must be satisfied with the approximation. Habit itself is steadying, but it requires some adjustment of our sight, some relinquishing of grief's pitiless vision. The inexact rhymes throughout the poem, and particularly in the final stanza echo the semantic content. Dickinson teases us with what seems to be an exact rhyme, sight/Midnight, but is not, since *Midnight* is stressed on the first syllable. The concluding off rhyme, sight/straight, limps a little, as does Life itself, an image that contradicts the statement of stanza 2, that we "meet the Road—erect—."

Thus, this poem gives us the heroic Dickinson, but with a difference. In a famous early poem, she writes:

To fight aloud, is very brave—
But *gallanter*, I know
Who charge within the bosom
The Cavalry of Wo—

(Fr 138, 1860)

She knew this internal gallantry from her own life and continued to celebrate "the giant" and "the king" within. In 1871 she declared:

We never know how high we are
Till we are asked to rise

(Fr 1197)

These are the unshadowed assertions of inner triumph that schoolchildren tend to memorize. But the Dickinson of "We grow accustomed to the Dark—" is the greater poet, the one who knew how victory and defeat coexist in every step we take within the clearing darkness.

See also "AFTER GREAT PAIN, A FORMAL FEELING COMES—," "I CAN WADE GRIEF—," "I FELT A FUNERAL, IN MY BRAIN," and "I TIE MY HAT—I CREASE MY SHAWL—."

FURTHER READING

Sharon Cameron. "Dickinson's Fascicles," in *Handbook*, Grabher et al., eds., 151; Vivian R. Pollak, *Anxiety of Gender*, 210; Cynthia Griffin Wolff, *Emily Dickinson*, 452–453.

"We play at Paste—" (1862) (Fr 282, J 320)

This single eight-line stanza, was one of the four poems Dickinson enclosed in her first letter to THOMAS WENTWORTH HIGGINSON, the literary eminence whom she asked to tell her whether her verse was alive. She clearly valued it and expected it to tell him something about her. One of Dickinson's many wisdom poems, it is a virtuoso demonstration of her dictum, "TELL ALL THE TRUTH BUT TELL IT SLANT—." Its "message" is straightforward: What we learn while playing with primitive "Paste" serves as the template for our later, more accomplished and sophisticated efforts; it is the medium of our

apprenticeship, until we are "qualified for Pearl." In the poem's delightful concluding images, Paste and Pearl (costume jewelry and real) reappear as Gem Tactics and Sands, suggesting a highly evolved skill and the raw material/practice from which it has evolved. Pearls, after all, accrete around grains of sand:

And our new Hands
Learned Gem Tactics
Practicing Sands—

But what, more specifically, is the poem about? Should we wish to go further, many underlying themes suggest themselves. In her poems Dickinson often alluded to her beloved girlhood friend and sister-in-law, SUSAN HUNTINGTON GILBERT DICKINSON, as a pearl. Is it possible then that her earlier loves for friends such as ABIAH PALMER ROOT and ABBY WOOD are the "paste" with which she practiced for her "play" with the rare, precious Sue?

It is possible. Yet, if we knew nothing of Dickinson's history, the poem might speak to us of love in general—or of some altogether different sphere of experience: mastering an art or skill, developing understanding and expertise in any arena, or in the art of life itself. Critic Charles R. Anderson has suggested that the poem is about the difference between Dickinson's early light verse and her later mature poetry (*Stairway*, 33).

Biographer Cynthia Griffin Wolff detects an echo of the traditional religious notion of God's Kingdom, the "Pearl of Great Price," "for which all of life's limited pleasures ought to be traded." She cautions, however, that "the force of the legend has become so diluted that the poem might more plausibly be taken as a wry homily concerning our impatience with the earlier stages of our development of any earthly skill" (*Emily Dickinson*, 459).

For scholar Robert Weisbuch, any specific interpretation is narrow and suspect. He cautions us to "resist the temptation to pin down a poetry which depends upon expansible meaning" (*Emily Dickinson's Poetry*, 56). Underscoring the "precise imprecision" of Dickinson's symbols, Weisbuch insists that the responsibility of readers is to "formulate a theme broad enough to support the poem's burden and to refuse to transform analogical illustration into factual statement, biography, or arbitrary dreamed-up allegory" (Ibid., 57).

See also "SHELLS FROM THE COAST MISTAKING—," "THE MALAY TOOK THE PEARL—," and "YOUR RICHES—TAUGHT ME—POVERTY."

FURTHER READING

Charles R. Anderson, *Stairway*, 33; Robert A. Weisbuch, *Emily Dickinson's Poetry*, 56–57; Cynthia Griffin Wolff, *Emily Dickinson*, 459.

"We thirst at first—'tis Nature's Act—" (1863) (Fr 750, J 726)

In this anatomy of human thirst, Dickinson identifies three interlocking manifestations: the physical thirst of infancy, by which we enter and grow into life; the physical/emotional thirst of the final hours, by which we cling to life; and the spiritual thirst for immortal life that underlies all our thirsts and overcomes us at the moment of death, by which we let go of life.

The thirst of the infant is "Nature's Act," a longing of the flesh decreed by physical laws. By phrasing it this way the speaker implies that such thirst is generated by forces that lie outside the essentially human. The thirst of the dying is minimal ("A little water") and it is as much a thirst for compassion, for the touch of "fingers going by" (a synecdoche that pulls us into the perspective of the dying) as for drink. The giving and accepting of water at the hour of death was a powerful moment for Dickinson, one she returned to in several poems. To be chosen for the final act of giving water was, for her, both privilege and proof of a sacred bond with the one who is dying. Thus, in Fr 491, she writes:

The World—feels Dusty
When We stop to Die—
We want the Dew—then
Honors—taste dry—

The "Dew" that we crave is love, a fan "Stirred by a friend's Hand," which has the power to cool "like the Rain." The speaker prays to be that friend:

Mine be the Ministry
When thy Thirst comes—

In this poem she imagines the exotic "balms" she will bring to the dying, but elsewhere in her poetry she expresses a sense of her inadequacy to satisfy these final needs. In an early poem, "I bring an unaccustomed wine" (Fr 126, 1859), her offering to the dying proves a "tardy glass" clasped in dead hands. In "A DYING TIGER—MOANED FOR DRINK—," transposing this same drama from the domestic plane to an exotic symbolic one, the speaker recounts her failure to return in time with water for the mighty dying beast. These poems express the speaker's sense of helplessness to ward off death, as well as suggesting her sense of emotional inadequacy. But in the "higher" form of thirst she evokes in the conclusion of "We thirst at first," the burden is lifted from her. At death we pass out of nature and come to understand our earthly thirst as an intimation of the soul's "finer want":

Whose adequate supply
Is that Great Water in the West—
Termed Immortality—

Dickinson is a poet who repeatedly paints a vision of heaven only to mock it, reject it as uncongenial, reproach it for excluding her, or deny its reality. But in this poem, developing an idea she briefly touched upon in an 1859 poem, "Water is taught by thirst" (Fr 93), she ends on a note of religious optimism: the faith that our spiritual thirst itself "intimates" the existence of that which can slake it.

See also "A LOSS OF SOMETHING EVER FELT I—," "BECAUSE I COULD NOT STOP FOR DEATH—," "GOD GAVE A LOAF TO EVERY BIRD—," "I HAD BEEN HUNGRY, ALL THE YEARS—," "THIS WORLD IS NOT CONCLUSION," and "VICTORY COMES LATE."

FURTHER READING

Vivian R. Pollak, "Thirst and Starvation in Emily Dickinson's Poetry," in *Critical Essays*, Judith Farr, ed., 62–75; Richard Wilbur, "Sumptuous Destitution," in *Critical Essays*, Judith Farr, ed., 53–71; Cynthia Griffin Wolff, *Emily Dickinson*, 209.

"What Inn is this" (1859) (Fr 100, J 115)

This well-known, early graveyard poem is based on the conceit that the speaker finds herself in a strange, unidentified place, questioning where she is and why things are the way they are. The entire poem is an extended metaphor, in which the graveyard becomes the "Inn" of the dead; its rooms are the individual graves. This use of the "Inn" metaphor allows the poet to starkly and ironically define Death as devoid of the warmth and pleasures of life; there are no maids, no fire in the hearth, no tankards of ale. By "Peculiar Traveller" Dickinson may be referring to one newly dead and buried; and the speaker may very well *be* that Traveller. In other famous poems, such as "BECAUSE I COULD NOT STOP FOR DEATH—" and "I DIED FOR BEAUTY—BUT WAS SCARCE," Dickinson vividly imagines her transition from life to death and arrival in the graveyard. In the former poem, the grave is "a House that seemed / A Swelling of the Ground—"; in the latter, she converses with an inhabitant of an "adjoining Room—."

In this poem, however, the arrival in the tomb is permeated by a sense of mystery and horror, possibly derived from the Gothic literature, of which Dickinson was fond. A reader of Mrs. Anne Radcliffe and the Brontë sisters, she was familiar with Gothic tales of the macabre and supernatural, which characteristically took place in haunted castles, graveyards, ruins, and wild picturesque landscapes. The haunted house that the traveler comes upon, the mysterious landlord, and the obsession with graveyards were staples of these tales.

Note that an "Inn" is a temporary resting-place, a way station on a journey, either to or from home. It is not the Scriptural "House of the Lord" or "Palace of God"—those reassuring visions of eternal peace and immortality. If we think of this poem as Dickinson's attempt to cast herself into a scenario that succeeds death, it becomes clear that her imaginative journey to a heavenly abode is cut short by an overwhelming vision of the material grave where the body is placed. Not only is the place wholly comfortless, but the one in charge, the Landlord, whom she calls upon not once but twice, will not show himself. Furthermore, the very identity of the Landlord is in question: Who is in charge of this establishment? the speaker asks. Two obvious answers are death and God, albeit an absent one. Dickinson did not hesitate to speak of the Christian God in unorthodox terms.

The previous year, she had written another poem, "I NEVER LOST AS MUCH BUT TWICE—," in which she refers to God as a tradesman—a banker, in a reproachful line that reads, in its entirety, "Burglar! Banker—Father!" In the poem under discussion, Dickinson's unorthodoxy goes a step further (some might call it blasphemy) when she identifies God with a practitioner of black magic, a necromancer, that is, one who communicates with the spirits of the dead in order to predict the future. If the reader has not yet guessed that the speaker is in a graveyard, he can have no doubt of it now.

Still, when the speaker asks in the final line, "Who are these below?" the line conveys a sense of horror at the presence of death. Although the poet knows the literal answer to the question, she is also asking, Who *are* the dead? What is the body without the soul? She would address this mystery explicitly, 17 years later, after her father died:

> I dream about Father every night, always a different dream, and forget what I am doing daytimes, wondering where he is. Without any body, I keep thinking. What kind can that be?
> (L 471, August 1876, to the Norcross cousins)

Dickinson gets no further than the questions in this early poem, though she never ceases to explore the theme.

See also "A COFFIN IS A SMALL DOMAIN" and "SAFE IN THEIR ALABASTER CHAMBERS—."

FURTHER READING

David T. Porter, *Early Poetry*, 93; Cynthia Griffin Wolff, *Emily Dickinson*, 323.

"What mystery pervades a well!" (1877) (Fr 1433, J 1400)

This poem, with its aphoristic conclusion about nature's unknowability, is a favorite of anthologists. As we shall discover, however, the neatly tied-up ending, uncharacteristic of Dickinson's best poems, may have originated in a poem, not about nature, but about *human* nature.

The first two stanzas are structured upon the contrast between language suggesting boundlessness (mystery, water, another world, distance, limitlessness, abyss) and language drawn from the bounded, domestic realm (neighbor, jar, lid, the homey expression "as often as you please"). Following the speaker's initial awed exclamation, she attempts to domesticate the mystery. The water is personified as "he," as the speaker strives to establish a manageable relationship to "him." She does not succeed, however, for the inescapable face of the abyss predominates.

In the next two stanzas, a second element of nature—the grass—is introduced, and the speaker explores the interrelationships of self, water, and grass. Note that it is only the watery realms that are mysterious and awe-inspiring. In contrast, the humble grass and sedge are more closely identified with the speaker. The only thing mysterious about them is that they do not stand in awe of the water as she does. She is forced to see this fearlessness as a sign that "Related somehow they [grass and well, sedge and sea] may be." As the grass surrounding the well in stanza 3 is transformed into the image of the sedge adjacent to the sea in stanza 4, the "abyss" grows vaster:

The sedge stands next the sea
Where he is floorless
And does no timidity betray—

The sea in Dickinson's work is associated with a rich cluster of interrelated meanings, including eternity, sexuality, terror of the unknown, and repressed irrational desires. In this poem, the characterization of the sea as "floorless" suggests that someone caught up in it could "fall," uncontrollably, for an indefinite time, to unimaginable depths.

The conjunction *But* initiating the fifth stanza implies a truth that is contrary to the one posited in the preceding stanza. Thus, it may mean that, unlike the fearless sedge standing next to the sea, which must "somehow" be related to it, "those who cite her [Nature] most," that is, those who speak of nature easily and familiarly, are *not* somehow related to her and don't know what they're talking about. These are the ones who "Have never passed her haunted house, / Nor simplified her ghost." The latter phrase contains an echo of the Christian doctrine that the divine spirit pervades nature. But, as Cynthia Griffin Wolff points out, terms such as "'abyss' and 'awe' have become detached from any connection with God, now signifying no more than that which inspires terror and respect" (*Emily Dickinson,* 486). The lines also reject the transcendental view put forth by Ralph Waldo Emerson in his essay, "The Poet," which asserts that nature is a sacred text, ready to reveal all if only we read it correctly.

Instead, the image of the haunted house, which derives from the Gothic literature Dickinson was familiar with, suggests unsuspected terrors. The year before she wrote this poem, Dickinson sent a one-line letter to her literary mentor, THOMAS WENTWORTH HIGGINSON: "Nature is a Haunted House—but Art—a House that tries to be haunted" (L 459A, 1876). Dickinson's analogy tells us that Nature's "haunted" quality, while chilling, is also a model for her. As an artist, she sees her task as recreating the experience of awe and mystery inherent in nature, by penetrating to the furthest limits of experience. But nature itself is impenetrable and its alien quality becomes only more apparent as one comes nearer to it.

In a sense, the same might be said about this poem: the challenge of "pinning it down" to a single meaning becomes more formidable the more we know about it. What we know is that Dickinson composed variants for the final two stanzas; they are written in the handwriting of 1877 and were sent to Dickinson's sister-in-law and intimate friend, SUSAN HUNTINGTON GILBERT DICKINSON, and signed "Emily—." In these two variant stanzas, sent as a separate poem, "Susan" replaces "Nature." It reads as follows (changes are in italics): "But *Susan* is a stranger yet; / The ones that cite her most / Have never *scaled* her haunted house, / Nor *compromised* her ghost." The existence of this variant raises an obvious question: Was the poem, in Dickinson's original conception, about nature or Susan? Based on evidence found in the poet's worksheets, Sewall believes that the original poem was about Susan, with whom the poet had a lifelong intimate relationship, which many scholars believe to have been one of passionate love, at least on Emily's part, and which caused her much pain and disappointment. This would explain why, Sewall claims, the last stanza of the version as it is usually printed "has the snap of a retort. . . ." He continues, "Much of the figurative language of the letters to Sue describe her as a force of nature ('Gulf Stream,' 'torrid Spirit,' 'Avalanche'), and for Emily it was an easy step from there to a poem about Nature and its mystery" (*Life*, I, 209). Alfred Habegger agrees, calling the poem "the definitive treatment of Sue as unknowable alien. . . . The haunted house that had come to stand for memory is in this instance Sue herself, who resists intimacy and rebuffs those who want to know her" (*My Wars*, 544).

Such an interpretation—the well and its mystery as a metaphor for the bottomless depth and mystery of *human* nature—is buttressed by an earlier poem, "ONE NEED NOT BE A CHAMBER—TO BE HAUNTED—." The haunted chamber in this poem stands at the center of Dickinson's exploration of the dangerous and labyrinthine pathways of the mind. It is worth noting, however, that given the characteristic lack of a specific "scene" in the well poem, that is, the fact that it is not built around a specific incident, it could refer to any number of mysteries that cannot be penetrated.

The image of the well intrinsically contains the notions of depth and unfathomableness. In addition, Habegger believes that the image is related to the 1844 suicide by drowning in a well of Martha Dwight Jenkins, age 62, the wife of a prominent Amherst citizen, which must have made a strong impression on the 14-year-old Emily (*My Wars*, 174).

See also "I STARTED EARLY—TOOK MY DOG—."

FURTHER READING

Joanne Feit Diehl, "Emerson, Dickinson, and the Abyss," in *Modern Critical Views*, Harold Bloom, ed., 145–159; Ellen Louise Hart and Martha Nell Smith, eds., *Open Me Carefully*, 208–209.

"When I hoped, I recollect" (1862) (Fr 493, J 768)

In this poem, Dickinson explores the journey from hope to despair as a process of increasing dependence on and identification with what she calls "Nature." In the first two stanzas, she restates a commonplace of romantic exaggeration, "love kept me warm," with the difference that it is hope, not love, that renders her impervious to the elements. Indeed, romantic love may or may not be the underlying cause of the speaker's hope. She may be referring to the hope of religious conversion, since "without hope" was the term used for those who could not find Jesus during the numerous REVIVALS that swept New England during Dickinson's youth. We could go on speculating. Hope of a publisher? Hope of some other life than her own? Like so many Dickinson poems, this one contains an "omitted center" that we can never identify with any certainty. Whatever it is the speaker hoped for, feared, and ultimately despaired of is absent from the poem. What we are given instead is an imagistic approximation of what it feels like to move from hope to hopelessness. The speaker is a body in a landscape, at first immune to nature, then overwhelmed by it.

In stanza 1, the basic statement, "When I hoped, Roughest Air—was good," is cut in two by the speaker's recollection of precisely where she stood. One effect of this "interruption" is to inject a "second voice" into the poem, one that insists upon what it remembers. The assertion that she was standing "at a window facing West" when she hoped, should be read symbolically, rather than literally. The speaker, when she hoped, faced the direction of the sunset, light's imminent fading. But the "West" for Dickinson can be a prelude to desire's fulfillment, as when the "Daisy" follows the "Sun" beyond its setting point: "Enamored of the parting West—/ The peace—the flight—the amethyst—Night's possibility!" (Fr 161). And Dickinson's "West" is often a glorious fading, "the Transit in the West" (Fr 285) to everlasting life ("When I go out of Time—/ To Take my Rank—by—in the West—" Fr 395). Facing in the direction of hope, be it amorous or religious, she is warmed by it, not by a Merino shawl, immune to the sleet and cold at stanza 2.

As the poem progresses, what the speaker recollects grows more cosmic, less precise. She remembers the exact spot she stood when she hoped. But she remembers only the day when she feared, and the landscape is growing more universal ("Worlds were lying out to Sun—"). Note, that in this second, fear scenario, nature is reasserting its power over the speaker, freezing "Icicles opon my soul." As in another poem of that same year, "I DREADED THAT FIRST ROBIN, SO," the speaker is silent in the face of Nature's general rejoicing. When she hoped, she was impervious to Nature's onslaughts; when she feared, Nature was indifferent to her state. Her diminished power is mirrored in her transformation from an "I" to a "Me" ("Only Me—was still—").

In the final stanza, in which she evokes "the Day that I despaired," the speaker recreates an alliance between herself and Nature. Note that if hope and fear bind her to the past ("I recollect") despair binds her to an endless future of remembering: "If I forget" (ever). Nature, in her relentless inability to "forget" that night follows day, comes to represent the speaker herself. The image of sunset recurs, but unlike the hope-imbued, enticing threshold suggested by the "Window facing West," this "sunset" is described as an act of violence, and the Night that follows it is a state of blindness. The image is closer to that of an eclipse than a sunset:

Darkness intersect her face—
And put out her eye—

In both her letters and poems, the motif of "seeing," "face-to-face," is pervasive. Both "eye[s]" and "face" are among Dickinson's key words, appearing in her work with notable frequency. They are associated with union and separation, as in her oft-repeated wish "to see [someone's] face again" and in her images of Death as the closing of the eyes or the loss of face. Biographer Cynthia Griffin Wolff speculates that the ultimate value of "seeing" for Dickinson may be connected to unsatisfied yearnings dating back to that early period of infancy when nonverbal, face-to-face (eye-to-eye) communication is primary (*Emily Dickinson,* 52–55). In the context of this poem, the face intersected by darkness and the eye that has been put out are stark images of disorientation and isolation:

And the Day that I despaired—
This—if I forget
Nature will—that it be Night
After Sun has set—
Darkness intersect her face—
And put out her eye—
Nature hesitate—before
Memory and I—

The speaker's state of inner fragmentation is reflected in the broken syntax of this stanza, with its lack of clear connections between phrases. A paraphrase might read: "If I forget This, that is, the Day that I despaired, then Nature will forget that it is Night after the Sun has set, that Darkness intersects her face and puts out her eye. Nature will hesitate (to remember) before Memory and I will." Note the use of the uninflected verb forms "be Night," "intersect," "put," and "hesitate" instead of the correct "is Night," "Darkness intersects," "And puts," and "Nature will hesitate." Dickinson's early critics simply assumed that her use of uninflected verbs was ungrammatical. While conceding that such usage *sounds* ungrammatical, scholar Cristanne Miller sees it as a tool with which Dickinson consciously experimented in order to convey meaning. Miller suggests that by leaving a verb unmarked for tense and person, Dickinson suggests a universal, ongoing action (*Grammar,* 65). And ongoing action is certainly the poem's ultimate assertion. In the final line, the speaker recovers a sense of self. The "Me" of the previous stanza has once more become an "I" and this "I" is now allied with, perhaps even one with, Memory.

See also "'HOPE' IS THE THING WITH FEATHERS—" and "I CANNOT LIVE WITH YOU—."

FURTHER READING

Cristanne Miller, *Grammar*, 59–75; Cynthia Griffin Wolff, *Emily Dickinson*, 52–55.

"Who never wanted— maddest Joy" (1877) (Fr 1447, J 1430)

In this poem Dickinson affirms the value of what she called the "piercing Virtue" of renunciation—a theme she addressed throughout her life, in poems such as "I HAD BEEN HUNGRY, ALL THE YEARS—," "UNDUE SIGNIFICANCE A STARVING MAN," and "GOD GAVE A LOAF TO EVERY BIRD—." Dickinson does not tell a story, as she does in earlier poems about hunger/desire and fulfillment, but, in a manner typical of her late style, declares her truth in highly compressed, elliptical, syntactically ambiguous language.

The use of dashes or no punctuation at all at the end of lines, instead of periods, leaves the reader in doubt about whether particular lines are end-stopped or flow into the next (enjambed). Thus, stanza 1 can be read in several different ways:

Who never wanted—maddest Joy
Remains to him unknown—

The first two lines might mean, "Maddest joy remains unknown to the person who has never wanted it." This reading implies that the wanting itself is what creates knowledge of "maddest Joy"—an idea that resonates with the poem's message that expectation is more powerful than possession. But it is also possible to see the first two lines as flowing into the next two:

The Banquet of Abstemiousness
Defaces that of Wine—

In this case the stanza may be paraphrased in one of two ways, depending on whether the "Banquet of Abstemiousness" is the direct object of "unknown"

or the subject of the verb "defaces." In a prime example of Dickinson's use of syntactic doubling, it is both. Thus, we may read: "He who has not wanted maddest Joy does not know the Banquet of Abstemiousness" or "does not know *that* the Banquet of Abstemiousness defaces the banquet of wine." In either case, the poem establishes a direct connection between desiring "maddest Joy" and appreciating the superiority of "Abstemiousness." Note that Dickinson uses the longest (five-syllable) word available to her in her parodoxical image, verbally making plenty out of scarcity. In Dickinson's lexicon, *abstemiousness* denotes the quality of being temperate or sparing in consumption of food or intoxicating drink. It is stronger than *temperance,* but not as extreme as *abstinence* (total refraining from consumption). Yet, to be moderate in "consumption" of "maddest Joy" is itself a contradiction—equivalent to not consuming it at all.

In the first two lines of stanza 2, the "Banquet of Abstemiousness" is described more specifically: a state of affairs in which the desired object is within reach, but not yet attained. This is "Desire's perfect goal." Reaching, desiring, are themselves exciting, and without the potential "hangover" of a "banquet of wine." In the final two lines the speaker warns both herself and the reader: "Don't go any further! If you do, the Actual (experiencing) of what you have so ardently desired will 'disenthrall thy soul—.'" When we desire "maddest Joy," attaining it can only lead to disappointment. The very act of desiring something magnifies it in our imagination, so that the reality will always be inadequate. For Dickinson, whose emotional neediness was equaled by her powerful imagination, the letdown was bound to be especially severe. Her life-defining decision to retire from most social intercourse, as well as individual acts of refusal to see friends to whom she had written of her passionate desire for a meeting, probably reflected this realization. She once explained her behavior by saying, "We shun because we prize."

Despite the poem's attempt to affirm the joy of renunciation, neither its overall imagery nor its conclusion are altogether triumphant. The wine, which the speaker renounces in this poem, is an intoxicant that Dickinson rejoices in consuming in other poems, such as "I TASTE A LIQUOR NEVER BREWED—."

Moreover, the word "deface," meaning to destroy or mar the surface of a thing, to obliterate, literally means to remove the face. But the desire to see the face of a beloved person is a persistent leitmotif in Dickinson's poetry, a supremely valued perception. For the "Banquet of Abstemiousness" to deface the banquet of wine is thus an act of depersonalization, taking away the individual "face" from "maddest Joy" and replacing it with something else.

For poet Richard Wilbur this "something else" was "the vaster economy of desire, in which the pain of abstinence is justified by moments of infinite joy, and the object is spiritually possessed, not merely for itself, but more truly as an index of the All" ("Sumptuous Destitution," 58). In this view, physical thirst or desire "intimates the finer want— / Whose adequate supply / Is that Great Water in the West—/ Termed Immortality—" (Fr 726).

This transcendent view, however, by no means exhausts the many approaches Dickinson's speaker takes toward desire and possession. Much of her poetry denies the unbridgeable gap between reality and desire posited in this poem. Dickinson's speakers also revel in the consummation of joys, sexual and otherwise, as in "COME SLOWLY—EDEN!" An entire spectrum of approaches to desire can be found within her oeuvre. Some of her poetic voices eat and drink with abandon. Others find that renunciation leads not to any banquet but to a frightening emotional impoverishment. In "Oh Sumptuous moment" (Fr 1186) she relishes fulfillment and admits, "'Twill never be the same to starve / Now I abundance see—." As Robert Weisbuch points out, "you cannot define Dickinson by what she believes but by what she keeps caring about, turning it this way and that. . . . The contradictions come together in complex understandings—we do sometimes get to a paradise, but as soon as we are there we find 'a further'" (Weisbuch, "Prisming," 197–223).

See also "GOD GAVE A LOAF TO EVERY BIRD—," "I HAD BEEN HUNGRY, ALL THE YEARS—," and "RENUNCIATION—IS A PIERCING VIRTUE—."

FURTHER READING

Joan Burbick, "Economics of Desire," in *Critical Essays,* Judith Farr, ed., 53–61; Vivian R. Pollak, "Thirst and Starvation," in *Critical Essays,* Judith Farr, ed., 62–75; Robert Weisbuch, "Prisming," in *Handbook,* Grabher et al., eds., 197–223; and Richard Wilbur, "Sumptuous Destitution," in *Critical Essays,* Judith Farr, ed., 53–61.

"Wild nights—Wild nights!"
(1861) (Fr 269, J 249)

Dickinson's first editor, THOMAS WENTWORTH HIGGINSON, had misgivings about publishing this poem, "lest the malignant read into it more than that virgin recluse ever dreamed of putting there" (Johnson, *Poems,* 180). Since Higginson reluctantly placed the verse before the public, his naïve notion of Dickinson as a pure, nonsexual being, cut off from the world, has been discredited; "the malignant" have come to include the majority of Dickinson's readers, who correctly recognize, in this most famous of her erotic poems, the voice of a woman who well knew the power of sexual passion.

A poem that instantly grips the reader by its music, Fr 269 begins with two dramatic spondees (metrical feet with two stressed syllables), evoking the wild turbulence of a storm.

Wild nights—Wild nights!
Were I with thee
Wild nights should be
Our luxury!

Shorter than Dickinson's more usual three- and four-foot iambs, the two-foot lines, most with only two stresses in them, explode with a "vitality [that] breaks out of the poet's characteristic restraint within the regular or near-regular line patterns of the hymn book" (Porter, *Early Poetry,* 72). Yet despite its direct impact on the reader, the poem is anything but straightforward in its structure and meaning. Central to its complexity is the connection between the three stanzas, which seem, at first reading, to contradict one another.

In stanza 1, although the "Wild nights" are only hypothetical—what the speaker and her lover *would* have *if* they were together (which they are not), the force of the speaker's imagining with its three repetitions of the phrase is such that they have the vivid impact of a lived experience. The word *luxury* suggests sensuous pleasure; in Dickinson's lexicon, it means "voluptuousness in the gratification of appetite . . . lust." Thus, the speaker of stanza 1 imaginatively plunges into "wildness" with joyful anticipation.

In the first two lines of stanza 2, however, which stands as a brief didactic hiatus between the passionate exclamations that precede and follow it, the speaker exalts the pleasure of being a "Heart in port." The turbulent "winds," which, semantically, belong to the "wildness" of stanza 1, are here declared, with satisfaction, to be "futile." Instead, she has achieved a secure repose, in which neither chart nor compass is necessary, since the destination has already been reached. A contented stasis has replaced the turbulence of stanza 1. Critics have pointed to the chart and compass as allusions to the image of God as ship pilot, which was popular at the time this poem was written; if this is the case, is Dickinson rejecting divine guidance in these lines? Perhaps the suggestion was there for readers of Dickinson's own time; to modern readers, however, the terms are more general symbols of external instruments for finding one's way. In possession of her own internal navigational signals, the speaker has no need of them. Yet, in their passionate, exclamatory nature, lines 7 and 8 deny the very stasis they seem to proclaim.

They lead directly into stanza 3, where the tension between dynamic movement and peaceful repose shifts again. The "wildness" of the first stanza reasserts itself in the first two lines as the safely moored heart of stanza 2 gives way to a rowboat in motion on the sea in the Garden of Eden. As Dickinson was well aware, there *was* no sea in the biblical Garden of Eden, only a river: "And a river went out of Eden to water the Garden" (Genesis 2: 10). In introducing a sea into her Eden, she merges two visions: The first is the myth of Eden, which had been revived by American painters such as Thomas Cole, founder of the Hudson River School, in paintings such as *The Garden of Eden* (1828) and *Expulsion from the Garden of Eden* (1827–28) (Farr, *Passion,* 226–227). The second is that of the little boat upon the waters. Images of betrothed 19th-century lovers depicted as rowing together were popular in Dickinson's time, as was the idea of the lone boat struggling on the high seas (Ibid., 230). Dickinson transports the rowing lovers to her own version of Eden, the lost paradise of unashamed sensuality. Whatever its dangers, the speaker's exclamation "Ah—the Sea!" expresses unalloyed pleasure in the vast waters. While the sea can symbolize many things in Dickinson's writing—freedom, wilderness, immortality, salvation—here it is surely what Farr calls "an image of primal—sexual—waters."

In the final two lines, the "static" image of the "Heart in port" returns in the speaker's wish, "Might I but moor—tonight—/ In thee!" This wished-for mooring, however, with its unavoidable sexual connotations, contains within it the passionate striving on the sea that precedes it. It expresses the speaker's desire to submerge herself, in the quest for escape and/or ecstasy, in another person or, perhaps, in another Power. Thus the final lines resolve the dialectic between wildness and serenity on which the poem is based.

On the physical level, the image of the speaker as a boat mooring in a harbor reverses the roles inherent in male and female anatomy. This observation has led some readers to a homoerotic interpretation. If the poem is about Dickinson's love for another woman (the most likely candidate would be her sister-in-law, SUSAN HUNTINGTON GILBERT DICKINSON), the problem is eliminated.

Still others have read the poem in a religious light, as expressing a desire for immersion in a greater power or transcendent reality. Porter seeks a compromise between secular and religious camps by suggesting that "the sea . . . may represent both lover and immortality. It is perhaps best interpreted as a fusion of the two in which there is an undefined convergence of earthly and divine love." This refusal to be pinned down to a single interpretation, while characteristic of most poetry, is rooted in the very nature of Dickinson's highly compressed, elliptical poetic language.

See also "COME SLOWLY—EDEN!" and HYMN FORM.

FURTHER READING

Joanne Feit Diehl, *Romantic Imagination*, 159; Judith Farr, *Passion*, 228–231; Thomas Johnson, *The Poems of Emily Dickinson*, 180; George Monteiro, "Pilot-God Trope," 42–51; David Porter, *Early Poetry*, 70–72; David S. Reynolds, "Emily Dickinson and Popular Culture," in *Cambridge Companion*, 188–289; Cynthia Griffin Wolff, *Emily Dickinson*, 384.

"You constituted Time—" (1862) (Fr 488, J 765)

In this brief but complex poem, the poet juggles the conventional categories of temporal and eternal, mortal and divine, relative and absolute. Using the language of abstract argument, she addresses an earthly beloved who "comprises the whole realm of temporal reality. . . . So imprisoned, [the speaker] could not even conceive of Eternity except as a projected image of the face of Now" (Anderson, *Stairway*, 198). For the speaker, Eternity is "a Revelation" of the beloved:

You constituted Time—
I deemed Eternity
A Revelation of Yourself—

The syntax of the poem allows for two very different readings. In the first, there is an enjambment between the last line of the first stanza and the first line of the second. The last five lines of the poem might be paraphrased: "The Deity, who is absolute, removed you, who are relative, so that I might turn my slow idolatry from you to Him." A jealous God deprives her of her earthly love because it supplanted her love of Him. Her idolatry is "slow," that is, slow to adjust, refocus on the Deity, because she only reluctantly relinquishes her idolatry of the beloved. Her use of the pagan term *idolatry* to describe her worship of the Christian God would have been shocking to Christians in her day and is only somewhat less so in ours. Dickinson's use of the word thus conveys a subterranean message of her continuing resistance to changing the object of her worship; at heart, she remains a pagan.

This interpretation is consonant with many poems in which the earthly beloved is dearer to her than the jealous deity. Perhaps her ultimate expression of this allegiance occurs in the great poem of renunciation she would write the following year, "I CANNOT LIVE WITH YOU—" (Fr 706, 1863). Here she tells the beloved that she could not be resurrected with him, "Because Your Face / Would put out Jesus.'" She has not served Heaven

Because You saturated Sight—
And I had no more Eyes
For sordid excellence
As Paradise . . .

In this and other poems, Dickinson expresses a sense of hubris: She is or will be punished for identifying the sacred with mere mortals, for loving this world more than the Heaven of God. But she never relinquishes her sense of where her deepest devotion lies. Eleven years later, she concludes another major expression of love and loss, "Because that you are going" (Fr 1314, 1874), with a challenge to the Deity:

Because he is a "jealous God"
He tells us certainly

If "All is possible with" him
As he besides concedes
He will refund us finally
Our confiscated Gods—

If God is omnipotent, then let him return to us "Our confiscated Gods," that is, those he has taken in death.

Critic Gary Stonum suggests another plausible interpretation of "You constituted Time," in which, instead of lines 5–8 describing the actions of a jealous God, "the two stanzas represent discrete stages of the same idolatrous moment. . . . the fourth line refers, not to God's jealous intervention, but to what the speaker had taken "Eternity" and "Yourself" to be a revelation of, i.e., the lover's divinity" (*Dickinson Sublime*, 270n4). In this reading, the poem might be paraphrased as follows: "You constituted Time and I could not envision Eternity as anything other than a revelation of yourself. Thus, (I knew) you were deity. You, the Absolute removed all that was relative in my life, so that I would slowly come to worship only you."

See also "I SHOULD HAVE BEEN TOO GLAD, I SEE—," "NOW I KNEW I LOST HER—," and REVIVALISM.

FURTHER READING

Charles R. Anderson, *Stairway*, 198–199; William H. Shurr, *Marriage*, 7, 112; Gary Lee Stonum, *Dickinson Sublime*, 159, 207n4.

"Your Riches—taught me— Poverty." (1862) (Fr 418, J 299)

When Emily Dickinson sent this poem over the hedge to her sister-in-law, SUSAN HUNTINGTON GILBERT DICKINSON, in 1862, she prefaced it with the salutation. "Dear Sue," as if to underline the character of the poem as a personal note. She followed it with the simple words: "Dear Sue—You see I remember. Emily." What Emily was "remembering"—and saying good-bye to in this poem was their girlhood romance, which, by 1862, had existed only in memory for quite some time. Sue, who had married Emily's older brother, WILLIAM AUSTIN DICKINSON, in 1856 was now a new mother, and Emily's passion was directed to an apparently male figure whom she addressed as Master (see MASTER LETTERS).

Dickinson would never write a "definitive" farewell to Susan. There had been many previous poems about Sue and there would be more in the future: evoking her love for Sue, the pain of losing her, her disappointment in this once revered woman, and her unbreakable bond with her. Here, however, she evokes the transition in Susan's life from a girl, capable of infatuation with another girl, to a woman who loves men ("You drifted your Dominions—/ A Different Peru—"), and the impact of that momentous shift on Emily's sense of self. Reversing their actual economic status in adolescence, Emily develops the image of Susan's wealth in contrast with her own poverty. Sue's wealth is associated with exotic, torrid regions (Buenos Aires, Peru, India, places she once found described in her school geography), not because

Sue's nature is passionate (by most accounts it was not), but because she possessed a quality that aroused passion in others. In this woman, with whom both she and her brother had fallen in love, Emily sensed a power, which not only deprived her of Susan, but also made her feel her own lack of a similar desirability. She had counted herself "—a Millionaire / In little Wealths, as Girls could boast," and, indeed, Emily the girl, with her sprightliness, her gift for friendships, and her excellent academic abilities, not to mention her socially esteemed, close-knit family, possessed the requisite "wealths" of girlhood. (It is revealing, in this context, to note how Dickinson creates contradictory myths of her childhood. Compare this poem to those in which she says she was starved, locked up, and deprived, such as "I WAS THE SMALLEST IN THE HOUSE—" and "IT WOULD HAVE STARVED A GNAT—"). Susan's "drift of Dominions" to tropical realms leaves her with the sense that, in comparison with her vanished life with Sue, what remains to her is meager ("And I esteemed all Poverty / For Life's Estate with you—"). Note that instead of wanting to be *like* Sue, she wishes she could possess her. But Sue is unattainable, distant in time, space, and essence from the speaker, the outsider whom "At least it solaces to know / That there exists—a Gold—." Reading this line it is impossible not to hear "there exists a God" and to remember the many instances in which Dickinson declared herself to be "Susan's idolater."

In stanza 3, she introduces "mine" imagery, with its merged, double connotations of the material wealth of precious gems and metals, and the rich depths of sexual knowledge.

> Of Mines, I little know, myself—
> But just the names, of Gems—
> The colors of the Commonest—
> And scarce of Diadems—

The speaker declares she knows little of mines; throughout she insists on her simplicity, her limited knowledge of gems (in fact, Dickinson knew a great deal about gems, as her poetry demonstrates), and inability to grasp the nature of such wealth. Despite the word play in stanza 5, with the double meaning of "mine" ("To have a smile for mine—each Day, /

How better than a Gem!") the speaker well knows the Susan-mine cannot be hers.

Sue is associated with breadth and depth, the speaker with narrowness, surface, and constriction. In stanza 4 she ponders, naïvely, "But this, must be a different Wealth—/ To miss it—beggars so—." The speaker knows something "rich" is missing in her life, only indirectly, through the poverty of its absence. Maintaining this "innocent" stance to the end, she realizes the worth of what she has lost only at the moment of losing it. Susan remains a distant treasure, a pearl of great price, "That slipped my simple fingers through—/ While just a Girl at school."

The poem irresistibly returns to their simple girlhood "at school." THOMAS WENTWORTH HIGGINSON pointed to this line as an example of Dickinson's strange refusal to easily create a conventional rhyme (pearl/girl) by changing her word order. But Dickinson apparently had a greater need to land on the compelling image of "at school" than to make a rhyme. "At school" is not meant literally, since Emily and Sue were never classmates, but designates a time of learning, that vestibule to adult life. Indeed, the speaker rules herself out from the beginning as a participant in the adult sexual world. One key to this stance appears in stanza 5:

I'm sure 'tis India—all Day—
To those who look on You—
Without a stint—without a blame,
Might I—but be the Jew—

If the speaker could be the Jew—an allusion to the common image of Jews as diamond-cutters and traders—she could look at Sue all day without blame. But there would be "blame" in the speaker's protracted looking, perhaps because, beyond girlhood, the homoerotic nature of her love for Susan would be considered scandalous.

The poem does not develop this theme of a "sinful" love, but it is present in the image of the diamond mines of Golconda in Brazil. Judith Farr notes that at the time Dickinson wrote this poem *Harper's* had an article about Golconda, which was also the name of a nearby, notorious fortress and prison. Since Sue and her circle would have associated Golconda with misery and deprivation, Farr

suggests, Emily may have been telling her that "To gaze at Sue is to be in prison" (*Passion*, 142–143). We may speculate further that what created this prison was Emily's inability to either possess Sue or to not desire her. In the condensed poetic truth of this poem, the speaker realizes Sue's value at the moment of losing her. In the documented history of Emily and Sue, however, there was a prolonged period before she "knew she lost her," when Dickinson was in love with Sue. Dickinson grew estranged from Sue and went on to love others. But, judging from the letters and poems she wrote to her until the end of her life, she never wholly relinquished the sense of Sue as infinitely rich and queenly, identifying her with no less a figure of exotic sexual allure than Cleopatra.

See also "NOW I KNEW I LOST HER" and "THE MALAY—TOOK THE PEARL—"

FURTHER READING

Joan Burbick, "Emily Dickinson and the Economics of Desire," in *Critical Essays*, Judith Farr, ed.; Judith Farr, *The Passion of Emily Dickinson*, 140–143; Vivian R. Pollak, *The Anxiety of Gender*, 133–156.

"You've seen Balloons set—Hav'nt You?" (1863) (Fr 730, J 700)

Symbolic narratives such as this one are rare in Dickinson's work, another notable example being "MY LIFE HAD STOOD—A LOADED GUN." Anyone familiar with that enigmatic poem will approach this poem warily. For the presence of a symbol in a Dickinson poem by no means promises a simple one-to-one relationship between the symbol and what it symbolizes. Though far simpler than "My Life had stood—a Loaded Gun," Fr 730 is nonetheless structured as a multivalent web of possibilities.

In its surface action, the poem belongs to a small number that evoke a community experiencing something memorable together, a storm, perhaps (Fr 1454, "It sounded as if the Streets were running—") or its aftermath (Fr 1518, "Glass was the

Street—in Tinsel Peril"). Here people watch a hot air balloon ascend until it is out of sight, then crash back down to earth. They are momentarily uplifted by witnessing the sublime balloon, an emblem of beauty and transcendence that rises above everyday concerns.

Familiarly addressing an unspecified "you"—perhaps only the reader—the poet speaks first of "balloons" in general and transforms them into beings not of this earth, indeed, superior to the world of humans, who are called to higher things:

It is as Swans—discarded You,
For Duties Diamond—

Dickinson creates lush imagery for the balloons' ascent:

Their Liquid Feet go softly out
Opon a Sea of Blonde—

In their use of water imagery for flight, these lines are reminiscent of a moment in "A BIRD CAME DOWN THE WALK—," when the bird "unrolled his feathers, / And rowed him softer Home—." Both convey the sense of the speaker's ecstasy, as well as her exclusion from the exalted medium into which the creatures move. As the balloons ascend the sun-drenched air becomes "a sea of Blonde." Then, in line 7, a subtle change of tone occurs, a faint but distinct note of mockery toward the haughty balloons, which portends the Icarus-like hubris about to befall them.

They spurn the Air, as 'twere too mean
For Creatures so renowned—

Sure enough, in the very next stanza, just beyond the view of the observer, the balloons get into trouble as they begin to lose altitude ("struggle—some—for Breath—," as the breathless image has it), while the audience on the ground applauds. At this point, Dickinson inserts an unexpected observation: "They would not encore—Death—." Perhaps she is implying that the audience mistakes the balloons' acrobatics for virtuosity, while in fact they signal their demise. The crowd is insensitive, failing to understand what the spectacle means.

The fall of the balloon (now singular) is evoked in a series of action verbs—*Strains, spins, trips, tears,*

and *tumbles*—whose sounds spin and tumble into one another. The balloon (now feminine) dies violently as she

Tears open her imperial Veins—
And tumbles in the Sea—

The royal balloon thus appears to be taking her own life, and perhaps she has, by overreaching. In the reference to the sea (there was none, of course, in AMHERST), Dickinson links the balloon's fate to that of Icarus, son of Daedalus, who flew with his wax-attached wings too close to the sun and plummeted to his death in the sea.

In the final stanza, the illusion of transcendence vanishes and the mundane world reassembles. As biographer Cynthia Griffin Wolff puts it, we experience "a fall from the mythic into the flat matter-of-fact" (*Emily Dickinson*, 439). The disappointed crowd curses and disperses, dust settles in the streets and "Clerks in Counting Rooms "—the unimaginative literalists—not only deny the possibility that they have seen—or hoped to see—anything out of the ordinary; they deny their disappointment: "'Twas only a Balloon'—."

So, what is the poem about? Wolff sees it as the story of Christ's death and resurrection turned upside down, with the transcendent being's ascension followed, rather than preceded, by her death. In another interpretation, she reminds us that the majestic swan, thought by the ancients to have prophetic powers, was best known for the "poignant clarity of its death cry," for which reason the dying swan came to represent the poet (Ibid., 440). Further, the phrase "Balloons set," she notes, with which the poem begins, suggests a form of sunset.

Critics Suzanne Juhasz and Cristanne Miller, focusing on the poem's gender distinctions, also come up with more than one reading. They note that the plural balloons that rise are "ungendered," while the single balloon that falls is female. From this, they hypothesize that the poem "may describe the progress of a woman's life as an undifferentiated communal childhood of swanlike ascent abruptly terminated by an adulthood of isolated vulnerability and disaster" ("Performances of Gender," 121). In another reading, they suggest that the speaker's tone toward both balloon and clerks is ironic, since the male clerks idealize the female, who cannot breathe in so exalted and artificial an atmosphere, and so must fall.

While there may be little in the poem to justify such far-fetched interpretations, neither is there anything to specifically refute them. Dickinson's homey image of townsmen standing about, momentarily carried away by a popular spectacle, stands in its own right, while the language of the poem is sufficiently resonant to support a number of readings. Might Dickinson's balloon not be a symbol of poetry and the poet as it/she approaches what she called CIRCUMFERENCE, the far limits of what can be known or experienced, only to be cast back

down into the prose of life? Might it not symbolize the short-lived illusion of a transcendent love? The glorious, fragile balloon might be almost any attempt to rise above one's limitations and leave earth behind, all destined to fail, both foolishly and heroically.

See also "I WOULD NOT PAINT—A PICTURE—."

FURTHER READING

Suzanne Juhasz and Cristanne Miller, "Performances of Gender in Dickinson's Poetry," in *Cambridge Companion*, 120–122; Robert Weisbuch, *Emily Dickinson's Poetry*, 41–43; Cynthia Griffin Wolff, *Emily Dickinson*, 439–440.

PART III

Related Persons, Places, and Ideas

A

Adams, Elizabeth C. (1810–1873) Emily's beloved "Miss Adams" was her favorite preceptress at AMHERST ACADEMY. Miss Adams was in charge during the idyllic period in 1844 when Emily made her first circle of intimate friends, whom she called "the five," whose other members were ABIAH PALMER ROOT, ABBY MARIA WOOD, SARAH SKINNER TRACY, and HARRIET MERRILL. Teachers at the academy, who were frequently quite young, were encouraged to form caring, personal relationships with their students, and Miss Adams appears to have taken a warm interest in the gifted and enthusiastic Miss Dickinson. Although the two corresponded after Miss Adams left, none of their letters have survived.

The woman whom Emily called "our dear teacher" was a native of Conway, Massachusetts. By the time she arrived at the academy she was 33 and had considerable experience as an educator. She was a seasoned teacher and administrator, who had served as principal of the female department of an academy in Syracuse, New York, from 1840 to 1842. She returned to Massachusetts in 1842 and taught for four consecutive terms at the academy. Although Emily was a student there at the time, she missed a lot of school during that period, due to poor health. If the time they spent together was brief, however, Dickinson long cherished the memory of Miss Adams, along with that of "the five," three of whom transferred to other schools at the same time as their teacher left the academy.

As is the case for the other members of "the five," Emily's only recorded comments on Miss Adams are to be found in her many surviving letters to Abiah. She wrote:

> I had a newspaper as large as life from Miss Adams our dear teacher. She sent me a beautiful little bunch of pressed flowers which I value very much as they were from her. How happy we all were together that term we went to Miss Adams. I wish it might be so again, but I never expect it (L 6, May 7, 1845)

Miss Adams's special interest in her former pupil is evident from the gift of flowers. Characteristically, Miss Adams is evoked as the reigning spirit of a paradise lost. Three months later, reporting to Abiah that she hasn't heard from Miss Adams in a while, she wonders whether she will ever see her again and fears she never will. The distance between her and Miss Adams now seems enormous. "She is so far away—," she tells Abiah (L 7, August 3, 1845). The following month, feeling the absence of her classmates, she wishes she were transferring to an out-of-town school—an opportunity her parents would not afford her, most probably because of their concerns about her fragile health. She has recourse to her old teacher's homey wisdom for comfort: "But as our dear teacher Miss Adams used to say, if wishes were horses, then beggars might ride" (L 8 to Abiah, September 25, 1845).

When the unexpected happens and Miss Adams returns to the academy for another term in 1846, Emily is frustrated by being kept from her presence. "Dear Miss Adams is teaching in Amherst & I am very anxious to attend the Academy last term on that account & did go for 11 weeks, at the close of which I was so unwell as to be obliged to leave school," she tells Abiah (L 13, September 8, 1846). In the postscript to the letter, however, describing the commencement week festivities at AMHERST COLLEGE, she is scarcely able to contain her nostalgic pleasure: "It seemed like old times to meet Miss Adams and Mr. Taylor [a former principal at the Academy] again. I could hardly refrain from singing Auld Lang Syne."

The reunion would be short-lived, with Miss Adams departing after one semester. Emily gives an enthusiastic description of a new preceptress, Miss R. Woodridge, then adds: "I am always in love with my teachers. Yet, much as we love her, it seems lonely & strange without 'Our dear Miss Adams.'"

She manages to express the proper sentiments with respect to Miss Adams's upcoming marriage to "a very respectable lawyer in Conway, Mass;" her good wishes for her teacher's happiness war with her poignant sense of bereavement:

> I cannot bear to think that she will never more wield the sceptre, & sit upon the thrown in our venerable schoolhouse, & yet I am glad she is going to have a home of her own & a kind companion to take life's journey with her. I am delighted that she is to live so near us, for we can ride up & see her often. (L 15 to Abiah, March 14, 1847)

These are Emily's last recorded thoughts on Miss Adams, who married Albert Clark of Conway on April 7, 1847.

Amherst The town where Dickinson was born, lived for the whole of her life, and was buried, Amherst, Massachusetts, was established in 1759 in

This 1840 lithograph of Main St. offers the earliest view of The Homestead, in the center background. *(Courtesy of the Jones Library, Inc., Amherst, Massachusetts)*

View of Main Street today, a few blocks from The Homestead *(Courtesy of Darryl Leiter)*

the northeast corner of the town of Hadley in the fertile CONNECTICUT RIVER VALLEY, by the descendants of Puritan settlers. It was named after Lord Jeffrey Amherst, who has the dubious distinction of having recommended that local native American tribes be "extirpated" by giving them smallpox-infected blankets. When Emily Dickinson was born in 1830, the area was heavily populated by Dickinsons, who had a local reputation for an eccentric, determined, stubborn quality known as "Dickinson grit." So numerous and prominent were the Dickinsons in the town's life that the *Boston Journal,* in its account of a Dickinson family reunion in Amherst on August 8, 1883, commented, "we may well doubt whether the Dickinsons belonged to Amherst or Amherst to the Dickinsons."

The Amherst of Emily's day was a bastion of Orthodox CONGREGATIONALISM and the site of numerous emotional REVIVALS when townsmen who declared their newfound belief in Jesus Christ

were accepted as full members of the FIRST CHURCH OF CHRIST. The town's intellectual beacon was AMHERST COLLEGE, which Emily's paternal grandfather, SAMUEL FOWLER DICKINSON, played a leading role in founding. Despite a high level of culture, living conditions in the mid-19th century were crude. The town's roads were unpaved and devoid of streetlights. Devastating fires, such as the one that destroyed the business district in 1879, occurred with some frequency. There was little insulation against extreme temperatures, floods or drought. Families were self-sustaining to a high degree, keeping their own horses, cows, and chickens, and maintaining private vegetable gardens and orchards. Townsmen drew their water from individual wells, and without the benefits of electricity, gathered with family members around an oil lamp at night.

In her 56 years, Emily Dickinson left Amherst only for a year of schooling at MOUNT HOLYOKE FEMALE SEMINARY in South Hadley, Massachusetts, a handful of trips to Boston and to visit New England friends, and a three-week stay in Washington, D.C. When she was away, her letters harped on the theme of Amherst's superiority to wherever she was at the time. Her home-centeredness was by no means typical of Americans at this time when the country was expanding both to the west and the south; many of Emily's friends traveled extensively both at home and abroad. Her behavior *was* typical, however, of the Dickinsons as a family, whose dislike of travel seemed to increase with each succeeding generation. For Emily, Amherst was synonymous with "home," a central element in her sense of who she was and where she belonged.

As a young girl of 20, during her most sociable period, she could write to her uncle "Amherst is alive with fun this winter!" (L 29, 1850), describing the sleigh rides, parties, and frequent visiting. But as early as 1854, a breach between Emily and the Amherst community is evident: Her failure to publicly accept Christ, as virtually all her friends and family eventually did, and her standoffish attitude toward Amherst piety and good works left her increasingly isolated. The rift grew greater over the years; by the time she was 30, Dickinson chose to withdraw from the daily life of the town, remaining within the confines of the family compound. Although she kept abreast of local events and regu-

Merchant's Row in the early 1860s. The white building on the right houses the post office. William and George Cutler's general store is in the leftmost building, with a crowd out front. *(Courtesy of the Jones Library, Inc., Amherst, Massachusetts)*

larly exchanged letters with Amherst people, few of the locals she corresponded with ever saw her.

FURTHER READING

Theodora Ward, *The Capsule of the Mind: Chapters in the Life of Emily Dickinson.*

Amherst Academy The private school where Dickinson studied from ages nine to 16 (1840–47) had a major formative influence on her intellectual and personal growth, creating memories and friendships she would cherish all her life.

Emily's grandfather, SAMUEL FOWLER DICKINSON, was among the Amherst leaders who set out to raise the level of education that was then available in the region. The institution they founded opened formally on December 6, 1814, and was soon recognized as among the best schools in New England. The academy had many strengths: It boasted a broad, up-to-date curriculum; its faculty and administration contained a mix of young enthusiasts and established scholars; it was closely allied with AMHERST COLLEGE, which was founded later and allowed academy students to attend its lectures and provided a major source of well-educated instructors; its advanced teaching philosophy emphasized arousing student interest rather than encouraging rote memorization; and it was ahead of its time in providing teacher training.

Girls were first admitted in 1838; when Emily, together with her sister LAVINIA (Vinnie), entered in the "English course" at the beginning of the fall term, September 7, 1840, there were about 100 girls enrolled. They were supervised by a "preceptress," who was responsible not only for her pupils' intellectual development but also for their moral, social, and religious welfare. Both preceptresses and instructors were encouraged to form nurturing personal relations with their students, a policy under which the young Emily thrived. She wrote to her beloved friend ABIAH PALMER ROOT: "You know I am always in love with my teachers." During her seven years at the academy, she studied under a number of women. Although Caroline D. Hunt was the main female instructor at the time, what Emily thought of her is unknown, since her academy letters were written when Helen Hum-

Amherst Academy, where Dickinson studied from 1840 to 1847 *(Courtesy of the Jones Library, Inc., Amherst, Massachusetts)*

phrey was in charge. She enjoyed a warm relationship with Helen, who was the older sister of Emily's close friend JANE HUMPHREY. Rebecca Woodridge was another "very pretty" 20-year-old preceptress of whom Emily wrote, "We all love her very much." Her favorite, however, appears to have been ELIZABETH C. ADAMS, a woman in her early 30s, "our dear Miss Adams," as Emily called her, without whom life at school seemed "lonely & strange."

Among her male teachers, Emily had an important, personal bond with LEONARD HUMPHREY, who became principal in 1846 upon graduating from Amherst College. The young man was the first of a small number of men in her life she would address as "Master," men older than herself to whom she turned for wisdom, counsel, or love. Humphrey and Dickinson were friends, but there does not appear to have been a romantic bond between them. His early death in 1850 after a brief illness devastated her.

The deepest and most enduring influence, however, was that of EDWARD HITCHCOCK, the president of Amherst College, who was the guiding spirit of the academy during Emily's time there. An eminent geologist and a poet, Hitchcock was a man of God and science, who believed that the evidence of science, rather than contradicting religion, provided evidence of God's existence. His inspirational love of nature and celebration of the New England landscape, that combined both a sense of its sublimity and precise observation, resonate with the nature poetry Dickinson would later write.

The academy years also saw the establishment of friendships with schoolmates, which Emily would hark back to and strive to keep alive. She was especially close to Abiah Root, with whom she conducted an important correspondence, with ABBY MARIA WOOD, who became her "particular friend," and with Olivia and ELIZA COLEMAN, Sara Porter Ferry, Helen Fiske, Mary E. Humphrey, Martha Gilbert, SARAH TRACY, and HARRIET MERRILL. Yet friendship was soon followed by nostalgia for them, for none of these girls, with the possible exception of Abby Wood, would remain at the academy for as long as Emily. Perhaps because of parental concerns about her health, she was kept close to home in Amherst, while the others transferred to schools elsewhere, to get a taste of the world. The Dickinsons were willing to let her siblings transfer, but Emily's frequent illnesses, which caused her to miss long periods of school, alarmed them.

Although she once confessed to envying a friend for being able to get away, she seems to have been content with her lot. Upon entering, she wrote to Jane Humphrey: "I am in the class that you used to be in in Latin—besides Latin I study History and Botany I like the school very much indeed." (L 3, May 12, 1842) Three years later, she wrote Abiah: "They [her studies] are Mental Philosophy, Geology, Latin, and Botany. How large they sound, don't they? I don't believe you have such big studies. . . . We have a very fine school" (L 6, May 7, 1845). An outstanding student, she began in the English course, but later enrolled in the esteemed classical course for two years. While she probably took additional courses, it is known that she took three and possibly four years of Latin, as well as history, ecclesiastical history, arithmetic, algebra and geometry, and required classes in composition and declamation.

If the academy offered Dickinson a stimulating intellectual and personal life, it also steeped her in an atmosphere of orthodox piety. Students were required to attend a Saturday evening Bible class and to attend religion observances. Both textbooks and teachers were expected to ground their teachings in the soil of Christian faith, consistently relating specific subject matter to man's spiritual dimensions. Thus, Isaac Watts, in his book *The Improvement of the Mind,* instructed students how to use their mind so as "to subordinate all to the service of God." This kind of instruction had something positive to offer the poet, fostering a sense of the sublimity inherent in the topics under study. However, in that the receptive student was expected to undergo a religious conversion, it was also the source of much anguish to her. During the winter of 1846, a major REVIVAL began in Amherst, and Emily, who was attending prayer meetings, wrote to Abiah of her inner turmoil: "I am sailing upon the brink of an awful precipice, from which I cannot escape & over which I fear my tiny boat will soon glide if I do not receive help from above" (L 11, March 28, 1846). In fact, her boat, without divine assistance, pursued its independent course.

Despite its religious conservatism, the influence of Amherst Academy on Dickinson's life was overwhelmingly positive. She found there a world of new knowledge and perspectives, the freedom to be herself and the discipline to accomplish her goals. Her final term ended on August 10, 1847, and was celebrated by an "Exhibition" with declamations, singing, and prayer. The next year, she became a student at MOUNT HOLYOKE FEMALE SEMINARY in South Hadley, Massachusetts, where both her intellectual development and struggle with orthodox religion would enter a new phase.

FURTHER READING

Sewall, *Life,* II, 337–357; Habegger, *My Wars,* 139–166.

Amherst College   Founded in 1821 by Amherst civic and religious leaders, notably including the poet's paternal grandfather, SAMUEL FOWLER DICKINSON, the college had as its goal educating young men of limited means within an institution imbued with the values of orthodox CONGREGATIONALISM. The Dickinson men, Emily's father, EDWARD DICKINSON, and her brother, WILLIAM AUSTIN DICKINSON, continued to take active roles in the development of the college. For Emily, the college was a vital lifelong presence, a source of intellectual and cultural stimulation and of enriching friendships.

Samuel and his coreligionists were encouraged to engage in their ambitious project by the success of AMHERST ACADEMY, which they had brought into being in 1812 and which was becoming one of the best private classical schools in western Massachusetts. To embody the founders' crusading spirit, Samuel persuaded fellow enthusiast Colonel Rufus Graves to join him in promoting the creation of an evangelical college that would surpass the only other state colleges of the time, Harvard University and Williams College. To an orthodox Calvinist such as Samuel, Harvard Divinity School, which had embraced UNITARIANISM, was anathema. He and his cofounders conceived Amherst College as a vital step in reversing this trend away from the faith of the fathers. Through its talented and pious graduates, enriched by a classical education, the new college would play its part in civilizing and evangelizing the world. When the Amherst leaders applied to the Massachusetts General Court for a charter, they were opposed by the Harvard Unitarians, who warned that the proposed institution would become a "priest factory." Nothing could have fanned their spiritual zeal more. Samuel was a confidence-inspiring advocate and fund-raiser for the college on whose first board of trustees he would serve. His voice was pivotal in helping Amherst win out over 37 other towns as the site of the new college.

However, his zeal for the project, to which he recklessly committed his own funds, eventually led to his financial ruin. Amherst College, too, was on the brink of bankruptcy and Samuel died in 1838, not knowing that the school for which he had sacrificed himself would survive.

Both his son, EDWARD, and grandson, WILLIAM AUSTIN, continued his efforts on behalf of the college. For Edward, the Amherst Collegiate Charity Institution, as it was called in its first years, represented a humiliating setback in his young life: When Samuel could not afford to send him back to Yale, he was forced to spend his full junior year there—the year of the school's founding. It seemed to him a sad comedown from Yale and he was glad to leave it. Fourteen years later, however, in 1835, Edward, who was already a successful attorney, became a trustee of the college and in August of that year succeeded John Leland as treasurer. When he tried to resign in 1872, after 37 years of devoted service, the surprised trustees persuaded him to stay on until a successor could be chosen. A political battle ensued over who would succeed him, culminating in Austin's election as treasurer in December 1873. Austin found his father's records in a state of chaos and had to hire a bookkeeper to straighten them out. In the long run, he was considered less effective than his father had been in building and maintaining influential contacts for the college.

Lithograph of Amherst's College Row, prepared for the trustees in 1828. Thirty years later, College Row at last looked like this. *(Amherst College Archives and Special Collections)*

Emily's life grew closely intertwined with the college when she became a pupil at Amherst Academy. The two educational institutes were thoroughly identified with one another. They followed the same educational policies. Academy students regularly attended lectures at the college and Amherst professors gave courses at the academy. The college's graduates formed a significant part of the corps of dedicated young teachers at the academy. Emily's early education was shaped by the principles and personality of EDWARD HITCHCOCK, the college's president from 1845 to 1854. Both a scientist and man of religion, Hitchcock viewed the discoveries of science as confirmations of God's divine plan; during the decade of his presidency, he managed to briefly link the Puritan past with progressive scientific inquiry. As an orthodox Calvinist, he encouraged the practice of REVIVALS that caused the young Emily so much spiritual anguish. The Great Revival of 1850, as well as major revivals in 1846, 1849, and 1853, took place during his administration. For many decades, even through the Civil War period, Amherst boasted that no student who completed the four-year course failed to witness a revival.

Upon completing her formal education, Emily found a continuing source of spiritual and intellectual nourishment in Amherst College. When she returned home from her year at MOUNT HOLYOKE FEMALE SEMINARY in South Hadley in 1848, the college offered a variety of public exercises for her to attend in others' company, from the recurring exhibitions, senior levees, and commencement ceremonies to onetime events like the dedication of Appleton Cabinet in 1848, a small museum attached to the college, or the library in 1853. The years 1849–50, when Austin was an upperclassman, were especially meaningful to her. During his senior year, Austin was a member of the Alpha Delta Phi fraternity, the school's leading "secret society." Most of the students and tutors who came to call on Emily and her younger sister LAVINIA (Vinnie) were members of the fraternity. The friendships Emily enjoyed with these young men, particularly those with GEORGE HENRY GOULD, HENRY VAUGHAN EMMONS, JOHN LONG GRAVES, and George Howland, stimulated her to read new books and think new thoughts.

Even when Dickinson was becoming reclusive, the college's yearly commencement exercises, with their familiar rituals and faces, "the speechmaking, the dusty booths on the Common, the hordes of curious onlookers mixed with returning alumni, many in clerical collars" (Habegger, *My Wars,* 319) drew her back into its web. The poet's parents were acknowledged social leaders, famous for their commencement receptions, the Dickinson teas that became annual features of commencement week. A relative's memoirs tell us, "At these gatherings Emily was accustomed at first, to take a daughter's place. Later she was seen for shorter and shorter times, until in the latter years, her appearance was but a prelude to her disappearance, after just a word to one or two favored friends." (Clara Newman Pearl, "My Personal Acquaintance with Emily Dickinson," Jones Library, Amherst). When Austin and his wife, SUSAN HUNTINGTON GILBERT DICKINSON, moved into The EVERGREENS, next door to the Edward Dickinson home, they frequently entertained eminent people, including Ralph Waldo Emerson in 1857, who gave lectures and sermons at the college. Although Emily did not meet Emerson, she took advantage of the opportunity to meet and converse with many of these prominent guests.

During Dickinson's lifetime, Amherst College began its evolution into the secular, coeducational institution it is today. Under William A. Stearns, a graduate of Unitarian-oriented Harvard College, who became president when Hitchcock resigned in 1854, the student body grew secularized, and by 1871 three-quarters of the graduating class went into some profession other than the ministry. During the 1860s, fraternities evolved from serious-minded literary organizations to mere social clubs. In 1874, the graduating class's decision to conclude its year with a public ball was a bellwether of the times. Twenty years earlier, when even dancing in private homes had not been countenanced in Amherst, this would have been unthinkable (Wolff, *Emily Dickinson,* 427–428).

FURTHER READING

Alfred Habegger, *My Wars,* 11–20, 317–319; Heman Humphrey, *Sketches of the Early History of Amherst College,* Northampton, Mass., 1905; Thomas Le Duc, *Piety and Intellect at Amherst College;* Cynthia Griffin Wolff, *Emily Dickinson,* 427–428.

Anthon, Catherine (Scott) Turner (1831–1917) A friend of Emily's during the early 1860s, Catherine Anthon's special interest to scholars revolves around speculation that the poet's feelings for her were of a passionate nature. The daughter of Henry Scott, of Cooperstown, New York, she became acquainted with the poet's future sister-in-law, SUSAN HUNTINGTON GILBERT (DICKINSON) in 1848 when they were both students at Utica Female Seminary. In 1855 she married Campbell Ladd Turner, a doctor whose tuberculosis was already at an advanced stage when the couple wed. A year and a half later, the young bride became a widow, when Campbell died at the age of 26. In January 1859, the beautiful, flirtatious Catherine, dressed in mourning, came to stay with her old schoolmate, Sue, now married to Emily's older brother, WILLIAM AUSTIN DICKINSON, at Austin and Sue's elegant Italianate villa, The EVERGREENS. During that first extended visit Catherine and Emily spent evenings in one another's company at the Evergreens that the poet would later call "blissful" and, by the time Catherine left in February 1860, the two women had developed a warm friendship. Catherine returned for two more extended stays in October 1861 and 1863.

In the reminiscences she wrote later, Catherine Anthon recalled her visits at the Evergreens, which Sue had made the social center of AMHERST, in ecstatic terms: "Those celestial evenings in the Library—the blazing *wood* fire—*Emily—Austin,*— the music—the rampant fun—the inextinguishable laughter, the uproarious spirits of our chosen—our most congenial circle." She remembered, "Emily with her dog, & Lantern! often at the piano playing weird and beautiful melodies, all from her own inspiration. . . ." There was an element of girlish frivolity in the blossoming relationship. One night she and Kate "clinging fast like culprit mice" fled to another room, as Emily wrote, "as is my custom" when the bell was rung by Reuben A. Chapman, a dignified family friend, renowned jurist, and social conserva-

Catherine (Scott) Turner Anthon, a friend of Emily's from the early 1860s

tive. Emily, humiliated and remorseful, apologized for her behavior. Describing the episode to her good friend ELIZABETH LUNA CHAPIN HOLLAND, she wrote: "I do not mind [offending] Mr. Hyde of Ware [whom, with Mr. Chapman, the Edward Dickinsons had entertained the evening before], because he does not please me, but Mr. Chapman is my friend, talks of my books with me, and I would not wound him" (L 202, about February 20, 1859).

When Kate returned to Cooperstown, she and Emily began a correspondence; Emily is known to have written five letters to her between 1859 and 1866 (1859: L 203, L 208, L 209; 1860: L 222; 1866: L 317) and to have sent her a few poems. Sharp-witted and intense in their expression of affection and fidelity, these letters follow a pattern characteristic of Emily's correspondence with close women friends. In the first, L 203, written in March 1859, she admits her to her circle of special intimates: "I never missed a Kate before—Two Sues—Eliza and a Martha, comprehend my girls. Sweet at my door this March night another Candidate-Go Home! We don't like Katies here!—Stay! My heart votes for you, and what am I indeed to dispute her ballot—?" In language that invites Katie to join her in a brave, rare existence, expressive of her growing sense of having a special calling, she challenges her new friend, "Dare you dwell in the East where we dwell? Are you afraid of the Sun?" With her next letter, L 208, written in 1859, she sent a pair of garters she had knit for Katie, together with a witty, courtly poem, Fr 49, that begins: "When Katie walks, this Simple pair accompany her side." The next letter, L 209, believed to have been written in late 1859, expresses her longing for "the Maid in black"—a reference to Katie's mourning dress. Emily writes, "Those were unnatural evenings.—Bliss is unnatural—How many years, I wonder, will sow the moss upon them, before we bind again. . . ."

Since the letters sent to Emily Dickinson were destroyed when she died by her sister LAVINIA, we cannot know what Catherine Anthon's half of the correspondence was like. However, Emily's letter, probably written in the summer of 1860 (L 222), indicates that Katie, when she finally wrote, had offered excuses for neglecting the correspondence. Emily replies in turn, "The prettiest of pleas, dear, but with a Lynx like me quite unavailable. . . . you do not yet 'dislimn,' Kate, Distinctly your face stands in its phantom niche—I touch your hand—my cheek your cheek—stroke your vanished hair. Why did you enter, sister, since you must depart? Has not its heart been torn enough but *you* must send your shred? Oh! our Condor Kate! Come from your crags again!" What began with passionate enthusiasm has evolved into reproaches and disappointment. Emily Dickinson seems always to have demanded more of her friends than they were willing and able to give.

Her last known letter to Katie, L 317, was written in early March 1866. It begins with an expression of relief that she has at last heard from her friend and the pathetic plea, "Please don't leave Emily again, it gnarls her character!" Emily has read about a fire in Katie's town and declares her anxiety for Katie's welfare in terms that inadvertently reveal the anger behind her concern: "'Katie is doubtless in *ashes*,' I thought, I'm much obliged to God for not burning you up."

Katie married John Anthon in 1866 and there is no record of a continuing friendship with Emily after that. When, many years later, Katie came to visit Emily, the poet refused to see her. Biographer Alfred Habegger believes that "I shall not murmur if at last" (Fr 1429) probably written in 1877, containing the line, "Why, Katie, Treason has a Voice—/ But mine—dispels—in Tears," is Emily's "tearful excuse for not seeing her." Habegger writes, "Treason is voluble, full of excuses and reassurances, but Emily, still inwardly faithful, dare not speak lest the explanation of her avoidance 'ravage' her friends" (*My Wars*, 536). He implies that the intensity of the poet's love for Katie would be shocking. A three-line poem, Fr 1430, written on the same sheet of paper, "We shun because we prize her Face," also suggests that intensity of emotion, rather than lack of it, lay behind Emily's refusal to see this friend of her youth. She addresses the issue yet again, Habegger suggests, in the undated poem Fr 1716, where she writes: "That she forgot me was the least / I felt it second pain / That I was worthy to forget / Was most I thought upon." Habegger attributes Emily's feeling that she was "worthy to forget" to "the poet's constant love, arousing a kind of shame in the other woman" (*My Wars*, 537).

In her 1951 book, *The Riddle of Emily Dickinson*, critic Rebecca Patterson put forth the theory, shocking in a period before feminist criticism had begun to explore Dickinson's bisexuality, that Kate Anthon was the great passion of her life and that most of her love poetry was written to and about Anthon. Patterson suggested that Elizabeth Holland destroyed Dickinson's letters to her dating from 1860–65 in order to shield Emily from their revelation of her passion for Anthon (*Riddle*, 156; Sewall, *Life*, II, 605–606n). Patterson interpreted Fr 451, "THE MALAY—TOOK THE PEARL—" as describing the triangle between the Earl (Dickinson herself), the Malay (John Anthon and the Pearl (Catherine). This theory did not gain widespread support and, like many others concerning the details of the poet's intimate life, remains firmly within the realm of speculation.

When the poet's niece, MARTHA DICKINSON BIANCHI, published a collection of poems, *The Single Hound*, in 1914, Anthon wrote to her:

The first poem "To Sue" is beautiful. I could have wept over it. Some are rather obscure—must read them many times.

Such genius and mysticism as Emily possessed often transcends mortal comprehension.

See also ABIAH PALMER ROOT and ABBY MARIA WOOD (MRS. BLISS).

FURTHER READING

Alfred Habegger, *My Wars,* 373–375, 536–537; Rebecca Patterson, *Riddle,* 156; Richard B. Sewall, *Life,* II, 442, 467, 479–480, 487, 533, and 605–606n.

B

Bianchi, Martha Gilbert Dickinson (1866–1943) Martha Gilbert Dickinson Bianchi was Emily Dickinson's only niece and the last of the family line descended from Emily's father, EDWARD DICKINSON. Herself a poet and novelist, her most vital contribution to literature was as family memoirist and editor of her aunt's poems. Publishing eight volumes of Dickinson's writings and the most extensive volume of memoirs written by anyone who knew the poet directly, she played a central role in creating the public's image of Dickinson and its perception of her poetry in the first half of the 20th century. Although she has been harshly judged for her distortions of both the poet's biography and her work, Bianchi's legacy to Dickinson readers and scholars is valuable and complex. Her memoirs, while unreliable in many respects, also contain priceless personal and anecdotal glimpses of the Dickinson household. And, while she doubtless mangled much of her aunt's writings, she was the first to attempt to reproduce Dickinson's lineation as it appeared in her original manuscripts.

The middle child and only daughter of Emily's brother, WILLIAM AUSTIN DICKINSON, and his wife, SUSAN HUNTINGTON GILBERT DICKINSON, she was born on November 29, 1866, and named after her mother's sister, Martha Gilbert, of Geneva. The child who would become known as "Mattie" to the world and was affectionately called "Mopsy" by her mother, was five years younger than her brother EDWARD DICKINSON ("Ned") and nine years older

Martha Dickinson Bianchi, daughter of Austin and Sue. Emily's niece "Mattie" is shown here at age six. *(By permission of the Houghton Library, Harvard University)*

than her brother THOMAS GILBERT DICKINSON ("Gib"). Both brothers would die prematurely, Gib at the age of eight, of typhoid fever, and Ned, at 37,

252

of heart failure. Mattie, the survivor, was known to possess her parents' drive for dominance and self-expression. At about age three, she was characterized by her Aunt Emily as "stern and lovely—literary they tell me—a graduate of Mother Goose and otherwise ambitious" (L 333, to Susan Dickinson, who was away in Geneva, autumn 1869). Martha was a leader of the pack of children who played in the Dickinson compound, often observed Emily tending her flowers, and was the recipient of sweets Emily would lower in a basket from her bedroom window to the children. Remembering the aunt of these childhood years, she would later say, "Aunt Emily stood for *indulgence*" (*Face to Face*, 6).

Given the tensions in her parents' marriage, Martha's childhood could hardly have been the idyllic one she evokes in her memoirs. By the time she was 16, her father had commenced a passionate romance with the young married woman who would be Emily Dickinson's first editor, the lovely, talented, and ambitious MABEL LOOMIS TODD. Since Martha's writings omit any reference to the affair, which lasted until Austin's death in 1895, we have no direct record of how she felt about the fact that Austin and Mabel often found a refuge at The HOMESTEAD, with the blessing of both Emily and Emily's sister LAVINIA DICKINSON. What we do know—just as Austin did—is that Mattie was her mother's ally in the prolonged and bitter family strife. Austin showed his awareness of his older children's loyalties when he wrote in his will, "I make no special mention of Ned and Mattie because they are practically one in interest and feeling with their Mother...." (Sewall, *Life*, I 192).

In the 1890s, when the first published volumes of Emily's verse, edited by Mabel Todd and THOMAS WENTWORTH HIGGINSON, were attracting a wide and astonished readership, Martha Dickinson began to publish her own poems in magazines. AMHERST historian Daniel Lombardo comments: "Growing up in the shadow of Emily Dickinson would have been tough for anyone. But for Emily's niece, Martha, life was especially bittersweet. Few took Martha's career as a poet seriously...." (*A Hedge Away*, 14). Yet her mother, Susan, was said to have taken a greater interest in her daughter's

Martha Dickinson Bianchi, daughter of Austin and Sue. Emily's niece "Mattie" brought out eight volumes of her aunt's poetry between 1914 and 1937 and wrote important memoirs. *(By permission of the Houghton Library, Harvard University)*

poems than in the great numbers of Emily's that were in her keeping. Another admirer was brother Ned, who assured her that Aunt Emily's verse looks "very wraith like, and impossible beside her stronger, and saner niece's" (Bianchi Collection). Biographer Alfred Habegger, citing Martha's 1897 poem "Indian Summer," a favorite theme of her aunt's, notes that the niece's poetry "sometimes looks like a meretricious version of Dickinson's." Martha wrote "The spurnèd bough reveals the path / Her bird has flown; as unaware / A gentle sense of aftermath,—/ Renunciation fills the air," (*My Wars*, 565n14).

Following Austin's death, Mattie and her mother traveled to Europe together, where, during a yearlong sojourn, she met Alexander E. Bianchi, supposedly of the Imperial Horse Guard of St. Petersburg, and married him on July 19, 1903. "Count" Bianchi, described as "some-sort-of-titled

Ukrainian" hailed from Odessa and was nearly eight years younger than the 36-year-old Martha. The count was transferred to Boston that same year and the couple moved into Mattie's childhood home, The EVERGREENS. In his lively account of the marriage, Daniel Lombardo records that, "When the Count was introduced to Amherst at a party, he supposedly grew bored and dropped out of the receiving line" ("Who Was Count Bianchi?" 14). Indeed, a photo of him shows a slender young officer with a dark mustache and a distinct look of boredom. The couple lived in Amherst, where the count became "the source of much local speculation, some of it spurious," allegedly using up all of his wife's money before seeking new horizons. He spent time in a New York jail on fraud charges in 1907, related to failure to repay money to a friend of Martha's, Charlotte Terry of New York. He abandoned his marriage to Martha on June 20, 1908; Martha filed for divorce in 1919, which was finalized in 1920.

Habegger comments, "After this costly misadventure, Martha took a keen interest in the royalties to be made from her aunt" (*My Wars,* 609n1). Sometime after 1899, when Lavinia died, Susan came into possession of her extensive manuscripts of the poems. After Susan's death, in 1913, Mattie embarked on her first editing venture and the following year published *The Single Hound.* This collection contained 142 poems taken, not from Lavinia's manuscripts, but from the stash of poems Emily had sent to Susan over the years. It included the full text of "One sister have I in our house" (Fr 5); Austin had completely inked over any mention of Susan in Mabel's copy. The poems were generally presented "in a faithful text" (R. W. Franklin, *Editing Emily Dickinson,* 34) and "showed the world a different Dickinson: a Dickinson to whom *The New Republic's* reviewer Elizabeth Shepley Sergeant could refer as an early Imagist" (Morse, "Bibliographical Essay," 258–259), that is, a predecessor of such modern poets as Ezra Pound and William Carlos Williams, whose work was characterized by short musical lines and clear precise imagery. Sergeant characterized the book as "surprising as a cold douche, as acute as the edge of a precipice, as lambent as a meteor cleaving the night."

After this contribution, Martha did not publish another volume of her aunt's poetry until 1924. The volume she entitled *Complete Poems* was not, in fact, complete, but consisted of the three volumes edited by Mabel Todd and Thomas Wentworth Higginson in the 1890s, as well as *The Single Hound,* and five previously unpublished poems. By making 597 poems available within a single cover, however, it contributed to the discovery of Dickinson as part of the American canon in the 1920s. She went on to publish *Further Poems* (1929) and *Unpublished Poems* (1935), edited with the assistance of her friend Alfred Leete Hampson and based mainly on Lavinia's manuscripts. Dickinson's foremost editor, Ralph Franklin, notes that the manuscripts handled by Bianchi and Hampson "have been shuffled, cut up, and generally dealt with roughly" (*Editing,* 34). He is highly critical of them as editors, commenting, "These two volumes . . . contained numerous misreadings of the manuscripts as well as conscious attempts to satisfy a new public taste by making Emily Dickinson's form even more eccentric than it was" (*Editing,* 115–116).

While recognizing these serious flaws in Bianchi's work, Jonathan Morse ("Bibliographical Essay," 259–60) sees her as "ahead of her time" in her attempt in the 1929 *Further Poems* to print the poems in the lineations of the original manuscripts. Todd and Higginson had regularized the lines into the quatrains of a New England hymnal, as for example, in the following:

> The sun, as common, went abroad;
> The flowers, accustomed, blew,

Bianchi printed these lines as they appear in Dickinson's handwritten original:

> The Sun—as Common—went
> abroad—
> The Flowers—accustomed—
> blew—

By calling attention to the visual expressiveness of Emily Dickinson's manuscripts she foreshadows the efforts of numerous contemporary scholars, such as Sharon Cameron and Martha Nell Smith.

As a memoirist, Martha's contribution to Dickinson scholarship is similarly mixed. Her firsthand descriptions of her aunt's life within the family compound, *Life and Letters* (1924) and *Emily Dickinson Face to Face* (1932), continue to provide an invaluable resource to biographers, who must, however, carefully distinguish between their facts and fictions. Determined to present a sentimentalized figure whose life contained nothing that might be "embarrassing" or compromising to the family name, Martha was a key contributor to the myth of Emily Dickinson, which obscured the sterner realities of her life and the complexities of her character. Biographer Richard B. Sewall writes: "Martha helped create the figure of whimsy and fun, fond of children, full of gnomic wisdom, and of barely sufficient awe, mystery, and talent to remain a poet . . ." (*Life*, I, 532).

Another aspect of the myth Martha helped to create was her sensational claim that Aunt Emily had "met the fate she had instinctively shunned" on a visit to Philadelphia, where she and a married man fell in love but agreed to renounce one another. Martha wrote, "There is no doubt that two predestined souls were kept apart only by her high sense of duty and the necessity for keeping love untarnished by the inevitable destruction of another woman's life" (*Life and Letters*, 46–47). When this story met with skepticism and scorn, Martha went on to amplify it in 1932, in *Face to Face*. The man in question was the REVEREND CHARLES WADSWORTH, whom Emily did, in fact, meet in Philadelphia in 1855 and with whom she established a friendship. Wadsworth remains a prime candidate for the man whom Emily loved and called "Master," so that, as Habegger observes, Martha's "story can't be swallowed whole, but it may have a factual basis" (471). Sewall, on the other hand, stresses that there is "little evidence to support it and much to call it into question. But its high romantic style and lofty sentiments have created an impression hard to dislodge" (*Life*, I, 8n).

A third major area in which Martha's testament grossly distorts the record is her account of her mother's relationship to Aunt Emily as "a girlish infatuation that developed . . . into lifelong devotion, with no rifts or seams" (Ibid., 263). Citing the inaccuracies of *Life and Letters* as the main reason for Martha's bad reputation among scholars, Jonathan Morse writes, "Was Emily Dickinson's relationship with Susan Dickinson . . . passionate at the beginning, sympathetic at the end, but indifferent or worse for at least fifteen years in between? No problem; Mme. Bianchi just postdated some of Aunt Emily's early letters to make the record more uniformly smiley" ("Bibliographical Essay," 259). He archly observes that "From book to book she got no better, either at reading her aunt's handwriting or at remembering the existence of Mabel Loomis Todd" (Ibid., 259). Among her "sins of omission" was the editing out of all passages with lesbian overtones from her aunt's letters to Sue. Thus, "Susie, will you indeed come home next Saturday, and be my own again, and kiss me as you used to?" was reduced to "Susie, will you indeed come home next Saturday?" in Bianchi's rendering.

Martha presents her mother as Emily's poetic alter ego, with a "sixth sense" for evaluating her poetry. "Her sister Sue recognized her genius from the first, and hoarded every scrap Emily sent her," she affirms (*Life and Letters*, 64). In a later account, she rhapsodizes:

> the varied sympathies always existing between Aunt Emily and my mother—from their first girlish wonderings about life, on through the books they shared, the flowers they tilled, the friends they loved, their culinary wizardry, their domestic crises, their absorption in us children, their fun and fears, their gay whimsies and childish realities; all their deepening experiences uniting to weld the confident and profound devotion enduring unto death. (*Face to Face*, 176)

Was this willful misrepresentation or simple misunderstanding on Martha's part? Citing "A WOUNDED DEER—LEAPS HIGHEST—" and its credo of not showing deep wounds to the outside world, Sewall speculates that, if the poem is about Sue's cruelties, it would explain the cheerful face Emily put on their relationship all her life—and thus Martha's view of that relationship. "It is possible," he writes, "that young Mattie never saw any other side, or was so dazzled by her aunt's play-acting that she concluded the other side was unimportant" (*Life*, I, 213).

In addition to perpetuating her aunt's legacy, Mme Bianchi continued to write poetry and fiction, spending winters in New York or abroad, and summers alone in Amherst. She played an active role in the outside world, doing heroic work for the Red Cross during World War I. In 1933, at its 110th Commencement, Martha Dickinson became the first woman to receive an honorary degree from AMHERST COLLEGE. For her work as a novelist, poet, and editor of eight volumes of Dickinson's writings, the honor of Doctor of Letters was bestowed on Bianchi. She died on December 21, 1943, thus ending the line descended from Edward and EMILY NORCROSS DICKINSON. Her will requested that her famous house, The Evergreens, be burned to the ground, perhaps because of the many family tragedies that had occurred within its walls. Fortunately, however, as Lombardo notes, "This final tragedy has been sidestepped only by complex legal maneuvering" ("Count Bianchi," 16). Martha left Dickinson's manuscripts to Alfred Leete Hampson, her companion and coeditor, who in 1950 sold them to Harvard University. As the result of subsequent legal battles, however, Harvard retained only the manuscripts that had belonged to Susan and Lavinia, while Amherst College received those that belonged to Mabel Todd.

EDITIONS OF EMILY DICKINSON'S POETRY EDITED BY MARTHA DICKINSON BIANCHI

The Single Hound: Poems of a Lifetime. Boston: S. J. Parkhill, 1914.
The Complete Poems. Boston: Little, Brown, 1924.
Further Poems of Emily Dickinson Withheld from Publication by her Sister Lavinia. Edited with Alfred Leete Hampson. Boston: Little, Brown, 1929.
The Poems of Emily Dickinson. Edited with Alfred Leete Hampson. Boston: Little, Brown, 1930.
Unpublished Poems of Emily Dickinson. Edited with Alfred Leete Hampson. Boston: Little, Brown, 1935.

Poems. Edited with Alfred Leete Hampson. Boston: Little, Brown, [1937] 1950.

OTHER BOOKS BY MARTHA DICKINSON BIANCHI

The Life and Letters of Emily Dickinson. Boston: Houghton Mifflin, 1924.
Emily Dickinson Face to Face: Unpublished Letters with Notes and Reminiscences. Boston: Houghton Mifflin, 1932.
Life before Last: Reminiscences of a Country Girl (forthcoming) Edited by Barton Levi St. Armand and Martha Nell Smith.

See also PUBLICATION AND EDITORIAL SCHOLARSHIP.

FURTHER READING
Millicent Todd Bingham, *Ancestor's Brocades*, 376–396; Betsy Erkkila, "The Emily Dickinson Wars," in *Cambridge Companion*, 14–16; R. W. Franklin, *The Editing of Emily Dickinson*, 14; Alfred Habegger, *My Wars*, 546–49, 565, 570–71; Daniel Lombardo, "Just Who Was Count Bianchi?" in *A Hedge Away*, 14–16; Polly Longsworth, *Mabel and Austin*; Jonathan Morse, "Bibliographical Essay," in *A Historical Guide to Emily Dickinson*, 258–262; Richard B. Sewall, *Life*, I, 162, 254–261, and II, 562; Elizabeth Shepley Sergeant, "An Early Imagist," in *The Recognition of Emily Dickinson*, 88–93.

Bowles, Samuel (1826–1878) Samuel Bowles, the crusading editor of *The Springfield Republican*, an abolitionist and supporter of women's rights, entered Dickinson's life in June 1858 when he came to AMHERST and was entertained by WILLIAM AUSTIN and SUSAN HUNTINGTON GILBERT DICKINSON at The EVERGREENS. Rapidly developing his friendship with Austin and Sue, he became their frequent guest at a time when Emily was an active participant in their lively social gatherings. The nature of the intense relationship she formed with "Mr. Bowles," as she always called him, continues to be the subject of scholarly debate. For biographer Richard B. Sewall, "If her words mean anything at all . . . she was deeply in love with him for several years and never ceased loving him, at a distance, for the rest of her life" (*Life*, II, 473). Biographer Alfred Habegger takes a more cautious view. While characterizing Bowles as "possibly her most dynamic, volatile, and fascinating male friend," he believes that what she felt for him "wasn't love, or love exactly, but whatever it was it brought out some of her most intense writing" (*My Wars*, 375–376).

The son of the founder of *The Springfield Republican*, Samuel succeeded his father as editor in 1851 and transformed the paper into a highly influential organ of liberal Republicanism. Before the Whig collapse of 1854, the paper backed EDWARD DICKINSON and other conservatives. Under Bowles, the paper practiced a principled form of journalism, rising above narrowly partisan interests. Bowles himself never ran for office but was close to those who did, on local, state, and national levels. He was a shrewd and powerful player in public life, using his paper and his widely read editorials to influence events.

While all the Dickinsons admired Bowles, he was most intimate with Austin and Sue, whose children called him "Uncle Sam." They received at least 163 letters from Bowles, who came to see them at regular intervals and kept them abreast of his hectic life. In light of their radically different backgrounds, Austin and Samuel were unlikely best friends. Unlike Austin, who earned both undergraduate and law degrees, Bowles worked from the age of 17 on and, to his enduring regret, never attended college. During his second year on the job, he persuaded his father to turn the paper into a daily. True to his word that he would assume main responsibility for the paper, he dedicated his life to it. Bowles came of Puritan, but more recent Unitarian, stock; his practical nature reflected the utilitarian side of the developing CONNECTICUT RIVER VALLEY culture. In his early youth, he had little time for philosophizing or excursions into teaching or literature, although he later read passionately and counted Ralph Waldo Emerson and Charles Dickens among his friends. Samuel traveled widely at home and abroad, as Austin never did. The two men shared a commitment to AMHERST COLLEGE, art collecting, and an up-to-date style of ease and privacy.

As for his friendship with Sue, it was one of several he established during his lifetime with dynamic, intellectual women. In 1848, Bowles was married to Mary Schermerhorn of Geneva, New York, a plain, withdrawn, hypersensitive woman who suffered from chronic asthma; they raised a large family. While Samuel was protective of his life partner, he frequently took his marital troubles to The Evergreens, discussing with Sue the temptations of infidelity. Seeing her as a masterful and fascinating woman, he addressed many of his letters to The Evergreens to her. The warmth of their relationship inspired rumors in the 1860s that Sue and Samuel were a good deal more than friends. Judith Farr sees Bowles as a masculine version of Sue, with his vibrancy and love of excitement, his dark good looks, and a "bearing that was impressive or, according to Dickinson, 'Arabian' (L 3.662), her word for sexually charming. . . . Sue's interest in

Samuel Bowles, the charismatic editor of the *Springfield Republican,* whom Emily loved *(By permission of the Houghton Library, Harvard University)*

him made Bowles doubly appealing to Emily" (*Passion*, 186–187). As for Mary, she detested Sue and seldom accompanied Bowles to The Evergreens.

Bowles biographer George Merriam describes him as "a man who could unite an entire and life-long loyalty to one woman . . . with intimately and mutually helpful friendships with other women" (*Life and Times*, 216–217). Merriam no doubt exaggerates the ease of this balancing act, since Mary Bowles was deeply resentful of at least one of the spirited and brainy women who attracted him, MARIA WHITNEY. Distantly related to his wife, whom she cared for on several occasions following childbirth, the highly accomplished Maria, a one-time instructor in languages at Smith College, was probably Bowles's closest female friend.

As Habegger notes, "He could be a thrilling companion for alert single women conscious of being denied a man's entrée into the world" (*My Wars*, 378). When Dickinson met him, he was still in his early 30s, four years older than she was, extremely handsome, and energetic. He was known for his unrestrained openness and his kindness to people in trouble. His ability to bring a sense of the times into the Dickinsons' parlors was a quality the reclusive Emily enjoyed in her friends; and, as editor of a distinguished newspaper, he might have been a channel to the publishing of her poems. In the latter respect he clearly failed her. *The Republican* did publish a handful of her poems: "I TASTE A LIQUOR NEVER BREWED—" as "The May Wine"; "SAFE IN THEIR ALABASTER CHAMBERS—" as "The Sleepers"; "BLAZING IN GOLD AND QUENCHING IN PURPLE"; and "A NARROW FELLOW IN THE GRASS" as "The Snake," which Sue pirated to him. Emily considered herself "robbed" of the latter poem by editorial meddling; as for Bowles, his only known reaction to the poem was to wonder, "How did that girl ever know that a boggy field wasn't good for corn?" (*Face to Face*, 270). She sent him two groups of poems: those incorporated into the letters, with formal salutation and valediction, and those copied on separate sheets to be enclosed with the letters. The latter may be seen more as samples of her work, rather than directed personally to him. All were superior to the ones the paper printed. Sewall believes that, had she asked him directly, which was not her way, he might have

published them. Habegger, taking this argument a step further, believes that, given Bowles's friendship with and encouragement of women writers, had Emily been less ambivalent about publishing, the *Republican* would have been open to her, especially when Fidelia Hayward Cooke, a writer whose poems and fiction the paper had been publishing, replaced the chauvinistic JOSIAH GILBERT HOLLAND as literary editor. As it was, unattuned to either her language or her concerns, Bowles never became her literary champion.

Yet in his liberalism on women's issues and support of women's writing he was well ahead of his times. In fact, he was well ahead of Emily. They were united in their love for Elizabeth Barrett Browning's *Aurora Leigh*, a revolutionary female epic tracing the growth of a woman writer, and the writings of Emily and Charlotte Brontë, especially the latter's *Jane Eyre*. But Emily apparently lacked his enthusiasm for the idea that women's civic freedoms had to be drastically enlarged, if only for the good of society. Once, when Samuel spoke in favor of women having more active public lives, Emily scoffed at the notion. In her letter of early August 1860, she apologizes, denigrating herself as "Mrs. Jim Crow"—a female version of the stock blackface role many whites found comic, and asks for forgiveness: "I am sorry I smiled at women. Indeed, I revere holy ones, like [prison reformer] Mrs. Fry and Miss Nightingale . . ." (L 223).

The emotional core of their relationship, however, is difficult to ascertain. None of his letters to her survive and the dating of the surviving 50 letters and 35 poems she sent to him and Mary is uncertain. Moreover, Dickinson's language in her letters to him is cryptic, even encoded at times, as in the letter in which she refers to herself as Austin. Not surprisingly, different scholars have come up with radically different versions of what transpired between them.

At the beginning, Emily is at pains to assure Mary and Samuel that she is open to their liberal Unitarian views on religious and social questions. Accepting a book from Mary by Theodore Parker, in which he presents Jesus as "a good man with a genius for religion," but not a Savior, Emily wrote: "I heard that he was 'poison.' Then I like poison very well" (L 213, after Christmas 1859). She tried to establish a separate connection to Mary, "sending the stolid woman some of her most confidential, ingenious and moving productions" (Habegger, 379) but received only occasional replies.

To Samuel, who, in a letter to Austin, February 4, 1859, referred to her as "the sister of the other house who never forgets my spiritual longings," Emily confides, "I write you frequently and am much ashamed" (L 205 April 1859). Following Mary's May 15 stillbirth—the second of three she would endure—Samuel thanked her, through Austin and Sue, for her "beautiful thought." For Emily, always drawn to "men of sorrow," such as the REVEREND CHARLES WADSWORTH, Samuel's sufferings, not only his wife's miscarriages but also his daunting health problems, including poor eyesight, sciatica, headache, indigestion, and insomnia, may have enhanced his attraction to her. Bowles visited with Mary that summer, after which Emily wrote that she was "sorry you came, because you went away. Hereafter, I will pick no Rose, lest it fade or prick me" (L 189). Later, writing about her anxiety for Mary's health, she voiced her chronic fear lest "in such a porcelain life . . . one stumble upon one's hopes in a pile of broken crockery" (L 193, probably late August 1858). On September 6, 1859, their 11th anniversary, she sent them a gift of a flower and a poem (Fr 60) in which she compares Mary to a rose, herself to mistletoe ("of the Druid") and boldly imagines what it would be like to trade places with the wife. What Mary and Samuel made of this strange tribute is not known.

In a letter dated "around 1860" she sent him "TWO SWIMMERS WRESTLED ON THE SPAR," a vision of deadly personal struggle and universal indifference. There is no salutation or valediction, only the prefatory words "I can't explain it, Mr. Bowles" (L 219). Then, in early 1862, she sent him "TITLE DIVINE, IS MINE!" (L 250). Again, there is neither salutation nor valediction, only the concluding words: "Here's—what I had to 'tell you'—You will tell no other? Honor—is it's own pawn—". Sewall suggests that the poem combines at least three interpretations that are not mutually exclusive: She is becoming Bowles's imagined wife, or sharing Calvary with him, or announcing her vocation to him,

in the aftermath of "the agonizing failure of [their] friendship" (*Life,* II, 485). If Emily intended any of these messages, Bowles apparently missed the point. He seems to have replied promptly, expressing anxiety about the unorthodox "marriage" the poem proclaimed, for in her next letter, she assures him she has not lost her "snow," that is, her sexual purity. Habegger sees this exchange as a clear indication that she was confiding to Bowles her love for someone else, specifically, that the "husband" of the poem was Wadsworth, the charismatic Presbyterian minister Emily had met in Philadelphia in 1855.

Bowles sailed to Europe in April 1862, just when Wadsworth sailed to San Francisco, compounding Emily's sense of desertion. She wrote a consolatory note to Mary after the sailing: "When the Best is gone—I know that other things are not of consequence—The Heart wants what it wants" (L 262). Was this an audacious admission of her feelings for Bowles, or, as Habegger thinks, her way of writing about her loss of Wadsworth? Indeed, the letter is full of her concern for Mary's ability to bear her husband's absence. In her letters to Bowles in Europe, she begs him to come home, and tells him, "it is a Suffering to have a sea—no care how Blue—between your Soul and you" (L 272, about August 1862). Evoking their shared passions, she asks Bowles, who traveled in distinguished literary circles, to report anything he heard about Mrs. Browning, and when he visited her grave in Florence, to "put one hand on the Head, for me—her unmentioned Mourner" (L 266). His only message to her from Europe was scribbled along the edge of a letter to Sue and Austin: "When next you write, tell Emily to give me one of her little gems! How does she do this summer?"

Remarkably, when Bowles returned to the United States in November and visited Amherst after Thanksgiving, Emily refused to see him. Her note of explanation claims that she nobly kept to her room so that the others could have more of him. Four days later, in a note to Austin, Bowles asked that he convey "to the Queen Recluse my especial sympathy—that she has 'overcome the world.'—Is it really true that they sing 'old hundred' & China [a hymn tune] perpetually in heaven—ask her; and are dandelions, asphodels, or *Maiden's vows* the standard flowers of the ethereal?" After this episode, Emily's correspondence with Bowles, then at its peak (she sent him 13 letters in 1862), decreased to a mere trickle; she sent hardly any poems and what letters survive revolve around brief, practical matters, her gratitude for his attentions following her father's death, and concern about his health. Sewall sees the cause of their estrangement as Emily's abandonment of hope in the relationship, conceding that *if* Emily saw the "Queen Recluse" note, she would have been deeply hurt by it. Habegger, assuming that she *did* see the note, believes that she would have interpreted the phrase "Maiden's vows" as a betrayal of confidence and belittling of her "ecstatic announcement of her excruciating 'marriage' to Wadsworth, 'Title divine, is mine!'" (*My Wars*, 447–448). As for Bowles, he may have been offering an indirect apology to Emily when he wrote to Austin and Sue in May 1863: "I have been in a savage, turbulent state for some time, indulging in a sort of chronic disgust at everything & everybody—I guess a good deal as Emily feels." Despite his unflagging professional activities, he was experiencing a growing sense of failure: "I see my friends falling away around me, withdrawing in disappointment, in unrealized idealism, in breaking expectation."

Although their friendship did indeed flag, her continued reverence for him is reflected in a brief letter she sent him, around 1877, perhaps acknowledging the receipt of a photograph: "You have the most triumphant Face out of Paradise—probably because you are there constantly, instead of ultimately—" (L 489). And there is a final recorded episode between them that strongly hints at an intense, enduring connection. When Bowles came to The HOMESTEAD and Emily refused to see him, he called up to her room, "Emily, you damned rascal! No more of this nonsense! I've traveled all the way from Springfield to see you. Come down at once." Emily obeyed and was a "fascinating" companion. Her subsequent letter, the last she wrote him, a year before his death, contains the poem, "I have no Life but this—" which ends with the lines, "Except through this extent / The love of you." She then adds, "It is strange that the most intan-

gible thing is the most adhesive." She signs herself, "Your 'Rascal.' I washed the adjective."

Samuel Bowles died in January 1878 at age 52, his health destroyed by a life of ceaseless exertions. At his funeral, he was eulogized as a martyr to justice and the public good. In Emily's letter to her devastated sister-in-law, she wrote: "His nature was Future—He had not yet lived." After his death she reached out to his widow, writing of "his beautiful face . . . graphic as a spirit's" and making herself an equal in grief. She offered consolation as well to Maria Whitney, as another who had loved him, and initiated a correspondence with his son, Samuel, Jr. Gradually she elevated him in her mind to a place beside her father, writing to Maria Whitney in June 1883, "The past is not a package one can lay away. I see my father's eyes, and those of Mr. Bowles—those isolated comets" (L 830). She identified him with the sun, and when George Merriam was preparing his biography of Bowles for publication, Emily envisioned it as "a Memoir of the Sun, when the Noon is gone—" (L 908).

As a leading candidate for the man Dickinson called "Master," Samuel Bowles has been championed by Richard B. Sewall, Judith Farr in *The Passion of Emily Dickinson*, David Higgins in *Portrait of Emily Dickinson*, and Ruth Miller in *The Poetry of Emily Dickinson*, among others. Farr makes her case eloquently:

> It can be no coincidence . . . that the "Master" of Dickinson's poems and letters and the "Mr. Bowles" to whom she writes as a redeemer and Christ figure are addressed in identical imagery; or that her concern for Master's health and good opinion so closely parallels the concerns of those letters full of sentiment, timidity, respect, and (at last) ardor that followed Bowles over the sea to England or Europe. (*Passion*, 183)

If she is right about this, then the "true" story of their relationship is to be found in the poems she identifies as belonging to the "Narrative of Master" in Dickinson's oeuvre. Habegger dismisses the possibility that Bowles was Master, on the grounds that the "generally accepted" date of the first of the MASTER LETTERS, based on both handwriting features and seasonal allusions, is spring 1858, just before Emily met him. Most recently, however, Farr, questioning the accuracy and methodology of dating of both the first Master letter and the entrance of Bowles into Dickinson's life, has kept the debate very much alive (*Gardens,* 34–39).

See also "A WIFE—AT DAYBREAK I SHALL BE—," and "MINE—BY THE RIGHT OF THE WHITE ELECTION!"

FURTHER READING

Martha Dickinson Bianchi, *Face to Face*; Judith Farr, *Passion,* 178–244, and *Gardens,* 34–41, 62–64, 197–199, 270, and 277–278; Alfred Habegger, *My Wars,* 375–385, 389, 442–451; George S. Merriam, *Life and Times,* 1885; Richard B. Sewall, *Life,* II, 463–511.

box of Phantoms   "My box of Phantoms" was Dickinson's metaphor for the receptacle of memory in which she placed her lost friendships. She used the term twice in letters written in the mid-1850s, in both instances to friends who appeared to be vanishing from her life, SUSAN HUNTINGTON GILBERT DICKINSON and JOHN LONG GRAVES. The image evokes both a coffin and a trunk of youthful relics, costumes or masks, perhaps. By the mid-1850s, many of the friendships of her early years had, if not wholly expired, become anemic shadows of their former robust selves.

The earlier letter, by editor Thomas Johnson's official dating (*Letters*), was the one written to Sue, in late January 1855, after a quarrel between the two friends the previous September. In a letter taut with anguish over Sue's failure to write from Michigan, where she is visiting family, Emily begs, "If it is finished, tell me, and I will raise the lid to my box of Phantoms and lay one more love in; but if it *lives* and *beats* still, still lives and beats for *me,* then say me *so,* and I will strike the strings to one more strain of happiness before I die." (L 177). In this context of life and death, reflecting the intensity of Emily's feelings for Sue, the metaphor is more evocative of the coffin or grave. It presages the future erratic course of their relationship, during which Emily would often wonder about the status of her unreciprocated passion for the woman who became her sister-in-law.

When her "box of Phantoms" appears again, in the letter to her cousin John—her last surviving written communication to him—it is surrounded by an aura of resignation and melancholy. On the basis of handwriting, Johnson dates it "about 1856," but concedes that it may have been written earlier. Johnson speculates that the letter, delivered by hand, was sent during the summer vacation when Graves, who graduated from AMHERST COLLEGE in 1855, visited Amherst at commencement in August. During his undergraduate years, John had been a frequent visitor to the Dickinson household, once staying at the house, as Emily and Sue's male protector, when the rest of the Dickinson family was away. The poet wrote:

Ah John—*Gone?*

Then I lift the lid to my box of Phantoms and lay another in, unto the Resurrection—Then will I gather in *Paradise,* the blossoms fallen here, and on the shores of the sea of Light, seek my missing sands.
Your Coz—Emilie (L 186).

Apart from its elegiac sadness, the letter reflects the increasing ease with which Dickinson learned to lift the lid to her receptacle of losses, as she became the poet who would write, in 1862, "I CAN WADE GRIEF—/ Whole Pools of it—/ I'm used to that—" (Fr 312).

FURTHER READING

Richard B. Sewall, *Life,* 168, 206, 410.

C

capitalization Together with her use of the short-lined iambic hymn meter and her ubiquitous dashes, capitalization is one of the essential elements of Dickinson's stylistic signature. A Dickinson poem is instantly recognizable by these three elements.

In transforming the handwritten manuscripts into print, editors have had to struggle with the fact that, like her PUNCTUATION, Dickinson's capitalization can be difficult to decipher. Although most of the letters in her manuscripts are clearly capital or small, some are of an in-between size. She capitalizes substantives (nouns and adjectives) more often than verbs. What is the effect of this practice? By capitalizing words that are not normally capitalized, the poet is pointing to them, lifting them up, as it were, in her hierarchy of importance. Moreover, they point to the guiding intelligence of the poet herself. As scholar Robert Weisbuch puts it, "they announce a personality deciding for itself what should be the philosophical stress" (*Emily Dickinson's Poetry*, 72).

Beyond this clear function of emphasizing the presence of the word within the poem, however, different conclusions may be drawn as to the effect of the capitalized words. Linguistic scholar Cristanne Miller points out that there may be two very different effects. On the one hand, because so many of the capitalized words are nouns and adjectives, ideas and things are given an added degree of substantiality. On the other hand, Miller observes, "a capitalized noun also seems to represent its class, and to that extent it func-

tions symbolically" (*Grammar*, 59). It may seem to allegorize things. Both effects are apparent in "AMPLE MAKE THIS BED–" (Fr 804), in which Dickinson simultaneously evokes the physicality of coffin and grave and makes of them symbols of the sleeping dead awaiting the resurrection. Here is the second stanza:

> Be it's Mattrass straight—
> Be it's Pillow round—
> Let no Sunrise's yellow noise—
> Interrupt this Ground—

While we see the grave, "Mattrass," and "Pillow" on which the deceased rests, we also see the place Dickinson creates in this poem within an eternal, sacred landscape. Capitalization, while by no means the only or even the primary agent of transformation, plays a distinct role in creating this double perception.

If we move from the question of what the *effect* of capitalization is to the somewhat different one of what the author *intended* by them we are in murkier waters. R. W. Franklin, the groundbreaking editor who reconstructed the original manuscripts and made them available in print, believes that the efforts of scholars, intent on finding meaning in the least feature of the poet's handwriting, are much ado about nothing. He writes, "Familiarity with the manuscripts should show that the capitals and dashes were merely a habit of handwriting and that Emily Dickinson used them inconsistently ... without special significance"

(*Editing,* 120–121). He points out that not only her poems but letters, household notes, a shopping list, several recipes, and passages she copied from other writers are replete with capitals and dashes. Franklin illustrates his point by applying theories of what such features mean to a recipe for Mrs. Carmichael's coconut cake that Dickinson wrote down. According to current theories, he notes, "the capitals are Emily's 'way of conferring dignity' upon the ingredients of Mrs. Carmichael's cake, or are her 'mythopoetic device' for pushing Butter, Flour, 6 Eggs, and a Cocoa Nut (grated) into 'the fertile domain of myth'" (121). Franklin's down-to-earth approach is a refreshing tonic to some of the more far-fetched, overly reverent approaches to the written manuscripts. Yet it takes a good deal away from Dickinson as a conscious artist, who continually revised her work, and for whom each linguistic element of her dense, concise poems carried weight. She may have capitalized every noun in her recipes, but the fact that only selected words are so treated in the poems points to a conscious artistic choice.

See also HYMN FORM and PUBLICATION HISTORY AND EDITORIAL SCHOLARSHIP.

FURTHER READING

R. W. Franklin, *Editing,* 120–121; Cristanne Miller, *Grammar,* 58; Robert Weisbuch, *Emily Dickinson's Poetry,* 72.

Carlo Carlo was the black Newfoundland dog EDWARD DICKINSON presented to his daughter Emily during the winter of 1849–50, perhaps as a way of protecting her when she was away from home. The name Carlo is the same as that of the dog belonging to St. John Rivers, the devout, dictatorial missionary in the Charlotte Brontë novel, *Jane Eyre,* that the poet read with intense excitement that winter. "Years later," writes biographer Alfred Habegger, "villagers recalled the large animal as the poet's frequent companion on walks and visits" (*My Wars,* 226).

Dickinson's first written reference to Carlo appears in the 1850 valentine published in the *Indicator,* an AMHERST COLLEGE student magazine:

"That's what they call a metaphor in our country. Don't be afraid of it, sir, it won't bite. If it was my dog *Carlo* now! The Dog is the noblest work of Art, sir. I may safely say the noblest—his mistress's rights he doth defend—although it bring him to his end—although to death it doth him send!" Within the polite society of a town the size of AMHERST, the mention of Carlo was a surefire way to reveal the identity of the would-be "anonymous" author of this zany, virtuoso piece.

Carlo's name turns up frequently in the poet's correspondence with the man she called her mentor, THOMAS WENTWORTH HIGGINSON. In her second letter to him, in which she "introduces" herself, she tells him, "You ask of my Companions Hills—Sir—and the Sundown—and a Dog—large as myself, that my Father bought me—They are better than Beings—because they know—but do not tell . . ." (L 261, April 25, 1862). In this striking passage, Carlo's knowing, silent companionship is presented as a comforting foil to the lonely picture she sketches of family life: "I have a Brother and Sister—My Mother does not care for thought—and Father, too busy with his Briefs—to notice what we do. . . ."

Two years later, when she wrote to Higginson from Cambridge, Massachusetts, where she was undergoing treatment for eye problems and repeatedly likened her situation to a prison, she apparently remembered how she had previously described her companions to him. She tells him, "Carlo did not come, because that he would die, in Jail, and the Mountains, I could not hold now, so I brought but the Gods—" (L 290, early June 1864). Here Carlo is the possessor of an unbounded freedom not available to the poet herself. This is one of several examples in which she employs Carlo's persona as a way of speaking about herself. Thus, in a letter to Higginson explaining her reasons for "shunning Men and Women," she writes "they talk of Hallowed things, aloud—and embarrass my Dog—He and I don't object to them, if they'll exist their side." Even when she goes on to describe his canine nature, he represents a positive idea; "I think Carl[o] would please you—He is dumb, and brave—" (L 271, August 1862). Carlo is an alter ego, a sharer of the poet's sensibilities, in another famous passage addressed to Higginson, "If fame belonged to me, I could not escape her—if she did not, the longest day would pass me on the chase—and the approbation of my Dog, would forsake me . . ." (L 265, June 7, 1862).

In other letters, when Emily wants to tell her correspondents that she misses them, she says that Carlo does. Writing to her favorite cousins, LOUISE AND FRANCES NORCROSS, she reports: "Nothing has happened but loneliness, perhaps too daily to relate. Carlo is consistent, has asked for nothing to eat or drink since you went away. Mother thinks him a model dog, and conjectures what he might have been, had not Vinnie 'demoralized' him . . ." (L 285, October 7, 1863). How Emily's sister LAVINIA, a passionate lover of cats, "demoralized" Carlo can only be surmised.

Similarly, in a letter to SAMUEL BOWLES, the charismatic journalist who many scholars believe was the man Dickinson called "Master," she uses Carlo as the vehicle for expressing her own longing for him: "The Hills you used to love when you were in Northampton, miss their old lover, could they speak—and the puzzled look—deepens in Carlo's forehead, as Days go by, and you never come" (L 272, about August 1862). In a poem she sent to Bowles, which begins, "What shall I do—it whimpers so—/ This little Hound within the Heart—," her love is a reduced, pathetic version of her canine alter ego. Carlo himself appears in the final lines, as the channel through which she asks Bowles to tell her whether he wants her love: "Shall it come? / Tell Carlo—/ He'll tell me!" (Fr 237, 1861). And in the first and longest of the MASTER LETTERS, she includes Carlo in a vision of idyllic togetherness, pleading, "Could'nt Carlo, and you and I walk in the meadows an hour—and nobody care but the Bobolink. . . ." The image of a dog occurs in the poem "I STARTED EARLY—TOOK MY DOG," as a liminal figure, accompanying the poet to the boundary between the known and the unknown. Another significant dog image occurs in the 1864 poem, "THIS CONSCIOUSNESS THAT IS AWARE," in which the dog's faithfulness is transformed into a stark existential reality, the utter loneliness of the Soul forever wedded to self-con-

sciousness: "Adventure most unto itself / The Soul condemned to be—/ Attended by a single Hound / It's own identity."

Carlo was Emily Dickinson's companion for 16 years, dying in the winter of 1865–66. She sent this terse death notice to Higginson, "Carlo died—E. Dickinson. Would you instruct me now?" According to Habegger, "Carlo's death marked the end of something for Dickinson, who, in summer 1866, admitted to Higginson 'I explore but little since my mute Confederate [died]'" (My Wars, 497–498).

See also GOULD, GEORGE HENRY.

FURTHER READING

Alfred Habegger, My Wars, 226, 497–498; Richard B. Sewall, Life, 5, 271, 331, 420n, 497, 512, 515–516, 522n. 542, 578, 634, and 678.

circumference, circumference poems   Among the key words in Dickinson's poetry, *circumference* occurs in 17 poems: Fr 233 (J 313), Fr 610 (J 354), Fr 633 (J 78), Fr 653 (J 515), Fr 571 (J 533) (unfinished draft), Fr 669 (J 552), Fr 601 (J 633), Fr 853 (J 798), Fr 858 (J 802), Fr 930 (J 883), Fr 1067 (J 889), Fr 890 (J 943), Fr 833 (J 967), Fr 1099 (J 1084), Fr 1297 (J 1343), Fr 1636 (J 1620), and Fr 1730 (J 1663) (Rosenbaum, *Concordance*). But perhaps the most famous instance of the poet's idiosyncratic usage of the word occurs in a letter she sent to her mentor, THOMAS WENTWORTH HIGGINSON in 1862: "Perhaps you smile at me. I could not stop for that—my business is circumference—" (L 268).

Dickinson wrote this during her most productive and inspired period, as a poet who would not be deterred from her task, even if others ridiculed her. Her use of the word "circumference" to describe the business of poetry expresses a belief that the periphery of the circle is the poet's proper domain. The term contains two concepts that were central to her idea of poetry. The first is slantness: the poet cannot reach the "center," that is, the Truth of human experience, head on, but must circle around it, exploring it indirectly from varying perspectives. She sometimes uses the word *circuit* to express this aspect of circumference. (See "TELL ALL THE TRUTH BUT TELL IT SLANT—.") The second meaning has to do with limitation: Circumference is the outer limit of the circle of human experience, the boundary separating what is knowable from what is unknowable. While recognizing the existence of such a boundary, the poet's "business" is to explore the far limits of what can be known, reaching within herself and employing all the resources of language to stretch that boundary a bit further. This is the role of the poet in the 1863 poem "I saw no Way—The Heavens were stitched—" (Fr 633), where she concludes:

> I touched the Universe—
>
> And back it slid—and I alone
> Went out upon Circumference—
> Beyond the Dip of Bell—

The poet is a solitary, intrepid explorer clinging to the perimeter of the circle/globe and peering out into the vast, unknown Universe.

In a famous 1865 "Circumference" poem, "THE POETS LIGHT BUT LAMPS," she uses the word to signify the essence of what the poet has discovered and embodied in her work. Here, poems are "Lamps," whose lasting "vital" light is disseminated differently by each age:

> Each Age a Lens
> Disseminating their
> Circumference—
>
> (Fr 930)

Similarly, in a famous quatrain of 1884, "Circumference" is addressed as "Thou Bride of Awe"—the prize itself, the "truth," which the poet has "dared to covet" (Fr 1636).

"Circumference" is wed to the "Awe" of the unknowable, and any poet/knight who aspires to possess her, that is, to draw her into the realm of the knowable, is himself possessed by her. The poet's imagination becomes one with the limits of what can be humanly perceived.

Like the meaning of all the key words Dickinson uses, the meaning of "Circumference" varies from poem to poem and must be interpreted within specific contexts. Sometimes, as in "A COFFIN IS A SMALL DOMAIN," she uses it in relation to death, which, like poetry, stands on the boundary line separating the knowable from the unknowable. Dickin-

son was obsessed by the transition from life to death, and some of her greatest poems are dedicated to the attempt to insinuate the imagination into what follows that transition (see "BECAUSE I COULD NOT STOP FOR DEATH—," and "I HEARD A FLY BUZZ—WHEN I DIED—"). But the boundary can never be fully overcome, leaving the mourner in a state of "Circumference without Relief—/ Or Estimate—or End—." The boundary of human perception is thus a place of transcendence *and* limitation, exhilaration *and* defeat.

Unlike the romantic poets and transcendentalists in the tradition of Ralph Waldo Emerson, Dickinson did not believe that humanity was capable of fully transcending material reality and merging with the sublime reality of God. Her acceptance of the limitations of even the poet's heightened ability to grasp the essential meaning of death and eternity has caused some scholars to view her as a forerunner of the modernist tradition, in which it is no longer possible to speak of unambiguous truth.

See also "CRISIS IS A HAIR" and "I SHOULD HAVE BEEN TOO GLAD, I SEE—."

FURTHER READING

Laura Gribbin, "Emily Dickinson's Circumference: Figuring a Blind Spot in the Romantic Tradition," *Emily Dickinson Journal*, 1–21; and Joseph Raab, "The Metapoetic Element in Dickinson," in *Handbook*, Grabher et al., eds., 273–295.

Coleman, Eliza M. (Mrs. John Langdon Dudley) (1832–1871) A close girlhood friend and admirer, as well as a distant cousin, Eliza was the daughter of LYMAN COLEMAN and MARIA FLYNT COLEMAN of Monson, a cousin of Emily's mother. Eliza was 12 when her family moved to AMHERST, where Dr. Coleman was principal of AMHERST ACADEMY between 1844 and 1846; he was Emily's German teacher at the academy. Although Eliza and Emily enjoyed a regular and enduring correspondence, none of their letters to one another have survived. There are, however, frequent mentions of Eliza in the poet's letters to others. Her name turns up to report a letter received from her, a visit with her, the interest shown in her by a certain law student of EDWARD DICKINSON's named John Emerson.

Eliza was prophetically described by an early acquaintance as "a beautiful and accomplished girl but [one who] is I fear destined to an early death." (Leyda, *Years and Hours*, 252). Like her older sister Olivia, remembered as a "real beauty," who died suddenly at age 20 of "galloping consumption" while riding in a carriage, Eliza suffered all her life from tuberculosis. Olivia died on September 28, 1847, in Princeton, New Jersey, where Dr. Coleman was teaching at the College of New Jersey (now Princeton), two days before Emily left for MOUNT HOLYOKE FEMALE SEMINARY. Six weeks later, she writes to her close friend ABIAH PALMER ROOT that Eliza has written her "a long letter giving me an account of [her sister Olivia's] death, which is beautiful and affecting" (L 18, November 6, 1847). Scholars have suggested that Dickinson's poem "BECAUSE I COULD NOT STOP FOR DEATH—", with its vision of the *transitus*, the moment of dying, as a carriage ride with Death, is based on the circumstances of Olivia's death.

Eliza's loving understanding of the poet comes through in the letter she wrote, on October 4, 1854, to Emily's frequent companion and distant cousin, JOHN LONG GRAVES: "*Emilie* . . . sends me beautiful letters and each one makes me love her more. I know you appreciate her & I think few of her Amherst friends do. They wholly misinterpret her, I believe—" (Leyda, *Years and Hours*, 319). Biographer Richard B. Sewall speculates that this may have been a "polite way of saying that they would not respond with the intensity she apparently demanded of everyone" (*Life*, II, 518). Eliza's own precarious health, the early death of her sister, and the sword continually hanging over her own head must have imbued her with a poignant sense of mortality akin to the poet's. Even in the mid-1850s, Dickinson "could see death lurking in Eliza Coleman's febrile beauty . . ." (Wolff, *Emily Dickinson*, 135).

Eliza stayed with the Dickinsons during the painful AMHERST COLLEGE commencement of August 1854, when HENRY VAUGHAN EMMONS, with whom Emily had shared an intimate and invigorating "literary friendship," graduated and left Amherst. Eliza showed her sensitivity to Emily's emotional turmoil (which may also have been related to a quarrel with

SUSAN HUNTINGTON GILBERT (DICKINSON), by making, in Emily's Bible, a pencil bracket around the eight verses of Psalm 121, which begins, "I will lift up mine eyes unto the hills, from whence cometh my help" (Habegger, *My Wars*, 319). When Eliza left, the poet wrote to Graves: "Eliza went yesterday morning. I miss her thoughtful eyes . . ." (L 170).

The following year, the Colemans were living in Philadelphia, where Dr. Coleman had taken over as head of Philadelphia's Presbyterian Academy, the school of choice for the denomination's "families of position." As Emily and her sister LAVINIA made preparations for their monthlong trip to Washington, D.C., and Philadelphia, Emily wrote to Sue: "Eliza writes every day and seems impatient for us" (L 178, 28 Feb 1855). The two-week stay with the Colemans proved a momentous one, for it was then that Emily met the REVEREND CHARLES WADSWORTH, the charismatic minister of the Arch Street Presbyterian Church. The poet began a long, furtive correspondence with Wadsworth, with whom she may have been in love and who is one of the leading candidates for "Master."

If Eliza was privy to the details of Emily's relationship with Wadsworth, she would likely have guarded them fiercely. Emily's confidence in Eliza as a protector is expressed in a letter she wrote to her cousins LOUISE AND FRANCES NORCROSS, after their mother died. Alluding to Eliza's having chaperoned the girls at commencement that August, she wrote: "I knew she would guard my children, as she has often guarded me, from publicity, and help fill the deep place never to be full" (L 225, mid-September 1860).

Eliza had come to that year's commencement on the arm of her fiancé, John Langdon Dudley, whom she introduced to Emily at that time. The couple were married on June 16, 1861, and lived for a while in Middletown, Connecticut, where Vinnie and Emily, despite the latter's dislike of travel, made brief visits to them during the early years of Austin and Sue's marriage. John Dudley became one of the most successful and controversial preachers of his day; he served as minister in Middletown until 1868, when he accepted a pulpit in Milwaukee. Habegger suggests (*My Wars*, 56) that Emily may have written her 1864 poem: "SHE

ROSE TO HIS REQUIREMENT—DROPT," for Eliza, who took on "the honorable Work/ Of Woman, and of Wife—" to a dynamic and demanding man.

If she managed to carry the burdens of marriage and motherhood, however, Eliza's health remained fragile. "Eliza wrote last week, faint note in pencil—dressed in blankets, and propped up, having been so sick—," Emily reports to the Norcross cousins in early February 1863 (L 279). In 1867 the Norcross cousins were staying with the sickly Eliza in Middletown, Connecticut, while her husband was in Europe and there was no male protector in the house. The discovery of a strange man under a bed on July 2, an incident that was reported in the *Hartford Courant* and soon reached Emily, prompted a letter to the cousins in which she called Eliza "the lamb, who shared her fleece with a timider, even Emily"—a reference to the way Eliza had protected her from dreaded publicity during Amherst commencements.

The Norcross cousins were again on the scene, offering their domestic and nursing services, when Eliza's health took a precipitous dive in the spring of 1870. The situation took on a double poignancy when Eliza's parents came to see their daughter once more; Mrs. Coleman, also a consumptive, took a sudden turn for the worse and died on January 11, 1871. She was soon followed by her only surviving daughter, who, pitifully wasted by her disease, died on June 3, 1871, at the age of 39. "Eliza was not with us, but it was owing to the trains. We know she meant to come. Oh! Cruel Paradise," Emily wrote in a letter to Louisa Norcross, speaking of the commencement just passed (L 362, mid-July 1871). Shortly after Eliza's death, her widower married Marion V. Churchill, a "strikingly progressive journalist and poet half his age" (Habegger, *My Wars*, 544).

The year of Eliza's death, Dickinson wrote the great elegiac poem that begins:

> Whatever it is—she has tried it—
> Awful Father of Love—
> Is not Ours the chastising—
> Do not chastise the Dove—
>
> (Fr 1200, J 1204)

Biographer Cynthia Griffin Wolff, who believes the poem was written for Eliza, points to the "elo-

quent, matter-of-fact directness" with which "unknowable, unavoidable death is greeted with the dignity of supreme resignation" (*Emily Dickinson*, 497). The blameless purity Dickinson associated with her friend finds expression once more, in a letter she wrote to the Norcross cousins the following year: "While I write, dear children, the colors Eliza loved quiver on the pastures, and day goes gay to the northwest, innocent as she" (L 372, early May 1872).

FURTHER READING

Alfred Habegger, *My Wars*, 56, 319; Jay Leyda, *Years and Hours*, I, 252, 319; Richard B. Sewall, *Life*, II, 518; Cynthia Griffin Wolff, *Emily Dickinson*, 135, 497.

Coleman, Lyman (1796–1882) and **Maria Flynt** (1801–1871) The Colemans were friends of the Dickinsons and parents of ELIZA M. COLEMAN, a longtime friend of the poet. Maria Flynt, who came from Monson, was a cousin of Emily's mother, EMILY NORCROSS DICKINSON, and the two cousins attended the same girls' school in New Haven, Connecticut. There were other early links between the Dickinsons and the Colemans: Lyman was a tutor at Yale when Emily's father, EDWARD DICKINSON, was a student there. When Edward was courting his future wife, he told her she could turn to Lyman as a character reference for him. And when Lyman was courting Maria, Emily Norcross wrote with arch amusement of his frequent trips from Belchertown, where he lived, to visit Maria in Monson: "We consider Mr. Coleman almost a resident. I imagine he thinks cousin Maria would make but little progress in her favorite study, divinity, without frequent lectures" (Vivian R. Pollak, ed., *A Poet's Parents*, 37).

By the time Lyman brought his family to AMHERST in 1844, to become principal of AMHERST ACADEMY, he had been a tutor at Yale, a minister at Belchertown, and an instructor in boys' schools. He had also pursued advanced studies in Germany. When he assumed his duties at the academy, the school was going through a turbulent period: The young and largely inexperienced teaching staff was in constant flux; the curriculum was prone to frequent, radical change; the prestige of the school was declining and students were transferring to rival schools. Lyman's predecessor as principal was a young man named Jeremiah Taylor, who had just graduated from AMHERST COLLEGE and who remained at the academy for only a year. The 48-year-old Coleman was determined to institute reforms but appears to have been misguided in his efforts. In a school where the female preceptress played an essential role for the female students, he attempted to do without one, hiring, instead, a young lady assistant.

His duties were heavy; in addition to running the academy, he taught German and Greek at the college, where Emily became his student during a semester when she was obliged to stay at home: "I don't go to school this winter except to a recitation in German. Mr. C has a very large class, and father thought I might never have another opportunity to study it," she wrote to her friend ABIAH PALMER ROOT (L 9, January 12, 1846).

Lyman Coleman's tenure at the academy was weakened, and eventually cut short, by his anxiety for the health of his older daughter Olivia, a beautiful and accomplished young woman, who suffered from tuberculosis, or "consumption," as it was then known. In March 1846 the desire to remove her from the severe New England climate prompted him to resign from the academy and accept a teaching position at the College of New Jersey (now Princeton). His efforts on behalf of Olivia proved fruitless: Olivia died suddenly, the following year, on September 28, 1847, at age 20, while on a carriage ride. It was the tragedy of the tall, good-looking, ruddy Coleman to outlive both his frail, beautiful, consumptive, daughters and his consumptive wife. Maria Coleman died on January 11, 1871, while visiting her dying daughter Eliza in Milwaukee. Eliza soon followed her mother, dying on June 3, 1871, at the age of 39. Lyman, who had found his teaching niche at Lafayette College, in Easton, Pennsylvania in 1861, as professor of ancient languages, spent the rest of his professional career there.

FURTHER READING

Alfred Habegger, *My Wars*, 144–147; Vivian R. Pollak, *Poet's Parents*, 37.

Congregationalism   The religion through which Dickinson's PURITAN HERITAGE came down to her, its name is based upon the structural principle that each congregation, or local church, has free control of its own affairs. Jesus alone is recognized as the head of each local congregation, which is joined to fellow congregations as members of one common family under God.

The movement, which grew out of what was originally called Puritanism, began in the 16th century as a revolt against the Church of England, when Robert Browne published the first theoretical exposition of Congregational principles in 1582. The first Congregational churches were established very early in the 17th century in Gainsborough and Scrooby, England, but were forced into exile in Holland by government persecution. The Pilgrims who carried Congregationalism to America in 1620 were members of the congregation in Holland, originally of Scrooby, led by John Robinson. The established church of the Massachusetts Bay Colony, Congregationalism flourished in New England. In 1648 in the Cambridge Platform, a summary of principles of church government and discipline was drawn up. Congregationalists took a leading part in the Great Awakening (see REVIVALISM) that, in New England, was started in 1734 by the preaching of JONATHAN EDWARDS. As the country expanded, Congregational churches were established in the newly opened frontier regions.

During the early part of the 19th century, when the UNITARIAN secession of more than 100 churches, centered in eastern Massachusetts, threatened to divide the denomination, Amherst remained a bastion of traditionalism. Like other Congregationalist churches in the CONNECTICUT RIVER VALLEY, the FIRST CHURCH OF CHRIST of Amherst defended a Trinitarian orthodoxy grounded in the tenets of the official Westminster Confession of 1680: divine sovereignty, original sin, justification by faith in Christ's atoning work at Calvary, and the role of grace, the inward force capable of converting and sanctifying the soul.

Emily Dickinson attended the First Church, which was an integral part of her community, until she was 29, but never made the public declaration of accepting Christ, a ceremony then known as "conversion", which would have allowed her to become a full-fledged member of the church. Her inability to do so, at a time when many of her friends and family did, was long a source of anguish to her. The language and concepts of the religion of her fathers were integral to her poetry, primarily as the source against which she defined her unique spirituality.

FURTHER READING

Jane Donahue Eberwein. "'Graphicer for Grace': Emily Dickinson's Calvinist Language"; Rowena Revis Jones, "A Royal Seal: Dickinson's Rite of Baptism"; A. A. Rouner, Jr., *The Congregational Way of Life* (1960).

Connecticut River Valley Dickinson's native town of AMHERST is situated in the center of this fertile western Massachusetts region. The area's original European settlers came to the Wethersfield area of Connecticut in 1635, traveling upriver the following year to found the town of Springfield, Massachusetts. Dickinson's ancestors NATHANIEL AND ANN GULL DICKINSON were among the dissident group of Wethersfield settlers who followed their minister, Reverend John Russell, and helped found the town of Hadley, east of Northampton, in 1659. This area was the site of savage warfare between the English settlers and Native American tribes, in which several Dickinson ancestors participated. Amherst was carved out of Hadley's eastern section a century later, in 1755. The Dickinsons flourished in the Connecticut River Valley, becoming one of the most numerous families in the region.

From the 17th century until Emily Dickinson's day, the region was characterized by a spirit of orthodoxy that formed the bedrock of her PURITAN HERITAGE. Two generations before JONATHAN EDWARDS launched the First Great Awakening in Northampton in 1740, the first of several waves of religious REVIVALS that would sweep the region over the next 130 years, his grandfather Solomon Stoddard waged an impassioned battle against the liberal tendencies he saw as menacing the true faith. In Dickinson's day, the Connecticut Valley remained a bastion of orthodox

CONGREGATIONALISM, as opposed to the religious liberalism that took the form of UNITARIANISM in the eastern part of Massachusetts.

Inherent in Edwards's brand of orthodoxy was an assertion of the sublimity and self-reliance of the soul in its struggle against worldly temptation and deception. This orientation expressed itself in the independence that characterized the region's political history as well. As the rebellion of the colonies against England gathered steam, the majority of Connecticut Valley towns were initially cautious about participating in military conflict. Shortly after independence was won, western Massachusetts became the site of Shays's Rebellion of 1786–87, the armed revolt of farmers against what they viewed as discriminatory economic practices resulting in the loss of their farms to Boston bankers.

In addition to its religious and political distinctiveness, the Connecticut River Valley was renowned for its physical beauty. Nineteenth-century American lithographers delighted in natural vistas such as the Ox-Bow of the Connecticut River at Northampton and the view from Mount Tom in Holyoke, as well as picturesque rural and village scenes. Washington Irving, writing in 1832, shortly after Dickinson was born, wrote, "I have had a most delightful excursion along the enchanting Valley of the Connecticut. . . . It is a perfect stream for a poet."

An address by EDWARD HITCHCOCK, renowned botanist, geologist, and one of Dickinson's influential teachers, is imbued with the lyricism the region inspired in her day:

> How rich the slopes of yonder distant mountains, that bound the Connecticut Valley on either side! How striking Mount Sugar Loaf on the north, with its red belted and green-tufted crown; and Mount Toby too, with its imposing outline of unbroken forest! Especially, how beautifully and even majestically does the indented summit of Mount Holyoke repose against the southern sky! What sunrises and sunsets do we here witness. . . . (*The Highest Use of Learning: An Address delivered at his Inauguration to the Presidency of Amherst College.* Amherst, Mass., 1845)

Dickinson loved the land and wrote passionately of it: "This—is the land—the Sunset washes—/ These—are the Banks of the Yellow Sea—" (Fr 297). In a poem of 1863, she addresses her "SWEET MOUNTAINS—YE TELL ME NO LIE—/ Never deny Me—/ Never fly" (Fr 745). She calls these unvarying presences in her life "My Strong Madonnas." Asking them to cherish "The Wayward Nun—beneath the Hill," she offers them a form of "Worship": "When the Day/ Fades from the Firmament Away—To lift her Brows on You." When she speaks of seeing "New Englandly," she is referring to *her* part of New England and affirming the centrality of the Connecticut Valley's natural life to her vision of the world. "Without the Snow's Tableau/ Winter were lie—to me—/Because I see—New Englandly" (Fr 256).

FURTHER READING

Edmund Delaney, *The Connecticut River: New England's Historic Waterway;* James C. O'Connell, *The Pioneer Valley Reader: Prose and Poetry from New England's Heartland.*

D

definition poems Dickinson's numerous definition poems may be viewed as a subcategory of what biographer Richard B. Sewall calls her "wisdom pieces." Comprising fully half her canon, these consist of "thoughts on life and living, sometimes exhortations, sometimes warnings, sometimes pure clinical analyses, as in her anatomizings of hope . . ." (*Life,* II, 712). From her first effort in this genre, "EXULTATION IS THE GOING" (1860), to what may have been her last, "A Letter is a joy of Earth—," (1885), Dickinson composed definition poems throughout her writing life. By far the greatest number were written after 1863. By the late 1860s they were a regular feature of her work and would continue to be so until her death.

For the poet, who once told her new correspondent, THOMAS WENTWORTH HIGGINSON, that her sole companion was her "Lexicon," the well-worn Webster's Dictionary she read as others might read a novel, the notion of a definition was clearly appealing. And yet Dickinson's is the poetry of anti-definition. As she remarks in one poem, "The Definition of Beauty is/ That Definition is none—" (Fr 797). The very essence of her poetics is a slantwise telling that works against a single, simple definition of the fundamental human emotions and experiences that are the subject of these poems. Thus, when Dickinson defines, she does so as the poet she was, through metaphor. Most often she defines an abstract noun with concrete language, turning idea into picture. Thus "Exultation is the

going / Of an inland soul to sea—" and "FOREVER— IS COMPOSED OF NOWS." In one of her most powerful definition poems, "Presentiment—is that long shadow—on the Lawn—/ Indicative that Suns go down—". Elsewhere, we learn that "Revolution is the Pod / Systems rattle from" (Fr 1044); "Experiment to me / Is every one I meet" (Fr 1081); and "All Circumstances are the Frame / In which His Face is set" (Fr 1113). As these examples suggest, more often than not the definitions themselves, dense and mysterious, require defining.

Frequently, what is being defined is an emotion, as in "GRIEF IS A MOUSE—" and "'HOPE' IS THE THING WITH FEATHERS—." Although the lyric "I" is missing from these poems, they are anything but cold or impersonal. The power and authenticity of the defining images convey a sense of lived, often anguished, experience, In this sense, the definition poems represent one of the strategies Dickinson discovered for "telling it slant," both revealing the emotional essence of her experience and cloaking the specific circumstances.

Scholar Judith Farr, who has written extensively on the influence of 19th-century American painting on Dickinson, finds a connection between the definition poems and the emblem tradition in British art, transmitted by the Puritans to the New England of her day. She writes:

The emblem writers/engravers . . . were noteworthy for giving symbolic expression to moral proverbs, adages, ideas, or beliefs. They would print a quatrain about hope, for example, illustrating it with the picture of a woman holding aloft an anchor. Such a poem as "Exultation is the going. . . ." with its boats, headlands, and symbolic traveler could be similarly seen to define by illustration ("Dickinson and the Visual Arts," 64).

See also "A COFFIN IS A SMALL DOMAIN," "CRISIS IS A HAIR," "CRUMBLING IS NOT AN INSTANT'S ACT," "EDEN IS THAT OLD FASHIONED HOUSE," "REMORSE—IS MEMORY—AWAKE—," and "RENUNCIATION IS A PIERCING VIRTUE—."

FURTHER READING

Judith Farr, "Dickinson and the Visual Arts," in *Handbook*, Grabher et al., eds., 64; Cristanne Miller, *Grammar*, 40–41: Richard B. Sewall, *Life*, II, 712; Robert Weisbuch, "Prisming," in *Handbook*, Grabher et al., eds., 216; Cynthia Wolfe, *Emily Dickinson*, 476.

Dickinson, Edward (1803–1874) The poet's father was born on New Year's Day, 1803, in AMHERST, where he would spend his entire life. Edward was the eldest of nine children, five boys and four girls, born to SAMUEL FOWLER and LUCRETIA GUNN DICKINSON. Squire Dickinson, as Samuel was called, bequeathed his first son a double heritage: on the one hand, a social and civic prominence based on his numerous contributions to town life, notably including the founding of AMHERST ACADEMY and AMHERST COLLEGE; on the other, a degree of financial insecurity and insolvency that had a profound influence on the ambitious young man as he launched himself into the world.

Edward took his secondary education at Amherst Academy, as Emily later would, and went on to college at Yale. After one semester, however, Samuel's financial problems necessitated a change of plans: Edward must sell his furniture and come home. After attending Amherst College during the year of its founding, Edward was able to return to Yale, when his father's fortune rebounded. He had to drop out a second time for the same reason, but was at last able to complete his undergraduate years at Yale, where he found a larger and more stimulating world than he had known in Amherst and enjoyed the companionship of talented classmates. An average student, when he graduated in 1823 he was offered only the last, relatively unprestigious commencement speech, a "dialogue" in which seven other graduates participated.

After reading law in his father's law office, and studying at the Northampton Law School, he was admitted to the Hampshire County Bar in 1826. Biographer Alfred Habegger notes, "This was a trying period for the young man, whose struggle to enter the world was jinxed by his father's growing troubles. What we see crystallizing is a certain kind of uncommunicative hardness, a principled severity based on determination and the shock of seeing what goes wrong when the man of the house proves an inadequate protector" (*My Wars*, 18).

Edward Dickinson, the poet's father, in 1853. This is his only extant photograph. *(By permission of the Houghton Library, Harvard University)*

Samuel had neglected his legal practice in his zeal to develop Amherst College, investing his personal funds in the project, as well. By 1833, he had lost The HOMESTEAD, the family mansion he had built in 1813, and the family broke up. Most of the children scattered widely, while Samuel, his wife, and two youngest daughters went into "exile" in Cincinnati, hoping to make a new life.

While his father's family was disintegrating, Edward was busy creating a new family of his own. In the winter of 1826, he met EMILY NORCROSS (DICKINSON), daughter of the leading citizen of Monson, 20 miles south of Amherst, where Edward was serving as a marshal in a military court. Seventy of the courtship letters he sent her during six months of correspondence have survived and offer a revealing look into his nature. "My life must be a life of business, of labor and application to the study of my profession," he wrote in the letter in which he proposed to her. Although he liked "the battle of business," he was more than a mere fortune hunter and was idealistic about law as a means of promoting the social good. He wrote, "Let us prepare for a life of rational happiness. I do not expect, neither do I desire a life of *pleasure*, as some call it—I anticipate pleasure from engaging with my whole soul in my business . . . and with my dearest friend. . . . May we be happy, useful, & successful." Biographer Richard B. Sewall observes that, rather than a dour Puritan as he has often been painted, Edward was a "typical success-oriented, work-oriented citizen of expansionist America," and "a child of the Enlightenment," who believed in Reason and social progress through good works and the improvement of social institutions (*Life,* I, 44).

To what degree his future wife shared these sentiments cannot be gleaned from her brief, infrequent letters, which dwelt on her daily domestic affairs. Never much of a letter-writer, Emily Norcross answered his daily letters only once a month. After accepting his proposal, she contrived to postpone the wedding plans to the point of testing Edward's patience. On May 6, 1828, they married, according to her wishes, in a quiet ceremony in Amherst. At the same time, Samuel went bankrupt, and the young couple learned they did not

Edward Dickinson, the poet's father, painted in 1840, when he was 37, by O. A. Bullard *(By permission of the Houghton Library, Harvard University)*

have secure possession to their new home, whose title Samuel owned. Rallying from what must have been a great shock, Edward began working on various real estate deals and, by 1830, on the eve of the poet's birth, succeeded in buying the west half of the Homestead from Samuel. As time went on, he would prosper, taking care not to repeat his father's errors. Although he sold his half of the Homestead in 1840 and moved his family to a house on North Pleasant Street, he would buy back all of it in 1855. But his early financial stresses injected an atmosphere of anxiety into the life of the growing family, which now included WILLIAM AUSTIN DICKINSON, born in 1829, and Emily, born in 1830. A third child, LAVINIA NORCROSS DICKINSON, would arrive in 1833.

Inheriting the mantle of "squire" from his now disgraced father, "a role that mixed property, privilege, and responsibility in a way that was starting to look archaic" (Habegger, 505). Edward followed in his father's devotion to public causes, without, however, sacrificing his law career or endangering

The Homestead in 1858. In April 1855, Edward Dickinson moved his family back to the family mansion, where the poet was born. *(The Todd-Bingham Picture Collectiion. Yale University Library)*

his personal fortune. During the 48 years that he practiced law, he became Amherst's leading citizen, participating in virtually every civic project of any importance. He became treasurer of Amherst College in 1835 and served until his resignation in 1872. He was a lifelong trustee of Amherst Academy. In the 1860s he succeeded in bringing Massachusetts Agricultural College to Amherst. Deeply involved in local affairs, he frequently served as moderator of the Town Meeting and was active in the Parish Committee of the FIRST CHURCH OF CHRIST, the Temperance Society, the Hampshire Colonization Society, the Agricultural Society, and the board of the Northampton Lunatic Asylum.

When Amherst suffered a disastrous fire in July 1851, Edward took charge. Emily wrote to Austin: "after the whole day was over, they gave 'three cheers for Edward Dickinson, and three more for the Insurance Company'!" (L49). He was an organizer of and shareholder in the Amherst and Belchertown Railroad. When this 19-mile line opened in 1853, bringing a crowd up from New London to celebrate, Emily wrote to Austin:

Father was as usual, Chief Marshal of the day, and went marching around the town with New London at his heels like some old Roman General, upon a Triumph Day. . . . (L 127)

The Dickinsons were acknowledged social leaders in Amherst, famous for their annual receptions during the college's commencement week. They hosted many renowned figures and entertained close friends such as JUDGE OTIS PHILLIPS LORD, ELIZABETH AND JOSIAH HOLLAND, and SAMUEL BOWLES. Indicative of the preeminence and respect in which "Squire Dickinson" was held in his hometown, during his funeral the shops closed and all business was suspended in his honor.

By the late 1830s, Edward had begun following his father's lead by engaging in state politics, becoming a representative in the General Court of Massachusetts in 1838–39. He entered the national political arena as a delegate to the National Whig Convention in Baltimore in 1852. The following year, at the peak of his political career, he was elected by a narrow margin as a representative to the 33rd Congress, serving from 1853–55 as a one-term Whig. The Whig Party, to which Abraham Lincoln had belonged, dissolved in the late 1850s,

The law offices of Edward and Austin Dickinson were housed on the second floor of this building on the Paler Block. *(Courtesy of the Jones Library, Inc., Amherst, Massachusetts)*

when its urban stronghold was usurped by the short-lived "Know-Nothing" Party with its anti-Catholic and anti-immigrant platform. In the 1854 elections, when all Whigs were swept from office, Edward lost his bid for reelection by a substantial margin. Unwilling to switch his allegiance to the newly formed Republican Party, primarily to keep slavery quarantined off in the South, Edward, who was antislavery but also pro-states' rights, isolated himself and ended his national political career.

In 1874 he again represented his district in the General Court of Massachusetts, in order to bring a larger railroad line to Amherst, since one of his passions was to link Amherst to other parts of the region and state. He died on June 16, 1874, in Boston, while attending the legislative session. The cause of death was given as "apoplexy," although his family believed it was the morphine administered to him that killed him.

In her "tender eulogy" his wife said simply, "I loved him so." Yet Edward Dickinson was anything but a simple man. Behind the public figure was a tormented private man, particularly in his later years. His relationships to his wife and children were a mixture of affection, concern, and emotional estrangement. "His failing," Samuel Bowles wrote in the *Springfield Republican,* "was he did not understand himself; consequently his misfortune was that others did not understand him. . . ."

The poet, too, is reported to have said, "I am not very well acquainted with father" (Leyda, *Years and Hours,* 482). In a letter to JOSEPH BARDWELL LYMAN, she reveals a moment in which Edward confided his painful awareness of the aridity of his private life: "Father says in fugitive moments when he forgets the barrister & lapses into the man, says that his life has been passed in a wilderness or on an island—of late he says on an island." (*Lyman Letters,* 70). She wrote to her cousins, LOUISE AND FRANCES NORCROSS, when he was ill and seemed to have lost the will to live, "You know, he never played, and the straightest engine has its leaning hour" (spring 1871, L 360). In truth, Edward *did* sometimes play; he went to concerts, took walks with his family, entertained friends, laughed at his son's letters. His poetic side is revealed in the incident of October 1851, when Edward was among the first to notice the spectacular display of colorful northern lights in the sky above Amherst and rang the church bell to call the townspeople's attention to it (L 53).

But his pervasive sense of life was somber. In an 1851 letter, Emily told Austin:

> We don't *have* many jokes tho' *now*, it is pretty much all sobriety, and we do not have much poetry, father having made up his mind that its pretty much all *real life*. Fathers real life and *mine* sometimes come into collision, but as yet, escape unhurt! (L 65)

There can be no doubt that he loved his wife and children, though his affection often took the form of a controlling anxiety that could be oppressive to them. He was often away on business and sent his wife messages that must have stressed as much as they soothed: "Keep your doors all safely locked, nights, tho' nothing is going to harm you." He believed that his wife exposed herself to needless risks, while she believed he worried too much. (Habegger, *My Wars*, 112–113). He was particularly worried about Emily's frail health and wrote her, "You must not go to school, when it is cold or bad going—You must be very careful, & not get sick."

Edward could be an irresistible force, as when he relentlessly plied his children with medicines. He had a temper and would argue vociferously with Austin. Some have attributed his failure to become a full member of the church by publicly accepting Christ until he was 47, during the 1850 revival, to a stubborn unwillingness to humble himself completely. He had the "almost pathological undemonstrativeness of [a] late-Puritan" (Sewall, *Life*, I, 61). Bending over his father's coffin, Austin kissed him on the forehead and is reported to have said, "There, father, I never dared do that while you were living." After meeting him during his first visit to Emily, THOMAS WENTWORTH HIGGINSON described him in a letter to his wife as "thin dry & speechless," but speculated that he "was not severe . . . but remote."

In his attitude toward women Edward Dickinson was less than progressive for his own time and a chauvinist by current standards. He was deeply interested in education for women and sent both daughters to postsecondary school seminaries. But he believed that women's sphere of action was totally different from men's, if just as important. His daughter Emily clearly resented the way he lionized Austin's literary gifts while ignoring hers. His strong conviction that women belonged in their homes and churches and decidedly not in public life may have been a factor in the lifestyle Emily adopted and in her shrinking from publication (Habegger, *My Wars*, 50).

The question that Dickinson scholars continue to wrestle with is the degree to which Edward Dickinson "thwarted" his older daughter's life. One school of thought is that he dominated her and was responsible for what is regarded as "the tragedy" of her life. Thus, Clark Griffith, in *The Long Shadow*, and John Cody, in *After Great Pain*, dwell on Edward's pathological side. For Cody, coming from the perspective of psychoanalytic theory, Edward's destructive impact on his daughter was multifaceted: He made her anxious by "exaggerating the malignancy of the world," infantilized her and encouraged her dependency, and increased her preoccupation with death. By disparaging femininity he made her reject her own and take on a masculine identification she could not fully acknowledge, thus preventing her from achieving any satisfying adult sexual orientation (Cody, *After Great Pain*, 101–102).

The legend of Emily Dickinson's dismal home and tyrannical father originated in the later reminiscences of her sister Vinnie, as confided to MABEL LOOMIS TODD and Mary Lee Hall. But Vinnie's tales of an oppressed girlhood in which all suitors were scared away were told when she was old and embittered. They clash not only with her own youthful accounts, but also with many others that indicate a different reality, such as those of family friend Joseph Bardwell Lyman and Edward's granddaughter MARTHA DICKINSON BIANCHI.

Rejecting the most damning interpretations of the father-daughter relationship, Sewall points to Edward's sensitivity in presenting Emily with her "shaggy ally," her dog CARLO, and in creating a nook for her among the trees behind their home, where she could sit out-of-doors unobserved, when her desire for seclusion had advanced. Sewall discerns in Emily an "amused tolerance, a touch of condescension arising from an entirely justified sense of intellectual superiority, a tender devotion that made her delight in serving him in many ways (baking his bread, mending his slippers, playing music for him)" (*Life*, I, 61–62).

From an early age, she was able to define herself in opposition to him and see him from an ironic distance, repeatedly making him the focus of her (mostly) fond but formidable satiric jibes. Along with Austin, she used humor as a defense against his mild authoritarianism, was not intimidated by him, and in some ways she seems to have done what she wished, without directly defying him. Thus, 20-year old Emily describes a confrontation with her irate father in a blithe, humorous tone:

> . . . after tea I went to see Sue—had a nice little visit with her—then went to see Emily Fowler, and arrived home at 9—found Father in great agitation at my protracted stay—and mother and Vinnie in tears, for fear that he would kill me. (L 42, June 8, 1851, to Austin)

She could write:

> Father [is] too busy with his Briefs—to notice what we do—He buys me many Books—but begs me not to read them—because he fears they joggle the Mind. (L 261, to Higginson, April 26, 1862)

Emily Dickinson continued to read her books.

Later she developed a deep pity for his lonely and austere life. Her description of their last afternoon together, to Higginson, in July 1874, reflects the spectrum of her complicated emotions for him:

> The last Afternoon that my Father lived, though with no premonition—I preferred to be with him, and invented an absence for Mother, Vinnie being asleep. He seemed peculiarly pleased as I oftenest stayed with myself, and remarked as the Afternoon withdrew, he "would like it not to end."
>
> His pleasure almost embarrassed me and my Brother coming—I suggested they walk. Next morning I woke him for the train [to Boston]—and saw him no more.
>
> His Heart was pure and terrible and I think no other like it exists.

> I am glad there is Immortality—but would have tested it myself—before entrusting him. (L 418)

Devastated by his death, she stayed in her room during the funeral and did not attend the memorial service. She was shocked at her own reaction, telling her Norcross cousins, "I thought I was strongly built, but this stronger has undermined me. . . . Though it is many nights, my mind never comes home" (L 414). Two years later, she told them, "I dream about father every night, always a different dream, and forget what I am doing daytimes, wondering where he is" (L 559). In death, he remained an immense internal presence, a focus for the great questions about death and immortality that obsessed her. Three years after his death, she wrote:

> Lay this Laurel on the one
> Too intrinsic for Renown—
> Laurel—vail your deathless Tree—
> Him you chasten—that is he—
>
> (Fr 1428)

See also "I LIKE TO SEE IT LAP THE MILES—," JOEL NORCROSS, PURITAN HERITAGE, and REVIVALISM.

FURTHER READING

Martha Dickinson Bianchi, *Face to Face*, 21–24, 63–64, 82–86; Millicent Todd Bingham, *Emily Dickinson's Home: Letters of Edward Dickinson and His Family*; John Cody, *After Great Pain*; 92–103; Alfred Habegger, *My Wars*, 44–50, 93–94, 110–14, 293–294, 344–346; Jay Leyda, *Years and Hours*; Vivian Pollak, *A Poet's Parents*; Richard B. Sewall, *Life*, I, 44–73.

Dickinson, Edward ("Ned") (1861–1898) "Ned" was Emily Dickinson's nephew, the eldest child of her brother WILLIAM AUSTIN DICKINSON and SUSAN GILBERT DICKINSON. He was born on June 19, 1861, during the first year of the Civil War and called "Jackey" or "Union Jack," for the first six months of his life. His mother, who had lost a sister in childbirth, was terrified of giving birth and had tried repeatedly to abort him, a fact she and Austin would later connect with his slow development and

Edward ("Ned") Dickinson, Emily's nephew, suffered from epilepsy and died of angina in May 1898 at age 37. *(By permission of the Houghton Library, Harvard University)*

poor health. He was a difficult baby who cried night and day and raised doubts about his normalcy and survival.

In 1874, he had a serious bout of rheumatic fever, after which the family was continually worried about cardiac complications. Then, at 15, he had the first of the grand mal epileptic seizures that would plague him all his life. Austin's diary records how, while Sue lay terrified in bed, he would run to Ned in the middle of the night and find his son in convulsions. Both parents kept the dread secret from him and tried to create as normal a life as possible for him. He was barred from rough sports but fished, rode horseback, and developed a love of reading. He pursued a partial course at AMHERST COLLEGE, received no grades and did not graduate with his class in 1884. He eventually became a librarian at the college and, in his 30s, became engaged to Alice Hall. But their marriage plans ended when Ned died of heart problems on May 3, 1898, at the age of 37.

When her nephew was born, Emily's first response was jealousy and resentment that Sue was engrossed with the new baby (see Fr 189). But as the child grew, he became a beloved companion, sharing her love of Charles Dickens and George Eliot. His sister, MARTHA DICKINSON BIANCHI, paints a moving picture of their intimacy:

> His love of books kept him near her, and his sense of humor delighted her. He saved all his funniest stories, his gift of mimicry, his power of offhand description for her; and if his Aunt Lavinia went to a neighbor's for an evening chat, Ned was usually to be found in front of the fire with his Aunt Emily, perched on the edge of a stiff-backed chair, the light of the flames flickering over her white dress, her hands crossed for permanence, but in easy position for flight should their talk be broken by an unwelcome knock. (*Face to Face*, 169)

When Ned was 21, he fell passionately in love with the talented, beautiful MABEL LOOMIS TODD, four years his senior, who had recently moved to town with her husband, David. Sue, who had taken the Todds under her social wing, at first encouraged her son's friendship with Mabel, who heedlessly led him on. When Mabel realized the extent of his feelings and severed their relationship, the hurt and embittered young man went to his mother and accused Mabel of seducing and then dropping him, and now going after Austin. The accusation was true, for Mabel and Austin were by then romantically involved. In the feud between his parents, Ned was his mother's staunch ally. When she supported his Aunt Lavinia in her legal suit against the Todds over a strip of Dickinson land the now deceased Austin had wanted to give them, Ned sat beside Vinnie at the trial, his mother's proxy. Sue and Vinnie enjoyed a legal victory, but the stressful trial took its toll, and Ned fell fatally ill the day the decision was handed down.

FURTHER READING

Martha Dickinson Bianchi, *Face to Face*, 167–171; Alfred Habegger, *My Wars*, 430–434, 608, 610, 564–565; Polly Longsworth, *Austin and Mabel*, 160–162; Richard B. Sewall, *Life*, I, 174–175, 189, 192–193; 257.

Dickinson, Emily Norcross (1804–1882)   The poet's mother was the daughter of JOEL and BETSEY

FAY NORCROSS of Monson, Massachusetts, 20 miles south of AMHERST. She was the third child among her six brothers and two sisters. Although her father was a prosperous farmer, businessman and investor, her girlhood was not one of leisure. As the eldest of only two daughters who lived to maturity (her sister Lavinia was eight years younger), she was her mother's mainstay in managing the large Norcross household. Nonetheless, she had a superior education, first attending the coeducational Monson Academy and then a highly regarded girls' boarding school in New Haven, Connecticut, from 1822–23, where she was commended for "punctual attendance, close application, good acquirements, and discreet behavior."

She met EDWARD DICKINSON, a Yale College graduate, in the winter of 1826 in Monson, where he was serving as a marshal in a military court. Edward, who wanted to marry and settle down into a life of "rational happiness," quickly identified her as a suitable mate, informing her that she was "a

Emily Norcross Dickinson, the poet's mother, painted by O. A. Bullard in 1840, when she was 35 *(By permission of the Houghton Library, Harvard University)*

person in whom so many of the female virtues are conspicuous" (Pollak, *A Poet's Parents,* 3). During six months of correspondence, he sent long, serious letters, which she answered with short apologetic ones, centering around her domestic life. Although she failed to respond to either his ideas or affection, he was in love and proposed the following June, offering to make her a "friend" for life. She put him off for a few months and then postponed the wedding for more than a year. On May 6, 1828, according to her wishes, they were married in a small ceremony in Amherst.

Biographer Richard B. Sewall sees the marriage as a happy and successful one, in which both partners naturally adapted to the traditional pattern of dominant husband and submissive wife (*Life,* I, 78). A story exists, perhaps apocryphal, that on the eve of the poet's birth, Mrs. Dickinson had a paper-hanger redo her bedroom, the only time she was known to defy her husband. But whether she was so abject as to seem degraded in the eyes of her children remains an open question. Her granddaughter, MARTHA DICKINSON BIANCHI, characterized her as a "fluttering little mother, always timorous, always anxious" (*Life and Letters,* 10). Certainly, her early life had given her cause for fearfulness. She had lost a baby brother, a young sister, and two brothers in their 20s; one of her brothers and her 52-year-old mother died the year that her first child was born. The new bride gave birth to three children within four years: Austin in April 1829, Emily in December 1830, and Lavinia in February 1833. She was sick after Lavinia's birth for a long time and sent Emily to stay with her sister, LAVINIA NORCROSS, in Monson for a month.

The young Mrs. Dickinson was variously described by acquaintances as "plaintive," "pleasant," and "sweet." Domestic by nature, she seldom left home except for brief visits to relatives in Monson or Boston. Yet she was more sociable than the "mousy" versions of her imply, attending social and community events, contributing her cooking and produce to the annual cattle show, doing good works, and attending church. In 1831 she was the first of the Dickinsons to accept Christ and join the church, and she had her children baptized. As a sign of their desire to be united, she and Edward continued to pray for his conversion, which would not occur until almost 20 years later. She was a fanatical housekeeper, who loved gardening and prepared excellent meals for her family. The poet once wrote, "My mother does not care for thought" (L 261). Although Mrs. Dickinson did read occasionally, she was inexpressive and hated writing letters, a trait the family joked about good-humoredly. This is one reason we know so little about her.

During Edward's frequent business trips, when she grew anxious about the children, his letters exhort her not to overdo and exhaust herself. Edward's protectiveness and his wife's vulnerability led to a family pattern of "sparing" Mrs. Dickinson "unnecessary" cares. This may explain the poet's revelation to THOMAS WENTWORTH HIGGINSON in 1870, "I never had a mother. I suppose a mother is one to whom you hurry when you are troubled" (L 324b). In 1874, she developed this theme of motherlessness: "I always ran Home to Awe when a child, if anything befell me. He was an awful Mother, but I liked him better than none" (L 405).

Was Dickinson exaggerating when she said she had no mother or was she recognizing a fundamental reality of her emotional life? For psychoanalytic critic John Cody, there is no doubt that Mrs. Dickinson was a failure as a mother to Emily, whose "voracious love-hunger" was never satisfied. In Cody's reconstruction, Emily felt cruelly rejected by her mother, grew up in repressed bitterness toward her, failed to make a proper female identification with this weak, uninspiring figure and identified with the males in her life, instead, and consequently never had a satisfying sex life. While none of this can be "proven," there are probably elements of truth in Cody's picture of Mrs. Dickinson's emotional inadequacy. Sewall remarks that, if Cody's description is true, "it makes of her life with her mother even more of a triumph of self-discipline, humor, patience and (however belated) love" (*Life*, I, 75).

The mother's inability to help her daughter in times of emotional need was evident when, in 1855, the family moved from the Pleasant Street house where they had lived for 15 years to The HOMESTEAD. Both Emily and her mother felt troubled and displaced, but it was the mother's distress

that had precedence. Emily wrote to her friend ELIZABETH LUNA CHAPIN HOLLAND, "Mother has been an invalid since we came *home*, . . . lies upon the lounge or sits in her easy chair, I don't know what her sickness is, for I am but a simple child, and frightened at myself." Mrs. Dickinson became increasingly listless and suffered for several years from a nonspecific illness that caused her family anxiety and added to her daughters' household burdens. The need to care for her mother may well have been a contributing factor in the poet's gradually increasing seclusion in her late 20s.

"God keep me from what they call *households*" (L 36), Emily Dickinson, who is generally assumed to have found her timid mother uninspiring, wrote at 19. But the relationship between mother and daughter was more complex. Like her mother, Emily made her home the stage of her life and eventually immersed herself in cooking, baking, and gardening—domestic skills at which her mother had excelled.

The poet's mother was undoubtedly limited; she had no insight into the inner life of her husband or children. On the other hand, she never tried to interfere with them, and thus may have indirectly spurred the poet's spiritual independence. She was loving and tender toward her children. Her daughter Vinnie summarized, "Father believed and mother loved." After her husband's sudden death, the poet records in a letter to Mrs. Holland, Mrs. Dickinson said, "I loved him so." Emily adds, "Had he a tenderer eulogy?" On June 15, 1875, Mrs. Dickinson suffered a paralytic stroke on the anniversary of her husband's death and, until her death on November 14, 1882, Emily largely assumed the care of the helpless invalid. She required almost constant attention for the last four years of her life. In 1880, Emily wrote to her Norcross cousins a loving account of caring for Mother, "Mother's dear little wants so engross the time,—to read to her, to fan her, to tell her health will come tomorrow, to explain to her *why* the grasshopper is a burden, because he is not so new a grasshopper as he was . . ." (L 666).

After her mother's death, Emily wrote to her friend Elizabeth Holland, "We were never intimate Mother and Children while she was our Mother— but Mines in the same Ground meet by tunneling and when she became our Child, the Affection came" (L792, mid-December 1882). Her letters contain no relief, only shock and grief and a heightened sense of what her mother meant to her. In a poem memorializing her, "To the bright east she flies" (Fr 1603), she characterizes life without her mother as "Homeless at home."

See also JOEL WARREN NORCROSS, SARAH VAILL NORCROSS, REVIVALISM.

FURTHER READING

Martha Dickinson Bianchi, *Face to Face*, 88–89; John Cody, *After Great Pain*, 40–42, 47–54, 66–69, 92–97, 481–490; Alfred Habegger, *My Wars*, 31–63, 70–72, 79–80, 90–93; 110–114, 341–344, 607–608; Vivian R. Pollak, ed., *A Poet's Parents: The Courtship Letters of Emily Norcross and Edward Dickinson*; Richard B. Sewall, *Life*, I, 74–90.

Dickinson, Lavinia Norcross (1833–1899) "One Sister have I in the house—/ And one a hedge away." Emily Dickinson wrote in 1858 (Fr 5). Although the poem becomes a celebration of her sister-in-law, SUSAN HUNTINGTON GILBERT DICKINSON, the "spiritual sister" who inspired many of her poems, the role of her younger sister Lavinia ("Vinnie") in her life and legacy, though different from Sue's, was equally if not more important. The poet's only sister, two years her junior, Lavinia lived with Emily all her life and was thus her closest associate for more than 50 years. She was "the uncomplicated Dickinson," the pragmatic, feisty survivor who ran the household and protected her sister from the unwanted incursions of the outside world. Utterly devoted to Emily during her lifetime, she transferred her fierce loyalty to her poems after Emily's death. Without her unwavering belief in the poems and relentless determination to publish them, Emily Dickinson's poetry might never have become known.

When Lavinia Norcross Dickinson was born, in AMHERST, on February 28, 1833, her household was in a period of stress. Her mother, EMILY NORCROSS DICKINSON, was taking an unusually long time to recuperate from the birth, while her father, EDWARD DICKINSON, was preoccupied with difficult business dealings concerning house owner-

Lavinia ("Vinnie") Norcross Dickinson, Emily's younger sister, in 1852 *(By permission of the Houghton Library, Harvard University)*

ship. To ease the household burden, two-year-old Emily was shipped off to stay for a few months with her mother's younger sister, Aunt LAVINIA NORCROSS, in Monson, where by all accounts she enjoyed a warm, pleasant sojourn with her adoring aunt. While modern concepts of child-rearing would lead us to suspect that such displacement of the older sister upon the arrival of the baby would lead to lifelong hostilities, such was not the case with Emily and Vinnie. There was the usual family bickering, including one recorded incident in which Vinnie told their big brother, WILLIAM AUSTIN, not to believe the stories Emily told about her. But the sisters appear to have been generally nurturing to one another. At first Emily took care of the younger child, but Vinnie, whose health was more robust than her sister's, concerned herself with Emily's welfare early in life.

Within the triangle of siblings, Emily and Austin's natural closeness, based in part on their superior intelligence and mutual literary leanings, made Lavinia the odd woman out. Their affinity with one another was apparent, and Emily once scolded her brother for his too-obvious favoritism. But Vinnie, however pained she was by this situation, was feisty and not easily put down. Once, when Austin complained about her handwriting, she retorted by telling him that *his* was illegible. Nonetheless, the older Dickinson children tended to pigeonhole her and as a matter of course expected her to handle the burden of household matters. This expectation extended even to correspondence; Emily once wrote rather condescendingly to Austin that she would leave "all the matter of 'fact' to our practical sister Vinnie" and reserve for herself the more interesting things to write about.

Vinnie attended AMHERST ACADEMY with Emily, on an intermittent basis, and then was allowed to go to boarding school at Ipswich Female Seminary during the 1849–50 academic year. She was a mediocre student, but a lively and popular one, whose talent for mimicry created much hilarity. Her roommate at Ipswich, Jane Hitchcock, wrote that Vinnie was the one who made life at the stuffy school bearable. While she could not compete with Emily academically, she managed to fulfill one expectation of seminary life that had eluded her sister. In 1850, during a religious REVIVAL, Vinnie converted, that is, publicly declared her acceptance of Christ. She wrote Austin: "At times, I desire religion above all things, & this world seems small indeed. . . . Does Emilie think of these things at all? Oh! That she might!" But Emily had already given a great deal of thought to such things, both as a student at Amherst Academy and at MOUNT HOLYOKE FEMALE SEMINARY and had resisted considerable pressure to make her own declaration of Christian faith.

Vinnie's willingness to convert may have been indicative of a pliant, conventional nature, more prone to give in to social pressures than was her sister's. For the rest of her life was not marked by any special religiosity. When she returned home to Amherst, she led an active social life and had many flirtations and romances. The best-documented of these, and perhaps the most important, was with JOSEPH BARDWELL LYMAN, a school friend of Austin's

from Williston Seminary, who first visited the Dickinson household in the mid-1840s. His surviving letters and diaries, published in 1965 as *The Lyman Letters,* reveal a hitherto unknown Lavinia. As Joseph deepened his intimacy with all the Dickinsons during regular subsequent visits, he became a close "Platonic" friend to Emily and a fond suitor to Vinnie. They were frequently alone together, playing "spoony," as one of Joseph's friends put it, and after Lyman left New England in 1851, he declared that he never forgot her kisses, which he described as "sweeter than anything on Earth." He would write of her repeatedly, in a nostalgic vein, to his fiancée Laura Baker, once recording a snatch of their conversation on his last afternoon in Amherst, at the annual sugaring-off party. In this account, pretty, devoted Vinnie, barely 18, says she wants to be with him, but Joseph holds back, saying that he wants to avoid gossip. Vinnie replies, "I know Joseph, but I love you, and I'm proud of you and of your love. . . ." When he departed for the Deep South a few weeks later, Vinnie writes tersely in her diary, March 26, 1851: "Walked with Joseph. Now he is gone! . . . Had maple Sugar. Joseph has gone, two years is a long time!"

In the picture of Vinnie that emerges from Lyman's letters to Laura, she is warm and pliant, gentle and affectionate. At the same time, however, he condescends to "poor little soft-lipped Vinnie" and plays her down somewhat callously, perhaps to rationalize his harsh rejection of her:

> I was very happy once in Vinnie's arms—very happy. She sat in my lap and pulled the pins from her long soft chestnut hair and tied the long silken mass around my neck and kissed me again & again. . . . Her skin was very soft. Her arms were fat & white, . . . but that was all. Vinnie hasn't brains at all superior. She is a proud, wilful, selfish girl . . . I never thought she would make me a good wife. (*Lyman Letters,* 50–51)

This was disingenuous of Joseph, since he had written to his mother, in 1854, and again in 1855, that he intended to marry her. But his meeting Laura and another remarkable girl, Araminta Wharton, in Nashville, in 1856, apparently altered his perspective. He characterizes Vinnie as unfit to be the wife of a self-made man like himself, since she is "only a 'milk white fawn' . . . who thinks too much of her fine house & carriage & roses. . . ."

Whatever her feelings about Joseph's departure, Vinnie didn't stay home and mope. The girl, whom at 18 Emily described as "*perter* and *more* pert day by day" (to Emily, the word *pert* meant lively, brisk, smart, saucy, bold, and indecorously free) recorded a whirlwind social life in the diary she was given on New Year's Eve 1851. Vinnie's social notes are remarkable, not for any literary value, but for the way they illuminate her sister's and her own social life. Biographer Alfred Habegger calls them "[a] kind of daily telegraph from the mid-nineteenth century to our time, [that] taps out Amherst's mundane social rhythm for us" (*My Wars*, 255). The diary records, among other things, the sisters' frequent attendance at a reading club for men and women. The chief activity, however, was calling on friends and neighbors, and it absorbed so much of Vinnie's time her parents repeatedly tried to rein her in. Once she made a day trip with her main boyfriend for the year, William Howland, without her parents' knowledge. In the first eight months of the year, her diary records a total of 35 social interactions with Susan Gilbert. Known for her unique wit and talented impersonations, Vinnie had the ability to enchant a circle of friends.

Nonetheless, by 1852, there were signs that she was undergoing a crisis. She recorded in her diary an offer of marriage from William Howland, which never came to anything. Lyman was in the Deep South and she felt he was losing interest in her. She wrote to Austin, "I've been thinking lately how easily I could become *insane*. Sometimes I feel as if I should be." It is hard to know whether Vinnie was merely indulging in the Dickinson propensity for dramatic rhetoric, especially since she gives no further account of her distress. All that is clear is that she felt herself approaching a breaking point, which she apparently avoided by keeping frantically busy, primarily with household and social activities.

When Joseph became engaged to Laura in 1856, Vinnie wrote him a gracious letter of congratulations, indicating that she still had marriage prospects and had promised to make a decision soon. "Perhaps I may give them all up," the proud 24-year-old adds with a touch of bravura. Whether Vinnie gave up her prospects, or the other way around, as was certainly the case with Lyman, is unknown. Neither is it clear that Joseph was the great, disappointing love of her life. All we know is that, like Emily, she gradually adopted her lifestyle, never marrying and centering her life on the family home. The great difference between the sisters, of course, was that Vinnie continued to have an active social life, making and receiving visits to the end, and even traveling to see out-of-town friends until she was well into middle age.

Lavinia once gave a terse and revealing characterization of her family: "As for Emily, she was not withdrawn or exclusive really. She was always watching for the rewarding person to come, but she was a very busy person herself. She had to think—she was the only one of us who had to do that. Father believed; and mother loved; and Austin had Amherst; and I had the family to keep track of" (Bingham, *Emily Dickinson's Home*, 413–414). Although she could write plaintively about her role, by age 20 she was already taking over the household. She loved her garden and her ubiquitous cats, captured by her niece Mattie (MARTHA DICKINSON BIANCHI) in her memoirs: "My Aunt Lavinia's cats—Tabby, Drummy-doodles, Buffy, and Tootsie—sat about the kitchen with an eye half open for trouble" (*Face to Face*, 3–4).

If Vinnie wanted more, no one seemed aware of it. Emily accepted her sister at face value and considered her "happy with her duties, her pussies, and her posies." As they grew older, she outgrew her, but loved her, respected her abilities, and relied on her both emotionally and practically. In a letter to Lyman, Emily wrote that, "if we had come up for the first time from two wells . . . her astonishment would not be greater at some things I say." She described her as "driven" and "under terrific headway," and wrote with a mixture of admiration and mockery to her good friend, ELIZABETH LUNA CHAPIN HOLLAND, in the election year of 1880, "Vinnie is far more hurried than Presidential Candidates—I trust in more distinguished ways, for *they* have only the care of the Union, but Vinnie the Universe—" (L 667).

As she grew older, Lavinia developed a reputation for shrewdness, blunt honesty and caustic wit. Her niece recalled an episode when a man came to the door selling a rodent and insect killer: "'Have you cockroaches, rats or mice, water-bugs, beetles or—' when Aunt Lavinia broke in with an assuring smile, 'No, we have not; but I don't think I will take any this morning, thank you'" (*Face to Face*, 12).

She was famous for her family loyalty and would brook no criticism of her immediate relatives or disagreement with their opinions. Above all, her protectiveness was directed toward Emily. During the years when the poet would not come to the door, Vinnie was her "vicarious representative," greeting all callers with a bland unfailing hospitality (*Face to Face*, 11–12) and turning wrathfully upon anyone who hurt her. While still in her 20s, Emily told a friend, "our practical sister Vinnie has been all, so long, I feel the oddest fright at parting with her for

Lavinia ("Vinnie") Norcross Dickinson, Emily's younger sister with one of her many beloved cats, in 1896, on the east porch of The Homestead *(By permission of the Houghton Library, Harvard University)*

an hour, lest a storm arise, and I go unsheltered." When their father died and Austin was prostrate with grief, it was Vinnie who took charge of practical arrangements, Vinnie who condoled with visitors while Emily stayed upstairs in her room. And in 1883, when Austin and Sue's beloved eight-year-old son, GILBERT ("Gib") died suddenly, it was Vinnie who ministered to the spirits of her devastated, suicidal brother.

The most moving account of Vinnie's protectiveness toward her sister is in a letter written by Emily to her cousins, LOUISE AND FRANCES NORCROSS, after a fire destroyed the business center of Amherst early in the morning of July 4, 1879. As Emily sees the conflagration from her bedroom window, Vinnie enters "soft as a moccasin, 'Don't be afraid, Emily, it is only the fourth of July.'" Emily knows better, but decides to go along: "I did not tell her that I saw it, for I thought if she felt it best to deceive, it must be that it was so." Vinnie leads her into their sleeping mother's bedroom, and when she steps out for a moment, Emily gets a true account of the fire from a servant. She continues, "And so much lighter than day it was, that I saw a caterpillar measure a leaf far down in the orchard; and Vinnie kept saying bravely, 'It's only the fourth of July.'. . . Vinnie's 'only the fourth of July' I shall always remember. I think she will tell us so when we die, to keep us from being afraid" (L 610). Near the end of her life, Emily wrote to a friend: "Your bond to your brother reminds me of mine to my sister—early, earnest, indissoluble. Without her life were fear and Paradise a cowardice, except for her inciting voice" (L 827, mid-June 1883, to Charles H. Clark).

When Emily died, Lavinia, who always honored her wishes, promptly followed her instructions to destroy her letters, a step she would later regret. However, it was customary to burn the letters of the dead at that time, and Lavinia had no way of knowing how important her sister's correspondence would be to the world until she discovered her poems. She knew that Emily wrote poems and had read some of them. Vinnie had been a reader in her youth and even composed over the years a series of poems, lacking in talent but exhibiting her characteristic honesty. She was not insensitive to poetry or oblivious to her sister's writing. But the sheer number of poems she found amazed her. Emily had left no instructions to destroy the poems and Vinnie preserved them. She had always considered her sister a genius and now she was determined to see the poems in print. She turned for help to her literary sister-in-law, Susan, but when Susan failed to respond with the alacrity Vinnie expected, she elicited the assistance of Susan's enemy, Austin's mistress, MABEL LOOMIS TODD, and Emily's great literary friend, THOMAS WENTWORTH HIGGINSON. As these two brought out the first three volumes of Dickinson's poetry, between 1890 and 1896, Lavinia was a constant presence, impatiently goading editors and publisher to hasten their important work. She apparently regarded Emily Dickinson and her poetry as her exclusive property and only reluctantly agreed to remunerate the editors for their considerable labors.

The end of Vinnie's life was marred by an 1898 lawsuit she brought against Mabel Todd and her husband for "falsely" claiming the right to a strip of Dickinson land. The case was pure fabrication, since Austin Dickinson, prior to his death in 1895, had instructed Vinnie to deed the land to the Todds; Vinnie had already taken steps in that direction before suddenly changing her mind. She perjured herself repeatedly during her testimony, won her case, but lost Mabel's collaboration on any future publications based on the manuscripts in her possession. The devastated Mabel put them aside and no more of Emily's poems were published in Lavinia's lifetime. Biographer Richard B. Sewall speculates that Vinnie's thoroughly uncharacteristic behavior in lying and betraying her brother's wishes may have been related to her fear of her sister-in-law Sue and the powerful family tensions that had existed for decades between the residents of The HOMESTEAD and The EVERGREENS. If this was the case it bespeaks yet another reversal in her character, for Vinnie had fearlessly stood up to Sue in the past, particularly with respect to decisions about publishing Emily's poems.

Mabel Todd's daughter, Millicent Todd Bingham, offers a physical description of the elderly (in her mid-sixties) Vinnie. Her portrait is grotesque and should be read in light of the fact that the Todds had every reason to remember Vinnie in the least complimentary way. Yet it also offers a fascinating glimpse of the transformation of the pretty, sensual young woman over a lifetime filled with care, loss, and disappointment:

> There she sat in her apple-green kitchen, or on the sheltered back porch, an uncompromising slender little figure in an [old-fashioned] black cashmere dress. . . . Her sour, shriveled face with its long nose was wrinkled like a witch of the fairytale, her hands twisted and knotted. . . . But her hair, her marvelous dark hair streaked with gray, seemed to concentrate all the juices of her wizened body—heavy, luxuriant, the focus of interest in her person. . . . (*Ancestor's Brocades,* 14)

By the end of her life, Vinnie could no longer be called "the uncomplicated Dickinson." She had been "the most outgoing, least inhibited member of the household" (Sewall, *Life,* I, 131), the one who never minced words, in contrast to the oblique style of the rest of the family. But in her later years, the forthrightness that had always characterized her seems to have abandoned her. Having outlived all her immediate family, Lavinia died on August 31, 1899, apparently of heart disease. She continued to have her friends and supporters. A eulogy, written by a friend of her later years, Professor Joseph Chickering of Amherst, and printed in the *Springfield Republican,* depicts her as "unique, rather than peculiar. She never said things as other people said them . . . she abhorred the commonplace . . . her views of life . . . were at once shrewd and amusing. . . ."

See also PUBLICATION AND EDITORIAL SCHOLARSHIP.

FURTHER READING

Millicent Todd Bingham, *Ancestor's Brocades,* 14, 27–30, 210–213, 297–299, 349–367; Bingham, *Emily Dickinson's Home,* 82–83, 490–492; *Martha* Dickinson Bianchi, *Emily Dickinson Face to Face,* 3–4, 11–12, 20, 23, 48–49, 69, 107–113; Alfred Habegger, *My Wars,* 97–98, 185–187, 253–257; Richard B. Sewall, *Life,* I, 128–157 and editor, *The Lyman Letters,* 19–55.

Dickinson, Lucretia Gunn (1775–1840)   Emily Dickinson's paternal grandmother was the second of 10 children born to Hannah Montague Gunn and Nathaniel Gunn in Montague, Massachusetts, 10 miles north of AMHERST. She married SAMUEL FOWLER DICKINSON on March 21, 1802, and the following year gave birth to the first of their nine children, EDWARD DICKINSON, the poet's father. The mother of four girls and five boys, none of whom died before her, she was unusually fortunate among women of her day. Her life with Samuel, however, was not an easy one and her difficult temperament estranged her from her children. Only a few letters from her, most addressed to Edward, survive; they reveal her as a woman who expressed herself bluntly on such practical matters as killing hogs. They also reflect her desire for Edward to make a public declaration of accepting Christ during the course of a REVIVAL in 1820, so that she would not have to lament that "Harvest is past the Summer is ended & you are not saved." (Habegger, 8–9). She herself did not join the FIRST CHURCH OF CHRIST until 1820, 20 years after her husband did.

She was the first mistress of The HOMESTEAD, the imposing first brick home on Main Street in Amherst that Samuel built for his growing family in 1813. Samuel's strained finances led him to sell half the house to Edward, who moved in with his wife and infant son AUSTIN in 1830. A few months later Emily was born. The two years the families spent together were less than idyllic. Samuel's investment of his personal resources in the building of AMHERST COLLEGE placed pressure on a household that Lucretia once described as "crazy." Lucretia's argumentative personality, which made many people, including her children, find her "impossible to tolerate," added to the tension. She was "by tradition of somewhat tart disposition, and was often referred to in moments of bad temper as 'coming out' in her high-strung grandchildren. If a door was banged—'It's not me—it's my Grandmother Gunn!' was an excuse glibly offered by the three small rascals (Emily, Austin, and LAVINIA)." (Bianchi, *Face to Face*, 87–88).

Samuel's finances continued to deteriorate and in 1833, when Emily was two, he sold his half of the

Lucretia Gunn Dickinson, the poet's paternal grandmother *(The Todd-Bingham Picture Collection. Yale University Library)*

Homestead and with Lucretia and their younger children moved to Ohio, first to Cincinnati and three years later to the isolated outpost town of Hudson. There, the woman one of her daughters described as slow "to form acquaintances or attachments" found herself lonely and friendless. Her husband died in 1838, leaving her in financial straits. When she returned east, none of her children were eager to take full-time responsibility for the contentious old woman. Edward refused to offer her a home. She went to live with her sister Clarissa Gunn Underwood and brother-in-law Kingsley Underwood in Enfield, Massachusetts, where her daughter Elizabeth, the youngest and only unmarried daughter, only 17 at the time, helped to care for her during the last months of her life. Emily and her sister Vinnie visited her there at least once, in

September 1838. Lucretia died at age 64 of consumption on May 11, 1840, in Enfield and was buried in Amherst.

FURTHER READING

Martha Dickinson Bianchi, *Face to Face*, 87–88; Alfred Habegger, *My Wars*, 8–9.

Dickinson, Nathaniel and Ann Gull Emily Dickinson's earliest paternal ancestors to settle in America, Nathaniel and Ann Gull Dickinson, were part of the Great Migration of between 14,000 and 21,000 English men and women who came to New England for economic and religious reasons between 1629 and 1640. The Dickinsons subscribed to the militant late-Reformation religious movement known as Puritanism, which rebelled against the domination and abuses of the Church of England and sought religious freedom in the New World. They were thought to have crossed the ocean in 1630 with John Winthrop, the Puritan leader and future governor of Massachusetts; however, new evidence was published in 1998, establishing the date of migration somewhere between 1636 and 1638. The couple made the journey from the parish of Billingsborough, in Lincolnshire, England, to the primitive British colony in Wethersfield, Connecticut, in whose records Nathaniel's name appears for the first time in 1637; he was admitted as a freeman.

Ann bore nine sons and two daughters in Wethersfield; it was common at the time for families to reach this size. When a church split occurred in 1659 they joined 58 other families in a move north to Massachusetts, where they founded the town of Hadley in the fertile CONNECTICUT RIVER VALLEY, just east of Northampton. A "man of muscle, as of mind," as the Dickinson patriarch would later be called by an admiring descendant, Nathaniel played a leading role in Hadley's municipal, military, religious, and educational affairs. He was a town magistrate and one of the first trustees of the Hopkins Grammar School of Hadley.

In addition to being civic leaders and capable administrators, educators, and homesteaders, the Dickinson men were also determined fighters: warriors for their faith, independence from Britain and economic equality When Nathaniel and all his sons took part in the fighting that broke out in 1675 between the English settlers and the native people of the region, three sons died in battle. Nathaniel and Anne's grandson Ebenezer Dickinson fought Indians at Deerfield after the Massacre of 1704, when Canadian Indians and their French allies destroyed Deerfield, killing 49 and marching more than 100 residents on snowshoes to a settlement near Montreal. Ebenezer's son and grandson, Nathan and Nathan, Jr., fought in the French and Indian War; the younger man went on to participate in the Revolutionary War, and Shays's Rebellion, the 1786 armed revolt of the farmers of western Massachusetts against what they viewed as discriminatory economic practices. As warriors for their faith, independence from Britain and economic equality, the Dickinson forebears constituted "a microcosm of the American experience as it sprang from the Puritan roots of New England" (Wolff, 13).

In 1745, Nathan and Nathan, Jr., who was Emily Dickinson's great-grandfather, moved their families to the eastern districts of Hadley, where in 1759 a new town would be established and named AMHERST, after Lord Jeffrey Amherst. There the Dickinson clan prospered as farmers and eventually became prominent local figures, forging an unbreakable link between the family's name and the town's.

Although Emily Dickinson took little interest in her early forebears per se, the PURITAN HERITAGE they left her, particularly as it was embodied in the faith of CONGREGATIONALISM, played a crucial role in the development of both her character and her poetry.

FURTHER READING

Frederick Dickinson, *To the Descendants of Thomas Dickinson*, Chicago, Ill., 1897, 13–18; Alfred Habegger, *My Wars*, 3; Stott, Clifford C., "The Correct English Origins of Nathaniel Dickinson and William Gull, Settlers of Wethersfield and Hadley," *New England Historical and Genealogical Register* 152 (April 1998) 159–178; Cynthia Griffin Wolff, *Emily Dickinson*, 13.

Dickinson, Samuel Fowler (1775–1838) Dickinson's paternal grandfather was born in AMHERST, the youngest son and seventh of eight children of Esther Fowler and Nathan Dickinson, Jr. Described by one of his daughters as "gentle and sensitive, and with more than ordinary mental gifts," he was favored by his siblings and encouraged by his parents to pursue his education. At 16, he entered Dartmouth College, which offered a solid classical curriculum, and four years later, in 1795, graduated second in his class. His salutatorian address, which dealt with civil government and manners, is permeated by the exaltation of Reason, a quality he strove to inspire others to cultivate in his new career as a teacher in New Salem, Massachusetts. He apparently found teaching to be too dependent upon the "whims" of constituents and abandoned it after a year. He suffered from lung problems and, after recovering from a bout of illness that year, formally declared his faith in Christ. He next considered becoming a minister, studying with Rev. Nathanael Emmons, a renowned New England Calvinist, whose teachings were grounded in the traditional doctrines of God's sovereignty and human depravity. Only four months sufficed to convince him he was unsuited to a religious career; however, he continued to revere Emmons and appears to have internalized his emphasis on the power of the will and the obligation to use it. At 21, he became a deacon of Amherst's FIRST CHURCH OF CHRIST.

From then on, he would return to the tradition of his Dickinson forebears and follow a secular career. Returning to Amherst, by 1797 he was reading law under the tutelage of Judge Simeon Strong, the town's leading lawyer. Like Judge Strong, he purchased a great deal of real estate, acquiring the nickname "the Squire," but found himself unable to keep up with the mortgages. This tendency to overreach would have a negative impact on his future enterprises and eventually undermine his considerable success as a loyal civic leader and legislator.

In 1802, Samuel married LUCRETIA GUNN (DICKINSON) of nearby Montague, who would bear him nine children, of whom EDWARD DICKINSON, Emily's father, was the oldest. Samuel was a father who showed deep concern for his children's health, setting his business affairs aside when they were sick, and who took a lively interest in the education of all his children, including his daughters. In 1813, by which time he and Lucretia had their first five children, he dealt with the family's need for more spacious quarters by building The HOMESTEAD, Amherst's first brick house, on Main Street. His granddaughter Emily would be born 17 years later in this graceful Victorian structure and live most of her life there.

This was the period in which he became involved in the work that would mark his most lasting contribution. Together with Judge Strong's son Hezekiah, in 1812, he began organizing the establishment of AMHERST ACADEMY, which would be one of the best private classical schools in western Massachusetts. Two years later the school, housed in a three-story brick structure, opened its doors to students of both sexes. The success of this project spurred Samuel to engage in one even more ambitious: the founding of AMHERST COLLEGE in 1821. In a crusading spirit, Samuel persuaded fellow enthusiast Colonel Rufus Graves to join him in promoting the creation of an evangelical college that would surpass Harvard and Williams, then the state's only colleges. To an orthodox Calvinist such as Samuel, Harvard Divinity School, which had embraced UNITARIANISM, was anathema. He and his cofounders conceived Amherst College as a vital step in reversing this trend away from the faith of the fathers. Its mission would be to "civilize and evangelize the world by the classical education of indigent young men of piety and talents" (Sewall, *Life,* I, 34). When the Amherst leaders applied to the Massachusetts General Court for a charter, they were opposed by the Harvard Unitarians, who warned that the proposed institution would become "priest factory." Nothing could have fanned their spiritual zeal more.

Samuel was a confidence-inspiring advocate and fund-raiser for the college on whose first board of trustees he would serve. His voice was pivotal in helping Amherst win out over 37 other towns as the site of the new college. In his work on the building committee, however, his fanatical obsession with the project led him to invest his own funds recklessly. By 1817, he was forced to mortgage the Homestead for $2,500 (today about $75,000), digging himself into a financial hole from which he would never emerge. When the college's funds ran low, he volunteered his own horses and laborers, boarded workers in his home at his own expense, and even occasionally paid their wages.

Eventually, the foundations of his stature as one of Amherst's most renowned citizens disintegrated. He had been elected as representative to the State House 10 times and once to the State Senate. But his 1828 run for a congressional seat ended in a crushing defeat after he opposed his district on a tariff issue. In his dedication to building the college, he had badly neglected his legal practice. The denouement came in 1833, when he was forced to sell the Homestead and leave Amherst with his wife and younger children for what must have seemed like exile in Cincinnati. His new position at Lane Theological Seminary, directing students in the manual labor required as part of the school's curriculum, was a steep comedown from his previous endeavors. In an 1835 letter to Edward, his daughter Catherine wrote that his "spirits are completely broken down & probably will never rise again." In 1836, he became treasurer and building supervisor at Western Reserve College in Hudson, Ohio, then an isolated frontier post. Neither he nor his family adjusted well. Depressed, in poor health, financially broken, and neglected by his children and former friends, he died there in 1838, when Emily was seven.

After his death, however, Samuel's strengths and achievements were properly recognized; his Amherst grave was heaped with flowers by the very relatives who had found him an embarrassment in the last years of his life. His idealism, apparently, "made him a nobler figure to history than to those who lived beside him" (Leyda, *Years and Hours*, II, 175). His grandson, Emily's beloved older brother, WILLIAM AUSTIN DICKINSON, in 1889 in an address prepared for celebration at the First Congregational Church, praised him for strength and character, while omitting his life's sad ending, of which the Dickinsons did not speak.

As for his influence on Emily, there are few overt references to Samuel in her writing, although Austin's knowledge of their grandfather's life and character is a reliable indicator that she, too, was familiar with them. Living in Amherst all her life,

the presence of the college would have served as a constant reminder of his finest achievement. She mentions him explicitly in a letter to her father's sister, CATHERINE SWEETSER, who once asked her to send Samuel's Bible. Emily replied that she was "reluctant to entrust anything so sacred to my Father as my Grandfather's Bible to public messenger" (L 828). It is also possible that a dream she reported to Austin when she was 16, in which her father had failed financially, their rye field "mortgaged to Seth Nims," the local postmaster, reflected an underlying specter of failure in the Dickinson household, connected to Samuel's experience (L 16). Whatever his *direct* influence may have been, "the go-for-broke zealotry of her grandfather fed into her life in complex and intimate ways" (Habegger, 13). She shared his inability to thrive outside of Amherst, a temperament prone to extremes of exultation and despair, and an absolute dedication to her chosen work.

FURTHER READING

Alfred Habegger, *My Wars*, 7–13, 15–21; Jay Leyda, *Years and Hours,* II, 175. Sewall, *Life*, I, 28–43.

Dickinson, Susan Huntington Gilbert (1830–1913) Beloved girlhood friend, sister-in-law, and lifelong correspondent, Susan Dickinson was a figure of supreme importance in Emily Dickinson's life. The poet sent her a total of 500 "writings," including letters, poems, and poem-letters, including about 400 poems, far more than she sent to any other correspondent. A complex woman, capable of arousing both devotion and enmity, she was a controversial figure in her lifetime and remains one for Dickinson scholars today. While most critics recognize that Emily Dickinson loved Susan, there is a continuing debate over the nature of that love (erotic, platonic), the manner in which it was reciprocated, and its evolution over the course of the two women's lives. Some feminist critics believe that, beginning with the testimony of her arch-rival, MABEL LOOMIS TODD, Susan's importance to Dickinson has been minimized and suppressed and her character vilified. Seeking to balance the record, they have made a case for Susan as Dickinson's "primary reader" and "her central source of inspiration, love, and intellectual and poetic discourse" (Hart and Smith, *Open Me Carefully*, xi).

Born in physical proximity and within nine days of one another, Emily and Sue had radically different beginnings. Susan Huntington Gilbert was born on December 19, 1830, in Greenfield, Massachusetts, just 20 miles north of AMHERST, the youngest of seven children of Harriet Arms and Thomas Gilbert. Both parents came of respectable CONNECTICUT RIVER VALLEY families, but the father was a drinker and unsuccessful tavern keeper, and the family was poor. In 1832, the year Gilbert moved to Amherst to become proprietor of a tavern and livery stable on Main Street, Sue's seven-year-old sister died. Four years later, when Susan was six, her mother died of consumption, a tragedy that led to the breakup of the family. Susan and her three sisters went to Geneva, New York, to be cared for

Susan Gilbert Dickinson, the girlhood friend with whom Emily was in love, and who later became her sister-in-law, c. 1850 *(The Todd-Bingham Picture Collection, Yale University Library)*

by their aunt and uncle, Sophia Arms and William Van Vranken. Her 19-year-old brother Frank went to live with the oldest brother, Dwight, who was already making his own living in Michigan. Five years later, Sue's father died in Greenfield, at age 48, reportedly of drink, and was listed as an "insolvent debtor" in the county records.

Although Sue was fond of Aunt Sophia and happy in Geneva where she lived for 10 years, the grief, loss, and uncertainty of those early years marked her indelibly. She wrote of missing her mother's love ("The memory of her goodness will never die. . . .") and firmly believed they would be reunited in heaven. But her father's memory was marred by shame and the gossip about his "dying upon charity" circulated in Amherst as late as the 1880s. Susan's ambivalence toward him is reflected in her dropping his name, Gilbert, when she married, but later naming her youngest son, THOMAS GILBERT DICKINSON ("Gib"), for him. When Susan returned to Amherst at age 16, she felt the onus of her father's lingering reputation and of her own humiliating status as an unwanted dependent in the home of her brother-in-law. All three younger Gilbert sisters, Sue, Martha ("Mattie"), and Mary, lived with their oldest sister, Harriet, and her husband, William Cutler, partner in Amherst's leading mercantile outlet, Sweetser and Cutler. Sue, who had a strong dislike for William, chaffed at her reliance on him and clung to the dream of leaving Amherst and making a home that would reunite her with her siblings. She felt especially close to Dwight and Mary, to whom she was temperamentally akin. Both Dwight, to whom she looked as a father, and Frank were financially successful and responsible older brothers, who generously helped meet their sisters' financial needs.

While Emily Dickinson was studying at MOUNT HOLYOKE FEMALE SEMINARY, Sue attended AMHERST ACADEMY, in 1846–47 before going on to spend two semesters at the well-respected Utica Female Seminary. There she developed both a passion for literature and considerable skill in her main subject, mathematics. This period of intellectual growth was abruptly interrupted, however, when her sister Mary, eight years older and like a mother to her, died on July 14, 1850, less than a month after giv-

Merchant's Row, on the Amherst common, in 1869. Susan Gilbert Dickinson's brother-in-law, George Cutler, with whom she lived before her marriage, owned the general store, to the left, with shovels on porch. *(Amherst College Archives and Special Collections)*

ing birth to a daughter in Grand Haven, Michigan. For Sue, who had dreamed of going to live with this beloved sister, the loss was especially deep and bitter. Having lost her mother and two sisters, she felt she must be "ready to die" and meet them in the next life. During the powerful religious REVIVAL that swept Amherst during the summer of 1850, she declared her acceptance of Christ and joined the FIRST CHURCH OF CHRIST. As a consequence of Mary's death Sue developed a terror of childbirth, which would lead to early frigidity in her marriage as well as a number of abortions.

It was during this period, with her sister Mattie still in Michigan and unable to comfort her, that she became friends with Emily and attracted several admirers among the AMHERST COLLEGE students, including Emily's older brother, WILLIAM AUSTIN DICKINSON. Emily's first letter to her, written the day of Mattie's return, cedes first rights to Sue to her

sister, while stating her own claims: "Don't forget all the little friends who have tried so hard to *be* sisters, when indeed you *were* alone!" (L 38, about December 1850). When Sue impulsively left for Baltimore the following September, to teach for a year at Mr. Robert Archer's School, Emily's tone of sisterly entitlement evolved into something more urgent and intimate. As Polly Longsworth notes, "Emily was quite literally in love with her" and what she sent her "were unmistakably love letters, more persistently and lyrically romantic than what she was writing to other friends [such as JANE HUMPHREY, ABIAH PALMER ROOT, and ABBY WOOD], although they did not far exceed the 19th-century tolerance for intimacy between unmarried females" (*Austin and Sue*, 92–93). In April 1852, she writes:

So sweet and still, and Thee, Oh Susie, what need I more, to make my heaven whole?

Martha ("Mattie") Gilbert, the older sister of Susan Dickinson, who was in love with Austin *(By permission of the Houghton Library, Harvard University)*

Sweet Hour, blessed Hour, to carry me to you, and to bring you back to me, long enough to snatch one kiss, and whisper Good bye, again.

I have thought of it all day, Susie, and I fear of but little else, and when I was gone to meeting it filled my mind so full, I could not find a *chink* to put the worthy pastor; when he said "Our Heavenly Father," I said "Oh Darling Sue.". . . (L 88)

As she waits feverishly for Sue to return, she says, in a tone of near-surprise, "Why, Susie, it seems to me as if my absent Lover were coming home so soon—and my heart must be so busy, making ready for him" (L 96). Here Dickinson assigns Susan the male role. Yet a little earlier she had written Sue the famous passage in which she contemplates the day when she and Mattie and Sue will be "yielded up" to marriage, comparing them to blossoms des-

tined to be consumed by the mighty sun: "They know what the man of noon, is *mightier* than the morning and their life is henceforth to him" (L 93). While this passage is generally cited as evidence of Dickinson's fear of heterosexuality, it exudes an excitement and craving for the dangerous intensity of marriage.

Emily's romantic obsession with Susan was conducted safely through the mails, and appears to have remained within the realm of fantasy. Judith Farr argues, "If we are to believe the persuasive evidence of the poems, this intense romance of the heart was never physically consummated" (*Passion,* 110). Moreover, there was never any question of Dickinson stepping outside the family and social boundaries that defined her daily life and provided her economic security. Nor would she be disloyal to her brother, Austin, who became engaged to Susan in the spring of 1853. She thus found herself, as Vivian Pollak writes, "pursuing mutually antagonistic goals . . . simultaneously attempting to create a female counterculture with Sue and to integrate her into the Amherst family circle" (*Anxiety of Gender,* 61). Pollack suggests that, while making a heroic effort "to maintain her ideal self-image as a facilitator of family harmony," "her desire to *be* Austin" was difficult to control (73–74).

As for Sue, her decision to marry Austin meant giving up her dreams of traveling and escaping Amherst with its painful memories. Knowing she could not support herself by teaching, she recognized that marriage was her only way to escape from dependency. Their courtship, which was troubled from the beginning, began in the spring of 1850, during his senior year in college. Three years later, the couple became engaged, shortly after their overnight tryst at the Revere Hotel in Boston on March 23, 1853, during which, in Austin's words, "we promised ourselves to each other." Sue continually put off the wedding, perhaps because Austin's "masculine expectations for love and the begetting of children began to rouse Sue's latent anxieties as the wedding date came closer" (Longsworth, *Austin and Mabel,* 85). She may also have been struggling with her feelings for Samuel Bartlett, a distant relative, whose married home became a haven for her between 1853 and 1856, and who stimulated her intellect and emotions.

In his letters to Sue, Austin focused on his dreams of the perfect love and joyous future they would share, seemingly unaware that she may not have shared his romantic expectations. Austin was tormented by doubt of her love, feeling himself to be at the mercy of her unpredictable moods, what he called the "tempestuous latitude" where she lived. Sue was ill for a year after agreeing to marry Austin, with what was termed a "nervous fever" and may have been depression.

They would not marry until July 1, 1856, six months after Austin had gratified Sue by at last declaring his faith and joining the church. The failure of any member of the Dickinson family to attend the wedding in Geneva, New York, at the home of Sue's Aunt Sophia, is puzzling, especially in light of the family's affection for the handsome, bright, and charismatic young woman who was joining their ranks. No letter of congratulations from Emily to the newlyweds has been preserved.

Susan's future father-in-law, EDWARD DICKINSON, who had been her fellow convert in 1850, particularly approved of the match and helped persuade the young couple to remain in Amherst by offering to build them an elegant home adjacent to The HOMESTEAD. The newlyweds moved directly into their Italianate villa, The EVERGREENS, directly after their wedding and lived there together until Austin's death 40 years later. On the surface, the household thrived. Sue threw herself into beautifying her home, cultivating her garden, and making the Evergreens into the center of Amherst's social life. In "Annals of the Evergreens," the long essay she wrote in 1893, she recapitulated the brightest moments of her marriage, when she entertained a long list of eminent visitors, including Ralph Waldo Emerson in 1857. *Springfield Republican* editor SAMUEL BOWLES, a close friend of Sue and Austin was a frequent visitor, and Sue apparently enjoyed a flirtatious relationship with this charming and worldly man, who resembled her in his sociability and love of excitement. One admirer described her as "a really brilliant and highly cultivated woman of great taste and refinement, perhaps a little too aggressive, a little too sharp in wit and repartee, and

a little too ambitious for social prestige . . ." (*Austin and Mabel*, 113–114).

Little is known about the quality of Sue and Austin's relationship during the early and middle years of their marriage. Austin's remark to MABEL LOOMIS TODD, made a quarter of a century later, that he "felt as if he were going to his own execution" on his wedding day, may be an exaggeration of the sort a married man makes to his mistress to justify his infidelity. His diary records Sue's ungoverned temper, her reluctance to have sex, and "morbid dread of having any children." He told Mabel that Sue had had three or four abortions prior to the birth of their son EDWARD DICKINSON ("Ned") in 1861. Sue had made sustained attempts to abort him—acts that both she and Austin held responsible for Ned's developing epilepsy. Whatever her fears, Sue gave birth to two more children, Martha ("Mattie") in 1866 (see MARTHA DICKINSON BIANCHI) and Gib in 1875.

Sue was disliked by many and had a reputation in the town for snobbery, arrogance, and petty cruelty. "Something in her backfired . . . she rejected the very adulation and warmth she attracted, and often found pleasure in small revenges," notes Longsworth (*Austin and Mabel*, 114). Austin feared her violent temper, saw her as selfish and pleasure-seeking, and gradually distanced himself from her unrelenting social activities. She was rumored to drink excessively. When he initiated his affair with Mabel Todd in 1882, he told her he had had no happiness before he met her. From then on Austin and Sue would maintain the outward fiction of their marriage, while living as hostile strangers.

The nature of Sue's relationship with Emily, once they were sisters-in-law, is equally complex and difficult to document. During the late 1850s and early 1860s, Emily was a frequent participant in Sue's soirées, joining in the stimulating conversation and hilarity, and striking up close friendships with Bowles and the vivacious young widow, CATHERINE (SCOTT) TURNER ANTHON. As her girlhood friends married and moved away, her social circle narrowed, and in 1859 she called Susan and Austin "my crowd." When Sue became a mother, Emily was jealous at first, but she later became a tender, devoted aunt, evincing a near-maternal tenderness to Sue's children. During the 30 years when they lived "across the hedge" from one another, they developed the daily intimacy of two householders, borrowing eggs and exchanging medications. But they also retained something of the personal intensity and literary verve of their girlhood intimacy, as Emily's side of their ongoing correspondence reveals. (Only a handful of Susan's letters survived).

Throughout her life, Emily sent dozens of brief, frequently encoded and enigmatic notes, poems and letter-poems to Susan, who apparently felt free to comment on them. In 1859, after Sue professed herself "not suited" with the second stanza of "SAFE IN THEIR ALABASTER CHAMBERS—," Dickinson wrote two alternates. Always eager to impress Sue, a sophisticated reader who herself wrote in many genres, she thanks her for her comments: "Your praise is good—to me—because I *know* it *knows*—and *suppose* it *means*—Could I make you and Austin—proud—sometime—a great way off—'twould give me taller feet" (L 238). Feminist scholar Martha Nell Smith believes that this interchange is representative of an ongoing "poetry workshop" between the two women, in which Sue played an important role in Dickinson's shaping of her work. Smith notes that Sue was the only one to whom Emily sent drafts of her poems and sees this as evidence that "at least sometimes Dickinson put her poetic performances through dress rehearsals by sending them to Sue" (*Rowing in Eden,* 152). However, as Smith admits, there is no direct evidence to support this idea. Moreover, Dickinson's comment to THOMAS WENTWORTH HIGGINSON in 1862, that she had no one else to ask, when she wrote asking for his opinion on her poems, casts into doubt Sue's role as satisfying literary mentor.

Much has been written about Emily and Sue's estrangement in later years. Mabel Todd reports LAVINIA NORCROSS DICKINSON's statement that she knew "Emily would die years before she ought owing to the cruelties practiced upon her" by Sue (cited in Sewall, *Life,* I, 196). It has also been alleged that, as she grew increasingly reclusive, Emily stopped coming to the Evergreens and set foot there for the first time in 15 years on the night that Sue's son Gib died (*Life,* I, 198). Smith strongly contests the idea that the women did not see one another for

Facsimile of letter to Sue Dickinson: "Dear Sue—With the exception of Shakespeare you have told me of more knowledge than anyone living—to say that sincerely is strange praise—" *(By permission of the Houghton Library, Harvard University)*

all those years, pointing to their correspondence as proof of uninterrupted contact, including frequent visits from Sue at the Homestead (*Rowing in Eden,* 156–157). In this view, it was only after Gib's death in 1883 and Austin's affair with Mabel, whom he often met at the Homestead, that Sue stopped coming there. Questions remain about how much Emily knew about the unhappiness of Austin and Sue's marriage and what Sue thought of Emily's apparent sanctioning of Austin's affair. There were other grounds for estrangement between the two women as well, notably Sue's disapproval of Emily's love affair with JUDGE OTIS PHILLIPS LORD.

Certainly the two women's lives moved in opposite directions, with Sue becoming an intensely social being, a "Cosmopolite," as Emily termed it, while she withdrew into her private world. In 1877, Dickinson sent Sue a letter poem that expressed her sense of the latter's fundamental inscrutability: "But Susan is a stranger yet; / The ones that cite her most / Have never scaled her haunted house, / Nor compromised her Ghost" (L 530). Yet, in a late letter to Sue, she says, "With the exception of Shakespeare, you have told me of more knowledge than anyone living—To say that sincerely is strange praise." The implication is that Sue revealed to Emily the full spectrum of human nature, from its heights to its depths. Several poems plumb those depths. As Farr astutely notes, "Love is not always—perhaps rarely—inspired by a suitable subject. Her poems prove how clearly Dickinson knew it" (*Passion*, 156). Dickinson evokes Sue's heedless cruelty in "She dealt her pretty words like Blades—." In another poem of disillusionment, "It dropped so low—in my Regard—," she blames herself "For entertaining Plated Wares / Upon my Silver Shelf". And in what is perhaps her most moving, eloquent poems of disillusionment, "Now I KNEW I LOST HER—" (about 1872), she sees Sue as "Alien, though adjoining / As a Foreign Race—."

No matter how disillusioned she may have been with her, however, there can be no doubt that Emily continued to love Susan and to hold her sacred. Until the end of her life, her letters affirm the uniqueness and endurance of their bond: "The tie between us is very fine, but a Hair never dissolves" (L 1024), she wrote in late 1885. As Farr notes in her illuminating discussion of "The Narrative of Sue," "Dickinson's passion for her sister-in-law resulted in a body of poems and letters that is as eloquent and complex as any written to 'Master'" (*Passion*, 109). Farr traces the intricate web of images and tropes through which Dickinson wrote of her unfulfilled love for Sue. She was Dickinson's idol, a Siren, her unattainable pearl, a lost Eden that "never capitulates" (L 584, about 1878), "the Woman whom I prefer," and with whom she felt as one, "Where my Hands are cut, Her fingers will be found inside . . ." (L 288, about 1864). At age 48 she wrote, "Susan, I dreamed of you, last night," and enclosed a carnation (L 585, about 1878). In the literary encoding of her letters, she reminded Sue that, beneath the veil of their conventional lives, Sue was her Cleopatra. She evoked her in terms of a powerful elemental warmth that was both

exciting and dangerous ("Sue fronts on the Gulf Stream"; she is "an Avalanche of Sun!"; "What depths of Domingo in that torrid Spirit!"). In 1884, she implores her, "Be Sue—while I am Emily—/ Be next—what you have ever been—Infinity" (L 912).

We know a great deal less about what Susan felt for Emily. There must have been some level of reciprocated affection that continued to elicit Emily's side of the correspondence. Yet it also seems probable that Emily's excessive demands on a woman struggling with marriage and motherhood could be oppressive. Susan valued Emily's writings enough to preserve them. It was she who performed the intimate ritual of dressing her for burial and

The path between The Homestead (in the background) and The Evergreens, across which Emily Dickinson and Susan Gilbert Dickinson continued to exchange messages, long after they had stopped visiting one another *(Courtesy of Darryl Leiter)*

who wrote the sensitive and heartfelt obituary that appeared in the *Springfield Republican*.

When Dickinson died in 1886, Sue was a deeply troubled woman. She had been devastated by the death of her eight-year-old son Gib of typhoid fever in 1883, a shared grief which evoked some of Emily's most exquisite letters to her. The strain of Austin's open affair had taken its toll, making her increasingly despotic and temperamental. In light of this, her failure to respond to Lavinia's request that she edit Emily's poems for publication may have reflected something other than indifference. Smith musters evidence to show that Sue was slowly working on a plan for a volume of Emily's writings that would have been far more inclusive of her work as

a whole than Todd and Higginson's conventional volumes of poems. Whatever the case, a letter she wrote to Higginson after the publication of *Poems* (1890) indicates her confidence that she and Emily knew each other perfectly: "I am told Miss Lavinia is saying that I *refused* to arrange them [the poems]. Emily knows that is not true."

After her husband's death in 1895, Sue continued to live at the Evergreens, making frequent trips to Europe with her daughter. She died on May 12, 1913, at age 82.

See also "Like eyes that look'd on Wastes—," "Of all the Souls that stand create—," "The Malay—took the Pearl—," "Your Riches—taught me—Poverty." and publication and editorial scholarship.

FURTHER READING

Martha Dickinson Bianchi, *Face to Face*, 92–104, 111–122; Millicent Todd Bingham, *Ancestor's Brocades*; Lillian Faderman, "Emily Dickinson's Letters to Sue Gilbert," *Massachusetts Review* 28, (Summer 1977); Judith Farr, *Passion*, 100–177; Alfred Habegger, *My Wars*, 264–278, 334–340, 436–441, 461–464; Ellen Louise Hart and Martha Nell Smith, *Open Me Carefully*; Polly Longsworth, *Austin and Mabel*, 67–124; Vivian Pollak, *The Anxiety of Gender*, 59–82; Agnieszka Salsa, "Dickinson's Letters," in *Handbook*, Grabher et al., eds., 167–171; Richard B. Sewall, *Life*, I, 161–169, 197–214; Martha Nell Smith, "Susan and Emily Dickinson: their lives, in letters," in *Cambridge Companion*, 51–73; Martha Nell Smith, *Rowing in Eden*, 129–220.

Dickinson, Thomas Gilbert (1875–1883) "Gib," as he was called, was the youngest of the three children of the poet's brother, William Austin Dickinson and Susan Huntington Gilbert Dickinson. He died suddenly of typhoid fever on October 5, 1883, barely aged eight, a blow from which his family never fully recovered.

Gib was the child of his parents' middle age and the only one of his siblings who was close to both of his emotionally estranged parents. His father's idol and the adored "playmate" of his Aunt Emily, he was loved by all of Amherst. His extraordinary

Susan Huntington Gilbert Dickinson, photographed in Berlin at age 80 *(By permission of the Houghton Library, Harvard University)*

obituary in the *Amherst Record* describes a child wise and giving beyond his years, self-reliant, gentle, and sensitive, with whom adults conversed for their own pleasure (Sewall, *Life,* I, 125).

Emily's "alliance" with the little boy is demonstrated by an episode in which a kindergarten teacher rebuked him for "lying" about an imaginary beautiful white calf and made him cry. His indignant aunt "besought them one and all to come to *her,* she would show them! The white calf was grazing up in her attic at that very moment!" ("Country Girl," 64–65, cited in Habegger, 548.). On the night he died, she rushed to be with him—the first time in 15 years she had set foot in The EVERGREENS. Later, she would tell ELIZABETH LUNA CHAPIN HOLLAND:

> "Open the Door, open the Door, they are waiting for me," was Gilbert's sweet command in delirium. *Who* were waiting for him, all we possess we would give to know—Anguish at last opened it, and he ran to the little Grave at his Grandparents' feet—All this and more, though *is* there more? More than Love and Death? Then tell me it's name! (L 873, late 1883).

Afterward, as her sister LAVINIA reported, "Emily received a nervous shock the night Gilbert died & was alarmingly ill for weeks" (cited in Sewall, *Life,* I, 146). Austin was in a suicidal despair for months, recovering his lease on life only through embarking on a passionate affair with MABEL LOOMIS TODD. The boy's mother, Susan, "would see no one, would not even be driven through the village for more than a year" (Bianchi, "Country Girl," 120).

Sewall speculates that, had he lived, "this remarkable child might have brought about some reconciliation between his parents" as well as between Emily and Susan (*Life,* I, 204). Emily did send the bereaved mother exquisite letters of "condolence," in which she celebrates the lost child. In them she makes "no reference to God and interprets Gib's death as his own transcendent achievement" (Habegger, *My Wars,* 617). Attempting to transform tragedy into victory, she evokes Gib as Ajax, the classical hero known for his strength.

Gilbert rejoiced in Secrets—
His life was panting with them. . . .

Thomas Gilbert ("Gib") Dickinson, son of Austin and Susan Dickinson, Emily's beloved nephew, at about six years old. His sudden death of typhoid fever at age eight, in early October 1883, was a devastating blow to the family. *(By permission of the Houghton Library, Harvard University)*

He knew no niggard moment—His life was full of Boon . . .
No crescent was this Creature—He traveled from the Full—
Such soar, but never set—
I see him in the Star, and meet his sweet velocity in everything that flies . . .
Without a speculation, our little Ajax spans the whole. . . . (L 886)

The letter ends with the poem, "Pass to thy Rendezvous of Light" (Fr 1624). A year after the boy's death, in a letter to Sue, she enclosed a poem (Fr 1666), which begins, "Some Arrows slay but whom they strike—/ But this slew all *but* him . . ."

After Gib's death, she continued to write notes to his little friends. For the poet, who had lost her mother the previous year, and would soon lose the man she loved, JUDGE OTIS PHILLIPS LORD, Gib's death was perhaps the most painful of the accumulated griefs that preceded—and may have led to—her own final illness.

See also: MARTHA DICKINSON BIANCHI and EDWARD ("NED") DICKINSON.

FURTHER READING

Martha Dickinson Bianchi, "Reminiscences of a Country Girl," 64–5, 120; Alfred Habegger, *My Wars*, 615–619; Richard B. Sewall, *Life*, I, 124–125n, 146–147, 204–206.

Dickinson, William Austin (1829–1895) Emily's beloved older brother, Austin, was the family member closest to her in temperament and sensibility, the one who shared her sense of humor, and conspired with her in youthful rebellion. When their parents left town for two days, 17-year-old Austin wrote a friend that he and Emily were "anticipating a fine time in the absence of the ancient people" (Sewall, ed., *Lyman Letters*, 11–13). They were in league, not only against parents, but also against whomever or whatever bored, irritated, saddened or threatened the other. It was "Austin and Emily against the world," as biographer Richard B. Sewall has put it (*Life*, I, 97).

Born on April 16, 1829, in AMHERST, Austin was the eldest child of EDWARD and EMILY NORCROSS DICKINSON. A year and eight months older than Emily, the intelligent, high-spirited boy formed a natural alliance with his intense, imaginative and witty sister. Their "down-to-earth" younger sister, Vinnie (LAVINIA NORCROSS DICKINSON), frequently felt excluded. While Austin lived at home, attending AMHERST ACADEMY, he and Emily enjoyed long, intimate talks and developed a private language. When, in April 1842, he left for Williston Seminary at age 13, she wrote him the first letter she is known to have written to anyone. "We miss you very much indeed you cannot think how odd it seems without you there was always such a Hurrah wherever you was," wrote the 11-year-old Emily. During a correspondence that would last until shortly before Austin's marriage in 1856, the

Daguerreotype of William Austin Dickinson taken in the early 1850s *(The Todd-Bingham Picture Collection, Yale University Library)*

hole left in her life by his absence would remain a constant theme.

Austin attended Williston from April to August 1842, and again for the 1844–45 academic year, returning home to Amherst in between in order to protect the females of the household during his father's frequent and often extended business trips. During the latter period, he met another talented and high-spirited boy, JOSEPH BARDWELL LYMAN, who would become his close friend, and a frequent visitor to the Dickinson home, where he would court Vinnie and form a close "platonic relationship" with Emily. As an undergraduate at AMHERST COLLEGE from 1846 to 1850, Austin, tall and straight with a head of unruly red hair, continued to enliven the household, bringing home classmates, such as HENRY VAUGHAN EMMONS, GEORGE

GOULD, and JOHN LONG GRAVES, with whom Emily established intimate friendships.

Austin graduated Phi Beta Kappa and was honored by being chosen to deliver a commencement speech, only the title of which, "Elements of Our National Literature," survives. After graduation he tried teaching, first in Sunderland, a village 10 miles north of Amherst, then in Boston for about a year (1851–52). The experiment proved unsuccessful; teaching bored him and he was often lonely and homesick. Between teaching stints, he read law in his father's office and in March 1853 entered Harvard Law School. After graduating in July 1854, he considered moving to Chicago, but accepted his father's offer of a partnership. He would practice law in Amherst for the rest of his life. By this time, he was engaged to SUSAN HUNTINGTON GILBERT (DICKINSON) and his father's offer to build an elegant home, The EVERGREENS, for the couple on the property adjoining The HOMESTEAD may have influenced his decision. Some commentators have seen Austin's decision as an act of capitulation to his father's will, while others have pointed out that he was passionately attached to New England. It is even possible that remaining near Emily may have been a consideration, since he continued to depend on her to counteract his tendency to brood and worry, and to bolster him in innumerable ways.

As Emily's letters reveal, she flattered and pampered him, assured him of the family's love and admiration, sent him foodstuffs, worried about his laundry and his health. How Austin responded to her ministrations and what he gave in return are less clear. Only two of Austin's letters to her survive; presumably, the others were destroyed by Vinnie, along with the rest of the correspondence in Emily's possession, after she died, in accordance with her wishes. Eighty-six of her letters to Austin survive, all but three written between 1842 and 1854, that is, from the time she was 11 until his return to Amherst to practice law. The greatest number date from 1851, 1852, and 1853.

The letters are fascinating in many ways. To mitigate her brother's loneliness, Emily re-created detailed scenes of life in the Dickinson household, inviting him to share in them. Writing to Austin brought out the high-spirited, witty, satirical Emily.

She poked fun at conventional notions, as when she tells him how she is "gaining correct ideas of female propriety & sedate deportment" at MOUNT HOLYOKE FEMALE SEMINARY. Tiresome relatives or ludicrous neighbors became the butt of her wit and Father was a favorite object of satire. In contrast with her letters of this time to ABIAH PALMER ROOT or JANE HUMPHREY, she rarely gave way to dark moods or engaged him on the great subjects of religion, death, and immortality. This reticence may reflect her desire to inject some cheer into what she persisted in thinking of as his exile in Sunderland, Cambridge, or Boston. At any rate, it indicates that, however close they were, there was much that she held back from him.

Beneath her devotion to him there may have been an undercurrent of resentment of the male child who was the object of her father's admiration, especially when it came to literary issues. She once called him "Brother Pegasus," while letting him know that she, too, was writing verses. Austin worked hard at his epistolary style, and Father, as Emily wrote, praised his letters as "altogether before Shakespeare." Moreover, Austin could apparently be critical, as when he told her he wanted a "simpler style" in her letters. Her letter of June 28, 1851, reflects both these issues, as well as her determination to mask her feelings behind the cloak of humor. After praising a letter from him as "*so funny*—we have all been laughing till the old house rung again at your delineations of men, women, and things," she writes:

> I feel quite like retiring in the presence of one so grand, and casting my small lot among small birds and fishes—you say you don't understand me, you want a simpler. *Gratitude* indeed for all my fine philosophy! . . . As *simple* as you please . . . I'll be a little ninny—a little pussy catty, a little Red Riding Hood. . . .

One "dark" reality she did not spare him was her own loneliness and desire for him to return. As her girlhood friends married and moved away, Austin increasingly became her mainstay. In 1851, a year when many of their young Amherst acquaintances died, she wrote to him of home as "a bit of Eden," "fairer . . . and *brighter* than all the world beside." "Home is a holy thing," she declared, and wished she could transmit to him at Harvard Law School the "blessed air" she breathed in Amherst. She seemed to know that none of this was what a sister trying to help her brother as he enters the world, would say: "If I am *selfish*, Austin, I tell you you *must come home*." That same year, she wrote, "I think we miss each other more every day that we grow older, for we're all unlike most everyone, and are therefore more dependent on each other for delight."

But two years later, in a letter of May 16, 1853, foreseeing that their intimacy was ending, she wrote: "I feel very sure lately that the years we have had together are more than we shall have—I guess we shall journey separately. . . ." While there is no doubt that Austin's marriage to Sue in 1856 marked the end of an era, the nature of Austin and Emily's subsequent relationship is largely unknown. Sewall finds it inconceivable that during all the years he lived next door at The Evergreens, she did not write to him as she did to Sue, who received no less than 128 letters from 1858 on. Assuming there were such letters, either Vinnie or Sue, who survived him by many years, could have destroyed them. In the likely event that the letters alluded to the estrangement between the residents of the two neighboring mansions and the unhappiness of Austin and Sue's marriage, it is easy to imagine why each would have done so.

The union of Austin and Sue was troubled from the beginning. Their courtship began in the spring of 1850, during his senior year in college; three years later, the couple became engaged, shortly after their overnight tryst at the Revere Hotel in Boston on March 23, 1853, during which, in Austin's words, "we promised ourselves to each other." They would not marry until another three years had passed, on July 1, 1856, six months after Austin had acceded to Sue's ardent wish that he join the church. When the couple wed in Geneva, New York, at the home of Sue's Aunt Sophia, not a single member of the Dickinson family attended. In light of the family's affection for the charismatic young woman who was joining their ranks, the Dickinsons' absence is puzzling. Father particularly approved of the match and, as for Emily, who loved Sue with an intensity

greater than any she had had for other girlhood friends, the union of the two people closest to her at first seemed a cause for rejoicing. Whether she was aware of the conflicts and misunderstandings that had characterized their courtship is uncertain.

But the correspondence between Austin and Sue reveals a turbulent relationship, rife with doubts and misunderstandings. Austin was undergoing a period of emotional, intellectual, and spiritual confusion, which he confided, interestingly enough, not to Sue, but to her sister, Martha Gilbert, a year older than Sue, less outgoing, and herself in love with Austin. While courting Sue, he wrote Martha letters full of intense romantic introspection, in which he speaks of himself as "a frightened child" awakening "for the first time, to consciousness of my existence," striving to understand both himself and the cosmos.

In his letters to the pious Sue, he skirted around his religious doubts, focusing instead on his dreams of the perfect love and joyous future they would share. He seems to have been unaware that Sue, orphaned in her early years and looking to marriage for financial security and social respectability, may not have shared his romantic expectations. Austin was tormented by doubt of her love, feeling himself to be at the mercy of her unpredictable moods, what he called the "tempestuous latitude" where she lived. In what Austin confessed to Martha was a love-hate relationship, they took turns wounding one another, considering breaking off, and then retreating. Scholar Polly Longsworth believes that Austin's mistake was to define Sue as the feminine aspect of himself, so that anything she said that failed to echo his sentiments "threw him into spasms of gloom" (*Austin and Mabel*, 98). He wrote her that he had "been brought up to the idea that it was not a man's part to *show* tenderness unless in sore distress. . . . I have never *before* received *any* from any*body* . . ." When his undemonstrative father died, Austin kissed him and said, "There, father, I never dared do that while you were living." Yet he had a desperate need for tenderness and turned to Sue to find it: "Love *me*, Sue—*Love* me—for its my life," he pleaded. Given his neediness, it is interesting that he was aware of her fear of sex, and reassured her that he would make no demands she was unwilling to meet. Was Austin unconsciously entering a union that would ensure a continued absence of the tenderness he consciously wanted?

A quarter of a century later, he would tell his mistress, MABEL LOOMIS TODD, that he "felt as if he were going to his own execution" on his wedding day. Austin may have been exaggerating; there is little evidence to suggest the quality of his married life. His diary records Sue's ungoverned temper, her reluctance to have sex, and "morbid dread of having any children" (one of Sue's sisters had died in childbirth). He told Mabel that Sue had had three or four abortions prior to the birth of their son Ned in 1861. Sue had made sustained attempts to abort Ned—acts which both she and Austin

William Austin Dickinson. c. 1890 *(The Todd-Bingham Picture Collection, Yale University Library)*

held responsible for his developing epilepsy. Whatever her fears, Sue gave birth to two more children, Martha in 1866 and Gilbert in 1875.

The young couple's life was complicated by the arrival of the orphaned adolescent Newman sisters, Clara and Anna, wards of Edward Dickinson, in 1858. Living at the Evergreens for 10 years, they helped Sue care for the children but were regularly humiliated by her and treated like poor relations. "Something in her backfired . . . she rejected the very adulation and warmth she attracted, and often found pleasure in small revenges," notes Longsworth (*Austin and Mabel*, 114). Sue threw herself into beautifying her home, cultivating her garden, and making the Evergreens into the center of Amherst's social life. She entertained a long list of eminent visitors, including Ralph Waldo Emerson in 1857, and was greatly admired for her charm and taste.

During the first few years of the marriage, Emily was a frequent visitor, striking up friendships with Austin and Sue's great friend SAMUEL BOWLES and the vivacious young widow, CATHERINE TURNER ANTHON, and joining in the stimulating conversation and hilarity that characterized evenings at the Evergreens. Austin was himself worldly and sociable, a lover of literary conversation and good theater. He took enormous pride in his fine horses and made a flamboyant figure in his light-colored driving coat, his yellow wide-brimmed planter's hat and orangewood cane. His passion for art took him on frequent trips to New York to buy expensive paintings. But as the years passed Austin was increasingly estranged from the goings-on of "Sue and her crowd." He spent so much time with his sisters at the Homestead that Emily remarked, "We almost forget that he ever passed to a wedded Home" (L 807, 1883).

He found compensation for his domestic unhappiness in an exhausting round of professional and civic activities. He continued his father and grandfather's tradition of service to community, church and college, which he carried out at times with a brusque manner that could create enemies. Unlike his forebears, he never entered politics. As treasurer of Amherst College for 22 years, he instructed presidents in their duty, as his father had. But he also supervised construction of new college buildings and campus landscaping. A passionate lover

Amherst Common as it appeared around 1870. Austin headed a campaign to beautify Amherst by draining and planting the Common. *(Courtesy of the Jones Library, Inc., Amherst, Massachusetts)*

of nature, he was inspired by a series of lectures by EDWARD HITCHCOCK to embark on a campaign of beautifying Amherst, draining and planting the village common. After the Civil War, as Amherst expanded, he took a leading role in the introduction of public water, sewage, lighting, and roads. During 1867-68, he promoted and supervised the construction of the new First Church; Emily, according to legend, "crept out one evening with her brother as far as a certain tree in the hedge in order to see the new church." In his final years, he threw himself into creation of the idyllic Wildwood Cemetery.

These are only some of the projects that Austin, the "indispensable man" in town, took on, in addition to his responsibility for both his own household and, after his father's death, the affairs of his ailing mother and unmarried sisters at the Homestead. Intriguingly, as late as 1893, this leading citizen of Amherst was contemplating a move to Omaha, Nebraska, and wrote of wishing to see more "men of the world, and affairs, which I greatly miss here, as did my father before me." Yet he was a New Englander to the core and uncomfortable anywhere else. In 1887, on a trip that took him as far as St. Louis, he wrote: "I wouldn't give a volume of Emerson for all the hogs in Mississippi."

The fantasy of moving may well have been spurred by the tensions in Amherst resulting from his long affair with MABEL LOOMIS TODD, who was 24 years old when she moved from Washington, D.C., to Amherst in 1881 with her husband David Todd, a new astronomy professor at the college. Petite and very pretty, vivacious and multitalented, Mabel painted, played the piano, sang, and wrote, all with a high degree of accomplishment. As the Todds were drawn into Sue's social world, Austin and Mabel were increasingly drawn to one another by their shared sensibilities and love of nature. The affair that began between them in 1882 would end only with Austin's death in 1895, though neither ever left his or her spouse. Their diaries and letters reveal an extraordinary relationship, characterized by a sustained passion. Although their affair was generally known, Austin's reputation remained intact, since "community sympathy seemed to endorse his solution to what was generally recognized as a difficult marriage to Sue" (*Austin and Mabel,* 121). The lovers would often meet at the Homestead and it is probable that Emily did not begrudge her brother the joy Mabel gave him, particularly in light of the grief he sustained in the early years of their relationship.

On October 5, 1883, Austin and Sue's youngest child, eight-year-old Gilbert, died suddenly of typhoid fever. The loss of this precocious, delightful little boy devastated the inhabitants of both houses, not least his adoring Aunt Emily, who never recovered from his death; shortly afterward she was stricken with the illness that would end her life two-and-a-half years later. For Austin, estranged from his wife and two older children who took their mother's side in the marital conflict, the blow was so staggering that both Vinnie and Mabel feared for his life. Mabel wrote in her diary, "Mr. D. nearly died too. Gilbert was his idol, and the only thing in his house which truly loved him, or in which he took any pleasure." What ultimately saved him was his love for Mabel.

Austin seems always to have been overwhelmed, even incapacitated, in the presence of death. When his friend Frazar Stearns was killed in the Civil War, Austin's state of mind alarmed even Emily, who urged Samuel Bowles to reach out to his stricken friend. Similarly, when his father died, Austin (like Emily) was incapable of dealing with funeral arrangements, which were left to the practical Lavinia. When Emily died in 1886, he had another terrible shock. He wrote to Mabel who, once more, would sustain him:

It was settled before morning broke that Emily would not wake again this side.

The day was awful. She ceased to breathe that terrible breathing just before the whistles sounded for six. . . .

I was nearby.

Austin would outlive her by nine years, succumbing to heart disease, exacerbated by exhaustion, on August 16, 1895. His relentlessly active life had taken its toll. Amherst shops were closed during the funeral, as they had been for his father's. The obituary published in the *Springfield Republican* captured the private man that not all could see in the take-charge, sometimes imperious public figure: ". . . his nature was all gentleness and refinement, and there was a shyness and reserve in his composition, coupled with an intensity of feelings, that were almost pathetic at times. . . ."

When Austin died, he left behind an interpersonal morass involving his widow, his sister Vinnie, and his mistress that had profound effects on the posthumous publication of Emily's poems. Vinnie, who had befriended Mabel, ultimately turned to her to edit the poems when Sue showed no interest in doing so. Together with THOMAS WENTWORTH HIGGINSON, Mabel brought out the three editions of *Poems* in the early 1890s that introduced Emily Dickinson to the world. Mabel also collected and published the first edition of the *Letters* and would almost certainly have continued her dedicated work, had Vinnie not betrayed their friendship by suing her over a strip of land Austin had directed her to transfer to the Todds after his death. Mabel, embittered by Vinnie's treachery and exhausted by the strain and humiliation of a public trial, abandoned the manuscripts in her keeping. Not until 1913, with the publication of *The Single Hound,* under the editorship of MARTHA DICKINSON BIANCHI, would additional Dickinson poems become known to the public.

Austin himself, though he played an important role in the publication of the poems, encouraging Mabel and supplying her with biographical insights, seems never to have fully appreciated them. In his thank-you note to Higginson after the publication of the first volume, he wrote: "Whether it was, on the whole, advisable to publish is yet with me a question. . . ." He recognized his sister's brilliance, her wit, sparkling imagination, courage, and honesty. Yet, unlike Mabel, who heard and resonated to the music of Emily's poetry, her "Brother Pegasus," as she had called him in their youth, seems to have had no ear for it.

See also EDWARD ("NED") DICKINSON, SAMUEL FOWLER DICKINSON, THOMAS GILBERT DICKINSON, FIRST CHURCH OF CHRIST, PUBLICATION AND EDITORIAL SCHOLARSHIP, and REVIVALISM.

FURTHER READING

Millicent Todd Bingham, *Ancestor's Brocades*, 349–400; Millicent Todd Bingham, *Emily Dickinson's Home*, 127–142, 160–175, 256–270; Polly Longsworth, *Austin and Mabel*; Richard B. Sewall, *Life*, I, 91–127, 161–229, 428–443.

E

Edwards, Jonathan (1703–1758) A great 18th-century preacher and religious thinker who was the central figure of the first major American revival of religion, the Great Awakening of 1735–41, Edwards was a central figure in Emily Dickinson's PURITAN HERITAGE. He influenced her both through his theology and his role in promoting the REVIVALISM that was still a vital force in her youth. Edwards, whose sermons and discourses express the essence of Calvinist/Puritan theology, believed fervently that the meaning of history as a whole, as well as of any specific event, is God's plan for human redemption through Christ. His thinking exemplified the dualism inherent in Puritanism. One pole of his worldview was a vision of human nature as innately depraved and a belief in the absolute reality of Evil and of Satan; he preached that people must not trust themselves, since even the best natural virtue was unacceptable to God. Perceiving fear as a means of repentance, he strove, at times only too successfully, to inculcate it in his listeners. His delivery of a 1741 sermon, "Sinners in the Hands of an Angry God," in Enfield, Connecticut, caused such moaning and distress among the congregants that he never got to finish it. A controversial, arrogant man, in 1750 he was dismissed by the Northampton congregation he had served for 23 years and banished to Stockbridge, Massachusetts, a wilderness, where his flock consisted of 12 white families who disliked him and 250 quarrelling Indians.

This was the preacher of hellfire whom Dickinson refers to in a note she sent in the 1880s to her nephew's teacher, contrasting his message with that of Jesus:

> "All Liars shall have their part"—Jonathan Edwards
>
> "And let him that is athirst come"—Jesus (L 712 about 1881)

For Dickinson and others, this Edwards, intolerant and unforgiving, was the epitome of Calvinist terror and, as such, inimical to her spirit. His heritage, as embodied in the religious revivals that were so prominent in the AMHERST of her youth, and in which she could not bring herself to participate, caused her inner turmoil.

In his thinking as well as in his personal life, however, there were other, more sympathetic and life-affirming aspects. A man of rich imagination, who loved nature and experienced moments of sublime rapture, he believed that a loving God meant to redeem sinful humanity and that, in the end, with piety on the rise, only a few would be damned. Moreover, he "had given the drama of the soul a flaming immediacy for the people who came under the influence of his teaching," preaching the "spirit of sublime self-reliance which was from the beginning a hidden but irresistible thrust of Puritanism" (Sewall, *Life,* I, 24). In this sense, Edwards's Puritan consciousness nurtured Dickinson's. His "negativity, his disciplined journey through conscious despair, humiliation, and the joy of submission to an arbitrary and absent ordering of the Universe, presaged hers." (Howe, *My Emily Dickinson*, 48–49). Dickinson's decision not to publish her poetry in her lifetime may be viewed as a gesture of Calvinist self-assertion, a transposition to *her* religious universe, in which Poetry reigned, of Edward's belief that recognition by the world is not recognition by God and is thus a delusion.

Among his most important writings are "A Faithful Narrative of the Surprising Work of God," "Thoughts of the Revival in New England," and his unfinished masterwork, "A History of the Work of Redemption."

FURTHER READING

Susan Howe, *My Emily Dickinson*, 45–57; George M. Marsden, *Jonathan Edwards: A Life*. New Haven, Conn.: Yale University Press, 2003; Richard B. Sewall, *Life*, I, 21–27.

Emmons, Henry Vaughan (1832–1912)   One of the group of AMHERST COLLEGE students who visited the Dickinson home in the early 1850s, Emmons established a vibrant friendship with Emily. Their mutual passion for literature, especially poetry, was at the core of the relationship. Emmons entered the poet's life in 1853, the year her first literary mentor, BENJAMIN FRANKLIN NEWTON, died. The two young people—Emmons was two years her junior—were deeply drawn to each other, spending long hours in conversation. Whatever romantic feelings existed between them, the pair apparently never reached the stage of discussing marriage. Emily knew of Henry's interests in other women and, ostensibly at least, gave him her blessing. The friendship lasted from 1853 to 1854, ending when Emmons, engaged by then, graduated and went his own way, leaving Emily to add him to her "BOX OF PHANTOMS."

Emily and Henry came from similar social worlds. His father, Williams Emmons, was a pious and highly respected judge in Hallowell, Maine, a Whig like Emily's father, and, like EDWARD DICKINSON, securely established in the local hierarchy of his town. Emmons's mother belonged to the learned Vaughan family, said to possess a private library four-fifths the size of Harvard's. His paternal grandfather, the Reverend Nathanael Emmons, had coached Emily's paternal grandfather, SAMUEL FOWLER DICKINSON, in Calvinist theology in the 1790s.

As the "bright, black-eyed son of Judge Emmons," Henry was a worthy representative of his family's traditions. Despite a youthful episode in which he had run away from home, he is described by a contemporary as "a young gentleman of an amiable disposition & engaging manners. He has promising talents, is a bright scholar, & sustains a fair moral & religious character." (William Gardiner Hammond, *Remembrance of Amherst*, 241–242). Entering Amherst in 1851, he proved himself a serious scholar, presenting a number of papers over the years on such weighty topics as "Sympathy in Action," "Influence of the Belief in a Resurrection on Law" and (at his graduation ceremonies) "Sources of Originality."

He also emerged as a leader at the college. When Daniel Webster died on October 24, 1852, Emmons was among the five students who drew up a set of resolutions in his honor, the college voting to wear a badge of mourning for 30 days.

Henry Vaughan Emmons, Emily's close literary friend, in an 1854 photograph *(Amherst College Archives and Special Collections)*

His most important initiative was the founding of the *Amherst Collegiate Magazine,* whose first editor he became. Arguing idealistically for the establishment of the magazine, he expressed his hope "to counteract the many adverse influences at work in the college tone" and correct the impression that Amherst lacked "cultivation—literary power—literary advantages. . . ." Comparing the school to Yale, he wrote that "the bees are always swarming there—and fill the air with their clamor—while here they are silently at work making honey."

Emmons, who was a prolific writer, if not necessarily an elegant one, published 11 of his "labored and earnest essays, all of them clogged with an unusually imagistic prose" in the magazine during its first year (Habegger, *My Wars,* 317). In one of these, "Poetry the Voice of Sorrow" (published in October 1853), drawing heavily on "A Vision of Poets" by Elizabeth Barrett Browning, he presents a view of poets as the selected few, appointed by God, who "listen to His voice more nearly than other men." Like Jacob, they "wrestle with the angel of sorrow until he leaves a blessing upon them," after which they "bring peace and beauty to common men." Emily, who revered Barrett Browning, doubtless resonated to these words. It may even have been she who brought "A Vision of Poetry," with its view of poets as saints and martyrs, which plays a key role in her own poetry, to Emmons's attention. In another essay, "The Words of Rock Rimmon" (1854), Emmons expresses a youthful dream of joining the ancient school of true poets. Although he would never do so, his ardor for poetry tells us all we need to know about the speed and intensity with which his friendship with Emily developed.

Emmons was introduced to the Dickinson household by his roommate and her cousin, JOHN LONG GRAVES. By February 1852, Emily knew him well enough, as she informed her brother AUSTIN, to ride with *"Sophomore Emmons"* "alone." (L 72, February 6, 1852). Two weeks later, his name appears in a list of young men who visit often (L 75, to Austin, February 18, 1852]. That same month she wrote to SUSAN HUNTINGTON GILBERT DICKINSON, confiding that she had found a "beautiful, new, friend." Of the notes and letters they exchanged over the next two years, 14 of Emily's to Henry have survived. They tell of "beautiful rides" and walks together, calls and sociable evenings in the Dickinson home, often in the company of John Graves, a gift of arbutus from Emmons, a valentine from Emily, an exchange of books and, most likely, manuscripts. They are all brief; some are invitations, some encoded notes, written in their private language:

Mr. Emmons—

Since receiving your beautiful writing I have often desired to thank you thro' a few of my flowers, and arranged the fairest for you a little while ago, but heard you were away—

I have very few today, and they compare but slightly with the immortal blossoms you kindly gathered me, but will you please accept them—the "Lily of the field" for the blossoms of Paradise, and if 'tis ever mine to gather those which fade not from the garden we have not seen, you shall have a brighter one than I can find today.

Emilie E. Dickinson [L 119, spring 1853]

Although Dickinson often sent her friends flowers, the ones she mentions here are almost certainly her poems; "immortal blossoms" are probably his "beautiful writing," and flowers that "fade not," the deathless poems she hopes to write—a rare, early admission of her poetic ambitions. Sewall suggests that "Lily of the field" may be poem Fr 559, "Through the Dark Sod—as Education—/The Lily passes sure—"; although dated 1862 by Johnson and 1863 by Franklin, it may have been in her portfolio before then (*Life,* 412).

Emily's notes also contain allusions to a special "friend" whom Emmons is spending time with, apparently a young woman Emily knew. Shortly before Amherst's commencement week, he informed her of his engagement to Susan Phelps of Hadley. Emily wrote to him, asking to meet Susan. After the meeting, she gives no sign of jealousy or hurt, assuming, instead, the role of delighted platonic friend: "My heart is full of joy, Friend." Saying she must see him, she asks to ride with him that afternoon, then adds, "Of her I cannot write, yet I do thank the Father who's given her to you and wait impatiently to speak with you—" (L 169).

Emmons graduated from Amherst on August 10, 1854, at which occasion he, his fiancée, and Emily spent the day "very sweetly" together. Judging from Emily's description of her last days with Emmons, his engagement was not interfering with his desire to be with Emily: "There was much that was sweet Commencement week—much too that was dusty, but my bee gathered many drops of the sweetest and purest honey. I had many talks with Emmons, which I will not forget, and a charming farewell ride, before he went away—he stayed more than a week after Commencement was done, and came to see me often. . . . I shall miss Emmons very much" (L 172, to Sue, late August 1854).

Before leaving, he sent her a literary gift of some kind. We know of it through the enigmatic thank-you and farewell letter she sent him:

I find it Friend—I read it—I stop to thank you for it, just as the world is still—I thank you for them all—the pearl, and then the onyx, and then the emerald stone.

My crown, indeed! I do not fear the king, attired in this grandeur.

Please send me gems again—I have a flower. It looks like them, and for its bright resemblance, receive it.

A pleasant journey to you, both in the pathway home, and in the longer way—*Then* "golden morning's open flowings, *shall* sway the trees to murmurous bowings, in metric chant of blessed poems"—Have I convinced you Friend?

Pleasantly, Emily (L 171: August 18, 1854).

The references to precious gems draw upon what Emily called "the Gem chapter," Revelation 21, where the gates of the New Jerusalem are said to be of pearl and the fourth and fifth foundations are adorned with emerald and sardonyx (Habegger, *My Wars*, 320). Emily was always hyperbolically appreciative of his gifts of words, and the "immortal blossoms" of her previous letter here become divine gems. Whatever the gift was, it has apparently endowed Emily with royalty ("my crown") and supreme self-confidence. In the next line, she tempers her triumphal tone, comparing her "flower" modestly to his "gems," but still insisting on their "bright resemblance." The quotation ("golden mornings . . .") is a graceful modification of a tercet from Barrett Browning's "A Vision of Poets," with which Emmons had concluded his "Rock Rimmon" essay. Precisely what she may have convinced him of, whether a literary or romantic matter, remains enigmatic, as does the oddly lukewarm valediction, "Pleasantly."

Five years later, on May 8, 1860, Emmons, who had been studying theology in distant Bangor Theological Seminary for three years, from 1856–59, and Susan Phelps broke off their engagement. Emily, who had kept in touch with Susan, wrote her a one-line note of solidarity that month: "'When thou goest through the Waters, I will go with thee.'" If she wrote to Henry as well, the letter has not survived. Emmons married Ann Shephard, daughter of George C. Shepard, longtime friend of the Dickinsons, on September 6, 1865, and continued on an active ministerial career until his retirement in 1902.

The Evergreens EDWARD DICKINSON, the poet's father, built the Italianate villa for WILLIAM AUSTIN and SUSAN HUNTINGTON GILBERT DICKINSON, the poet's older brother and sister-in-law just west of the Dickinson HOMESTEAD, at the time of their marriage in 1856. The first named house in AMHERST, it was called the Evergreens because of Austin's interest in tree planting and landscaping. Edward paid for the house and retained ownership, but placed Austin in charge of design. With substantial input from the well-known Northampton architect William Fenno Pratt, Austin built the earliest and one of the finest examples of Italianate domestic architecture in Amherst. He strove to make the villa, with its flat-roofed tower and wide porch, a place of "superior comfort or refinement." His intentions were reflected in the banishment of the kitchen to an older, pre-existing house hidden behind and joined to the new structure. The rooms of the Evergreens were smaller than those of the more stately Homestead; they "aimed at an up-to-date jewel-box effect—an exhibition of privacy and comfort organized around high-definition kitsch, including a statuette of Cupid and Psyche in rapturous embrace" (Habegger, 429–430). The house's exterior was distinguished by smooth stone-

The Evergreens, home of Susan and Austin Dickinson, in winter *(Courtesy of the Jones Library, Amherst, Massachusetts)*

colored siding and bright green shutters, and by the scattering of rhododendrons under the trees.

Together, the Homestead and the Evergreens formed a family compound, where Emily Dickinson lived her life "within the hedge." There, Austin and Sue raised their three children, EDWARD AUSTIN DICKINSON (NED) (1861–98), MARTHA DICKINSON BIANCHI (Mattie) (1865–1943), and THOMAS GILBERT DICKINSON (Gib) (1875–83), his Aunt Emily's precocious favorite, whose tragic death of typhoid fever at age eight changed the lives of the entire family. While Austin pursued his legal career and civic projects, Sue turned the Evergreens into a center of social and cultural life in Amherst. Socially ambitious and adroit and deeply interested in culture, Sue thrived in her role as hostess, opening the house to a succession of prominent literary and political visitors. When Ralph Waldo Emerson spoke in Amherst in 1857,

he was entertained at the Evergreens. Sue gave a vivid account of the visit (from which Emily stayed away) in her draft essay about her prominent guests, "Annals of the Evergreens," a 25-page typewritten document (Dickinson Papers, Houghton Library, Harvard) written for her children as a memorial of the great days in the Evergreens. (See Sewall, *Life*, I, Appendix I, 247–248, for excerpts.) Over the years, her guest list included the writer Bret Harte, abolitionist Wendell Phillips, and Anna Dickinson, the pioneering woman orator during and after the Civil War. Sue and Austin's drawing room served as something akin to a literary salon for Emily, providing a setting for lively talk and interaction with minds capable of stimulating her. Not least important among those Sue introduced her to was SAMUEL BOWLES, the dynamic editor of the *Springfield Republican,* who would join that select company of older men the poet called "Master."

While the lives of the Dickinsons at each house were closely intertwined, over the years, as her seclusion increased, Emily rarely visited the Evergreens, a notable exception, a plausible legend has it, being the night of her beloved nephew Gib's death. Relations between the two households were complex and often hostile. "The war between the houses," as it is referred to in Dickinson scholarship, was a multifaceted, ongoing set of conflicts, whose primary antagonists were Emily, sister LAVINIA, Austin, Sue and, after 1882, Austin's mistress and Emily's future literary executrix, MABEL LOOMIS TODD. The estrangement had its roots in Austin's troubled courtship of Sue and in Emily and Sue's turbulent friendship;

Rear view of The Evergreens today, open to visitors as part of the Emily Dickinson Museum. Happily, the wish of Martha Dickinson Bianchi, that the house be burned after her death, was not honored. *(Courtesy of Darryl Leiter)*

it reached new depths of bitterness when Austin became involved with Mabel; after Emily's death, hostilities swirled around issues of property and the posthumous publication of the poet's work.

Austin and Sue lived at the Evergreens until their respective deaths in 1895 and 1913. Their only surviving child, Martha, continued to live in the house and preserve it, without change, until her own death in 1943. Her efforts, as well as those of her heirs, Alfred Leete and Mary Landis Hampson, succeeded in preserving the house intact. However, her will stipulated that it be burned to the ground, possibly to "exorcise" the family tragedies the house had witnessed. Fortunately, this wish was not honored. Today it is still completely furnished with Dickinson family furniture, household accoutrements, and décor selected and displayed by the family during the 19th century.

In 2002, ownership of the Evergreens was transferred from the Martha Bianchi Trust to Amherst College. It was subsequently merged with the Homestead into a single museum, called The Emily Dickinson Museum, devoted to the interpretation of the life of the poet and her family and the community in which she lived.

Front view of The Evergreens, the Italianate villa Edward Dickinson built for Austin and Susan Dickinson. Susan made it into Amherst's leading social salon. *(Courtesy of Darryl Leiter)*

FURTHER READING

Alfred Habegger, *My Wars*, 429–30; Richard B. Sewall, *Life*, I, 161–234.

F

The First Church of Christ Established in 1739, when AMHERST was known as the Third Precinct of Hadley, Massachusetts, the First Church was the CONGREGATIONALIST assembly the Dickinson family attended. In a system in which a town was both a political and religion entity, the church was finely interwoven with the very founding of Amherst: The first town meetings were held in the church building and town revenues supported the church's ministers until 1833. The original wooden meetinghouse near College Hill that Emily attended in her childhood and youth was replaced in 1867 by an impressive new structure at 165 Main Street, where it stands today, across from The EVERGREENS, where Emily's brother and his wife, WILLIAM AUSTIN and SUSAN HUNTINGTON GILBERT DICKINSON, lived. Austin played a leading role in promoting the construction of the church's Pelham granite edifice. Designed by the architect George Hawthorne, its tall spire, massive grace, and stained-glass windows bestowed a distinction on the Dickinson quarter of Amherst. (Habegger, 506–507). According to LAVINIA DICKINSON, Emily, already a recluse, ventured out with Austin one evening as far as a certain tree in the Evergreens' hemlock hedge in order to see the new church. Although by then she had not attended church services for close to 20 years, the church was a lifelong presence in her community and her inner life.

From its pre-Revolutionary beginnings to Emily Dickinson's time, the First Church remained

The First Church of Christ of Amherst, completed in 1867 on Main Street, across from the Dickinson mansion *(Courtesy of the Jones Library, Amherst, Massachusetts)*

faithful to its Puritan/Calvinist orthodox stance, fiercely opposed to the "heretical," liberal positions of UNITARIANISM, which was continuing to gain supporters in eastern Massachusetts. For Emily's grandfather, SAMUEL FOWLER DICKINSON, and fellow church elders, opposition to Unitarianism was a primary motivation for the founding of AMHERST

COLLEGE as a Calvinist educational institution to rival Harvard Divinity School, a bastion of Unitarianism.

From childhood to early adulthood Emily attended services at the church, where she heard the preaching of Reverend Aaron Merrick Colton, whose pithy, humorous, understated sermons provided her with a lesson in the power of language. Her early letters are replete with accounts of events during church services. Emily's family was actively involved in church matters, albeit on different levels. Austin and Emily's father, EDWARD DICKINSON, participated in many decisions made by the congregation. Edward spoke at the dedication of the new building in 1868 and Austin delivered an address at the 150th anniversary celebration in 1889. At the time, it was possible to be a member of a Congregational *parish*, which was in charge of finances, without being a full member of the *church*, which required a public profession of faith in Christ. Thus, on July 3, 1831, when Emily was seven months old, her mother, EMILY NORCROSS DICKINSON, joined the church by profession of faith, part of a wave of fresh converts, in a year when REVIVALISM was shaking New York and New England. Emily's father worked for the parish for 20 years while his wife was a church member, professing his faith only on August 11, 1850, on the same day that his future daughter-in-law Susan converted. Vinnie, too, joined the church during that year of revivals. Emily, "estranged from certain aspects of things spiritual and temporal in her small, self-conscious community" (Sewall, II, 688), never did. In 1861, she wrote:

Some keep the Sabbath going to Church—
I keep it, staying at Home—
With a Bobolink for a Chorister—
And an Orchard, for a Dome—

(Fr 236, J 324)

See also PURITAN HERITAGE.

FURTHER READING

250 Years at First Church in Amherst (1739–1989), Amherst, Mass.: First Congregational Church in Amherst, 1990; Alfred Habegger, *My Wars*, 124–28; Richard B. Sewall, *Life*, I, 118–22 and II, 618.

Fowler, Emily Ellsworth (Mrs. Gordon Lester Ford) (1826–1893)   A childhood friend, whom Dickinson included in a list of girls who were "very dear" to her, Emily Fowler was beautiful, cultured, and at ease in the public spotlight. She was the daughter of William Chauncy Fowler, professor of rhetoric and oratory, and English literature at AMHERST COLLEGE (1838–1843), and Harriet W. Fowler, daughter of Noah Webster, who compiled the *American Dictionary of the English Language* that Dickinson used and cherished. Four years older than Dickinson, Emily Fowler attended AMHERST ACADEMY during the early 1840s, when the poet was a student there. With her mother's expert coaching, Emily Fowler did well at public exams. But tragedy befell the family when she was in her teens. In the fall of 1842 her small brother died, to be followed two years later, in the spring of 1844, by her mother, who had been suffering from consumption, as tuberculosis was then called, for many years. Emily Fowler had no choice but to withdraw from school in order to take charge of her surviving siblings and run the household.

Some of what is known of the friendship of Emily Dickinson and Emily Fowler derives from the 14 letters the poet wrote, beginning in the spring of 1850, and extending briefly beyond Fowler's marriage in December 1853. Richard B. Sewall has called these letters "as vacuous a correspondence as Emily ever conducted" (*Life*, II, 375). And, indeed, eight letters are little more than excuses for not coming to visit; one included a lock of hair, and one a flower. Although Dickinson expresses adoration and longing for her older friend, she does not open up to her. The lack of closeness between the two young women may have been rooted in the divide that opened between the poet and those friends who were carried away in the religious REVIVALS that swept through Amherst during her youth. Emily Fowler was an early convert, joining the church on profession of faith at age 16. During the powerful revival of 1850, she sent the poet and her brother, AUSTIN, a lengthy letter, in which she assured them that they would eventually be blessed with "the sense of sin, the joy of pardon, the holy strength, the happiness" that came with accepting Christ. In Austin's reply to this letter, he

Emily Fowler Ford, a close girlhood friend of the poet's

said that he presumed his sister would not answer, since "She is rather too wild at present." Dickinson had experienced a number of revivals, in her school days at both Amherst Academy and MOUNT HOLYOKE FEMALE SEMINARY, and, despite much soul-searching, had proven immune to their appeal. But she did eventually write to Fowler, in terms that implied she was undergoing a difficult religious struggle: "I wanted to write, and just tell you that *me* and *my spirit* were fighting this morning." She wrote this affectionate letter on a day when a snowstorm provided the perfect excuse for not visiting (L 32, early 1850). In subsequent letters, Dickinson could be playful and inventive in making her excuses. In one, she pretends to be writing as she stands at the door, resisting the temptation to knock and go in, since then she would be so happy, she would never leave (L 78, about 1852). In another, she writes, "I come and see you a great many times every day, though I don't bring my body with me, so perhaps you don't know I'm there" (L 111, spring 1853).

Nonetheless, the two young women *did* socialize. The social diary of Dickinson's younger sister LAVINIA records that Emily Fowler called no fewer than 18 times in 1851. In the memoirs that she wrote after the poet's death, she provides some arresting descriptions of Dickinson in her early 20s. "She loved with all her might," writes Fowler Ford, "there was never a touch of the worldling about her." Describing the Shakespeare club that Fowler organized, she writes: "[Dickinson] once asked me, if it did not make me shiver to hear a great many people talk, they took all the clothes off their souls'. . . ." She recalls Dickinson's reaction when one of the young men in the club suggested inking out the Bard's bawdier passages: "(Dickinson) took her departure, saying, 'There's nothing wicked in Shakespeare, and if there is I don't want to know it.'" Fowler further notes, "She mingled freely in all the companies and excursions of the moment and the evening frolics . . . Emily was not beautiful yet she had great beauties. Her eyes were lovely auburn, soft and warm, and her hair lay in rings of the same color all over her head, and her skin and teeth were good . . ." (Leyda, *Years and Hours*, 1, 133, 135).

In the fall of 1851, Fowler was going through a difficult time. As her brothers grew up and went their ways, the Fowler's family home was breaking up. Professor Fowler did not approve of his daughter's fiancé, Francis Edward March, and when March's lungs hemorrhaged, he sailed south, releasing Fowler from her engagement. During this period, Dickinson wrote consolingly to Fowler and remarked in a letter to Austin, "I wonder how she endures all her numberless trials." Although March recovered his health, Fowler decided to marry her father's choice, Gordon Lester Ford, the wealthy former partner of her ex-fiancé and a promising lawyer. The couple left AMHERST on December 16, 1853, and made their home in Brooklyn, New York, where Gordon Ford became a successful business executive.

Emily's letter to the new Mrs. Ford, less than a week after the marriage, is particularly interesting for its description of the wedding as a kind of death: ". . . when . . . hidden by your veil you stood before us all and made those promises, and when we kissed you, all, and went back to our homes, it seemed to me translation, not any earthly thing, and if a little after you'd ridden on the wind, it would not have surprised me" (L 146, December 21, 1853). The word *translation*, as Dickinson uses it here, refers to "the removal of a person to heaven without subjecting him to death" (Noah Webster, *Dictionary*). The passage suggests something of the young Dickinson's view of marriage, as both exultation and removal from the world. Despite this extravagant vision of loss, Dickinson made no special efforts to hold on to the friendship. Fowler Ford became an author in her own right and the mother of two sons who would become well-known writers. She had some influence in the literary world and might have helped Dickinson get her work into print. Instead, she recounts in a letter to MABEL LOOMIS TODD, she advised JOSIAH HOLLAND, editor of *Scribner's*, who was considering some of Dickinson's poems, that her old friend's poetry was "beautiful, so concentrated, but they remind me of orchids, air-plants that have no roots in the earth." Sewall blames Mrs. Ford for confirming the editor's doubts and thus preventing publication of Dickinson's work at a time in her life when she was still willing to be published. He character-izes Mrs. Ford's poems, stories and essays as "so deeply rooted in the moral and religious platitudes of the day as to have little life of their own" (*Life*, II, 378). In 1882, a full 10 years after Mrs. Ford published her collection *My Recreations*, she sent a copy to Dickinson, who replied with a three-sentence acknowledgment of the gift. In July of that year, when Ford visited Amherst, Emily, who rarely received visits by then, refused to see her.

After Dickinson's death and the triumph of her first posthumous collection of the *Poems*, Mrs. Ford shared her girlhood memories of the poet in the reminiscences she sent to Mrs. Todd. Describing their girlhood excursions, gathering wildflowers, she paints a sentimental image of the poet as nature lover, a flower among the flowers, while offering little insight into the realities of Dickinson's early life. In 1891 she published a poem in the *Springfield Republican*, called "Eheu! Emily Dickinson!" in which she perpetuated the myth of the recluse who shrank from life.

FURTHER READING

Jay Leyda, *Years and Hours*, I, 133–35; Richard B. Sewall, *Life*, 375–379.

G

Gould, George Henry (1827–1899) A close friend of Emily's brother, WILLIAM AUSTIN, who visited the Dickinson household from around 1849 until at least 1852. George Gould was one of the group of outstanding young men, Austin's classmates at AMHERST COLLEGE, including HENRY VAUGHAN EMMONS and JOHN LONG GRAVES, who made the winter of 1849–50 "alive with fun" for 19-year-old Emily. Gould was a lanky young man of six foot eight, with a lean face, a beaked nose, and a ready wit. Although he had no money and was forced to rely on the Charity Fund to pay his college bills, this in no way impeded his active and successful college career. A member of Austin's illustrious fraternity (Alpha Delta Phi), he was an editor of *The Indicator,* the college's literary monthly. Known as an excellent public speaker, he often competed with Austin on rhetorical platforms; it was Gould's commencement speech ("Relation of Self Reverence to Christianity"), rather than Austin's, that was lauded in *The Hampshire and Franklin Express,* which said it "abounded in glowing thought." Gould would go on to become a respected minister, who settled in Worcester in 1872.

There is no doubt that Emily and George enjoyed an intimate friendship. Like Emmons and BENJAMIN FRANKLIN NEWTON, he was the type of sensitive, idealistic young man with whom she could share her enthusiasms and, possibly, her poetry. Gould's invitation to Emily to attend a candy-pulling with him has survived; the poet preserved it

and 25 years later, drafted a poem (Fr 1389) about winter's approach on the back. Beyond this, however, Gould's role in her life remains a matter of speculation.

He is generally thought to be the recipient of Emily's notorious valentine that was published in *The Indicator* in 1850. The editor whose comments accompany the valentine was Henry Shipley; it is not known whether he published the work with the poet's consent. "I wish I knew who the author is. She must have some spell, by which she quickens the imagination, and causes the high blood to run frolic through the veins," wrote Shipley, who essentially gave away the author's identity by appending the valentine with the abbreviation "Q.E.D." (used to indicate that a mathematical proposition has been proven). Selected from the pile of valentines from female admirers that inundated *The Indicator,* the bold prose composition was a virtuoso demonstration of Dickinson's wit, sense of hilarity, and verbal mastery. After a flight of euphonious Latinate nonsense ("Magnum bonum, 'harum scarum,' zounds et zounds, et war alarum. . . ."), she proposes a meeting with the young man she is addressing, saying she wants "a chat sir, or a tête-à-tête, a confab, a mingling of opposite minds. . . ." While she never suggests more than this intellectual union, her anticipation of it is tongue-in-cheek ecstatic: "Our friendship, sir, shall endure till sun and moon shall wane no more, till stars shall set, and victims rise to grace the final sacrifice." Declaring that she is "Judith

The 1850 commencement photograph of George Gould, Emily's intimate friend and probable recipient of her first publication, a comic valentine letter *(Amherst College Archives and Special Collections)*

the heroine of the Apocrypha" and the young man "the orator of Ephesus," she reassures him, "That's what they call a metaphor in our country. Don't be afraid of it, sir, it won't bite. If it was my dog *Carlo* now!" (Dickinson knew, of course, that by mentioning CARLO, she was giving herself away.) In her invocation of a glorious union, she alludes to the social activism of the radical reform movement of the 1840s, but with a wild hyperbolic twist: "We'll build Alms-houses, and transcendental State prisons and scaffold—we will blow out the sun, and the moon, and encourage invention. Alpha shall kiss Omega—we will ride up the hill of glory—Hallelujah, all hail!" What response Gould had to the valentine is unknown. Nor is there any record of the reaction of Emily's father, EDWARD DICKINSON, who believed that women should stay out of the public spotlight and could hardly have

been pleased by his daughter's flamboyant literary debut.

The second mystery surrounding Emily and George concerns the nature of their relationship and Edward's role in it: Were they in love and did Edward forbid them to marry? Was George the friend, mentioned in the letter to Abiah, whom Emily loved "*so* dearly," but with whom she resisted the temptation to go for a ride? Was he the "golden dream" she was dreaming that winter? Dickinson's most recent biographer speculates "that Edward took some sort of disciplinary step to arrest his 19-year-old daughter's involvement with the impoverished editor who had connived at her exposure in print" (Habegger, *My Wars*, 239). It seems highly improbable that George Gould was Emily's great love and the reason she wore white later in life—a thesis that formed the basis of Genevieve Taggard's 1930 biography. Sewall notes that Emily was strong-minded enough by this stage in her life to have married George, had she truly wanted him. In a letter to MABEL LOOMIS TODD, dated February 8, 1894, Gould wrote, "I had quite a cherished batch of Emily's letters myself kept sacredly in a small trunk . . . which some fifteen years ago mysteriously disappeared . . ." (*Ancestor's Brocades*, 254). Had they survived, they undoubtedly would have solved the riddle.

FURTHER READING

Millicent Todd Bingham, *Ancestor's Brocades*, 254–255; Alfred Habegger, *My Wars*, 234–239; Richard B. Sewall, *Life*, II, 419–422; Genevieve Taggard, *The Life and Mind of Emily Dickinson*, (New York: Alfred A. Knopf, 1930).

Graves, John Long (1831–1915) "Cousin John," as Emily liked to call him, was a distant cousin, related to the Amherst Dickinsons through the family of LUCRETIA GUNN DICKINSON, the poet's paternal grandmother. Born in Sunderland, Massachusetts, John was a year younger than Emily. Arriving in town for his freshman year at AMHERST COLLEGE, he promptly introduced himself to the Dickinson household on Pleasant Street, becoming a frequent visitor and special friend of Emily's from then on, until he graduated in 1855. The poet's eight surviving letters to him, five of which are brief, lively notes, indicate that Emily went to a concert with him, knitted wristlets for him (to thank him for the gift of an aeolian harp), played the piano for him, and asked him in, together with his roommate HENRY VAUGHAN EMMONS, for currant wine.

Her witty poem-invitation to him conveys the tone of the relationship:

A little poem we will write unto our Cousin John,
to tell him if he does not come and see us very soon,
we will immediately forget there's any such a man,
and when he comes to see us, we will not be "at home."

(L 117, spring 1853)

But there was another, deeper side to their friendship. If this strikingly handsome and intelligent cousin was not romantically involved with Emily, he appears to have keenly valued her uniqueness. In a letter to John on October 4, 1854, the poet's childhood friend ELIZA M. COLEMAN wrote, "I know you appreciate her & I think few of her Amherst friends do." At a time when other, earlier friendships were fading, John and Henry Emmons, who shared Emily's passion for literature, filled an important gap in her life.

A memorable episode in their friendship occurred in April 1854, when the other Dickinsons were visiting Washington, D.C., and John was recruited to stay at the Pleasant Street house to protect Emily and SUSAN HUNTINGTON GILBERT (DICKINSON). Two years later, when John was serving as a school principal in Orford, New Hampshire, Emily harked back nostalgically to "those triumphant days—Our April." She recalls one haunting night when she played the piano for him: "I play the old, old tunes yet, which used to flit about your head after honest hours—and wake dear Sue, and madden me, with their grief and fun—How far from us, that spring seems—" (L 184, late April 1856). Cousin John was among the few to hear Emily play; apparently the compositions she performed were original. Many years later, Graves's daughter recalled: "Oftentimes

father would be wakened from his sleep by heavenly music. Emily would explain in the morning, 'I can improvise better at night'" (cited in Leyda, *Years and Hours,* from an article by Gertrude M. Graves in the Boston *Sunday Globe,* January 12, 1930).

In that same letter, Emily expresses her concern for John's welfare and desire to have him confide in her: "Are you very happy? Why didn't you tell me so before you went away? . . . You know what I mean, dont you, and if you are so happy, I kneel and thank God for it, before I go to sleep." Since the next two paragraphs are about John's reconciliation with Emmons, after an extended quarrel, John's "happiness" may have been related to this episode; or Emily may have been alluding to a romantic interest of John's.

It was only toward the end of their relationship, after John had graduated with high honors in August 1855, giving the philosophical oration at commencement (on "Philological Philosophy"),

John Long Graves, Emily's distant cousin and special friend in the early 1850s, when he was a student at Amherst College *(By permission of the Houghton Library, Harvard University)*

that Emily's letters allow him access to her deeper feelings. Her old friend is now principal of Orford Academy in New Hampshire. Writing in late April 1856, on a Sunday when she has declined to attend church with her family, she attempts a vivid tableau of the arriving spring, which quickly gives way to an elegy on things past and passing:

> Much that is gay—have I to show, if you were with me, John upon this April grass—then there are *sadder* features—here and there, *wings* half gone to dust, that fluttered so, last year—a mouldering plume, an empty house, in which a bird resided. Where last year's flies, their errand ran, and last year's *crickets fell!* We, too, are flying—fading, John—and the song "here lies," soon upon lips that love us now—will have hummed and ended. (L 184)

Making an effort to wrench herself from these morbid musings, she raises what she calls "no schoolboy's theme!"—the promise of resurrection. Her thoughts, however, are anything but consoling. Writing to this future minister, during the Easter season, Dickinson has no qualms about regaling him with a mocking send-up of the life to come:

> It is a jolly thought to think that we can be Eternal—when air and earth are *full* of lives that are gone—and done—and a conceited thing indeed, this promised Resurrection! *Congratulate* me—John—Lad—and "here's a health to *you*"—that we each have a *pair* of lives, and need not chary be, of the one "that *now* is"—
>
> "Ha—ha—if any can afford—'tis *us* a roundelay!

This manic outburst soon gives way to melancholy. Congratulating John on his engagement to Fanny Britton, daughter of one of the founders of Orford Academy, she says she is "glad indeed to see—if in your heart, *another* lies, bound one day to me," but cannot help adding, "Mid your momentous cares, pleasant to know that 'Lang Syne' has it's own place—that nook and cranny still retain their accustomed guest." Relegated to the obscure corners of his life, she identifies herself with nature's

last year's discards that she has described earlier. Like other important friends, such as Emmons, who disappeared from her life when he graduated in 1854, John was moving on and marrying, while she stayed behind.

Emily's last surviving written letter to John consigns him to her BOX OF PHANTOMS, a metaphor she also used in a letter written around the same time to Sue. On the basis of handwriting, Johnson dates it "about 1856," but concedes that it may have been written earlier. Johnson speculates that the letter, delivered by hand, was sent during the summer vacation when Graves, who graduated from Amherst College in 1855, visited Amherst at commencement in August.

> Ah John—*Gone?*
>
> Then I lift the lid to my box of Phantoms and lay another in, unto the Resurrection—Then will I gather in *Paradise*, the blossoms fallen here, and on the shores of the sea of Light, seek my missing sands.
>
> Your Coz—Emilie (L 186).

If she wrote to him again after this terse, resigned farewell, the correspondence has not survived. John married Frances on September 1, 1858, and was ordained pastor of the new Congregationalist Church in Boston in 1860. He gave up this position a few years later and went into business. When EDWARD DICKINSON died suddenly in Boston in 1874, John traveled to Amherst to assist the bereaved family and share with them what he could about the circumstances of the death. If he saw Emily at that time, as is not unlikely, there is no record of such a meeting. John's daughter wrote that whenever he spoke of Emily Dickinson in later years "there was about him a kind of glow," and he would say, "unlike anyone else—a grace, a charm. . . ." (Millicent Todd Bingham, *Emily Dickinson's Home*, 400–401).

FURTHER READING

Millicent Todd Bingham, *Emily Dickinson's Home.* 400–401; Alfred Habegger, *My Wars*, 295–296; Richard B. Sewall, *Life*, II, 404–410.

H

Higginson, Thomas Wentworth (1823–1911)
"Mr. Higginson," Emily Dickinson wrote on April 15, 1862, "Are you too deeply occupied to say if my Verse is alive? The Mind is so near itself—it cannot see distinctly—and I have none to ask— " (L 260). The 31-year-old poet had decided to write to this eminent man of letters after reading his article, "Letter to a Young Contributor," in the April 1862 *Atlantic Monthly*. The article offered witty, practical advice to young writers, pointedly including women, and spoke of the glory of language and the power and mystery of the individual word—ideas that resonated with Dickinson's own sense of her craft. She enclosed with her note four poems: "We play at Paste," "SAFE IN THEIR ALABASTER CHAMBERS—," "The nearest dream recedes unrealized," and "I'll tell you how the Sun rose." When Higginson responded, critiquing her work and asking to know more about her, the two began a rich, lifelong correspondence that played a vital role in the poet's life.

Ironically, Higginson, famous in his lifetime as social activist, revolutionary Abolitionist and influential writer, is now remembered chiefly for his friendship with a poet whose work he never wholly embraced. This "radical Brahmin" (*My Wars*, 452) was the youngest of the 10 children of Stephen and Louisa Storrow Higginson. He graduated from Harvard College in 1841 and went on to earn a degree from Harvard Divinity School (1847). He married his cousin, Mary Elizabeth Channing, who later became permanently confined due to a mus-

cle ailment that may have been multiple sclerosis. Using his pulpit to criticize society's ills, he served as the radical pastor of the First Religious Society (Unitarian) in Newburyport (1847–52), and then at the Free Church at Worcester (1852–61). In his inaugural sermon there, he said: "We need more radicalism in our religion and more religion in our radicalism."

A man of action as well as words, he twice tested the new Fugitive Slave Law in Boston, once in a conspiracy that failed in 1851, and again in 1854 in a violent attempt to protect the fugitive slave Anthony Burns. In that action, Higginson was wounded and one man was killed. He was a member of the "Secret Six" who conspired to provide financial backing for John Brown's raid on the federal arms depot in Harper's Ferry on October 16, 1859. When it failed, Abolitionism was briefly in retreat and Higginson turned his energies elsewhere.

Resigning from the ministry, Higginson rose rapidly in the literary world through his fine essays for the *Atlantic Monthly*, including a series of sensitive nature essays that focused on the seasonal changes and flowering plants of New England. Dickinson, who was a regular reader of the *Atlantic*, most probably read these and was drawn to the man who spoke of the inadequacy of literature or art to describe "one summer day." Nature would be a vital part of the bond they formed.

Dickinson was aware of Higginson's political activism, but seems to have taken little interest in

Thomas Wentworth Higginson, the eminent writer whom Dickinson sought out as her literary mentor. After her death, he became her first editor. *(By permission of the Houghton Library, Harvard University)*

this aspect of his life. When the Civil War broke out, he left literature behind and accepted a position in the Union Army that not every soldier would have found attractive: colonel of the First South Carolina Volunteers, the first regiment recruited from former slaves (1862–64). Writing to him then, Emily says only that she wished she had seen him before he became "improbable," adding "War seems to me an oblique place." Biographer Richard B. Sewall observes that, in her surviving letters to Higginson, "she all but ignored the stirring events of the time and said nothing at all about the great national causes with which he had for years been publicly identified—Abolition, women's rights, the plight of the Northern poor" (*Life*, II, 535). While he fought for the Union, she was in the midst of her period of "flood creativity," writing hundreds of her finest works.

Dickinson reached out to Higginson at a moment when two other key figures in her life were leaving for other shores. REVEREND CHARLES WADSWORTH, the married Presbyterian minister whom some believe to have been her great love, was on the point of sailing to San Francisco. At the same time, SAMUEL BOWLES, the crusading editor of the *Springfield Republican,* with whom she shared an intimate friendship, had embarked for several months in Europe. Both men were mentors of sorts to Emily— religious and spiritual confidants. Now she turned to Higginson in the hope of finding in him a literary mentor. More than 70 of her letters to him have survived, and, despite a certain amount of posing, they are among her most revealing. Highly literary, thoughtful, and candid about the spiritual and artistic problems of her middle and later years, they tell us much of what we know about her. Although Higginson's letters were destroyed, we can infer some of his advice, requests, and comments from her replies. We also have a handful of letters, to his wife and sisters, sharing his impressions of her after each of his two visits.

Her first letter, with its breathless request for an opinion on her poetry, was terse and mysterious. Higginson wrote back at once to find out who she was. She answered with what he later called an ability to evade "with a naïve skill such as the most experienced and worldly coquette might envy." (*Atlantic Monthly,* October 1891, 445). "You asked how old I was? I made no verse—but one or two—until this winter—Sir—" (L 261, April 25, 1862). This was simply untrue. She had written hundreds of poems since 1858, including some of her greatest. Throughout, the second letter is a mixture of honest confession and half-truth. She confides, "I had a terror—since September—I could tell to none—and so I sing, as the Boy does by the Burying Ground—because I am afraid—." The "terror" may refer to her learning about Wadsworth's imminent departure, or to the first hint of her subsequent eye troubles, or to some frightening nervous or mental disturbance. Yet to cite this specific fear as *the* explanation for why she "sang" was surely misleading. She is disingenuous, too, when she describes her reading, mentioning "Mr.

Ruskin" and "Sir Thomas Browne," writers Higginson recommended in his article, while omitting Emerson and her beloved Shakespeare.

She presents herself as a loner, whose companions are "the Hills—Sir—and the Sundown—and a Dog—" and depicts herself as isolated within an uncongenial family:

> I have a Brother and Sister—My Mother does not care for thought—and Father, too busy with his Briefs—to notice what we do—He buys me many Books—but begs me not to read them—because he fears they joggle the Mind.

Biographer Alfred Habegger cautions the reader not to take such claims at face value, while recognizing that "they offer powerful insights into her conception of her situation" (My Wars, 455). Thus, her famous self-portrait in a subsequent letter is less a description than a vision of herself: "I . . . am small, like the Wren, and my Hair is bold, like the Chestnut Bur—and my eyes, like the Sherry in the Glass, that the Guest leaves—" (July 1862, L 268).

Dickinson's most persistent fiction in the early letters, however, is her self-presentation as the novice she was not. She asks: "Could you tell me how to grow—or is it unconveyed—like Melody—or Witchcraft?" And yet she had already grown immensely on her own. The three poems she enclosed with her second letter ("THERE CAME A DAY—AT SUMMER'S FULL—," "Of all the Sounds despatched abroad," and "South winds jostle them") amply demonstrated that she had been initiated into the mysteries of both melody and witchcraft.

The "surgery" Higginson had already performed on her poems, for which she thanked him, doubtless expressed his rigidly time-bounded sense of poetic form: insistence on exact rhyme, standard punctuation, correct grammar, and titles. Dickinson humbly acknowledged his criticism of her "spasmodic gait" and "uncontrolled" style. When he later praises some poems highly, she replies: "I have had but few pleasures so deep as your opinion, and if I tried to thank you, my tears would block my tongue" (L 265). She begs him to be her "Preceptor" (teacher) and sends him a poem

comparing him to the dawn coming into her dark life. When he advises her to delay publishing, she assures him that publishing is "foreign to my thought, as Firmament to Fin—" (L 265, June 1, 1862). Since she had written to him in response to an article advising young poets on how to publish, her disavowal is not quite credible. By the next letter (L 268, July 1862), she promises him obedience and signs herself "Your Scholar."

The next month, she is all humility as she confesses the source of her failure to "control" her verse:

> I had no Monarch in my life, and cannot rule myself, and when I try to organize—my little Force explodes—and leaves me bare and charred—
>
> I think you called me "Wayward." Will you help me improve?" (L 271, August 1862)

A few lines later, however, she can scarcely disguise her dismay that Higginson was proving no different from others:

> You say 'Beyond your knowledge.' You would not jest with me, because I believe you—but Preceptor—you cannot mean it? All men say 'What' to me, but I thought it a fashion—

Despite the deference she expresses in her letters, Emily Dickinson never paid the least attention to his poetic advice. She was disturbed as to why she was "the only Kangaroo among the Beauty" and wanted him to help her understand and change this. Yet, even as she strove to please him, she could not deny her sense of inner rightness: "Perhaps you smile at me. I could not stop for that. My Business is Circumference—." Circumference, a key concept in her poetics, signified the utmost of the poet's reach into the unknown (see CIRCUMFERENCE POEMS). Despite her desire for a mentor and Higginson's willingness to play the role, the difference between their temperaments doomed the attempt from the outset. As Sewall points out, he had none of her "inquiring, groping, experimental spirit" (Life, II, 550). He was never haunted by the doubts that tormented and inspired her, but instead devoted his life to fighting for what he knew was just.

If Higginson ultimately failed Dickinson as a literary critic, he nonetheless played a vital role in her life, providing her with a literary friend she could talk to. She read all his articles, which served as a point of departure for their literary discussions. It was to Higginson that she expressed what became her most famous remark on literature: "Nature is a Haunted House—but Art—a House that tries to be haunted" (1876, probably spring). And she apparently found wisdom in his larger literary precepts. In 1877 she wrote him:

Often, when troubled by entreaty, that paragraph of your's has saved me—"Such being the Majesty of the Art you presume to practice, you can at least take time before dishonoring it. . . ."

He was a loyal correspondent, who recognized that she was a poet, perceived something "remarkable" in her, and was interested enough in her to come to Amherst to meet her.

In the spring of 1869, he invited her to come to Boston to attend meetings of either the Radical Club or the Women's Club, the two leading intellectual societies open to women. He wrote: "I have the greatest desire to see you, always feeling that perhaps if I could once take you by the hand I might be something to you; but till then you only enshroud yourself in this fiery mist & I cannot reach you, but only rejoice in the rare sparkles of light" (L 330a). But Emily refused: "Could it please your convenience to come so far as Amherst I should be very glad, but I do not cross my Father's ground to any House or Town" (L 330). She continued, "You were not aware that you saved my Life. To thank you in person has been since then one of my few requests."

Higginson arrived at The HOMESTEAD on August 16, 1870, a day later than she expected him. That night, from his room at Amherst House, despite his fatigue, he followed his custom of writing a detailed letter to his invalid wife, to alleviate her sense of isolation. His account provides a unique portrait of the poet in her 40th year:

A step like a pattering child's in entry & in glided a little plain woman with two smooth bands of reddish hair and a face . . . with no good feature—in a very plain and exquisitely clean white pique & blue net worsted shawl. She came to me with two day lilies which she put in a sort of childlike way into my hand & said, "These are my introduction" in a soft frightened breathless childlike voice—& added under her breath Forgive me if I am frightened; I never see strangers and hardly know what to say—but she talked soon & thenceforward continuously. . . . (L 342a and L 342b)

He goes on to cite many of the remarkable things she said, including:

"Women talk: men are silent: that is why I dread women."

"If I read a book [and] it makes my whole body so cold no fire ever can warm me I know *that* is poetry. If I feel physically as if the top of my head were taken off, I know *that* is poetry. These are the only way I know it. Is there any other way."

"How do most people live without any thoughts. . . . How do they get the strength to put their clothes on in the morning."

"Truth is such a *rare* thing it is delightful to tell it."

"I find ecstasy in living—the mere sense of living is joy enough."

"Is it oblivion or absorption when things pass from our minds?"

Although clearly fascinated by her, he concludes: "I never was with anyone who drained my nerve power so much. Without touching her, she drew from me. I am glad not to live near her." Twenty years later, in an October 1891 article he wrote in the *Atlantic Monthly*, Higginson would express the same reservations about Dickinson's extreme emotional demands, while admitting his inability to fully understand her:

The impression undoubtedly made on me was that of an excess of tension, and of an abnormal life. . . . She was much too enigmatical a being for me to solve in an hour's interview, and an instinct told me that the slightest attempt at direct cross-examination would make her withdraw into her shell. . . .

When he visited her for the second and last time, in 1873, on a lecture trip to Amherst, he recorded only one of her remarks: "She says, 'there is always one thing to be grateful for—that one is one's self and not somebody else.'" In a letter to his sisters afterward, he described her as "my eccentric poetess" and cited his wife's exclamation, "Oh, why do the insane so cling to you?" as applying to Dickinson's case. This kind of condescension "after two visits, fifty-two poems, and twenty-one letters" suggests that Higginson "too, was posing a bit with his sisters. When he told Mary of the things Emily had said that 'you would have thought foolish & I wise,' his admiration seems to have been genuine" (Sewall, *Life,* II, 566). His affectionate follow-up letter to Emily speaks of "the beautiful thoughts and words you have sent me" and expresses the hope that they will continue to correspond with trust, honesty, and love.

Indeed, their intimate correspondence continued, with Emily sending him a large number of poems, until her death. She still occasionally asked for more instruction and about 1874 reverted to signing herself "Your Scholar" and began to call him "Master." But he had also become the friend to whom, in 1874, she wrote the beautiful letter about her last afternoon with her father. She became more and more solicitous about his family affairs, especially during his wife's illness in the mid-1870s. On September 2, 1877, following his wife's death, she offered, as a veteran of loss, to guide him through his grief: "The Wilderness is new—to you. Master, let me lead you" (L 517). She sent him four letters of consolation, two of them signed "Your Scholar." Yet it was she who was instructing him. "Do not try to be saved—but let Redemption find you—" (L 522, early autumn 1877).

In February 1879, when Higginson married a second tine, to Mary Potter Thacher, Dickinson rejoiced, "To congratulate the Redeemed is perhaps superfluous for Redemption leaves nothing for Earth to add. . . ." (L 593, February 1879). In the years ahead, they would console one another over the loss of their mutual friend, HELEN FISKE HUNT JACKSON. And in early May 1886, desperately ill herself, she addressed him a two-line poem-note, asking whether her "friend" still "breathes" (L 1045). When Dickinson died the following month, Higginson attended the funeral, reading Emily

Brontë's "Last Lines," one of her favorite poems, at the ceremony.

In the years immediately following her death, Higginson became a key figure in the publication of a body of poetry he had not considered worthy of seeing print during the poet's lifetime. Although MABEL LOOMIS TODD originally provided the necessary enthusiasm and eventually did the lion's share of work on the pioneering editions of the poetry they brought out in the early 1890s, without Higginson's influence in the literary world, she might not have found a publisher for Dickinson's work. After her sensitive reading aloud of several poems, he agreed to be her coeditor. As the work progressed, he wrote to her on November 25, 1889:

> I can't tell you how much I am enjoying the poems. There are many new to me which take my breath away & which have *form* beyond most of those I have seen before. . . . (*Ancestor's Brocades,* 34)

Thomas Wentworth Higginson and daughter Margaret on a tricycle, c. 1884 *(The Todd-Bingham Picture Collection, Yale University Library)*

His confidence in the poems steadily soared, until, on November 12, 1890, when copies of the First Series of *Poems* by Emily Dickinson arrived, he wondered: "How could we ever have doubted about them" (*Ancestor's Brocades,* 72).

Yet Higginson seems never to have abandoned his lifelong doctrine of form, even after Dickinson's poems achieved astounding popularity. In his *Reader's Dictionary of American Literature* (1903), he wrote: "Emily Dickinson never quite succeeded in grasping the importance of poetic form." Rather than dismiss him as hopelessly retrograde, however, Habegger provocatively suggests that Higginson "still embodies the sympathetic bafflement and even dismay of more sophisticated readers" (*My Wars,* 458).

See also PUBLICATION AND EDITORIAL SCHOLARSHIP.

FURTHER READING

Millicent Todd Bingham, *Ancestor's Brocades*; Tilden G. Edelstein, *Strange Enthusiasm: A Life of Thomas Wentworth Higginson*; Alfred Habegger, *My Wars,* 451–459, 522–524; Suzanne Juhasz and Cristanne Miller, "Performances of Gender in Dickinson's Poetry," in *Cambridge Companion,* 107–128; Richard B. Sewall, *Life,* II, 532–576; Anna Mary Wells, *Dear Preceptor: The Life and Times of Thomas Wentworth Higginson* (1963).

Hitchcock, Edward (1793–1864) An eminent geologist and educator, Hitchcock, as president of AMHERST COLLEGE, exerted a strong influence on Dickinson when she was a student at the college's sister institution, AMHERST ACADEMY. Hitchcock graduated from what was then Yale College in 1818 and in 1821, married Orra White of AMHERST, who shared his life until her death, a year before his, on May 26, 1863. He became the first professor of chemistry at Amherst College in 1825. Twenty years later, on April 14, 1845, he was elected president of the college, a post he held until November 22, 1854, serving the college as an able administrator during its most crucial years.

Internationally recognized for his books on geology, Hitchcock was a giant in the Amherst community. In his funeral eulogy, William S. Tyler

Edward Hitchcock, eminent scientist and educator, whose thinking influenced Emily Dickinson as a student at Amherst Academy

described him in terms that demonstrate the reverence he inspired: "He was a large man. His frame was large, his mind was large, his heart was large. He sympathized with all, because he comprehended all; and he comprehended all . . . because he had all in himself" (cited in Sewall, *Life,* II, 342).

Amherst College and the academy, which had given birth to it, were closely allied; the college permitted academy students to attend its lectures and provided a major source of well-educated instructors. Thus, during Emily's time at the academy, between 1840 and 1847, Hitchcock's philosophy of religion and education was pervasive in the school's curriculum. His religion was of the orthodox Calvinist variety, placing him staunchly behind the spirit of religious piety that permeated every aspect of education at the academy when Emily was a student. Teachers were expected to be religious, and textbooks, no matter what the subject matter, were firmly grounded in Christian beliefs.

The essence of Hitchcock's diverse teachings was that science and religion were not in conflict, but mutually illuminated one another. For this scientist and man of God, science actually proved religion; the wonders of nature, which he sought to understand with the most up-to-date scientific knowledge of natural processes and structures, were for him demonstrations of the sublimity of the creation and its creator. He was the type of professor who, not content with talking to his students about the subject at hand, enthusiastically led them on botanical and geological field trips.

Hitchcock's reverence for creation undoubtedly influenced, or, at the least, reinforced, Dickinson's evolving perception of the natural world; the poetry she later wrote would express a similar sense of sublimity in nature. Years later, she gave some indication of the significance of Hitchcock's work to her when she wrote to THOMAS WENTWORTH HIGGINSON: "When Flowers annually died and I was a child, I used to read Dr. Hitchcock's Book on the Flowers of North America [possibly a reference to his *Catalogue of Plants Growing . . . in the Vicinity of Amherst* (1829)]. This comforted their Absence—assuring me they lived" (L 488, early 1877). Hitchcock was himself a poet who, in his 1845 inaugural address, paid lyric tributes to the CONNECTICUT RIVER VALLEY in terms akin to her own feelings for the New England landscape she would later celebrate in her poems.

Emily would surely have read, even if she did not attend, Hitchcock's 1850 series of lectures, *Religious Lectures on Peculiar Phenomena in the Four Seasons.* Many passages in these lectures, which characterized each season's unique beauty and meaning, as well as its own chemistry and physics, resonate with her own poetry, including those dealing with the seasons, in which the sense of sublimity coexists with a precise knowledge of chemical processes, botany, and geology. Hitchcock's book on geology was especially influential. The numerous earthquakes and volcanoes that appear in her poetry testify to the impact of his geological studies on her imagination. Equally prominent, Dickinson's poems are studded with gems, minerals, plain rocks, and even alloys, in ways that reveal the poet's knowledge of their properties and how they were formed.

Hitchcock's personal example and scholarship nourished the young Emily. At the same time, Sewall points out the irony that Hitchcock, in his views on poetry, represented an attitude fundamentally opposed to the kind of work Dickinson would produce. Using the criterion of orthodoxy to define good poetry, he declared himself the enemy of "wantonness and indecency" and distrusted "artists of the beautiful." This attitude was common among inhabitants of the Connecticut River Valley and contributed to the guilt Dickinson felt as she embarked on the career of poet.

FURTHER READING

Edward Hitchcock, *Catalogue of Plants Growing Without Cultivation in the Vicinity of Amherst College,* Amherst, Mass., 1829; *The Highest Use of Learning: An Address delivered at his Inauguration to the Presidency of Amherst College,* Amherst, Mass., 1845; *Religious Lectures on Peculiar Phenomena in the Four Seasons,* Amherst, Mass., 1850; Richard B. Sewall, *Life,* II, 342–357.

Holland, Elizabeth Luna Chapin (1823–1896) and **Josiah Gilbert** (1819–1881)   The Hollands entered Emily Dickinson's life when she was 22, during the August 1853 Commencement Week celebrations of AMHERST COLLEGE, during which EDWARD and EMILY NORCROSS DICKINSON held their famous receptions. The couple came to dine with the Dickinsons in their Pleasant Street home and had, as Emily wrote to her absent brother, WILLIAM AUSTIN, "Champagne for dinner and a very fine time. . . ." Together with her sister, LAVINIA, Emily made a brief visit to the couple's Springfield home in September 1853. She enjoyed herself so well that, despite her growing reluctance to travel, she accepted a second invitation the following September. So began a sustaining lifelong friendship, especially with Elizabeth Holland, who became her closest friend.

When Emily met the Hollands, they had been married for nine years and had been living in Springfield since 1849, when SAMUEL BOWLES hired Josiah Holland as literary editor of the *Springfield Republican.* At 30, "Dr. Holland," as Josiah was called, after a brief attempt at a medical career, had tried a stint at journalism and a period of teaching in the south, which led to his writing *Sketches of Plantation Life,* published in the *Republican* by Bowles. In his 20 years at the *Republican,* Holland transformed it into a medium for serious discussion of literary, religious, and moral affairs. While differing with Bowles on

Elizabeth Luna Chapin Holland, the nurturing, longtime friend Emily called "Little Sister" *(By permission of the Houghton Library, Harvard University)*

many issues, as part owner of the paper, he was free to express his views. Unlike Bowles, he was an antifeminist who opposed women's rights to own property and to vote. In an unsigned essay "Women in Literature" (1858) he developed the familiar idea that men express principles while women express fancies, dismissing two of Emily's (and Bowles's) most beloved works, Charlotte Brontë's *Jane Eyre* and Elizabeth Barrett Browning's *Aurora Leigh*. His opinion of Walt Whitman is clear from the title of the review he ran: "'Leaves of Grass'—Smut in Them."

In addition to his journalistic work, Josiah was a prolific author. In 1855, he published his *History of Western Massachusetts*. Yet his greatest fame was as an essayist. Under the pen name of Timothy Titcomb, he wrote a series of short articles that amounted to lay sermons on moral matters. Dickinson biographer Alfred Habegger calls him "a preacher at heart" with "a sure grasp of mass-market tastes," a "polished simplifier" with a larger following in the Midwest than in New York or

Boston (*My Wars*, 308). He became something of a national institution and lectured throughout the country. In 1870 he moved to New York and founded *Scribner's Monthly*, later the *Century Magazine*, and remained its editor until his death.

Given his literary opinions and the simplified level of his own writings, we may well ask what attracted Emily to Dr. Holland. We know that he considered her poems "too ethereal" for publication. He and Elizabeth, whose literary tastes were conventional, seem to have valued the 31 poems she sent them less as literature than as unique expressions of their cherished friend. But if Emily resented this "blind spot" in their understanding of her, there is no evidence of it in her letters. The Hollands offered her not literary validation

Josiah Gilbert Holland, husband of Emily's great friend, Elizabeth. He was cultural editor of the *Springfield Republican* and later editor of *Scribner's Monthly*. *(By permission of the Houghton Library, Harvard University)*

but something she needed as much, if not more, at that juncture of her life. At a time when she was feeling the loss of many girlhood friends, as well as the growing constraints created by her mother's precarious health, she found in them both affection and a liberating spiritual companionship.

She reveled in the free-spirited atmosphere of their home, markedly in contrast with her own, reverberating with laughter, literary talks, and the harmony of Elizabeth's piano accompanying Josiah's fine tenor. According to Theodora Ward, the Hollands' granddaughter, they "must have seemed the perfect young married couple—he tall, dark, likened by one of his friends to an Indian chief; she little, lively, and radiant, the perfect mother and hostess" (cited in Sewall, *Life,* II, 596). Elizabeth has been described as the "typical womanly woman," attractive and gracious, putting her husband's concerns first. Habegger points out that Dickinson was deeply attracted to the spectacle of "the dark man with the doll-wife," or "the Angel Wife," as she characterized them years later, and, in several poems of the early 1860s, pictured herself in just such a relationship:

Forever at His side to walk—
The smaller of the two! . . .

(Fr 264)

Of equal importance was the Hollands' relaxed brand of religiosity. Like Dickinson, Dr. Holland rejected doctrine and his way of putting beliefs to the test of feelings authorized Emily to go on trusting her own feelings. Years later, after Josiah's death, she wrote his widow: "I shall never forget the Doctor's prayer, my first morning with you—so simple, so believing. *That* God must be a friend— *that* was a different God—and I almost felt warmer myself, in the midst of a tie so sunshiny" (L 731, October 1881). Her first letter, after the September 1853 visit, reveals the spiritual release she felt just thinking about them: "I love to write to you—it gives my heart a holiday and sets the bells to ringing" (L 133). In her early letters, she expresses embarrassment at writing too much of her joy in them. In March 1855, writing from Philadelphia, she calls them "these darling friends, for whom I would not count my life too great a sacrifice.

Thank God there is a world, and that the friends we love dwell forever and ever in a house above" (L 179). With the Hollands she could flaunt her religious irreverence and at the same time dream of a heavenly reunion with them. Later, she could write confidently, "Perhaps you laugh at me! Perhaps the whole United States are laughing at me too! *I* can't stop for that! *My* business is to love!" (L 269).

Ninety-four of the letters that Emily wrote to the Hollands have survived, most of them to Elizabeth, seven years her senior, whom by 1860, she called "Sister," "Little Sister," and "Loved and Little Sister." Of the friendship, biographer Richard B. Sewall observes, "It has no flavor of crisis, no sudden intensity of feeling or purpose only to diminish decorously over the years" (*Life,* II, 594). Perhaps the sole note of irritation came when Emily reproached her friend for writing a joint letter to her and Vinnie, advising her: "A mutual plum is not a plum . . ." (L 321, probably late November 1866).

With Elizabeth Holland, an excellent listener, Emily found a rapport she lacked with her own mother and turned to her for motherly advice on all kinds of issues: the anxiety she felt after listening to a sermon about perdition; the ordeal of moving from the house on Pleasant Street to The HOMESTEAD; Vinnie's headache; the tribulations of keeping house during her mother's illness; her distress at inadvertently offending her friend Mr. Chapman. With the notable exception of the quality and role of her poetry in her life, Mrs. Holland seems to have understood Emily best, becoming her true spiritual sister.

There is an unexplained five-year gap in their correspondence, between 1860 and 1865, crucial years in the poet's life, the years of her "flood creativity," when she was experiencing emotional crises, the nature of which have never been wholly clarified. Scholars have advanced many theories to explain why Emily might not have written or why the Hollands might have destroyed the letters she *did* write. Sewall believes it is inconceivable that she did not turn to Elizabeth during these years and Theodora Ward doubted there was any break in the friendship. In 1862 and 1864, she sent them four poems, and the important L 269 has been variously dated 1859, 1861, and 1862.

After 1865, Emily's letters are generally more objective, replete with references to the world of nature and affairs, and to books, and liberal with quotations from the Bible. Their sharp wit and tendency toward aphorism are remarkable, as in this letter of early May 1866:

> Friday I tasted life. It was a vast morsel. A circus passed the house—still I feel the red in my mind though the drums are out. . . .
>
> The lawn is full of south and the odors tangle and I hear today for the first the river in the tree.
>
> You mentioned spring's delaying—I blamed her for the opposite. I would eat evanescence slowly.
>
> Vinnie is deeply afflicted in the death of her dappled cat, though I convince her it is immortal, which assists her some. . . . (L 318)

This same letter begins with another striking passage, which reveals the evolution in Dickinson's understanding of the reality of friendship from the days when she had longed for a perfect unity with such girlhood intimates as ABIAH PALMER ROOT and JANE HUMPHREY. It eloquently expresses her essential paradoxical belief that fulfillment depends on deprivation:

> After you went, a low wind warbled through the house like a spacious bird, making it high but lonely. When you had gone the love came. I supposed it would. The supper of the heart is when the guest has gone.
>
> Shame is so intrinsic in a strong affection we must all experience Adam's reticence.

In other letters, she insisted to the worldly Hollands that true life is internal. When they returned from five months in Europe in May 1870, she wrote them: "To shut our eyes is Travel." Two years later, when her aversion to travel caused her to refuse to visit them in Springfield, she defended herself in metaphor: "In adequate Music there is a Major and a Minor. Should there not also be a Private?" (L 370). There was much that was private—her relationships with Bowles, REVEREND CHARLES WADSWORTH, or JUDGE OTIS PHILLIPS LORD—that she chose not to share with Mrs. Holland. But she

shared her own griefs—the deaths of her father in 1874, her mother in 1882, and her eight-year-old nephew THOMAS GILBERT DICKINSON in 1883—and supported her "Little Sister" through such traumas as the loss of an eye following surgery in the summer of 1872, assuring her: "Be secure of this, that whatever waver—her Gibraltar's Heart is firm" (L 377). She wrote movingly to her when Josiah died in 1881.

Despite their awareness of grief and transience, the Holland letters are imbued with a spirited love of life. Emily seems never to have lost either her intense interest in the affairs of Mrs. Holland, her children and grandchildren, or her deep affection for this lifelong friend. In her last letter to her, written in early spring 1886, just before her death, when Elizabeth was in Florida for her rheumatism, she affirms: "Emily and Vinnie give the love greater every hour" (L 1038).

See also "WHO NEVER WANTED—MADDEST JOY," CATHERINE TURNER ANTHON, CONGREGATIONALISM, PURITAN HERITAGE, and REVIVALISM.

FURTHER READING

Alfred Habegger, *My Wars,* 307–310, 563–564; Richard B. Sewall, *Life,* II, 593–625; Theodora Van Wagenen Ward, *Emily Dickinson's Letters to Dr. and Mrs. Josiah Gilbert Holland.*

Holland, Sophia (1829–1844) Sophia Holland was the close childhood friend whose early death had a devastating impact on the young Emily. Sophia was the daughter of Seneca Holland, a leading Amherst businessman, and Emily's second cousin, a granddaughter of Lucinda Dickinson, a sister-in-law of Emily's paternal grandfather, SAMUEL FOWLER DICKINSON. She was 15 when she died at home, of typhus, on April 29, 1844. Emily, who was 13 at the time, kept watch at her friend's deathbed and was allowed to see her as she lay unconscious just before she died. Afterward, Emily became ill and was sent to Boston by her concerned parents, to spend a month with her favorite aunt, LAVINIA NORCROSS NORCROSS. She returned in better health and better spirits. Emily's first written mention of Sophia occurs in a letter to ABIAH PALMER ROOT, informing her that Sophia's father seemed cheered since adopting his niece "in Sophia's place"; the niece was precisely Sophia's age and strongly resembled her (L 9, January 12, 1846). Emily reports this matter-of-factly, giving no indication of her reaction to her friend being "replaced" in this manner.

She apparently kept her grief to herself, unburdening herself only two years later, in a remarkable passage in a letter to Abiah. Trying to comfort Abiah for the loss of her friend E. Smith, she gave a vivid account of her own anguish:

> She was too lovely for earth & she was transplanted from earth to heaven. I visited her often in sickness and watched over her bed. But at length Reason fled and the physician forbid any but the nurse to go into her room. Then it seemed to me I should die too if I could not be permitted to watch over her or even to look at her face. At length the doctor said she must die & allowed me to look at her for a moment through the open door. I took off my shoes and stole softly to the sick room.
>
> There she lay mild & beautiful as in health & her pale features lit up with an unearthly—smile. I looked as long as friends would permit & when they told me I must look no longer let them lead me away. I shed no tear for my heart was too full too weep, but after she was laid in her coffin & I felt I could not call her back again I gave way to a fixed melancholy. (L 11, March 28, 1846)

Scholars differ over the "normalcy" of Emily's involvement in this death scene. Cynthia Griffin Wolff believes that, given the hold of death and death scenes on the Victorian imagination and the frequency with which people died at home, the adults present found her "persistence and curiosity" wholly understandable: "The vigil over Sophia Holland constituted a part of Emily Dickinson's training for womanhood in mid-nineteenth century Amherst." (*Emily Dickinson*, 77). Judith Farr disagrees: "Although Victorian culture encouraged pious contemplation of death and eternity, Dickinson's absorption seems to have struck people as dangerously excessive." (*Passion*, 5). Whatever the judgment of the adults present, there can be no doubt about either the intensity of the young poet's

response to this loss or her resiliency, that is, her ability to be drawn back into the circle of life.

The passage is also important for what it shows about her growing literary prowess and anticipates about the nature of her mature poetry. Despite a handful of phrases drawn from the lexicon of sentimental Victorian death scenes ("I trust," "Reason fled," "fixed melancholy"), the writing is spare, dramatic, and searingly honest. While attesting to extreme emotions—the sense that she, too, would die if she could not see Sophia's face—there is a dignity and stoicism to her response. She avoids the easy comfort of healing tears or a neat religious resolution to her anguish.

A number of themes that would be central to her poetry are found here: the woman "too lovely for earth"; the urgent desire to look at other faces ("What would I give to see his face?" Fr 266); the gnawing of a grief that is suppressed and leads to depression ("GRIEF IS A MOUSE—," Fr 753); the admonition to bear grief silently; and the searing loss of a loved one who will be waiting in heaven (Farr, *Passion*, 5).

FURTHER READING

Judith Farr. *Passion*, 45; Cynthia Griffin Wolff, *Emily Dickinson*, 76–77.

The Homestead Said to be AMHERST's first brick residence, The Homestead was built by Emily Dickinson's paternal grandfather, SAMUEL FOWLER DICKINSON, in 1813, to house his growing brood of children. Emily was born in this house, also called the "Mansion," and lived in it for the first nine and last 30 years of her life. The spacious center hall structure is located at 280 Main Street, about three blocks east of the Amherst village center. "It has all the grace and symmetry of the pre-Victorian American style" but as a landmark has nothing to make it distinctive (Wolff, *Emily Dickinson*, 3). A symmetrical hip-roofed dwelling in the Federal style, it had two stories, each containing four rooms. Over the years it underwent extensive additions and remodeling. A one-story wooden "office" (no longer standing) was attached to the west wall. In 1817, Samuel mortgaged the house for $2,500 (about $75,000 today), the beginning of financial

Emily Dickinson's family home, The Homestead, in 1886 *(By permission of the Houghton Library, Harvard University)*

woes from which he would never succeed in extricating himself.

In 1830, as Samuel's fortunes declined and his own rose, EDWARD DICKINSON, the poet's father and Samuel's oldest son, bought the western half of the Homestead for $1,500. Edward, his wife, EMILY NORCROSS DICKINSON, together with their young son, WILLIAM AUSTIN, moved in. Later that year, on December 10, Emily Elizabeth Dickinson was born. In March 1833 Samuel, whose career had reached its low point (AMHERST COLLEGE, which he had played a leading role in founding, was in deep financial straits), sold his half of the Homestead to David Mack, owner of a general store in Amherst, and moved to Cincinnati, Ohio. The Edward Dickinson family continued to live at the Homestead with the Mack family for seven more years. The Dickinsons built a brick addition on the back of the house for the kitchen and laundry, embellished the roof with a stylish cupola, erected a veranda on the western side of the house, and built a conservatory (no longer extant) for the poet's exotic plants. To

the north of the house stood a huge barn for carriage, sleigh, and harness room, stalls for two horses and two cows, and a toolhouse with a room for the hired man on the second floor.

Rear view of The Homestead today, open to visitors as part of the Emily Dickinson Museum *(Courtesy of Darryl Leiter)*

Edward sold his half of the Homestead to David Mack in April 1840 and moved his family to a clapboard house (no longer standing) on North Pleasant Street. In April 1855, following the death of David Mack, he bought it back and in mid-November of that year the Dickinson family moved back. The following year he built a house adjacent to the Homestead, to the west; his son, Austin, brought his new bride, SUSAN HUNTINGTON GILBERT DICKINSON, to live there, and they named it The EVERGREENS. Together, these properties, set back from the street with a tall hedge of hemlocks, which afforded additional privacy, would form the geographical limits of Emily's world in the latter half of her life. Her bedroom was on the second floor; two of its windows faced Main Street, and two, the Evergreens.

Emily and her sister, LAVINIA NORCROSS DICKINSON, remained at the Homestead for the rest of their lives. After Emily's death in 1886, Lavinia lived on at the Homestead until she died in 1899. At that time, the property was inherited by Austin's daughter, MARTHA DICKINSON BIANCHI, and leased to tenants until 1916, when it was sold to the Parke family. In 1963, in response to the growing popularity of Emily Dickinson, the house was designated a National Historic Landmark. In 1965, the Parke family sold the house to the trustees of Amherst College. Today the house is operated as a museum dedicated to educating the public about the life and work of one of America's greatest poets. To many, it has become a place of pilgrimage, where readers go "as if to a saint's shrine, seeking some ineffable truth" (Wolff, *Emily Dickinson*, 3).

FURTHER READING

Polly Longworth. "The World of Emily Dickinson"; Homestead Web site, available online, URL: http://www.emilydickinsonmuseum.org/pressinco.html, accessed January 10, 2006; Richard B. Sewall, *Life*, II, 321–322, 442–443; Cynthia Griffin Wolff, *Emily Dickinson*, 3, 29–30.

Humphrey, Jane (1829–1908)   A girlhood friend, to whom Dickinson wrote two important and revealing letters when she was 19 years old, Jane was the daughter of Dr. Levi W. Humphrey of Southwick, Massachusetts, and the sister of Helen Humphrey,

who became a preceptress at AMHERST ACADEMY in 1842, when Emily was a pupil there. The girls met when Jane, who was a year older than Emily, came to attend the academy for a brief time and lived with the Dickinsons. When she departed, 11-year-old Emily wrote her a chatty letter about school matters and mutual friends, laced with tender nostalgia:

> I miss my beloved Jane—I wish you would write to me—I should think more of it than of a mine of gold . . . what good times we used to have jumping into bed when you slept with me. (L 3, May 12, 1842)

The childhood friends were reunited in 1847, when both were students at MOUNT HOLYOKE FEMALE SEMINARY in South Hadley, Massachusetts. Unlike Emily, who left after 10 months without earning her certificate, Jane graduated in 1848 and became a teacher. Her first position was as preceptress at Amherst Academy, where she served for five terms. Although she and Emily must have seen a great deal of one another during this period, there is no written documentation of their friendship at this time. Later, however, when Jane had left Amherst for other teaching positions, Emily would remind her of that time together, identifying it with moments of simple, shared delight in nature:

> I think I love you *more* when spring comes—you know we used to sit in the front door, afternoons after school, and the shy little birds would say chirrup, chirrup, in the tall cherry trees, and if our dresses rustled, hop frightened away. . . . You won't forget it, Jennie, Oh no, I'm sure you wont, for when you are old and gray, it will be a sweet thing to think of, through the long winter's day! (L 86, about April 1852)

During the early 1850s, as Jane's teaching career took her to Warren, Massachusetts, and to Willoughby, Ohio, the two young women corresponded. Five of Emily's letters have survived; the most important of these are L 30 and L 35, both written in 1850, the year of the great REVIVAL that swept through Amherst. Nineteen-year-old Emily, finding herself in the midst of a religious fervor that would claim her father and her sister

LAVINIA, felt free to reveal her iconoclastic side to Jane. In her January letter, in what Sewall calls "her Manifesto against the Age, or New England Piety, or . . . MARY LYON's doctrine of Work" (*Life*, II, 392), she shows off a burgeoning gift for social satire, lampooning the passion for good works that surrounded her:

> The halt—the lame—and the blind—the old—the infirm—the bed-ridden—and superannuated—the ugly, and disagreeable—the perfectly hateful to me—all *these* to see and be seen by—an opportunity rare for cultivating meekness—and patience—and submission—and for turning my back to this very sinful, and wicked world. Somehow or other I incline to other things—and Satan covers them with flowers and I reach out to pick them. (L 30, January 23, 1850)

Her spirit of rebelliousness is evident as well in her comments about BENJAMIN FRANKLIN NEWTON, her father's former law clerk who had been her literary mentor. Telling Jane about the beautiful copy of Ralph Waldo Emerson's poems that Newton had sent her, she declares, "I can write him in about three weeks—and I *shall*." The words imply that her parents had forbidden her to write before then and that Jane is aware of this situation. Unlike her letters to her pious friend, ABIAH PALMER ROOT, in which she also wrote about her "wickedness," but in a far more restrained tone, punctuated with contrition and self-doubt, the letters to Jane, written to an emotional ally, let her blow off steam. She writes, "I love to be surly—and muggy—and cross—and then I remember you—and feel that I do a kind of justice to you—and myself—which eases my conscience wonderfully."

Her next letter, written in April, begins on a more somber note; Jane's father is dying and Emily, who cannot offer her religious consolation, offers the solace of her love instead. She then goes on to make an extraordinary "revelation":

> I have dared to do strange things—bold things, and have asked no advice from any—I have heeded beautiful tempters, yet do not think I am wrong. Oh I have needed my trusty Jane—my friend, encourager, and sincere counciller, my rock and strong assister!

Her "confession" is more of an ingenious exercise in concealment, in which she speaks of "an experience, bitter and sweet" that has beguiled her and given her life "an aim," and of the past winter as "all one dream" from which she has no wish to awaken. Continuing to employ her awakening gift for original metaphor, she goes on to set Jane a riddle, which has bedeviled Dickinson scholars ever since:

> What do you weave from all these threads, for I know you hav'nt been idle the while I've been speaking to you, bring it nearer the window, and I will see, it's all wrong unless it has one gold thread in it, a long, big shining fibre which hides the others—and which will fade away into Heaven while you hold it, and from there come back to me.

Some scholars have interpreted the "golden thread," which is echoed in May of that year in a letter to Abiah, where she writes of "dreaming a golden dream, with eyes all the while wide open," as a love affair. Others believe she was referring to her discovery of her poetic vocation. That year she wrote her first known poem; in February, a prose valentine of hers had been printed in an AMHERST COLLEGE literary journal, marking her first appearance in print. "Nobody *thinks* of the joy, nobody *guesses* it, to all appearance old things are engrossing, and new ones are not revealed, but there *now* is nothing old, things are budding, and springing, and singing . . .," she wrote tantalizingly. What Jane's reaction to this letter was and whether she later became privy to Emily's secret are unknown. Jane gave up teaching in 1858, when she married William H. Wilkinson, a harness manufacturer, and went to live with him in Southwick. If there was further correspondence between the two friends after Jane's marriage, it has not survived.

See also GEORGE HENRY GOULD.

FURTHER READING

Alfred Habegger, *My Wars*, 129–130, 133–135, 228–230; Richard B. Sewall, *Life*, II, 390–399.

Humphrey, Leonard (1824–1850)   A principal
of AMHERST ACADEMY, Humphrey was the first man
whom Emily referred to as "Master," the term she
applied to a small number of men older than herself
whom she revered and turned to for counsel, wisdom, and, sometimes, love. Described by the historian of the academy as "a young man of rare talents
and great promise" (Tuckerman, *Amherst Academy,*
214), Humphrey took over the leadership of the
school while still in his senior year at AMHERST
COLLEGE. Appointed in 1846, he managed to
restore confidence among students and staff, undermined during a period of weak administration, while
completing his studies with highest honors. Emily
boasted to her friend ABIAH PALMER ROOT that "we
have an excellent Principal in the person of Mr.
Leonard Humphrey, who was the last valedictorian
[at Amherst College]" (L 14, late autumn 1846).

Humphrey and Dickinson established their
friendship during her final year at the academy.
When she went on to MOUNT HOLYOKE FEMALE
SEMINARY the following year, he visited her there
during her first winter, bringing Emily's AMHERST
friend MARY WARNER, for what Emily called a
"delightful" visit. Although they doubtless corresponded, none of their letters have been found.
There is no evidence of a romantic bond between
them; in fact, Humphrey's correspondence with
a friend reveals that he was interested in several
other Amherst girls.

One of the things they had in common was
precarious health; both had frequently withdrawn
from school during periods of illness. Still, his
early death, on November 13, 1850, at his home
in North Weymouth, after a brief illness, came as
a devastating, unexpected blow to her. The whole
community was shocked and honored him with
many eulogies. The impact of Humphrey's loss on
Emily was profound. Highly vulnerable to each
new death among her family and friends, and feeling a close, personal dependency on her beloved
teachers, she plunged into melancholy thoughts
about the grave and what might lie beyond. She
poured out her grief to Abiah: ". . . the hour of
evening is sad—it was once my study hour—my
Master has gone to rest, and the open leaf of
the book, and the scholar at school *alone,* make

Leonard Humphrey, the young principal of Amherst
Academy and the first man Emily referred to
reverentially as "Master"

the tears come, and I cannot brush them away; I
would not if I could, for they are the only tribute
I can pay to the departed Humphrey." (L 39, late
1850). In the same letter, she calls Humphrey's
death her "first affliction," although this was not
in fact the case: Six years earlier, she had been
deeply shaken by the death of her friend SOPHIA
HOLLAND.

Her adoption of the term "Master" may
have been related to her recent, avid reading of
Charlotte Bronte's *Jane Eyre,* since "master" was
Jane's habitual form of address for Rochester. She
was also reading a lot of sentimental literature, in
which the appellation was often used (Habegger,
My Wars, 150).

FURTHER READING

Alfred Habegger, *My Wars,* 150; Richard B. Sewall,
Life, II, 340–341; Frederick Tuckerman, *Amherst
Academy,* 214.

hymn form (prosody) Emily Dickinson composed the overwhelming majority of her 1,789 known poems in hymn form, also known as common meter. Thoroughly familiar with the rich and varied Western metrical tradition, the rhythms of John Donne and George Herbert, her beloved Shakespeare and Elizabeth Barrett Browning, William Wordsworth, John Keats, Henry Wadsworth Longfellow, and Edgar Allen Poe, she chose a different path. Her model was the hymnologist to New England Congregationalism, Isaac Watts, whose name was a household word in Dickinson's time, and whose work was basic to the New England vocabulary of rhythm and verse. The psalms and hymns of Watts were as familiar to New Englanders as the Bible. Emily's mother owned *Watts' Hymns*, and the family library housed copies of his *Church Psalmody* and *Psalms, Hymns and Spiritual Songs of the Reverend Isaac Watts*. As a child, Emily sang his hymns in church each Sunday

Hymn form traces its genealogy from the "fourteener," a line of seven iambic feet that was popular in the 13th century. (An iambic foot is a set of two syllables in which the accent falls on the second syllable: da *dum*. A line of seven iambic feet would therefore contain 14 syllables, and every other syllable would be accented.) When it evolved into the "ballad measure," the seven iambs became separated into a line of four iambs followed by a line of three iambs. A syllabic pattern of 8-6-8-6 resulted, with the even lines always rhyming and the odd lines often rhyming. Hymn form has the same structure.

While the ballad characteristically combines the narrative and lyric modes, the hymn is rarely narrative but is instead imbued with a devotional tone.

Dickinson never speaks of Watts in her letters, but she points to him in some of her poems, by echoing his lines. Thus, at the end of Fr 114, "Where bells no more affright the morn—", she cites Watts's lines:

Could we but climb where Moses stood,
And view the landscape o'er.

In the poem, they appear in quotation marks:

"Oh could we climb where Moses stood,
And view the landscape o'er."

While the poem has an undertone of longing for the bliss of heaven, its predominant tone is playful and irreverent. We are led to a fundamental question: Why did the frequently irreverent Dickinson, who refused to attend church after the age of 30, choose a form associated with conventional piety to express the language of her soul?

The issue can be approached on many levels. Linguistic scholar Cristanne Miller suggests that Watts may have attracted her with his frequent use of irregular rhymes and harsh-sounding phrases (usually involving vocabulary considered neither poetic nor religious) and with the extraordinary variety of sounds and themes he used within a simple rhythmical frame. She notes that Dickinson's own rhythms, loose rhymes, and abbreviated metaphors of description sound less unusual when placed beside Watts's hymns than when compared with the work of her contemporaries (*Grammar*, 142).

Some feminist scholars propose that Dickinson's avoidance of iambic pentameter, the fundamental meter of the Western tradition, constitutes a deliberate rejection of the established norms of a patriarchal literature. But, if that was her motivation, why then did she adopt a form associated with yet another patriarchal system, and one far less congenial to her than Western literature? Further, does a poet make such a fundamental choice on the basis of social/political issues, particularly when she never espoused them in a more direct fashion?

Critic David Porter comes closer to the core of the matter when he suggests that Dickinson may not have decided to use the form consciously. The hymn form embodies her central theme of aspiration and its cadence came to frame her thoughts in her early years. When she began to write poems, she recreated her "inner drama of anguish and aspiration" in the metrical form she already possessed:

The rhythm of the articulating voice within her moved in the meter and in the line length and syntactical concision of the hymn. Through it she refracted the special light of her own beliefs. (*Early Poetry*, 61)

By using a form expressive of religious faith for a poetry of struggling and questing, Porter suggests,

Dickinson incorporated in her work a powerful source of dynamic tension that functions at both the metrical and philosophical levels:

> The hymn form reinforces with artistically subdued persuasion the aspiring quest for consummation. The form also provides for an ingenious complexity arising from the persistent secularity of attitude and language in counterpoint to the devotional schema. Hymnody, that is, provides constant occasion for irony. (Ibid., 55)

Using the vehicle of orthodox belief, she expresses her stubborn love of this world, rebellion against doctrine, and habitual religious skepticism. When Dickinson is whimsical, the result is parody; when she is more serious, the effect is ironic. At other times, "it is an act of profound insight into the personal dilemma of faith" (Ibid., 68).

For Dickinson, with her penchant for brevity, the hymn form with its short four- and three-foot lines was an ideal vehicle for her disjunct, elliptical style; her use of it may have pushed her further in that direction. It is difficult to imagine how she could have achieved with a longer line the effects made possible by short ones. She did experiment beyond the hymn form, writing more than 50 early poems in thoroughly mixed meters, some of which are so unpatterned as to qualify as free verse (Porter, 55). In a poem such as "WILD NIGHTS—WILD NIGHTS!" for example, the intensity of her impulse demanded an even more concise form than the hymn allowed.

Dickinson did not merely use the hymn form; she transformed it into what Richard B. Sewall calls "a new, often staccato music of her own" (*Life*, II, 714). Only in her weaker poems does she slavishly follow a regular meter, as in Fr 228 "My Eye is fuller than my vase—," when the bouncing rhythm reveals the inherent shortcomings of hymnody. Such instances are the exception, however, rather than the rule. In most of her work, Dickinson defies the expectation built into the hymn form. She fractures and stretches out the lines with her injection of dashes and undermines the complacency of rhyme with her slant rhymes. Rather than the comforting or exalted closure of period or exclamation mark, her dash-ended poems stand open to uncertainty.

See also CONGREGATIONALISM, PUBLICATION AND EDITORIAL SCHOLARSHIP, PUNCTUATION, PURITAN HERITAGE, and REVIVALISM.

FURTHER READING

James Davidson, "Emily Dickinson and Isaac Watts" *Boston Public Library Quarterly* 6 (1954): 141–149; A. R. C. Finch, "Dickinson and Patriarchal Meter: A Theory of Metrical Codes," *PMLA* 102 (1987), 166–176; Thomas Johnson, *Emily Dickinson: An Interpretive Biography*, 86–88; Cristanne Miller, *Grammar*, 141–143; David Porter, *Early Poetry*, 54–74; Richard B. Sewall, *Life*, II, 714.

J

Jackson, Helen Fiske Hunt (1830–1885)   Helen Fiske Hunt Jackson was the single figure of literary stature who recognized Emily Dickinson's genius during her lifetime. Although they were born in AMHERST in the same year, the two girls were not close neighbors, attended different schools, and had little to do with one another as children. Helen was a robust tomboy, who resisted discipline and was sent away to boarding school at age 11. Her mother, Deborah Vinal Fiske, died of consumption in 1844; three years later, her grieving father, Nathan Welby Fiske, professor of moral philosophy and metaphysics at AMHERST COLLEGE, died of dysentery in Jerusalem, where he had traveled to restore his health. Helen, then at Ipswich Seminary, was orphaned at 16. With characteristic courage and resourcefulness, she went to live happily in the home of John Abbott, a friend of the family, and attended his progressive institute for girls in New York City.

She married Edward Bissell Hunt, an army engineer, in 1852, and lived with him, first in Washington, D.C., then in Newport, Rhode Island. Their family was destined for tragedy. A first son, Murray, lived only 11 months. In 1863, Major Hunt accidentally blew himself up while working to perfect an early form of submarine. Then, Helen's beloved son Rennie died, at age nine, in 1865, of diphtheria.

During her long period of recovery from these crushing disasters, she turned to writing. While living in a literary boardinghouse in Newport, Rhode Island, she met fellow boarder THOMAS WENTWORTH HIGGINSON, who became her mentor, guiding her writing and advancing her career. Unlike Emily, who called Higginson "mentor" but followed her independent creative path, Helen strove to change her verse to suit him. By 1869 her poems began appearing in the *Atlantic Monthly*; by the 1870s "H. H.," as she signed her first volume, *Verses,* (1870) was acclaimed a leading poet by such luminaries as SAMUEL BOWLES and Ralph Waldo Emerson. She made her greatest reputation in prose, however, publishing a novel, *Mercy Philbrick's Choice,* and two works on America's treatment of the Indians, *A Century of Dishonor* (1881) and *Ramona* (1884), both of which stirred the national conscience.

In 1870, after Higginson showed Helen some of Emily's poems, the two women began corresponding and soon developed a warm, late-blossoming friendship. When Helen married William S. Jackson in 1875, moving with him to Colorado Springs, Emily sent her a congratulatory verse:

> Who fleeing from the Spring
> The Spring avenging fling
> To Dooms of Balm—
>
> (L 444)

The lines, which allude to Helen's return to life's joys in her second marriage, mystified their recipient, who honestly confessed, "I do wish I knew just what 'dooms' you meant, though" (L 444a). Later she would recognize that "part of the dimness must

Helen Fiske Hunt Jackson, the well-known novelist and Indian rights advocate who told Dickinson she was a "great poet" and urged her to publish *(By permission of the Houghton Library, Harvard University)*

have been in me" (L 476c). On March 20, 1876, she wrote:

> You are a great poet—and it is wrong to the day you live in, that you will not sing aloud. When

you are what men call dead, you will be sorry you were so stingy.

The two women would meet twice in person, in 1876 and 1878, and continue to correspond until Helen's death. Throughout their friendship, Helen pressed Emily to publish. She succeeding in getting her to contribute a poem, "SUCCESS IS COUNTED SWEETEST," to a volume of anonymous poetry, *A Masque of Poets,* published by Thomas Niles, as part of the anonymous series brought out by Roberts Brothers. When Dickinson sent Niles two additional poems, he suggested publishing a volume of her verse. She answered evasively and nothing came of it.

In June 1884, Helen suffered a badly broken leg in Colorado Springs. In reply to Emily's sympathetic letter, she asked to be made her literary executor. Emily ignored the offer and Helen, absorbed by her own troubles, gave up. She died of stomach cancer on August 12, 1885. In her stunned grief, Emily wrote to Higginson (L 1043), thanking him for giving her Helen and enclosed a verse (Fr 1684), in which Helen is associated with "The Might of Human Love.—"

See also PUBLICATION AND EDITORIAL SCHOLARSHIP.

FURTHER READING

Alfred Habegger, *My Life,* 555–559; Evelyn I. Banning, *Helen Hunt Jackson,* 1973; Vivian R. Pollak, "The Example of Helen Hunt Jackson," in *Handbook,* Grabher et al., eds., 323–341; Richard B. Sewall, *Life,* II, 577–592.

L

letters The importance of Emily Dickinson's letters, both for their intrinsic artistry and as revelations of both her psychological and artistic evolution, cannot be overestimated; they are her only surviving prose. Dickinson was a prolific and passionate correspondent, who wrote her first known letter at age 11 to her brother WILLIAM AUSTIN DICKINSON and her last to her cousins, LOUISE AND FRANCES NORCROSS, just before her death. Since she neither kept a diary nor wrote memoirs, we must look to her letters for the fullest record of her conscious life. Primary sources for understanding her loves, friendships, family and other social relations, the letters also frequently supply contexts for enigmatic poems. Dickinson transformed the genre of the intimate letter, making it a vehicle in which her distinctive prose and her poems intertwined. Recent scholarship has examined the letters as art forms, focusing on the fine line distinguishing her poetry from her prose. In light of her habit of including poems in her letters, some critics have suggested that Dickinson thought of her correspondents as the primary audience for her poetry and of letter writing as her chosen method of publication.

In spite of all they tell us about her life and work, however, Dickinson's letters open only a partial view onto the complex landscape of her emotional and interpersonal life. Since virtually all the letters sent to her were burned, according to her wishes, when she died, we have only her side of her many correspondences. And we have only some of her letters. The 1,049 letters in Thomas Johnson's 1958 three-volume edition, written to 93 known correspondents, several of whom she wrote to often and for years, plus 12 unknown correspondents, represent "only a fraction, and probably a small one" of Dickinson's letters (Sewall, *Life*, II, 750–751).

And yet, even this fraction might not have survived. MABEL LOOMIS TODD, Dickinson's first editor, resolved to collect and publish the letters only after a chance meeting with ABIAH PALMER ROOT, Emily's close girlhood friend, who offered to share her invaluable cache of letters. "The letters, scattered here, there, and everywhere, had to be lured from their hiding places after they were discovered" (*Ancestor's Brocades*, 188). Together with Emily's sister, LAVINIA, Mabel worked for several years at this arduous task, locating recipients and then persuading them to surrender their letters. Many were reluctant, believing it was sacrilege for others to read them. Other possessors of rich, extensive correspondences, such as the Norcross cousins, agreed to hand over copies of their letters only after they had censored the originals. Mabel and Vinnie's persistence, plus the larger view of some correspondents, who saw the literary value of the letters, made the volumes possible. With Vinnie and Austin's help, and guided by handwriting and stylistic changes, Mabel tried to piece together "a consecutive story." Yet the result of their labors was anything but a balanced sampling of Emily's correspondence; for Lavinia, Austin, and Mabel, who was Austin's longtime mistress, all had reasons for wishing to minimize the role of Austin's wife, SUSAN HUNTINGTON GILBERT DICKINSON, in

Facsimile of Emily Dickinson's earliest extant letter, written to her brother Austin, in 1842 *(By permission of the Houghton Library, Harvard University)*

Emily's life. Thus they heavily censored and mutilated the poet's most extensive correspondence of all, the one to Susan.

When the first volumes of letters appeared in 1894, the general audience found little to interest them and few copies were sold. Not until 12 years later, when the letters were reissued as a single volume, was interest in them aroused. The "letters are caskets of jewels," wrote a reviewer for the *Boston Transcript,* "Not a shell, but contains its pearl. There are phrases that are poems in epitome."

The 1894 volumes were followed by publication of selected letters edited by Austin and Sue's daughter, MARTHA DICKINSON BIANCHI, by Mabel's daughter, Millicent Todd Bingham, and

others. Then in 1958, Thomas H. Johnson and Theodora Ward published their landmark three-volume *Letters,* which remains the most complete extant collection of the correspondence. Among the most important missing correspondences are those with her early literary mentor, BENJAMIN FRANKLIN NEWTON and with REVEREND CHARLES WADSWORTH, reputed to be one of her great loves.

Both before and after she became a recluse in the early 1860s, letter writing was an imperative of Emily Dickinson's nature, her preferred way of establishing and nourishing intimate bonds. She wrote to her immediate and extended family, to schoolmates, friends, friends of friends, neighbors, and Amherst acquaintances. In the 1840s and early 1850s, she wrote regularly to Austin, her adored older brother, whenever he was away from home. She corresponded with the friends of her girlhood, such as ABIAH PALMER ROOT, JANE HUMPHREY, EMILY FOWLER, and ABBY WOOD, until they married and drifted away. In her early 20s, she began a correspondence with her future sister-in-law, Sue Gilbert, which would last a lifetime. Apart from letters to distant friends, she sent frequent notes to neighbors and almost daily notes across the lawn to Sue or her children. In 1853, she began a lifelong correspondence with her new friends ELIZABETH AND JOSIAH HOLLAND. In the late 1850s, she began writing to SAMUEL BOWLES and his wife, Mary, and when Samuel, whom she loved, died, she began writing to his son, Samuel, Jr., and to Bowles's close friend, MARIA WHITNEY. The rich correspondence with her "Little Cousins," Louise and Frances Norcross, began in 1859. Somewhere between 1858 and 1861, she composed the three extraordinary letters to an unknown beloved, which came to be known as the MASTER LETTERS. After 1862, she broadened her circle of correspondents, reaching out to eminent writers THOMAS WENTWORTH HIGGINSON and HELEN FISKE HUNT JACKSON, and to Thomas Niles, the editor of Roberts Brothers publishers of Boston. When Wadsworth died in 1882, she corresponded with his friends, the Clark brothers, James Dickson and Charles. Between 1878 and 1883, she wrote a series of joyous and poignant letters to JUDGE OTIS PHILLIPS LORD, the final love of her life, and when Lord died in 1884, she wrote to his cousin Benjamin

Kimball. In her last years, she wrote to Mrs. Todd, whom she had never met.

Dickinson's letter-writing style underwent a dramatic change over the years. As an adolescent, she would set aside whole mornings or afternoons for the composition of her long, expansive, affectionate, and sometimes overwritten missives. Her letters to Austin and to absent girlfriends show her taking her time in painting a scene; she can be ebullient or melancholy, reflective, and not infrequently melodramatic and self-consciously "literary," borrowing from conceits drawn from her own reading. She is both absorbed in the present as she enthusiastically progresses with her studies and already haunted by the mystery of death, the sense of time passing, and the fear of losing touch with those she loves. Her letters declare her abiding loyalty and, all too frequently, her disappointment in others for not writing as often and as fully as she desires. However she might chide and bully them, few could meet her demands and, like Abiah Root or Sue Gilbert, her friends tended to withdraw from the excessive pressure she placed on them. Ironically, the anguish of losing them provoked some of her best writing.

Although their primary purpose was communication, these early letters were also ideal vehicles for Dickinson to explore her sense of life and to develop skills to express it artfully. Scholar Jane Eberwein sees the letters written in the 1850s as a "stylistic workshop," in which Dickinson shaped her poetry by way of her prose (*Strategies of Limitation*, 47–55). "It was through the process of writing letters," she comments, "that Dickinson first explored her literary resources and identified the themes, tone, self-image, and artistic strategies that would characterize her poetry" (Ibid., 47). Her strategies included "puns and wordplay," "startling imagery," "play on literary and scriptural allusions," and the inclusion of "brief or extended fantasies" in the letters (Ibid., 48–50).

Dickinson's epistolary style undergoes a marked change in the Master letters she wrote between 1858 and 1862, to an unknown beloved. Her technique of reducing both herself and her beloved to roles by referring to him as "Master" and to herself as "Daisy" is not something she carried forward into other correspondences. But it does point to her need "for distancing experience, for controlling intensity through a formalized stylization of expression . . ." in her letter writing (Salska, "Dickinson's Letters," 174). Instead of the expansiveness of her earlier letters, Dickinson relies here on suppression to convey intensity of feeling; making extensive use of metonymy, she pares down her language, finding that the power of negation and omissions spoke more eloquently than open declaration. Both in her letters and her poems, she was learning the art of telling the truth "slant." Critic Cristanne Miller notes that in both genres:

> Dickinson's language is densely compressed, metaphorical, disjunctive; syntax is inverted; words are coined and used ungrammatically. . . . Both letters and poems balance informality and formality, colloquialism and complexity, intimacy and distance. (*Grammar*, 5)

Thus, as she gradually withdrew from society in the early 1860s and letters assumed a heightened importance to her, these strategies gave Dickinson powerful tools for controlling relationships. As Johnson notes,

> The degree and nature of any intimacy was hers to choose. Henceforth the letters are composed with deliberation. . . . The letters are briefer because the thought is tersely ordered. Many, if not most of them, were now written first in rough draft and then recopied. (*Letters*, xiii)

After 1866, her poetic production decreased, and letters became her primary genre. They were her vehicles for cultivating intimacy with those who led their lives outside the boundaries of the household to which she had confined herself, a psychic space in which she could enjoy the sense of an exclusive bond with each correspondent. In a poem of 1863, "The Way I read a Letter's—this—" (Fr 700), she recounts her rituals for closeting herself in absolute privacy, without the presence of even a mouse, before engaging in her hidden "Heaven"—the reading of a letter. She was deeply offended when Elizabeth Holland wrote a joint letter to her and Vinnie. "A mutual plum is not a plum," she rebuked her (L 321). Yet Emily herself sometimes addressed her letters to two people at once (Samuel and Mary Bowles, Frances and Louise Norcross). And the "intimacy" she offered in her letters was not always truthful, that is, representative of who she really was. A striking example of this is her initial correspondence with Higginson, in which the 31-year-old woman who had already written more than 400 poems presented herself as a childlike novice and signed herself "Your Scholar." We have no difficulty in believing Austin when he asserts that "Emily definitely posed in those letters" (Sewall, *Life,* II, 538). Just as Dickinson advised Higginson that "the speaker of my poems is not myself, but a certain person," so the "I" of her letters is often a literary construct, designed to seduce its recipient.

In the case of Higginson, Dickinson's pose was probably based on her intuition of the most likely way to engage the interest of this renowned man of letters, who had just published an article of advice to beginning writers. Her decision to reach out to him in 1862 and ask him to be her literary mentor represented a watershed in her life as a poet. From then on, letters would keep her connected, not only to her "select society," but also to the intellectual and literary circles of the New England of her time. She "let it be known in the competent and influential literary circles outside her immediate family and friends that she was seriously a poet" (Salska, "Dickinson's Letters," 168). Moreover, as she increasingly enclosed and incorporated poems in her letters, she created her own audience for them. Martha Nell Smith argues that Dickinson in effect became her own publisher, creating through her letters her highly exclusive "limited editions" (*Rowing in Eden,* 11).

Some scholars argue, however, that viewing the letters as mere "containers" for the poetry creates a rigid boundary between prose and verse, when in fact it is quite fluid. This is particularly true of the letters she wrote after the early 1860s, which "both in style and rhythm begin to take on qualities that are so nearly the quality of her poems as on occasion to leave the reader in doubt where the letter leaves off and the poem begins" (Johnson, *Letters,* xv). Scholar Judith Farr believes that

Dickinson herself "did not always sharply distinguish between the uses of her art," "writing letters that scan, enclosing poems in letters, composing poems that are letters, revising and rerevising both" (*Passion,* 16). Critic William Shurr (*New Poems by Emily Dickinson*) has gone so far as to present selected prose fragments of the letters as "newly discovered poems," on the basis of metrical criteria, a view that has been greeted skeptically as "much too mechanical for the modern sense of the nature of poetry" (Salska, "Dickinson's Letters," 179, n5).

Scholar Sarah Wider takes a more moderate approach. Pointing out that Dickinson wrote many of her verses specifically for her letters, she maintains that they form part of an artistic whole, linked by syntax and imagery, from which neither poetry nor prose can be extracted. The fact that in the holographs of the poems (Dickinson's handwritten originals), as opposed to the printed versions, there is no spatial separation between poetry and prose suggests that Dickinson herself thought of them in this way. Wider identifies a dialogue within the poems, in which "prose answers poetry; poetry, prose." Sometimes a poem serves as an unconventional closing to a letter and may even be addressed to someone other than the addressee, as in a letter to Elizabeth Holland that ends with a poem addressed to her recently deceased husband, Josiah. "Shall we wish a triumphant Christmas to the brother withdrawn? Certainly he possesses it," she tells Elizabeth. In the verse that follows, she tells Josiah, "thou hast borne a universe / Entirely away" (L 742). The poem does not repeat the message of the prose, but instead offers a somewhat different view of Josiah's death, stressing what has been lost in his departure. Thus, as Wider notes, rather than a "one-to-one correspondence between the poem and the prose, the reader is left with several possibilities for connecting the varied expressions of a related thought" ("Corresponding Worlds," 13).

Dickinson often sent her poems as gifts to her correspondents, sometimes to replace what she could not give. When their father died, she wrote to her Norcross cousins "Let Emily sing for you because she cannot pray," and enclosed "'Tis not that dying hurts us so,—" (L 278, Fr 528). When Mrs. Todd sent her a panel of Indian pipes that she had painted, she replied, "I cannot make an Indian Pipe but please accept a Humming Bird," followed by her poem "A ROUTE OF EVANESCENCE" (L 770). This way of speaking of a poem in a letter—as a metaphor for an object she would like to enclose—also occurs in L 802 in which she sends Mrs. Holland her "Portrait," in the poem "To see her is a Picture" (Fr 1597). One of the interesting facts about these two examples is that Dickinson sent the same poems to other correspondents. The "Hummingbird" was sent out five times (L 602, 627, 675, 770, 814), the "Portrait" twice (L 802, 809).

Dickinson's regular practice of sending the same poem in personal letters to more than one correspondent has been interpreted by some scholars as evidence of her "posing." For Miller, it "serves as a warning to her twentieth-century readers that poems mailed in letters may be deceptively personal; they were not conceived in the light of a single friendship" (*Grammar*, 13). As her prime example, she cites a poem found in two clean copies after Dickinson's death. Both written on embossed stationery and folded as if they had been put in envelopes, one begins "Going to Him! Happy letter!" (Fr 277), the other: "Going—to—Her! / Happy—Letter!" In the first, the pronoun "Him" occurs throughout, in the second "Her." The poem consists of a series of instructions to the "Happy letter," of what to tell the recipient about its own creation—a playful conceit whereby the speaker indicates the painstaking effort and emotion that have gone into writing the letter. It ends flirtatiously, with the speaker forbidding the letter to tell where it is currently hidden—presumably in her bosom. Given the poem's lack of any personal reference, it could easily be transferred from one context to another, sent to a beloved man—or woman.

Another striking example of Dickinson's multiple mailings is the tormented poem, "Through the strait pass of suffering—," which she sent to Samuel Bowles in a letter attempting to reassure him that her "Snow" (purity) is still intact. Before sending it, she made a fair copy for herself. Later, she sent a copy to Sue Dickinson. Miller concludes:

> The multiple copies suggest that the poet's primary intent in writing the poem was not to present herself as a martyr to Bowles or to point toward any single occasion, whatever the impetus for sending him the poem might have been. In the letter to Sue, the poem would seem to have a different reference. (Ibid., 13)

Thus, the poems are "private messages universalized" (15). They speak both to the letter's recipient and to the world at large. Dickinson alludes to this when she writes to Higginson, "A Letter always feels to me like immortality because it is the mind alone, without corporeal friend" (L 330, June 1869).

Dickinson never lost sight of the primary, private dimension of letter writing, however. She had a keen appreciation of the power of letters to wound as well as heal. "We bruise each other less in talking than in writing, for then a quiet accent helps words themselves too hard" (L 332). Elsewhere, she noted that "a Pen has so many inflections and a Voice but one" (L 470). Still later, she put this idea even more strongly: "An earnest letter is or should be life-warrant or death-warrant, for what is each instant but a gun, harmless because 'unloaded,' but that touched 'goes off'?" (L 656). On the evidence of those that have come down to us, it is clear that her own letters were in virtually every case "life-warrants," messages designed to affirm her love and concern for a particular individual and, in however oblique a fashion, to share herself with another.

As a 20-year-old, she anticipated the joy of rereading old letters "when years have flown":

> To hold a letter to the light—
> Grown Tawny—now—with time—
> To con the faded syllables
> That quickened us like Wine."
> ("In Ebon box when years have flown,"
> Fr 180, 1860)

A late fragment, written the year before she died, indicates that the ability to experience the unique, intense pleasures of a letter was for her a not inconsiderable consolation for the limitations of the human condition:

> A Letter is a joy of Earth—
> It is denied the Gods—
>
> (Fr 1672, 1885)

For discussions of individual correspondences see CATHERINE TURNER ANTHON, SAMUEL BOWLES, ELIZA M. COLEMAN, SUSAN HUNTINGTON GILBERT DICKINSON, WILLIAM AUSTIN DICKINSON, HENRY VAUGHAN EMMONS, EMILY FOWLER FORD, GEORGE HENRY GOULD, JOHN LONG GRAVES, THOMAS WENTWORTH HIGGINSON, ELIZABETH AND JOSIAH HOLLAND, JANE HUMPHREY, HELEN FISKE HUNT JACKSON, OTIS PHILLIPS LORD, JOSEPH BARDWELL LYMAN, LOUISE AND FRANCES NORCROSS, JOEL WARREN NORCROSS, LAVINIA NORCROSS NORCROSS, ABIAH PALMER ROOT, CATHERINE SWEETSER, and MARIA WHITNEY.

See also "TELL ALL THE TRUTH BUT TELL IT SLANT," "THIS IS MY LETTER TO THE WORLD," and PUBLICATION AND EDITORIAL SCHOLARSHIP.

FURTHER READING

Dickinson Electronic Archives, "Letter-Poem: A Dickinson Genre," available online, URL: http://www.emilydickinson.org/letter/letintro.htm, accessed January 10, 2006; Martha Dickinson Bianchi, *Life and Letters* and *Emily Dickinson Face to Face*; Millicent Todd Bingham, *Ancestor's Brocades*, 188–323, *Emily Dickinson's Home: Letters of Edward Dickinson and his Family*, and *Emily Dickinson: A Revelation*; Jane Eberwein, *Dickinson: Strategies of Limitation*, 1985, 47–55; Judith Farr, *Passion*, 16, 109, 199, 213; Ellen Louise Hart and Martha Nell Smith, *Open Me Carefully: Emily Dickinson's Intimate Letters to Susan Huntington Dickinson*; Thomas H. Johnson and Theodora Ward, eds., *Letters*, 1958; Thomas H. Johnson, ed., *Selected Letters*; Suzanne Juhasz, "Reading Emily Dickinson's Letters," *ESQ: A Journal of the American Renaissance* 30 (1984): 170–192; Cristanne Miller, *Grammar*, 5–19; Agnieska Salska, "Dickinson's Letters," in *Handbook,* Grabher et al., eds., 163–180; Richard B. Sewall, *Life*, II, Appendix V: "A Note on Missing Correspondences," 750–751; William Shurr, ed., *New Poems of Emily Dickinson*; Martha Nell Smith. *Rowing in Eden,* 11–16; Sarah Wider, "Corresponding Worlds: The Art of Emily Dickinson's Letters," *EDJ*, I.I. (1992), 10–38; Cynthia Griffin Wolff, *Emily Dickinson*, 126–128; 575–576, note 62.

Lord, Judge Otis Phillips (1812–1884) "Oh, had I found it sooner! Yet Tenderness has not a Date—it comes and overwhelms," wrote Emily Dickinson to Judge Otis Phillips Lord, on April 30, 1882 (L 750). Eighteen years her senior and her late father's best friend, the portly, white-haired judge, feared and disliked by many for his ferocity in the courtroom, seems an unlikely amorous choice for the poet, who was in her late 40s when their romance began. Although numerous questions as to the nature of their relationship remain unanswered, Dickinson's surviving letters leave no doubt that she loved Lord and was loved in return.

He was born on July 11, 1812, in Ipswich, Massachusetts, to the Honorable Nathaniel and Eunice Kimball Lord. After graduating from AMHERST COLLEGE in 1832, he studied law at Harvard and was admitted to the bar in 1835, first in Ipswich, and then in 1844 in Salem, where he resided for the rest of his life. In 1843 he married Elizabeth Wise Farley, a descendant of Harvard President Leverett. The couple would have no children. As a lawyer, Lord established a lucrative and wide-ranging practice, and during the 1840s and 1850s, he turned to politics, serving in the Massachusetts legislature and State Senate. In an article of March 29, 1853, the *Springfield Republican* called him "the acknowledged leader of the House, a man of vigorous intellect ... force of character ... a powerful and pungent debater," who is "severe in his logic, blighting in his sarcasm, and audacious in his denunciations...." With the establishment of the Superior Court in 1859 he was appointed an associate justice and served until 1875, when he was promoted to the state Supreme Judicial Court.

Like his best friend, EDWARD DICKINSON, who was 10 years older than he, Lord was a die-hard Whig. By the 1850s he had established himself as the leading Whig in Massachusetts and famously proclaimed that "The great heart of Massachusetts is Whig to the core." With his gift for pithy oratory and his sly and stinging wit, he might have enjoyed a brilliant political career, but for the disintegration of the Whig Party. Neither he nor Edward were willing to switch allegiances and remained men without a party. But Lord was nonetheless an influential figure. A champion of the Civil War, the

Judge Otis Phillips Lord, of Salem. He and Emily fell in love in the late 1870s. *(By permission of the Houghton Library, Harvard University)*

Union, and the Constitution, he harped upon the need to return to the values of the past. He often became the center of controversy, as, for instance, when he sentenced a Catholic witness to jail for refusing to kiss the Bible and preferring to take the oath by lifting his hand. Known as a judge of stern principles and harsh sentences, he was notoriously hard on divorce-seekers.

In private life, however, he was known for his kindness, generosity and lively conversation with intimates and kindred spirits. Certainly, in an uncongenial setting, he could be awkward. According to anecdote, while a guest of WILLIAM AUSTIN and SUSAN HUNTINGTON GILBERT DICKINSON at The EVERGREENS, he rose to his feet and recited from memory a grim song by hymnist Isaac Watts on "damnation and the dead," to which the other guests responded with nervous laughter.

With Emily, however, there was ease and connection. She called him "My lovely Salem," "my Darling," "My Sweet One," "my Church." Unfazed by his conservatism, she accepted him without reservations. Critic Betsy Erkkila has suggested that his conservatism, which retained "the older gentry values of the past against the liberal, progressive, and democratizing politics of the ante- and post-bellum years" was what drew her to him ("Art of Politics," 163). Erkkila intriguingly argues that the poet sought to create with Lord, whom she called "my native Land—my Darling" (L 615), "a kind of fantasy republic of love grounded in the values of patriotism, self-sacrificing virtue, and freedom that had been lost to American history."

Like Emily, he rejected religious doctrine and did not belong to a church. She wrote, "While others go to Church, I go to mine, for are you not my Church, and have we not a Hymn that no one knows but us?" (L 790, December 3, 1882). She reveled in his wit and sense of fun, telling him, "You have a good deal of glee in your nature's corners. . . ." (L 695, scrap 2, probably 1881). Emily's niece MARTHA DICKINSON BIANCHI recalled how "They saved scraps of current nonsense for each other, and these clippings flew back and forth between [them]. . . . There was a certain kind of wit she labelled 'the Judge Lord brand'" (*Life and Letters*, 69). Their shared love for Shakespeare was a strong bond between them. In 1880 he presented her with an expensive and sensitive gift: a marbled Shakespeare concordance.

Biographer Richard B. Sewall suggests that Lord may have admired in Emily the quality of "common sense," which he revered and defined as "wisdom applied to conduct." He may also have recognized in her a gift he once called knowledge of "the subtle and more mysterious workings of the human mind." He was also a man who understood that a certain kind of public reserve, which he called "inertia" often reflected a state of intense mental activity (*Life*, II, 650–652).

There is insufficient evidence to establish when their intimate relationship began. Judge Lord was a frequent guest at The HOMESTEAD when Edward Dickinson was alive and continued to visit the Dickinsons after Edward's death. In October 1875 the Lords spent a week in Amherst. Emily and her mother, probably with the judge's supervision, made their wills, with Mrs. Lord serving as witness. An 1877 letter from Lord to the poet's sister, LAVINIA DICKINSON, reveals his concern for Emily and sensitivity to her nature. He asks Vinnie for the truth about Emily's health: "knowing how unselfish she is, how unwilling to disclose any ailment, I fear that she has been more ill, than she has told me." After his wife, "a woman of power as well as of unusual beauty" (Bingham, *A Revelation,* 57), died of cancer on December 10, 1877 (Dickinson's 47th birthday), he continued to visit for a week or so at a time during the early 1880s, staying with his nieces at the Amherst House.

That we know anything more than this about Emily and Judge Lord is due to the remarkable survival of some of her letters to him. (His from her were apparently burned after his death.) In her 1954 account of how she came by the letters, Millicent Todd Bingham describes how Austin gave the letters, all in one envelope, to her mother, MABEL LOOMIS TODD, in the early 1890s, with an indication that they were "very special and personal." How he obtained them, whether Emily entrusted them to him or whether he, for whatever reasons, rescued them from the fire that consumed the rest of her correspondence, remains a mystery. It was probably Austin who censored the letters, cutting out substantial portions. Mabel Todd, Dickinson's first editor as well as Austin's longtime mistress, never considered including them in the collection of Dickinson's letters she was then preparing. She put them away in her camphorwood box, along with the rest of her invaluable cache of Dickinson documents. The brown envelope would be opened by Mrs. Bingham only in 1932, following her mother's death (Ibid., 1–35).

The letters present great textual difficulties. Only 15 letters, some mere scraps, survive, and there is no way to know which among the drafts and fair copies were mailed. Only three can be dated precisely, the first of which was written on April 30, 1882. How long had the correspondence been going on? On the basis of handwriting, scholars have attributed the first five of the 15 to sometime in 1878, the year after Mrs. Lord died. But Dickinson's latest biographer, Alfred Habegger, believes this dating is probably incorrect and offers evidence supporting the thesis that the first letters weren't written until 1880. He comments, "It seems impossible that this [L 563, an amorous fragment] could have been written a few months after Elizabeth Lord died" (*My Wars,* 587).

Sewall, however, explains the depth of feeling in a letter written so soon after the judge lost his wife by assuming that the lovers' feelings had begun developing well before Mrs. Lord's death. He notes that, while there are phrases that indicate that Emily and Otis had a long past, other sentences indicate that love had come suddenly and recently. He surmises that their feelings for one another had grown over a long period of time, but were given release only by Mrs. Lord's death.

Placing the affair within the context of Emily's situation in the late 1870s, Sewall speculates that Lord "brought a release of spirit at a difficult time in her life, with her father gone, her mother a hopeless invalid . . . Bowles dead, Sue apparently long since lost . . . Austin overworked and depressed, and her literary production and ambition well beyond their peak." (*Life,* II, 654). Indeed, the first letter (L 559, about 1878) begins with a sense of exhilarating new freedom:

> My lovely Salem smiles at me. I seek his Face so often—but I have done with guises.
>
> I confess that I love him—I rejoice that I love him—I thank the maker of Heaven and Earth— that gave him me to love—the exultation floods me. I cannot find my channel—the Creek turns Sea—at thought of thee—

Yet, in the next letter (L 560, about 1878), she is aware of the need to stem the flood of feeling. She begs him, "Oh, my too beloved, save me from the idolatry that would crush us both—." After a life of principled renunciation, she may have felt that her personal integrity was threatened by complete abandonment to her love. Indeed, in a subsequent letter attributed to 1878 (L 562), she appears to be refusing her sexual favors on the grounds, frequently asserted in her poetry, that longing is superior to fulfillment:

Dont you know you are happiest while I with-
hold and not confer—dont you know that "No"
is the wildest word we consign to Language?

> . . . It is Anguish I long conceal from you to
let you leave me, hungry, but you ask the divine
Crust and that would doom the bread.

Alfred Habegger places this renunciation in perspective, however, when he notes: "She . . . appears
to assume that 'no' is not 'no' but a basis for additional play, intimacy, confession" (*My Wars*, 590).
Before we interpret the above as Dickinson's final
refusal of a sexual relationship with Lord, we should
recall that it was written at the very beginning of
their affair. Mrs. Todd reports Susan Dickinson's
caution to her that the Dickinson sisters "have not,
either of them, any idea of morality. . . . I went in
there one day, and in the drawing room I found
Emily in the arms of a man." If there is any truth
to the scene Susan draws, then we know there was
a physical side to their love, whether or not it was
consummated.

We know that Emily played with the idea of
marriage and that Lord, in fact, made an offer. He
had apparently called her "Jumbo" after she told
him that a long letter she had written to him on
thick paper and concealed under her clothes had
aroused suspicion. In a letter of about November
1882, she wrote: "Emily 'Jumbo'! Sweetest name,
but I know a Sweeter—Emily Jumbo Lord. Have I
your approval?" (L 780). The following month, on
December 3, 1882, in the aftermath of her mother's
death on November 14, she refers to his proposal:
"You said with loved timidity in asking me to your
dear Home, you would 'try not to make it unpleasant'—so delicate a diffidence, how beautiful to
see!" (L 790).

After years of nursing her mother, Emily's grief
must have been mingled with relief. In the same
letter, she wrote Lord, "Speaking of you as I feel,
Dear, without that Dress of Spirit must be worn for
most, Courage is quite changed." She loved him,
she could be herself with him, but they never married, no doubt, in large part because of the judge's
failing health. The previous May he had suffered a
serious "attack" of uncertain nature, which forced
him to resign from the bench in December 1882,

the same month Emily mentions his proposal. From
then on, he lived in the knowledge that he could
die suddenly at any moment, and Emily seems to
have loved him with greater desperation. In a poem
of 1884, Fr 1654, she wrote: "Still own thee—still
thou art / What Surgeons call alive—/ Though
slipping—slipping—I perceive / To thy reportless
Grave—". He died of a stroke on March 13, 1884,
aged 72.

Shortly after his death, she wrote to Benjamin
Kimball, a cousin of Lord's entrusted with settling
the judge's estate: "Abstinence from Melody was
what made him die. Calvary and May wrestled in
his Nature" (L 968). The lines strikingly echo what
she wrote of her father after his death: "He never
played and the straightest engine has its leaning
hour."

Paradoxically, however, if Lord could not sing,
he enabled Dickinson to do so. The letter continues: "to sing in his presence was involuntary,
thronged only with Music, like the Decks of Birds."
One of the unanswered questions about their relationship is the extent to which Lord knew her
poetry or was aware of the depth of her commitment to her art. While she must have sent others, in the surviving letters she sent him only two
poems: Fr 1622, "The summer that we did not
prize," about the late coming of tenderness, and
Fr 1557, "How fleet—how indiscreet an one," a
whimsical treatment of the theme of love and guilt.
Nowhere in the letters does she speak of poetry or
of herself as poet. Yet he may have moved her to
write many of the great poems of her later years. At
the conclusion of *A Revelation*, Bingham prints 23
poems, with little comment, which she presumably
thought were connected to this late experience.
These include: Fr 1447, "WHO NEVER WANTED—
MADDEST JOY"; Fr 1473, "I thought the Train would
never come—"; Fr 1528, "The Thrill came slowly
like a Boon for"; and Fr 1653 "So give me back to
Death—." His death inspired one of her finest elegies, "Though the great Waters sleep," (Fr 1641,
1884).

Whatever facts are missing from our understanding of Emily Dickinson's love affair with Otis
Lord, her sister, at least, well knew how important
it had been to her. When Emily died, as THOMAS

WENTWORTH HIGGINSON recorded in his diary: ". . . Vinnie put in [the coffin] two heliotropes by her hand 'to take to Judge Lord.'"

See also "RENUNCIATION—IS A PIERCING VIRTUE."

FURTHER READING

Martha Dickinson Bianchi, *Life and Letters*, 69–70; Millicent Todd Bingham, *Emily Dickinson: A Revelation*; Betsy Erkilla, "Dickinson and the Art of Politics," in *Historical Guide*, 163; Alfred Habegger, *My Wars*, 584–593; Richard B. Sewall, *Life*, II, 642–667.

Lyman, Joseph Bardwell (1829–1872) Joseph Bardwell Lyman was a close girlhood friend of the poet and the suitor of her sister, LAVINIA NORCROSS DICKINSON ("Vinnie"). Much of what we know about his relationship to the Dickinson family comes from a cache of letters and journals that were put into the hands of biographer Richard B. Sewall in 1961 by Joseph Bardwell Lyman III and subsequently published as *The Lyman Letters*. This important set of documents, which contains excerpts of the poet's letters to Lyman, proved to be a vital contribution to Dickinson scholarship. In addition to giving us new words from Emily herself, they illuminate Vinnie's life, giving her a separate existence from that of her famous sister, and cast a humanizing light on the Dickinson home, which was traditionally portrayed as grim and forbidding.

Joseph Bardwell Lyman was born on October 6, 1829, in Chester, Massachusetts, 40 miles west of Amherst, the son of Timothy and Experience Bardwell Lyman. His father died when Joseph was eight, leaving a wife and eight children with limited financial resources. Writing about his childhood, Joseph portrayed himself as a frail, timid boy with a great thirst for books. He often referred to the poverty of his youth, the necessity of having to earn the money for his own education, and later, his pride in being a successful self-made man.

His family was related by marriage to Emily's mother, EMILY NORCROSS DICKINSON, through the Lyman Colemans, who moved to AMHERST in 1844. This connection may explain how he came to invite Emily's brother, WILLIAM AUSTIN DICKINSON, to room with him at Williston Seminary (now Academy) in Easthampton, Massachusetts, where they were both students. But Austin was obliged to return home, since his father, EDWARD DICKINSON, who was often away on business at the time, insisted that a male "guard" be present to protect the women of his household. The disappointed Austin was allowed to invite his schoolmate for a two-month visit before Joseph resumed his education at Williston.

This visit, the first of many, had a profound impact on the talented and high-spirited Joseph. Sewall speculates, "To a sensitive, impressionable and poor boy, who had been considered a little strange in his own home, a 'queer chicken' with his precocious intellectual curiosities, this household must have represented what he dreamed of in warmth, charm, and conversation" (*Lyman Letters*, 7). The Dickinsons welcomed him into their home, treating him almost as family. He and Austin became close friends and, during his 1846 visit, he began an intense love affair with Vinnie and a deep and lasting relationship with Emily. For the next four years, while a student at Yale, Joseph continued to regularly visit what he described to his mother as "that charming second home of mine in Amherst," maintaining and deepening his connections with the Dickinsons. His later reminiscences of those days stress "the warmth of the Dickinson circle, its integrity and harmony . . ." and counter "the persistent notion of the bleakness of the Amherst scene and of the Dickinson family as joyless and introverted, unworldly, of little appeal to gay, full-blooded, and talkative youth" (Ibid., 8).

His most intense relationship was his romance with pretty, "soft-lipped," plump-armed Vinnie, whom he courted and held on his lap while they exchanged sensual kisses. At one point Joseph believed he would marry Vinnie, and he kept her memory vivid for many years after they were no longer involved. Smugly—and condescendingly—sure of her love for him, he dangled her image before his fiancée, Laura Baker, now as an example of how he wished Laura were more affectionate, as Vinnie had been, now to assure Laura that he could never have married Vinnie, because she lacked Laura's character, intelligence, and belief in him.

If Joseph was Vinnie's suitor, he was purely a friend to Emily, whom he described as "Platonic." Elsewhere he called her "rather morbid and unnatural," by which he may have meant that she showed no interest in a romantic, sexual relationship with him. (The physically appealing young man, accustomed to easily attracting women, once called Laura "morbid" when she was cold to him). Emily was 16, Joseph 17 when they met. During his visits to the Dickinsons in the 1840s, they walked and talked together frequently, read German plays together and sat side by side looking up words in the same dictionary. Sewall speculates that their main bond may have been literary and that Joseph may have given the young Emily literary encouragement. He found her "spiritual" and mentioned her, in a letter to his older brother in 1849, as an exception to the rule that women don't know how to make conversation: "Em. Dickinson is a year younger it is true but older . . . in mind & heart." Their spiritual connection would prove more enduring than his sensual infatuation with Vinnie.

Each in her own way, both sisters mourned when Joseph left New England in 1851 and went south. Emily wrote to her beloved friend and future sister-in-law, SUSAN HUNTINGTON GILBERT (DICKINSON), who had gone to teach in Baltimore, "Dear Susie, Dear Joseph; why take the best and dearest and leave our hearts behind?" For the next few years Joseph lived a peripatetic, bachelor life that included teaching and traveling in Connecticut, Tennessee, and Mississippi. He studied law in Nashville from 1853 to 1855 and completed his legal education in New Orleans in 1856. Throughout his wanderings he continued to correspond with the Dickinsons, seemingly more frequently than with his own family. When he arrived in New Orleans in 1855, he wrote to his mother, "The Dickinson people still remember me and write me letters. They have been the truest of all my New England friends." He continued to cherish the memory of them and wrote in January 1858, "I like them better than I do my own family. . . ."

In New Orleans, Joseph established himself as an aggressive young lawyer and man about town.

Emily, far from being put off by the increasingly worldly and ambitious Joseph, "saw the 'arrow in his hand'—his ambition—and rather relished the world-shine he acquired" (Sewall, *Life*, II, 423). He was one of many close friends who lived out in the world, including THOMAS WENTWORTH HIGGINSON, SAMUEL BOWLES, JOSIAH HOLLAND, CATHERINE TURNER ANTHON, and JUDGE OTIS PHILLIPS LORD, and who kept her in touch with larger events. Joseph gave up his New Orleans life, however, to fight for the Confederacy in the Civil War and, upon his return, abandoned his career as a lawyer and embarked on a busy career as a writer and journalist in New York City. An astute observer of the social world, he wrote for many publications and became an editorialist and feature writer for *The New York Times*.

After breaking off his romance with Vinnie and engaging in a number of other amorous adventures, he became engaged to Laura Baker, whom he met during a visit home in 1856, and they married in 1858. During the course of a happy and productive marriage, they had seven children. In 1867 they collaborated on what became a popular book, *The Philosophy of Housekeeping*. Laura became a writer in her own right and supported their children by her writing after Joseph's early death, on January 28, 1872, of smallpox, at his home in Richmond Hill, Long Island.

Perhaps the most valuable part of Joseph Bardwell Lyman's legacy to the world of literature are the excerpts from Emily Dickinson's letters that he transcribed and saved; they are all that remains of their long correspondence, which was interrupted by his marriage and the Civil War, but resumed when he came north again after the war. He transcribed them after the Civil War, apparently revising as he wrote. In the passages he saved from her letters, "Emily appears at her best, not posing, talking neither up nor down nor in riddles." (Sewall, *Life*, II, 423). The seven passages, or "snatches," as he called them, saved from her letters were clearly selected because of their striking style and opinions, often on literary topics, such as Shakespeare, the Bible, and the power of words. Their wide subject range and style have suggested to some scholars, that Joseph, the professional journalist, may have been planning to use them in some kind of literary project. While most of the "snatches" date from their later friendship, one was probably written in the late 1840s. In it, Emily offers a rare, intimate portrait of whiling away a Sunday at home with Austin, indulging in "merry talk" about bumblebees and improvising a bumblebee duet. In the midst of this frivolity, their straitlaced father enters the room and says that "he was glad to see the little people enjoy themselves."

When she had become a poet, she shared with Joseph the transformation in her sense of language:

> We used to think, Joseph, when I was an unsifted girl and you so scholarly that words were cheap & weak. Now I don't know of anything so mighty. There are [those] to which I lift my hat when I see them sitting princelike among their peers on the page. Sometimes I write one, and look at his outlines till he glows as no sapphire. (*Lyman Letters*, 78)

As she made deeper excursions into her imagination, she confided to him:

> So I conclude that space & time are things of the body & have little or nothing to do with our selves. My country is Truth. . . . I like Truth—it is a free Democracy.

Joseph also wrote a brief sketch of her sometime between his return from the Civil War and his death, worth quoting in full:

Emily

"Things are not what they seem"

NIGHT IN MIDSUMMER

A Library dimly lighted, three mignonettes in a little stand. Enter a spirit clad in white, figure so draped as to be misty[,] face moist, translucent alabaster, forehead firmer as of statuary marble. Eyes once bright hazel now melted & fused so as to be two dreamy, wondering wells of expression, eyes that see no forms but gla[n]ce swiftly to the core of all thi[n]gs—hands small, firm, deft but utterly emancipated from all claspings of perishable things, very firm strong little hands absolutely under control of the brain, types of

quite rugged health[,] mouth made for nothing and used for nothing but uttering choice speech, rare thoughts, glittering, starry misty figures, winged words.

The sketch implies that Joseph actually saw Emily again, and, indeed, the description of the poet dressed in white corresponds to her habit in those years. But there is some evidence that there was no face-to-face meeting and that the episode is fanciful. A note from Laura, written after the poet's death, states: "Mr. Lyman didn't really see her, tho' he talked with her." For biographer Alfred Habegger, the sketch is proof that, in the 1860s, "Hidden as she was and relatively quiescent, Dickinson was emphatically not in retreat from life." He speculates, "What Lyman may have meant by 'rugged health' was her obvious and amazing vitality. Maybe that was why he headed his sketch, 'Things are not what they seem'" (*My Wars*, 518–519).

What is clear is that the two old friends retained their importance to one another. Joseph was one of the very few friends of her youth who did not abandon Emily when he went away, and Emily remained a vivid presence in his inner life. When the poet died in 1886, his widow Laura wrote, "I wonder if they have met up yonder. . . ."

See also "A SOLEMN THING—IT WAS—I SAID," HENRY VAUGHAN EMMONS, GEORGE HENRY GOULD, JOHN LONG GRAVES, and ABIAH PALMER ROOT.

FURTHER READING

Alfred Habegger, *My Wars*, 283–287, 514–519; Richard B. Sewall, ed., *The Lyman Letters: New Light on Emily Dickinson and Her Family*; Sewall, *Life*, II, 422–427.

Lyon, Mary (1797–1849)   A pioneer in women's education, Mary Lyon was the founder and guiding spirit of MOUNT HOLYOKE FEMALE SEMINARY in South Hadley, Massachusetts, where Emily Dickinson was a student from September 30, 1847, to August 3, 1848. The school she founded evolved into Mount Holyoke College, one of the leading women's colleges in the country.

Mary Lyon was born on February 28, 1797, on a remote farm in Buckland, a hill town in western

Massachusetts. The family was devout but poorly educated. When her father died, her mother was left to raise seven children and manage a 100-acre farm on her own. Mary, who was five at the time, learned from her mother a vast array of culinary and housekeeping skills. At the same time, she managed to keep up her education, begun at age four at the village school, sometimes lodging with relatives or local families. She obtained a better education than most girls of her time, despite having to leave school at age 13 when her mother remarried and went to live with her new husband. Mary became self-supporting, earning one silver dollar a week as a housekeeper for her brother Aaron.

She was offered a position teaching school at age 17—no formal certification was required—on the basis of her reputation as a first-rate student. While supporting herself in this way, she managed to continue her own education and became a student at AMHERST ACADEMY in 1818, where her great intellectual powers were stimulated. She studied science

Mary Lyon, founder of Mount Holyoke Female Seminary, in an 1845 daguerreotype *(Mount Holyoke College Archives and Special Collections.)*

with EDWARD HITCHCOCK in the 1820s and formed an important friendship with that eminent man of science and religion, who would be the dominant influence at the academy when Emily Dickinson was a student there in the 1840s.

During her 20 years of teaching in Massachusetts and New Hampshire, notably at Ipswich Female Seminary, Mary Lyon became famous for her high standards of scholarship, discipline, and piety. As she became an authority on women's education, she conceived her plan for organizing a college for higher education for women. After three years of exhausting fund-raising and involvement in every aspect of the new school's philosophy, curriculum and physical facilities, she opened the doors of Mount Holyoke Female Seminary in 1837.

Hitchcock supported and guided her throughout this process and his influence was apparent in the character of the new institution. Lyon and Hitchcock were at one in their dedication to both science (she taught chemistry) and religion. Both strove to expose their students to the latest scholarship—and to convert them to Christ. A similar philosophy guided both Hitchcock's Academy and Lyon's Seminary—but the missionary spirit was far more prominent at Mount Holyoke. In her desire to make women's higher education the equal of men's and to make them emissaries of Christianity to the world at large, Mary Lyon was a revolutionary; but the evangelical religion she championed was highly conservative. The seminary's existence depended upon the support of dedicated evangelicals, who shared Lyon's dream of converting the next generation of mothers and teachers in their youth (Habegger, *My Wars*, 197).

As the school's principal for 12 years, Lyon was engaged in everything from administration, teaching, and addressing assemblies to kitchen work (at first she did much of the cooking herself). She saw herself as a "mother" to her poorly paid, devoted staff—her "family." There were no hired servants; together, students and staff pitched in to do the domestic chores. Coming under the sway of this remarkable woman, there was much that Emily Dickinson might have found inspiring in her: her hatred of "empty gentility," her belief that women had the power to "become almost what we will," her emphasis on meditative discipline, her injunction never to "write a foolish thing in a letter or elsewhere: "what is written is written"—a sentiment that resonated with Dickinson's own belief that "A Word dropped careless on a Page" can exert either a destructive or positive influence that is long-lasting. In short, she gave the young Emily "the example of a brilliant and loving woman who had found her work and given her life to it" (Sewall, *Life*, II, 367).

However, apart from the curious fact that later in life Dickinson always wore white, as Mary Lyon had done, there is no evidence that she was a role model. Although her name occurs often in Emily's letters from Mount Holyoke, there are no extended passages about her. Emily's early remarks to her pious friend ABIAH PALMER ROOT during her second month there are positive: "One thing is certain, & that is that Miss. Lyon & all the teachers, seem to consult our comfort & happiness in everything they do & you know that is pleasant" (L 18, November 6, 1847). Lyon's witty, soft-spoken manner could cause merriment among her students. But a distinctly ironic, mocking tone characterizes Emily's remarks to brother WILLIAM AUSTIN, with whom she was more likely to share her rebellious side. In one letter, she makes fun of Miss Lyon's emphasis on self-reliance: "Do you know of any nation about to besiege South Hadley ... I suppose Miss Lyon, would furnish us all with daggers & order us to fight for our lives, in case such perils should befall us" (L 16, October 21, 1847). A few months later, she is chafing at "*Mistress* Lyon's" rules and delighting in her pleasure in flouting them. She writes Austin that Lyon had forbidden the sending of valentines, but the

girls who were there the previous year, "knowing her opinions, were sufficiently cunning to write & give them into the care of Dickinson ..." (L 16, October 21, 1847). The seminary had endless rules, which students were not allowed to challenge. On the contrary, one of their duties was to inform on one another's infringements. Despite her desire to conform, Emily must have resented such pressures. Nor would she have been drawn to a teacher like Miss Lyon, who warned "no-hopers" such as herself (those who could not accept Christ) that they were exposing themselves to "a miserable eternity."

During Emily's year at the seminary, Lyon was ill and depressed by the fact that 30 girls were still "without hope" when the school year ended. She died just seven months after Emily left Mt. Holyoke, at age 52, in the prime of her career. Among the broad community that grieved her, foremost was Edward Hitchcock, who, in August 1851, published a memorial compilation, *The Power of Christian Benevolence Illustrated in the Life and Labors of Mary Lyon*—a book that appears on the list of books in Edward Dickinson's library. If Emily read it, she would have made the surprising discovery that her former schoolmistress saw herself as rebellious and world-loving (terms very similar to the way the young Emily viewed herself) and as a woman who did not expect to see heaven herself, but hoped to prepare others for it.

FURTHER READING

Alden Green, *Mary Lyon and Mount Holyoke;* Mount Holyoke, "Opening the Gates," available online, URL: http://www.mtholyoke.edu/marylyon/, accessed January 11, 2006; Richard B. Sewall, *Life,* II, 358–367.

M

Master letters Since their first publication in 1955, almost a century after they were written, the drafts of three letters to an unidentified individual Emily Dickinson called "Master" have been the subject of intensive study and speculation. Scholars continue to take sides in a heated debate that is unlikely ever to be settled about the identity of the person to whom these desperately passionate love letters were addressed. Biographer Richard B. Sewall calls them "extraordinary human documents, at once baffling and breathtaking" (*Life*, II, 513), while pioneering editor R. W. Franklin believes that they "stand near the heart of her mystery" (*Master Letters*, 5). Yet these letters, with their uncertain history of discovery, publication, dating, and transcription, are themselves a mystery.

The first riddle they present is how and why they survived. Since they were clearly not with Dickinson's correspondence, which her sister, LAVINIA NORCROSS DICKINSON, destroyed after her death, they may have been in the box of poems Lavinia found in a locked box on May 15, 1886. Although Dickinson's first editor, MABEL LOOMIS TODD, knew of them by the early 1890s, she chose to excerpt only six brief sentences both in her 1894 edition of the *Letters* and her 1931 revision of the earlier volume. Only in 1955, when Todd's daughter, Millicent Todd Bingham, inherited the manuscripts from her mother, were they published in full, in *Emily Dickinson's Home*. Subsequently they became widely available when Thomas Johnson included them in his 1958 three-volume *Letters*. However, neither Bingham's nor Johnson's versions adhered strictly to the manuscripts or dealt adequately with the sequence of the letters. Jay Leyda's versions, in his *Hours and Years*, were also interpretive.

Then, in 1986, R. W. Franklin published new, authoritative versions, based on close scrutiny of the original documents, which are currently housed in the Emily Dickinson Collection of the Amherst College Library. Striving to render the manuscripts as completely and literally as possible, Franklin offered line by line transcriptions and published facsimile reproductions on the facing pages of the typed version. Another revolutionary aspect of his versions is the reordering of the letters' sequence, with letters 2 and 3 changing place. Franklin's dating method relies on analysis of Dickinson's handwriting as it evolved from year to year, for example, her transition from writing the article "the" in two parts, as "t" and "he" to writing it as a linked unit "the" in 1861.

Franklin stresses that none of the surviving documents, two in ink with pencil and/or ink corrections, one entirely in pencil, were in "suitable condition" to be sent out. There is no evidence that they were ever recopied and mailed, nor any reason they would not have been. Certain that they represent fragments of an extensive correspondence, Franklin believes they "indicate a long relationship, geographically apart, in which correspondence would have been the main means of communication" (Ibid., 5).

Letter 1, which Franklin assigns to the spring of 1858, is the earliest of the three and the briefest. Evidently responding to a letter from Master, Dickinson begins by saying that she is ill, but is more concerned that Master has been ailing. Her tone is respectful and gracious: "I thought perhaps you were in Heaven, and when you spoke again, it seemed quite sweet, and wonderful, and surprised me so. . . ." She then invokes the Spring outside her door, wishing she were "Mr. Michael Angelo" and could paint it for him. Yet her own "painting" of the scene is visionary, transferring Heaven to earth: "Indeed it is God's house—/ and these are gates / of Heaven. . . ." She continues: "You ask me what my flowers said—then they were disobedient—I gave them messages." While pretending to blame "the flowers," that is, her poems, which he has failed to understand, she gently takes him to task: "They say what the lips in the West say, when the sun goes down, and so says the dawn . . .," that is, they say what nature says. "Listen again, Master . . .," she implores, eager for him to understand more than he does. She then tells him it is Sabbath and reintroduces the motif of heaven by musing on future Sabbaths when they may "meet on shore. . . ."

The tone of Letter 2 (previously thought to be Letter 3, but assigned by Franklin to early 1861) is radically different: defensive, frantic, and impassioned. Written entirely in pencil, with numerous cancellations and substitutions, it begins, in reply to Master's accusation:

> Oh—did I offend it—
> (Didn't it want me
> to tell it the truth),
> Daisy—Daisy—offend it—who
> bends her smaller life to
> his it's meeker lower every day—

In the 19th century "Master" was the appropriate address of servant, slave or pupil to the man in charge, and this letter, of all three, most starkly reveals a depth of psychological and sexual servility. Yet, as Cynthia Griffin Wolff astutely notes, the writer's abject self-humiliation barely conceals her rage as she begs for forgiveness for an offense she does not understand. By her chilling use of the impersonal pronoun "it," instead of "you" or "him," a usage found in such poems as "IF I MAY HAVE IT, WHEN IT'S DEAD," she depersonalizes Master and dismisses him to the realm of the dead (*Emily Dickinson*, 411). Her offense was probably to tell him the truth that she loves him with "A love so big it scares her, rushing among her small heart—." She is an offender and a blunderer, who kneels "Low at the knee that bore her once unto [royal] wordless rest. . . ." She will submit to any punishment but banishment and promises to be his "best little girl." Her only defense of herself is that she is "Daisy—who never flinched thro' that awful parting, but held her life so tight he should not see the wound—." She does not spare him this time, however, evoking her present wound as a "stab," more painful than a bee's sting, or her cough "as big as a thimble" or the "Tomahawk in my side." Yet, she wants nothing more than to be with this punishing deity, since "Heaven will only disappoint me—" because it will not be "so dear" as Master, a theme developed in such great love lyrics as "I CANNOT LIVE WITH YOU—" ("Your Face / Would put out Jesus'").

The third and longest letter, written in summer 1861, responds to Master's apparent lack of belief in what she has been professing:

> If you saw a bullet
> hit a Bird—and he told you
> he was'nt shot—you might weep
> at his courtesy, but you would
> certainly doubt his word—
> One drop more from the gash
> that stains your Daisy's
> bosom—then would you *believe?*

She defends her love by asserting the mystery of her own nature:

> God made me—[Sir]—Master—I did'nt
> be—myself—[He] I dont know how
> it was done—He built the
> heart in me—Bye and bye
> it outgrew me—and like
> the little mother—with the
> big child—I got tired
> holding him—

Judith Farr's identification of the mother-child image with a passage in one of Dickinson's favorite novels, Charlotte Brontë's *Jane Eyre,* shows the consciously literary dimension of these letters. Jane has a dream before her impending marriage, in which she carries a little child that she can't put down anywhere, no matter how tired her arms grow. "The child is Jane herself and represents her past. . . . So what Dickinson is saying to Master is that she too has outgrown the child's pose; that she now writes to him as an amorous woman" (*Passion,* 198–199).

She reminds him that she asked him for "Redemption," and that he gave her "something else," a vague enough phrase to accommodate various interpretations, including sexual fulfillment. In any case, it replaced her previous longing: "I forgot the Redemption / (in the Redeemed—." Assuring him that "I am older—tonight, Master—/ but the love is the same—," she expresses her anguish at their separation and her irrepressible wish, though she knows it is not "God's will," to have "the Queen's place." In reply to his reproach that "I do not tell you all"—she insists that she has "confessed." She compares herself to both "Vesuvius"— the volcano—and Pompeii—the city it destroyed. Pompeii heard Vesusius's "syllable" "and "hid forever," implying that after "erupting" once, she has retreated in frightened silence at the violence of her passion. To his request, "Tell [me] of the want," she replies in a series of images that suggest mingled desires for a painful cure, the transcending of limits, and the exhilaration of proximity to vast depths:

> —you
> know what a leech is, dont
> you—and (remember that) Daisy's arm is
>   small—
> and you have felt the Horizon—
> hav'nt you—and did the
> sea—never come so close as
> to make you dance?

She then launches into a series of fantasies, of walking with him in the woods with her dog, CARLO; of being with him in heaven; and being

with him when they are both old. She asks if he could come to New England this summer.

Perhaps referring to the integrity of her confession, of her passion for him, or of her virginity, she asks,

> What would you do with me
> if I came "in white"?
> Have you the little chest—to
> put the alive—in?

The image suggests, chillingly, that he might bury this great gift alive, in the "little chest," that is, the coffin. In the final, poignant line, a sense of resigned hopelessness reigns, as she notes, "you / did'nt come to me 'in white'—/ nor ever told me why—."

Noting that the Master of these letters is unreal and remote, without a single descriptive phrase to pin him with any certainty to any of the men in Dickinson's life we know anything about, some scholars have suggested that he was a fantasy figure, and that the letters are "fictional." Franklin is among those who reject this notion, arguing that Dickinson did not write letters as a fictional genre. Judith Farr defends the reality of the addressee on the basis that the letters "reflect turmoil, like that of a person tortured by the problem of what to say to somebody important" (*Passion,* 199). Vivian Pollak takes an intermediary position, arguing that "although Master has some of the attributes of an actual person, he exists primarily as a function of Dickinson's need for an eroticized father figure" (*Anxiety of Gender,* 95).

For those who believe that Master was a real person, the leading candidates are REVEREND CHARLES WADSWORTH, the charismatic Presbyterian minister Dickinson met in Philadelphia in 1855, and SAMUEL BOWLES, the worldly, crusading editor of *The Springfield Republican,* who was a close friend of the Dickinsons from 1858 on. Cynthia Griffin Wolff considers both Bowles and Wadsworth unlikely candidates, and suggests that Master could have been any one of a number of distinguished men who came to Amherst. Feminist scholars such as Rebecca Patterson and Martha Nell Smith raise the possibility that Master is a woman, with

Smith putting forth SUSAN HUNTINGTON GILBERT DICKINSON as the likely candidate.

Dickinson's latest biographer, Alfred Habegger, asserts that Bowles could not have been Master, since the generally accepted dates of Emily's first "Master" draft is spring 1858. Like Pollak and Polly Longsworth, among others, he votes for Charles Wadsworth, who (like Bowles) was married and totally inaccessible, lived far from her, had at least one face-to-face meeting with her, and possessed the religious authority Dickinson seems to invest in Master, since she asks him for redemption. Sewall, however, notes that Dickinson often used the word "redemption" in a secular way. He believes that Bowles was Master, citing the similarities between the Master letters and poems she sent Bowles, the fact that Emily often wrote him about his poor health, that his pet name for her was Daisy, and that he, more so than Wadsworth, himself a poet, would have been more likely not to understand her poetry. Above all, he notes the intensity of the letters Emily was writing at this time to Bowles, whom she clearly loved. She could not, in Sewall's estimation, have loved both him and Wadsworth "at the same time at such a pitch" (*Life*, II, 528).

Judith Farr is probably Bowles's most interesting and persuasive advocate. She argues that the letters must be understood within the context of Bowles's favorite writer, Charlotte Brontë, and especially of *Jane Eyre*. Pointing to numerous verbal and imagistic echoes from that novel, "the kind of encoded communication Bowles would have understood," she notes that "Master" is what Jane calls Rochester, the man she loves, but cannot marry because he is already wed. Even more persuasively, Farr writes, "It can be no coincidence ... that the 'Master' of Dickinson's poems and letters and the 'Mr. Bowles' to whom she writes as a redeemer and Christ figure are addressed in identical imagery ..." (*Passion*, 183). In addition to the image of Christ, who is called "Master" by his disciples in the New Testament, she identifies as central components of the "Narrative of Master" the images of the Sun god, Apollo, the light-bearer; the alternate image of Master as Promethean fire; and images of the sea, representing love, sexuality, terror, and eternity.

No matter whom they espouse as Master, most scholars concede that his identity can never be "proven" and that it is, after all, of secondary importance. Some have seen the letters' deeper significance in terms of what they indicate about Dickinson's fundamental psychological stance, in which passion and separation are linked, and the reunion of the lovers can take place only in heaven. For Sewall, the truly important thing is what they reveal about her devastating love experience, about "the intensity, depth, and power of her love and the agony of its frustration" (*Life*, II, 513).

Equally important, however, is their relevance to her poetry. Highly literary and crafted, despite their genuine desperation, they show an artist at work. "It is by no chance," writes Sewall, "that these three letters are the seedbed, the matrix, of dozens of poems" and that these poems are in a sense the "final drafts" of the letters (*Life*, II, 520). Agnieszka Salska concurs, noting that the stylistic lessons of the Master letters were crucial to the poetry:

> It seems as if in the Master letters all her earlier exercises in intensity brought her to some edge beyond which the realization or intuition came that language does not render intensity by expansiveness and description but through concentration and suppression. ... Thus it seems only natural that her most creative time as a poet should coincide with and immediately follow developments in style traceable to the Master letters ("Dickinson's Letters," 174–175).

See also "I SHOULD HAVE BEEN TOO GLAD—I SEE—," "TITLE DIVINE—IS MINE," and "WILD NIGHTS—WILD NIGHTS!"

FURTHER READING

Judith Farr, *Passion*, 178–344; R. W. Franklin, ed., *Master Letters of Emily Dickinson*; Alfred Habegger, *My Wars*, 416–421; Vivian Pollak, *Anxiety of Gender*, 83–102; Agnieszka Salska, "Dickinson's Letters," in *Handbook*, Grabher et al., eds., 174–175: Richard B. Sewall, *Life*, II, 512–531; Martha Nell Smith, *Rowing in Eden*, 17–18 Cynthia Griffin Wolff, *Emily Dickinson*, 406–412.

Merrill, Harriet   Harriet was a member of the small group of close friends, all classmates at AMHERST ACADEMY, who came together in 1844, under the tutelage of Emily's favorite preceptress, ELIZABETH C. ADAMS. The other members of this intimate circle, whom Emily dubbed "the five," were ABBY MARIA WOOD, ABIAH PALMER ROOT, and SARAH SKINNER TRACY. Little is known about Harriet, who was a daughter of Calvin Merrill, one of the original trustees of Amherst Academy and active in the founding of AMHERST COLLEGE. Like Abiah and Sarah, by 1845 she had transferred to another school, possibly a girls' school in Pittsfield, and later she would teach, first at Amherst Academy and then at Pittsfield.

Nothing has survived of Emily's correspondence with Harriet, which was, in any case, almost wholly one-sided, with Emily doggedly keeping up her end of the conversation in the face of Harriet's silence. In a letter to Abiah, offering one-line sketches of the old crowd, Emily writes, "Hatty is making fun as usual" (L 5, February 23, 1845). Whatever the nature of the "fun" Harriet created, whether it was witty irreverence or just plain hilarity, Emily loved and missed her and only reluctantly gave up on the relationship. Writing to Abiah of changes taking place in AMHERST, she is moved to a metaphoric flight by Harriet's departure:

> ". . . but the worst thing old Time has done here is he has walked so fast as to overtake Harriet Merrill and carry her to Hartford on last week Saturday. I was so vexed with him for it that I ran after him and made out to get near enough to him to put some salt on his tail, when he fled and left me to run home alone. . . ." (L 6, May 7, 1845)

All of Emily's subsequent mentions of Harriet in the letters to Abiah bemoan her failure to write to Emily, her other friends, or even her aunt of the same name, an aristocratic single lady who kept student lodgers. (In the last year of her life, Emily wrote of the death of Harriet's aunt, under mysterious circumstances: "Miss Harriet Merrill was poisoned by a strolling Juggler, and to be tried in the Supreme Court next week. . . . Poor, romantic Miss Merrill!" [L 1041, April 17, 1886]). Reply-ing to Abiah's disappointment in not hearing from Harriet, Emily advises her to "heap coals of fire upon her head by writing to her constantly until you get an answer." (L 7, August 3, 1845). This was Emily's technique, but it rarely proved effective in Harriet's case. Emily continued to obsess on the reasons for Harriet's silence, speculating that "procrastination has carried her off" (L 8, September 25, 1845). In her postscript, she enumerates the letters and gifts she has sent (including "a very handsome book mark") and how little she and Abby and her aunt, Mrs. Merrill, have received in return. She opines, "I really can't help thinking she has forgotten the many happy hours we spent together, and though I try to banish the idea from my mind, for it is painful to me." The following year, she writes Abiah: "Have you yet heard from Dear Harriet? I have not. Miss Merrill has written to Harriet and Frances inviting them to spend Thanksgiving. I need not tell you how much I wish to see her & learn the cause of her long silence" (L 14, late autumn 1846).

Emily's comments on Harriet reveal not only the tenacity with which she clung to old friendships, but how inconceivable it was to her that someone she loved could be swept away by another life and value the past less than she did. Harriet's ability to do so continued to pose a mystery to her. All this is evident in her final mention of the young woman she continues to refer to by the affectionate name "Hatty":

> Mrs. Merrill . . . thinks Hatty so busy that she cant get time to write any of us. But if so busy why does she not send us a paper or speak of us when she writes her grandmother? There is a mystery about her silence to me. I hope she is happy. . . . (L 15, March 14, 1847)

Mount Holyoke Female Seminary   Dickinson attended this school for higher education, located in South Hadley, Massachusetts, nine miles south of AMHERST, for 10 months, from September 30, 1847, to August 3, 1848. Founded in 1837 by MARY LYON, a pioneer in women's education, the school evolved into Mount Holyoke College, the outstanding women's college that today enrolls about

2,000 students from all over the United States and the world.

When Emily Dickinson arrived, the seminary housed 235 girls and 12 teachers in a large, four-story brick building. Designed by Miss Lyon to resemble a house and thus foster a family-like feeling among the girls, the building contained both living and academic facilities under a single roof. The day, which began at 6 A.M., was divided into half-hour periods, devoted to academic studies, prayer and private meditation, domestic chores, calisthenics, and meetings of various sorts. The school was governed by no fewer than 70 rules concerning student conduct, health, protection of the building, safety, visits home, correspondence, and communication with the opposite sex. Although teachers were friendly, they enforced the strict rules, which forbade such things as occasional visits home on Sundays or meeting a young man anywhere but in the parlor, in the presence of a teacher. This lack of physical privacy coexisted with the pressure to conform to stringent religious norms. Although the school was not affiliated with any single religious denomination, its mission, as conceived by the founders, was to prepare the next generation of devout wives, mothers, and servants of the church. As much as any academic goal, its aim was to convert young women to the word of Christ and give them a role in spreading it to the world. During this embryonic stage of women's education, when women had extremely limited access to the professions, Mount Holyoke emphasized dedication to religion and rules, rather than objective critical judgment.

For 16-year-old Emily, who had just completed seven enriching years at AMHERST ACADEMY, Mount Holyoke held out the prospect of broadening her world and she eagerly looked forward to beginning her stay there. Most of what we know about this last stint of formal education is drawn from her letters from South Hadley: seven to her brother, WILLIAM AUSTIN, and three to her close friend and former academy schoolmate, ABIAH PALMER ROOT. The story that emerges from these letters is one of determined efforts to adjust and succeed, repeated bouts of homesickness and, ultimately, high hopes disappointed.

Mount Holyoke Female Seminary in South Hadley, Massachusetts, which Emily attended during the school year 1847–48 (*Mount Holyoke College Archives and Special Collections*)

Academically, she was a success, entering on the Junior level and, within six weeks, passing her entrance exam to the Middle level. (There was a third, Senior level, upon the completion of which students received a certificate.) She studied ancient history, chemistry, physiology, algebra, astronomy, and rhetoric, evoking both envy and irritation among fellow students by her original compositions. She told Austin she was much "engrossed in the history of Sulphuric Acid!!!!!" and she boasted about acquiring skills in balancing her account book.

Her emotional adjustment was more complex. From the outset of her stay at Mount Holyoke, Emily, who felt a great responsibility not to disappoint her father, seems determined not to complain and to make a go of things: "I had a great mind to be homesick after you went home, but I concluded not to & therefore gave up all homesick feelings. Was not that a wise determination?" she writes to Austin, after he had visited her, three weeks into the semester (L 16, October 21, 1847). Despite such wisdom, she demands to know when she will see him again and orders him to return soon with more goodies in hand. Feeling cut off from the world, she asks him the name of the candidate for president and if the Mexican war has terminated. An ironic attitude toward Miss Lyon is already apparent: "Do you know of any nation about to besiege South Hadley? . . . I suppose Miss Lyon. [sic] would furnish us all with daggers & order us to fight for our lives, in case such perils should befall us."

Her first letter to Abiah from South Hadley (L 18, November 6, 1847), after she had been there for about six weeks, declares that she has overcome her initial, intense homesickness: "I am now contented & quite happy, if I can be happy when absent from my dear home & friends . . . you must remember that I have a very dear home. . . ." She expresses herself as pleased with her roommate, her cousin Emily Lavinia Norcross, and with the school's homelike atmosphere, and gives a sketch of her packed daily schedule consisting of religious devotions, academic studies, calisthenics, piano practice and "advice from Miss. Lyon in the form of a lecture." She finds nothing to complain of in her light domestic duties (clearing away the knives and washing them) or in the food, which she finds "wholesome and abundant." Even her classmates, whom she expected to have "rough & uncultivated manners," prove a pleasant surprise: ". . . on the whole, there is an ease & grace a desire to make one another happy, which delights . . . me. I find no Abby [Wood], or Abiah, or Mary [Warner], but I love many of the girls. . . ."

In this same letter, however, in which she sings her school's praises, she gives a touching account of her joy when her parents pay her a surprise visit and tells Abiah that she cannot wait to go home for Thanksgiving. For the rest of her stay at Mount Holyoke, Emily's feelings would continue to seesaw between homesickness and acceptance of her new life—a typical enough pattern for a young person away from home for the first time. Two months after returning from Thanksgiving holidays, she relates the visit in ecstatic detail to Abiah, playing with orthography to convey the joy of being back "my *own* DEAR HOME" (L 20, January 17, 1848). Once again, she says she was very homesick at first, then got wrapped up in her studies. She professes herself happy at the seminary, but admits that she has found no friends like those she had at the academy. To Austin, she writes that she is lonely but takes comfort in the decision that her father had already made not to send her back for a second

year, and that she will be home in only 22 weeks. Her rebellion against the school's regulations is revealed in a description of how, although "*Mistress* Lyon" forbade the sending of valentines, the girls who were there the previous year, "knowing her opinions, were sufficiently cunning to write & give them into the care of Dickinson," who contrived to mail them (L 2, February 17, 1848).

Despite all this, when, in March, her parents learned that she had a bad cough and insisted she come home to be nursed, she resisted strenuously. If school was confining, being mercilessly medicated by her father was another kind of prison. During her six-week stay at home (which included spring vacation), she kept up with her studies. She recovered and returned on May 11 for the summer semester.

Among those aspects of seminary life that distressed her—her homesickness, the lack of privacy, the endless regulations—one of the most pervasive was the continual religious pressure at the school. From the day a girl entered, she was obliged to declare her status as either Christian, "Hoper," or "No-Hoper." Emily Dickinson was a "No-Hoper" from start to finish. Different accounts have been given of her lone rebellion against the coercive campaigns that took place; but, while she seems to have dissented in some forthright manner, she did not stand alone. Thirty of the 230 students with whom she finished out the year were also "No-Hopers." Furthermore, although she had already experienced—and resisted—REVIVALS in her hometown, her feelings on the painful subject of devoting her life to Christ were conflicted. She went to the assemblies at which Miss Lyon spoke to the students three times a week and attended sermons, experiencing a range of reactions from ecstasy to boredom, depending on the speaker. Her pious roommate, cousin Emily of Monson, wrote of her, "She says she has no particular objection to becoming a Christian and she says she feels bad when she hears of one and another of her friends who are expressing a hope but still she feels no more interest." In her final semester, writing to her pious friend Abiah, Emily admits, "I have neglected the *one thing needful* when all were obtaining it. . . . I am not happy and I regret that last term, when that golden opportunity was mine, that I did not give up and become a Christian. It is not now too late . . . but it is hard for me to give up the world" (L 23, May 16, 1848).

Thus, despite her sister LAVINIA's later account to MABEL LOOMIS TODD, that

"there were real ogres at South Hadley then," "if she felt bullied by the 'ogres' or harassed by Miss Lyon's piety, there is little in . . . her *own* record to show it" (Sewall, *Life,* II, 367). Her return home after only one year of study may have had little to do with religious bullying or other hardships. More often than not, students left after a single year. The seminary did not offer a baccalaureate degree; and its student body, most of whom moved on to domestic, teaching or missionary lives, had no need for the certificate conferred on completion of the Senior level. Moreover, Dickinson, who, as far as we know, seems to have left quite willingly, may have gotten all she could from the school's curriculum, which overlapped what she had already studied at Amherst Academy. Her hometown of Amherst, with its college and frequent eminent visitors, offered greater opportunities for intellectual stimulation. And in her home library, she found what she called a "feast in the reading line."

In all, Dickinson's experience at Mount Holyoke was not a defeat. She proved that she could overcome her homesickness and survive among strangers, work hard, succeed in her studies, and hold on to who she was. The institution and its values failed, however, to show her a path more appealing than returning to her parents' home, where, her formal education at a close, she would remain for the rest of her life.

See also CONGREGATIONALISM and PURITAN HERITAGE.

FURTHER READING

Alfred Habegger, *My Wars,* 191–212; Richard B. Sewall, *Life,* II, 357–367.

N

Newton, Benjamin Franklin (1821–1853) Ben Newton was one of Dickinson's earliest and most important spiritual and intellectual mentors. She met him in her mid-teens, when he came to AMHERST from his native Worcester to work in her father's law office for two years (1847–49). A member of Worcester's second UNITARIAN society, the Church of the Unity, he was the first person she knew who belonged to the other side of the social divide separating orthodox CONGREGATIONALISTS from the liberal Unitarians. During his two years in Amherst, Newton, who was nine years older than Emily, visited the Dickinsons frequently and became her "gentle, yet grave Preceptor, teaching me what to read, what authors to admire, what was most grand and beautiful in nature, and that sublimer lesson, a faith in things unseen, and in a life again, nobler and much more blessed—" (L 153, 1854). Newton's belief in life's inherent dignity and in the ability of the sovereign mind's ability to transcend nature offered her a vision of immortality far more congenial than the Calvinist precepts of human depravity and an eternity dependent on the judgment of a wrathful God.

Shortly before returning to his law studies in Worcester, in August 1849, Newton wrote in her album, with characteristic modesty and wit: "All can write autographs, but few paragraphs; for we are mostly no more than *names*." After his departure, they kept up a steady correspondence, none of which has been found. The loss of these letters is particularly unfortunate, in that they almost certainly would have shed light on Dickinson's development into a poet. Encouraging her poetic sensibility, Newton sent her a copy of Ralph Waldo Emerson's *Poems* (1847), Emerson's first volume of collected verse. A comment she made to THOMAS WENTWORTH HIGGINSON nine years later alludes to Newton's faith that her vocation was to be a poet: "My dying Tutor told me that he would like to live till I had been a poet . . ." (L 265, 1862). His death was a profound loss, depriving her of her only source of literary guidance and encouragement in those years. There is no evidence that the deep friendship she felt for him developed into romantic love.

Dickinson's first recorded response to Newton's death on March 24, 1853, of tuberculosis consists of a terse postscript to an otherwise cheerful letter to her brother: "Oh, Austin, Newton is dead. The first of my own friends. Pace" (L 110, March 1853). Nine months later, however, she addressed a letter, striking in its earnestness and naiveté, to Edward Everett Hale, the eminent Unitarian minister, whom she believed to have been present at Newton's deathbed. In it she gives her fullest extant description of his benevolent influence on her spiritual development and humbly begs to know how he died: "He often talked of God, but I do not know certainly if he was his Father in Heaven—Please, Sir, to tell me if he was willing to die, and if you think him at Home, I should love so much to know certainly, that he was in Heaven." (L 153, 1854). Hale passed this letter on to the Reverend Alonzo Hill, the pastor who actually attended Newton during his last moments. Although the reply has not been found, we know from a subsequent note from Emily to Hale that it reassured her about his spiritual victory: "I thank you when you tell me that he was brave and patient—and that he dared to die. I thought he would not fear, because his soul was—valiant—but that they met, and fought, and that my Brother conquered, and passed on triumphing, blessed it is to know" (1854, newly discovered, not in *Letters*).

Twenty-two years later, he was still present in her thoughts: "My earliest friend wrote me the week before he died 'If I live, I will go to Amherst—If I die, I certainly will.'" (L 457, 1876, to Higginson). In the context of their original correspondence, Newton's words apparently refer to his belief in her as a poet and certainty of witnessing her future glory, whether before his death or afterward (Habegger, 222).

FURTHER READING

Alfred Habegger, *My Wars*, 216–222, 315–315; Diana Wagner and Marcy Tanter, "New Dickinson Letter Clarifies Hale Correspondence," *EDJ* 7.1 (1998): 110–117.

Norcross, Betsey Fay (1777–1829) Betsey Fay Norcross was the poet's maternal grandmother; she died at the age of 51, the year before Emily Dickinson was born. This grandmother, whom Dickinson never knew, exerted an important, indirect influence on her life.

She was the first wife of JOEL NORCROSS, a prosperous farmer, businessman, and investor, and the first citizen of the town of Monson, located 20 miles south of AMHERST. Despite the financial security and social prestige she enjoyed, her life was far from pampered. Betsey had nine children and lived to bury four of them, including her two oldest, Hiram and Austin, who both died in their 20s. Hiram probably died of tuberculosis. She lost a son, Ely, at age two, and a daughter, Nancy, at age

six. Only two of her daughters lived to adulthood: EMILY NORCROSS DICKINSON, the poet's mother, and LAVINIA NORCROSS, the poet's favorite aunt. Since mothers of Betsey's generation relied on their daughters to carry out the considerable burdens of housekeeping, this relative paucity of grown daughters placed even heavier responsibilities on her. The Norcross residence was huge, a converted tavern that required a great deal of care. The Norcrosses kept boarders, who needed to be looked after, and brought in only one "hired girl."

Betsey's life was dedicated to her household affairs, with all its losses and hardships. Her minister, Alfred Ely, wrote in his obituary for her, "Humble and retiring in her disposition, it was in the bosom of her family, and among those who observed her in domestic life, that her prudence and affectionate regard to the happiness of all around her appeared most conspicuous." For biographer Alfred Habegger, this passage might also apply to both Emily Dickinson's mother and to the poet herself. "There were vital continuities between Betsey, her daughter Emily, and her gifted granddaughter," he writes. "Prominent among them was a strong and exclusive adhesiveness to house and family. The poet's love of home derived in part from her mother's and grandmother's unusually 'retiring' domesticity" (*My Wars*, 27–28).

Habegger's point of view counterbalances the tendency in previous Dickinson scholarship to see the influence of the poet's maternal forebears as negligible. Thus, Betsey's evangelical commitment may be seen as another vital part of Emily Dickinson's maternal inheritance. She was a member of the Praying Circle, begun in 1827 in Monson by Hannah Porter, the dynamic wife of the town's second leading citizen (after Joel). The single largest contingent of members of this organization belonged to the Norcross clan by blood or marriage. Members of this exclusive ladies' group dedicated themselves to bringing about a religious revival, which took place in 1829, as Betsey lay on her deathbed. This same Hannah Porter who worked with Betsey to spread the true religion later concerned herself with Emily Dickinson's spiritual welfare when the 17-year-old future poet was a student at MOUNT HOLYOKE FEMALE SEMINARY. Under the direction of the evangelical educator, MARY LYON, the school placed considerable pressure on its students to publicly declare their acceptance of Christ—a pressure to which the poet never succumbed. But Hannah Porter "seems to have organized an informal circle of concern around the future poet . . ." making her a focus of prayer and pressure (*My Wars*, 30). This incident makes clear that the conventional religiosity Emily Dickinson resisted all her life came from both paternal *and* maternal lines.

Betsey Fay Norcross was cared for in her final illness primarily by her daughter Lavinia, who sent this piteous letter to her sister:

> [Mother] is not able to sit up but a few minutes & not able yet to turn herself in bed. I cannot think you realize how feeble she is—should any disorder attract her, but little would bring her to the grave, you can have no idea how emaciated she is . . . she is very anxious to see you wishes after commencement is over to have your husband fetch you down you must not disappoint her. . . . (Dickinson family papers, Houghton Library, Harvard University)

Quite possibly, Betsey's anxiety to see her oldest daughter was related to the fact that she had not yet declared for Christ. Her husband, EDWARD DICKINSON, was apparently loath to part with her, however, and Emily Norcross Dickinson arrived, with her infant son, just a few hours before her mother's death, in the early hours of September 5. A month or so after Betsey's death, Lavinia Norcross went through a searing spiritual ordeal that culminated in her accepting Christ. Emily Norcross Dickinson, not yet converted, seems to have been overwhelmed by grief and guilt. She had let her mother die without the consolation that they would meet in heaven.

With two children still at home to be cared for, Betsey's widower, Joel Norcross, took a second wife, SARA VAILL NORCROSS, less than a year and a half after her death.

See also CONGREGATIONALISM, PURITAN HERITAGE, and REVIVALISM, REVIVALS.

FURTHER READING
Alfred Habegger, *My Wars*, 27–31, 65–66.

Norcross, Joel (1776–1846) Emily Dickinson's maternal grandfather, Joel Norcross, was a pillar of society in the town of Monson, 20 miles south of Amherst. He and his first wife, BETSEY FAY NORCROSS, had nine children; the poet's mother, EMILY NORCROSS DICKINSON, was the third among her six brothers and two sisters. The Norcrosses were churchgoing, literate farmers, who strongly believed in education.

A highly successful businessman and investor, Joel Norcross's prosperity stands in contrast to the reckless financial dealings of the poet's paternal grandfather, SAMUEL FOWLER DICKINSON. The poet's father, EDWARD DICKINSON, had an unusually close and confidential relationship with his father-in-law. When he needed advice about purchasing a house in 1828, he turned to Joel rather than to his own impecunious father. Biographer Alfred Habegger describes how Joel responded with a "mix of sound Yankee advice and kindly diplomacy," expressing his faith that Edward knew best what was right for his family (*My Wars*, 68–69).

There was no aspect of Monson's public life in which Joel Norcross did not play a preeminent role. He was a mainstay of Monson's First Congregational Church and a major supporter of Monson Academy, one of western Massachusetts's finest academies prior to its decline in the 1830s. As Habegger points out, "One of the most important things to bear in mind about Emily Dickinson is that *both* her grandfathers dug deep in their pockets for education" (*My Wars*, 27). If Samuel Fowler Dickinson's investments in AMHERST COLLEGE brought him to financial ruin, however, Joel's investments in education were both effective and prudent. When he died at age 69, the principal of Monson Academy candidly observed of this shrewd and public-spirited man, whose bluntness seems to have won him his share of enemies, that it was "pretty generally conceded that Monson has lost a benefactor in Mr. Norcross though many hated him heartily while he lived" (cited in Habegger, 27).

Less than two years after the death of his first wife in 1829, Joel married for the second time, on January 6,1831, just after the poet's birth. His new wife, SARAH VAILL NORCROSS, who came from an eminent clerical family, took over the care of his children still at home, Lavinia, Alfred, and Joel Warren.

Little is known about the poet's relationship with her maternal grandfather. At age two, she was sent to stay with her aunt LAVINIA NORCROSS, following the birth of her sister, LAVINIA NORCROSS DICKINSON. Aunt Lavinia, who adored the little girl, wrote to her brother-in-law, Edward, that Grandfather Joel was "much amused by her sports" and in church, where she behaved well for a two-year-old, he would "pat her"—but gently—the few times she spoke aloud. Biographer Richard B. Sewall quotes Aunt Lavinia's letter as follows: "Once in a while she would speak loud but not to disturb any one—she sit between Pa & me—he would slap her a little occasionally when she was doing wrong—not to hurt her or make her cry—" (*Life*, II, 324). According to Habegger, however, "slap" is an erroneous transcription of the word "pat" (*My Wars*, 85). In her surviving correspondence, Emily Dickinson makes only one reference to Joel: "We expect Grandpa Norcross . . . up here this week" (L 5, to Austin, May 1, 1842). He died when she was 16, on May 5, 1846.

FURTHER READING

Alfred Habegger, *My Wars*, 25–27, 68–71; Richard B. Sewall, *Life*, II, 324.

Norcross, Joel Warren (1821–1900) "Uncle Joel" was the son of JOEL and BETSEY FAYE NORCROSS of Monson and the youngest brother of Emily's mother, EMILY NORCROSS DICKINSON. He was only nine years older than the poet, who, in her letters, sometimes refers to him simply as "Joel." His name first turns up in Emily's 1851–52 letters to her brother, WILLIAM AUSTIN, who was teaching school in Boston. Joel had established himself there as an importer of cutlery and fancy goods and the Dickinsons addressed all letters to Austin in care of Joel, 31 Milk Street, Boston. Joel traveled frequently to Europe on buying trips and, as the "first Norcross

to notice the world of fashion, he impressed some as eccentric, self-important, vain." (Habegger, *My Wars*, 228). This was certainly the reaction of Emily's younger sister, LAVINIA. She wrote to Austin in 1853, "Joel has made us a visit & I'm glad its over, for I have got tired of hearing about *Ego altogether*. He is never informed on any other subject" (Bingham, *Home*, 297).

The poet, however, writing to him three years earlier, seems to have placed rather a high value on communication with Uncle Joel. During a visit to AMHERST he had apparently promised to write to her. When she failed to hear from him, she wrote her famous letter to him, L 29, January 11, 1850, that begins with the salutation, "Dearest of all dear Uncles." In this extravagant piece of writing, she creates a prophetic dream vision of apocalypse and retribution, in which Uncle Joel is horribly punished for the supreme crime of breaking a promise to his niece. She must tell him about this vision, she informs him, because it is not too late for him to do right. But she seems less interested in saving him than in detailing his punishment and calls down all manner of maledictions on him, for the crime of not writing the long letter to her he had promised, although he *has* sent a letter to her father. She inveighs:

> I call upon all nature to lay hold of you—let fire burn—let water drown—and light put out—and tempests tear—and hungry wolves eat up—and lightening strike—and thunder stun—let friends desert—and enemies draw nigh and gibbets *shake* but never *hang* the house you walk about in . . . Would you like to try a duel—or is that too quiet to suit you—at any rate I shall kill you—and you may dispose of your affairs with that in view.

Biographer Richard B. Sewall regards this letter as primarily a stylistic experiment of the budding poet, "a gorgeous bit of fooling and the most sustained bit of virtuoso writing (of what survives) she had yet done" (*Life*, II, 384). But he adds, "More important, she seems to have found a way to structure certain thoughts that to express otherwise would have left her vulnerable in a way she was increasingly trying to avoid" (Ibid., 385).

And, indeed, not only "certain thoughts," but also certain powerful feelings seem to be taking refuge behind the heavy-handed humor. Reading this letter, it is difficult to avoid the suspicion that, beneath its playfulness, there must have been a good deal of real rage. Yet Dickinson, as she would do in her poetry, here "tells it slant." She continues her mock-tirade with an intriguing passage about the killing of a person "by a loaded gun" and how it was wrong to execute the gun's owner for the crime—an ingenious way of metaphorically separating the murderer (herself in this fantasy) from her murderous instincts. John Cody, in his psychoanalytic study of Dickinson, sees the letter as "an example of the hostile humor whose heaviness betrays her suppressed and underlying earnestness" (*After Great Pain*, 273).

As always in Dickinson scholarship, critics disagree on the nature and extent of the poet's "dark" feelings. While biographer Alfred Habegger insists that the letter is "all in fun," and that, "it would be naïve to read her violent language as an expression of rage," he too admits that the humor is "over the top" and that "anyone receiving such a letter would feel uneasy" (*My Wars*, 229). He believes that the impetus for the letter is the young woman's frustration at not being able "to reach the world of men that has been disclosing itself" and portrays the 19-year-old Emily as being "in a state of eruption, throwing off the rules her elders had pounded into her" (230). Yet, neglect by women provoked similar feelings. In a letter she wrote to her close friend JANE HUMPHREY that same year (L 30), Emily similarly gave vent to violent fantasies of punishing someone for deserting her by not writing:

> Gone *how*—or *where*—or *why*—who saw her go
> . . . hold—bind—and keep her—put her into
> States-prison—into the House of Correction—
> bring out the long lashed whip—and put her
> feet in the stocks—and give her a number of
> stripes and make her repent her going!

However far she might venture into such punitive imaginings, however, the young Emily Dickinson knew how to adroitly extract herself and resume a balanced, cheerful voice. Thus, she continues her letter to Uncle Joel with a down-to-earth account

of how "Amherst is alive with fun this winter." And she ends by writing, humbly and humorously, "Will you write me before you go hence? Any communications will be received gratefully. Emilie—I believe."

As for the real Uncle Joel, despite his niece's threats, he went on to live until the ripe old age of 79. His first wife, Lamira F. Jones of Chicago, whom he married on January 17, 1854, died on May 3, 1862. His second wife was Maggie P. Gunnison of Roxbury, whom he married on April 24, 1866. He had two children by the first marriage, and one by the second. In a letter of consolation written to Joel when Lamira died of consumption in a New York hotel, at age 29, leaving behind her two children, Emily wrote to him as a sober adult, reminding him of his parental responsibilities and expressing the hope that they would be closer, for the sake of the deceased woman.

See also "MY LIFE HAD STOOD—A LOADED GUN," "TELL ALL THE TRUTH—BUT TELL IT SLANT—," and ABIAH PALMER ROOT.

FURTHER READING

Millicent Todd Bingham, *Emily Dickinson's Home*, 297; John Cody, *After Great Pain*, 273–275; Alfred Habegger, *My Wars*, 228–229, 395; Polly Longsworth, "Upon Concluded Lives: New Letters of Emily Dickinson," *EDIS Bull* 7, no. 1 (May/June 1995), 2–4; Richard B. Sewall, *Life*, II, 384–385.

Norcross, Lavinia (1812–1860)   Lavinia Norcross was Emily Dickinson's favorite aunt. Eight years younger than the poet's mother, EMILY NORCROSS DICKINSON, Lavinia was a lover of books and a whiz at memorizing; she was high-spirited and unconventional enough to marry the first cousin she loved. More outgoing and adept at expressing her feelings and opinions than her older sister, she became the "delegated intermediary" between AMHERST and the Norcrosses in Monson (Habegger, *My Wars*, 60).

Twenty-one year old Aunt Lavinia took charge of the two-year-old Emily for about a month when she was sent to Monson following the birth of her sister, LAVINIA. The baby was "difficult," Mrs. Dickinson ailing, and her husband engrossed in stressful business dealings; so Lavinia agreed to take on the "burden" of little Emily and found it an unalloyed joy. On the trip to Monson, there was a thunderstorm and the toddler Emily called it "the fire"—her first recorded comment on nature. Aunt Lavinia apparently knew how to comfort the initially frightened child. In her letters to her sister, which contain the first description we have of the poet, she appears as a model child:

Emily is perfectly well & contented—She is a very good child & but little trouble—She has learned to play on the piano—she calls it the *moosic.* She does not talk much about home— sometimes speaks of *little Austin* but does not moan for any of you—She has a fine appetite & sleeps well & I take satisfaction in taking care of her. . . . There never was a better child. . . . She is very affectionate and we all love her very much—She dont appear at all as she did at home—& she does not make but very little trouble.

The child, probably receiving more lavish affection than she got at home, was thriving with her substitute mother. Lavinia missed her acutely when she returned home and remembered that "whenever any thing went wrong she would come to me."

Unfortunately, due to the loss of their letters, little is known about the subsequent relationship of aunt and niece. Aunt Lavinia remained a resource in times of trouble, for when Emily became seriously depressed after her young friend SOPHIA HOLLAND died, in April 1844, her worried parents sent her to stay with Lavinia for a month.

Lavinia married Loring Norcross (1808–63) on November 4, 1834, overcoming her own misgivings about the union. Loring was her first cousin and almost a brother, who, as her father's ward, had lived in the Norcross home for extended periods. Residing in Boston, where Loring became a dry goods commission merchant, they had three children: Lavinia, the eldest, who died at age four, and LOUISE AND FRANCES NORCROSS, the poet's favorite cousins. When Loring's business failed and he filed for bankruptcy in 1851, Lavinia stood by him. Her inheritance was protected in a trust drawn up by her father and allowed the family to live comfort-

ably. Since the family was reticent about Loring's ongoing financial problems, Emily may have had only a dim idea of what was going on. Loring, whose poor judgment embroiled him in further dubious financial and legal dealings, died on January 17, 1863, aged 55.

His wife died of consumption three years earlier, on April 17, 1860, aged 48. Emily's letters to her cousins, "Loo" and "Fanny," when their mother was dying show that her bond with Aunt Lavinia was as strong as ever, "perhaps as close as any Emily established with the outer family circle" (Sewall, *Life,* I, 35). Emily wrote to her sister, Vinnie, who had cared for their aunt during her final illness:

Blessed Aunt Lavinia now; all the world goes out and I see nothing but her room, and angels bearing her into those great countries in the blue sky of which we don't know anything. (L 217)

See also BETSEY FAYE NORCROSS, JOEL NORCROSS, and SARAH VAILL NORCROSS

FURTHER READING

Alfred Habegger, *My Wars,* 60–65, 6, 82–86, 263–264, 344–345, 396–397; Jay Leyda, *Years and Hours,* 20–22; Richard B. Sewall, *Life,* II, 323–326; 534–535.

Norcross, Louise (Louisa) (1842–1919) and **Frances Lavinia** (1847–1896) Emily Dickinson's beloved "Little Cousins," "Loo" and "Fannie" were the daughters of her maternal aunt, LAVINIA NORCROSS, and uncle, Loring Norcross. As children, Loo and Fanny were welcome frequent visitors at the Dickinson home. Louise, small, dainty, fanciful, and impractical, was considered to be most like Emily and had been her special friend. Bright and charming Frances would grow into a tall and stylish woman, the one who dealt with worldly issues. When their mother, Emily's favorite aunt, died in 1860, the poet transferred her affection to them. She told her sister, LAVINIA, who was with them: "Poor little Loo! Poor Fanny! You must comfort them . . ." and sent them a conciliatory poem, "'Mama' never forgets her birds," (Fr 130). Assuming the role of mother, she offered them complete, uncritical love: ". . . always I have a chair for you in the smallest parlor in the world, to wit, my heart" (L 225, mid-September 1860). They adored her in return.

Louise was 21 and Frances 15 when, three years later, their father died. Emily tried to comfort them, asking, "Wasn't dear papa so tired always after mama went, and wasn't it almost sweet to think of the two together these new winter nights?" (L 278) Papa's disastrous business dealings would have left them penniless, if not for their mother's real-estate investments. The sisters, neither of whom married, lived together in comfort until Fanny's death. Emily stayed with them in Cambridge when she underwent treatment for her eye problems for several months in 1864 and 1865 and called them "solid Gold" in their care for her. From time to time, they cared for other needy relatives. When Uncle JOEL WARREN NORCROSS's wife, Aunt Lamira, died in 1862, they tended Joel's children and ran the household. Later, they spent two years in Milwaukee, living with relatives John and ELIZA M. COLEMAN Dudley through a painful time when Eliza died and John remarried. They returned to Massachusetts in 1872, resided at Boston's Berkeley Hotel for about a year, and then settled in nearby Concord, where they joined Ralph Waldo Emerson's liberal First Parish. Thus, withdrawal from the orthodox religion of their forebears was a point in common with their cousin Emily. They made many friends, including Emerson's daughter and Emily's friend, MARIA WHITNEY. The poet took pleasure in hearing of their social activities and was solicitous about their reading, quoting freely to them from the Bible, Shakespeare and current literature. They were a resource to her, "adoring, uncritical, but perceptive enough to delight in her wit and understand (up to a point) her problems" (Sewall, *Life*, II, 638).

Emily's correspondence with them began in 1859 and continued until a few weeks before she died. All of the poet's letters were destroyed when Fanny died. What survives derives from transcripts supplied to MABEL LOOMIS TODD when she was preparing the first published volume of the poet's *Letters*, issued in 1894. Mabel considered the Norcross cousins to be "geese"—fussy, silly, dull, and

commonplace—and wondered what Emily had seen in them. But she was biased by her frustrating experience with them, for the sisters refused to let anyone see the letters directly and insisted on editing out numerous passages they deemed too intimate to share.

Seventy-seven letters are included in Thomas Johnson's collection, dating from 1859 to 1886. Even in their censored form, they constitute a treasure trove of Dickinson's epistolary art and contain priceless insights into the fluctuations of her inner life. Although the poet did not discuss her creative life with them, she sent them a substantial number of poems. Thus, when their father died, she wrote, "Let Emily sing for you because she cannot pray," and enclosed "'Tis not that dying hurts us so,— " (L 278, Fr 528). Her motherly concern for her "little children" pervades the correspondence. She encouraged them to grow and to appreciate the glories of the world around them. Writing with humor and wisdom, she "chatted and joked with her 'little children' as blithely as if there were no clouds at all in her sky" (*Life*, II, 634). Biographer Richard B. Sewall suggests that her motherly encouragement to the girls may have been partly self-encouragement (*Life*, II, 633). She regaled them with some of her best satiric sketches of household members, relatives, or near acquaintances, as when she described her pious and portly neighbor, Mrs. Luke

"Called Back," the inscription on Emily Dickinson's gravestone. The poet's final letter, sent to her "Little Cousins," Louise and Frances Norcross, consisted of these words. *(Courtesy of Darryl Leiter)*

Sweetser: "she gets bigger, and rolls down the lane to church like a reverend marble" (L 339).

At times, however, she allowed herself to express her doubts and anguish to the cousins. When Aunt Lamira died, she wrote, "I wish 'twas plainer, Loo, the anguish in this world. I wish one could be sure the suffering had a loving side" (L 263). Twenty years later, she sent them the most moving of her letters after her mother's death, in which faith, doubt, and pain contend: "I believe we shall in some manner be cherished by our Maker—that the One who gave us the remarkable earth has the power still farther to surprise that which He has caused. Beyond that all is silence. . . ." (L 785).

Among the memorable letters to the cousins is the one dealing with the death of Frazar Stearns, the son of AMHERST COLLEGE's president, who was killed in the Civil War in 1862. Her intense feeling and attention to detail demonstrate that she was anything but indifferent to the war. In another prose masterpiece, she describes the great 1879 fire, in which Vinnie heroically reassures her, "It's only the fourth of July" (L 610). Perhaps the most famous, however, is the final one, the last letter Emily is known to have written: "Little Cousins, Called back. Emily" (L 1046, May 1886).

See also CONGREGATIONALISM and PURITAN HERITAGE.

FURTHER READING

Alfred Habegger, *My Wars*, 394–400, 544–545; Richard B. Sewall, *Life*, II, 626–641.

Norcross, Sarah Vaill (1788–1854)   Sarah Vaill Norcross was Emily Dickinson's stepgrandmother. She married JOEL NORCROSS, the poet's maternal grandfather, on January 6, 1831, 16 months after the death of his first wife, BETSEY FAY NORCROSS. Three of the nine children of Joel and Betsey still remained at home and a woman's organizing hand was needed to tend to them and to run the large Norcross home in Monson, Massachusetts, 20 miles south of AMHERST.

Sarah Vaill Norcross came from an eminent clerical family. Her father was the shrewd and humorous Reverend Joseph Vaill, pastor for 50 years of a Connecticut church; in 1839, he became

the subject of a full-length biography. Sarah herself had been a teacher and was generally respected as a woman of intellect and ideas. When she died, on April 25, 1854, she bequeathed Emily two books on the subject of pioneering women educators.

According to biographer Alfred Habegger, "Sarah's extant letters, pleasant but a little starchy, are those of someone who made a constant point of being temperate, refined, helpful, good-humored" (*My Wars*, 70). In preparation for the arrival of so estimable a lady, the immense Norcross house was given a top-to-bottom cleaning and her future stepdaughter, LAVINIA NORCROSS, agonized over what to call her. She wrote to her sister EMILY NORCROSS DICKINSON, the poet's mother, "What shall I call her? Can I say Mother. O that I could be far away from here—Emily you may depend I want to be with you." This plaintive letter was written on December 6, 1830, four days before the poet's birth.

Stepgrandmother Sarah seems to have been more of a presence in Emily Dickinson's life than either of the grandmothers to whom she was related by blood. Emily's surviving letters record two visits by "Grandmother," as she calls her, to Amherst, in fairly close succession, suggesting that she saw her with relative frequency. In these accounts, the young Emily displays an affectionate yet ironic attitude toward her socially conservative Monson relatives, who surely included Grandmother Norcross. Both visits provided occasions for her to exercise her wit. "We had a very pleasant visit from the Monson folks—they came one noon and stayed till the next," she wrote to her brother, WILLIAM AUSTIN, on May 16, 1853. "They agree beautifully with Father on the 'present generation.' They decided that they hoped every young man who smoked would take fire. I respectfully intimated that I thought the result would be a vast conflagration, but was instantly put down" (L 123).

The second mention occurs less than two months later. In a July 1, 1853, letter to Austin she reports that Grandmother has been visiting and has just left, leaving the Dickinson family "tired." When Sarah arrived, the poet's father, EDWARD DICKINSON, had just returned from a visit with Austin in Boston.

Emily is eager to ask him about the hippodrome they had visited, but doesn't dare to do so. She explains that "he came home so stern that none of us dared ask him, and besides Grandmother was here, and you certainly don't think I'd allude to a *Hippodrome* in the presence of that lady!" The incongruity of horseracing and her regal, proper grandmother spurred her to good-natured, youthful hyperbole. She continues, "I'd as soon think of popping fire crackers in the presence of Peter the Great!" (L 130).

See also LUCRETIA GUNN DICKINSON.

FURTHER READING

Alfred Habegger, *My Wars*, 8, 70–71.

P

prosody See HYMN FORM.

publication and editorial scholarship Dickinson's ambivalence toward entering the literary marketplace, whatever its reasons, resulted in the publication of only 10 poems in her lifetime, seven of them in the *Springfield Republican,* all of them anonymous, and none at her own instigation. In the early 1860s, she still nourished the hope of a larger poetic success, telling her sister-in-law and then primary reader and critic, SUSAN HUNTINGTON GILBERT DICKINSON, "Could I make you and Austin—proud—sometime—a great way off—'twould give me taller feet" (L 238, 1861). Yet the following year, in a letter to her new literary mentor, THOMAS WENTWORTH HIGGINSON, she denied any desire to publish.

Despite the unorthodoxy of her poems, with such close friends as SAMUEL BOWLES, editor of the *Springfield Republican,* and JOSIAH G. HOLLAND, literary editor of the *Republican* and founder of *Scribner's,* there is no doubt she could have published, had she wished to do so. HELEN FISKE HUNT JACKSON, one of the leading women writers of the time, told her she was a great poet and repeatedly reminded her of her social obligation to make her work known to the public, while Thomas Niles, editor of Roberts Brothers in Boston, asked her to send him a manuscript of her verse. Yet Dickinson took advantage of none of these opportunities.

She may have internalized the conservative philosophy of her father, who believed that public exposure of a woman's achievements was unseemly. Moreover, as she would write in her famous poem, "PUBLICATION—IS THE AUCTION," compromising one's vision to please the public was anathema to her. Thus, by choosing not to publish she gained artistic freedom at the expense of social validation.

Yet Dickinson did share her poetry with a "select society" of family members and friends. She recited her poetry aloud to her family and she enclosed more than one-third of her poems in her voluminous correspondence, with the greatest number of poems going to her sister-in-law, Sue. Some scholars, such as Martha Nell Smith, believe that this was Dickinson's consciously chosen method of publication, based on a principled rejection of traditional printing distribution methods (*Rowing in Eden,* 11–49).

From 1858 to 1864, she made copies of more than 800 of her poems, gathered them into 40 groups, and sewed each of these groups together with string to form booklets or "fascicles," as they are generally called. If, as some have suggested, this was a form of self-publication, it was publication without distribution. There is no evidence that she showed these bound booklets to anyone. After this, she organized nearly 400 sheets of poems more haphazardly and did not bind them; these groups are now known as "sets."

When the poet died in May 1866, her sister, LAVINIA NORCROSS DICKINSON ("Vinnie"), discovered among her papers not only these fascicles and

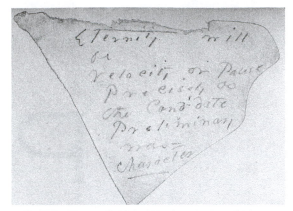

"Eternity will be . . .": Facsimile of draft of second stanza of "Two lengths has every Day—" (Fr 1354, 1875) *(By permission of the Houghton Library, Harvard University)*

Was she indifferent or hostile to publishing Dickinson's work, as biographer Richard B. Sewall suggests? Or, as feminist scholar Martha Nell Smith asserts, did she have a plan for a volume of Emily's writings, what she called "The Book of Emily," combining poems and prose (letters) that she considered more representative of Dickinson than Mrs. Todd's conventional volumes of poems? Sue herself vehemently denied the charge of indifference. In a letter to Higginson, she both defended herself and expressed confidence that the spirit of Emily, with whom she shared a perfect mutual understanding, was in possession of the true facts: "I am told Miss Lavinia is saying that I *refused* to arrange them [the poems]. Emily knows that is not true."

Whatever the case, late in 1887, Mabel Todd began the arduous task of transcribing the poems

sets but also miscellaneous fair copies, semifinal drafts, and worksheet drafts written on odds and ends of papers—the backs of envelopes and discarded letters, bits of wrapping paper, and edges of newspapers. Vinnie had honored her sister's wishes and promptly burned her letters, as was customary at the time, a step she would later bitterly regret. Yet Lavinia had no way of knowing how important her sister's correspondence would be to the world until she discovered her poems. Although she knew that Emily wrote poems and had read some of them, the sheer number of poems she found amazed her. Whether or not Emily had asked her sister to destroy them (there is an unattested legend that she did), Vinnie, who had always considered her sister a genius, made the decision to preserve them. Determined to see the poems in print, she turned for help to her literary sister-in-law, Susan. When Susan failed to respond with the alacrity Vinnie expected, she elicited the assistance of Susan's enemy, Mabel Louis Todd, the mistress of her husband, Austin (WILLIAM AUSTIN DICKINSON). Vinnie had formed a close friendship with both Mabel and her husband, David Peck Todd, and knew that Mabel had faith in the poems.

Was Susan more interested in the poetic career of her daughter Mattie (MARTHA DICKINSON BIANCHI)?

Mabel Loomis Todd in 1883. She would become Dickinson's first editor. *(The Todd-Bingham Picture Collection. Yale University Library)*

on her typewriter, consulting frequently with Austin on editing issues. Early poems to Sue, such as "One sister have I in the house" were scribbled over and obscured, probably by Austin, in the materials Mabel was given to edit. Similarly, when Mabel later edited Dickinson's letters for publication, Sue and Emily's close early correspondence was omitted. Austin and Mabel's personal hostility toward Sue, the obstacle to their sharing a life together, is reason enough for these omissions, but the lovers may also have been motivated by their belief that Sue had changed toward Emily and was thus unworthy of a place in her literary debut.

In early November 1889, Mabel met with Higginson, Emily's renowned literary friend, who had discouraged her from publishing, finding Dickinson's thoughts dazzling but her form "crude." He changed his mind after Mabel read him a number of poems, amazed that there were "so many in passably conventional form" and asked her to prepare A, B, and C lists of the most acceptable for him to look over. Thus their historical collaboration began. In 1890 and 1891, Roberts Brothers publishers of Boston, under the supervision of Thomas Niles, brought out *Poems* and *Poems, Second Edition,* edited by Mabel Todd and Higginson. Mabel then took on the daunting task of collecting Emily's letters, which she brought out in two volumes in 1894. In 1896, she brought out *Poems, Third Series.*

Mabel's editing of the poems has long been disparaged by scholars who criticize her for her editorial license in changing words "to make them flow smoother," conventionalizing rhyme and grammar, and, at Higginson's insistence, adding titles. The two editors also had a preference for Dickinson's more sentimental poems. Thus, as Jonathan Morse notes, the 1890 Todd-Higginson collection, "bound in virginal white with Mabel's painting of white flowers on the cover, originates the perennial image of the poet as fey vestal and cute little girl" ("Bibliographical Essay," 257–258).

Nonetheless, the value of Mrs. Todd's work cannot be overestimated. As Sewall reminds us, ". . . she heard Emily's music as others did not. In a day that sought message and uplift and the charm

of lilting meters, she was ahead of her time in sensing and articulating the rhythmic and melodic qualities that, among other things, make Emily's poems remarkable. It is notable that Higginson was not converted to the poems until he heard her read them aloud" (*Life,* I, 226). While her versions of Dickinson may not have conveyed the whole Emily, they gave enough to secure a readership and a recognition that, despite their fitful starts and stops, continued to grow.

Mabel Todd's work ceased in 1898 when Vinnie successfully sued the Todds over a bequest of land from Austin, a three-foot-wide strip of meadow that ran along the east side of the Dell. After Vinnie blatantly perjured herself to achieve her end, Mabel, humiliated and heartbroken, stopped working on the hundreds of Dickinson poems and letters in her possession. She reopened the camphorwood box in which they were stored only in 1931, the year before her death. That year, assisted by her scholarly daughter, Millicent Todd Bingham, Mabel brought out an expanded version of her 1894 *Letters.* Todd Bingham later mined her mother's papers and the poems and Dickinson letters in the box, and wrote *Ancestor's Brocades* (1945), a fascinating and detailed account of the process of editing the 1890 volumes. The work is marred, however, by the absence of any clue as to the real nature of her mother's relationship with Austin. When she died, Mabel charged her daughter to "set the record straight," but Millicent could not bring herself to write of her mother's illicit liaison. Millicent's publication of *Bolts of Melody,* in 1945, which contained 668 poems that had been withheld from readers since the 19th century, caused a sensation.

Meanwhile, the antagonism between Mabel and Susan was being perpetuated, as Susan's daughter (and Emily's niece), Martha Dickinson Bianchi, brought out a series of "rival" collections. A year after Susan's death in 1913, she published a volume of poems, *The Single Hound,* based on manuscripts, not from Lavinia's holdings, but from the stash of poems Emily had sent to Susan over the years, including the full text of "One sister have I in our house." The poems were generally presented "in a faithful text" (R. W. Franklin, *Editing*

Millicent Todd Bingham, daughter of Mabel Loomis Todd, who published *Bolts of Melody,* in 1945, which contained 668 poems that had been withheld from readers since the 19th century *(The Todd-Bingham Picture Collection. Yale University Library)*

umes, *The Single Hound,* and five additional poems. While far from "complete," the volume brought 597 poems together within a single cover and stimulated the growing appreciation of Dickinson in the 1920s as one of the great American poets. Bianchi subsequently edited and published *The Life and Letters of Emily Dickinson,* 1924; *Further Poems of Emily Dickinson Withheld from Publication by her Sister Lavinia,* 1929, in which she attempted to reproduce Dickinson's original lineation; *The Poems of Emily Dickinson,* 1930; *Emily Dickinson Face to Face: Unpublished Letters with Notes and Reminiscences,* 1932; *Unpublished Poems of Emily Dickinson,* 1935; and *Poems,* 1937, a second attempt at a collected edition.

Thus, by the 1940s, Dickinson, although firmly a part of the American literary canon, was represented by a bewildering array of discrepant collections. Readers could have only limited confidence that the printed versions approximated the poems as originally written. Her manuscripts remained the subjects of legal dispute. In 1950, Bianchi's companion and heir, Alfred Leete Hampson, sold them to Harvard University. Todd Bingham, however, challenged Harvard's claim to ownership and possession of all Dickinson's work. She won her case and the manuscripts were again divided, between the Houghton Library at Harvard, which now owns the manuscripts of Susan and Lavinia, and the Amherst College Library, which owns the manuscripts that belonged to Mabel Todd.

A giant step forward in establishing Dickinson's authentic texts was taken in 1950, when Harvard University Press enlisted the textual scholar Thomas Johnson to edit the complete poems on the basis of surviving manuscripts housed at Harvard's Houghton Library, Boston Public Library, and Amherst College Library. Using changes in Dickinson's handwriting in her letters to suggest approximate dates for the poetry, Johnson brought out the three-volume variorum edition, *Poems of Emily Dickinson,* in 1955, followed by the three-volume *Letters of Emily Dickinson,* coedited by Theodora Ward, in 1958. In addition to establishing chronology, Johnson retained Dickinson's idiosyncratic spelling and punctuation, and provided variant readings of the poems. In 1960 Johnson's *Complete Poems,* a reading edition (without vari-

Emily Dickinson, 34). They showed the world a different Dickinson, a poet whom *The New Republic's* reviewer, Elizabeth Shepley Sergeant, called "an early Imagist," that is, a predecessor of such modern poets as Ezra Pound and William Carlos Williams, whose work was characterized by short musical lines and clear precise imagery.

In 1924, Bianchi brought out *The Complete Poems,* consisting of the three Todd-Higginson volants) was published, followed by his selected poems, *Final Harvest,* in 1961. Johnson's *Selected Letters* came out in 1971. For 40 years, these editions stood alone as the standard, reliable version of Dickinson's oeuvre, more truly representative of her originality, depth, and breadth than any of the previous, partial collections.

In the Todd–Higginson, Todd Bingham, and Bianchi editions, the poems were arranged according to organizing principles, primarily "thematic," devised by the editors. Johnson, on the other hand, in his 1955 variorum, attempted to identify the poet's original arrangement in her fascicles. Then Ralph W. Franklin, in his 1967 *Editing of Emily Dickinson,* the book that opened a new era of textual scholarship, and in a series of subsequent articles, revised Johnson's ordering and added a number of missing poems.

But the poet's original arrangement was not fully restored until 1981, when Franklin, who had better access to the manuscripts than Johnson, brought out *The Manuscript Books of Emily Dickinson.* Franklin reconstructed the fascicles' original state by examining imperfections in the stationery, smudge patterns, and puncture marks where the poet's needle had pierced the paper to bind them. Readers now had available for the first time facsimiles of the 40 fascicles just as Dickinson had assembled them. Franklin explained the rationale for his work:

> A facsimile edition is of particular importance to Dickinson studies, for the manuscripts of this poet resist translation into the conventions of print. Formal features like her unusual punctuation and capitalization, line and stanza divisions, and display of alternate readings are a source of continuing critical concern. Because she saw no poems through the press and left her manuscripts unprepared for print, judgments must be informed by the manuscript conventions themselves. Perhaps no less important, interest has developed in the fascicles as artistic gatherings. . . . [Johnson's edition] translated the mechanics of the poems into conventional type and, in presenting them chronologically, obscured the fascicle structure. Such an edi-
> tion, though essential, does not serve the same purpose as a facsimile of the fascicles. (*Manuscript Books,* ix)

As Martha Nell Smith notes, "Editing is always interpretation, and one of the primary values of facsimile reproductions is that, as editions, they leave more decisions—about the poet's intentions and what counts as poetic technique—up to individual readers than do print translations" ("Dickinson's Manuscripts," 128). Thus, for example, while Franklin believes that such features as Dickinson's capitals and dashes "were merely a matter of handwriting," others see them as conscious techniques for creating nuances of meaning.

Franklin published his variorum edition, *The Poems of Emily Dickinson,* in 1998 and his reading edition by the same name, now the standard scholarly editions, in 1999. But a reading edition involves editorial choice; and the artificiality of making *any* choice among Dickinson's variants has been emphasized by critics such as Sharon Cameron, who argues that "since Dickinson refuses to choose among the variants, she disallows us from doing so" ("Dickinson's Fascicles," 145). This line of thinking sees Dickinson's variants, not as alternate choices that the poet was considering, but as part of a revolutionary, inclusive poetic structure in which the poet strove for enhanced meaning by incorporating all her variants. In a related vein, critics such as Susan Howe, Jerome McGann, Ellen Louise Hart, and Martha Nell Smith stress the inadequacy of any reading edition and believe that only the manuscripts can render Dickinson's poems authentically, with all their irregularities of grammar, punctuation, and capitalization, and line and stanza divisions ("The Dickinson Wars," 17).

Franklin's groundbreaking scholarship has also allowed researchers to examine the question of what, if any, organizing principles guided Dickinson in the creation of her fascicles. Some scholars, including Franklin himself, believe that the fascicles, which contain most of the poems written between 1858 and 1864, have no significant order, but were simply a means for the poet to organize her burgeoning production, allowing her to bind them chronologically as she wrote them.

But others have argued that one or all of the booklets focus upon a particular aesthetic or thematic principle. Sharon Cameron has argued persuasively that Dickinson assembled the fascicles on the basis of principles other than chronology, showing how some fascicles are composed of poems that Dickinson copied in different years (Oberhaus, *Emily Dickinson's Fascicles*, 1–3). By examining the fascicles as "units of sense," in which individual poems reflect upon and argue with one another, scholars are attempting to find "larger statements" within Dickinson's oeuvre than that contained in any one poem.

Finally, in the 21st century, the capabilities of electronic publishing as a means of adding new dimensions to our perception of Dickinson's work are being explored. In 1992, the Dickinson Editing Collective was formed; one of its primary functions was to facilitate the development of a hypermedia archive of all of Dickinson's writing. The *Dickinson Electronic Archives* were created in order to allow those unable to go to the special collections in which Dickinson's manuscripts are housed the opportunity to examine them. They will include for the first time, "all her drawings, cutouts, and visual manipulations of paper shape and type and assembly (from stationery to shopping bags, to affixed stamps and illustrations scissored from other books" (Smith, "Dickinson's Manuscripts," 132).

See also "A NARROW FELLOW IN THE GRASS," "I'M NOBODY! WHO ARE YOU?," "SAFE IN THEIR ALABASTER CHAMBERS—," "SUCCESS IS COUNTED SWEETEST," "THIS IS MY LETTER TO THE WORLD," and LETTERS.

FURTHER READING

Millicent Todd Bingham, *Ancestor's Brocades*; Sharon Cameron, *Choosing Not Choosing*, and "Dickinson's Fascicles," in *Handbook*, Grabher et al., eds., 138–160; Paul Crumbley, *Inflections of the Pen: Dash and Voice in Emily Dickinson*; Dickinson Electronic Archives, available online, URL: http://www.emilydickinson.org, accessed July 17, 2006; Betsy Erkilla, "The Emily Dickinson Wars," in *Cambridge Companion*, 11–29; Ralph W. Franklin, *Editing of Emily Dickinson*; Susan Howe, *Unsettling the Birth-Mark: Unsettling the Wilderness in American Literary History*; Jerome G. McGann, *The Visible Language of Modernism*; Jonathan Morse, "Bibliographical Essay," in *Historical Guide*, 255–283; Dorothy Huff Oberhaus, *Emily Dickinson's Fascicles*; Martha Nell Smith, *Rowing in Eden* and "Dickinson's Manuscripts," in *Handbook*, Grabher et al., eds., 113–137; Marta Werner, *Emily Dickinson's Open Folios: Scenes of Reading, Surfaces of Writing*.

punctuation   Dickinson's unconventional punctuation, particularly her extensive and "ungrammatical" use of the dash, is a prime element of her stylistic signature. Together with her idiosyncratic use of capitals and her virtually exclusive use of the hymn meter, they make a Dickinson poem difficult to mistake for anyone else's.

Of all her "irregularities," Dickinson's punctuation is the feature most editors have had little compunction in regularizing. In some instances, where irregular punctuation adds nothing to the tone or content of a poem, the practice seems justified. The prime example is her consistent adding of an apostrophe to the possessive *its* and her use of a premature apostrophe in contractions: ca'nt, did'nt, etc. Thomas Johnson omitted them, while editor R. W. Franklin, in what is now considered the authoritative version of the poems, has chosen to include them. They may add a certain "authenticity" to the poems, but little is lost when they are omitted.

It is a different story altogether when other elements of punctuation, particularly the ubiquitous dash, are eliminated or replaced by commas and periods. Without the dashes, the poems are distinctly flattened. Compare, for instance, the version of "MUCH MADNESS IS DIVINEST SENSE—" published by MARTHA DICKINSON BIANCHI in 1924 with the first lines of Franklin's version:

> Much madness is divinest sense
> To a discerning eye;
> Much sense the starkest madness.
> 'Tis the majority
> In this, as all, prevails.
> Assent, and you re sane;
> Demur,—you're straightway dangerous,
> And handled with a chain.

> (Bianchi)

Much Madness is divinest Sense—
To a discerning Eye—
Much Sense—the starkest Madness—

(Franklin)

The Bianchi version is quieter, saner. The offending dashes are omitted or replaced by more sensible semicolons, a comma, and a period; in the one instance in which the editor included a dash, she apparently felt uncomfortable enough to preface it with a comma, thus creating her own irregularity. Bianchi also changes Dickinson's capitals to lowercase letters and even corrects her grammar, replacing the uninflected form of the verb, "prevail," with the inflected "prevails." The overall effect is of a disjunction between the poem's (tame) form and (rebellious) content. The message is stated calmly, logically. By contrast, the dash-ridden Franklin version is both emphatic and breathless, conveying the speaker's agitation. It does not end with a neat period, but trails off with a dash that suggests an absence of rest or completion, the continued ferment in the speaker's mind.

Toward the end of her life, Dickinson wrote:

What a hazard an Accent is! When I think of the Hearts it has scuttled or sunk, I almost fear to lift my Hand to so much as a punctuation. (variant of L 1011)

The importance she attached to punctuation in her poems is illustrated by her letter to her literary mentor, THOMAS WENTWORTH HIGGINSON, about her poem, "A NARROW FELLOW IN THE GRASS," which had been published, without her knowledge, as "The Snake" in *The Springfield Republican*. After explaining to Higginson, whom she had assured of her lack of interest in publishing, that the work had been "pirated," she tells him that she was "defeated too of the third line by the punctuation" (L 316). Dickinson's second and third lines are as follows:

You may have met Him—did you not
His notice instant is—

In the *Republican*, they were printed:

You may have met him—did you not?
His notice instant is.

The *Republican* version unambiguously separates the two lines. But the manuscript version allows for two possibilities. The first is that the two lines are distinct. "Did you not?" means simply, "You *have* met him, haven't you?" If, however, lines 3 and 4 are read together, form reinforces meaning. Without the aid of punctuation at the end of line 3 or a transitional phrase such as "let me tell you," line 4 springs upon the reader with the suddenness of the snake's appearance.

Dickinson's direct testimony that the distinction was crucial to her makes it difficult to justify a stance such as Franklin's, which sees her most prominent punctuation mark—the dash—as a mere feature of the poet's handwriting. Since Dickinson inserted dashes into everything she wrote, letters, household notes, even cake recipes, Franklin denies the possibility that she used them in any purposeful way in her poems. Weisbuch, who notes that Dickinson's dashes are borrowed from the common punctuation of 19th-century letters, disagrees, arguing that while she may have used them habitually in all her writings, she used them *consciously* in her poems.

On the other end of the spectrum from Franklin are those critics who believe that not only are the dashes meaningful but that differently formed dashes have different meanings. They have attempted to divide her slanting lines into angular slants, vertical slants, elongated periods, stress marks, and half-moon marks, and to differentiate them according to their position above, at, or below the writing line. But no one has argued convincingly that these distinctions affect meaning and so far all editors have simply represented them as dashes (Miller, *Grammar*, 50).

Even a cursory survey of Dickinson's use of the dash indicates the central role it plays in her poetics. A vital instrument in creating ambiguity, dashes are essential in "syntactic doubling," in which a word or phrase has a dual relationship to what has come before and what will come afterward. As Weisbuch notes, the dashes are like hinges, allowing lines to refer backward and forward:

The dash typically forces the reader continually to reinterpret meanings. It gives a quality of immediacy to the poems, makes them seem to develop before our eyes[;] . . . it serves as a syntactical equivalent to Dickinson's dictum, "The Soul should always stand ajar." (*Emily Dickinson's Poetry,* 75–76)

Another defining feature of her work, compression, could hardly have been achieved without the dashes, which serve as marks of ellipsis. Commas, periods and semicolons would be inappropriate and confusing if superimposed on her disjunct syntax. Rhythmically, they were essential to the syncopated disruption of Dickinson's hymn meter, which might otherwise have become monotonous.

Cristanne Miller notes that sometimes dashes merely replace ordinary punctuation, but often they occur where a comma or any other punctuation would be unnecessary or wrong. She indicates the ways in which they convey the speaker's inner state, suggesting pauses for breath or deliberation or signs of an impatient eagerness that cannot be bothered with the formalities of standard punctuation. "Overall," Miller writes, "they create a suggestion that the mind at work in the text is unfettered by normal rules of logical procedure" (*Grammar,* 51). In addition, they emphasize words by isolating them, create suspense, slow the reader's progress through the poem, and reflect semantic content, such as fumbling or hesitating.

Dickinson's patterns of punctuation were not static. In her important essay, Kamilla Denman describes how the poet moved from the conventional punctuation of her earliest poems "through a prolific period where punctuation pulled apart every normal relationship of the parts of speech, to a time of grim redefinition punctuated by weighty periods, on to a final stage where language and punctuation are minimal but intensely powerful" ("Volcanic Punctuation," 195). While Dickinson's themes remained constant, her changing punctuation contributed significantly to the change in the tone of her poems over time.

During 1858 and 1859 the distinguishing feature of Dickinson's punctuation was the overuse of the exclamation mark in both poems and letters. Employing them to implement dramatic intention or control, she used them to evoke a spectrum of intense moods, ranging from joy to pain, pleasure,

satire, and exultant discovery. Dickinson was more likely to conclude her poems with exclamation points and question marks than with periods, which appear infrequently, and are most often encountered in her very early and late poetry. Exclamation marks contribute to the impression that the voice is spontaneous and intimate.

By 1862, however, the exclamation mark was rare. The period between 1860 and 1863 was marked by the rampant, anarchic use of dashes, in letters as well as poems. In the poems, the dash replaces almost every other mark of punctuation and is placed between almost every one of the parts of speech. Writing to SAMUEL BOWLES, she complained, "The old words are *numb*—and there *an't* any *new* ones" (L 252). "In the absence of new diction," writes Denman, "she sought to define words through dislocating marks of punctuation" (191).

Scholars have speculated that, during these years of "flood creativity," Dickinson's excessive use of dashes was an expression of great stress, possibly even a mental breakdown. Radiating an extreme of emotion or psychological distress, the dashes unsettle many readers, who find them somewhat jarring. Others, however, responding to their aural and rhythmic effects, have posited musical theories of her punctuation. Dickinson, who was an accomplished pianist, often equates her poetry with music, identifying herself with a singer and a robin. In a poem of 1862, she sees herself as a translator of music into language: "Better—than Music! For I— who heard it—/ I was used—to the Birds—before— / This—was different—'Twas Translation—/ Of all tunes I knew—and more—." Like music, Denman notes, Dickinson's punctuation expands the space and pitch in which words are uttered, underlines or undercuts words, blends words or dislocates them from their context ("Volcanic Puncuation," 198– 199). Composers, aware of the musical potential of her verse, have been setting it to music since the end of the 19th century.

After 1863 there is a distinct shift in tone, diction and punctuation, as Dickinson's work is increasingly imbued with nostalgia. Instead of disrupting syntax through punctuation, "Dickinson's assault on language takes the form of redefining words [in her many DEFINITION POEMS] rather than the disruption of syntax through punctuation" (Ibid., 200). The absence of any punctuation in a number of poems written from 1870 on indicates that it was no longer an indispensable part of composition at this stage.

In both its presence and its absence, Denman writes, Dickinson's punctuation affirms

> the silent and the nonverbal, the spaces between words that lend resonance and emphasis to poetry. In the punctuation of her poetry, Dickinson creates a haunting, subversive, impelling harmony of language, wordless sound (emotional tonality and musical rhythms), and silence. Like songs set to music, Dickinson's poems are accompanied by a punctuation of varying pauses, tones, and rhythms that extend, modify, and emancipate her words, while pointing to the silent places from which language erupts. (Ibid., 189)

See also CAPITALIZATION, HYMN FORM, and PUBLICATION AND EDITORIAL SCHOLARSHIP

FURTHER READING

Sharon Cameron, *Lyric Time*, 13–14; Paul Crumbly, *Inflections of the Pen: Dash and Voice in Emily Dickinson*; Kamilla Denman, "Volcanic Punctuation" in *Critical Essays*, Judith Farr, ed., 187–205; Roland Hagenbüchle, "Precision and Indeterminacy in the Poetry of Emily Dickinson," *ESQ* (1974), 33–56; Brita Lindberg-Seyersted, *Emily Dickinson's Punctuation*; Cristanne Miller, *Grammar*, 49–57; Martha Nell Smith, *Rowing in Eden*, 80–82; Gary Stonum, *Dickinson Sublime*, 22–39; Robert Weisbuch, *Emily Dickinson's Poetry*, 72–76.

Puritan heritage   Essential to understanding her life and poetry, Dickinson's Puritan heritage was one of the primary sources of her passionate exploration of God, faith, and the human condition. Whether she was rejecting or embracing its tenets, Dickinson was deeply influenced by the worldview of New England Puritanism. The Puritan concepts of divine immanence, providential history, the sense of "election," and Redemption permeate her work as "fixed points in her spiritual navigation" (Sewall, *Life*, I, 25). Many of her great themes—the

nature of God, death, and what she called "the Flood subject" of immortality—flow directly from this spiritual heritage.

Dickinson's first American ancestors, NATHANIEL AND ANN GULL DICKINSON, were among those Puritans, who rebelled against the perceived corruption of the Church of England, created a religion meant to "purify" its beliefs and practices, and came to the New World in the 1630s to find religious freedom. The line of Dickinson forebears that sprang from these early Puritans were practical men and women, involved in the affairs of this world: settling and defending their new home, bearing and nurturing large families under severe conditions, becoming landowners and farmers, educators, lawyers, and civic leaders. Thus Dickinson's sense of Puritan theology, as embedded in the CONGREGATIONALISM into which it evolved, came from her reading, the sermons she heard at the FIRST CHURCH OF CHRIST, which she attended until her late 20s, and from her interactions with family, friends, and teachers. The CONNECTICUT RIVER VALLEY, where JONATHAN EDWARDS had preached his stern brand of Calvinist/Puritan theology a century before Dickinson's birth, was a stronghold of uncompromising Puritanism. In the religiously conservative AMHERST of Dickinson's youth, the REVIVALISM Edwards had initiated was enjoying a lively comeback.

Dickinson's inability to convert to Christianity, as many of her friends and relatives were doing, caused her pain. She was not a respecter of doctrines and the Calvinist doctrine of innate sin, with its belief in a vindictive God lording it over a depraved humanity, was always repugnant to her. However, despite her formal estrangement from the church, her way of life reflected basic Puritan ideals. She embraced the virtues of simplicity, austerity, hard work, and denial of the flesh. She cultivated these ways, however, not in the spirit of repentance, but because they suited her intrinsic nature. "Consider the lilies was the only commandment I ever obeyed," she wrote to a friend two years before her death (Sewall, *Life*, I, 23). Puritan habits of mind, including constant vigilance over the soul and fierce introspection, were fundamental to her.

Perhaps more than any other American poet, she embodies the basic Puritan belief that value and meaning are to be discovered within. In Dickinson, however, what is found within is as likely to exhilarate as to appall:

> Exhiliration—is within—
> There can no Outer Wine
> So royally intoxicate
> As that diviner Brand
>
> (Fr 645)

The Puritan drama of the soul, with its vacillation between ecstasy and despair and urgent sense of a reckoning at hand, are prominent in her writings. The Puritan was commanded to keep a diary and engage in a constant inner dialogue between flesh and spirit, soul and self. Although she defined the poles of her own dialogue differently, Dickinson was similarly engaged in an intense, ongoing inner dialogue.

Like the Puritan, she had a deep sense of the "ontological gap between God and man and the absolute importance of this divide" (Stonum, "Dickinson's Literary Style," 255). The thrust of many of her poems is the assertion of an unbridgeable separation of time and eternity or earth and heaven:

> I know that He exists.
> Somewhere—in Silence—
> He has hid his rare life
> From our gross eyes.
>
> (Fr 365)

> Prayer is the little implement
> Through which Men reach
>
> Where Presence—is denied them.
>
> (Fr 623)

The influence of Connecticut Valley Puritanism is also evident in Dickinson's adaptation of the "spirit of sublime self-reliance," stressed by Jonathan Edwards (see "ON A COLUMNAR SELF—"). In Dickinson's work, the sense of inner sufficiency and rightness, independent of the opinions of the crowd, is linked to her affirmation of herself as poet. While she rejected the Puritan concept of predestined, unconditional grace, which only God could bestow, she had her own concept of a "white election," related to her sense of chosenness in the kingdom of poetry, which occupied the most exalted position in her spiritual hierarchy (see "I RECKON—WHEN I COUNT AT ALL—").

Finally, many of the formal aspects of her poetry—her colloquial diction and urgent tone, the logical construction of her rhetoric, and her metrical HYMN FORMS—are all traceable to her Puritan heritage.

FURTHER READING

Karl Keller, *The Only Kangaroo among the Beauty: Emily Dickinson and America*; Richard B. Sewall, *Life*, I, 17–27; Susan Howe, *My Emily Dickinson*, 45–57; Perry Miller, *The Puritan Mind*; Gary Lee Stonum, "Dickinson's Literary Background," in *Handbook*, Grabher et al., eds., 55–58.

R

revivalism, revivals The AMHERST of Emily Dickinson's youth was a town swept by no fewer than eight religious revivals: ritualistic communal events in which congregants struggled to surrender themselves to the will of an all-powerful Christian God. Known as conversion, such individual spiritual transformations, declared in public and celebrated by the community, were seen as crucial rites of passage. While people of all ages underwent conversions, they were particularly prevalent among the young, for whom they signified a passage from carefree youth to sober adulthood. For women, who could not look to careers for adult status, conversion bestowed a special distinction. Throughout her formative years Emily Dickinson's inability to convert was a source of anguish for her. Despite her own inner urgings, as well as public pressures, however, she could not declare what she did not feel.

The history of revivalism in the CONNECTICUT RIVER VALLEY began with the Great Awakening of 1735 to 1741, led by the fiery Calvinist preacher of Northampton, JONATHAN EDWARDS. Thousands came under the spell of his teaching that the meaning of history as a whole, as well as of any specific event, is God's plan for human redemption through Christ. Believing in the absolute reality of Evil and of Satan and in the innate depravity of human nature, Edwards preached that people must not trust themselves, since even the best natural virtue was unacceptable to God. Perceiving fear as a means of repentance, he strove to inculcate it in his listeners.

The Second Great Awakening of 1815 to 1835 was a wide-ranging conservative reaction to the liberal humanistic spirit of UNITARIANISM as well as to the increasing influence of secularism. Revivals were nurtured by new institutions such as Sabbath Schools and societies for distributing Bibles and tracts, commissioning missionaries, and launching powerful advocacy campaigns for temperance. Revivalism continued to play a vital role in late-Puritan communities throughout the next two decades; by the early 1870s, however, society had changed sufficiently to make them a thing of the past.

At the heart of the experience of conversion was the agony of wrestling with God and one's own conscience, as exemplified by Jacob's wrestling with the angel at Peniel: "And Jacob was left alone; and there wrestled a man with him. . . . And he said, I will not let thee go, except thou bless me" (Genesis 32; 24, 26). Revivalists returned to this moment repeatedly, wrestling for high stakes: release from the terrors of disease and death and the promise of resurrection. The price they paid for these blessings was the fundamental revision of the sense of self that accompanied submission to a will greater than their own.

Dickinson's first confrontation with revivalism came when she was a student at AMHERST ACADEMY. In a letter written to her friend ABIAH PALMER ROOT during the revival of 1846, she described an earlier experience when she was "almost persuaded to be a christian. . . . I never enjoyed such perfect peace and happiness as the short time in which I felt I had found my savior" (L 10, January 31, 1846). Her bliss was short-lived, however. Afterward, she told Abiah, she "cared less for religion than ever" and refused to attend revival meetings during the winter of 1845, fearing that her susceptible imagination would once more mislead her. Nonetheless, she asserted her belief that "I shall never be happy without I love Christ."

The following year, Dickinson became a student at MOUNT HOLYOKE FEMALE SEMINARY in South Hadley, Massachusetts, whose visionary founder, MARY LYON, believed that the crucial step in preparing the next generation's mothers and teachers was to convert them in their youth. The school's annual awakenings were tense, emotional affairs, where the silence of deadly earnestness was broken by the uncontrollable weeping of girls too overwrought to eat. It was the custom to rank students according to their spiritual state. When Dickinson participated in the 1847–48 revival, she was classed with those who did not yet "have hope" that they could be saved and were thus "impenitent." Frequent meetings were convened for those without hope. In a well-coordinated campaign to convert Emily, Hannah Porter, an evangelical figure who was active in the revival, received reports on her from her roommate and cousin Emily Lavinia Norcross; from Sarah Jane Anderson, another student; and from Mary C. Williams, a teacher. It is not known "to what extent Emily knew she was the target of a devout and determined group of women" (Habegger, 202–205). Although Emily wrote in her letters that she knew she ought to "give up & become a Christian," she apparently expressed her revolt against the coercive proceedings in some conspicuous way.

Back home in Amherst during the unusually fervent Great Revival of 1850, the 19-year-old Emily wrote to her childhood friend JANE HUMPHREY, "Christ is calling everyone here, all my companions have answered." (L, 94, April 3, 1850). That year saw the conversion of her father, EDWARD DICKINSON, and her beloved younger sister LAVINIA, as well as her close friends EMILY FOWLER, SUSAN HUNTINGTON GILBERT

(DICKINSON), ABBY WOOD, MARY WARNER, and Jane Hitchcock. In this letter, Emily expressed a mixture of envy and sadness at her inability to join the ranks of the saved, as well as resentment of the revival spirit: "I am standing alone in rebellion, and growing very careless. . . . How strange is this sanctification, that works such a marvellous change, that sows in such corruption, and rises in golden glory, that brings Christ down, and shews him, and lets him select his friends! . . . [The converted] seem so very tranquil, and their voices are kind, and gentle, and the tears fill their eyes so often, I really think I envy them."

No amount of envy, however, was sufficient for her to make the complete abnegation of self that conversion demanded. She could never testify to that direct visitation of the spirit that was required for membership in the church and the concept of herself as a sinner in the hands of an angry God was alien to her. Unable to relinquish her personal vision for the orthodox one, or to subjugate language to religious ends, she found herself increasingly isolated within her close circle of family and friends. The 1856 conversion of her brother WILLIAM AUSTIN, who had been her chief ally in irreverence, was especially painful for her. By the age of 30 she had stopped attending church altogether.

FURTHER READING

Alfred Habegger, *My Wars*, 202–205; Alan Heimart and Perry Miller, eds., *The Great Awakening*, Indianapolis and New York: Bobbs-Merrill, 1967.

Root, Abiah Palmer (Mrs. Samuel W. Strong) (b. 1830) Abiah was Dickinson's beloved school friend and recipient of a unique set of surviving early letters, in which the voice of the young Emily is heard in a variety of moods and stages of development. The two friends met in 1844 when Emily was 13, Abiah 14, and both were students at AMHERST ACADEMY. Abiah came into her life just as Emily was returning to school after a period of illness and depression brought on by a number of devastating deaths the previous year, including that of her lovely young cousin, SOPHIA HOLLAND, who preceded Abiah as an intimate. In a letter written when she was 20, Emily recalled her delight at first seeing Abiah, an attractive and self-possessed girl, ascending the stairs "bedecked with dandelions, arranged, it seemed for curls" There was an immediate rapport between them and Abiah soon became one of "the five" classmates, who constituted the poet's first close circle of friends, which coalesced in the fall of 1844 when Emily's beloved ELIZABETH C. ADAMS was preceptress. The other members were ABBY WOOD, HARRIET MERRILL, and SARAH TRACY.

Hailing from Feeding Hills, a hamlet near Springfield, Abiah was the daughter of a well-regarded merchant and Congregational deacon. The dandelions in her hair and the fact that she was involved in the unconventional and ambitious act of writing a romance are indications of the "free spirit" Emily admired in her at first. In 1845, after only two terms together, they were sepa-

Abiah Palmer Root, Emily's cherished girlhood friend and recipient of an extraordinary group of letters from the poet *(The Todd-Bingham Picture Collection. Yale University Library)*

rated when Abiah left Amherst for a school closer to home, enrolling in Miss Campbell's school in Springfield. Emily saw her infrequently from then on, although their correspondence lasted for 10 years. From 1845 to 1854, Emily wrote to her friend 22 times. The numbers of her letters in Johnson's 1958 edition are 5–15, 18, 20, 23, 26, 31, 36, 39, 50, 69, 91, and 166. These include the 10 letters extant for 1845 and 1846 and five of the 12 for 1847 to 1848, when her only other surviving correspondence was with her brother WILLIAM AUSTIN. These early, frequent letters are lengthy and often playful, full of youthful high spirits, as well as sober reflection. They constitute a unique record of the young Dickinson as she recounts her interests, concerns, and enthusiasms, and demonstrate her growing command of language during her school years.

The first five letters are filled with what Emily warned would be "a long siege in the shape of a bundle of nonsense from friend E": flights of inspired silliness, gossip, poetic flourishes, quotations from Shakespeare and the Bible, and professions of eternal friendship. Only with the sixth letter did Emily linger on solemn matters. Along with Abby Wood, Abiah became the recipient of Emily's anguished thoughts on her spiritual condition, a subject that obsessed the young women during this time of frequent and fervent religious REVIVALS. Since Abby's letters from Emily have not survived, these letters to Abiah have become the chief source revealing the poet's struggles over what she called the "all-important subject." On January 31, 1846, Emily wrote to Abiah describing a previous incident, in which she felt she had "found my savior," only to discover the ephemeral nature of her belief, which had filled her with "perfect peace and happiness." She follows this revelation with a passage on the dreadful thought of eternity and her utter inability to imagine her own death scene (which she then goes on to imagine).

When next she wrote Abiah, on March 28, 1846, her friend had taken the great step and made her own public declaration of belief. Emily expressed her wish that she herself "had found the peace which has been given to you." Recalling the fleeting period of belief described in her January letter, she confesses, "But the world allured me & in an unguarded moment I listened to her syren song. From that moment I seemed to lose my interest in heavenly things by degrees." She acknowledges that she "ought now to give myself to God & spend the springtime of life in his service," but finds herself once more resisting the pressures of the latest revival underway in Amherst. She devotes the rest of the letter to the deaths of mutual acquaintances, giving a striking description of the death of Sophia Holland two years earlier.

Abiah's acceptance of a religious stance that Emily found untenable created an inevitable gulf of sympathy between the friends. From this point on, Emily no longer confides her spiritual struggle. In her letter of June 26, 1846, she reaches out to Abiah through memories of their brief period at school together under the tutelage of Miss Adams, who is once more Emily's teacher. But the letter is permeated by her excitement at the prospect of entering MOUNT HOLYOKE FEMALE SEMINARY in South Hadley in the fall. She devotes most of her letter sent from Boston on September 8 of that year to an account of her experiences in that city, describing the "City of the dead" on Mount Auburn and going into much detail on her visit to the Chinese Museum. When she does broach the subject of religion, to which "you have so frequently and so affectionately called my attention in your letters"—a hint that Abiah may have been hounding her on the subject—it is to say that she has yet to find God and remains "a stranger—to the delightful emotions which fill your heart." A letter later that autumn is filled with anticipation of her delayed move to South Hadley.

In the three letters written to Abiah from South Hadley during 1847 and 1848, Emily gives a vivid account of her one year of higher education. (Together with the seven letters she wrote to Austin, they constitute the only record of this period). Despite setbacks in health, which required extended absences, and the spells of homesickness which only intensified over time, the picture that emerges is that of a successful, enthusiastic student, proud of her school, adjusting well to her studies and opening herself to new friendships. She does not speak to Abiah about religion again

until January 17, 1848, when she mentions the current revival at South Hadley in a brisk postscript. Then, on May 16, as she prepares to leave the seminary, she writes Abiah of her regret at losing the "golden opportunity" to "give up and become a Christian." What Abiah's responses to these words were remains unknown; but Emily's last, brief letter to her in that year reveals that a serious estrangement has occurred between the two. Abiah, who had not answered Emily's letter, appeared at Mount Holyoke's commencement exercises, but ignored Emily, who glimpses her in the crowd. Emily's letter is full of her anguish—and anger—at this snub: "Why did you not come back that day, and tell me what had sealed your lips toward me? . . . [I]f you don't want to be my friend any longer, say so, & I'll try *once* more to blot you from my memory."

Although the friendship survived this crisis, there would be no more than seven more letters from Emily to Abiah from 1848 to 1855, when the correspondence breaks off altogether. In her first letter after the rift (L 31, January 29, 1850), Emily reels off an extended, virtuoso fantasy on the cold from which she is suffering. She seems to be struggling to find a topic. In the next breath, she wonders why they didn't talk more the last time they met: "it wasn't for want of a subject, it never *could be* for that." Her professions of affection for Abiah seem forced and she signs herself, "Your very sincere and *wicked* friend."

When next she writes on May 7 and 17, 1850 (L 36), she addresses Abiah as "Dear Remembered," excusing her failure to write sooner by the fact that she has been tending her sick mother and performing extra household duties. She recounts a minor triumph of self-denial: her refusal to go out riding with a "a friend I love *so* dearly" and writes wistfully of Abby Wood's conversion, while she herself remains "one of the lingering bad ones. " Mysteriously, she adds, "I tell you I have been dreaming a *golden* dream, with eyes all the while wide open," possibly an allusion to her emerging dream of becoming a poet. In the same paragraph, however, she declares herself a "martyr" to household cares and exclaims, "God keep me from what they call *households*, except that bright one of faith!" She ends by asking Abiah to "scatter a fragrant flower in this wilderness life of mine by writing me. . . ."

Abiah's dignified, proper life increasingly becomes a foil for Emily's vision of her own wild one. Thus, in late 1850, she writes: ". . . You are growing wiser than I am, and nipping in the bud fancies which I let blossom—perchance to bear no fruit, or if plucked, I may find it bitter. The shore is safer, Abiah, but I love to buffet the sea—I can count the bitter wrecks here in these pleasant waters, and hear the murmuring winds, but oh, I love the danger! You are learning control and firmness. Christ Jesus will love you more. I'm afraid he don't love me *any!* . . ." (L 39). She may have been alluding to romantic interests, to the development of "unorthodox" ways of thinking, or indirectly hinting at the life of the poet she was envisaging. To be a poet meant a bitter break with the "sweet girl christian" life she was brought up to live (Sewall, *Life,* II 389). At this point in her life, Emily was turning to SUSAN HUNTINGTON GILBERT (DICKINSON) as her new intimate.

But, despite her differences from Abiah, the letter still clings to the bonds of the past: "the golden links, though dimmed, are no less golden, and I love to hold them up, and see them gleam in the sunshine." She returns to this theme of the sacredness of memory in subsequent letters, writing, in January 1852, that she knows her letter will make Abiah happy "if school-day hearts are warm and school-day memories precious!" (L 69). In her letter of May 1852, recalling the first time she saw Abiah, with dandelions twined in her hair, she exclaims: "Oh, Abiah, you and the early flower are forever linked to me . . ." (L 91). She professes her belief that "the friendship formed at school was no warmer than now, nay more, that *this* is warmest—they differ indeed to me as morning differs from noon—one may be fresher, cheerier, but the other fails not."

This was no more than wishful thinking, however; for, if Emily could not relinquish her idyllic early memories of Abiah, neither could she reconcile herself to Abiah's evasiveness in the present. In August 1851 and again in January 1852, Abiah repeated her behavior of 1848 in South Hadley, when she quietly left town, without granting Emily the heart-to-heart talk on which she had counted. Emily does not disguise her anger and disappointment with their brief imperfect meetings, writing on August 19, 1851, "allow me to remark that you have the funniest manner of popping into town, and the most *lamentable* manner of popping *out* again of anyone I know." (L 50): In January 1852, she reproaches Abiah for not paying a farewell visit: "Why did you go away and not come to see me? I felt so sure you would come, because you promised me, that I watched and waited for you, and bestowed a tear or two upon my absentee. How very sad it is to have a confiding nature, one's hopes and feelings are quite at the mercy of all who come along . . ." (L 69).

Significantly, Emily devotes a good part of her final letter to Abiah (L 166, July 1854) to the illness and recovery of Sue, who has replaced Abiah as her closest confidante. Refusing Abiah's invitation to visit, she explains, "I don't go from home, unless emergency leads me by the hand," adding archly, "I'm so old fashioned, Darling, that all your friends would stare. . . ."

While Emily comes out better in standard interpretations of why the friendship ended—she was more complex than Abiah, more brilliant, more independent-minded and skeptical—the differences in the girls' sexual development was probably another important factor.

As Judith Farr writes, "By twenty, Abiah Root was clearly heterosexual. She had moved from the girlish world of best friends, shared friends, and crushes on the headmistress. . . . In 1854 she made a happy marriage with the Reverend Samuel W. Strong of Westfield. Absorbed in love for a new husband, why would Abiah wish to continue answering Emily's letters, which rebuke her for not caring enough, not writing?" (*Passion* 107)

The correspondence from Emily to Abiah has had textual problems that stem from the 19th century: By late 1891, when MABEL LOOMIS TODD met Mrs. Samuel W. Strong, Abiah's letters to Emily had already been destroyed, but Emily's to Abiah survived, and it was Abiah's offer to make them available that set Todd to preparing the edition of letters published in 1894. Mrs. Todd writes of how "a little lady in a black bonnet" approached her and introduced herself as Emily's old schoolmate, saying "she had never forgotten her extraordinary compositions, and *where* might she read some of Emily's prose?" (Todd, *Letters*, 1931, xv–xvi). In the process of copying and editing the letters to Abiah for publication, there were deletions, corrections and other alterations, resulting in a number of incomplete and inaccurate texts. With the discovery of new sources, Dickinson's most eminent current editor, R. W. Franklin, has succeeded in making the most complete reconstruction of these letters to date.

FURTHER READING

R. W. Franklin, "Emily Dickinson to Abiah Root: Ten Reconstructed Letters," *The Emily Dickinson Journal*; Judith Farr, *Passion*, 104–107; Richard B. Sewall, *Life*, Vol. II, 379–390.

S

Sweetser, Catherine Dickinson (1814–1895) "Aunt Katie," her father's sister, was a favorite aunt of Emily's throughout her life. Along with her sister Elizabeth, she accompanied her parents, SAMUEL FOWLER and LUCRETIA GUNN DICKINSON, when Samuel's disastrous finances necessitated a move from his native AMHERST to Cincinnati. In her letters of this period, Katie wrote of Samuel's despair and decline and her belief that it was "*wrong* for people so old, to go from their first home & find another." After Samuel died in 1838, she shrewdly guessed that depression had brought on his death. Now married and in a home of her own, she was stricken with guilt and regretted that neither she nor her siblings had provided a home for their parents.

In 1835 she married Joseph A. Sweetser, the brother of Luke Sweetser, a prominent Amherst merchant and a lifelong neighbor of the Dickinsons. The couple lived in New York City. The marriage ended mysteriously with Joseph's disappearance almost 40 years later. On January 21, 1874 he left their apartment at the Madison Square Hotel to attend a committee meeting at the Madison Square Presbyterian Church, across the street. Since he had previously slipped on the ice and injured his head, the family feared his mind had been affected and he had harmed himself. Although they placed a personal ad in the *New York Herald,* nothing was heard of him again. Shaken by the event, Emily wrote to Katie (L 408, late January 1874) and enclosed a poem that begins:

> Death's Waylaying not the sharpest
> Of the thefts of Time—
> There Marauds a sorer Robber—
> Silence—is his name—
>
> (Fr 1315)

She had consoled her aunt four years earlier upon the death of her eldest son, Henry Edwards, a journalist of 33, after a long illness. Presenting Henry as a prisoner who coveted liberty, she wrote, "There are no Dead, dear Katie, the Grave is but our Moan for them" (L 338, late February 1870).

Katie, a master gardener with her own conservatory, had shown young Emily her first mignonette. Much of the poet's surviving correspondence with her centers on flowers and gardening—perhaps their greatest common interest. In 1880, she wrote, "I trust your Garden was willing to die. I do not think that mine was—it perished with beautiful reluctance, like an evening star" (L 66). She would thank "Sweet and Gracious Aunt Katie" for sending her "beloved lilies" and, in 1885, noted that "Aunt Katie never forgets to be lovely, and the sweet clusters of yesterday only perpetuate a heart warm so many years" (L 991).

Emily once wrote of enjoying her aunt's company, "as do new found *girls*" (L 190, 1858 to Uncle Joseph), yet Katie could also appear to her as the ideal mother. She once wrote, "I congratulate you on your children and they upon you. To have had such Daughters is sanctity—to have had such a Mother, divine. To *still* have her, but tears forbid me. My own is in the Grave" (L 892, early spring 1884).

See also EDWARD DICKINSON.

FURTHER READING

Alfred Habegger, *My Wars*, 104–108, 587–588; Richard B. Sewall, *Life*, 19n, I, 37–38.

T

Todd, Mabel Loomis (1856–1932)   Mabel Loomis Todd entered the world of the Dickinsons of AMHERST late in Emily's life, in 1881, when the poet had only five more years to live, yet she came to play a crucial role in perpetuating her legacy. As the mistress of Emily's brother, WILLIAM AUSTIN DICKINSON, she brought the "war of the houses," which had long divided the residents of The HOMESTEAD and The EVERGREENS, to new levels of estrangement. But her devotion to Austin and feeling for Emily's poems spurred her to edit the first three volumes of poems and the first volume of letters, in the 1890s, thus introducing Emily Dickinson to the world. Without her devotion, talent, and discrimination, Dickinson's oeuvre might never have reached the reading public.

She was born on November 10, 1856, the only child of Mary Alden Wilder and Eben Jenks Loomis. Mabel took pride in a New England lineage she traced through Puritan ministers to Priscilla Alden. But she was raised in straitened circumstances in a series of boardinghouses in Concord, Cambridge, and Washington, D.C., by parents who, despite their attachment, spent much time apart. Eben was self-educated and scholarly, but never acquired formal academic training or achieved professional standing. He worked for 50 years as an assistant in the Nautical Almanac Office in Washington, D.C., though he had higher aspirations. He wrote poems and essays on nature and was a friend of Henry Thoreau. Mabel loved walking with him, absorbed his love of nature, and turned to him for spiritual and moral inspiration, much as she would later lean on Austin, who was the same age as her father. Mabel's adoring mother was the practical one, who managed the household and finances, and removed her only child from Washington's heat to spend summers in New England in a series of inexpensive rented rooms. Mabel attended Georgetown Female Seminary for three years, thriving in its ambitious academic program, before moving to Boston to study at the New England Conservatory of Music in 1875. Back in Washington in 1877 and enjoying a stimulating social life, she met David Peck Todd, an up-and-coming young astronomer. Her diary entry of his first call records his blond good looks, charm, and, significantly, his flirtatiousness. Mabel evidently knew David was a philanderer before they married on March 5, 1879.

The couple arrived in Amherst in September 1881, when David, who had graduated from AMHERST COLLEGE six years earlier, accepted a position as astronomy professor at his alma mater. Twenty-four-year-old Mabel had left her year-and-a-half-old daughter, Millicent, with her mother in Washington until she could "get settled." Mabel knew little of housekeeping and disliked the little she knew. Petite and very pretty, vivacious and multitalented, Mabel painted, played the piano, and sang, and wrote, all with a high degree of accomplishment. She responded with exuberance to the town's "quiet elegance," natural beauty, and cultural and social amenities, becoming a leading figure in musical and theatrical activities. She was the lead soloist of First Church, a lead singer of Handel's *Esther* in an 1887 performance, and played the star role in Frances Hodgson Burnett's *A Fair Barbarian.* She held musical evenings and gave music lessons. She had a love of nature and a flair for painting it, as exemplified in the panel of Indian Pipes, one of Dickinson's favorite flowers, she sent to the poet in 1882. Emily responded by sending Mabel her hummingbird poem, "A ROUTE OF EVANESCENCE." Mabel's Indian Pipes would later appear on the cover of Emily's first published volumes of poetry.

Mabel Loomis Todd in Japan in 1896 *(The Todd-Bingham Picture Collection. Yale University Library)*

Inevitably the scintillating newcomers were adopted by the town's leading hostess, SUSAN HUNTINGTON GILBERT DICKINSON. Deeply impressed by the older woman, Mabel at first described her as "the most of a real society person here. . . . Her presence filled the room with an ineffable grace and elegance." At their first meeting, Sue's husband, Austin, struck Mabel as "fine (& very remarkable) looking—& very dignified & strong and a little odd." The Dickinsons became her "ideal people" and, for about a year and a half, relationships between the Todds and the Austin Dickinsons were close and cordial. Then, in March 1882, Sue and Austin's eldest son, 21-year-old EDWARD DICKINSON ("NED"), fell in love with Mabel, who had carelessly led him on. When she realized the extent of his passion, she turned him away. Sometime in late fall of 1882 or early winter 1883, the wounded young man went to his mother, not only with his own complaints about Mabel, but with tales of her involvement with Austin. Ned's stories were well founded, since Mabel and Austin were by then deeply committed to one another.

Austin and Mabel's love letters, given to Yale in 1968, and published, along with their diary entries, in Polly Longsworth's *Austin and Mabel,* provide a remarkable record of an idealistic passion, sustained over the course of 13 years, until Austin's death in 1895. In the summer of 1882, Austin began appearing more regularly at family social occasions and escorting Mabel home. During rides in the countryside around Amherst, they discovered their shared sensibilities and love of nature. On one of these excursions they looked deeply into one another's eyes and admitted their love. Austin signaled this fateful crossing into new emotional territory by writing the word "Rubicon" in his diary on September 11, 1882.

It may be significant that Austin was able to take this step on the night he first brought Mabel to the Homestead, where she was warmly welcomed by sisters Emily and Vinnie (LAVINIA NORCROSS DICKINSON). Earlier, Mabel had been intrigued by the rumors surrounding Emily, "a lady whom the people call the *Myth.* . . . She has not been outside of her house for fifteen years," dressed only in white and had a "perfectly wonderful mind." She encoun-

"The Shutesbury School of Philosophy," as the members of Susan Dickinson's camping trip dubbed themselves, photographed after their return. Mabel Loomis Todd is standing, in wide-brimmed hat. Sue is seated to the right, her arms around Gib. Sue's daughter Mattie is to the right, in a straw hat. Ned Dickinson is lying in front with his tennis racket, while Mabel's husband, David Todd, is crouched behind him, in straw bowler. *(The Todd-Bingham Picture Collection, Yale University Library)*

tered the Myth on the night she first came to the Homestead and played the piano for its inhabitants. Emily remained invisible, listening from the shadows of the hall. Mabel wrote:

> When I stopped Emily sent me in a glass of rich sherry & a poem ["Elysium is as far as to / The very next room"] written as I sang.... She is very brilliant and strong, but became disgusted with society & declared she would leave it when she was quite young.

Although Mabel would never meet Emily face to face, she would come to know her better through the affectionate correspondence that sprang up between them and their indirect contacts at the Homestead, which became Austin and Mabel's most frequent meeting place. Their diaries reveal that they consummated their love at the Homestead, on the evening of December 13, 1883, in the dining room where they often met before the fire. Later, Mabel's daughter, Millicent, would write: "The effect on Emily? She was glad that Austin had found some comfort after his all but ruined life. In my mother's words, 'Emily always respected real emotion.'"

There seems never to have been a dearth of real emotion in the letters the lovers sent to one another, faithfully, obsessively, devising intricate systems of secrecy, over the years. For Austin, the affair revived his youthful dreams, unrealized with Sue, of a "perfect love." In early 1884, declining to relive the miseries of the past, he declares:

> Is it not better, and enough, for me to say, simply, what I have said so many times before, that I love you, love you, love you with all my mind, and heart, and strength! . . . That in you I have found the sweetest, richest dream of my boyhood, youth and manhood more than realized! That I have found in you what a woman may be to a man, hope, courage, joy, inspiration, rest, peace, religion! That in you I have found my perfect soul-mate, for time and eternity. . . .

As for Mabel, she was 27 years younger than Austin, whom she revered and called "My King." Just as in girlhood she had looked to her father to bring out the best in her, she now told Austin:

> You have deepened my life and broadened it, and exalted it. . . . [A]ll the best in my soul stretches forth its hands to you. And what has always seemed to me like the dear God's love is embodied to me in yours—magnificent, all-embracing; true and noble and divinely tender.

In an era when divorce was not to be thought of, Mabel continued to live as David's wife, often traveling abroad with him for extended periods, while Austin lived like a stranger at the Evergreens with the furious and estranged Sue, who insisted he maintain appearances. If Sue reacted in the expected manner of a betrayed wife, however, David appeared to accept his wife's passion for another man with equanimity, tolerating Austin's regular presence in his home. The two men worked together in the late 1880s, building and landscaping the Dell, the Queen Anne's cottage where the Todds would live for many years, on a road Austin had cut through his meadow. David considered the older man his best friend and declared, years later, "I loved him more than any man I ever knew." Austin seemed to return his feelings of friendship. As treasurer of Amherst College, he looked out for the young professor's affairs and several times had his salary raised.

But what David really felt remains an enigma. Much later, he told his daughter that adultery had ruined his life. He was probably referring as much to his own adulteries, which began three years after their marriage, as to Mabel's. Likening him to "a sweetly immoral child," Mabel tolerated his romances to a point, but her social snobbery drove her to fury when he gave himself to "low women." For most of her life, Mabel kept her silence about his behavior to protect "dear David, " whom she continued to love.

During her years with Austin, she prided herself on her ability to love two men, in defiance of conventional morality. Naïvely, she bemoaned the scorn and condemnation such behavior earned her in straitlaced Amherst. For, if Austin's stature in the town protected him from open public censure, Mabel was frequently embarrassed by Sue's animosity and shunned by her supporters. If Austin avoided confronting Sue about this, he nonetheless took enormous risks within the relationship. By 1887 Mabel was wearing his wedding ring on her left hand, and during 1888 they attempted to conceive a child, an effort they called "the experiment." They may have contemplated leaving Amherst together, but the plan never materialized. In the latter half of their relationship, from 1887 on, Austin and Mabel frequently consulted on the editing and preparation of Emily's poems for publication. Vinnie, who had found the huge cache of poems after her sister's death, prevailed upon Mabel to take on the task after trying in vain to enlist Sue. Vinnie had formed a close friendship with both Todds and knew that Mabel had faith in the poems. Indeed, Mabel's conviction that the poems should be published stands in contrast to Sue's apparent indifference and Austin's ambiguity about the poems' worth. Late in 1887, when Mabel began transcribing the poems on her typewriter, her own suffering and social isolation in Amherst led her to feel a growing spiritual kinship with the poems:

> The poems were having a wonderful effect on me, mentally and spiritually. They seemed to open the door into a wider universe than the little sphere surrounding me which so often

hurt and oppressed me—and they helped me nobly through a trying time.

In early November 1889 she met with THOMAS WENTWORTH HIGGINSON, Emily's renowned literary friend, who had discouraged her from publishing, finding her thoughts dazzling but her form "crude." He changed his mind after Mabel read him a number of poems, amazed that there were "so many in passably conventional form." In 1890 and 1891, Roberts Brothers publishers of Boston, under the supervision of Thomas Niles, brought out *Poems* and *Poems, Second Edition,* edited by Mabel and Higginson. Mabel then took on the daunting task of collecting Emily's letters, which she brought out in two volumes in 1894. In 1896, she brought out *Poems, Third Series.* As interest in Emily Dickinson grew, Mabel, who had a great talent for public speaking, developed a thriving second career giving lectures on the poet's life and work.

Mabel's editing of the poems has long been disparaged by scholars who criticize her for her editorial license in changing words "to make them flow smoother." Nonetheless, the value of her work cannot be overestimated. As Sewall reminds us, "[S]he heard Emily's music as others did not. In a day that sought message and uplift and the charm of lilting meters, she was ahead of her time in sensing and articulating the rhythmic and melodic qualities that, among other things, make Emily's poems remarkable. It is notable that Higginson was not converted to the poems until he heard her read them aloud" (*Life,* I, 226). While her versions of Dickinson may not have conveyed the whole Emily, they gave enough to secure a readership and a recognition that, despite their fitful starts and stops, continued to grow.

In the midst of Mabel's labors on behalf of his sister's work, Austin died on August 16, 1895, of heart disease. She was able to bid him good-bye and place in his casket a token of their love, through the kindness of Ned, who quietly let her in at a side door, while Sue and the rest of the family were at the dining table. Mabel, who considered herself his true wife, wore mourning for him. She wrote, "The whole town weeps for him.

Yet I am the only mourner." Her grief was extreme and prolonged.

Three years later, bitterness was added to grief when Vinnie betrayed her long-standing friendship with Mabel and David. Abetted by Susan, whom she apparently feared, in 1898 Vinnie successfully sued the Todds over a bequest of land from Austin, a three-foot-wide strip of meadow that ran along the east side of the Dell. After Vinnie blatantly perjured herself to achieve her end, Mabel, humiliated and heartbroken, stopped working on the hundreds of Dickinson poems and letters in her possession. She reopened the box in which they were stored only in 1931, the year before her death. That year, assisted by her daughter, Millicent Todd Bingham, a Harvard Ph.D. who taught French at Vassar and Wellesley, Mabel brought out an expanded version of her 1894 *Letters.* Millicent later mined her mother's papers and the poems and Dickinson letters in the box, and wrote *Ancestor's Brocades* (1945), which gives a fascinating and detailed account of the process of editing the 1890 volumes, which is marred, however, by the absence of any clue as to the real nature of her mother's relationship with Austin. When she died, Mabel charged her daughter to "set the record straight," but Millicent could not bring herself to write of her mother's shameful sin. Millicent also wrote *Emily Dickinson's Home* (1955), an important literary history of Emily Dickinson's milieu, and *A Revelation,* an account of Emily's love affair with JUDGE OTIS PHILLIPS LORD. Her publication of *Bolts of Melody,* in 1945, which contained 668 poems that had been withheld from readers since the 19th century, caused a sensation.

Mabel and David remained in Amherst, moving in 1898 to Observatory House, the rent-free residence of the college astronomer. They led active lives, teaching, writing, and raising funds for the new observatory, which was completed in 1904. In 1913, the year that Susan died, Mabel had a cerebral hemorrhage. She was 56 and never regained full use of her right hand and foot. She lectured extensively, despite this, and accompanied David on several astronomical expeditions. David's behavior grew increasingly erratic during his late 50s; he was eased off the faculty into early retirement in

1917. He was institutionalized in 1922 and spent his last 17 years in a series of hospitals and nursing homes.

See also MARTHA DICKINSON BIANCHI, PUBLICATION AND EDITORIAL SCHOLARSHIP.

FURTHER READING

Millicent Todd Bingham, *Ancestor's Brocades*; Polly Longsworth, *Austin and Mabel*; Jonathan Morse, "Bibliographical Essay," in *A Historical Guide to Emily Dickinson*, 253–262; Richard B. Sewall, *Life*, I, 170–185, 215–228, 252–301.

Tracy, Sarah Skinner Sarah was one of "the five," Emily's inner circle of classmates at AMHERST ACADEMY, all of the same age, which also included ABBY MARIA WOOD, ABIAH PALMER ROOT, and HARRIET MERRILL. Apart from Abiah, Sarah was the only girl who was not from AMHERST, and who lived as a boarder during her academy terms. In the pantheon of philosophers whose identities the girls adopted, Sarah was the "Virgil" of the group (Abiah was "Plato" and Emily "Socrates").

The daughter of a minister, by 1846 Sarah had publicly declared her acceptance of Christ and become a formal member of the CONGREGATIONAL-IST church. She transferred to another school, shortly after Abiah did, probably to a school for girls in Pittsfield, Massachusetts (Johnson, *Letters*, 26). Apart from these meager facts, little is known about the circumstances of her life.

The five girls whose friendships coalesced in 1844, when Emily's beloved ELIZABETH C. ADAMS was preceptress, were already traveling separate paths the following year, when Abiah, Sarah, and Harriet transferred to other schools. The idyllic period of their solidarity, what Emily, as early as 1846, called the "ancient picture," would remain a precious memory to her, and her letters to Abiah are replete with nostalgic longing. "Oh Abiah. If Sarah, Hatty, and yourself were only here this summer what times we should have," she writes (L 7, August 3, 1845). She made a valiant effort to keep the friendships alive through letters. Although no letters between Emily and Sarah have survived, we know, through Emily's letters to Abiah, that they *did* correspond, at least through 1846, and saw one another again in 1851, when Sarah visited Amherst. Sarah appears to have been an erratic correspondent, judging from Emily's seesawing reports, now complaining that she considers Sarah and Harriet "lost sheep," now exulting "I hear from Sarah Tracy often." More often than not, it is Emily who makes the unreciprocated effort: "I send them [Harriet and Sarah] a paper every week on Monday, but I never get one in return" (L 9, January 12, 1846).

Apart from her disappointment when she does *not* hear from Sarah, the theme that she sounds repeatedly in her mentions of her friend is the girl's unchanging, noble serenity. "Sarah alias Virgil is as consistent and calm and lovely as ever," she writes Abiah (L 5, February 23, 1845). "I think if there is one in the world, who deserves to be happy, that one is Sarah. She is a noble girl and I love her much," she writes later that year (L 8, September 25, 1845).

In one instance, even when Sarah deprives Emily of a visit, the latter finds virtue in it. Sarah had been invited to come to Amherst at a time when Miss Adams would be there, but deferred to her father's wish that she stay home and attend a family reunion. Emily, whose loyalty to her own father remained staunch, appears to be justifying Sarah's action to Abiah: "You know Sarah is an obedient daughter! & she preferred to gratify her father rather than to spend the summer with her friends in Amherst" (L 12, June 26 1846).

When the two at last meet again, in 1851, Emily writes with astonishment of Sarah's unchanging serenity and purity:

Isn't it very remarkable that in so many years Sarah has changed so little—not that she's stood still, but has made such *peaceful* progress—her thot's tho' they are *older* have all the charm of youth—have not yet lost their freshness, their innocence and peace—she seems so pure in heart—so sunny and serene, like some sweet Lark or Robin ever soaring and singing— I have not seen her much—I want to see her more—." (L 50, August 19, 1851)

It is as if Sarah has become the embodiment of that youthful joy and purity that Emily associates with the lost days of the "five." For the poet, who was by then well along the path that would continue to separate her from old friends and community values, and whose spiritual progress was anything but peaceful, the riddle of Sarah's serenity must have been tantalizing.

U

Unitarianism The secession of more than 100 churches from the main body of orthodox, Calvinist-based CONGREGATIONALISM in the early part of the 19th century to found Unitarianism formed a social divide that defined relationships in the New England of Emily Dickinson's day. Although raised in the orthodox tradition, in a family affiliated with AMHERST's FIRST CHURCH OF CHRIST, she had important friendships with Unitarians. In her aversion to the darker aspects of Calvinist/Puritan theology, such as the doctrines of a punishing God and the essential depravity of human nature, she was in tune with the new liberal form of Christianity. Not surprisingly, when the first volume of her poems was published posthumously, the most enthusiastic reviews came from the Unitarian press.

Unitarianism denied the doctrine of the Trinity, believing that God exists only in one person and viewing Jesus not as equal, but subordinate to God: a human model for the sacred life, but not the Divine Savior. Rejecting the Calvinist notion of divine election, it was anti-revivalist and stressed the role of the individual in bringing about his/her own redemption through reason and conscience. Celebrating the power of reason, Unitarians applied it to the study of biblical texts. Their belief in innate human goodness created a religion of serenity, based on a life of rational virtue, wholly alien to the terror and psychic violence that orthodox Calvinists accepted as necessary in a fallen world.

The war between the two interpretations of Protestants reached a new level of acrimony when, in 1805, Harvard's divinity school defected to Unitarianism, appointing a Unitarian to the Hollis Chair of Divinity. Emily's grandfather, SAMUEL FOWLER DICKINSON, was prominent among those defenders of Calvinist orthodoxy who were moved by this betrayal to found AMHERST COLLEGE with the intention of making it into the kind of evangelical educational institution Harvard was originally intended to be.

The first Unitarian Emily knew and admired was BENJAMIN FRANKLIN NEWTON, a member of Worcester's second Unitarian society, the Church of the Unity. Nine years her elder, he worked at her father's law firm for two years in the late 1840s. When he died in his early 30s, in 1853, she wrote to the pastor of his church, the prominent Unitarian clergyman Edward Everett Hale, asking for details of his last moments, so that she might know "whether he sleeps peacefully." In her tribute to Newton, she calls him her "gentle, yet grave Preceptor," crediting him, among other things, with teaching her "a faith in things unseen, and in a life again, nobler, and much more blessed." In the following years, she would develop intense relationships, carried out mainly through letters, with two other Unitarian "Preceptors." The first was SAMUEL BOWLES, editor of *The Springfield Republican*, and a leading candidate for recipient of the MASTER LETTERS. Samuel and his wife, Mary, were Unitarians who held liberal views on religious and social questions. Emily assured them that she spurned her pastor's teaching that "we are a Worm" (natural depravity). When Mary gave her a book by the controversial Unitarian leader Theodore Parker, she replied "I heard that he was 'poison.' Then I like poison very well." The book is believed to have been *The Two Christmas Celebrations,* which explains that Jesus was a "good man with a genius for religion" (Habegger, *Life,* 376–377). Another central figure in her life, THOMAS WENTWORTH HIGGINSON, to whom she sent her poems, and on whom she relied as her literary mentor, had been a divinity student at liberal Harvard and then a radical Unitarian minister in Newburyport, Massachusetts, from 1847 to 1852.

The influence of Unitarianism, as of any "ism," is difficult to specify in the work of so original and independent a poet as Dickinson. When a clergyman of the old school described her posthumously published poem "GOD IS A DISTANT, STATELY LOVER" as "one of the most offensive pieces of insistent Unitarianism ever published," he was using the term in a general way to connote a heretical departure from tradition. Dickinson may have joined Unitarians in rejecting the tenets of a punishing God and human depravity; but her poetry, with its anguish and urgent questioning, reflects little of Unitarian serenity and its sanitizing of death in the hope of the Resurrection.

See also PURITAN HERITAGE.

FURTHER READING

Alfred Habegger, *My Wars,* 376–377; Rowena Revis Jones, "'A Taste for Poison': Dickinson's Departure from Orthodoxy"; David Robinson, *The Unitarians and the Universalists.* Westport, Conn.: Greenwood Press, 1985.

W

Wadsworth, Reverend Charles (1814–1882)
Charles Wadsworth was the inspired Presbyterian
minister Emily Dickinson met when she was 24
and with whom she maintained, mostly through
letters, an "intimacy of many years" until his
death in 1882. The nature of that intimacy has
long been the subject of dispute between scholars.
Was Wadsworth Emily's great love and the source
of her love poems, an idealized figure of fantasy, or
a platonic spiritual adviser? In the absence of new
evidence, these questions can never be resolved,
yet Wadsworth remains a leading candidate for
the man Emily called "Master" and to whom she
addressed her extraordinary MASTER LETTERS.

Even the fact that she met Wadsworth in Philadelphia in March 1855 has been proved only
by circumstantial evidence. Emily and her sister, LAVINIA NORCROSS DICKINSON, arrived from
Washington, where they had spent three weeks
with their father, EDWARD DICKINSON, who was
then a member of the House of Representatives, around March 14, 1855, to stay with the
Colemans, whose sole surviving daughter, ELIZA
M. COLEMAN, was Emily's close friend. Edward
escorted them there, then continued on to
AMHERST. Although Emily makes no mention of
it in her only surviving letter from Philadelphia,
to ELIZABETH LUNA CHAPIN HOLLAND, since the
Colemans were Presbyterians and belonged to the
Arch Street Church, it is unlikely that she did not
attend with them during her two-week stay and
hear the famous minister.

Born in 1814 in Litchfield, Connecticut, into
a prominent industrial family, Charles enjoyed a
privileged life until 1830, when his father, Henry,
died insolvent, and everything he owned had to
be sold to pay his debts. His widow, Mary, with
whom Charles seems to have been very close,
remarried in 1834. The boy left Litchfield for
upstate New York, where he attended a number
of schools, including the well-respected Oneida
Institute for intended ministers. He graduated
from Union College in 1832, by which time
he had a reputation as a poetic prodigy, writing gloom-filled verses that express a sense of
early initiation into life's sorrows. For unknown
reasons, he soon renounced poetry to become
a minister and turned instead toward the modern practical world and applied religion. In an
1852 sermon, he declared the steam engine was
a "mightier epic than the Paradise Lost [of Mil-
ton]". He also celebrated the victory of Anglo-
Saxon Christianity over the "Heathenism" of the
Indians. Biographer Alfred Habegger points to
the irony in Emily's turning "to a man who went
public at an early age with his precocious verse
and then found success by repudiating poetry and
the past, and celebrating the triumph of modern
industrial Protestantism" (*My Wars*, 334).

His career was devoted to building up weak,
disintegrating congregations. He spent two years
at the Princeton Theological Seminary and was
pastor of the Second Presbyterian Church of Troy,
New York, from 1842–50. He came to Phila-

delphia in 1850 and in a few years transformed the Arch Street Church from a tiny, dwindling congregation of about 12 families to a thriving, prominent institution. His preaching was ranked second only to that of Henry Ward Beecher, and his popularity in Philadelphia was comparable to Beecher's in Brooklyn. In April 1862, he accepted a call from the Calvary Presbyterian Society in San Francisco, returning to Philadelphia in 1869. He was apparently happily married to Sarah Jane Locke for 36 years, and had three children, one of whom, Charles, Jr., became a famous preacher and national leader. He died suddenly of pneumonia on April 1, 1882, at age 68. Many of his sermons were published, in pamphlet form, in periodicals, and collected in four volumes, two during his lifetime (1869 and 1882) and two after his death (1884 and 1905).

A plain man with dark, intense eyes, Wadsworth delivered his sermons in deep bass tones, marked by great moral fervor, boldness, forceful intellectual argument, and beauty of imagery. He gave the impression of one who knew suffering through deep personal experience. Yet he also had a "roguish" style that Mark Twain commented on, an irreverent humor that would have appealed to Emily who wanted a preacher who did not make "the love of God . . . seem like Bears."

While we may speculate on the many points of spiritual and expressive affinity between them, the facts of their relationship are sparse. They seem to have corresponded from the 1850s on, although all that remains of their correspondence is a single unsigned and undated note from Wadsworth that somehow escaped burning with the rest of the letters in Emily's possession when she died. It is an earnest, but formal pastoral reply, addressed to "Miss Dickenson," expressing concern about some unspecified "affliction" she has written him about and asking to learn more of her "trial." While caring and affectionate, it contains no trace of sexual passion. Millicent Todd Bingham, who first published it in *Emily Dickinson's Home*, believed it must have been written at least a few years after their 1855 meeting, since the friendship appears to have been well-established.

Reverend Charles Wadsworth, Emily Dickinson's "beloved Clergyman," who many believe was the man she called "Master"

We also know that, after Philadelphia, he came to see her at The HOMESTEAD at least twice, once in March 1860, after his mother's death, and again in August 1880, many years after his return to Philadelphia. According to a tradition in the Holland family, Emily sent letters to Wadsworth, from his return to Philadelphia in 1869 until his death, furtively, through her close friend Elizabeth Holland.

Around such meager certainties, a legend was created that Charles Wadsworth and Emily Dickinson fell in love at first sight, but renounced one another since Wadsworth was a married man. In despair, the legend goes, Emily returned to Amherst, wrote her anguished love poems and, soon after, became a recluse, the lady in white. It was Emily's niece, MARTHA DICKINSON BIANCHI, who propagated this sensational claim that Aunt Emily had "met the fate she had instinctively shunned" on a visit to Philadelphia. Martha wrote, "There is no doubt that two predestined souls were kept apart only by her high sense of duty and the necessity for keeping love untarnished by the inevitable destruction of another woman's life" (*Life and Letters*, 46–47]. When this story met with skepticism, Martha went on to amplify it in 1932, in *Face to Face*. For Habegger, Martha's "story can't be swallowed whole, but it may have a factual basis" (*My Wars*, 471). Habegger believes that "the terror since September [1861]" Emily told THOMAS WENTWORTH HIGGINSON about may very well refer to Wadsworth's imminent departure for San Francisco in 1862. He resolves the discrepancy in dates by assuming that Wadsworth told her of his intentions earlier.

Biographer Richard B. Sewall, on the other hand, doubts the veracity of the legend, stressing that there is "little evidence to support it and much to call it into question. But its high romantic style and lofty sentiments have created an impression hard to dislodge" (*Life*, I, 8n). He points out that Dickinson only began writing the poems of frustrated love four or five years after the Philadelphia visit. But his greatest objection to Martha's legend, shared by Bingham and other more recent scholars, is that Emily's withdrawal from the world was neither abrupt nor dramatic, but a gradual evolution of her need for creative solitude. Sewall concedes that she was capable of being greatly moved by sermons and that a single sermon by the gifted, somewhat mysterious Wadsworth could have had a deep and lasting effect.

Other scholars, such as William Robert Sherwood in his study *Circumference and Circumstance*, believe that Wadsworth was never Emily's actual lover but grew into an obsessive and creatively fruitful fantasy for her. In this view, Emily returned home to cherish the image of her idealized and inaccessible 41-year-old preacher and to "live in her imagination through the whole course of love fulfilled and unfulfilled." He thus became her Muse, the source and inspiration of her great love poetry (Sewall, *Life*, II, 449). This theory is rejected by the many readers and scholars who feel that Dickinson's love poems could only have been written from genuine experience.

Both the depth and the limitations of Dickinson's "intimacy" with Wadsworth are revealed in 21 letters she sent to his friends, the Clark brothers, after his death, beginning in August 1882; the first six are to James Dickson Clark, the remaining 15 to Charles Clark, beginning in April 1883, when James was stricken with the illness from which he died in June. It was James who initiated the correspondence, sending her a volume of Wadsworth's sermons. Emily responded eagerly. One of the themes of her letters is that Wadsworth was a mystery to her. In her first letter, she wrote of the reclusive and scholarly minister:

> In an intimacy of many years with the beloved Clergyman, I have never before spoken with one who knew him, and his Life was so shy and his tastes so unknown, that grief for him seems almost unshared.
>
> He was my Shepherd from 'Little Girl'hood and I cannot conjecture a world without him, so noble was he always—so fathomless—so gentle. (L 766)

In a letter to James in late 1882, she wrote,

> The Griefs of which you speak were unknown to me, though I knew him a 'Man of sorrow,' and once when he seemed almost overpowered by a spasm of gloom, I said 'You are troubled.' Shivering as he spoke, 'My life is full of dark secrets,' he said. He never spoke of himself, and encroachment I know would have slain him. He never spoke of his Home. . . . (L 776)

We never learn the source of this perceived sorrow, which contrasts strikingly with the story contained in the Wadsworth family letters. In addition to at least two volumes of sermons the Clarks sent her, Emily asked for Wadsworth's picture and James sent one. She asked for the pictures of his children, but never mentioned his wife. She knew his personal life so little, she had to ask the Clarks whether he had a sister or a brother.

Her letters to the Clarks suggest that what she found in him was, above all, a fellow sufferer, who bore his pain in silence. She may have seen in him "the spiritual insight and integrity that she was coming to believe only suffering could give . . ."

(Sewall, *Life,* II, 460). Her vision of him as one who had earned an immortality comparable to Christ's is evident in the lines (previously sent to Higginson) she enclosed in a letter to the Clarks:

'Twas Christ's own personal Expanse That bore him from the Tomb. (Fr 1573)

Certainly, there are numerous poems in which Dickinson conflates the image of a lover with that of Christ, lending fuel to the argument that Wadsworth was indeed her "Master" and great love. For Dickinson's latest biographer, in possession of the latest information about the dating of her manuscripts, Wadsworth is, indeed, the "only . . . candidate who matches what we infer about the unknown correspondent," but he adds the caveat that "the evidence remains so circumstantial and conjectural, it is wisest to hold back" (Habegger, *My Wars,* 421). Sewall, who believed that SAMUEL BOWLES was Master, offers an alternate view of Wadsworth's probable role in the poet's life:

Meanwhile, all we can say with confidence is that she needed someone all her life with whom she could share her spiritual problems and disbeliefs honestly. . . . And at a crucial point . . . she would have been especially susceptible to the kind of Christianity Wadsworth preached and to the kind of man he was. (*Life,* II, 462)

See also "I LIKE A LOOK OF AGONY," "I SHOULD HAVE BEEN TOO GLAD, I SEE—," "THERE CAME A DAY—AT SUMMER'S FULL—," and "TWO SWIMMERS WRESTLED ON THE SPAR—."

FURTHER READING

Martha Dickinson Bianchi, *Face to Face,* 47–53, and *Life and Letters,* 46–47; Millicent Todd Bingham, *Home,* 368–373; Alfred Habegger, *My Wars,* 330–334, 418–421; Vivian Pollak and Marianne Noble, "A Brief Biography," in *Historical Guide,* 45–49; Richard B. Sewall, *Life,* II, 444–462; William Robert Sherwood, *Circumference and Circumstance;* George Whicher, *This Was a Poet,* 99–112.

Warner, Mary (Mrs. Edward Crowell) (1830–1903) A member of Emily's early group in AMHERST and one of her dearest friends outside "the five" AMHERST ACADEMY schoolmates she identified as her inner circle. Mary was the daughter of Aaron Warner, professor of rhetoric and oratory, and English literature at AMHERST COLLEGE (1844–53).

As she began her year away from home, at MOUNT HOLYOKE FEMALE SEMINARY in South Hadley, Emily, writing to ABIAH PALMER ROOT, included Mary in her "short list" of exceptional friends: "I find no Abby or Abiah or Mary [Warner], but I love many of the girls" (L 18, November 6, 1847). In Emily's letters from Mount Holyoke, to Abiah or to her brother WILLIAM AUSTIN, she frequently sends her love to Mary; if Mary writes her a long letter, or fails to respond to one of her own, Emily reports this. We know that they exchanged books, including Henry Wadsworth Longfellow's *Kavanagh.* Writing to Abiah, she rejoices, "Mr. Humphrey brought Mary Warner over to see me the other day & we had a delightful time, you well know." (L 20, January 17, 1848).

When Emily returned to Amherst in August 1848, their friendship resumed its former rhythms.

Mary Warner, a close girlhood friend of the poet *(Amherst College Archives and Special Collections)*

The first indication that Mary is following a different course in her life appears in a letter to another early friend, JANE HUMPHREY, in which Emily describes the intensity of the religious REVIVAL gripping Amherst in 1850: "Abby [Wood], Mary, Jane [Hitchcock], and farthest of all my Vinnie have been seeking, and they all believe they have found" (L 35, April 3, 1850).

In addition to being pious, Mary was attractive and popular. In the diary of William Hammond, an Amherst student who was a year and a half older than Mary, and who wrote a vivid account of Amherst life in the 1840s, we find an enthusiastic portrait of the young woman. Hammond, who courted her and came close to proposing marriage, called her "Le Bijou" (the Jewel) and describes her as "a pretty, modest, pleasant girl with beautiful hair." He praises her as a musician, chess player, and good cook. In an account of a sleigh ride that ended with both of them tumbling into a snowbank, Hammond admits that he kept his gaze on Mary instead of the horse; her high spirits and tousled curls only heightened his admiration of her.

Hammond was one of several beaux. Later his friend Edward Olcott proposed to her three times. John Sanford, Austin's friend, proposed to her once. She was also courted by Benjamin E. Thurston, who was an Amherst senior. When Emily describes a scene from this courtship in a letter to Austin, her tone is ironic: "Mary Warner and Thurston are getting along nicely, spent last Monday evening, sliding down Boltwood's hill—the very last phase of flirtation." In the next lines, she feels the need to reassure her brother that she is not being catty about Mary's diminished appearance, but the message is clearly that Mary (from too much courting, perhaps?) has lost her bloom: "Mary dont seem very flourishing just now—everybody seems to get the idea she's a little gone by and faded. Dont be roused by this into the former furie, for Mary and Vinnie and I are on the pleasantest terms in the world" (L 71, January 28, 1852). Apparently there had been some unpleasantness recently.

Six months later, her comments to Austin on this courtship are similarly arch, with a dash of scolding thrown in. The girls have not been seeing each other, and Emily has received this anecdote through the grapevine. Emily implies that Mary has not been monogamous in bestowing her favors:

I hav'nt seen Mary Warner since you went away—the last time I *heard* of her, she had Thurston and Benjamin, *weeding her flower garden. That's* romantic, is'nt it—she better have her heart wed, before she weeds her garden! (L 95, June 20, 1852)

The following spring, when Mary's younger sister Anna Charlotte is ill and dying, Emily tells Austin, "Mary is at present incarcerated, and becomes in the public eye, more and more of a martyr daily" (L 108, March 18, 1853). Once more the tone is ironic, the implication being that for the sociable Mary, incarceration at home is martyrdom.

Several years would pass before Mary at last "wed her heart" and married Edward Payson Crowell, on August 13, 1861. An 1853 graduate of Amherst, he was professor of Latin in the college from 1864 to 1908. The degree to which the old friends' relationship had cooled by then is reflected in the one-line note Emily sent her on that occasion: "Dear Mary, You might not know I remembered you, unless I told you so—Emily—" (L 236, about August 1861).

Only two other letters to Mary have survived. The first was written in 1856, to commemorate the third anniversary of Mary's younger sister's death. Emily copied out for her the 10 anguished stanzas of John Pierpont's popular elegy for his son, containing such lines as "I cannot make him dead! / His fair sunshiny head / Is ever bounding round my study chair." Dickinson, who had a puzzling liking for bad, sentimental poetry, found the elegy "very sweet" and was sure Mary would love the verses: "They make me think beside, of a Little Girl at *your* house, who stole away one morning, and tho' I cannot find her, I'm sure that she 'is there'" (L 183, about April 20, 1856). Judith Farr notes that, despite the comforting ending, in which the father meets his dead child in heaven, "it might have been more merciful to Mary" had Dickinson chosen a poem less obsessed with recalling the events of death and burial as if they had just taken place (*Passion*, 14).

The last of the three surviving letters to Mary, written at the time of Mary's departure for Europe and a year before Emily's death, confirms that the poet kept abreast of her friend's life, and retained an affectionate interest in it. In the opening line of this "bon voyage" note, Emily asks whether it is "too late," that is, whether Mary has already departed; but beneath this surface meaning, she seems to be casting a wistful last glance at the girl-friend intimacy they shared:

Is it too late to touch you, Dear?

> We this moment knew
> Love Marine and terrene—
> Love celestial too—

I give his Angels charge—
> Emily (L 975, early March 1885)

FURTHER READING

Judith Farr, *Passion*, 14. William Gardiner Hammond, *Remembrance of Amherst: An Undergraduate's Diary, 1846–1848*, George Frisbie Whicher, ed.

Maria Whitney, Samuel Bowles's intimate friend. Dickinson befriended her after Bowles's death.

Whitney, Maria (1830–1910) Maria Whitney was the intimate friend of SAMUEL BOWLES, the reform-minded editor of *The Springfield Republican*, whom Emily Dickinson loved and revered. The poet initiated a correspondence with Whitney in 1878, following Bowles's premature death at age 51.

Attractive, worldly, and highly intelligent, Maria was the daughter of Josiah Dwight Whitney, a wealthy Northampton banker. In this cultivated family, one brother taught philology at Yale, another was a Harvard geologist, and a third was director of the Boston Public Library. Related to Bowles's wife Mary through the Dwight family, the unmarried Maria stayed with the Bowleses on several occasions between 1863 and 1867, assisting Mary following childbirth. Yet Mary, rather than feeling grateful, resented Maria and, in the spring of 1868, fanned scandalous rumors about her relationship with Samuel.

Although Maria, who had a deep sense of duty, was alarmed and deeply offended by the rumors, they had a strong underpinning of truth. Whether or not there was a sexual dimension to their intimacy, it is clear that Maria loved Samuel, whom she called "my dearest friend," and was close to him for many years. On his part, handsome, charismatic Samuel seemed to cherish Maria above any of the other intellectual, spiritual women who were drawn to him and whose company he relished. He called her his "fair logician" in deference to her discursive, academic mind, which resembled his own. In his vibrant letters to her, he propounded his views on ambition, progress, and what Sewall calls his "uninspired religious thinking," that focused on "growing in goodness" and leaving "theories and faith to time" (Sewall, *Life*, II, 473). Neither he nor Maria, who took a scholarly interest in religions, pondered the tormenting spiritual questions that obsessed Emily.

Samuel, who "had an ego that demanded perfect loyalty from women, and was not above exploiting Maria's devotion to secure her care of his wife and children" (Habegger, *My Wars*, 579), was jealous of the rich, independent life of her own that Maria led. His last illness coincided with her return from Paris and the beginning of her work at Smith College, where she taught languages in the late 1870s. Starting a new, stressful job and the strain of "keeping up" during his last weeks caused her immense anguish.

In spring of 1862, Maria first visited The EVERGREENS, having returned to her father's house in Northhampton after a year in New York teaching impoverished German girls. During the 16 years of Maria's friendship with WILLIAM AUSTIN and SUSAN HUNTINGTON GILBERT DICKINSON, there is no evidence that Emily and Maria met. However, Emily sent her poems written expressly for her during this time, including Fr 430, "A Charm invests a face / Imperfectly beheld—" (1862), proclaiming the superior charm of a face that remains hidden behind a veil. Apparently, though, the poet had held open the prospect of seeing Maria. For when the grieved woman left for California in 1864, to care for her dead sister's children, Emily sent her a poem via Austin, Fr 813, "How well I knew her not" in which she mourns the loss of "A Bounty in prospective" and develops her paradoxical theme of "the parting of those that never met."

When Samuel Bowles died of overwork on January 16, 1878, Emily boldly wrote to Maria, addressing her as a fellow mourner:

I have thought of you often since the darkness,—though we cannot assist another's night. I have hoped you were saved. That he has received Immortality who so often conferred it, invests it with a more sudden charm. . . . (L 537, early 1878)

Maria's side of the correspondence was destroyed, according to her wishes, after her death, but Emily's words indicate that she responded affectionately to the poet's overture. Seventeen letters from Emily have survived, in which the revered and painfully missed figure of Bowles stands at the center. While offering consolation to Maria, Emily confessed her own longing for a reunion with Bowles in heaven. When HELEN FISKE HUNT JACKSON and her husband visited Mrs. Bowles, Emily passed on the news that Samuel's widow, formerly hostile to Maria, had spoken of her "with peculiar love" (L 573, late 1878). Maria came to Amherst twice in 1880: in late March

and on July 31, when she had resigned her position at Smith and was about to sail for Germany. On one of these occasions, she saw Emily, who wrote afterward that Maria's "recollecting" was "a haunting picture." "One sweet sweet more—One liquid more—of that Arabian presence!" (L 643). Seven years after Bowles's death, Emily was still writing to Maria about him with undiminished intensity. "I fear we shall care very little for the technical resurrection," she confessed, "when to behold the one face that to us comprised it is too much for us, and I dare not think of the voraciousness of that only gaze and its only return" (L 969, probably early 1885).

The exchange between the two women, founded on Samuel's death, eventually took on a life of its own. Emily wrote Maria about her mother's death and, in a letter of 1883, in which she apologized for not receiving her on a visit to Amherst, enclosed her eulogy for Mrs. Dickinson, "To the bright east she flies." (L 815). That same year, Maria went to California to care for her brother Josiah's baby, following his wife's death. Biographer Alfred Habegger suggests that the learned, sophisticated Maria was plagued by a "nagging sense of homelessness and unfulfillment, [which] she tried to assuage in her nursing stints" (My Wars, 58). When Maria unsuccessfully tried to break the baby's nightly dependence on the wet nurse, Emily asked, "Is there not a sweet wolf within us that demands its food?" (L 824, probably May 1883). And when Maria had withdrawn from this disappointing attempt at mothering, Emily wrote in the voice of mature wisdom, "I am glad you accept rest. Too many disdain it" (L 860, summer 1883). Thus, despite her deep, prolonged grief for the man who may have been her great love, the Dickinson of the Whitney correspondence, now in her 40s and 50s, comes across as a high-spirited woman, confident and eager to ease others' sufferings, even as she endured her own.

See also "MASTER LETTERS" and LOUISE AND FRANCES NORCROSS.

FURTHER READING

Alfred Habegger, *My Wars*, 461–463, 578–583; Richard B. Sewall, *Life*, II, 471–474 509–510.

Wood, Abby Maria (Mrs. Daniel Bliss) (1830–1915)   An Amherst girl, born the same year as the poet, Abby was a close friend of Emily's from childhood through young womanhood. She was a daughter of Joel and Abby Moore Sweetser Wood of Westminster; when her father died in 1833, however, she came to live with her uncle Luke Sweetser, on the hill just north of the Dickinson HOMESTEAD. Although the Dickinsons moved away to the house on West Street in 1840, Emily and Abby were probably good friends by then. That year both girls entered AMHERST ACADEMY. They shared the same table and there is a surviving school edition of Virgil with both girls' names inscribed in it. (Emily apparently presented this book to Abby as a gift, when she and her husband sailed for Beirut in 1855). In 1845 they spent their free time with each other during a term when both were obliged to be at home. They became part of an intimate circle of schoolmates dubbed by Emily "the five," that came together, under Emily's favorite preceptress ELIZABETH C. ADAMS. The other members were ABIAH PALMER ROOT, HARRIETT MERRILL, and SARAH TRACY. The short-lived circle fell apart, when all the girls but Emily and Abiah transferred to other schools.

Although Emily would cherish this time of close girlhood intimacy for the rest of her life, she would eventually grow estranged from her early friends. The correspondence between Emily and Abby has not survived. All we have of the poet's letters to Abby, some of which must have been sent from MOUNT HOLYOKE FEMALE SEMINARY in South Hadley when Emily was resisting the pressure of intense religious REVIVALS, is the response of Abby's son after reading them in 1913, "I see that 'Emily' was very early a rebel." Fortunately, however, the story of their friendship—and its decline—can be pieced together from Emily's letters to others, primarily those to Abiah.

The earliest mention of Abby is in a letter to Abiah, who has transferred to a school in Springfield, in which Emily offers capsule characterizations of the old crowd: "Abby goes to school and is storing her mind with knowledge as the bee sips the nectar from the flowers" (L 5, February 23, 1845). A few months later, she reports "Abby Wood & I sit together and have real nice times" (L 6, May 7, 1845). Emily frequently sends love from Abby and once calls her "our particular friend, and the only particular friend among the girls" (L 8, September 25, 1845).

In their relationship with the absent Abiah, Emily speaks for Abby as though they were one. Thus, when Abiah is deciding whether to accept Christ, she writes, "Abby and I shall be in a state of suspense until we hear from you and know what choice you have made . . ." (L 10, January 31, 1846). Later, she and Abby rejoice that Abiah is in the fold and hope that they may soon follow (L 11, March 28, 1846). When Abiah fails to make a promised visit to Amherst, Emily writes of how deeply disappointed she and Abby were (L 12, June 26, 1846). In March 1846 Emily and Abby hear of Abiah's conversion. (By now Sarah Tracy had also been saved). While happy for Abiah, they are anxious for their own spiritual fate and hope that the revival underway at AMHERST COLLEGE will result in their own conversions.

The bond between the two girls was warmly upheld during Emily's year at Mount Holyoke. In a letter to her brother, WILLIAM AUSTIN, she says she hears often from Abby and is pleased she has not been forgotten (L 17, November 2, 1847). Writing to Abiah about the new friends she is making at the seminary, she says, "I find no Abby or Abiah or Mary [Warner], but I love many of the girls." She reports that Abby has visited, along with Austin and their sister LAVINIA, two weeks earlier, and that it made her happy to hear them say they were "*so lonely*" without her (L 18, November 6, 1847).

The two friends begin to go their own ways as Abby moves along the path to her own religious conversion. Emily tells Abiah:

> I had quite a long talk with Abby while at home and I doubt not she will soon cast her burden on Christ. She is sober, and keenly sensitive on the subject, and she says she only desires to be good. How I wish I could say that with sincerity, but I fear I never can. But I will no longer impose my own feelings even on my friend. Keep them sacred, for I never lisped them to any save yourself and Abby. (L 23, May 16, 1848)

Abby would not convert, however, until the powerful Amherst revival of 1850, which also claimed the poet's father, EDWARD DICKINSON, her sister, Vinnie, and close friend SUSAN HUNTINGTON GILBERT DICKINSON. Shortly before this, as Emily wrote to their mutual friend, JANE HUMPHREY, Abby was in the throes of a painful loss: "Abby Wood is in Athol. Her only brother is very low—and probably cannot recover. I pity the child with my whole heart—she is too young to suffer so." (L 30, January 23, 1850). A few days later, she wrote to Abiah: "[Abby] must be very sad and need all comfort from us. She will be left *alone*—won't she?" (L 31, January 29, 1850). The italics indicate the terror this thought held for Emily, who valued her intact family above all else.

Writing to Abiah five months later, when Abby has already accepted Christ, Emily now sees her old friend as her virtuous foil. Speaking of herself as "one of the lingering *bad* ones," she describes Abby with a mixture of admiration and estrangement:

> she makes a sweet, girl christian . . . full of radiance, holy, yet very joyful. She talks of herself quite freely, seems to love Lord Christ most dearly, and to wonder, and be bewildered, at the life she has always led. It all looks black, and distant, and God, and Heaven are near, she is certainly much changed. (L 36, May 7 and 17, 1850)

In her next letter, she puts herself and her old friend into wholly different realms:

> We take different views of life, our thoughts would not dwell together as they used to when we were young—how long ago that seems! She is more of a woman than I am, for I love so to be a child—Abby is holier than me—she does more good in her lifetime than ever I shall in mine—she goes among the poor, she shuts the eye of the dying—she will be had in memorial when I am gone and forgotten. (L 39, late 1850)

If Emily was less than prophetic in her view of which of the two would achieve immortality, her comparison reveals much of how she now viewed herself and her past. Although only 20, she feels herself to be far removed from her youth. She had new friends, many of them drawn from Austin's college circle, who were opening her mind to progressive books and ideas. She was probably aware by now that she would never convert and felt increasingly isolated among family and friends who had. Conversion was viewed by the community as a sign of maturity, especially for women; by accepting Christ, Abby had moved into her womanhood, while Emily clung determinedly to the sense of herself as a child—an image that included the qualities of freedom, playfulness, commitment, and perhaps, a state of pre-sexuality.

Inevitably the friendship faltered. At the Sweetsers' annual after-dinner Thanksgiving gathering in 1851, Emily went so far as to leave the room while Abiah was singing for the guests. By the following year, however, in a letter to Abiah in which she expresses serious concern about Abby's health, there has been some revival of friendship: "I often see Abby—oftener than at sometimes when friendship drooped a little. Did you ever know that a flower, once withered and freshened again, becomes an immortal flower . . . ?" (L 91, to Abiah, about May 1852).

On November 23, 1855, Abby became a missionary's wife, when she wed the Reverend Daniel Bliss, a former Amherst College student. She traveled to Beirut with him, where she helped him found the Syrian Protestant College (American University). Emily, who counted on her friends who traveled to keep her in touch with the world, exchanged letters with her during the years of her foreign adventures. At one point, Abby sent her specimens for her herbarium and a section of polished olivewood from Syria.

When she returned to visit Amherst in 1873, Abby discovered that Emily "had become the "village mystery, inaccessible to all but an elect few, who were admitted to the sanctuary with appropriate preliminaries and ceremonies" (Daniel Bliss, *The Remembrances of Daniel Bliss*. 62, New York: Revell, 1920). Unwilling to treat "her old crony as a Sibyl," Abby insisted on being "received on the old basis." Emily complied, and, after the visit, wrote a poem (Fr 1304, J 1267) that is thought to record the occasion. In a brief dramatic exchange, the poet, who *does* see the "Flake" in her visitor's hair, nonetheless tells her she hasn't changed. The visitor, however, with "valor / Sagacious of my mistake," does not return the insincere compliment: "Have altered—Accept the pillage / For the prog-ress' sake." Dickinson humbly accepted this piece of wisdom from her childhood friend.

FURTHER READING

Alfred Habegger, *My Wars,* 141, 148, 179–180, 205–206, 535–536; Richard B. Sewall, *Life,* II, 387–389, 532.

PART IV

Appendices

CHRONOLOGY

c. 1636

Nathaniel and Ann Gull Dickinson, the poet's earliest paternal ancestors to settle in America, migrate from England to Wethersfield, Connecticut.

1775

October 9: Samuel Fowler Dickinson, paternal grandfather, is born.

Lucretia Gunn Dickinson, paternal grandmother, is born.

1776

Joel Norcross, maternal grandfather, is born.

1777

Betsey Faye Norcross, maternal grandmother, is born.

1803

January 1: Edward Dickinson, father, is born.

1804

July 3: Emily Norcross (Dickinson), mother, is born.

1813

Samuel Fowler Dickinson builds the Homestead on Main Street, Amherst, where the poet was born.

1814

Amherst Academy, where the poet studied, is founded.

1821

Amherst College is founded.

1828

May 6: Edward Dickinson and Emily Norcross are married.

1829

April 16: William Austin Dickinson ("Austin"), brother, is born.

September 5: Betsey Faye Norcross, maternal grandmother, dies.

1830

April 3: Father buys half of The Homestead from his father, Samuel Fowler.

Father, mother and baby brother move into The Homestead.

December 10: Emily Elizabeth Dickinson, the poet, is born.

December 19: Susan Huntington Gilbert (Dickinson) ("Sue") is born.

1831

January 6: Joel Norcross, maternal grandfather, marries Sarah Vaill.

The poet's mother becomes a member of the First Church of Christ after professing her faith.

1833

February 28: Lavinia Norcross Dickinson ("Vinnie"), sister, is born.

May–June: Two-year-old Emily stays with her aunt, Lavinia Norcross, in Monson.

Samuel Fowler Dickinson, bankrupt, leaves Amherst for Cincinnati, Ohio.

1834

Lavinia Norcross, the poet's aunt, marries her first cousin, Loring Norcross.

1835

August 4: Father becomes treasurer of Amherst College.

September 7: Emily begins four years at a primary school.

1837

Mary Lyon establishes Mount Holyoke Female Seminary.

1838

January: Father begins first term as elected representative to Massachusetts General Court.

April 22: Samuel Fowler Dickinson dies in Hudson, Ohio, isolated, depressed, and with finances in disarray.

1840

April: Father sells his half of The Homestead to General Mack. The family moves to the North Pleasant Street house.

September 7: Emily and Vinnie begin their first year at Amherst Academy.

1842

January: Father begins first term as senator in the Massachusetts legislature.

April: Emily writes her first extant letter to Austin at Williston Academy.

1843

Father is elected to second term as senator in the Massachusetts legislature.

1844

April 29: Sophia Holland, Emily's 15-year-old friend, dies.

May: Emily's parents send her to visit Aunt Lavinia in Boston, to lift her spirits.

June: Emily meets Abiah Palmer Root at Amherst Academy, and their close friendship begins.

December: Religious revival sweeps through Amherst; Emily does not attend meetings.

1845

February: Abiah Root leaves Amherst; she and Emily begin to correspond.

Edward Hitchcock is inaugurated as president of Amherst College.

1846

spring: Austin's schoolmate, Joseph Lyman, lives with the Dickinsons for two months, while father is away on business; beginning of friendship with Emily and romance with Vinnie.

spring: Another religious revival takes place in Amherst; Emily does not participate. May 5: Joel Norcross, grandfather, dies.

August 25: Emily visits Aunt Lavinia in Boston, remains until mid-September.

August: Austin enters Amherst College

1847

Beginning of Emily's friendship with Benjamin Franklin Newton, her father's law clerk, who acts as a spiritual and intellectual mentor.

August 10: Emily finishes seventh year at Amherst Academy

August?: Abiah Root visits Amherst.

September 28: Olivia Coleman, sister of Emily's close friend Eliza M. Coleman dies at age 20.

September 30: Emily enters Mount Holyoke Female Seminary.

c. December: Emily sits for daguerrotype at Mount Holyoke.

Charlotte Brontë's *Jane Eyre* and Emily Brontë's *Wuthering Heights*, novels Emily loved, are published.

1848

May–August: Emily completes last semester at Mount Holyoke and returns to Amherst, after father decides not to send her to school the following year.

August 3: Abiah Root attends commencement at Mount Holyoke and snubs Emily.

October 29: Emily writes letter to Abiah expressing hurt and sense of rejection.

December 19: "Gigantic Emily Brontë" dies.

1849

Emily writes satiric valentine letter to William Cowper Dickinson, valedictorian of Amherst College, class of 1848.

March 4: Mary Lyon dies.

May: Longfellow's *Kavanagh* published (Austin brings it home).

August: Benjamin Franklin Newton leaves Amherst.

c. December: Father presents Emily with black Newfoundland dog, Carlo, her companion for next 16 years.

1850

January: Benjamin Franklin Newton sends Emily Ralph Waldo Emerson's *Poems*.

February: Emily publishes a comic valentine letter ("Magnum bonum"), her first known publication, in *The Indicator,* a new Amherst College student literary magazine.

March: Emily sends her first known poem ("Awake ye muses"), a comic valentine, to father's law partner, Elbridge Gerry Bowdoin.

March–August: Religious revival sweeps through Amherst; Emily "stands alone in rebellion."

spring: Austin and Sue begin courtship.

summer: Beginning of Emily's intense friendship with Sue, after Sue's sister dies in childhood.

August 8: Austin graduates from Amherst College.

August 11: Father and Sue join First Church of Christ after professing faith.

Austin begins teaching at Sunderland.

November 3: Vinnie joins First Church of Christ after professing faith.

November 30: Leonard Humphrey, principal of Amherst Academy and Emily's first "Master," dies, age 27.

Publication of Ik Marvel's *Reveries of a Bachelor* and Nathaniel Hawthorne's *The Scarlet Letter.*

1851

June 7: Austin begins teaching Irish immigrants in Boston.

July 3: The Dickinsons attend Jenny Lind's recital in Northampton.

July 26: Major fire in Amherst.

September 6–22: Emily and Vinnie visit Boston, where Emily consults a homeopathic physician.

September: Sue begins teaching in Baltimore; Emily sends her a love letter.

September 29: Father rings Amherst church bells when aurora borealis appears.

Herman Melville's *Moby-Dick* is published.

1852

Emily's "Sic transit" valentine is published in *Springfield Republican.*

July 26: Austin returns home from Boston; gives up teaching career.

December 7: Father elected to U.S. House of Representatives on Whig ticket.

Harriet Beecher Stowe's *Uncle Tom's Cabin* is published.

1853

March 9: Austin enters Harvard Law School.

March 23: Austin and Sue become engaged.

March 24: Benjamin Franklin Newton dies, age 32.

May 9: Amherst-Belchertown Railroad opens.

June 9: New railroad is celebrated in Amherst ("New London Day").

early September: Emily and Vinnie visit Elizabeth and Josiah Holland in Springfield.

1854

March 31: Death of Charlotte Brontë.

April: Emily stays with Sue and cousin John Long Graves at The Homestead when the Dickinson family is in Washington, D.C.

July: Austin graduates from Harvard Law School.

September 19–20: Emily and Vinnie pay second visit to the Hollands.

c. late September: Emily and Sue are estranged; Sue leaves town for seven months; Emily writes, telling her she can "go or stay."

1855

c. early February: Emily and Vinnie go to Washington, D.C., for several weeks and visit Mount Vernon.

March: Emily and Vinnie visit Eliza M. Coleman in Philadelphia; Emily probably met Reverend Charles Wadsworth, who may have been the recipient of her Master letters, and heard him preach.

April: Father buys back The Homestead from General Mack.

October 31: Father and Austin form law partnership.

Father defeated in second run for Congress on Whig ticket.

mid-November: Family moves into The Homestead, where Emily will live for the rest of her life.

November: Mother's extended depressive illness begins.

Walt Whitman publishes *Leaves of Grass*, a book Emily never read; she "was told he was disgraceful." Henry Wadsworth Longfellow publishes *Hiawatha*.

1856

January 6: Austin becomes a member of the First Church of Christ after professing his faith. Emily is now the only member of her family who refuses to join.

July 1: Austin and Sue marry in Geneva, New York, and move into The Evergreens, which becomes a center of cultural and social life in town.

October 17: Emily's bread wins second prize at Agricultural Fair.

1857

December 16: Emerson gives a lecture in Amherst titled "The Beautiful in Rural Life" and is entertained at The Evergreens. Emily does not meet him.

Very little documentation of poet's life for this year.

1858

spring: Emily writes first Master letter.

c. June: First letter to Samuel Bowles, editor of *Springfield Republican*.

First year of "flood creativity," Emily writes 43 poems.

Emily organizes her poems into the first booklets, or fascicles, a practice she would continue until 1864.

1859

January 9: First letter to Louise Norcross.

January–February: Emily meets Catherine Scott Turner Anthon ("Kate") when she visits Sue at The Evergreens. They become fast friends, enjoying evenings of music and merriment.

Charles Darwin publishes *Origin of Species*.

Emily writes 82 poems.

1860

mid-March?: Reverend Charles Wadsworth pays an unexpected call on Emily.

April 17: Aunt Lavinia Norcross dies; Emily reaches out to her daughters, cousins Louise and Frances Norcross ("Lou" and "Fanny")

October: Emily and Vinnie visit Eliza Coleman in Middletown.

Emily writes 54 poems.

1861

Early winter: Emily drafts second Master letter.

May 4, 11: *Springfield Republican* prints Emily's poem "I taste a liquor never brewed—," under title "The May-Wine."

June 19: Edward Dickinson, "Ned," Sue and Austin's first child, is born.

June 29: Elizabeth Barrett Browning, Emily's favorite poet, dies.

summer: Emily writes third Master letter.

September: Emily experiences a mysterious "terror," which has been attributed to either a physical or psychological crisis.

December: Emily and Sue exchange letters on "Safe in their Alabaster Chambers—."

Emily writes 88 poems.

1862

March 1: *Springfield Republican* publishes "Safe in their Alabaster Chambers—."

March 14: Frazar Stearns, son of Amherst College president, is killed in Civil War.

April: Samuel Bowles sails to Europe.

April 15: Emily writes first letter and encloses four poems to Thomas Wentworth Higginson, after reading his article, "Letter to a Young Contributor," in *Atlantic Monthly*.

May 1: Reverend Charles Wadsworth leaves Philadelphia, sails with family to San Francisco.

May 6: Henry David Thoreau dies.

November 16: Samuel Bowles returns from Europe; Emily refuses to see him.

December 4: Higginson becomes colonel of a regiment of former slaves.

Emily writes 227 poems

1863

January 17: Uncle Loring Norcross dies; Emily comforts her "little cousins," Louise and Frances Norcross.

Emily writes 295 poems, her greatest output in a single year.

1864

March 12: *Round Table*, New York publication, prints Emily's poem, "Some keep the Sabbath going to Church—."

February–March: Three poems appear in *Drum Beat*, a short-lived Brooklyn newspaper designed to raise money for medical care for Union soldiers.

March 30: *Springfield Republican* publishes Emily's poem, "Blazing in Gold and quenching in Purple."

April: "Success is counted sweetest" is published in the *Brooklyn Daily Union*.

late April: Emily goes to Boston, where she receives eye treatment; stays with solicitous Norcross cousins in roominghouse in Cambridgeport.

May 13: Austin is drafted, pays $500 for substitute.

May 19: Nathaniel Hawthorne dies.

November 28: Emily returns from Cambridge not wholly recovered but able to resume some household chores.

Emily writes 98 poems.

1865

April: Emily returns to Boston for further eye treatment; remains for seven months.

Last year of period of flood creativity; Emily writes 229 poems.

1866

January 27: Emily's dog Carlo dies.

February 14, 17 *Springfield Republican* publishes Emily's poem, "A narrow Fellow in the Grass."

November 29: Austin and Sue's second child, Martha ("Mattie") (Martha Dickinson Bianchi) is born.

1867

No information available for this year.

1868

May 25: The Hollands leave for two years in Europe.

September 23: Father dedicates the new church.

1869

May 11: Emily refuses Higginson's invitation to literary salon in Boston, explaining "I do not cross my Father's ground to any House or Town."

1870

August 16: Higginson visits Emily at The Homestead for first time.

1871

June 3: Emily's childhood friend Eliza Coleman Dudley dies, age 31.

George Eliot publishes *Middlemarch*, one of Emily's favorite novels.

1872

January 27: Joseph Lyman dies.

July 10: Father resigns as treasurer of Amherst College.

1873

c. May: At Father's request, Jonathan Jenkins, pastor, examines Emily and finds her theologically sound, despite failure to attend church

c. August: Abby Wood (Mrs. Daniel Bliss), close girlhood friend, returns from Beirut, where she and husband have established American University, and visits Emily.

November 5: Father is once more elected to Massachusetts General Court.

December 1: Austin is elected treasurer of Amherst College.

December 3: Higginson lectures in Amherst and pays his second (and last) visit to Emily.

1874

June 16: Father dies suddenly in Boston hotel room, after injection of morphine; family suspects medical malpractice.

1875

June 15: Mother stricken with paralysis following a stroke on the anniversary of her husband's death.

Emily signs her own will, which contains no instructions about her manuscripts.

August 1: Austin and Sue's third child, Thomas Gilbert Dickinson, "Gib", is born.

1876

March 20: Helen Hunt Jackson ("H. H.") writes to Emily, "You are a great poet—and it is a wrong … that you will not sing aloud."

August 20: "H. H." invites Emily to contribute to anonymous poetry anthology, "No Name Series," published by Roberts Brothers.

October–November: Austin suffers a bout of malaria.

George Eliot begins publishing *Daniel Deronda*, "That wise and tender Book."

December: Sue gives Emily *Of the Imitation of Christ* by Thomas à Kempis.

1877

June 28: Bowles visits Emily, who at first refuses to see him.

September 2: Death of Higginson's first wife, Mary Elizabeth Channing.

October: Bowles is ill.

December 10: Mrs. Otis Lord dies.

1878

January 16: Bowles dies.

October 24: "H. H." visits Emily with her husband.

November 20: Emily's poem "Success is counted sweetest" is published anonymously in Roberts

Brothers's *A Masque of Poets*. Readers attribute it to Emerson.

Emily begins her romance with Judge Otis Phillips Lord, her father's closest friend.

1879

February: Higginson marries Mary Potter Thatcher.

July 3–4: Amherst suffers its worst fire. Vinnie protectively tells Emily "It is only the fourth of July."

1880

early August: Wadsworth pays Emily an unexpected visit, tells her, "I am liable at any time to die."

December 24: George Eliot dies.

December 25: Judge Otis Phillips Lord gives Emily a concordance to Shakespeare.

Sue gives Emily ("whom not seeing I still love") Disraeli's *Endymion*.

1881

March 15: Judge Otis Phillips Lord falls ill.

April 17: Lord, now recovered, visits The Evergreens.

August 31: Mabel Loomis Todd moves to Amherst with husband, Professor David Peck Todd.

October 12: Josiah Holland dies.

1882

April 1: Reverend Charles Wadsworth, "my closest earthly friend," dies.

April 16: Judge Otis Phillips Lord visits Emily.

April 24: Thomas Niles, editor at Roberts Brothers, unsuccessfully solicits a manuscript of Emily's poems.

April 27: Ralph Waldo Emerson dies.

May 1: Judge Otis Phillips Lord becomes critically ill.

July 15: Emily refuses to see close girlhood friend Emily Fowler Ford.

September 10: Mabel Loomis Todd comes to The Homestead, sings for invisible Emily.

September 11: "Rubicon": Mabel and Austin declare their love for one another.

September–October: Mabel sends Emily painting of Indian pipes. Emily reciprocates by sending her "Humming Bird" ("A Route of Evanescence").

November 14: Mother, long bed-ridden, dies.

1883

January: Mabel and Sue have a crucial confrontation.

October 5: Emily's beloved eight-year-old nephew Gib dies suddenly of typhoid fever. Emily collapses after going to the Evergreens on the night of his death. Sue remains secluded for the next year.

October 7: Austin, devastated by son's death, falls ill with malaria.

December 13: Austin and Mabel consummate their romance in The Homestead dining room.

1884

March 13: Judge Otis Phillips Lord dies after an extended illness.

June 14: Emily has first attack of her final extended illness.

1885

August 12: Emily is "unspeakably shocked" by the death of Helen Hunt Jackson, who had asked to be her literary executor.

November: George S. Merriam's *The Life and Times of Samuel Bowles*, eagerly awaited by Emily, is published.

1886

January 12: Mabel's diary records that Emily was "taken very ill."

early spring: Emily's last known letter to Elizabeth Holland: "Emily and Vinnie give the love greater every hour."

spring: Emily writes her last known letter to Higginson.

early May: Emily writes her last letter to Norcross cousins:

> Little Cousins,
>> Called back.
>>> Emily.

May 13: Emily loses consciousness.

May 15: Emily Dickinson dies at around 6 o'clock in the evening. The cause of death was presumed to be a liver ailment, Bright's disease, but was probably hypertension.

May 18: Sue's obituary for Emily is published in *Springfield Republican*.

May 19: Emily Dickinson is buried in the West Cemetery. Higginson reads Emily Brontë's "Last Lines" ("No coward soul. . . .")

Sue's obituary for Emily is reprinted in *Amherst Record*.

1890

November 12: *Poems* by Emily Dickinson, edited by Mabel Loomis Todd and T. W. Higginson, is published by Roberts Brothers, Boston.

Eleven editions are published by the end of 1892.

1891

November 9: *Poems* by Emily Dickinson, second series, edited by T. W. Higginson and Mabel Loomis Todd, is published by Roberts Brothers; fifth edition, 1893.

1894

November 21: *Letters of Emily Dickinson*, edited by Mabel Loomis Todd is published in two volumes.

1895

August 16: Austin dies of heart failure.

1896

September 1: *Poems* by Emily Dickinson, third series, edited by Mabel Loomis Todd, published by Roberts Brothers; second edition, 1896.

1898

November 16: Vinnie sues the Todds over Austin's land bequest to them; wins her case in April 1898.

Mabel stops editing Emily's manuscripts; puts them aside.

1899

August 31: Vinnie dies.

1913

May 12: Sue dies.

1914

The Single Hound, edited by Martha Dickinson Bianchi, is published.

1924

The Life and Letters of Emily Dickinson, edited by Martha Dickinson Bianchi, is published.

The Complete Poems of Emily Dickinson, edited by Martha Dickinson Bianchi and Alfred Leete Hampson, is published.

1929

Further Poems by Emily Dickinson, edited by Martha Dickinson Bianchi, is published.

1931

Letters of Emily Dickinson, edited by Mabel Loomis Todd, is published.

1932

Emily Dickinson Face to Face: Unpublished Letters with Notes and Reminiscences, Martha Dickinson Bianchi, is published.

October 14: Mabel Loomis Todd dies.

1935

Unpublished Poems of Emily Dickinson, edited by Martha Dickinson Bianchi and Alfred Leete Hampson, is published.

1937

Poems by Emily Dickinson, edited by Martha Dickinson Bianchi and Alfred Leete Hampson, is published.

1945

Bolts of Melody: New Poems of Emily Dickinson, edited by Mabel Loomis Todd and Millicent Todd Bingham, is published.

1951

Emily Dickinson's Letters to Dr. and Mrs. Josiah Gilbert Holland, edited by Theodora Van Wagenen Ward, is published.

1955

The Poems of Emily Dickinson, variorum edition, edited by Thomas H. Johnson, in three volumes, is published.

1958

The Letters of Emily Dickinson, edited by Thomas H. Johnson and Theodora Ward, in three volumes, is published.

1960

The Complete Poems of Emily Dickinson, edited by Thomas H. Johnson, is published by Little, Brown.

1981

The Manuscript Books of Emily Dickinson, edited by R. W. Franklin, is published in two volumes by Harvard University Press.

1986

The Master Letters of Emily Dickinson, edited by R. W. Franklin, is published.

1998

The Poems of Emily Dickinson: Variorum Edition, edited by R. W. Franklin, is published in three volumes by Harvard University Press.

Bibliography of Dickinson's Works

Works Published Anonymously during the Poet's Lifetime

"Magnum bonum," prose valentine, *The Indicator*, late February 1850.

"'Sic transit gloria,'" valentine, *Springfield Republican*, February 20, 1852.

"Nobody knows this little rose," *Springfield Republican*, August 2, 1858.

"I taste a liquor never brewed" (under the title "The May Wine"), *Springfield Republican*, May 4, 11, 1861.

"Safe in their Alabaster Chambers" (under the title "The Sleeping"), *Springfield Republican*, March 1, 1862.

"Blazing in gold and quenching in purple" (under the title "Sunset"), *Drumbeat* (Brooklyn, N.Y.). February 29, 1864; (under the title "Sunset") *Springfield Daily Republican*, March 30, 1864; *Springfield Weekly Republican*, April 2, 1864.

"Flowers—Well—if anybody" (under the title "Flowers"), *Drumbeat*, March 2, 1864; *Springfield Daily Republican*, March 9, 1864; *Boston Post*, March 16, 1864.

"These are the days when Birds come back—" (under the title "October"), *Drumbeat*, March 11, 1864.

"Some keep the Sabbath going to Church—" (under the title "My Sabbath"), *Round Table* (New York), March 12, 1864.

"Success is counted sweetest" (with no title), *Brooklyn Daily Union*, April 27, 1864; *A Masque of Poets*, Boston: Roberts Brothers, 1878.

"A narrow Fellow in the Grass" (under the title "The Snake"), *Springfield Republican*, February 14, 17, 1866.

Posthumous Editions of Emily Dickinson's Poems and Letters (in chronological order)

Dickinson, Emily. *Poems by Emily Dickinson*. Edited by Mabel Loomis Todd and Thomas Wentworth Higginson. Boston: Roberts Brothers, 1890. Dickinson's first appearance in book form contained 115 poems, with titles and other editorial "improvements," such as conventional rhyme, grammar, and vocabulary. Selections show a bias toward Dickinson's more sentimental poems. Now in the public domain, along with the "Second series" and "Third series," they continue to propagate a skewed image of the poet as cute little girl and eccentric virgin.

———. *Poems by Emily Dickinson*, second series, Edited by T. W. Higginson and Mabel Loomis Todd. Boston: Roberts Brothers, 1891.

———. *Letters of Emily Dickinson*. 2 vols. Edited by Mabel Loomis Todd. Boston: Little, Brown, 1894. The first collection of Dickinson's letters, painstakingly collected by Todd from frequently reluctant correspondents.

———. *Poems by Emily Dickinson*, third series. Edited by Mabel Loomis Todd. Boston: Roberts Brothers, 1896.

———. *The Single Hound: Poems of a Lifetime*. Edited by Martha Dickinson Bianchi. Boston: S. J. Parkhill, 1914. Containing 142 poems in the possession of the editor's mother, Susan Dickinson, it presented a more complex Dickinson to the world than the earlier Todd-Higginson volumes had. One critic saw this Dickinson as "an early Imagist," that is, a predecessor of such modern poets as Ezra Pound and William Carlos Williams, whose work was characterized by short musical lines and clear precise imagery.

———. *The Complete Poems of Emily Dickinson*. Edited by Martha Dickinson Bianchi. Boston: Little Brown, 1924. Not really complete, consists of the three Todd–Higginson volumes plus five previously unpublished poems. The volume brought 597 poems together within a single cover and stimulated the growing appreciation of Dickinson in the 1920s as one of the great American poets.

———. *Selected Poems of Emily Dickinson.* Edited by Conrad Aiken. London: Cape, 1924. Aiken's introductory essay contained new theoretical approaches to the poet's work that continue to be important.

———. *Further Poems of Emily Dickinson Withheld from Publication by her Sister Lavinia.* Edited by Martha Dickinson Bianchi with Alfred Leete Hampson. Boston: Little, Brown, 1929. Notable for the editors' attempt to print the poems in the lineations of the original manuscripts.

———. *The Poems of Emily Dickinson.* Edited by Martha Dickinson Bianchi with Alfred Leete Hampson. Boston: Little, Brown, 1930.

———. *Letters of Emily Dickinson.* Edited by Mabel Loomis Todd. New York: Harper & Brothers, 1931. An expanded version of the 1894 *Letters.*

———. *Unpublished Poems of Emily Dickinson.* Edited by Martha Dickinson Bianchi with Alfred Leete Hampson. Boston: Little, Brown, 1930.

———. *Poems by Emily Dickinson.* Edited by Martha Dickinson Bianchi with Alfred Leete Hampson. Boston: Little, Brown, 1937.

———. *Bolts of Melody: New Poems by Emily Dickinson.* Edited by Mabel Loomis Todd and Millicent Todd Bingham. New York: Harper and Brothers, 1945. Contained 668 poems that had been withheld from readers since the 19th century. Caused a sensation and was called "the most stunning surprise in the history of American literature."

———. *The Poems of Emily Dickinson: Including Variant Readings Critically Compared with All Known Manuscripts.* Edited by Thomas H. Johnson. Cambridge, Mass.: Harvard University Press, 1955. The first scholarly, comprehensive edition of Dickinson's poetry, containing 1,775 poems. Johnson used changes in Dickinson's handwriting in her letters to suggest approximate dates for the poetry, retained Dickinson's idiosyncratic spelling and punctuation, and provided variant readings of the poems.

———. *The Letters of Emily Dickinson.* 3 vols. Edited by Thomas H. Johnson and Theodora Ward. Cambridge, Mass.: The Belknap Press of Harvard University Press, 1958. Containing 1,049 letters, 124 prose fragments, and extensive notes, they provide the closest thing we have to an autobiography of the poet. Fascinating, essential reading for anyone who wants to know Dickinson.

———. *The Complete Poems of Emily Dickinson.* Edited by Thomas H. Johnson. Boston: Little, Brown, 1960. The one-volume reading edition of the poems. The standard authoritative version of Dickinson's poems for almost 40 years, until R. W. Franklin published his versions.

———. *Final Harvest: Emily Dickinson's Poems.* Selection and Introduction by Thomas H. Johnson. Boston: Little, Brown, and Company, 1960. A superb selection of 575 of Dickinson's greatest poems. This is an excellent place for the reader to begin.

———. *The Manuscript Books of Emily Dickinson.* Edited by R. W. Franklin. 2 vols. Cambridge, Mass.: Harvard University Press, 1981. This groundbreaking work made facsimiles of the 40 fascicles and 15 unbound sets available to readers for the first time. Franklin reconstructed the fascicles' original state by examining imperfections in the stationary, smudge patterns, and puncture marks where the poet's needle had pierced the paper to bind them.

———. *Emily Dickinson: Selected Letters.* Edited by Thomas H. Johnson. Cambridge, Mass.: The Belknap Press of Harvard University Press, 1985. An excellent selection for those not ready to tackle all 1,000-plus letters.

———. *The Master Letters of Emily Dickinson.* Edited by R. W. Franklin. Amherst: Amherst College Press, 1986. The three mysterious letters to an unknown individual the poet called "Master," newly edited and dated. This elegantly printed edition also contains an envelope of facsimiles of the letters.

———. *The Letters of Emily Dickinson.* 1 vol. Edited by Thomas H. Johnson and Theodora Ward. Cambridge, Mass.: The Belknap Press of Harvard University Press, 1986. This is a less expensive, digital reprinting of the 1958 *Letters.*

———. *New Poems of Emily Dickinson.* Edited by William H. Shurr with Anna Dunlap and Emily Grey Shurr. Chapel Hill: University of North Carolina Press, 1993. This highly controversial volume presents selected prose fragments of the letters as "newly discovered poems," on the basis of metrical criteria.

———. *Open Me Carefully: Emily Dickinson's Intimate Letters to Susan Huntington Dickinson.* Edited by Ellen Louise Hart and Martha Nell Smith. Ashfield, Mass.: Paris Press, 1998. A compilation of the poet's 36-year correspondence to her next-door neighbor and sister-in-law.

————. *The Poems of Emily Dickinson: Variorum Edition.* Edited by R. W. Franklin. 3 vols. Cambridge, Mass.: Harvard University Press, 1998. Franklin had better access to the manuscripts than Johnson. His appendices offer tables of poems added to or deleted from the canon, single poems separated into multiple poems and vice versa. Apart from this, the new authoritative variorum does not differ radically from Johnson's 1960 edition.

————. *The Poems of Emily Dickinson: Reading Edition.* Edited by R. W. Franklin. Cambridge, Mass.: The Belknap Press of Harvard University Press, 1999. Currently the standard scholarly edition of Dickinson's poems.

BIBLIOGRAPHY OF SECONDARY SOURCES, WITH PARTIAL ANNOTATION

Bibliographies and Source Materials

Blake, Caesar R., and Carlton F. Wells, eds. *The Recognition of Emily Dickinson: Selected Criticism since 1890*. Ann Arbor: University of Michigan Press, 1964. An important selection of review articles, including 16 essays published in the 19th century and 29 published from 1900 to 1960.

Boswell, Jeanetta. *Emily Dickinson: A Bibliography of Secondary Sources*, with Selective Annotations, 1890 through 1987. Jefferson, N.C.: McFarland, 1989. Organized alphabetically by author's name, this compilation provides brief summaries of each critical work.

Buckingham, William J. *Emily Dickinson: An Annotated Bibliography, 1850–1968*. Bloomington: Indiana University Press, 1970. A collection of 600 articles, including documents difficult to obtain.

———, ed. *Emily Dickinson's Reception in the 1890s: A Documentary History*. Pittsburgh, Pa.: University of Pittsburg Press, 1989.

Clendinning, Sheila T. *Emily Dickinson: A Bibliography 1850–1966*. Kent, Ohio: Kent State University Press, 1968. Provides a short summary of Dickinson's early editorial history and biographical criticism.

Dandurand, Karen. *Dickinson Scholarship: An Annotated Bibliography, 1969–1985*. New York: Garland, 1988.

Duchac, Joseph. *Poems of Emily Dickinson: An Annotated Guide to Commentary Published in English*. Boston: G. K. Hall, 1979 (vol. 1) and 1993 (vol. 2). Volume 1 covers the period from 1890 to 1977. Volume 2 covers the period from 1988 through 1989. Brief critical excerpts are given for the poems, listed alphabetically.

Lubbers, Klaus. *Emily Dickinson: The Critical Revolution*. Ann Arbor: University of Michigan Press, 1968. The most comprehensive development study of Dickinson's critical reception.

Messmer, Marietta. "Dickinson's Critical Reception." In *The Emily Dickinson Handbook*, edited by Gudrun Grabher, Roland Hagenbüchle, and Cristanne Miller, 299–322. Amherst, Mass.: University of Massachusetts Press, 1998. An up-to-date survey and analysis of Dickinson criticism. Emphasizes the impact of psychoanalytic, New Historicist, linguistic, and feminist perspectives on reading Dickinson.

Morse, Jonathan. "Bibliographical Essay." In *A Historical Guide to Emily Dickinson*, edited by Vivian R. Pollak, 255–283. Oxford and New York: Oxford University Press, 2004. A succinct, up-to-date, and insightful essay on the history of publication of Dickinson's work, including discussion of textual scholarship and computer technology.

Myerson, Joel. *Emily Dickinson: A Descriptive Bibliography*. Pittsburgh: University of Pittsburgh Press, 1984.

Sewall, Richard B., ed. *Emily Dickinson: A Collection of Critical Essays*. Englewood Cliffs, N.J.: Prentice Hall, 1963. A selective collection of review articles that concentrates on post-1924 criticism.

Woodress, James. "Emily Dickinson." In *Fifteen American Authors before 1900: Bibliographical Essays on Research and Criticism*, edited by Earl N. Harbert and Robert A. Rees, 185–229. Madison: University of Wisconsin Press, 1984. Excellent essay-length study of Dickinson's critical reception.

Concordances

MacKenzie, Cynthia J., with Penny Gilbert. *Concordance of the Letters of Emily Dickinson*. Boulder: University of Colorado Press, 2000.

Roseblum, S. P. *A Concordance to the Poems of Emily Dickinson*, Ithaca, N.Y.: Cornell University Press, 1964. An essential tool for exploring the frequency and contexts of the words in Dickinson's poetry.

Biographical Works

Benfey, Christopher. *Emily Dickinson: Lives of a Poet.* New York: Braziller, 1986.

Bianchi, Martha Dickinson. *Emily Dickinson Face to Face: Unpublished Letters with Notes and Reminiscences by Her Niece, Martha Dickinson Bianchi.* Boston: Houghton Mifflin, 1932. Another firsthand description of her aunt's life within the family compound, it continues to provide an invaluable resource to biographers but presents a sentimentalized portrait of the poet, creating the myth of the childlike, innocent poet.

————. *The Life and Letters of Emily Dickinson.* Boston: Houghton Mifflin, 1924. Contains valuable firsthand reminiscences of the poet by her only niece, but Bianchi presents a distorted, idealized version of the poet's relationship to Bianchi's mother, Susan Dickinson.

Bingham, Millicent Todd. *Ancestor's Brocades: The Literary Debut of Emily Dickinson: The Editing and Publication of Her Letters and Poems.* New York: Harper & Brothers, 1945. A fascinating and detailed account of the process of how Bingham's mother, Mabel Loomis Todd, and Thomas Wentworth Higginson edited the first volumes of Dickinson's poems and letters in the 1890s. The work is marred, however, by the absence of any clue as to the real nature of her mother's relationship with Austin Dickinson.

————. *Emily Dickinson: A Revelation.* New York: Harper & Brothers Publishers, 1954. The first publication of Dickinson's letters to Judge Otis Phillips Lord and an account of their love affair.

————. *Emily Dickinson's Home: Letters of Edward Dickinson and His Family, with Documentation and Comment.* New York: Harper & Row, 1955. An important literary history of Dickinson's milieu.

Capps, Jack L. *The Life of Emily Dickinson.* New York: Farrar, Straus & Giroux, 1974.

Chase, Richard. *Emily Dickinson.* American Men of Letters Series. New York: Sloane, 1951. Placing Dickinson within the Puritan tradition, Chase uses a biographical approach to explicate a selection of poems.

Cody, John. *After Great Pain: The Inner Life of Emily Dickinson.* Cambridge, Mass.: Harvard University Press, 1971. The controversial psychoanalytic study that develops the theory that Dickinson suffered a psychotic breakdown in the early 1860s, caused by her lack of maternal nurturing.

Gelpi, Albert. *Tenth Muse: The Psyche of the American Poet.* Cambridge, Mass.: Harvard University Press, 1975. Incorporating the aspect of gender into a Freudian/Jungian approach, Gelpi argues that Dickinson internalized the psychological burden of the 19th-century woman in general.

Griffith, Clark. *The Long Shadow: Emily Dickinson's Tragic Poetry.* Princeton, N.J.: Princeton University Press, 1964. A vision of the poet as a "Transcendentalist-in-reverse" whose tragic outlook took the form of angst and terror. Griffith sees her psychological problems as rooted in a rejection of her own femininity.

Habegger, Alfred. *My Wars Are Laid Away in Books.* New York: Random House, 2001. Rather than organizing his biography around the important figures in her life (as Sewall's biography does) this recent major study traces the poet's life from year to year, suggesting what her daily life was like and identifying the stages of her personal and poetic development.

Johnson, Thomas H. *Emily Dickinson: An Interpretive Biography.* Cambridge: Harvard University Press, 1955. A companion to his groundbreaking variorum editions of the poems and letters. Focuses on the poet's family, friends, and religious environment and analyzes her prosody with respect to the hymns of Isaac Watts.

Leyda, Jay. *The Years and Hours of Emily Dickinson.* 2 vols. New Haven, Conn.: Yale University Press, 1960. The indispensable compilation of events, observations and records related to Dickinson, arranged chronologically and drawn from a multitude of sources. Its wealth of raw data has been mined by every biographer since 1960.

Liebling, Jerome. *The Dickinsons of Amherst.* Photographs by Jerome Liebling. Essays by Christopher Benfey, Polly Longsworth, and Barton Levi St. Armand. Hanover, N.H.: University Press of New England, 2001. A beautiful coffee-table book with interesting essays.

Longsworth, Polly. *Austin and Mabel: The Amherst Affair and Love Letters of Austin Dickinson and Mabel Loomis Todd.* New York: Farrar, Straus & Giroux, 1984. A revealing account of the love affair between Dickinson's brother and the woman who became her first editor.

————. *The World of Emily Dickinson.* New York: Norton, 1990. A full and fascinating pictorial record of the poet, the people in her life, and the Amherst milieu.

Patterson, Rebecca. *The Riddle of Emily Dickinson,* Boston: Houghton Mifflin, 1951. Significant for its assertion of the importance of women in the poet's life. Speculating that Catherine Scott Anthon was the woman Dickinson loved, this was the first study to discuss Dickinson's possible lesbian relations.

Pollak, Vivian R., ed. *A Poet's Parents: The Courtship Letters of Emily Norcross and Edward Dickinson.* Chapel Hill: University of North Carolina Press, 1988. Sheds important light on Dickinson's maternal heritage and modifies commonly accepted notions of male dominance and female submission patterns in Dickinson's family.

Pollak, Vivian R., and Marianne Noble. "Emily Dickinson 1830–1886: A Brief Biography." In *A Historical Guide to Emily Dickinson,* edited by Vivian R. Pollack. Oxford and New York: Oxford University Press, 2004. A succinct, up-to-date introduction.

Pollitt, Josephine. *Emily Dickinson: The Human Background of Her Poetry.* New York, Harper, 1930. An early, highly speculative but refreshing narrative account of the poet's life and loves. Suggests that Helen Fiske Hunt Jackson's husband, Major Hunt, was the secret man in her life.

Sewall, Richard B. *The Life of Emily Dickinson.* 2 vols. New York: Farrar, Straus & Giroux, 1974. The classic biography, insightful, engaging and comprehensive. Counters the notions of Dickinson as highly disturbed and of her home as unduly oppressive and gives the story of Austin Dickinson's love affair with Mabel Loomis Todd for the first time. Generally fair-minded and generous, but considered to be biased toward the point of view of Mabel's daughter, Millicent Todd Bingham, who made important materials available to him. A substantial part of this work is devoted to Dickinson's immediate family and important friends.

————, ed. *The Lyman Letters: New Light on Emily Dickinson and Her Family.* Amherst: University of Massachusetts Press, 1965. These letters, by Emily's close friend and her sister Lavinia's suitor, offer unique glimpses of the poet and present the Dickinson household as warm and intellectually stimulating.

Taggard, Genevieve. *The Life and Mind of Emily Dickinson.* New York: Knopf, 1930. Engagingly written but conjectural early study that attempts to give a sense of the poet's life as she actually lived it. Suggests that George Gould was the secret man in her life.

Walsh, John Evangelist. *The Hidden Life of Emily Dickinson.* New York: Simon and Schuster, 1971.

————. *This Brief Tragedy: Unraveling the Todd-Dickinson Affair.* New York: Grove Weidenfeld, 1991. Interprets the love affair of Mabel Loomis Todd and Austin Dickinson and speculates that the poet may have committed suicide by taking strychnine.

Ward, Theodora. *The Capsule of the Mind: Chapters in the Life of Emily Dickinson.* Cambridge, Mass.: Harvard University Press, 1961. Taking a Jungian approach, Ward pioneered psychobiographical studies of Dickinson. She sees the poet's writings as self-revelations, rooted in dream and fantasy.

Whicher, George Frisbie. *This Was a Poet: A Critical Biography of Emily Dickinson.* New York: Charles Scribner's Sons, 1939. The first biography to reliably discuss the poet's cultural and social world, stressing the important influences of Puritanism and Yankee humor.

Wolff, Cynthia Griffin. *Emily Dickinson.* New York: Alfred A. Knopf, 1986. This comprehensive feminist psychobiography is heavily weighted toward interpretation of the poetry in terms of Dickinson's inner life. Views Dickinson as deeply conflicted and negatively affected by her emotionally aloof parents. Wolff's provocative focus on Dickinson's "wrestling with God" and with gender expectations produces some brilliant interpretations, as well as some quirky ones.

Other Secondary Sources

Ackmann, Martha. "Biographical Studies of Dickinson." In *The Emily Dickinson Handbook,* edited by Gudrun Grabher, Roland Hagenbüchle, and Cristanne Miller, 11–23. Amherst: University of Massachusetts Press, 1998. An excellent survey of Dickinson biographies and biographical research.

Anatharam, Priyamvada Tripathi. *Sunset in a Cup: Emily Dickinson and Mythopoeic Imagination.* New Delhi: Cosmo, 1985.

Anderson, Charles. "Despair." In *Modern Critical Views: Emily Dickinson,* edited by Harold Bloom, 9–35. New York: Chelsea House Publishers, 1985.

————. *Emily Dickinson's Poetry: Stairway of Surprise.* New York: Holt, Rinehart and Winston, 1960. A sensitive thematic study of the poems that also extensively treats Dickinson's stylistic features, including her wit, puns, eccentric grammar, and prosody.

Banning, Evelyn I. *Helen Hunt Jackson.* New York: Vanguard Press, 1973.

Baker, Wendy. *Lunacy of Light: Emily Dickinson and the Experience of Metaphor.* Carbondale: Southern Illinois University Press, 1987.

Baym, Nina. "God, Father, and Lover in Emily Dickinson's Poetry." In *Puritan Influences in American Literature,* edited by Emory Elliott, 193–209. *Illinois Studies in Language and Literature* 65. Urbana: University of Illinois Press, 1979. Discusses Dickinson's use of the child persona as a means of denouncing God as an insensitive father.

Benfey, Christopher. *Emily Dickinson and the Problem of Others.* Amherst: University of Massachusetts Press, 1984.

Bennett, Paula. *Emily Dickinson: Woman Poet.* Iowa City: University of Iowa Press, 1990. The critic who has most strongly advanced the theory that Dickinson's poetry is homoerotic, Bennett offers the poet's "clitorocentrism" as an explanation for such features of her work as her paradoxality, insistence on autonomy and stylistic and thematic emphasis on "little/bigness."

———. My *Life a Loaded Gun: Female Creativity and Feminist Poetics.* Boston: Beacon Press, 1986. Explores Dickinson's romantic child-persona in relation to her rejection of the traditional New England model of the self-denying female, which allowed her to adopt the "self-indulgence" of the writing life.

Budick, E. Miller. *Emily Dickinson and the Life of Language: A Study in Symbolic Poetics.* Baton Rouge: Louisiana State University Press, 1985. Interprets Dickinson's decision to withdraw from social life as a retreat to the symbolic realm of language.

Burbick, Joan. "Emily Dickinson and the Economics of Desire." In *Emily Dickinson: A Collection of Critical Essays,* edited by Judith Farr, 76–88. Upper Saddle River, N.J.: Prentice-Hall, 1996.

Cameron, Sharon. *Choosing Not Choosing: Dickinson's Fascicles.* Chicago: University of Chicago Press, 1992. An influential study that stresses the importance of viewing Dickinson's poems within the context of the fascicles. Cameron argues that the fascicles give the poems contexts that counteract the view that they are enigmatic and culturally incomprehensible. She argues against narrative readings of the fascicles, seeing the poems within each fascicle as variants of one another. She shows that by refusing to make textual and thematic choices in her poems, the poet challenged the idea of limits or boundaries.

———. "Dickinson's Fascicles." In *The Emily Dickinson Handbook,* edited by Gudrun Grabher, Roland Hagenbüchle, and Cristanne Miller, 138–160. Amherst: University of Massachusetts Press, 1998.

———. "'A Loaded Gun': The Dialectic of Rage." In *Modern Critical Views: Emily Dickinson,* edited by Harold Bloom, 99–128. New York: Chelsea House Publishers, 1985.

———. *Lyric Time: Dickinson and the Limits of Genre.* Baltimore: Johns Hopkins University Press, 1979. Discusses Dickinson's poetry in terms of the fact that the lyric as a genre rejects the limitations of narrative and objective concepts of time.

Capps, Jack L. *Emily Dickinson's Reading, 1836–1886.* Cambridge, Mass.: Harvard University Press, 1966. Traces the sources of Dickinson's literary allusions to the Bible, Shakespeare, the metaphysical poets, Burns, Emerson, Elizabeth Barrett Browning, Robert Browning, and others.

Coghill, Sheila, and Thom Tammaro, eds. *Visiting Emily: Poems Inspired by the Life and Work of Emily Dickinson.* Iowa City: University of Iowa Press, 2000.

Crumbley, Paul. "Dickinson's Dialogic Voice." *The Emily Dickinson Handbook,* edited by Gudrun Grabher, Roland Hagenbüchle, and Cristanne Miller, 93–109. Amherst: University of Massachusetts Press, 1998.

———. *Inflections of the Pen: Dash and Voice in Emily Dickinson.* Lexington: University of Kentucky Press, 1997. A perceptive study of Dickinson's punctuation, based on "dialogic criticism," which focuses on the existence of more than one voice in the poems.

Cunningham, J. V. *Dickinson: Lyric and Legend.* Los Angeles: Sylvester & Orphanus, 1980.

———. "Sorting Out: The Case of Dickinson," *The Southern Review* 5, no. 2 (Spring 1969): 436–456.

Dandurand, Karen. "New Dickinson Civil War Publications." *American Literature* 56 (March 1984): 17–27. An important revelation of previously unknown publications of the poet's work during her lifetime.

Davidson, James, "Emily Dickinson and Isaac Watts." *Boston Public Library Quarterly* (1954): 141–149.

Delaney, Edmund. *The Connecticut River; New England's Historic Waterway.* Chester, Conn.: Globe Pequot Press, 1983.

Denman, Kamilla. "Emily Dickinson's Volcanic Punctuation." In *Emily Dickinson: A Collection of Critical Essays*, edited by Judith Farr, 187–205. Upper Saddle River, N.J.: Prentice-Hall, 1996. This excellent article is the place to begin for those interested in understanding the effects of Dickinson's punctuation and its evolution over time.

Dickie, Margaret. "Feminist Conceptions of Dickinson." In *The Emily Dickinson Handbook*, edited by Gudrun Grabher, Roland Hagenbüchle, and Cristanne Miller, 342–355. Amherst: University of Massachusetts Press, 1998. This excellent summary of feminist writings on Dickinson is the place to start for those who want to understand the dominant critical approach to Dickinson for the past 20 years.

———. *Lyric Contingencies: Emily Dickinson and Wallace Stevens*. Philadelphia: University of Pennsylvania Press, 1991. This study examines the importance of gender in Dickinson's sense of a discontinuous self that looks forward to the modernist poetry of Wallace Stevens and to feminist conceptions of the decentered self.

Dickinson, Frederick, *To the Descendants of Thomas Dickinson*, Chicago, Ill.: 1897.

Dickinson Editing Collective. *Dickinson Electronic Archives*. Available online. URL:http://jefferson-village.virginia.edu/dickinson/. This revolutionary Web site has the ambitious goal of establishing a hypermedia archive with online reproductions of all existing Dickinson-related documents and their publication histories.

Diehl, Joanne Feit. *Dickinson and the Romantic Imagination*. Princeton, N.J.: Princeton University Press, 1981. This study proposes that Dickinson subverted the tradition of Wordsworth, Shelley, Keats, and Emerson. Argues that, excluded from this tradition as a woman, Dickinson used her sense of estrangement as a source of poetic power. Posits that her primary divergence from the romantic tradition lies in her gender, which led her to have a male muse.

———. "Emerson, Dickinson, and the Abyss." In *Modern Critical Views: Emily Dickinson*, edited by Harold Bloom, 157–159. New York: Chelsea House Publishers, 1985.

———. *Women Poets and the American Sublime*. Bloomington: Indiana University Press, 1990. This study develops the idea that Dickinson created a "counter-Sublime" that converted renunciation of power into a force equally as grand as the Sublime. Feit Diehl traces this concept through the work of Marianne Moore, Elizabeth Bishop, Sylvia Plath, and Adrienne Rich.

Dobson, Joanne. *Dickinson and the Strategies of Reticence: The Woman Writer in Nineteenth-Century America*. Bloomington: Indiana University Press, 1989. Analyzes Dickinson's ambivalent relationship to the 19th-century view of womanhood. Discusses both the poet's "slant" style and her decision not to publish as they reflect her internalization of her culture's norms for femininity.

Doriani, Beth Maclay. *Emily Dickinson, Daughter of Prophecy*. Amherst: University of Massachusetts Press, 1996. This study demonstrates how, by drawing on the stance, style, and structures of the prophets of the bible, Dickinson took on a prophetic voice.

Eberwein, Jane Donahue. "Dickinson's Local, Global, and Cosmic Perspectives." In *The Emily Dickinson Handbook*, edited by Gudrun Grabher, Roland Hagenbüchle, and Cristanne Miller, 27–43. Amherst: University of Massachusetts Press, 1998.

———. *Dickinson: Strategies of Limitation*. Amherst: University of Massachusetts Press, 1985. This study examines the ways in which the poet overcame or evaded the cultural limitations of her time.

———. "Emily Dickinson and the Calvinist Sacramental Tradition." In *Emily Dickinson: A Collection of Critical Essays*, edited by Judith Farr, 89–104. Englewood Cliffs, N.J.: Prentice-Hall, 1996. This is an essential essay for understanding Dickinson's transformation of language from the Calvinist tradition in creating her own sacred universe.

———. *An Emily Dickinson Encyclopedia*. Westport, Conn.: Greenwood, 1998.

———. "'Graphicer for Grace': Emily Dickinson's Calvinist Language." *Studies in Puritan American Spiritually* I (1990): 170–201.

———. "'Is Immortality True?'" In *A Historical Guide to Emily Dickinson*, edited by Vivian R. Pollack, 67–102. Oxford and New York: Oxford University Press, 2004. This excellent article examines Dickinson's spiritual quest in the context of changes in New England's religious culture during her lifetime.

Edelstein, Tilden G. *Strange Enthusiasm: A Life of Thomas Wentworth Higginson*. New Haven, Conn., and London: Yale University Press, 1968.

Emily Dickinson Museum. Available online. URL: http:www.emilydickinsonmuseum.org. Accessed March 20, 2006.

Erkkila, Betsy. "Dickinson and the Art of Politics," in *A Historical Guide to Emily Dickinson,* edited by Vivian R. Pollack, 133–174. Oxford and New York: Oxford University Press, 2004.

———. "The Emily Dickinson Wars." In *The Cambridge Companion to Emily Dickinson,* edited by Wendy Martin, 11–29. Cambridge: Cambridge University Press, 2002. A fascinating essay on the consequences for Dickinson's literary heritage of the conflict between Susan Dickinson and Mabel Loomis Todd.

———. *The Wicked Sisters: Women Poets, Literary History, and Discord.* New York: Oxford University Press, 1992. Arguing against feminist views that maternalized and sentimentalized the relations between women writers, Erkilla views Dickinson in the context of her race, class, and ethnic environment. She concludes that Dickinson's radical poetics were joined to her conservative, sometimes reactionary, political stances.

Faderman, Lillian. "Emily Dickinson's Letters to Sue Gilbert," *Massachusetts Review,* 28, (Summer 1977): 197–225.

———. *Surpassing the Love of Men: Romantic Friendship and Love between Women from the Renaissance to the Present.* New York: Morrow, 1981. Proposes that the recipient of the Master letter is a woman.

Farr, Judith. "Dickinson and the Visual Arts." In *The Emily Dickinson Handbook,* edited by Gudrun Grabher, Roland Hagenbüchle, and Cristanne Miller, 61–92. Amhrest: University of Massachusetts Press, 1998.

———. *The Passion of Emily Dickinson.* Cambridge, Mass.: Harvard University Press, 1992. An important, insightful study of Dickinson's love poetry to Susan Gilbert Dickinson and Samuel Bowles, whom Farr identifies as the great female and male passions of her life. The second major aspect of the book is a reading of Dickinson's work in the context of nineteenth-century visual arts.

———, with Louise Carter. *The Gardens of Emily Dickinson.* Cambridge, Mass.: Harvard University Press, 2004. This beautifully produced and illustrated book contains a wealth of detail about the poet and her second greatest passion, along with Farr's fine insight into Dickinson's flower poems.

Farr, Judith, ed. *Emily Dickinson: A Collection of Critical Essays.* Upper Saddle River, N.J.: Prentice-Hall, 1996. This outstanding collection of essays by leading lights of Dickinson criticism focuses on Dickinson's themes, poetics, and language.

Fast, Robin Riley, and Christine Mack Gordon, eds. *Approaches to Teaching Emily Dickinson's Poetry.* New York, MLA, 1989. This wide-ranging collection presents a full spectrum of approaches available to the student of Dickinson's work.

Ferlazzo, Paul. *Emily Dickinson.* Boston: Twayne, 1976.

Finch, A. R. C. "Dickinson and Patriarchal Meter: A Theory of Metrical Codes." *PMLA,* 102 (1987): 166–176.

Ford, Thomas W. *Heaven Beguiles the Tired: Death in the Poetry of Emily Dickinson.* Tuscaloosa: University of Alabama Press, 1966.

Franklin, R. W. *The Editing of Emily Dickinson: A Reconsideration.* Madison: University of Wisconsin Press, 1967. The book that opened the modern era of Dickinson textual scholarship questions the principle that a final, definitive version of the poems, representing the author's intentions, can be established.

———. "Emily Dickinson to Abiah Root: Ten Reconstructed Letters." *Emily Dickinson Journal* 4, No. 1 (1995): 1–43.

Freeman, Margaret H. "A Cognitive Approach to Dickinson's Metaphors." In *The Emily Dickinson Handbook,* edited by Gudrun Grabher, Roland Hagunbüchle, and Cristanne Miller, 258–272. Amherst: University of Massachusetts Press, 1998.

Fulton, Alice. "Her Moment of Brocade: The Reconstruction of Emily Dickinson." *Parnassus: Poetry in Review* 25, no. 1 (Spring 1989): 9–44.

Gelpi, Albert. "Emily Dickinson and the Deerslayer: The Dilemma of the Woman Poet in America." *Shakespeare's Sisters: Feminist Essays on Woman Poets,* edited by Sandra M. Gilbert and Susan Gubar, 122–34. Bloomington: Indiana University Press, 1979.

———. *Emily Dickinson: The Mind of the Poet.* Cambridge, Mass.: Harvard University Press, 1966. Discusses Dickinson in relation to 19th-century New England, transcendentalism, and romanticism.

Gibson, Andrew. "Emily Dickinson and the Poetry of Hypothesis." In *Essays in Criticism* 33.3 (July 1983): 220–237.

Gilbert, Sandra M. "The Wayward Nun Beneath the Hill: Emily Dickinson and the Mysteries of Womanhood." In *Emily Dickinson: A Collection of Critical Essays,* edited by Judith Farr, 20–39. Upper Saddle River, N.J.: Prentice-Hall, 1996.

Gilbert, Sandra M., and Susan Gubar. *The Madwoman in the Attic: The Woman Writer and the Nineteenth-Century Literary Imagination.* New Haven, Conn.: Yale University Press, 1979. This monumental study of the woman writer and the 19th-century literary imagination sparked a feminist reinterpretation of Dickinson's sources of creativity and of her reasons for going into seclusion. The Dickinson the authors perceive is the enraged, emotionally divided 19th-century woman, torn between domestic and creative roles: half angel in the house, half madwoman in the attic.

Gohdes, Clarence L. "Emily Dickinson's Blue Fly." *New England Quarterly* 51, no. 3 (September 1978): 423–431.

Grabher, Gudrun. "Dickinson's Lyrical Self." In *The Emily Dickinson Handbook,* edited by Gudrun Grabher, Roland Hagenbüchle, and Cristanne Miller, 224–239. Amherst: University of Massachusetts Press, 1998.

Grabher, Gudrun, Roland Hagenbüchle, and Cristanne Miller, eds. *The Emily Dickinson Handbook,* Amherst: University of Massachusetts Press, 1998. A superb recent collection of essays by leading Dickinson scholars, covering a broad spectrum of bibliographical, textual, and historical issues.

Gribbin, Laura. "Emily Dickinson's Circumference: Figuring a Blind Spot in the Romantic Tradition." *Emily Dickinson Journal.* Vol. 2, no. 1, (1993): 1–21.

Hagenbüchle, Roland. "Dickinson and Literary Theory." In *The Emily Dickinson Handbook,* edited by Gundrun Grabher, Roland Hagenbüchle, and Cristanne Miller, 356–384. Amherst: University of Massachusetts Press, 1998.

———. "Precision and Indeterminacy in the Poetry of Emily Dickinson." *Emerson Society Quarterly* 20 (1974): 33–56. This influential article traces the difficulties of Dickinson's language to her reliance on metonymy rather than metaphor.

———. "Sing and Process: The Concept of Language in Emerson and Dickinson." *Dickinson Studies,* no. 58 (Bonus 1986): 59–88. This influential article describes Dickinson's differences from Emerson. If Emerson connected man to the eternal through nature, Dickinson saw words as the connection.

Hammond, William Gardiner. *Remembrance of Amherst: An Undergraduate's Diary, 1846–1848.* Edited George Frisbie Whicher New York: Columbia University Press, 1946.

Hecht, Anthony. "The Riddles of Emily Dickinson." In *Emily Dickinson: A Collection of Critical Essays,* edited by Judith Farr, 149–162. Upper Saddle River, N.J.: Prentice-Hall, 1996.

Heimart, Alan, and Perry Miller, eds. *The Great Awakening.* Indianapolis and New York: The Bobbs-Merrill Co., 1967.

Heman Humphrey, *Sketches of the Early History of Amherst College.* Northampton, Mass.: 1905.

Hesford, Walter. "The Creative Fall of Bradstreet and Dickinson," *Essays in Literature* 14, no. 1 (Spring 1987): 81–91.

Higgins, David. *Portrait of Emily Dickinson: The Poet and Her Prose.* New Brunswick: Rutgers University Press, 1967.

Hitchcock, Edward. *Catalogue of Plants Growing without Cultivation in the Vicinity of Amherst College.* Amherst, Mass.: 1829.

———. *The Highest Use of Learning: An Address delivered at his Inauguration to the Presidency of Amherst College.* Amherst, Mass.: 1845.

———. *Religious Lectures on Peculiar Phenomena in the Four Seasons.* Amherst, Mass.: 1850.

Hoffman, Tyler B. "Emily Dickinson and the Limit of War." *Emily Dickinson Journal* 3. no. 2 (1994): 1–18.

Homans, Margaret. *Women Writers and Poetic Identity: Dorothy Wordsworth, Emily Brontë, and Emily Dickinson.* Princeton, N.J.: Princeton University Press, 1980. A study of how the work of these poets represents feminine reactions to the masculine romantic tradition, influencing the very nature of their nonmimetic language.

Horan, Elizabeth. "To Market: The Dickinson Copyright Wars." *Emily Dickinson Journal* 5, no. 1 (1996): 88–120.

Howe, Susan. *The Birth-Mark: Unsettling the Wilderness in American Literary History.* Hanover, N.H.: University Press of New England, 1993. This study casts doubt on any interpretation of the poems through the fascicles, arguing that their original order was broken by the poet's friends and first editors.

———. *My Emily Dickinson.* Berkeley, Calif.: North Atlantic Books, 1985. A creative response to Dickinson by a poet and scholar. Howe engages Dickinson's voice in a dialogue with other writers and critics.

Johnson, Greg. *Emily Dickinson: Perception and the Poet's Quest.* Tuscaloosa: University of Alabama Press, 1985.

Jones, Rowena Revis. "A Royal Seal: Dickinson's Rite of Baptism." *Religion and Literature* 18, no. 3 (Fall 1986): 29–51.

———. "A Taste for 'Poison': Dickinson's Departure from Orthodoxy." *Emily Dickinson Journal,* 2, no. 1 (1993): 47–64.

Juhasz, Suzanne. ed. *Feminist Critics Read Emily Dickinson.* Bloomington: Indiana University Press, 1983.

———. "'The Landscape of the Spirit.'" In *Emily Dickinson: A Collection of Critical Essays,* edited by Judith Farr, 130–140. Upper Saddle River, N.J.: Prentice-Hall, 1996.

———. *Naked and Fiery Forms: Modern American Poetry by Women: A New Tradition.* New York: Harper & Row, 1976.

———. "Reading Emily Dickinson's Letters." *ESQ: A Journal of the American Renaissance* 30 (1984): 170–192.

———. *The Undiscovered Continent: Emily Dickinson and the Space of the Mind.* Bloomington: Indiana University Press, 1983. Develops the thesis that Dickinson withdrew from society in order to choose the life of the mind and be a woman poet on her own terms.

Juhasz, Suzanne, and Cristanne Miller. "Performances of Gender in Dickinson's Poetry." In *The Cambridge Companion to Emily Dickinson,* edited by Wendy Martin. Cambridge: Cambridge University Press, 2002: 107–128.

Juhasz, Suzanne, Cristanne Miller, and Martha Nell Smith. *Comic Power in Emily Dickinson.* Austin: University of Texas Press, 1993. This study discusses the importance of the audience for Dickinson's "performative" poetry, focusing on comic strategies to undermine the authority of patriarchal institutions.

Keller, Karl. *The Only Kangaroo among the Beauty: Emily Dickinson and America.* Baltimore: Johns Hopkins University Press, 1979. The most comprehensive early analysis of the poet in the context of 19th-century culture.

Kher, Inder Nath. *The Landscape of Absence: Emily Dickinson's Poetry.* New Haven, Conn.: Yale University Press, 1974. This study stresses the importance of silence and negation in the poetry.

Knapp, Bettina L. *Emily Dickinson.* New York: Continuum, Frederick Ungar, 1989.

Lease, Benjamin. *Emily Dickinson's Readings of Men and Books: Sacred Soundings.* New York: St. Martin's Press, 1990. Identifies Dickinson's "Master" as Charles Wadsworth, showing how the Master letters echo passages from Wadsworth's sermons.

Leder, Sharon, and Adrea Abbott. *The Language of Exclusion: The Poetry of Emily Dickinson and Christina Rossetti.* Contributions in Women's Studies, no. 83. New York: Greenwood, 1987.

Le Duc, Thomas. *Piety and Intellect at Amherst College.* New York: Columbia University Press, 1946.

Lee, A. Robert. "'This World Is Not Conclusion': Emily Dickinson and the Landscape of Death." *Anglo-American Studies* 2 (1982): 217–232.

Lindeberg-Seyersted, Brita. *Emily Dickinson's Punctuation.* Oslo, Norway: University of Oslo, 1976.

———. *The Voice of the Poet: Aspects of Style in the Poetry of Emily Dickinson.* Cambridge, Mass.: Harvard University Press, 1960. An important early linguistic study that identifies colloquialness, indirection, and idiosyncrasy as Dickinson's governing principles.

Loeffelholz, Mary. *Dickinson and the Boundaries of Feminist Theory.* Urbana: University of Illinois Press, 1991. This review of feminist scholarship emphasize the close relationship among feminist, deconstructionist, and psychoanalytic works. The author recognizes the need for feminist scholars to develop a model for a countertradition in women's writing that does not idealize it.

Lombardo, Daniel. *A Hedge Away: The Other Side of Emily Dickinson's Amherst.* Northampton, Mass.: Daily Hampshire Gazette, 1997.

———. *Tales of Amherst: A Look Back.* Amherst, Mass.: Jones Library, Inc., 1986.

Longsworth, Polly. "Upon Concluded Lives: New Letters of Emily Dickinson." *Emily Dickinson International Society (EDIS) Bulletin* 7, no. 1 (May/June 1995): 2–4.

Loving, Jerome. *Emily Dickinson: The Poet on the Second Story.* Cambridge: Cambridge University Press, 1986.

Lowenberg, Carlton. *Emily Dickinson's Textbooks.* Lafayette, Calif.: Lowenberg, 1986.

Marsden, George M. *Jonathan Edwards: A Life.* New Haven, Conn.: Yale University Press. 2003.

Martin, Wendy. *An American Triptych: Anne Bradstreet, Emily Dickinson, Adrienne Rich.* Chapel Hill: University of North Carolina Press, 1984.

———, ed. *The Cambridge Companion to Emily Dickinson.* Cambridge: Cambridge University Press, 2002. This recent collection of 11 first-rate essays looks at Dickinson in terms of biographical and publication issues, elements of her poetics, and cultural contexts.

McGann, Jerome J. *Black Riders: The Visible Language of Modernism.* Princeton, N.J.: Princeton University Press, 1993. This study focuses on Dickinson's deep interest in the visual aspects of her writing, asserting that it was not written for a print medium.

———. "Emily Dickinson's Visible Language." In *Emily Dickinson: A Collection of Critical Essays,* edited by Judith Farr, 248–259. Upper Saddle River, N.J.: Prentice-Hall, 1996.

McIntosh, James. *Nimble Believing: Dickinson and the Unknown.* Ann Arbor: University of Michigan Press, 2000.

Merriam, George S. *The Life and Times of Samuel Bowles,* 2 vols. New York: 1885.

Messmer, Marietta. "Dickinson's Critical Reception." In *The Emily Dickinson Handbook,* edited by Gudrun Grabher, Roland Hagenbüchle, and Cristanne Miller, 299–322. Amherst: University of Massachusetts Press, 1998. An excellent summation of the vast body of Dickinson criticism from 1890 to the late 1990s.

———. *"A vice for voices": Reading Emily Dickinson's Correspondence.* Amherst: University of Massachusetts Press, 2001.

Miller, Cristanne. "Approaches to Reading Dickinson." *Women's Studies* 16, nos. 1–2 (1989): 223–228.

———. "Dickinson's Experiments in Language." In *The Emily Dickinson Handbook,* edited by Gudrun Grabher, Roland Hagenbüchle, and Cristanne Miller, 240–257. Amherst: University of Massachusetts Press, 1998.

———. *Emily Dickinson: A Poet's Grammar.* Cambridge, Mass.: Harvard University Press, 1987. The best, most comprehensive study of Dickinson's language. Miller examines the poet's use of indirection, compression, and fragmentation and analyses such characteristics of Dickinson's grammar as nonrecoverable deletions, disjunctive syntax, and semantic doubling. She sees gender as the key factor in the development of her compressed, disruptive style.

———. "How 'Low Feet' Stagger: Disruptions of Language in Dickinson's Poetry." In *Feminist Critics Read Emily Dickinson,* edited by Suzanne Juhasz, 134–135. Bloomington: Indiana University Press, 1983.

———. "The Sound of Shifting Paradigms, or Reading Emily Dickinson in the Twenty-first Century." In *A Historical Guide to Emily Dickinson,* edited by Vivian R. Pollack, 201–234. Oxford and New York: Oxford University Press, 2004.

Miller, Ruth. "'A letter is a joy of earth': Dickinson's Communication with the World." *Legacy: A Journal of Nineteenth Century Women Writers* 3, no. 1 (Spring 1986): 29–39.

———. *The Poetry of Emily Dickinson.* Middletown, Conn.: Wesleyan University Press, 1968. The first study to focus on the structure of the fascicles. Miller identified a narrative pattern for them, from acceptance through suffering and rejection to resolution.

Mitchell, Domhnall. "Emily Dickinson and Class." In *The Cambridge Companion to Emily Dickinson,* edited by Wendy Martin, 191–214. Cambridge: Cambridge University Press, 2002.

———. *Emily Dickinson: Monarch of Perception.* Amherst: University of Massachusetts Press, 2000.

Moers, Ellen. *Literary Women: The Great Writers.* Garden City, N.J.: Doubleday, 1976.

Monteiro, George. "The Pilot-God Trope in Nineteenth-Century American Texts." *Modern Language Studies* 7, no. 2 (Fall 1977): 42–51.

Morris, Timothy. "The Development of Dickinson's Style." *American Literature* 60, no. 1 (Mar 88): 26–41.

Mossberg, Barbara Antonina Clarke. "Emily Dickinson's Nursery Rhymes." In *Feminist Critics Read Emily Dickinson,* edited by Suzanne Juhasz, 45–66. Bloomington: Indiana University Press, 1983.

———. *Emily Dickinson: When a Writer Is a Daughter.* Bloomington: Indiana University Press, 1982. This study views the poetry somewhat narrowly, as a response to the poet's relationship with her parents.

Mount Holyoke College. Mary Lyon. Available online. URL http://www.mtholyoke.edu/marylyon. Accessed March 20, 2006.

Mudge, Jean McClure. *Emily Dickinson and the Image of Home.* Amherst: University of Massachusetts Press, 1975.

Mulvihill, John. "Why Dickinson Didn't Title." *Emily Dickinson Journal* 5, no. 1 (1996): 71–87.

Noble, Marianne. *The Masochistic Pleasures of Sentimental Literature.* Princeton, N.J.: Princeton University Press, 2000.

Oberhaus, Dorothy Huff. *Emily Dickinson's Fascicles: Method and Meaning.* University Park: Pennsylvania State University Press, 1995. Focusing on the 40th fascicle, Oberhaus finds that it contains a deep structural and thematic unity, centered in a spiritual pilgrimage from renunciation to illumination.

———. "'Tender Pioneer': Emily Dickinson's Poems on the Life of Christ." In *Emily Dickinson: A Collection of Critical Essays,* edited by Judith Farr,

105–118. Upper Saddle River, N.J.: Prentice-Hall, 1996.

O'Connell, James C. *The Pioneer Valley Reader: Prose and Poetry from New England's Heartland.* Stockbridge, Mass.: Berkshire House, 1995.

Orzeck, Martin, and Robert Weisbuch, eds. *Dickinson and Audience.* Ann Arbor: University of Michigan Press, 1996.

Ostriker, Alicia Suskin. *Stealing the Language: The Emergence of Women's Poetry in America.* Boston: Beacon Press, 1986.

Paglia, Camille. *Sexual Personae: Art and Decadence from Nefertiti to Emily Dickinson.* New Haven, Conn.: Yale University Press, 1990. Paglia identifies instances of erotic sadism throughout Dickinson's poetry.

Patterson, Rebecca. *Emily Dickinson's Imagery.* Edited by Margaret H. Freeman. Amherst: University of Massachusetts Press, 1979.

Petrino, Elizabeth. *Emily Dickinson and Her Contemporaries: Women's Verse in America, 1820–1885.* Hanover, N.H.: University Press of New England, 1998.

Pollak, Vivian R. "American Women Poets Reading Dickinson: The Example of Helen Hunt Jackson." In *The Emily Dickinson Handbook,* edited by Gudrun Grabher, Roland Hagenbüchle, and Cristanne Miller, 323–341. Amherst: University of Massachusetts Press, 1998.

———. "Dickinson and the Poetics of Whiteness." *The Emily Dickinson Journal* no. 2 (2000): 84–95.

———. *Dickinson: The Anxiety of Gender.* Ithaca, N.Y.: Cornell University Press, 1984. Blending biographical and feminist approaches, this major study definitively established the importance of gender in Dickinson's life and career. It compellingly examines poems in light of Dickinson's biography, with a focus on the impact of Emily Norcross Dickinson's failure as a mother. Pollak sees loss and renunciation as the sources of the poet's creativity. She suggests that the rift between the rebellious and the submissive woman in the poetry was never bridged.

———, ed. *A Historical Guide to Emily Dickinson.* Oxford and New York: Oxford University Press, 2004. An excellent recent collection of essays by leading scholars on different aspects of "Dickinson in her time."

———. "Thirst and Starvation in Emily Dickinson's Poetry." In *Emily Dickinson: A Collection of Critical Essays,* edited by Judith Farr, 62–75. Upper Saddle River, N.J.: Prentice-Hall, 1996.

Porter, David. *The Art of Emily Dickinson's Early Poetry.* Chicago: University of Chicago Press, 1966. Focusing on poems written before 1862, in Johnson's dating, this was the first strictly formalistic study. Porter examines the use of meter, rhyme, imagery, diction, personae, and the irony inherent in Dickinson's use of the hymn form to express a skeptical world view.

———. "The Crucial Experience in Emily Dickinson's Poetry." *Emerson Society Quarterly: A Journal of the American Renaissance* 20 (1974): 280–290.

———. *Dickinson: The Modern Idiom.* Cambridge, Mass.: Harvard University Press, 1981. Concentrates exclusively on Dickinson's elliptical language and identifies her as the first practitioner of an American modernism characterized by alienation from the sociocultural environment.

———. "The Early Achievement." In *Modern Critical Views: Emily Dickinson,* edited by Harold Bloom, 65–80. New York: Chelsea House Publishers, 1985.

———. "Searching for Dickinson's Themes." In *The Emily Dickinson Handbook,* edited by Gudrun Grabher, Roland Hagenbüchle, and Cristanne Miller, 183–196. Amherst: University of Massachusetts Press, 1998.

———. "Strangely Abstracted Images." In *Emily Dickinson: A Collection of Critical Essays,* edited by Judith Farr, 141–148. Upper Saddle River, N.J.: Prentice-Hall, 1996.

Privratsky, Kenneth L. "Irony in Emily Dickinson's 'Because I could not stop for death.'" *Concerning Poetry* 11, no. 2 (Fall 1978): 25–30.

Raab, Josef. "The Metapoetic Element in Dickinson." In *The Emily Dickinson Handbook,* edited by Gudrun Grabher, Roland Hagenbüchle, and Cristanne Miller, 273–295. Amherst: University of Massachusetts Press, 1998.

Reynolds, David S. *Beneath the American Renaissance: The Subversive Imagination in the Age of Emerson and Melville.* New York: Knopf, 1988. Analyzes Dickinson's writing with respect to the interrelationship of popular and elite culture and the subversive potential of 19th-century American "women's literature."

———. "Emily Dickinson and Popular Culture." In *The Cambridge Companion to Emily Dickinson,* edited by Wendy Martin, 167–190. Cambridge: Cambridge University Press, 2002.

Rich, Adrienne. "Vesuvius at Home: The Power of Emily Dickinson." In *Shakespeare's Sisters: Feminist Essays on Women Poets,* edited by Sandra M. Gilbert and Susan Gubar, 99–102. Bloomington: Indiana University Press, 1979. This influential essay revolutionized the view of Dickinson, revealing her as the enraged poet. Rich discussed Dickinson's strategic use of the child persona in relation to male authority figures as an attempt to conceal her power and viewed her poetry as a form of aggression. She argued that a previously ignored poem, "My Life had stood—a Loaded Gun—" was central to understanding Dickinson and turned it into the key poem for feminist critics.

Robinson, David. *The Unitarians and the Universalists.* Westport, Conn.: Greenwood Press, 1985.

Rosenthal, M. L., and Sally M. Gall. *The Modern Poetic Sequence: The Genius of Modern Poetry.* New York: Oxford University Press, 1983.

St. Armand, Barton Levi. "The Art of Peace." In *Emily Dickinson: A Collection of Critical Essays,* edited by Judith Farr, 163–172. Upper Saddle River, N.J.: Prentice-Hall, 1996.

———. *Emily Dickinson and Her Culture: The Soul's Society.* Cambridge: Cambridge University Press, 1984. An important study of Dickinson in relationship to Victorian American culture. St. Armand demonstrates how her work integrated elements from popular culture, including women's scrapbooks, journals, folk art, and landscape painting.

St. Armand, Barton Levi, and George Monteiro. "Dickinson's 'Hope' is the thing with feathers." *The Explicator* 47, no. 4 (Summer 1989): 34–37.

Salska, Agnieszka. "Dickinson's Letters." In *The Emily Dickinson Handbook,* edited by Gudrun Grabher, Roland Hagenbüchle, and Cristanne Miller, 163–180. Amherst: University of Massachusetts Press, 1998.

———. *Walt Whitman and Emily Dickinson: Poetry of the Central Consciousness.* Philadelphia: University of Pennsylvania Press, 1985.

Sandeen, Ernest. "Delight Deferred by Ecstasy: Emily Dickinson's Late-Summer Poems." *New England Quarterly,* 40 (December 1967): 483–500.

Sergeant, Elizabeth Shepley. "An Early Imagist." In *The Recognition of Emily Dickinson: Selected Criticism since 1890,* edited by Caesar R. Blake and Carlton F. Wells, 88–93. Ann Arbor: University of Michigan Press, 1964.

Sherwood, William R. *Circumference and Circumstance: Stages in the Mind and Art of Emily Dickinson.* New York: Columbia University Press, 1968.

Shurr, William H. *The Marriage of Emily Dickinson: A Study of the Fascicles.* Lexington: University Press of Kentucky, 1983. Shurr's analysis of the fascicles yields the hypothesis that Dickinson married, became pregnant, and may have had an abortion.

Small, Judy Jo. "A Musical Aesthetic." In *Emily Dickinson: A Collection of Critical Essays,* edited by Judith Farr, 206–225. Upper Saddle River, N.J.: Prentice-Hall, 1996.

———. *Positive as Sound: Emily Dickinson's Rhyme.* Athens: University of Georgia Press, 1990. A study of Dickinson's rhymes as structural principles marking stanzaic regularity, but argues that regular rhymes cannot always be associated with stability and irregular rhymes with instability.

Smith, Martha Nell. "Dickinson's Manuscripts." In *The Emily Dickinson Handbook,* edited by Gudrun Grabher, Roland Hagenbüchle, and Cristanne Miller, 113–137. Amherst: University of Massachusetts Press, 1998.

———. "Heavenly Rewards: Recontextualing Emily Dickinson's 'Checks.'" In *After A Hundred Years,* 219–238. Kyoto, Japan. Apollon-sha, 1988.

———. "The Importance of a Hypermedia Archive of Dickinson's Creative Work." *Emily Dickinson Journal* 4, no. 1 (1995): 75–85.

———. *Rowing in Eden: Rereading Emily Dickinson.* Austin: University of Texas Press, 1992. This provocative feminist study challenges the idea that Dickinson wrote in isolation and suggests that she found an alternative way of "publishing" her poems in her letters. Smith discusses the role of Susan Dickinson as Dickinson's primary reader and collaborator and offers a view of the Master letters as imaginative exercises.

———. "Susan and Emily Dickinson: Their Lives in Letters." In *The Cambridge Companion to Emily Dickinson,* edited by Wendy Martin. Cambridge: Cambridge University Press, 2002: 51–73.

Stocks, Kenneth. *Emily Dickinson and the Modern Consciousness.* London: Macmillan, 1988. A study of Dickinson's "modern" consciousness and responses to the "abyss" of the new scientific, technological, and economic order.

Stonum, Gary Lee. "Dickinson against the Sublime." In *University of Dayton Review* 19, no. 1 (Winter 1987–1988): 31–37.

———. "Dickinson's Literary Background." In *The Emily Dickinson Handbook,* edited by Gudrun Grabher, Roland Hagenbüchle, and Cristanne Miller,

44–60. Amherst: University of Massachusetts Press, 1998.

———. *The Dickinson Sublime*. Madison: University of Wisconsin Press, 1990. This is a comprehensive examination of Dickinson's fascination with the power inherent in the Sublime. Drawing a picture of Dickinson as a powerful poet, he argues against the thesis that Dickinson's aesthetics are author-centered and discusses her commitment to a rhetoric of stimulus.

Stott, Clifford C. "The Correct English Origins of Nathaniel Dickinson and William Gull, Settlers of Wethersfield and Hadley." *New England Historical and Genealogical Register* 152 (April 1998): 159–178.

Thomas à Kempis. *Imitation of Christ*. Chicago: Moody Press, 1958.

Tuckerman, Frederick. *Amherst Academy: A New England School of the Past, 1814–1861*, Amherst, Mass. 1929.

Turco, Lewis Putnam, edited by *Emily Dickinson: Woman of Letters*. Albany: State University of New York, 1993. Scholarly and creative essays on Dickinson's correspondence.

250 Years at First Church in Amherst (1739–1989). Amherst, Mass.: First Congregational Church in Amherst, 1990.

Vendler, Helen. "The Unsociable Soul." *New Republic* August 3, 1992: 34–37.

Wagner, Diana and Marcy Tanter. "New Dickinson Letter Clarifies Hale Correspondence," *Emily Dickinson Journal* 7, no. 1 (1998): 110–117.

Walker, Cheryl, ed. *American Women Poets of the Nineteenth Century*. New Brunswick: Rutgers University Press, 1982.

———. *The Nightingale's Burden: Women Poets and American Culture before 1900*. Bloomington: Indiana University Press, 1982. This study seeks to see Dickinson's work as transcending that of her contemporaries among women poets, who took up the "nightingale's burden" to sing of secret sorrow and forbidden live.

Wallace, Ronald. *God Be with the Clown: Humor in American Poetry*. Columbia, Mo.: University of Missouri Press, 1984. Examines Dickinson's humorous approaches to God as a paradoxical strategy of gaining power through powerlessness.

Ward, Theodora Van Wagenen. *Emily Dickinson's Letters to Dr. and Mrs. Josiah Gilbert Holland*. Cambridge, Mass.: Harvard University Press, 1951.

Wardrop, Daneen. "Emily Dickinson and the Gothic in Fascicle 16." In The Cambridge Companion to Emily Dickinson, edited by Wendy Martin, 142–164. Cambridge: Cambridge University Press, 2002.

———. *Emily Dickinson's Gothic: Goblin with a Gauge*. Chicago: University of Chicago Press, 1996.

Webster, Noah. *American Dictionary of the English Language*. New York: S. Converse, 1828.

Weisbuch, Robert. *Emily Dickinson's Poetry*. Chicago: University of Chicago Press, 1975. Places Dickinson within the context of her cultural heritage of Puritan Calvinism, Emersonian transcendentalism, and 19th-century romanticism.

———. "The Necessary Veil: A Quest Fiction." In *Modern Critical Views: Emily Dickinson*, edited by Harold Bloom, 81–98. New York: Chelsea House Publishers, 1985.

———. "Prisming Dickinson; or, Gathering Paradise by Letting Go." In *The Emily Dickinson Handbook*, edited by Gudrun Grabher, Roland Hagenbüchle, and Cristanne Miller, 197–223. Amherst: University of Massachusetts Press, 1998. This is a key article that brilliantly expounds how attempting to assign a Dickinson poem "to one aspect of experience will rob it of its vitality."

Wells, Anna Mary. *Dear Preceptor: The Life and Times of Thomas Wentworth Higginson*. Boston: Houghton Mifflin, 1963.

Werner, Marta, ed. *Emily Dickinson's Open Folios: Scenes of Reading, Surfaces of Writing*. Ann Arbor: University of Michigan Press, 1995.

White, Fred D. "Emily Dickinson's Existential Dramas." In *The Cambridge Companion to Emily Dickinson*, edited by Wendy Martin, 91–106. Cambridge: Cambridge University Press, 2002.

Wider, Sarah. "Corresponding Worlds: The Art of Emily Dickinson's Letters." *Emily Dickinson Journal*, I.I. (1992), 10–38.

Wilbur, Richard. "Sumptuous Destitution." In *Emily Dickinson: A Collection of Critical Essays*, edited by Judith Farr, 53–61. Upper Saddle River, N.J.: Prentice-Hall, 1996.

Wolff, Cynthia Griffin. "[Im]pertinent Constructions of Body and Self: Dickinson's Use of the Romantic Grotesque." In *Emily Dickinson: A Collection of Critical Essays*, edited by Judith Farr, 119–130. Upper Saddle River, N.J.: Prentice-Hall, 1996.

Wolosky, Shira. *Emily Dickinson: A Voice of War*. New Haven, Conn.: Yale University Press, 1984. A pioneering study of the impact of the Civil War on Dickinson's writing, demonstrating how the trauma of the war caused and reinforced the poet's metaphysical conflicts and questioning of religion.

————. "Emily Dickinson: Being in the Body." In *The Cambridge Companion to Emily Dickinson,* edited by Wendy Martin, 129–141. Cambridge: Cambridge University Press, 2002.

————. "Public and Private in Dickinson's War Poetry." In *A Historical Guide to Emily Dickinson,* edited by Vivian R. Pollack, 103–131. New York: Oxford University Press, 2004.

————. "A Syntax of Contention." In *Modern Critical Views: Emily Dickinson,* edited by Harold Bloom, 161–185. New York: Chelsea House Publishers, 1985.

INDEX